The Christian Tradition

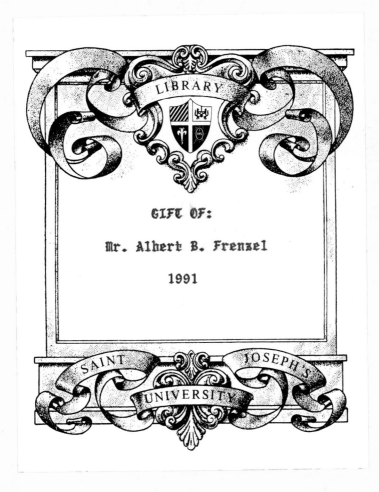

The Christian Tradition
A History of the Development of Doctrine

Jaroslav Pelikan

1

The Emergence of the Catholic Tradition (100–600)

BT
21.2
P42
V.1

The University of Chicago Press

Chicago and London

International Standard Book Number: 0–226–65370–6 (*clothbound*);
    0–226–65371–4 (*paperbound*)
Library of Congress Catalog Card Number: 79–142042

THE UNIVERSITY OF CHICAGO PRESS, CHICAGO 60637
THE UNIVERSITY OF CHICAGO PRESS, LTD., LONDON

87 86 85 84 83 82 81 80   7 8 9 10 11
Printed in the United States of America

Cor ad cor loquitur.
Heart speaketh unto heart.
  Cardinal Newman's coat of arms

Veni Creator Spiritus.
Come, Creator Spirit.
  Adolf von Harnack's epitaph

Contents

CONTENTS

Preface

The Emergence of the Catholic Tradition begins the publication of my history of Christian doctrine, which I hope to complete in five volumes within the next decade. In this volume I have sought to set down the development of what the Christian church believed, taught, and confessed between 100 and 600. The second volume of *The Christian Tradition* will cover the history of Christian doctrine in its Greek, Syriac, and early Russian forms from 600 to 1700 (although, strictly speaking, its account of the "non-Chalcedonian" churches will begin before 600) and will bear the title, *The Spirit of Eastern Christendom*. In *The Growth of Medieval Theology* I shall carry the story of Christian teaching in the Latin church from 600 to 1300. Volume 4, also confined to the West, will be called *Reformation of Church and Dogma, 1300–1700*. Then in the final volume, *Christian Doctrine and Modern Culture*, I plan to put the Eastern and the Western developments back together, as they once more faced a common situation.

The Christian Tradition is, therefore, a five-volume work with a single overall concept guiding its composition and organization. At the same time each of its volumes is designed to be a self-contained unit, independent in its presentation from any of the others. If, for example, a student of medieval art or Reformation politics wants to find the doctrinal background for his field, he should be able to use the appropriate volume of this set as a book unto itself. Each volume carries its own title and, hopefully, its own message. Nevertheless, the work as a whole is intended to take on the audacious and yet necessary task of starting at the beginning of the history of Christian doctrine and continuing to the twentieth century. As the author of articles and even entire monographs on subjects which have received a sentence or two in this account, I am acutely aware of the dangers in any such enterprise. But that awareness is outweighed by the conviction, which I share with Sir Steven Runciman, "that the supreme duty of the historian is to write history, that is to say, to attempt to record in one sweeping sequence the greater events and movements that have swayed the destinies of man. The writer rash enough to make the attempt should not be criticized for his ambition, however much he may deserve censure for the inadequacy of his equipment or the inanity of his results" (*A History of the Crusades* [New York, 1964–67], 1:xi).

This volume is based on a study of the primary sources in the original languages—Greek, Syriac, and Latin. To cite these, I have devised a system of marginal annotation which will, I hope, serve the interests of the scholar and the needs of the student simultaneously, without intruding the apparatus of erudition on the reader who is not interested (not yet interested or no longer interested) in the footnotes. I have, of course, consulted the sources in translation as well and have felt free to adopt and to adapt these as seemed suitable. The book has also derived much benefit from secondary works, a small number of which are indicated in the Bibliography, where I have given preference to the books from which I have learned the most and to those books which will take the reader to the next level of specialization.

With the reader in mind I have sought, even when technical theological terms were unavoidable, to define them upon their first significant appearance; the index will serve as a guide to such definitions. The index will also serve as a means of identifying the proper names that are quoted or cited in the text. By using the index and by working his way through the narrative, even someone who knows no church history and no theology should be able to follow the plot and watch its movement. In this way I strive to meet the needs of the two sets of readers to whom I have, with equal interest, addressed this book: students of theology and church history, who are concerned with the history of Christian doctrine because it is Christian; students of intellectual history, who are concerned with the history of Christian doctrine because it contains important and influential ideas. Being at one and the same time a historian of ideas and a historian of the church, I hope that both groups will be able to read this book and to benefit from it.

I wish I could thank everyone who has helped me on the way, but there are a few whom I simply must thank: my *Doktorvater*, Wilhelm Pauck, who was a student of Adolf von Harnack and has been my mentor; my students in the history of doctrine during almost a quarter-century, who have watched this exposition develop; the National Endowment for the Humanities, whose grant of a senior fellowship enabled me to do the job; publishers of my previous works, who have granted me permission to quote myself; colleagues at various universities, especially Daniel J. Boorstin, with whom I discussed the conception of the work as a whole; hearers and readers, some of them anonymous, whose evaluations and criticisms compelled me to improve the book; and Mrs. Margaret Schulze, my former secretary and editorial assistant, who saw the project through almost to the point of completion.

Primary Sources

Authors and Texts

Ath.   Athanasius of Alexandria
  Apol.Const.   *Apology to Constantius*
  Apol.sec.   *Second Apology against the Arians*
  Ar.   *Orations against the Arians*
  Decr.   *On the Decrees of the Synod of Nicea*
  Dion.   *Defense of Dionysius*
  Ep.Aeg.Lib.   *Epistle to the Bishops of Egypt and Libya*
  Ep.Afr.   *Epistle to the Bishops of Africa*
  Ep.fest.   *Festal Epistles*
  Ep.Serap.   *Epistles to Serapion*
  Fug.   *Apology for His Flight [Apologia de fuga sua]*
  Gent.   *Against the Heathen [Contra gentes]*
  Inc.   *On the Incarnation of the Logos*
  Syn.   *On the Synods of Ariminum and Seleucia*
  Tom.   *Tome to the Antiochenes*
  V.Ant.   *Life of Antony [Vita Antonii]*
Ps.Ath.   Pseudo-Athanasius
  Apoll.   *On the Incarnation against Apollinaris*
  Ar.4   *Fourth Oration against the Arians*
  Exp.fid.   *Exposition of the Faith [Expositio fidei]*
Athenag.   Athenagoras of Athens
  Leg.   *Supplication for the Christians [Legatio pro Christianis]*
  Res.   *On the Resurrection of the Dead*
Aug.   Augustine of Hippo
  Anim.   *On the Soul and Its Origin [De anima et eius origine]*
  Bapt.   *On Baptism against the Donatists*
  Civ.   *City of God [De civitate dei]*
  Conf.   *Confessions*
  Corrept.   *On Rebuke and Grace [De correptione et gratia]*
  Doctr.christ.   *On Christian Doctrine*
  Duab.anim.   *On Two Souls against the Manicheans [De duabus ani-mabus contra Manichaeos]*
  Enchir.   *Enchiridion*
  Ep.   *Epistles*
  Ep.fund.   *Against the Epistle of Manicheus Called Fundamental*
  Ep.Joh.   *Exposition of the First Epistle of John*
  Ev.Joh.   *Exposition of the Gospel of John*
  Faust.   *Against Faustus the Manichean*
  Fid.et.symb.   *On Faith and the Creed [De fide et symbolo]*
  Fort.   *Against Fortunatus*
  Gen.ad litt.   *Exposition of Genesis according to the Letter [De Genesi ad litteram]*
  Gest.Pelag.   *On the Proceedings of Pelagius [De gestis Pelagii]*
  Grat.   *On Grace [De gratia]*
  Grat.Christ.   *On the Grace of Christ [De gratia Christi]*
  Haer.   *On Heresies*
  Jul.   *Against Julian*
  Jul.op.imperf.   *Incomplete Work against Julian [Contra secundam Juli-ani responsionem opus imperfectum]*
  Mag.   *On the Teacher [De magistro]*
  Mor.Manich.   *On the Morals of the Manicheans*

Nat.bon.	On the Nature of the Good against the Manicheans [*De natura boni contra Manichaeos*]
Nat.et grat.	On Nature and Grace [*De natura et gratia*]
Nupt.et. concup.	On Marriage and Concupiscence [*De nuptiis et concupiscentia*]
Parm.	Against the Epistle of Parmenianus
Pecc.merit.	On the Merits and the Remission of Sins [*De peccatorum meritis et remissione*]
Pecc.orig.	On Original Sin [*De peccato originali*]
Pelag.	Against Two Epistles of the Pelagians
Perf.just.	On Man's Perfection in Righteousness [*De perfectione justitiae hominis*]
Persev.	On the Gift of Perseverance
Petil.	Against the Letters of Petilian
Praed.sanct.	On the Predestination of the Saints [*De praedestinatione sanctorum*]
Ps.	Exposition of the Psalms
Retract.	Retractations
Serm.	Sermons
Soliloq.	Soliloquies
Spir.et litt.	On the Spirit and the Letter [*De spiritu et littera*]
Trin.	On the Trinity
Vera relig.	On True Religion [*De vera religione*]
Bab.*Un.*	Babai of Kashkar. *On the Union*
Barn.	Epistle of Barnabas
Bas.	Basil of Caesarea
Ep.	Epistles
Eun.	Against Eunomius
Hom.	Homilies
Spir.	On the Holy Spirit
Ps.Bas.*Eun.4*	Pseudo-Basil. *Fourth Book against Eunomius*
Bed.*H.e.*	Bede. *Ecclesiastical History*
Boeth.	Boethius
Cons.	Consolation of Philosophy
Divin.	Whether Father, Son, and Holy Spirit May Be Substantially Predicated of the Divinity
Eut.	Against Eutyches and Nestorius
Fid.cath.	On the Catholic Faith [*De fide catholica*]
Herm.sec.	Commentary [Second] on Aristotle "On Interpretation" [*In librum Aristotelis περὶ ἑρμενείας editio secunda*]
Trin.	On the Trinity
Bon.II.*Ep.Caes.Arel.*	Boniface II. *Epistle to Caesarius of Arles*
Caes.Arel.*Grat.*	Caesarius of Arles. *On Grace* [*De gratia*]
Cassian	Cassian
Coll.	Conferences [*Collationes*]
Nest.	On the Incarnation of the Lord against Nestorius
Cassiod.*Inst.div.*	Cassiodorus. *On the Institution of Divine Letters*
CAraus.(529)	Council of Orange [Concilium Arausicanum]
Can.	Canons
Def.fid.	Definition of Faith [*Definitio fidei*]
CChalc.*Act.*	Council of Chalcedon. *Acts*

CCP(553)	Second Council of Constantinople
Anath.	*Anathemas*
Can.	*Canons*
Sent.	*Sentences*
CEph.(431)	Council of Ephesus
Act.	*Acts*
Anath.	*Anathemas*
Ep.Cael.	*Epistle of Celestine*
Gest.Orient.	*Proceedings of the Orientals* [*Gesta Orientalium*]
CTrull.*Can.*	Trullan Council. *Canons*
Chrys.*Sac.*	John Chrysostom. *On the Priesthood* [*De sacerdotio*]
Cic.*Div.*	Cicero. *On Divination*
1 Clem.	*First Epistle of Clement*
2 Clem.	*Second Epistle of Clement*
Clem.	Clement of Alexandria
Exc.Thdot.	*Excerpts from Theodotus*
Paed.	*Tutor* [*Paedagogus*]
Prot.	*Exhortation to the Greeks* [*Protrepticus*]
Q.d.s.	*Who Is the Rich Man That Is Saved?* [*Quis dives salvetur*]
Str.	*Stromata*
Clem.*Recogn.*	*Clementine Recognitions*
Comm.*Instr.*	Commodianus. *Instructions*
Const.*Or.s.c.*	Constantine I. *Oration to the Assembly of the Saints* [*Oratio ad sanctorum coetum*]
Const.*App.*	*Apostolic Constitutions*
Cypr.	Cyprian of Carthage
Domin.orat.	*On the Lord's Prayer* [*De dominica oratione*]
Donat.	*To Donatus*
Ep.	*Epistles*
Laps.	*On the Lapsed*
Test.	*Testimonies*
Unit.eccl.	*On the Unity of the Church* [*De unitate ecclesiae*]
Cyr.	Cyril of Alexandria
Apol.Thdt.	*Apology against Theodoret*
Chr.un.	*That Christ Is One* [*Quod unus sit Christus*]
1 Cor.	*Exposition of 1 Corinthians*
Dial.Trin.	*Dialogues on the Trinity*
Ep.	*Epistles*
Ep.Nest.	*Epistles to Nestorius*
Inc.unigen.	*On the Incarnation of the Only-Begotten* [*De incarnatione unigeniti*]
Is.	*Exposition of Isaiah*
Joh.	*Exposition of the Gospel of John*
Luc.	*Exposition of the Gospel of Luke*
Thds.	*To Theodosius*
Cyr.H.*Catech.*	Cyril of Jerusalem. *Catechetical Lectures*
Cyr.S.*Sab.*	Cyril of Scythopolis. *Life of Sabas*
Dant.*Inf.*	Dante Alighieri. *Inferno*
Didym.	Didymus of Alexandria
Spir.	*On the Holy Spirit*
Trin.	*On the Trinity*

Did.	Didache
Diogn.	Epistle to Diognetus
Dion.Ar.	Pseudo-Dionysius the Areopagite
C.h.	Celestial Hierarchy
D.n.	On the Divine Names
Ep.	Epistles
E.h.	Ecclesiastical Hierarchy
Myst.	On Mystical Theology
Dion.Hal.*Ant.Rom.*	Dionysius of Halicarnassus. *Roman Antiquities*
Ephr.	Ephraem Syrus
Carm.Nis.	Poems of Nisibis [Carmina Nisibena]
Serm.	Sermons
Epiph.*Haer.*	Epiphanius of Salamis. *Against Eighty Heresies*
Eus.	Eusebius of Caesarea
E.th.	Ecclesiastical Theology
Ep.Caes.	Epistle to the People of Caesarea
H.e.	Ecclesiastical History
P.e.	Preparation for the Gospel [Praeparatio evangelica]
V.C.	Life of Constantine [De vita Constantini]
Eust.Mon.*Ep.*	Eustathius the Monk. *Epistle on the Two Natures against Severus*
Euther.*Confut.*	Eutherius of Tyana. *Confutations*
Ev. Phil.	Gospel of Philip [Evangelium Philippi]
Ev.Thos.	Gospel of Thomas [Evangelium Thomae]
Ev.Ver.	Gospel of Truth [Evangelium Veritatis]
Evagr.*H.e.*	Evagrius. *Ecclesiastical History*
Faust.Rei.*Grat.*	Faustus of Riez. *On Grace [De gratia]*
Ps.Fel.*Ep.Petr.Full.*	Pseudo-Felix. *Epistle to Peter the Fuller*
Fulg.*Ep.*	Fulgentius of Ruspe. *Epistles*
Gennad.*Vir.ill.*	Gennadius. *Lives of Illustrious Men [De viris illustribus]*
Gr.M.	Gregory the Great [Gregorius Magnus]
Ep.	Epistles
Dial.	Dialogues
Ev.	Homilies on the Gospels [In evangelia homiliae]
Ezech.	Homilies on Ezechiel
Mor.	Moral Discourses on Job
Past.	Pastoral Rule
Gr.Naz.	Gregory of Nazianzus
Carm.	Poems [Carmina]
Ep.	Epistles
Or.	Orations
Gr.Nyss.	Gregory of Nyssa
Anim.et resurr.	On the Soul and the Resurrection [De anima et resurrectione]
Apoll.	Against Apollinaris
Ep.	Epistles
Eun.	Against Eunomius
Maced.	Against the Macedonians
Or.catech.	Catechetical Orations
Tres dii	That There Are Not Three Gods [Quod non sint tres dii]
V.Macr.	Life of Macrina [De vita Macrinae]
V.Mos.	Life of Moses [De vita Mosis]

Gr.Presb.*V.Gr.Naz.*	Gregory the Presbyter. *Life of Gregory of Nazianzus* [*De vita Gregorii Nazianzeni*]
Herm.	Hermas
Mand.	*Mandates*
Sim.	*Similitudes*
Vis.	*Visions*
Hier.	Jerome [Hieronymus]
Ep.	*Epistles*
Hom.Orig.in Luc	*Homilies of Origen on the Gospel of Luke*
Jovin.	*Against Jovinian*
Pelag.	*Against the Pelagians*
Rufin.	*Against Rufinus*
Vigil.	*Against Vigilantius*
Vir.ill.	*Lives of Illustrious Men* [*De viris illustribus*]
Hil.	Hilary of Poitiers
Const.	*To Constantius Augustus*
Ps.	*Exposition of the Psalms*
Syn.	*On the Councils* [*De synodis*]
Trin.	*On the Trinity*
Hipp.	Hippolytus of Rome
Antichr.	*On Antichrist*
Dan.	*Exposition of Daniel*
Haer.	*On Heresies*
Noët.	*Against Noetus*
Trad.ap.	*Apostolic Tradition*
Horm.*Ep.*	Hormisdas. *Epistles*
Ign.	Ignatius of Antioch
Eph.	*Epistle to the Ephesians*
Mag.	*Epistle to the Magnesians*
Phil.	*Epistle to the Philadelphians*
Rom.	*Epistle to the Romans*
Smyrn.	*Epistle to the Smyrneans*
Trall.	*Epistle to the Trallians*
Ildef.*Vir.ill.*	Ildefonsus of Toledo. *Lives of Illustrious Men* [*De viris illustribus*]
Iren.	Irenaeus of Lyons
Dem.	*Proof of the Apostolic Preaching* [*Demonstratio apostolicae praedicationis*]
fr.	*Fragments*
Haer.	*Against Heresies*
Jac.Bar.*Ep.*	Jacob Baradaeus. *Epistles*
Joh.Ant.*Ep.Cyr.*	John of Antioch. *Epistles to Cyril*
Joh.D.	John of Damascus
F.o.	*On the Orthodox Faith*
Haer.	*On Heresies*
Jos.	Flavius Josephus
Ant.	*Antiquities of the Jews*
Ap.	*Against Apion*
Jul.	Julian the Emperor
Caes.	*Caesars*
Ep.	*Epistles*
Gal.	*Against the Galileans*

Just.	Justin Martyr
1 Apol.	*First Apology*
2 Apol.	*Second Apology*
Dial.	*Dialogue with Trypho*
Justn.	Justinian I
Conf.	*Confession of the True Faith against the Three Chapters*
Ep.Thdr.Mops.	*Epistle against Theodore of Mopsuestia*
Monoph.	*Against the Monophysites*
Or.	*Against Origen*
Sev.	*Sacred Constitution against the Severians*
Juv.*Sat.*	Juvenal. *Satires*
Lact.*Inst.*	Lactantius. *Divine Institutes*
Leo M.	Leo the Great [Leo Magnus]
Ep.	*Epistles*
Serm.	*Sermons*
Tom.	*Tome*
Leont.B.*Nest.et Eut.*	Leontius of Byzantium. *Against the Nestorians and Eutychians*
Ps.Leont.B.*Sect.*	Pseudo-Leontius of Byzantium. *On the Sects*
Leont.H.*Nest.*	Leontius of Jerusalem. *Against the Nestorians*
Mar.Vict.*Ar.*	Marius Victorinus. *Against Arius*
Marc.*fr.*	Marcellus of Ancyra. *Fragments*
M.Polyc.	*Martyrdom of Polycarp*
Mel.*fr.*	Melito of Sardis. *Fragments*
Meth.	Methodius of Olympus
Res.	*On the Resurrection of the Dead*
Symp.	*Symposium*
Ps.Meth.*Palm.*	Pseudo-Methodius. *Sermon on the Palm Branches*
Min.Fel.*Oct.*	Minucius Felix. *Octavianus*
Nest.	Nestorius of Constantinople
Baz.	*Bazaar of Heraclides*
Capit.	*Chapters [Capitula]*
Ep.Cael.	*Epistle to Celestine*
Ep.Cyr.	*Epistle to Cyril*
fr.	*Fragments*
Hist.	*History*
Hom.in Heb. 3:1	*Homily on Hebrews 3:1*
Null.det.	*None Worse [Nulla deterior]*
Serm.	*Sermons*
Serm.Theot.	*Sermons on the Theotokos*
Nov.*Trin.*	Novatian. *On the Trinity*
Optat.*Donat.*	Optatus of Mileve. *Against Parmenianus the Donatist*
Or.	Origen of Alexandria
Cant.	*Exposition of the Song of Solomon [Commentarius in Cantica Canticorum]*
Cels.	*Against Celsus*
Ex.	*Homilies on Exodus*
Is.	*Homilies on Isaiah*
Joh.	*Commentary on the Gospel of John*
Jos.	*Homilies on Joshua*
Lev.	*Homilies on Leviticus*
Luc.	*Homilies on the Gospel of Luke*

Matt.	*Commentary on the Gospel of Matthew*
Orat.	*On Prayer* [*De oratione*]
Princ.	*On First Principles*
Rom.	*Commentary on Romans*
Ov.*Met.*	Ovid. *Metamorphoses*
Pass.Perp.	*Passion of Perpetua and Felicitas*
Paul.Ant.*Ep.syn.*	Paul of Antioch. *Synodical Epistle*
Paul.Sil.*Soph.*	Paul the Silentiary. *Sancta Sophia*
Pelag.*Rom.*	Pelagius. *Exposition of Romans*
Petr.Lomb.*Sent.*	Peter Lombard. *Sentences*
Ph.*Qu.om.pr.lib.*	Philo of Alexandria. *That Every Righteous Man Is Free* [*Quod omnis probus liber sit*]
Philox.	Philoxenus of Mabbug
Hom.	*Homilies*
Inc.	*On the Incarnation*
Trin.	*On the Trinity*
Phot.*Cod.*	Photius of Constantinople. *Codices*
Pist.Soph.	*Pistis Sophia*
Pl.	Plato
Leg.	*Laws* [*Leges*]
Ti.	*Timaeus*
Plin.*HN*	Pliny the Elder. *Natural History*
Plin.*Ep.*	Pliny the Younger. *Epistles*
Procl.*Arm.*	Proclus of Constantinople. *Tome to the Armenians*
Prosp.	Prosper of Aquitaine
Auct.	*Official Pronouncements of the Apostolic See on Divine Grace and Free Will* [*Praeteritorum episcoporum sedis apostolicae auctoritates de gratia dei et libero voluntatis arbitrio*]
Coll.	*Against Cassian the Lecturer* [*Contra collatorem*]
Ep.Aug.	*Epistle to Augustine*
Ep.Ruf.	*Epistle to Rufinus*
Resp.Gall.	*Response to the Objections of the Gauls*
Resp.Gen.	*Response to the Extracts of the Genoese*
Resp.Vinc.	*Response to the Vincentian Articles*
Sent.	*Sentences from Augustine*
Vocat.	*Call of All Nations* [*De vocatione omnium gentium*]
Radb.*Corp.*	Radbertus. *On the Body and Blood of the Lord* [*De corpore et sanguine Domini*]
Ratr.*Corp.*	Ratramnus. *On the Body and Blood of the Lord* [*De corpore et sanguine Domini*]
Rufin.*Symb.*	Rufinus. *Commentary on the Apostles' Creed* [*Commentarius in symbolum apostolorum*]
Sacr.Gelas.	*Gelasian Sacramentary*
Scot.Er.*Praed.*	John Scotus Erigena. *On Predestination*
Serv.Lup.*Ep.*	Servatus Lupus. *Epistles*
Sev.Ant.	Severus of Antioch
Ep.	*Epistles*
Ep.Thds.	*Epistle to Theodosius of Alexandria*
Socr.*H.e.*	Socrates Scholasticus. *Ecclesiastical History*
Soz.*H.e.*	Sozomen. *Ecclesiastical History*
Suet.*Tib.*	Suetonius. *Tiberius*

Sulp.Sev.*Mart.*	Sulpicius Severus. *Life of Martin*
Symb.Ant.	Creed of Antioch [*Symbolum Antiochenum*]
Symb.Ath.	Athanasian Creed [*Symbolum Athanasianum*]
Symb.Chal.	Creed of Chalcedon [*Symbolum Chalcedonense*]
Symb.Nic.(325)	Creed of Nicea [*Symbolum Nicaenum*]
Symb.Nic.–CP	Niceno-Constantinopolitan Creed [*Symbolum Nicaeno-Constantinopolitanum*]
Syn.Sel. (585)	Synod of Seleucia-Ctesiphon
Syn.Carth. (418)	Synod of Carthage
Tat.*Or.*	Tatian. *Oration to the Greeks*
Tert.	Tertullian of Carthage
Anim.	*On the Soul* [*De anima*]
Apol.	*Apology*
Bapt.	*On Baptism*
Carn.	*On the Flesh of Christ* [*De carne Christi*]
Castit.	*Exhortation to Chastity*
Coron.	*On the Crown* [*De corona*]
Cult.fem.	*On the Dress of Women* [*De cultu feminarum*]
Fug.	*Flight in Persecution* [*De fuga in persecutione*]
Hermog.	*Against Hermogenes*
Idol.	*On Idolatry*
Jejun.	*On Fasting* [*De jejunio*]
Jud.	*Against the Jews* [*Adversus Judaeos*]
Marc.	*Against Marcion*
Monog.	*On Monogamy*
Nat.	*To the Nations*
Orat.	*On Prayer* [*De oratione*]
Paenit.	*On Penitence*
Praescrip.	*Prescription of Heretics*
Prax.	*Against Praxeas*
Pudic.	*On Modesty* [*De pudicitia*]
Res.	*On the Resurrection*
Scap.	*To Scapula*
Scorp.	*Scorpiace*
Spect.	*On the Spectacles*
Test.anim.	*Testimony of the Soul* [*De testimonio animae*]
Virg.vel.	*On the Veiling of Virgins* [*De virginibus velandis*]
Ps.Tert.*Haer.*	Pseudo-Tertullian. *Against All Heresies*
Thdr.Mops.	Theodore of Mopsuestia
Col.	*Exposition of Colossians*
Eph.	*Exposition of Ephesians*
fr.	*Fragments*
fr.inc.	*Fragments on the Incarnation*
Gal.	*Exposition of Galatians*
Gen.	*Exposition of Genesis*
Hom.catech.	*Catechetical Homilies*
Joh.	*Exposition of the Gospel of John*
Pecc.orig.	*On Original Sin* [*De peccato originali*]
Phil.	*Exposition of Philippians*
Ps.	*Exposition of the Psalms*
1 Tim.	*Exposition of First Timothy*

Thds.Al.	Theodosius of Alexandria
Ep.	*Epistles*
Or.	*Orations*
Thdt.	Theodoret of Cyrrhus
Eran.	*Dialogue [Eranistes]*
H.e.	*Ecclesiastical History*
Theoph.*Autol.*	Theophilus of Antioch. *To Autolycus*
Thos.Aq.*S.T.*	Thomas Aquinas. *Summa Theologica*
Tim.CP*Haer.*	Timothy of Constantinople. *On the Reception of Heretics*
Ven.Fort.*Carm.*	Venantius Fortunatus. *Poems [Carmina]*
Verg.	Vergil
Aen.	*Aeneid*
Ecl.	*Eclogues*
Vinc.Ler.*Comm.*	Vincent of Lérins. *Commonitory*

Editions and Collections

ACO	*Acta conciliorum oecumenicorum.* Strasbourg, 1914–.
ACW	*Ancient Christian Writers.* Westminster, Maryland, 1946–.
Bedjan	Bedjan, P., ed. *Le livre d'Héraclide de Damas.* Paris, 1910.
Beek	Beek, C.I.M.I. van, ed. *Passio Sanctarum Perpetuae et Felicitatis.* Bonn, 1938.
Bihlmeyer	Bihlmeyer, K., ed. *Die apostolischen Väter.* Tübingen, 1924.
Brink	Brink, J. N. Bakhuizen van den, ed. Ratramnus. *De corpore et sanguine Domini.* Amsterdam, 1954.
Brooks	Brooks, E. W., ed. Severus of Antioch. *Sixth Book of Letters.* London, 1902–4.
CCSL	*Corpus christianorum. Series latina.* Turnhout, Belgium, 1953–.
Chabot	Chabot, J. B., ed. *Synodicon Orientale ou recueil de synodes nestoriens.* Paris, 1902.
Cross	Cross. F. L., ed. *Athanasius de Incarnatione.* London, 1939.
CSCO	*Corpus scriptorum christianorum orientalium.* Paris, 1903–.
CSEL	*Corpus scriptorum ecclesiasticorum latinorum.* Vienna, 1866–.
Funk	Funk, F. X., ed. *Didascalia et constitutiones apostolorum.* Paderborn, 1905.
GCS	*Die griechischen christlichen Schriftsteller der ersten drei Jahrhunderte.* Berlin, 1897–.
Goodspeed	Goodspeed, E. J., ed. *Die ältesten Apologeten.* Göttingen, 1915.
Grant	Grant, R. M., and Freedman, D. N., eds. *The Secret Sayings of Jesus.* Garden City, N. Y., 1960.
Grobel	Grobel, K., ed. *The Gospel of Truth: A Valentinian Meditation on the Gospel.* New York, 1960.
Harvey	Harvey, W. W., ed. *Sancti Irenaei . . . Adversus Haereses.* Cambridge, 1857.
Hennecke	Hennecke, E., ed. *Neutestamentliche Apokryphen.* 2d ed. Tübingen, 1924.

Hussey	Hussey, R., ed. Socrates Scholasticus. *Historia ecclesiastica.* Oxford, 1853.
Jaeger	Jaeger, W., ed. *Gregorii Nysseni Opera.* Berlin and Leiden, 1921–.
LCL	*Loeb Classical Library.* Cambridge, Mass., 1912–.
Lietzmann	Lietzmann, H., ed. *Apollinaris von Laodicea und seine Schule.* Tübingen, 1904.
Loofs	Loofs, F., ed. *Nestoriana: Die Fragmente des Nestorius.* Halle, 1905.
Mansi	Mansi, J. D., ed. *Sacrorum conciliorum nova et amplissima collectio.* Florence, 1759–98.
MGH	*Monumenta Germaniae historica: Epistolae.* Berlin, 1891–.
Morin	Morin, G., ed. *Sancti Caesarii arelatensis Opera omnia nunc primum in unum collecta.* Maredsous, Belgium, 1937–42.
Moxon	Moxon, R. S., ed. Vincent of Lérins. *Commonitorium.* Cambridge, 1915.
Mynors	Mynors, R. A. B., ed. Cassiodorus. *Institutiones.* Oxford, 1937.
Nairn	Nairn, J. A., ed. *"De Sacerdotio"* of St. John Chrysostom. Cambridge, 1906.
Opitz	Opitz, H. G., et al., eds. *Athanasius' Werke.* Berlin, 1934–.
PG	*Patrologia graeca.* Paris, 1857–66.
Pitra	Pitra, J. B., ed. *Analecta sacra spicilegio solesmensi parata.* Paris, 1876–91.
PL	*Patrologia latina.* Paris, 1878–90.
Reischl-Rupp	Reischl, W. K., and Rupp, J., eds. Cyril of Jerusalem. *Opera.* Munich, 1848–60.
SC	*Sources chrétiennes.* Paris, 1940–.
Schaff	Schaff, P., ed. *Creeds of Christendom.* 6th ed. New York, 1919.
Schmitt	Schmitt, F. S., ed. *Sancti Anselmi opera omnia.* Seckau, Rome, Edinburgh, 1938–61.
Souter	Souter, A., ed. Pelagius. *Expositions of the Thirteen Epistles of St. Paul.* Cambridge, 1922–31.
ST	*Studi e testi.* Rome, 1900–.
Swete	Swete, H. B., ed. Theodore of Mopsuestia. *Commentary on the Epistles of St. Paul.* Cambridge, 1880–82.
TU	*Texte und Untersuchungen zur Geschichte der altchristlichen Literatur.* Leipzig, 1882–.
Weyer	Weyer, H., ed. Novatian. *De Trinitate.* Düsseldorf, 1962.
Wilson	Wilson, R. M., ed. *The Gospel of Philip.* New York, 1963.

Some Definitions

1 Cor. 13:13

What the church of Jesus Christ believes, teaches, and confesses on the basis of the word of God: this is Christian doctrine. Doctrine is not the only, not even the primary, activity of the church. The church worships God and serves mankind, it works for the transformation of this world and awaits the consummation of its hope in the next. "Faith, hope, love abide, these three; but the greatest of these is love"—love, and not faith, and certainly not doctrine. The church is always more than a school; not even the age of the Enlightenment managed to restrict or reduce it to its teaching function. But the church cannot be less than a school. Its faith, hope, and love all express themselves in teaching and confession. Liturgy is distinguished from ceremonial by a content that is declared in the Credo; polity transcends organization because of the way the church defines itself and its structure in its dogma; preaching is set apart from other rhetoric by its proclamation of the word of God; biblical exegesis avoids antiquarianism because it is intent on discovering what the text teaches, not merely what it taught. The Christian church would not be the church as we know it without Christian doctrine.

All this is, strictly speaking, a description rather than a definition of Christian doctrine. And since this history deals with the development of Christian doctrine, the definition of doctrine, which has itself developed, should perhaps be postponed to the end and formulated a posteriori. For "doctrine" has not always meant the same, not even formally. In fact, the word is used in the parlance of the church (and will be used in this book)

1

in a sense different from the sense it has in the Bible (and in books on biblical theology). When the Old Testament speaks about "instruction" or the New Testament about "the doctrine," this includes teaching about both confession and conduct, both theology and ethics. A separation between them is fatal, a distinction unavoidable, just as in the New Testament itself "faith" and "works" are distinguished without being separated. Indeed, at the risk of oversimplification, the specification of what is meant here by Christian doctrine may tentatively be said to proceed from such New Testament distinctions. When it is said that "even the demons believe" and presumably believe aright, it is their "doctrine" in the churchly sense of the term that is being referred to. But when the New Testament speaks of "doctrines of demons," it seems to be referring chiefly to distortions of the standards of Christian conduct. An ancient Christian collect addresses God as the one "in knowledge of whom standeth our eternal life, whose service is perfect freedom," distinguishing between the knowledge of God and the service of God. Christian doctrine may be defined as the content of that saving knowledge, derived from the word of God.

Already in the early centuries, Christian thinkers began to distinguish between that instruction which was intended "to make known the word concerning Christ, and the mystery regarding him" and that instruction which was intended "to point to the correction of habits." At least in part, the distinction was suggested by the procedure of the New Testament itself. Theodore of Mopsuestia noted that both in the Epistle to the Romans and in that to the Ephesians the apostle Paul first set forth "dogmatic sermons," defined as "sermons which contain an account of the coming of Christ and indicate the blessings which he has conferred upon us by his coming," and then went on to "ethical exhortation." The great commission in Matthew 28:19 likewise was seen as a division of Christian discipline into two parts, "the ethical part and the precision of dogmas," the former being contained in the commandments of Jesus and the latter in the "tradition of baptism." This meant that "the method of godliness consists of these two things, pious doctrines and virtuous practice," neither of which was acceptable to God without the other. Both

Prov.1:7
Acts 2:42

Rom.3:27-28
James 2:18

James 2:19

1 Tim.4:1

Sacr.Gelas.3.56 (PL 74:1217-18)

Ath.Ep.fest.11.3 (PG 26:1405)

Thdr.Mops.Eph.arg. (Swete 1:114)

Gr.Nyss.Ep.24.2 (Jaeger 8–II:75)

Cyr.H.Catech.4.2 (Reischl-Rupp 1:90)

forms of instruction belonged in the pulpit and in books about Christian teaching. The standard manual of doctrine in Greek Christianity, the *Orthodox Faith* of John of Damascus, discussed not only the Trinity and christology,

Joh.D.*F.o*.2.15–17 (*PG* 94:932–33)

but also such matters as fear, anger, and the imagination. Its later counterpart in the Latin church, the *Sentences* of

Petr.Lomb.*Sent*.3.36–40 (*PL* 192:1087–90)

Peter Lombard, included in its third book a treatment of the virtues created by grace. The two branches of theology were not permanently separated until the work of the seventeenth-century Protestant theologian, Georg Calixtus, but the distinction between doctrine and life had been in force long before that division of labor was effected.

Our opening definition requires more detailed specification. Christian doctrine is the business of the church. The history of doctrine is not to be equated with the history of theology or the history of Christian thought. If it is, the historian runs the danger of exaggerating the significance of the idiosyncratic thought of individual theologians at the expense of the common faith of the church. The private beliefs of theologians do belong to the history of doctrine, but not simply on their own terms. For one of the most decisive differences between a theologian and a philosopher is that the former under-

Or.*Lev*.1.1 (*GCS* 29:281); Or.*Jos*.9.8 (*GCS* 30:353); Or. *Is*.7.3 (*GCS* 33:283)

stands himself as, in Origen's classic phrase, "a man of the church," a spokesman for the Christian community. Even in his theological speculations and in his polemic against what may have been public teaching in the church of his time, a theologian such as Origen knew himself to be accountable to the deposit of Christian revelation and to the ongoing authority of the church. His personal opinions must be set into the context of the development of what the church has believed, taught, and confessed on the basis of the word of God. It is usually difficult, and sometimes impossible, to draw the line of demarcation between the teachings of the church and the theories of its teachers; what the teachers thought often reflected an earlier stage in the development or anticipated a later one. Yet it is this development of church doctrine that will be the special object of our investigation here.

Doctrine is what is believed, taught, and confessed. Ever since its emergence as a distinct field of investigation in the eighteenth century, the history of doctrine has concentrated on what is confessed, that is, on dogmas as the normative statements of Christian belief adopted by various ecclesiastical authorities and enforced as the official teaching of the church. The history of dogma has claimed to pay attention to the doctrinal development before or after the formulation of such normative statements only for the sake of the relation of this development to dogma. In practice, however, the histories of dogma have tended to expand beyond their self-imposed limitations, whose arbitrariness becomes especially evident in the terminus ad quem assigned to the study: the last (or the latest) council or confessional document of a particular branch of the church. Since most of Protestantism had concluded its confessional development by the middle of the seventeenth century, there could not be a history of Protestant dogma, but only a history of Protestant theology. Yet there was more to the history of doctrine within Protestantism than the sequence of its theological systems.

By relating what is confessed to what is believed and to what is taught, this history seeks to take account of how doctrines have developed. Without setting rigid boundaries, we shall identify what is "believed" as the form of Christian doctrine present in the modalities of devotion, spirituality, and worship; what is "taught" as the content of the word of God extracted by exegesis from the witness of the Bible and communicated to the people of the church through proclamation, instruction, and churchly theology; and what is "confessed" as the testimony of the church, both against false teaching from within and against attacks from without, articulated in polemics and in apologetics, in creed and in dogma. Creeds and decrees against heresy will bulk large in our documentation, as they do in that of the histories of dogma; for what the church confesses is what the church has believed and taught—or at least part of what the church has believed and taught. In the history of dogma, what the church believes and teaches apart from its normative statements of faith is important as a commentary on creed and dogma. In the present history of the development of doctrine, the creed and dogma are important as an index to what the church believes, teaches, and confesses. We shall, to some extent, have to read back from what was confessed to what was taught to

Dilthey (1923) 167

what was believed; for as Count Yorck once wrote to Wilhelm Dilthey, the difference between history and antiquarianism is that history must be "regressive," moving from the present to the past.

The relation between believing, teaching, and confessing also implies that both the subject matter and the source material for the history of the development of doctrine will shift, gradually but steadily, as we trace it through the history of the church. This is not intended to say that a doctrine, once formulated, stops developing and becomes fixed; not even the dogma of the Trinity has stood perfectly still since its adoption and clarification. It does mean that having developed from what was believed to what was taught, and perhaps even to what was confessed, a doctrine gradually became part of the authorized deposit of the faith. To trace its further development we shall have to look, increasingly though by no means exclusively, to its professional expositors, the theologians, as they speculated on it both in their philosophy and in their mystagogy, as they studied it and criticized it, as they used it to interpret the very Scriptures on which it was supposedly based, and as they expanded and revised it. In later volumes of this history, therefore, the history of doctrine will move into, but will never quite become, the history of theology. A graphic sign of this shift through the centuries is contained in the evolution of the theologian's vocation. During the years 100 to 600, most theologians were bishops; from 600 to 1500 in the West, they were monks; since 1500, they have been university professors. Gregory I, who died in 604, was a bishop who had been a monk; Martin Luther, who died in 1546, was a monk who became a university professor. Each of these life styles has left its mark on the job description of the theologian, but also on the way doctrine has continued to develop back and forth between believing, teaching, and confessing.

The writings of theologians will, of course, be prominent as a source throughout our history of doctrine, as they are for the history of theology. If the theologians are indeed the responsible spokesmen of the church, one would expect their books to provide most of the information about the development of doctrine. But it is not only to their treatises on systematic theology that we must turn for such information. Even in these treatises, moreover, they acted not only as refuters of heresy or formulators of dogma or defenders of the faith, but as interpreters of Scripture. For example, Athanasius's *Orations against the Arians* consist of his explanations of a series of biblical passages over which the Arian and the Nicene parties had engaged in controversy; Thomas Aquinas was rightly known as a "master of the sacred page"; and Martin Luther, in the apt phrase of Heinrich Bornkamm, was really a professor of Old Testament exegesis. Because, as our definition states, Christian doctrine is based on the word of God, we shall be turning to the exegetical works of Christian theologians as well as to their dogmatic and polemical writings. We shall also examine the doctrinal implications drawn from certain proof texts of Scripture. The history of biblical interpretation and the development of hermeneutics deserve study on their own merits and are not our direct concern here.

Viewing Christian doctrine as what the church believes, teaches, and confesses on the basis of the word of God, this history will not deal with the doctrinal content of the Old Testament and the New Testament in their own terms either. These constitute fields of research unto themselves, and for our purposes the theology of the New Testament is not what Jesus and the apostles may have taught but what the church has understood them to have taught. This is an ongoing process rather than a given product. There are also practical reasons for beginning with the second century, as suggested by the story, probably apocryphal, of the German historian of dogma who each year supplied more and more background material until in his final year of lecturing on *Dogmengeschichte* he concluded the semester with the christology of the Epistle to the Hebrews. Our very insistence on the centrality of biblical exegesis in the development of doctrine makes it unnecessary or undesirable to preface this history with an epitome of New Testament teaching—not because we want to "sneak past" the problem of "kerygma and dogma," but because that problem must be worked out in the development of the Christian tradition. Friedrich Schleiermacher identified the twofold character of the New Testament as "on the one hand, the first member in the series, ever since continued, of presentations of the Christian faith" and as, on the other hand, "the norm for all succeeding

Ath.*Ar.*1–3 (*PG* 26:12–468)

Bornkamm (1948) 6

Wolf (1956) 807

Schleiermacher (1960) 2:288

presentations." For our purposes here—and for the outlook of the men and movements whom we shall be studying—the latter function is the decisive one.

The form which Christian doctrine, so defined, has taken in history is tradition. Like the term "doctrine," the word "tradition" refers simultaneously to the process of communication and to its content. Thus tradition means the handing down of Christian teaching during the course of the history of the church, but it also means that which was handed down. We shall have occasion in this volume to examine the concept of tradition as it was formulated over against ancient heresy, and repeatedly in later volumes we shall be referring to the formal issue of tradition, particularly when it became a matter of doctrinal controversy or a factor in doctrinal development. But we shall be dealing not so much with the formal as the material issue of tradition, that is, with the changes and with the continuities of various Christian doctrines as they shaped history and were shaped by it. Because it is with tradition that we are dealing, we shall be interested not only in change but also in continuity, not only in conflict but also in agreement. The pedigree of heresy—for example, the pre-Christian and extra-Christian history of Gnosticism or even the apparently insoluble debate over whether Paul of Samosata or Lucian of Antioch is to be regarded as the ancestor of Arianism—will not be central to our inquiry. For the same reason, the various theological parties, some of them described by contemporaries and others invented by nineteenth-century historians, will, more often than not, be mentioned only in passing instead of being permitted to determine most of our chapter headings. On the other hand, the history of such questions as the meaning of salvation will receive proportionately more space here than it does in most histories of dogma.

There is a sense in which the very notion of tradition seems inconsistent with the idea of history as movement and change. For tradition is thought to be ancient, hallowed by age, unchanged since it was first established once upon a time. It does not have a history, since history implies the appearance, at a certain point in time, of that which had not been there before. According to the *Ecclesiastical History* of Eusebius, orthodox Christian doctrine did not really have a history, having been true

Eus.*H.e*.1.1.1 (*GCS* 9:6)

Eus.*H.e*.7.30.4; 31.1(*GCS* 9:706; 716)

eternally and taught primitively; only heresy had a history, having arisen at particular times and through the innovations of particular teachers. Roman Catholic polemics has frequently contrasted the variations of Protestantism with the stable and unchanging doctrine of Roman Catholicism. It seems that theologians have been willing to trace the history of doctrines and doctrinal systems which they found to be in error, but that the normative tradition had to be protected from the relativity of having a history or of being, in any decisive sense, the product of a history. In the epigram of Page Smith, it was only when "tradition had lost its authority" that history was "pressed into service."

P. Smith (1964) 55

Upon closer examination, however, the problem of tradition and history is seen to be more complex. Even the most doctrinaire traditionalist must be concerned with such questions as the authenticity of works ascribed to an ecclesiastical writer or of decrees attributed to a council; he must trace the origin and transmission of quotations that appear in the documents of the church; he must investigate the social setting of his texts, to understand the very meaning of the words. All of these are historical assignments, some of them with far more subtle implications than the need of simply checking dates or verifying texts. The history of historical theology as a discipline of study demonstrates that the acceptance of orthodox tradition has not necessarily been incompatible with critical history, even though this acceptance has often led to an anachronistic reading of the history of doctrine. Such a reading accommodated early stages of development to later dogmatic definitions by means of the assumption that what eventually came to be confessed must have been believed, if not taught; that it must have been, as Cardinal Newman said, "really held every-

ap.O.Chadwick (1957) 235

where from the beginning." It is also evident that with the rise of the modern critical method of historical research has come nothing less than a new genetic way of viewing tradition and of making the location in time of a particular doctrinal formulation an essential element in the understanding of that formulation.

The development of Christian doctrine is both an issue in the study of Christian theology—perhaps the most important issue in contemporary Christian thought—and a chapter in intellectual history, and it must be studied by the methods and examined by the criteria of both fields. If it is read only as a branch of theology, as it usually has been, its role in the history of ideas, both as a continuation of pre-Christian lines of development and as a persistent object of intellectual curiosity, may well be subordinated to the interests of a confessional, dogmatic authority or of a speculative, individual system of Christian divinity. If it is read only in the context of the history of ideas, its indispensable setting within the worship, devotion, and exegesis of the Christian community will be sacrificed to a historical treatment anrlogous to that employed by the history of philosophical systems; as Étienne Gilson has noted, "the general tendency among historians of medieval thought seems to have been to imagine the middle ages as peopled by philosophers rather than theologians." But this is to neglect those elements in the history of doctrine which have been, at one and the same time, the most creative and the most reactionary, namely, those that have come from the faith and the life of the church.

Tradition without history has homogenized all the stages of development into one statically defined truth; history without tradition has produced a historicism that relativized the development of Christian doctrine in such a way as to make the distinction between authentic growth and cancerous aberration seem completely arbitrary. In this history we are attempting to avoid the pitfalls of both these methods. The history of Christian doctrine is the most effective means available of exposing the artificial theories of continuity that have often assumed normative status in the churches, and at the same time it is an avenue into the authentic continuity of Christian believing, teaching, and confessing. Tradition is the living faith of the dead; traditionalism is the dead faith of the living.

The very concentration on continuity obliges this history to be sensitive to the processes by which doctrine has or has not moved from being believed to being taught to being confessed and back again, and in the course of its exposition of development to contrast one stage with another. Thus both the variety of Christian teachings within history and their possible unity within tradition are integral to the subject matter of this book, as well as to its theological position. The theological presupposition of this history, a presupposition which is in turn based

Gilson (1957) 156

upon a particular reading of history, is the variety of theologies and the unity of the gospel—the unity as well as the variety, and the unity within the variety. It is based on an acceptance of genuine novelty and change in Christian history and on an affirmation of true development and growth. "Credo unam sanctam catholicam et apostolicam ecclesiam."

1

Praeparatio Evangelica

To interpret the development of doctrine in the ancient church, it is necessary to pay primary attention to the condition and growth of the church's faith and worship, to its exegesis of the Bible, and to its defense of the tradition against heresy; most of this book is based on a study of materials used for such purposes. Yet it would be a mistake to concentrate on these materials so completely as to ignore the relation of the theology of the church to the Jewish thought out of which it came and to the pagan thought which it sought to convert; for when the church confessed what it believed and taught, it did so in answer to attacks from within and from without the Christian movement. The relations of the church fathers to Judaism and to pagan thought affected much of what they had to say about the various doctrinal issues before them. The development of the doctrine of the person of Jesus Christ in relation to the Father must be studied largely on the basis of writings drafted against heresy, against Judaism, and against paganism. In the case of most of the so-called apologists, only writings of these kinds have survived, even though we know that some of them wrote other books addressed specifically to their fellow Christians. We must therefore attempt to determine what they were believing and teaching on the basis of what they confessed.

The risks involved in this procedure are obvious. If the sermon of Paul on the Areopagus were the only surviving scrap of evidence about his teaching, it would be impossible to extrapolate the theology of his epistles from this pericope. The character of the evidence has

Acts 17:22–31

constrained many histories of the development of doctrine
in the first three centuries to rely on such extrapolation,
and hence to underemphasize or even to distort the doctrine being taught within the church of the time. Therefore the discovery of even so slight a tract as the *Paschal
Homily* of Melito of Sardis compels a deeper sensitivity
to the relation between apologetics and proclamation.
There is also reason to believe that while treatises against
heresy and defenses of the faith against Jewish and pagan
thought were written down in order to be circulated,
among the faithful and perhaps among the gainsayers,
much of the positive instruction of the people was confined to oral presentation. Even though the written sources
in their present state do not always make this explicit,
many of the same fathers carried on the apologetic and
the expository and the polemical responsibilities of
theology at the same time. The apologetic work of those
fathers is an important key—in the case of so decisive a
figure as Justin Martyr, the only key we have left—to how
they thought about the faith and doctrine of the church.

In addition, the relation of Christian doctrine to Jewish
and to pagan thought is a subject worthy of investigation
for its own sake. The very legitimacy of the development
of Christian dogma has been challenged on the grounds
of its supposed hellenization of the primitive message;
the contrast between Greek and Hebrew ways of thought
has been used to explain the distinctiveness of Christian
doctrine. These are only modern versions of an ancient
debate. The early church as a community and its theologians were obliged to clarify, for friend and foe alike,
how the gospel was related to its preparations and antic-
ipations in the nation where it arose as well as in the
nations to which it was being borne.

The True Israel

According to tradition, only one of the writers of the
New Testament, Luke, was not a Jew. As far as we know,
none of the church fathers was a Jew, although both
Hermas and Hegesippus, for example, may have been;
Justin Martyr was born in Samaria but was a Gentile.
The transition represented by this contrast had the most
far-reaching of consequences for the entire development
of Christian doctrine.

Iren.*Haer*.4.34.2 (Harvey 2:270)

Matt.5:17
Tert.*Marc*.4.7.4; 4.9.15; 4.12.14 (*CCSL* 1:554; 561; 571)
Tert.*Marc*.5.14.14 (*CCSL* 1:708); *Act.Archel*.40 (*PG* 10: 1492–93)

Iren.*Haer*.3.12.5 (Harvey 2:58)

Stauffer (1952) 193–214

Just.*Dial*.47.2 (Goodspeed 145)

Acts 6–7

Aug.*Ep*.82.4–22 (*CSEL* 34—II: 355–75)
See pp. 79, 112–13 below

Acts 15:6—21

The earliest Christians were Jews, and in their new faith they found a continuity with the old. They remembered that their Lord himself had said that his purpose was to fulfill, not to abolish, the law and the prophets; and it was useless for heretics to deny this saying. From the early chapters of the Book of Acts we get a somewhat idealized picture of a Christian community that continued to follow the Scriptures, the worship, and the observances of Jewish religious life. The members of the church at Jerusalem, which Irenaeus called "the church from which every church took its start, the capital city [μητρόπολις] of the citizens of the new covenant," followed James, who, as "the brother of the Lord," was a kind of "caliph," in refusing to acknowledge a fundamental cleavage between their previous life and their new status. Clearly, they recognized that something new had come—not something brand-new, but something newly restored and fulfilled. Even after the fall of Jerusalem in A.D. 70, these "Nazarenes" maintained continuity with Judaism; they "wish to observe the ordinances which were given by Moses . . . yet choose to live with the Christians and the faithful." But especially in the period before A.D. 70, the tensions within Jewish thought were reflected also in the beginnings of Christian theology. The party headed by James manifested significant analogies with Palestinian Judaism, while the missionary party which eventually came to be identified with Paul, as well as the Christian apologetics of the second century, reflected certain affinities with the Jewish thought of the Hellenistic diaspora.

More fundamental than these parallels, however, is the conflict between Hellenistic Jews and Hellenistic Jewish-Christians over the question of the continuity of Christianity with Judaism. After A.D. 70 that conflict marked the relations between Christian and Jewish thought everywhere. The extent and the scope of the continuity produced controversy between Peter and Paul, and this controversy went on troubling the church. Various practical solutions were designed to meet immediate problems of cultic and dietary observance, but these did not issue in a consistent way of interpreting the theological question: What is new about the new covenant? Whatever else they may mean, the differences between the way this question was answered in Acts 15 (with its crucial

Gal.2:11–14

Rom.9:1–5

ap.Or.*Cels*.6.78 (*GCS* 3:149);
Or.*Cels*.5.50 (*GCS* 3:55)

Cochrane (1944) 266
Jul.*Gal*.43A (*LCL* 3:320)

See pp. 77–78 below

Barn.14.3–4 (Bihlmeyer 27–28)

Tert.*Marc*.5.20.2 (*CCSL* 1:724)

Rom.4:11
Aug.*Civ*.15.1 (*CCSL* 48:453–54)

textual variants) and the way Paul discussed it in Galatians do suggest the continuing difficulty which the church faced. The leaders of both sides were Christians of Jewish origin; despite their differing answers, they asked the question of continuity between Judaism and Christianity with a deep personal poignancy.

As converts began coming more from pagan than from Jewish ranks, the poignancy lessened and the obverse side of the question became more prominent. For Jewish Christians, the question of continuity was the question of their relation to their mother; for Gentile Christians, it was the question of their relation to their mother-in-law. What was offensive about Christianity in the eyes of Gentiles was, to a considerable extent, what it had inherited from Judaism. Celsus and other pagan critics ridiculed the claim that God had put in an appearance at, of all places, "some corner of Judea somewhere"; and the emperor Julian scored the Jewish and Christian conception of God as "essentially the deity of a primitive and uncivilized folk," even while he chided the "Galileans" for forsaking Judaism. Not only the Gentile critics of Christianity, but also the Gentile converts to Christianity demanded a decision about just how much of the Jewish tradition they were obliged to retain. The attitude of Marcion was a heretical instance of what may have been a rather widespread resentment also among orthodox believers; for the *Epistle of Barnabas,* while not going as far as Marcion in its rejection of the Old Testament, did claim that the original tablets of the covenant of the Lord were shattered at Sinai and that Israel had never had an authentic covenant with God. Tertullian's declaration, in opposition to Marcion, that "today" there were more who accepted the authority of the Old Testament than rejected it raises the question of whether the number of those rejecting it may not at one time have been considerable.

This struggle over the authority of the Old Testament and over the nature of the continuity between Judaism and Christianity was the earliest form of the quest for a tradition that has, in other forms, recurred throughout Christian history. The Christian adoption of Abraham as "father of the faithful" and the Christian identification of the church, the city of God, with the heritage of Abel are illustrations of this quest. When the church formu-

Eus.*H.e.*1.4.6 (*GCS* 9:40);
Aug.*Pel.*3.4.11 (*CSEL* 60:497–
98)

lated its quest for a tradition in a doctrine of correction-
and-fulfillment, it was enabled to claim as its own all the
saints and believers back to Abraham and even to Adam.
That doctrine of correction-and-fulfillment likewise
helped to set a pattern for the treatment of the problem
of tradition in subsequent centuries. Athanasius could
claim to have the tradition on his side despite the heretical-

Ath.*Dion.*14 (Opitz 2–I:56)

sounding language of many of the fathers; Augustine
could seek to exonerate the Greek fathers of the charges

See p. 280 below

See p. 330 below

of Pelagianism; the orthodox opponents of Gottschalk
in the ninth century could seek to exonerate Augustine
in turn; the arguments between the Greek East and the
Latin West turned on the testimony of tradition; and the
Protestant Reformers could affirm their loyalty to the
catholic tradition despite their separation from Rome. All
these arguments followed the outline of the appropriation
of the Jewish tradition by the Christians of the first and
second centuries.

Primary evidence for the development of that appropriation is a genre of Christian literature devoted
to a comparison of Christianity with Judaism. Within
this genre "there is no dialogue . . . which is conducted

A.L.Williams (1935) 42

on quite so high a level of courteousness and fairness" in
the early church as the *Dialogue with Trypho* of Justin
Martyr; and Justin's treatise was only one of many. Virtually every major Christian writer of the first five centuries either composed a treatise in opposition to Judaism
or made this issue a dominant theme in a treatise devoted
to some other subject. Scholars are generally agreed that
Justin's work represented the literary form of an actual
interview, but that it was composed many years after the
fact and reflected the author's hindsight on the debate.
But it is equally clear that many of the later treatises
"adversus Judaeos" neither reflected nor envisaged such
interviews. Rather, the dialogue with Judaism became a
literary conceit, in which the question of the uniqueness
of Christianity in comparison with Judaism became an
occasion for a literary exposition of Christian doctrine
for a non-Jewish audience of Christian readers. When,
for example, Peter Abelard wrote his *Dialogue between*

PL 178:1611–82

a Philosopher, a Jew, and a Christian, he may have incorporated some of the subjects still being treated in face-
to-face encounters between Jews and Christians, for these
were probably more frequent, even in the twelfth cen-

tury, than the textbooks usually suggest. But Abelard primary purpose was a dialectical one; he was writin to make Christians think, not to make philosophers c Jews accept Christianity.

Comparison of the treatises against the Jews from the first three centuries has disclosed the recurrence of certain biblical passages and conflations of biblical passages, certain historical references, and certain forms of argumentation. Thus, early in the twentieth century, the discovery of the long-lost text of the *Proof of the Apostolic Preaching* of Irenaeus in an Armenian version provided additional support for the theory that there existed a compilation "of Scriptural texts grouped under argument-headings, intended to convince the Jews out of the Old Testament itself that the Old Law was abolished, that its abolition was foreseen in the Old Testament, and that its purpose had been to prepare and

J.Smith (1952) 31

prefigure the New Law of Christ." This commonplace in Christian literature, aimed at demonstrating that the church had now become the new and the true Israel, may well have antedated the Gospels themselves. From the traditional title of such treatises as Cyprian's *To Quirinus: Three Books of Testimonies against the Jews,* this set of commonplaces has acquired the title "testimonies." The literature of the dialogue with Judaism provides important data about the developing self-understanding of Christian theology, as well as about its understanding of the differences between Christianity and Judaism.

Cypr.*Test.* (CSEL 3:35–184)

A prominent element in this literature of the dialogue was, inevitably, the issue of the continuing validity of the Mosaic law. The Old Testament had declared that the law was as permanent as the covenant with Israel; but the

Cypr.*Test.*2.1 (CSEL 3:63)

Just.*Dial.*10.4 (Goodspeed 102)

Christians, "treating this covenant with rash contempt, spurn the responsibilities that come with it." This appeared to Jewish thought to be a repudiation of both the law and the covenant. Justin replied to Trypho's charge by, in effect, stratifying the Old Testament law. The Christians retained whatever in the law of Moses was "naturally good, pious, and righteous"—usually

Just.*Dial.*45.3 (Goodspeed 142)

whatever conformed to a reductionistic conception of the natural law. Even among Jews, Christians insisted, the law of nature took precedence over the law of Moses, as for example when a woman gave birth to a child on the Sabbath. This implied that "the providence which long ago

Amph.*Mesopent.* (PG 39:121)

gave the law [of Moses], but now has given the gospel of Jesus Christ, did not wish that the practices of the Jews should continue." Christians were not bound by anything that had been addressed to the old Israel as a people. Such a stratification of moral, civil, and ceremonial elements in the Mosaic law proved very difficult to maintain with any consistency, and the fathers could not make it stick. Irenaeus, for example, celebrated the superiority of Christian doctrine and life to all of the law, including the Decalogue, even though he also affirmed that "the words of the Decalogue" had undergone "extension and amplification" rather than "cancellation" by Christ's coming in the flesh.

A more effective way than stratification for coping with the law of the Old Testament was provided by allegorical and typological exegesis. Here again the *Epistle of Barnabas* went further than most. To the question "Is there not a commandment from God which forbids the eating" of ceremonially unclean animals, it replied: "Yes, there is, but Moses was speaking in spiritual terms." The same was true of the circumcision of Abraham. Less drastic in his spiritualization of the Old Testament commandments, Tertullian argued that a "new law" and a "new circumcision" had replaced the old, which had been intended only as a sign or type of what was to come. Drawing directly on sources in Hellenistic Judaism, Origen put his interpretation of the Mosaic law into the context of an allegory on the exodus from Egypt; "with Origen the allegory of Philo [on the life of Moses and the exodus] will be incorporated into Christian tradition, and become part of the traditional typology." A special feature of the typology of the exodus was the anticipation of baptism by the miracle of the Red Sea; baptism was, in turn, set in opposition to the circumcision of the Old Testament. It is certainly an exaggeration to say that "by transforming the Gospel into a New Law the Apostolic Fathers returned to the impossible situation" of man without Christ, for the term "new law" and related terms such as "under the law of Christ [Χριστόνομος]" were not devoid of the evangelical content which "law" sometimes bears in the usage of the New Testament. At the same time it is evident that as moralism and legalism manifested themselves in Christian theology, much of the edge was removed from the argument of Christian apologetics against

Or.*Cels*.7.26 (*GCS* 3:177)

Iren.*Dem*.96 (*ACW* 16:106)

Iren.*Haer*.4.16.4 (Harvey 2:191–92)

Barn.10.2 (Bihlmeyer 21–22)
Barn.9.7 (Bihlmeyer 21)

Tert.*Jud*.3.8 (*CCSL* 2:1346)

Daniélou (1960) 219

Just.*Dial*.29.1 (Goodspeed 123)

Torrance (1959) 134

Ign.*Rom*.inscr. (Bihlmeyer 97)

Rom.3:27

what was taken to be the "Pharisaical" conception of the law.

Although the law and the prophets belonged together in the language of Jewish theology, Christian theology identified its cause with that of the prophets against the law. Ignatius argued that the prophets had observed Sunday rather than the Jewish Sabbath. Christian apologetics was even more assiduous in looking for proofs that Jesus was the fulfillment of the prophetic promises than it was in finding indications that he was the "end of the law." The beginnings of this process are evident already in the New Testament, especially, of course, in books such as the Gospel of Matthew and the Epistle to the Hebrews, but also in the Gospel of Luke, the one New Testament writer who has traditionally been identified as a Greek; it is in this Gospel that the risen Christ "beginning with Moses and all the prophets interpreted to them in all the [Old Testament] Scriptures the things concerning himself." The New Testament formula "that the Scripture might be fulfilled" may sometimes refer to a result rather than a purpose, but the translation "in order that [by divine decree] it might be fulfilled" suggests that the precise distinction between purpose and result is not really applicable. Irenaeus summarized the teaching of the New Testament and of early Christian tradition generally when he declared: "That all these things would come to pass was foretold by the Spirit of God through the prophets, that those who served God in truth might believe firmly in them."

The two purposes of the testimonies were: to show that Judaism, with its laws, had had its day; and to prove that "he who had been foretold has come, in accordance with the Scriptures" of the Old Testament. To this end the testimonies compiled those passages that were most readily applicable to Jesus as the Christ. The rebellion of the nations against Yahweh, as described in Psalm 2, was fulfilled in the suffering of Christ: "The heathen were Pilate and the Romans; the people were the tribes of Israel; the kings were represented in Herod, and the rulers in the chief priests." The psalms that spoke of enthronement could be applied to the resurrection of Christ, by which he had been elevated to the status of lordship; already in the New Testament, Psalm 110 was a favorite proof text for this claim. The other favorite proof text

Ign.*Mag*.9.1 (Bihlmeyer 91)

Rom.10:4

Luke 24:27

Funk (1961) 198

Iren.*Dem*.42 (*ACW* 16:75)

Cypr.*Test*.pr. (*CSEL* 3:36)

Tert.*Marc*.4.42.2 (*CCSL* 1:659)

Acts 2:34–35; Just.*Dial*.32.6 (Goodspeed 127)

Acts 8:30–35

Or.*Cels*.1.55 (*GCS* 2:106)

Just.*Dial*.89.3 (Goodspeed 203–4)

Just.*Dial*.49.2 (Goodspeed 147); Tert.*Apol*.21.15 (*CCSL* 1:125); Or.*Cels*.1.56 (*GCS* 2:107); Clem.*Recogn*.1.49.2–5 (*GCS* 51:36); Lact.*Inst*. 4.12.14–15 (*CSEL* 19:313)

Tert.*Marc*.3.7.1–4 (*CCSL* 1:516–17)

Just.*Dial*.29.2 (Goodspeed 123)

Just.*Dial*.71.2 (Goodspeed 181)
Just.*Dial*.66–67 (Goodspeed 173–74)

Matt.1:23

Barn.5.13 (Bihlmeyer 16); Iren.*Dem*.79 (*ACW* 16:97); Cypr.*Test*.2.20 (*CSEL* 3:87)

Just.*Dial*.97.4 (Goodspeed 212)

was the description of the suffering servant in Isaiah 53. The rabbis who disputed with Origen contended that it "referred to the whole people [of Israel] as though a single individual," but the text was interpreted so unanimously and unambiguously as Christian Scripture that even Trypho was constrained to admit that the Messiah was to suffer, though not that he was to be crucified. The "coming of the Lord" in later Jewish prophecy and apocalyptic also referred to Jesus as the Christ; but now it had to be divided into two comings, the first already accomplished in the days of his flesh and the second still in the future. Beyond the difference between humiliation and glory it was not always clear what the basis was for this division, which neither Judaism nor the anti-Judaistic Marcionites would accept. The assurance with which this interpretation was set forth indicates that Christian doctrine took the christological meaning of these passages for granted.

What the Christian tradition had done was to take over the Jewish Scriptures as its own, so that Justin could say to Trypho that the passages about Christ "are contained in your Scriptures, or rather not yours, but ours." As a matter of fact, some of the passages were contained only in "ours," that is, in the Christian Old Testament. So assured were Christian theologians in their possession of the Scriptures that they could accuse the Jews not merely of misunderstanding and misinterpreting them, but even of falsifying scriptural texts. When they were aware of differences between the Hebrew text of the Old Testament and the Septuagint, they capitalized on these to prove their accusation that the Jews had "taken away many Scripture passages from the translations carried out by the seventy elders." Of special importance was the Septuagint translation "virgin [$\pi\alpha\rho\theta\acute{\epsilon}\nu\sigma\varsigma$]" in Isaiah 7:14, which had been adopted by the New Testament and was canonized by early Christian writers. In Psalm 22:16 there may have been two Hebrew readings transmitted in the Jewish tradition: "they have pierced my hands and my feet" and "like a lion are my hands and my feet." Christian teachers, following the Septuagint, read "pierced" and applied this verse, together with the entire psalm, to the crucifixion; their Jewish opponents "maintain that this psalm does not refer to the Messiah."

In addition to these variant readings and canonized

Daniélou (1964) 88–107

Ps.96:10; Ven.Fort.*Carm*.2.7
(*PL* 88:96)
Just.*Dial*.73.1 (Goodspeed
182); Just.*1 Apol*.41.4 (Goodspeed 55)

Eus.*H.e*.1.11.7–8 (*GCS*
9:78–80); Hier.*Jovin*.1.39 (*PL*
23:265)

Eus.*H.e*.2.7–8 (*GCS* 9:144)

Matt.23:15

translations there developed a group of Christian additions to the text of the Septuagint or, as Daniélou has
termed them, Christian targumin and midrashim, which
paraphrased and expanded passages from the Old Testament in ways that substantiated Christian doctrine. Justin
Martyr accused the Jews of mutilating the passage "The
Lord reigned from the tree," to delete the obvious reference to the crucifixion of Christ. The Christian exegetical
tradition claimed to find other such deletions and mutila-
tions in the Jewish tradition of interpretation. It was perhaps a part of the same process of appropriation when the
Christian historian Eusebius ascribed to the Jewish historian Josephus a paragraph confessing the messiahship
and the divinity of Jesus; or when the same Christian
writer supposed that Philo's *On the Contemplative Life*
was describing the early Christians rather than a community of Jewish ascetics. The growing ease with which
appropriations and accusations alike could be made was in
proportion to the completeness of the Christian victory
over Jewish thought.

Yet that victory was achieved largely by default. Not
the superior force of Christian exegesis or learning or
logic but the movement of Jewish history seems to have
been largely responsible for it. It has been suggested that
by its rise the Christian movement deprived Judaism of
some of its earlier dynamic, especially of the proselyting
zeal that had marked Jewish thought in the Hellenistic
diaspora and even in Palestine, where Jews were said to
"traverse sea and land to make a single proselyte." There
were several translations of the Hebrew Bible into Greek
by Jews (as well as perhaps one or more by Christians).
By the end of the second and the beginning of the third
century of the Christian era, when Latin gradually began
to displace Greek in the western part of the Roman Empire, the situation within Judaism itself had changed.
The Septuagint seems to have been called forth by the
inability of younger Jews in the diaspora to read Hebrew
and by the desire to present the case for Judaism to the
Greek-speaking world. But it seems that neither of these
factors produced any translation of the Old Testament
into Latin by a Jew; when the Hebrew Bible began to
come out in Latin versions, these appear to have been
the work of anonymous Christian translators and finally
of Jerome. After the sack of Jerusalem in A.D. 70 and its

desecration during the following years, Jewish polemic against Christianity was increasingly on the defensive, while Christian doctrine felt able to go its own way, without engaging the rabbis in a continuing dialogue.

Or.*Cels*.1.55; 2.31 (*GCS* 2:106; 159)

Hier.*Vir.ill*.54 (*TU* 14–IA:32–33)

Eus. *H.e*.6.16.1 (*GCS* 9:552–54)

Hier.*Rufin*.3.6 (*PL* 23:462)

Aug. *Pecc.merit*.3.6.12 (*CSEL* 60:138–39)

Didym.*Trin*.1.18 (*PG* 39:345); Didym.*Spir*.15 (*PG* 39:1047)

Origen seems to have been one of the few church fathers to participate in such a dialogue. Origen may also have been the first church father to study Hebrew, "in opposition to the spirit of his time and of his people," as Jerome says; according to Eusebius, he "learned it thoroughly," but there is reason to doubt the accuracy of this report. Jerome, however, was rightly celebrated as "a trilingual man" for his competence in Latin, Greek, and Hebrew, and Augustine clearly admired, perhaps even envied, his ability to "interpret the divine Scriptures in both languages." The testimony about the knowledge of Hebrew by other church fathers—for example, Didymus the Blind or Theodore of Mopsuestia—is less conclusive. But it seems safe to propose the generalization that, except for converts from Judaism, it was not until the biblical humanists and the Reformers of the sixteenth century that a knowledge of Hebrew became standard equipment for Christian expositors of the Old Testament. Most of Christian doctrine developed in a church uninformed by any knowledge of the original text of the Hebrew Bible.

Whatever the reasons, Christian theologians writing against Judaism seemed to take their opponents less and less seriously as time went on; and what their apologetic works may have lacked in vigor or fairness, they tended to make up in self-confidence. They no longer looked upon the Jewish community as a continuing participant in the holy history that had produced the church. They no longer gave serious consideration to the Jewish interpretation of the Old Testament or to the Jewish background of the New. Therefore the urgency and the poignancy about the mystery of Israel that are so vivid in the New Testament have appeared only occasionally in Christian thought, as in some passages in Augustine; but these are outweighed, even in Augustine, by the many others that speak of Judaism and paganism almost as though they were equally alien to "the people of God"—the church of Gentile Christians.

Aug.*Ps*.94.7 (*CCSL* 39:1336–37)

Aug.*Ev.Joh*.16.3 (*CCSL* 36:166–67)

Dix (1953) 109

But the "de-Judaization of Christianity" was not expressed only by the place accorded to Judaism by Christian theologians. A more subtle and more pervasive effect of this process is evident in the development of various Christian doctrines themselves. Among these, the doctrine of God and the doctrine of man bear marks of de-Judaization. In Judaism it was possible simultaneously

1 Sam.15:11

1 Sam.15:29

to ascribe change of purpose to God and to declare that God did not change, without resolving the paradox; for the immutability of God was seen as the trustworthiness of his covenanted relation to his people in the concrete history of his judgment and mercy, rather than as a primarily ontological category. But in the development of the Christian doctrine of God, immutability assumed the status of an axiomatic presupposition for the discussion of other doctrines. Hence the de-Judaization of Christian thought contributed, for example, to the form taken by the christological controversy, in which both sides defined the absoluteness of God in accordance with the principle of immutability even though they drew opposite christo-

See pp. 229–32 below

logical conclusions from it.

Similarly, the course taken by the development of the Augustinian tradition has been affected by the loss of contact with Jewish thought, whose refusal to polarize the free sovereignty of God and the free will of man has frequently been labeled Pelagian. But the label is not appropriate, for Judaism has a Pelagian doctrine of nature but an Augustinian doctrine of grace. Augustine accused the Pelagians of "putting the New Testament on the same level with the Old" by their view that it was possible for

Aug.Gest.Pelag.5.15 (CSEL 42:67)

Hier.Pelag.3.14; 16 (PL 23:583; 586)

man to keep the law of God, and Jerome saw Pharisaism in the Pelagian notion that perfect righteousness was attainable within man's life here on earth. The development of Christian theology in the East, especially in the Antiochene school, manifested other ways of transcending the antitheses prevalent in the West and of setting forth "a doctrine which cannot properly be called either

Norris (1963) 186

Augustinian or Pelagian." But it, too, formulated the question in a manner alien to the Jewish tradition, even as it sought to find the answer for the question in the Jewish Bible.

Because the victory of Christian theology over Jewish thought came more by default than by conquest, the question of the relation between the two covenants has returned over and over to claim Christian attention. The significance of Jewish thinkers for Christian theologians —for example, of Moses Maimonides for Thomas Aqui-

nas, of Spinoza for Friedrich Schleiermacher, or of Martin
Buber for both Protestant and Roman Catholic theology
in the twentieth century—is not simply part of the continuing interaction between theological and secular
thought. In spite of the philosophical cast of these Jewish
thinkers, Christian theologians have hearkened to them
more as relatives than as strangers. At the same time, the
less philosophical and more biblical elements of the Jewish theological tradition have failed to play a similar role
in Christian history. But whenever individual theologians
have seemed to be going too far in their denigration of
the Old Testament, as Marcion in the second century and
biblical criticism in the nineteenth century did, they were
denounced for relegating the larger part of the Christian
Bible to a sub-Christian status. One of the most reliable
indices of the interpretation of Judaism in Christian
thought is the exegesis of Romans 9–11. The history of
this exegesis is the record of the church's struggle to give
theological structure to its intuitions regarding the relation between the covenants, or to reestablish the sense of
continuity-with-discontinuity evident in the language of
the New Testament about Israel as the chosen people.
Repeatedly, therefore, we shall be turning to this exegesis,
as well as to the doctrinal implications of the litanies and
collects of the church, which sometimes preserved such
a sense more faithfully than did its formal dogmatics.

It was apparently from Jewish sectarianism that some
of the earliest forms of Christian heresy came. According
to Irenaeus, "all the heresies are derived from Simon of

Iren.*Haer*.1.23.2 (Harvey
1:191)

Samaria," and one of the oldest catalogs of Christian
heretics, that of Hegesippus as preserved by Eusebius,
listed Simon first among those who came from "the
seven sects among the [Jewish] people" to "corrupt

ap.Eus.*H.e*.4.22.5 (*GCS*
9:370)

[the church] by vain teachings." Eusebius himself termed

Eus.*H.e*.2.13.6 (*GCS* 9:136)

Simon "the prime author of every kind of heresy" and
identified him with the Simon of Acts 8:9–25. Cyril of

Cyr.H.*Catech*.6.14 (Reischl-
Rupp 1:174)

Jerusalem, too, called him "the inventor of all heresy."
But the primary source of information about the heresy
of Simon is Justin Martyr, himself a native of Samaria.
According to Justin, Simon was acknowledged by his ad-
herents "as the First God," and they said that a certain
"Helen . . . was the First Thought which he brought into

Just. *1 Apol*.26.3 (Goodspeed
43)

existence." The concept of the First Thought seems to
have been derived at least partly from Jewish speculations

R.Grant (1959) 92

about the personal Wisdom of God. "Simonian gnosis arose out of Judaeo-Samaritan sectarianism," and through it contributed to the beginnings also of Christian Gnosticism. Like other forms of Gnosticism, Simonianism was radically pessimistic in its view of the created world, apparently carrying the implication of the doctrine of the two spirits in the Dead Sea Scrolls all the way to the point of an ontological dualism.

Not all the heretical forms of Jewish Christianity, however, manifested this dualism. Irenaeus reported that "those who are called Ebionites agree [with Jewish and Christian orthodoxy] that the universe was made by God." Where they diverged from Christian orthodoxy was in their view of Christ. According to Origen, there were "two sects of Ebionites, the one confessing as we do that Jesus was born of a virgin, the other holding that he was not born in this way but like other men." The first of these sects seems to have been made up of the orthodox Christians of Jewish origin mentioned earlier, who continued to observe the regulations of the Mosaic law even after they had accepted the messiahship and divine sonship of Jesus; it seems likely that they were identical with the "Nazarenes." The second group of Ebionites taught that though born as other men are, Jesus was elected to be the Son of God, and that at his baptism Christ, an archangel, descended on him, as he had on Adam, Moses, and other prophets. Jesus, too, was no more than the "true prophet." The distinction between Jesus and Christ was also used by Cerinthus and was to figure in various Gnostic Christian systems, but among the Ebionites it seems to have reflected Essene teaching. In addition, the heretical Ebionites "use the Gospel according to Matthew only, and repudiate the apostle Paul, maintaining that he was an apostate from the law." Their name seems to have been derived, not, as some of the fathers thought, from a founder called Ebion, but from the Hebrew word for "poor." The Ebionites may have been those descendants of the Essenes who remained Christian after the year 70. Like the Ebionites, the Elkesaites regarded Jesus as "a man like every other man" and as one of the prophets; to this extent they, too, bear marks of the heretical forms of Jewish Christianity.

Perhaps the most important implication of the Dead Sea Scrolls for the history of the development of Chris-

Iren.Haer.1.26.2 (Harvey 1:212)

Or.Cels.5.61 (GCS 3:65)

Epiph.Haer.30.16.3–4 (GCS 25:353–54)
Iren.Haer.1.26.1 (Harvey 1:211)

Iren.Haer.1.26.2 (Harvey 1:213); Tert.Praescrip.33.5 (CCSL 1:214)

Tert.Carn.14.5 (CCSL 2:900)

Hipp.Haer.9.14.1 (GCS 26:252)

tian doctrine after the New Testament is the clarification
of connections between sectarian Judaism and the beginnings of heretical Christianity. With the help of such
additional sources, the less familiar aspects of the Jewish
heritage of early Christian teaching are being illumined,
and it is becoming possible to check more accurately the
various reports of the fathers about the influence of heretical Jewish ideas upon heretical Christian theology. There
were also influences in the opposite direction, as Manda-
ism and other heretical species of Judaism absorbed elements of Christian heresy; and so it came about that both
Jewish and Christian heresy contributed to the origins of
Islam.

Within the mainstream of orthodox Christianity, however, the Jewish heritage remained visible in other ways.
The growth of the cultic, hierarchical, and ethical structures of Christianity led to the Christianization of many
features of Judaism. While much of that growth does not
belong directly to the history of the development of doctrine, it is important because of this "re-Judaization" of
Christianity. Justin argued that one of the differences between the old covenant and the new was that the priesthood had been superseded and "we [the church as a
whole] are the true high-priestly race of God." In the
New Testament itself the concept of "priest" referred
either to the Levites of the Old Testament, now made
obsolete, or to Christ or to the entire church—not to the
ordained ministry of the church. But Clement, who was
also the first to use the term "layman [λαικός]," already
spoke of "priests" and of "the high priest" and significantly related these terms to the Levitical priesthood; a
similar parallel occurred in the *Didache* and in Hippolytus. For Tertullian, the bishop was already "the high
priest," and for his disciple, Cyprian, it was completely
natural to speak of a Christian "priesthood." And so by
the time of Chrysostom's treatise *On the Priesthood* it
seems to have become accepted practice to refer to Aaron
and Eli as examples and warnings for the priesthood of
the Christian church. Chrysostom also spoke of "the Lord
being sacrificed and laid upon the altar and the priest
standing and praying over the victim," summarizing the
sacrificial language about the Eucharist which had also
become accepted practice. Therefore the apostles, too,
were represented as priests.

Just.*Dial*.116.3 (Goodspeed 234)

1 Clem.40.5 (Bihlmeyer 57)

1 Clem.32.2; 40.5 (Bihlmeyer 52; 57)
Did.13.3 (Bihlmeyer 7);
Hipp.*Trad.ap*.3 (*SC* 11:28)
Tert.*Bapt*.17.1 (*CCSL* 1:291)

Cypr.*Ep*.63.19 (*CSEL* 3:716)

Chrys.*Sac*.4.1.357 (Nairn 101)

Chrys.*Sac*.3.4.177 (Nairn 52)

Epiph.*Haer*.29.4.4 (*GCS* 25:324)

But this re-Judaization does not indicate any recovery of close association between Judaism and Christian theology; on the contrary, it shows how independent Christian doctrine had become of its Jewish origins and how free it felt to appropriate terms and concepts from the Jewish tradition despite its earlier disparagement of them. Now that Christian theologians were no longer obliged to engage in serious dialogue with Judaism, they were able to go their own Christian way in formulating the universal claims of Christianity. Not only the Jewish Scriptures and the Levitical priesthood, but other prerogatives and claims of the chosen people were consistently transferred to the church—a practice which was both an index to and a cause of the isolation of Gentile Christian thought from the Judaism contemporary with itself as well as from the Jewish Christianity out of which it had originally come.

The church, therefore, was the inheritor of the promises and prerogatives of the Jews. "Just as Christ is Israel and Jacob, so we who have been quarried out from the bowels of Christ are the true Israelitic race," the "third Israel" spoken of in Isaiah. Likewise, the church was now "the synagogue of God," "those who believe in" Christ having become "one soul, and one synagogue, and one church." Not the old Israel, but the church had the right to call Abraham its father, to style itself "the chosen people," and to look forward to inheriting the promised land. No title for the church in early Christianity is more comprehensive than the term "the people of God," which originally meant "the new Israel" but gradually lost this connotation as the Christian claim to be the only true people of God no longer had to be substantiated.

This appropriation of the Jewish Scriptures and of the heritage of Israel helped Christianity to survive the destruction of Jerusalem and to argue that with the coming of Christ Jerusalem had served its purpose in the divine plan and could be forsaken. It also enabled Christianity to claim an affinity with the non-Jewish tradition as well as with the Jewish and to formulate such doctrines as the Trinity on a more inclusive basis than that provided by Jewish monotheism alone. These and other advantages were cited by the defenders of Christianity against Judaism; they did not usually mention, even though they often exhibited, the impoverishment that came from the suppo-

Just.*Dial*.135.3 (Goodspeed 257)
Just.*Dial*.123.5 (Goodspeed 243)
Iren.*Haer*.3.6.1 (Harvey 2:22)

Just.*Dial*.63.5 (Goodspeed 169)

Just.*Dial*.119.5 (Goodspeed 238)

Iren.*Haer*.4.4.1 (Harvey 2:151–52)

See pp. 66–67 below

sition that in the Old Testament and in the Jewish elements of the New Testament the Christian church had as much of the tradition of Judaism as it would ever need.

The Christian Dispute with Classical Thought

The apologetic war of the early church was fought simultaneously on two fronts, for the theologians also addressed themselves critically to the other chief component of their thought world, classicism. For their dispute with Judaism they had extensive precedents in the New Testament, where most of the arguments had appeared, at least in seminal form. But the audience to which Christian thought was directed increasingly, and then almost exclusively, during the second and third centuries was one to which very little of the New Testament had been addressed. Except for fragmentary reports like those in Acts 14:15–17 and 17:22–31 and discussions such as that in Romans 1:19–2:16, theologians had almost no biblical precedent for their apologetic to pagan thought. Therefore these few passages from the New Testament have been called upon to provide the apologetic enterprise in every age with some sort of biblical justification for its work. Faced with this situation, the defenders of Christianity could take the Apocalypse of John as their model and repudiate pagan thought with all its works and all its ways, just as they unanimously repudiated the imperial cult; or they could seek out, within classicism, analogies to the continuity-discontinuity which all of them found in Judaism. The theologians of the second and third centuries combined these two emphases, but in varying proportions.

This they did in a series of apologetic treatises, the most comprehensive and profound of which was *Against Celsus* by Origen. Some of the elements in the Christian self-defense and self-definition against Judaism also provided ammunition for the theologians who sought to define similarities and differences between the Christian faith and classical thought. But in other respects the two apologetic cases were radically different, and the Christian writers against paganism took over arguments that had been standard in the apologias for Judaism, as well as other arguments from Greek philosophers. Here again, Justin is important not only for the intrinsic value of his treatises in interpreting the apologetic conflict of the early church, but also for the insights his works provide into the relation between the two fronts of that conflict. The earliest apology for Christianity (that of Quadratus), the most brilliant apology (that of Origen), and the most learned apology (that of Eusebius) were all written in Greek; nevertheless, the Latin writers "Tertullian, Lactantius, and Augustine outweigh all the Greek apologists." We shall, of course, draw upon both bodies of apologetic literature in this interpretation.

Much of the attack from pagan classicism, and therefore much of the defense from Christianity, was not principally doctrinal in nature. In the correspondence between Pliny and Trajan, and in much of the apologetic literature to follow until the tracts of the emperor Julian, two of the charges that constantly recurred were those of encouraging civil disobedience and of practicing immorality. But in the midst of arguments about these charges, which are not of direct concern to us, doctrinal issues continually arose. For example, one of the most widespread calumnies against the Christians was the charge, "most impious and barbarous of all, that we eat human flesh" or "loaves steeped in blood." The basis of this accusation was the language used by Christians about the Eucharist, for they seem to have spoken about the presence of the body and blood of Christ so realistically as to suggest a literal cannibalism. In the midst of rather meager and ambiguous evidence about the doctrine of the real presence in the second and third centuries and well beyond that period, these slanders would seem to be an important source of information in support of the existence of such a doctrine; but it is also important to note that the fathers, in defending themselves, did not elaborate a doctrine of the real presence.

One doctrinal element in the pagan attack was the claim that the Christians taught absurd myths. The theogonies of Hesiod and the tales of Homer had gradually been allegorized and spiritualized by the leaders of classical thought, who "ennobled what is base," until they were able to speak of "the divine" (neuter) and of "being" in language that only rarely betrayed the ancestry of their ideas in classical Greek and Roman mythology. This process of refinement and spiritualization, in which Socrates and others had been martyred for their criticism of the mythical picture of the gods, had largely accomplished

Geffcken (1907) 277

Plin.*Ep*.10.96–97

Theoph.*Autol*.3.4 (*SC* 20:212)
Tert.*Nat*.1.7.10 (*CCSL* 1:18)

See pp. 166–68 below
See pp. 304–6, 356 below

Arnob.*Nat*.5.43 (*CSEL* 4:211–12)

its purpose by the time of the conflict between pagan thought and Christian doctrine. And just when the leaders of pagan thought had emancipated their picture of the divine from the crude anthropomorphism of the mythological tradition, the Christians came on the scene with a message about one who was called "Son of God." It is not surprising, when "the most learned and serious classes . . . are always, in fact, the most irreverent toward your

Tert.*Nat.*1.10.36 (*CCSL* 1:28)

gods," that these classes should also have been the ones who vehemently resisted this message, which seemed to

Dix (1953) 77

be a relapse into "a physical meaning of a gross kind," the very thing from which, after such a hard struggle, they had been rescued. Therefore they made fun of such biblical narratives as those dealing with the virgin birth

Or.*Cels.*1.28 (*GCS* 2:79–80)

and the resurrection. In Theophilus's defense of Christianity, the assertion that God had a Son was not meant "as

Theoph.*Autol.*2.22 (*SC* 20:154); Lact.*Inst.*4.8.3 (*CSEL* 19:295)

the poets and writers of myths talk of the sons of gods begotten of intercourse [with women]." These and other parallels between the Christian and the pagan criticisms of ancient mythology were intended to show that, even in speaking of Jesus as the Son of God, "we tell no in-

Or.*Cels.*6.8 (*GCS* 3:78)

credible tales when we explain the doctrines about Jesus."

Sometimes the pagan attacks struck at the very heart of the Christian gospel. Despite the ambiguity that seems to be present in the fathers of the second and third centuries on the questions of justification, grace, and forgiveness, they did have to deal with these questions in the attacks of their pagan opponents. Celsus was the spokesman for much of paganism when he attacked the gospel of forgiveness as cheap grace: "Those who summon people to the other mysteries make this preliminary proclamation: 'Who has pure hands and a wise tongue.' . . . But let us hear what folk these Christians call. 'Whoever is a sinner,' they say, 'whoever is unwise, whoever is a child, and, in a word, whoever is a wretch, the kingdom of God will

Or.*Cels.*3.59 (*GCS* 2:253–54)

Jul.*Caes.*336B (*LCL* 2:412)

receive him.' " Julian expressed a similar judgment about the promise of forgiveness in baptism. Such attacks prompted even some fathers whose doctrine of grace was not very profound to see that if "you compare the other deities and Christ with respect to the benefits of health [or salvation] given by them," it would be recognized that "aid is brought by the gods to the good and that the misfortunes of evil men are ignored," while, by contrast, "Christ gave assistance in equal measure to the

Arnob.*Nat*.1.49 (*CSEL* 4:33)

good and the evil." More perhaps than they themselves could recognize, these spokesmen for Christianity pointed to the distinctive character of the Christian message as a promise of health and rescue based not upon worthiness but upon need; here as elsewhere, the pagan critics of Christianity seem sometimes to have been more profound in their identification of this distinctive character than were the defenders of Christianity.

In the same way, the pagan critics acknowledged the distinctiveness of Jesus Christ in a manner that was sometimes more trenchant than the theology of the Christian apologists and that thus called forth a more profound statement of Christian doctrine than would have appeared without the challenge. It was not only the story of the resurrection of Christ that drew the fire of pagan critics

Or.*Cels*.2.55 (*GCS* 2:178)

as a fable or the report of a hysterical woman, but the significance attached to the resurrection by Christian theology. Nowhere is that significance more unequivocally expressed than in the polemic of some Christian theologians against the pagan doctrine of the immortal soul. "The soul is not in itself immortal, O Greeks, but mortal. Yet

Tat.*Or*.13 (*TU* 4–I:14)

it is possible for it not to die." In these words Tatian voiced the doctrine that life after death was not an accomplishment of man, much less his assured possession, but a gift from God in the resurrection of Christ. Even

See pp. 123–32 below

when the apocalyptic vision had been eclipsed and the immortality of the soul had become a standard element

See pp. 51–52 below

in Christian teaching, this stress on the divine initiative in the achievement of life everlasting continued to act as a check on the more drastic implications of these changes. In these and other ways the attacks of pagan authors on the Christian message left their mark on the church's doctrines long after their external challenge had lost its effectiveness.

The reply of the apologists to that challenge has also continued to affect the development of Christian doctrine both directly and indirectly. It was at least partly in response to pagan criticism of the stories in the Bible that the Christian apologists, like their Jewish predecessors, took over and adapted the methods and even the vocabulary of pagan allegorism. Not even the most shocking of biblical narratives could match the crudity and "blasphemous nonsense" of the Greek myths, in which the gods were depicted as being superhuman not in virtue but in en-

Athenag.*Leg*.21.3 (Goodspeed 337)

Cypr.*Donat*.8 (*CSEL* 3:10)

Theoph.*Autol*.1.9 (*SC* 20:76–78); Clem.*Prot*.2.39.1 (*GCS* 12:29)

Tat.*Or*.21 (*TU* 4–I:23–24)

Tert.*Apol*.14.6 (*CCSL* 1:113)

R.Grant (1957) 28

ap.Eus.*H.e*.6.19.8 (*GCS* 9:560)

Or.*Cels*.1.42 (*GCS* 2:92)

Arnob.*Nat*.5.33 (*CSEL* 4:203); Tert.*Nat*.2.12.17 (*CCSL* 1:61–62)

Tert.*Anim*.20.1 (*CCSL* 2:811)

Just. 2 *Apol*.10.8 (Goodspeed 86)

durance, "not more superior in dominion than in vice." The apologists recited lengthy catalogs of the amorous exploits of the gods, taking care to note that these pornographic details were being quoted from the pagan authors themselves. Those who held to such shameful accounts of the divine had no right to reproach the Christian narrative of "the birth of God in the form of a man. . . . For it is not permissible even to compare our conception of God with those who are wallowing in filth and mud." If the myths were true, they should not be admitted in public; if they were false, they should not be circulated among religious people. A common way out of this difficulty among sophisticated pagans was allegorical exegesis. A sophisticated pagan such as Celsus "claims that his own exegesis of ancient writers is in harmony with their intention of handing down the truth in veiled form, to be uncovered by philosophical exegesis, while Jewish and Christian exegesis is merely defensive"; Porphyry accused Origen of misapplying Hellenistic allegory to the Jewish Scriptures. In his reply to Celsus, Origen was willing to concede at least some validity to the allegorical exegesis of the Homeric poems. Most Christian writers, however, denounced Stoic and other allegory as "the veneer of sophistic disputes by which not the truth but its image and appearance and shadow are always sought after." At one and the same time the apologists cited the pagan philosophers against pagan religion and denounced them for the artificiality of their efforts to square their teachings with Homer and Hesiod. Seneca was "often in agreement with us"; but Socrates was the most important of all, because he had refrained from allegorizing Homer and had banished him.

The reason for this importance was that Christ had been "known in part even by Socrates." As the apologists came to grips with the defenders of paganism, they were compelled to acknowledge that Christianity and its ancestor, Judaism, did not have a monopoly on either the moral or the doctrinal teachings whose superiority Christian apologetics was seeking to demonstrate. To some extent this acknowledgment was a tacit admission of the presence within Christian thought of doctrines borrowed from Greek philosophy. To account for the presence of such teachings in pagan philosophy, the apologists drew upon several devices. Justin sought to draw a connection between the philosophers and the preexistent Logos. It was the seed of reason (λόγος σπερματικός) in man which enabled pagan thinkers like Socrates to see dimly what came to be clearly seen through the revelation of the Logos in the person of Jesus. As the Logos had been adumbrated in various ways during the history of Israel, so also what paganism had learned about God and about the good life could be traced to the universal functioning of the Logos. The Stoics, the poets, and the historians all "spoke well in proportion to the share [they] had of the seminal Logos." But now that the seminal Logos had come in person, those who had been under his tutelage could find the fuller meaning of their intuitions. For Origen, too, the "Logos who came to dwell in Jesus . . . inspired men before that." The apologists' use of the idea of the Logos in their dispute with classicism certainly helped to establish this title in the Christian vocabulary about Christ, but other factors were no less important.

Tertullian's explanation of the presence of noble and good elements in paganism employed the idea of natural law rather than that of the seminal Logos. For him these elements included knowledge of the existence, the goodness, and the justice of God, but especially the moral precepts flowing from that knowledge. This law of nature agreed with Christian revelation in its condemnation of moral evil. Even in his Montanist phase Tertullian could appeal to "the law of the Creator," apparently with this law of nature in mind. In opposition to Jewish teaching about the law of Moses, Tertullian argued that the primordial natural law, which had been given in an unwritten form to Adam and Eve and thus to all nations, had now been "reformed for the better." Origen used the familiar Stoic distinction between "the ultimate law of nature" and "the written code of cities" to justify the Christian refusal to obey the idolatrous laws of the nations, including Rome; he was "apparently the first to justify the right to resist tyranny by appealing to natural law." But the Christian acceptance of the pagan idea of natural law did not compel a Christian theologian such as Origen to be oblivious of the relativity in the laws of the nations. Most of the history of Christian thought about natural law belongs to the development of Christian social ethics rather than to the history of doctrine; but

Just. 2 Apol.8.3 (Goodspeed 84)

Just. 2 Apol.13.3 (Goodspeed 88)

Or.Cels.8.54 (GCS 3:270)

See pp. 186–89 below

Tert.Coron.6.2 (CCSL 2:1047)

Tert.Marc.5.15.3 (CCSL 1:709)
Tert.Monog.1.1 (CCSL 2:1229)

Tert.Jud.2.9 (CCSL 2:1343)

Or.Cels.5.37 (GCS 3:40–41)

H.Chadwick (1953) 7

Or.Cels.5.27 (GCS 3:27–28)

natural law did play a role in the effort of early theologians to deal with paganism, and it went on to "provide the daughter churches of Western Catholicism, Lutheranism and Calvinism, with the means of regarding and shaping themselves as a Christian unity of civilization." Only in the new apologetics of the Enlightenment did this definition of the natural law meet with fundamental opposition.

Probably the most widespread theory proposed by the fathers to account for the truth in paganism was the suggestion that it had come from the Old Testament. Here they were following a precedent set by Jewish apologists. Aristobulus claimed that both Plato and Pythagoras had read Moses; Philo traced various Greek doctrines to a biblical origin; and Josephus maintained that the Jewish Bible was the source of many of the most profound insights in pagan thought. In the same spirit, Justin saw Moses as the source for the doctrine of creation in Plato's *Timaeus*, adding, however, that among Christians the confession of this and related doctrines was not confined to the learned but was present also among illiterates. Plato's *Phaedrus* was likewise traced to the Bible by Origen, who professed to have received this explanation from other writers. Theophilus of Antioch extended the claim to the Greek poets as well as the philosophers, who "plagiarized from the Scriptures to make their doctrines plausible." Minucius Felix took the various philosophical notions of the conflagration awaiting the world as proof that the "divine proclamations of the prophets" had provided the philosophers with the basis of their correct, even though "corrupted," insight. Characteristically, Tertullian, while conceding the possibility that the philosophers may have studied the Scriptures, insisted that their prepossessions had prevented them from understanding biblical truth. Augustine, too, considered the possibility, which he had learned from Ambrose, that Plato had become acquainted with the Bible while both he and Jeremiah were in Egypt; later on, Augustine withdrew this explanation on historical and chronological grounds, but continued to feel that at least some acquaintance with the Bible was the only possible explanation for Plato's cosmology and ontology.

Clement of Alexandria also maintained that the doctrines of Plato's *Timaeus* came "from the Hebrews," but

---

Marginal references (left column):

Troeltsch (1960) 160

Clem.*Prot*.6.70.1 (*GCS* 12:53); Cassiod.*Inst.div*.28.3 (Mynors 70)

ap.Clem.*Str*.1.22.150.1 (*GCS* 52:92–93) Ph.*Qu.om.pr.lib*.8.57 (*LCL* 9:42)

Jos.*Ap*.2.36.256–57 (*LCL* 1:394–96)

Just. 1 *Apol*.59–60 (Goodspeed 68–70)

Or.*Cels*.6.19 (*GCS* 3:89–90)

Theoph.*Autol*.1.14 (*SC* 20:90)

Min.Fel.*Oct*.34.1–4 (*CSEL* 2:48)

Tert.*Nat*.2.2.5 (*CCSL* 1:42)

Aug.*Doctr.christ*.2.28.43 (*CCSL* 32: 63)

Aug.*Civ*.8.11 (*CCSL* 47:227–28)

Clem.*Prot*.6.70.1 (*GCS* 12:53)

he had several other explanations for the parallels between philosophy and revelation. "He begins with the possibility that the truth contained in philosophy is to be ascribed to an accident involved in God's providential economy. He continues with explanations attributing the element of truth in philosophy to the general revelation, or even making the Greek philosophers prophets similar to those of the Old Testament. And he ends by indicating that philosophy owes its existence to a reflection of the eternal truth itself, and that the philosophers have beheld God—an imperfect, vague, unclear yet true vision." It is, of course, true that many of the ideas that seemed so similar to philosophical teachings were being read into the Old Testament rather than being found there; for example, Clement's doctrine of creation in some ways owed more to Plato than to Moses, even though he claimed to find that doctrine in the latter rather than in the former and had to explain the embarrassing parallel.

Molland (1936) 71

This effort to demonstrate that the truth of revelation, which was also being affirmed by the pagan philosophers, had occurred first in the Old Testament was not merely a way of finding biblical support for one or another doctrine. It was also part of the campaign to prove the superiority of Christian doctrine on the grounds of its antiquity. Antiquity was widely regarded in pagan thought as lending authority to a system of thought or belief. Celsus attacked Christianity in the name of "an ancient doctrine which has existed from the beginning, which has always been maintained by the wisest nations and cities and wise men." Christ was spurned by the pagans as "only of yesterday," as one who had not "been known by name" until his own time. Or, as Arnobius paraphrased the case for paganism on the basis of its supposed antiquity, "your [that is, the pagans'] religious observances precede the one we espouse by many years, and for that reason are truer because fortified by the authority of age." Because the Christian message was based not simply on some timeless truth, but on the historical events of the life, death, and resurrection of Jesus under Pontius Pilate, it appeared to be discredited as an innovation.

ap.Or.*Cels*.1.14 (*GCS* 2:66–67)

ap.Tert.*Apol*.37.4 (*CCSL* 1:148); ap.Eus.*H.e*.1.4.1 (*GCS* 9:38)

Arnob.*Nat*.2.72 (*CSEL* 4:106)

But the proclamation of those events was not the whole of the Christian message; or, rather, the apologists, together with the whole church, believed that those events were announced beforehand in the Sacred Scriptures of the Old Testament. On the basis, then, of Homer and of Moses, "the one being the oldest of poets and historians, and the other the founder of all barbarian wisdom," Tatian proceeded to prove "that our doctrines are older, not only than those of the Greeks, but than the invention of letters." Tatian's teacher, Justin, who argued the case for Christian innovations against Judaism, had argued earlier that the Old Testament, which was "now in the possession of all Jews throughout the world" but which actually belonged to Christianity, was "of greater antiquity than the Greek writers." Tertullian exclaimed: "Moses and God existed before all your Lycurguses and Solons. There is not a single later age that does not derive from primitive sources." Expanding upon these arguments, Clement of Alexandria demonstrated, in the summary words of Eusebius, "that Moses and the Jewish race went back further in their origins than the Greeks." In reply to the sneers of Celsus about the recent and outlandish origins of Christian teaching, Origen, too, maintained that "Moses and the prophets . . . are not only earlier than Plato but also than Homer and the discovery of writing among the Greeks. They did not say these things, as Celsus thinks, 'because they misunderstood Plato.' How could they have heard a man who had not yet been born?"

Ambrose appears to have been one of the few defenders of Christianity to admit, in his dispute with Symmachus, that this argument from antiquity did not hold; for "not the antiquity of years, but that of morals is laudable. It is not shameful to move on to something better." Nor was this claim to antiquity compromised in the mind of most of the apologists by the circumstance, sometimes noted in the writings of their pagan opponents, that some of the doctrines whose antiquity they demonstrated from the Old Testament were not explicitly stated there, but had come into Christian theology by way of Greek philosophy and only then were discovered in the Jewish Scriptures.

Although Clement of Alexandria told the Greeks that for the ideas in Plato's *Timaeus* they were "indebted to the Hebrews," he was himself indebted to the *Timaeus*. Nevertheless, he joined with the other apologists in defending what he understood to be the biblical view of creation against the cosmogonies of the philosophers, including the cosmogony of the *Timaeus*. When "the chorus

---

Tat.*Or*.31 (*TU* 4–I:31)

Just. *1 Apol*.31.5–6 (Goodspeed 46)
Just. *1 Apol*.59.1 (Goodspeed 68)

Tert.*Marc*.2.17.3 (*CCSL* 1:495)

Eus.*H.e*.6.13.7 (*GCS* 9:548); Aug.*Civ*.18.39 (*CCSL* 48:634)

Or.*Cels*.6.7 (*GCS* 3:76)

Ambr.*Ep*.18.7 (*PL* 16:974)

Clem.*Prot*.6.70.1 (*GCS* 12:53)

of the philosophers" were guilty of "deifying the universe" instead of "seeking the Creator of the universe," they needed to be told that "the sheer volition [of God] is the making of the universe. For God alone made it, because he alone is God in his being [ὄντως]. By his sheer act of will he creates [δημιουργεῖ]; and after he has merely willed, it follows that things come into being." In opposition to the Platonic idea of the demiurge, then, Clement asserted that God himself was the demiurge of all things. On the basis of this and similar statements, E. F. Osborn has concluded that "Clement is the first person to state and give reasons for the doctrine of creation *ex nihilo*."

But Clement's contemporary, Tertullian, elaborated the doctrine of creation out of nothing more fully in his *Against Hermogenes*. To some extent he seems, both here and elsewhere, to have been dependent on Theophilus of Antioch, who had taught, in opposition to the Platonic idea of the coeternity of God and matter, that "the power of God is manifested in this, that out of things that are not he makes whatever he pleases" and that therefore "nothing is coeternal with God." Conceding that creation out of nothing was not explicitly stated in the Bible but only implied, Tertullian argued from silence that "if God could make all things out of nothing, Scripture could quite well omit to add that he had made them out of nothing, but it should have said by all means that he had made them out of matter, if he had done so; for the first possibility would be completely understandable, even if it was not expressly stated, but the second would be doubtful unless it was stated." Apologists like Clement, Theophilus, and Tertullian recognized that the coeternity of God and matter was inconsistent with the sovereignty and freedom of God. In spite of the difficulties raised by the doctrine of creation ex nihilo for any attempt to cope with the problem of evil, the alternatives to this doctrine appeared to be a pantheism which taught that "God and matter are the same, two names for one thing" or a dualism that could be resolved, if at all, by denying that God the Creator "made all things freely, and by his own power, and arranged and finished them, and his will is the substance of all things."

According to Irenaeus, God the Creator "is discovered to be the one and only God who created all things, who

Clem.*Prot*.4.63.3 (*GCS* 12:48)

Osborn(1957) 33

Theoph.*Autol*.2.4; 2.10 (*SC* 20:102; 122)

Tert.*Hermog*.21.2 (*CCSL* 1:415)

Tert.*Hermog*.21.3 (*CCSL* 1:415)

Athenag.*Leg*.15.1 (Goodspeed 329)

Iren.*Haer*.2.30.9 (Harvey 1:367–68)

Iren.*Haer*.2.30.9 (Harvey 1:368)

alone is omnipotent, and who is the only Father founding and forming all things, visible and invisible." In answer both to mythological polytheism and to the doctrine of the coeternity of God and matter, the apologists asserted divine transcendence and strict monotheism (or, in their usual word, "monarchy"). They "apply the word nearly always to the absolute monarchy of God, and its primary sense is omnipotence. But since the whole significance of omnipotence is that it can be wielded only by one ulti-

Prestige (1956) 95

mate power, it really comes to mean monotheism." So long as the challenge to Christian doctrine was coming from classical polytheism or from philosophical pantheism or even from Gnosticism, this stress on the "monarchy" seemed to align the apologists with the Old Testament doctrine of God, in spite of their divergence from Judaism. But when Christian thought was called upon to vindicate its language about the divine dispensation ("economy") in Christ as consistent with monotheism, it took on the far more subtle assignment of demonstrating that its doctrine of "the Trinity . . . in no respect challenges the monarchy, while it conserves the quality of the

Tert.*Prax*.8.7 (*CCSL* 2:1168)

economy."

In their defense of the biblical view of creation, the apologists were also obliged to take up the question of the meaning of history. Greek historical thought had been impressed by the constantly recurring elements in human history; one of the means, though not the only one, by which the Greeks interpreted history was a theory of cycles. Among the Romans, their own sense of manifest destiny prompted a revision of this theory; it was asserted that although previous events had foreshadowed the com-

Verg.*Aen*.8.626–731

ing of Rome, as Vergil said, the fall of previous civilizations did not indicate the inevitable course of empire, so

Verg.*Aen*.1.278–79

long as Rome remained true to the ideals of its past. In declaring the loyalty of the Christians to the empire while repudiating the deification of the emperor, apologetic theologians were compelled to clarify their reasons for differing from these theories of history. It was a necessary presupposition of the Christian proclamation that historical events were unrepeatable; otherwise "it is inevitable that according to the determined cycles Moses will always come out of Egypt with the people of the Jews, [and] Jesus will again come to visit this life

and will do the same things he has done, not just once
but an infinite number of times according to the cycles."
In opposition to Roman claims, Tertullian asserted that
"all nations have possessed empire, each in its proper
time . . . until at last almost universal dominion has
accrued to the Romans," adding ominously: "What
[God] has determined concerning [the Roman Em-
pire], those who are closest to him know."

When a theology was dominated, as Tertullian's sometimes was, by a vivid futuristic eschatology, it could share
the Roman belief that the empire represented the final
phase of human accomplishment, but always with the
proviso that now it was time for the final phase of divine
intervention. When that intervention did not come, at
least not in the form in which many had expected it, the
apologists had to deal with the possibility that the world
would continue even without the empire as they had
known it. They often fell back upon a more general conception of "the providence of God, which regulates
everything according to its season." Such a view of
providence, like the monotheism of which it was a
corollary, seriously complicated the problem of evil and
of free will, as the formula of Origen suggests: "As a
result of [God's] foreknowledge the free actions of every
man fit in with that disposition of the whole which is
necessary for the existence of the universe." The doctrine
of divine providence became the standard rubric under
which theologians considered the problem of history. It
remained for Augustine to clarify the Christian conviction that because of Christ and despite "all appearances,
human history does not consist of a series of repetitive
patterns, but marks a sure, if unsteady, advance to an
ultimate goal."

Concerned as they were with ethical questions as much
as with doctrinal issues, the apologists also sought to
prove and defend the superiority of the Christian ethic.
Of the devices employed in this defense, the most important doctrinally was their interpretation of the Christian
gospel as a "new law." When Barnabas spoke of "the
new law of our Lord Jesus Christ, which is without a
yoke of necessity," he set a pattern followed by many
later theologians. Justin called Christ "the new lawgiver," and Origen termed him "the lawgiver of the
Christians"; by Cyprian's time such phrases as "the

Or.Cels.4.67 (GCS 2:337)

Tert.Nat.2.17.19 (CCSL 1:75)

Tert.Jejun.4.1 (CCSL 2:1260)

Or.Orat.6.3 (GCS 3:313)

Cochrane (1944) 484

Barn.2.6(Bihlmeyer 11)

Just.Dial.18.3 (Goodspeed 111)

Or.Cels.3.7 (GCS 2:208)

Cypr.*Ep*.27.4; 36.2 (*CSEL* 3:544; 574)

evangelical law" or "the law of the gospel" seem to have become a standard designation for the Christian message. As Moritz von Engelhardt has urged, such phrases "passed over into Christian language without necessarily indicating an inclination to a Jewish-Christian way of thinking. And something that could otherwise be interpreted in this sense acquires, in the context, a different and evangelical meaning." The "new law" implied new demands (the knowledge of Christ, repentance, and a sinless life after conversion) as well as new promises (forgiveness of sins and immortality). But when the Jewish context of such terms as "covenant" became less evident to Christians, "new law" also shed some of its earlier connotations.

Engelhardt (1878) 381

As Christianity became more respectable socially, its apologetics became more respectable philosophically. Long after the official adoption of Christianity by the emperor and eventually by the law of the empire, Christian theologians still went on writing apologetic treatises. The *Summa against the Gentiles* of Thomas Aquinas was written at a time when there were certainly very few "Gentiles," that is, pagans, left in western Europe and when those for whom it was ostensibly composed could not have understood it. But the tone of that *Summa,* and of apologetic treatises for some centuries preceding it, indicates that the war was decided even though it was not over. The statement of proofs for the existence of God became a part of the Christian theological enterprise only when it was no longer necessary for apologetic purposes, as though to assure that the triumph of revelation had not been won too cheaply. Conversely, one could afford to give reason its due when its subordination to revelation had been secured. Like the dialogues "adversus Judaeos," apologetics against classicism became more and more a function of churchly theology and continued to be this in most of the great systems in the history of Christian thought until the Enlightenment, when Christian doctrine found itself on the defensive again and was obliged to reconsider the meaning of its earlier victory in the dispute with classical thought. Then it was that the apologetic approach of works such as Origen's once more commended itself to the attention of theologians.

The victory of Christian apologetics was celebrated and documented in two ways, represented by Eusebius and

Lightfoot (1880) 331

Eus.P.e.1.3.7 (GCS 43:11)

Eus.H.e.2.pr.1 (GCS 9:102)

Eus.P.e.2.5.2 (GCS
43:88–89)

See pp. 34–35 above

Aug.Civ.2.2 (CCSL 47:35)

by Augustine. Eusebius, to whose learning and industry later centuries are indebted for much of what has been preserved about the early history of Christian apologetics, devoted a large part of his immense literary output to a defense of Christianity. His treatise in two parts, *Praeparatio evangelica* and *Demonstratio evangelica*, has been called "with all its faults . . . probably the most important apologetic work of the early church." In it he summarized and elaborated most of the arguments we have been detailing here, but he also set his own work apart from that of his predecessors by criticizing their preoccupation with "dialectical arguments [λόγοι]" at the expense of "historical facts [ἔργα]." To redress this balance, Eusebius composed historical works, first a *Chronicle* and then his *Ecclesiastical History*, both of which attempted to prove, by historical facts rather than merely by dialectical arguments, that Christianity and Christ possessed great antiquity and that the history of Christianity was a universal history. This he did in response to the repeated pagan charge that the Christian message was too recent and too provincial to merit serious consideration. He cast his apologetic in the form of a historical account and thereby laid the foundations for ecclesiastical history. As he was writing the *Ecclesiastical History*, the political need for Christian apologetics was removed with the conversion of Constantine; he nevertheless continued to provide the materials for the apologia to the intellectuals, which remained necessary longer than the apologia to the empire.

It was the lag between these two kinds of apologia that provided the occasion for the definitive exposition of the Christian case against classical thought, the *City of God* of Augustine. This work was an "endeavor to reply to those who attribute the wars by which the world is being devastated, and especially the recent sack of Rome by the barbarians, to the religion of Christ." The *City of God* repeated many of the arguments against paganism and for Christianity that had become commonplaces of the apologetic literature, but it organized them into an interpretation of world history in which the eternal purpose of God was borne by the city of God. Some earlier apologists had argued that, far from being the threat to Rome which its opponents called it, Christianity was ac-

Tert.*Apol*.30 (*CCSL*
1:141–42)

Aug.*Civ*.15.1 (*CCSL*
48:453–54)

Aug.*Civ*.5.21 (*CCSL*
47:157–58)

Aug.*Civ*.18.47 (*CCSL*
48:645–46)

Aug.*Civ*.20.17 (*CCSL*
48:727–29)

Aug.*Civ*.22.30 (*CCSL*
48:862–66)

tually the support of righteous governments. This argument Augustine took up into his schematization of world history as a conflict between the spiritual descendants of Abel and those of Cain, claiming that the collapse of the Roman ideal was due to the failure of the empire to recognize the true source of its strength. Both in the history of his chosen people and in the lives of "holy pagans" God had made his city known among men. Its ultimate destiny was that of the heavenly Jerusalem, which, in Augustine's description at the conclusion of the *City of God,* united and transformed many of the themes of early Christian apocalypticism. Like Eusebius, Augustine translated apologetics into history; but the history was not merely the account of the succession of the church from the apostles, but the whole way of divine providence.

The subsequent influence of the *Ecclesiastical History* and the *City of God* helped to assure the arguments of the apologists a permanent place in the development of Christian doctrine, in addition to an important role in other areas of Christian thought and practice. Christian theologians viewed classical thought, at least until the Renaissance, as the apologists of the early church had taught them to view it.

The Triumph of Theology

The closing of the philosophical school at Athens by the emperor Justinian in 529 is usually interpreted as the victory of Christian theology over classical thought. According to Gibbon, this was a time when Christian theologians had "superseded the exercise of reason, resolved every question by an article of faith, and condemned the infidel or sceptic to eternal flames. In many a volume of laborious controversy they exposed the weakness of the understanding and the corruption of the heart, insulted human nature in the sages of antiquity, and proscribed the spirit of philosophical inquiry, so repugnant to the doctrine, or at least to the temper, of an humble believer."

Gibbon (1896) 4:265

The closing of the Athenian academy was more the act of a coroner than an executioner. The establishment of the imperial University of Constantinople by Theodosius II, or perhaps by Constantine himself, had already transferred the center of Greek learning from Athens to the new capital of the Hellenic world, and so the pagan school in Athens "had already outlived its purpose" and "was no longer of great import in a Christian empire." The pagan professors emigrated from Athens to Persia but eventually returned to the empire, having obtained a promise of safe-conduct from Justinian. Teachers of philosophy, then, were regarded as both unwanted and harmless. From that interpretation it would be an easy step, though a wrong one, to conclude that theology had eliminated philosophy from the attention of thoughtful men: "Philosophy branched off from theology. It became its handmaid and its rival. It postulated doctrines instead of investigating them. It had to show their reasonableness or to find reasons for them. And for ages afterwards

philosophy was dead."

It is true that the formal study of Greek philosophy declined with the rise to authority of orthodox Christian theology. Of the writings of Aristotle it seems that only his *Categories* and *On Interpretation* had been translated into Latin by the close of our period; not even the rest of the treatises belonging to the *Organon,* much less the ethical and metaphysical writings, were put into a form that would have made them accessible to Western theologians. Boethius, the translator of these treatises, had intended to render all of Aristotle and Plato into Latin, and thereby "to bring them into harmony and to demonstrate that they do not disagree on everything, as many maintain, but are in the greatest possible agreement

on many things that pertain to philosophy." But the two logical treatises were all that he completed, or at any rate all that was preserved, and apparently were all of Aristotle that was known to the Christian West until the early part of the twelfth century. Only then did Western thinkers turn once more to a concerted study of classical philosophical systems, and that primarily as a result of external provocation as well as internal theological necessity. It was as theologians that they studied Aristotle. It seems as though philosophy and matters philosophical disappeared from the attention of Christian thinkers for half a millennium or more.

Yet this same Boethius, whose translation of Aristotle delineates the end of classical thought as much as does the nearly contemporary closing of the school at Athens, was also the author of a book which seriously qualifies any such interpretation of the triumph of theology. His *Consolation of Philosophy,* "the noblest literary work of the final period of antiquity," played a unique role in the history of medieval literature and devotion. Manuscripts of the work are widely distributed among the libraries of Europe; it was translated by King Alfred, by Chaucer, and perhaps by Queen Elizabeth I; and it provided comfort to Dante Alighieri in his bereavement over the death of Beatrice. Languishing in prison for treason and presumably for his fidelity to trinitarian orthodoxy in defiance of an Arian emperor, Boethius turned his hand to an old genre of classical literature, the consolatory discourse or "consolatio," which had been adapted from Greek models by Cicero. Boethius seems to have been the first Christian theologian to employ the "consolatio," but the result was a form of consolation which pictured the operation of the divine in the affairs of men without any unmistakable reference to the Christian doctrine of God, either Arian or Nicene. The basic theme of the book was a defense of free will and of the goodness of divine providence, under whose sovereignty fate was permitted to function. In a dialogue with philosophy personified, Boethius expounded his doctrine of God as "the constant foreknowing overseer . . . [whose] sight moves in harmony with the future nature of our actions as it dispenses rewards to the good and punishments to the bad."

Is this doctrine of God proof that "although doubtless a professing Christian," Boethius had sentiments which "were those of pagan philosophy"? Or is it more accurate to maintain that "the picture of God drawn there is so warm and authentic in a Christian sense that even if there were no decisive external proof available for the Christian confession of the last of the Romans, one would be justified in regarding Boethius as a Christian thinker"? On the basis of content alone, there seems reason to doubt the traditional account that the *Consolation* was written by a Christian theologian. It seems plausible to conclude that the author of the *Consolation* could not have been the Boethius to whom five treatises on Christian doctrine, including a polemic against Nestorius and Eutyches and an influential exposition of the doctrine of the Trinity, were attributed. But closer examination of the thought and the language of the Boethian corpus shows that both

Norden (1898) 2:585

Boeth.*Cons*.5.6.45 (*CCSL* 94:105)

H.Taylor (1938) 1:89

Grabmann (1957) 1:163

the *Consolation* and at least four of the theological treatises came from the same man. This would suggest that in the *Consolation* Boethius was pressing reason to the very boundaries of faith, and that this apologetic aim "explains why there is not a trace of anything specifically Christian or Biblical in the entire work." But this does not explain why at least one orthodox theologian, in the hour of utmost need, found solace more in philosophical contemplation based on natural reason than in the Christian revelation to which his theological works pointed.

Rand (1929) 178

In many ways, Boethius's *Consolation of Philosophy* only dramatizes a more general problem. The victory of orthodox Christian doctrine over classical thought was to some extent a Pyrrhic victory, for the theology that triumphed over Greek philosophy has continued to be shaped ever since by the language and the thought of classical metaphysics. For example, the Fourth Lateran Council in 1215 decreed that "in the sacrament of the altar . . . the bread is transubstantiated into the body [of Christ], and the wine into [his] blood," and the Council of Trent declared in 1551 that the use of the term "transubstantiation" was "proper and appropriate." Most of the theological expositions of the term "transubstantiation," beginning already with those of the thirteenth century, have interpreted "substance" on the basis of the meaning given to this term by such classical discussions as that in the fifth book of Aristotle's *Metaphysics;* transubstantiation, then, would appear to be tied to the acceptance of Aristotelian metaphysics or even of Aristotelian physics.

Mansi 22:982

Mansi 33:82

Yet the application of the term "substance" to the discussion of the eucharistic presence antedates the rediscovery of Aristotle. In the ninth century, Ratramnus spoke of "substances visible but invisible," and his opponent Radbertus declared that "out of the substance of bread and wine the same body and blood of Christ is mystically consecrated." Even "transubstantiation" was used during the twelfth century in a nontechnical sense. Such evidence lends credence to the argument that the doctrine of transubstantiation, as codified by the decrees of the Fourth Lateran and Tridentine councils, did not canonize Aristotelian philosophy as indispensable to Christian doctrine. But whether it did so or not in principle, it has certainly done so in effect; as natural law has come to be equated

Ratr.*Corp*.11 (Brink 36)

Radb.*Corp*.4.1 (*PL* 120:1277–78)

with a particular ecclesiastical formulation of what ought to be natural, so substance has come to be defined as a particular philosophical theology has defined it.

Transubstantiation is an individual instance of what has been called the problem of "the hellenization of Christianity." The charge that one's theological opponent has subordinated the truth of divine revelation to the philosophy of the Greeks is a common one in the history of theological polemics. The *Little Labyrinth,* probably written by Hippolytus, attacked the adoptionism of Theodotus and Artemon because, among other errors, these heretics had "deserted the Holy Scriptures of God"

ap.Eus.*H.e.*5.28.13–14 (GCS 9:504)

and given themselves to a study of Euclid and Aristotle; and Nestorius accused his opponents in the fifth-century christological controversies of being "led astray by the

Nest.*Ep.Cyr.*2.7 (*ACO* 1–I–1:31)

mentality of the Greeks." The accusation recurred in the attacks of the Reformers on medieval scholasticism, but it was in modern times that the idea of dogma as the hellenization of Christianity became a widely circulated explanation of the development of early Christian doctrine. Taken as it stands, "hellenization" is too simplistic and unqualified a term for the process that issued in orthodox Christian doctrine. Nevertheless, it is true that in its language and sometimes in its ideas orthodox Christian doctrine still bears the marks of its struggle to understand and overcome pagan thought, so that what later generations of the church (including those generations that were themselves ignorant of antiquity) inherited in the dogma of the church included more than a little of Greek philosophy as well. Victory over classical thought there assuredly was, but a victory for which some Christian theologians were willing to pay a rather high price.

How high a price is evident from the writings of the apologists. Even when the reader makes due allowance for the task of the apologists as the interpreters of the church to the Gentile world—and due allowance would mean more allowance than many historians of doctrine have been willing to make—the fact remains that "their attitude toward ancient culture is contradictory. On the one hand, the zeal of battle prompts them to look for contrasts and to accentuate them sharply, purposely to bring out the shadows, to create a dark background for the bright beam of Christianity, and not to be ashamed of using evil means for that end. On the other hand, the deepest contrasts are often concealed and veiled from them, because they have already taken up the gospel into the conceptual forms and ideas of the time and have blended it with them. They claim to be fighting for the new faith against the old world; in fact, they are partly continuing the battle of intellectual currents which were already at war in the ancient world, only adding to them

Wendland (1907) 159

some new issues and weapons." In various ways they joined to assert the thesis that Christ had come as the revealer of true philosophy, ancient and yet new, as the correction and also the fulfillment of what the philosophical mind had already grasped.

That thesis received its most authoritative exposition in the apologetics of Clement of Alexandria. Like other apologists, Clement has been represented as a thoroughgoing hellenizer, who trimmed the Christian faith to suit the presuppositions of an alien philosophy, because "the tradition of the church [was] a foreign thing to him

Harnack (1931) 1:642

both in its totality and in every detail." Hence his writings have been interpreted as primarily or even exclusively apologetic in intent. But the dominant theme of his authorship was clearly "the problem of training the

H.R.Niebuhr (1951) 126–27

immature wisely" in Christian doctrine and even more in the Christian life, as was explicit in the *Tutor* and implicit throughout the *Miscellanies*. But in the *Exhortation to the Greeks* Clement addressed an appeal to his philosophical colleagues to complete their world view

H.Chadwick (1966) 31–65

by accepting Christ. What they had already grasped of the ultimate nature of reality he called a slender spark, capable of being fanned into flame, a trace of wisdom,

Clem.*Str*.6.17.149.2 (*GCS* 52:508)

and an impulse from God. He chided them for being satisfied with a religious outlook that pictured deity as their religions did, while their philosophical outlook had far transcended these crude pictures. Their representations of Zeus were "an image of an image," but the true image of God was in the Logos; therefore the authentic

Clem.*Str*.5.14.94.5 (*GCS* 52:388)

"image of the image" was the human mind itself, not the crude statues whose inadequacy their philosophers had

Clem.*Prot*.10.98.4 (*GCS* 12:71)

taught them to recognize. He portrayed in glowing terms the intellectual and moral superiority of the Christian way to anything that even the noblest paganism had been able to discover. For "that which the chief of philosophy only guessed at, the disciples of Christ have both appre-

Clem.*Prot*.11.112.2 (*GCS* 12:79)

hended and proclaimed." Therefore he appealed to them,

blending Scripture and Homer: "Philosophy is a long-lived exhortation, wooing the eternal love of wisdom, while the commandment of the Lord is far-shining, 'enlightening the eyes.' Receive Christ, receive sight, receive your light, 'in order that you may know well both God and man.' " Clement did not feel obliged to refute the charges of immorality and irrationality still being directed against Christian life and doctrine. He wrote as an evangelist among the Greeks.

The importance of philosophy for his doctrine is not to be sought primarily in his complimentary remarks about the persons or even about the ideas of the philosophers, especially about Socrates and Plato, but rather in the influence of Middle Platonism upon his thinking about such crucial Christian doctrines as the nature of man and the person of Christ. Man he pictured as a dual being like the centaur of classical myth, made up of body and soul; it was the lifelong task of the Christian "philosopher gnostic" to cultivate the liberation of the soul from the chains of the body, in preparation for the ultimate liberation, which was death. This conception appeared even in Clement's profoundest statements of the Christian doctrine of man as creature and sinner, and was reflected in his accommodations to the Platonic doctrine of the preexistence of the soul. A similar ambivalence was evident in his christology. He repeatedly affirmed the historicity of the incarnation and the reality of the flesh of Jesus; but because his definition of what constituted true humanity labored under the handicaps just described, his christological statements frequently came to formulations that sound docetic. It seems evident that Clement was not in fact a docetist, but he did blur the distinction between the Logos and the soul in a way that could lead in that direction. Not the history of the life, death, and resurrection of Jesus Christ, but the divine Logos who appeared in that history was the motif of Clement's christology. He seems to have spoken with greater ease about the mode of existence peculiar to the resurrected Lord than about the mode manifest in his sufferings. One reason for this lay in Clement's concept of the resurrection itself, whether Christ's or the Christian's. The Middle Platonic view of the immortal soul sometimes seemed for Clement to be equated with resurrection, despite other indications that he did not consider

Clem.*Prot*.11.113.1–2 (*GCS* 12:79)

Clem.*Str*.4.22.144.2 (*GCS* 52:312)

Clem.*Str*.4.3.9.4 (*GCS* 52:252)

Clem.*Str*.4.3.12.5 (*GCS* 52:253–54)

Clem.*Prot*.11.111.2 (*GCS* 12:78–79)

Grillmeier (1965) 160–61

the soul to be naturally immortal. This was no simple hellenization of the gospel, as his polemics against Gnosticism for just such hellenization made clear; but it was less of a victory of Christian doctrine over Greek thought than it appeared to be.

Origen, too, has been represented as a consistent hellenizer; one of his pagan contemporaries said of him that "while his manner of life was Christian and contrary to the law, he played the Greek, and introduced Greek ideas into foreign fables." From a study of Origen's massive works on the Bible it is evident that he relied far less than did Clement on the notion of secret tradition and that he was even more intent than Clement on keeping his speculations within the confines of tradition. Therefore the tension between biblical and philosophical doctrine was, if anything, even more acute in Origen than in Clement. An apt illustration of the tension is Origen's doctrine of the resurrection, to which he devoted two books and two dialogues (all of them lost, except for fragments). The doctrine of a literal resurrection of the physical body was one that was "preached in the churches . . . for the simpleminded and for the ears of the common crowd who are led on to live better lives by their belief." But Origen regarded this literal doctrine as an allegory for the teaching that "in the body there lies a certain principle which is not corrupted from which the body is raised in corruption"—not the same body that died, but a body appropriate to the new and immortal life. Origen was quite willing to acknowledge, meanwhile, that he shared the doctrine of the immortality of the soul with pagan philosophers. He also taught "that the life of the soul did not begin when the soul was joined to the body" but that the soul had preexisted and had fallen in that earlier state. To another Christian of the third century, this was "the trifling of some who shamelessly do violence to Scripture, in order that their opinion, that the resurection is without flesh, may find support; supposing rational bones and flesh, and in different ways changing it backwards and forwards by allegorizing." The pagan philosopher failed to grasp what Origin believed to be the true meaning of the Christian doctrine of the resurrection, while the Christian literalist regarded that meaning as a betrayal of the biblical message to Platonic

ap.Eus.*H.e.*6.19.7 (*GCS* 9:560)

Hanson (1954) 182–92

ap.Meth.*Res.*3.17.2–5 (*GCS* 27:413–14)

Or.*Cels.*5.18–19 (*GCS* 3:19–20)

Or.*Cels.*5.23 (*GCS* 3:24)
Or.*Cels.*7.32 (*GCS* 3:182–83)

Or.*Cels.*3.81 (*GCS* 2:271–72)

Daniélou (1955) 289

Meth.*Res.*1.39.2 (*GCS* 27:282)

spiritualism. Eliminating either pole of Origen's thought from his system would make him more consistent; but it would be an oversimplification and a distortion of his thought, for biblical doctrine and philosophical speculation are both essential components of his theology.

Biblical doctrine and philosophical speculation were also intermingled in the theology of Tertullian, though in different proportions. His question, "What has Athens to do with Jerusalem?" and the resoundingly negative answer he repeatedly provided to that question have sometimes obscured the philosophical elements in his thought. The very issues whose significance we have examined in Origen, the resurrection and the soul, illustrate Tertullian's aversion to philosophy and his dependence upon it. His treatise on the resurrection acknowledged a degree of affinity between Christian doctrine and the teachings of some philosophers, but proceeded to expound various biblical passages about the flesh in antithesis to the philosophers and the heretics; he gave special attention to 1 Corinthians 15. The treatise on the soul opened with a similar attack on philosophical doctrines, specifically on the doctrine of the soul in Plato, whom he later called "the caterer to all these heretics." Once more he had to acknowledge parallels between biblical truth and philosophical teaching, but he was intent upon "freeing, on the one hand, the sentiments held by us in common with them from the arguments of the philosophers, and of separating, on the other hand, the arguments which both parties employ from the opinions of the same philosophers."

In theory Tertullian owed loyalty only to the Bible and to the "most frequent admonitions" of the Montanist Paraclete; "what we are ourselves, that also the Scriptures are (and have been) from the beginning." But it was by no means obvious what the Scriptures and the tradition of the church (or even the Paraclete) taught about the origin and nature of the human soul. Therefore he felt obliged to "call on the Stoics also to help me, who, while declaring almost in our own terms that the soul is a spiritual essence (inasmuch as breath and spirit are in their nature very near akin to each other), will yet have no difficulty in persuading [us] that the soul is a corporeal substance." By the time Tertullian had finished

Tert.*Praescrip*.7.9 (*CCSL* 1:193)

Tert.*Res*.1–3 (*CCSL* 2:921–25)

Tert.*Res*.4 (*CCSL* 2:925–26)

Tert.*Res*.48–60 (*CCSL* 2:987–1009)

Tert.*Anim*.1.2–6 (*CCSL* 2:781–83)

Tert.*Anim*.23.5 (*CCSL* 2:815)

Tert.*Anim*.2.1 (*CCSL* 2:783)

Tert.*Anim*.2.5 (*CCSL* 2:784)

Tert.*Anim*.58.8 (*CCSL* 2:869)

Tert.*Praescrip*.38.5 (*CCSL* 1:218)

Tert.*Anim*.5.2 (*CCSL* 2:786)

vindicating the biblical doctrine of the soul against the philosophers, he had invoked not only the Stoics, but Aristotle (whom he does not seem to have cited anywhere else) and other philosophical sources ranging from the pre-Socratics Heraclitus and Democritus to the philosophical scholar of the Augustan age, Arius Didymus. For his doctrine of the resurrection and of the simultaneous origin of soul and body, Tertullian could not avoid quoting the very philosophy against whose pretensions he had spoken so violently. Thus while Origen may be said to illustrate the modification of philosophical concepts by continuing exposure to biblical motifs, Tertullian may be said to illustrate the continuing and unavoidable, if not always acknowledged or even conscious, influence of philosophical ideas on Christian doctrine. Each shows that there was indeed a victory of theology over classical philosophy, but also that the victory was by no means as one-sided as the spokesmen for Christian doctrine claimed it was.

Lest the examples of Origen and Tertullian be dismissed as unrepresentative on the grounds that both have been condemned as heretics, the unimpeachable doctrinal rectitude of a Gregory of Nyssa may be taken as evidence for the thesis that the tension between biblical and philosophical doctrine continued to characterize the orthodox theology of the catholic tradition. Even if it is not accurate to maintain that his doctrine of the Trinity was rescued from tritheism by a Middle Platonic concept of essence, his view of the doctrines we have examined in Clement, Origen, and Tertullian, the doctrines of the soul and of the resurrection, reinforces the thesis, as the very title of his treatise, *On the Soul and the Resurrection*, suggests. It, too, insisted that "while [pagan philosophy] proceeded, on the subject of the soul, as far in the direction of supposed implications as the thinker pleased, we are not entitled to such license, namely, of affirming whatever we please. For we make Sacred Scripture the rule and the norm of every doctrine. Upon that we are obliged to fix our eyes, and we approve only whatever can be brought into harmony with the intent of these writings." Yet Gregory, like his mentor Origen, could not altogether escape the dominance of Platonic philosophy; in form and even in content, his treatise

Tert.*Anim.*12.3; 43.2 (*CCSL* 2:798; 845)

Tert.*Anim.*15.3–5 (*CCSL* 2:801–802)

Tert.*Anim.*54.2 (*CCSL* 2:861)

Gr.Nyss.*Eun.*3.2.98–99 (Jaeger 2:79)

See pp. 221–22 below

Gr.Nyss.*Anim.et res.* (*PG* 46:49)

on the soul repeatedly betrayed its ancestry in the *Phaedo,* just as his mystical theology documented both his involvement in and his transcendence of Platonic thought.

Gr.Nyss.*Anim.et res.* (*PG* 46:108)

Two Christian doctrines are perhaps the most reliable indications of the continuing hold of Greek philosophy on Christian theology: the doctrine of the immortality of the soul and the doctrine of the absoluteness of God— "God and the soul, that is what I desire to know, nothing more," in Augustine's familiar formula. The idea of the immortal and rational soul is part of the Greek inheritance in Christian doctrine; Thomas Aquinas and Philip Melanchthon are only two of the many theologians to compose treatises with the title *On the Soul* whose content was determined more by philosophical than by biblical language about the soul.

Aug.*Soliloq.*1.2.7 (*PL* 32:872)

Indeed, the idea of the immortality of the soul came eventually to be identified with the biblical doctrine of the resurrection of the body, a doctrine one of whose original polemical targets was the immortality of the soul. The pagan or heretical equation of the soul with life and the claim of natural immortality apart from the action of God the Creator were rejected by Christian thinkers on the grounds that "the soul itself is not life, but participates in the life conferred upon it by God," by whose will alone the soul received the capacity to endure eternally. Therefore "the soul participates in life because God wills it to live; thus it will not even have such participation when God no longer wills it to live." Tatian's statement that "in itself the soul is not immortal, but mortal" was based on his assumptions concerning the relation between time and eternity and between body, soul, and spirit. Yet it did give voice to the insistence on the doctrine of the resurrection in opposition to natural immortality.

Iren.*Haer.*2.34.4 (Harvey 1:383)

Tat.*Or.*13 (*TU* 4–I:14)

The basis for this insistence was the Christian doctrine of creation. Because only God was without beginning and everything else had been "brought into existence by the Framer of all things above, on this account we believe that there will be a resurrection of bodies after the consummation of all things." Athenagoras argued at length that the confession of God as the Creator required a doctrine of resurrection as the completion of the divine purpose, and that "the reason for [man's] coming to be

Tat.*Or.*5–6 (*TU* 4–I:6)

Athenag.*Res*.13 (*TU* 4-II:63)

See pp. 337–38 below

Ambr.*Exc.Sat*.2.65 (*CSEL* 73:285)

Ambr.*Exc.Sat*.2.50–52 (*CSEL* 73:275–76)

guarantees his resurrection, for without this he would not be permanent as man." But the argumentation of Athenagoras, in contrast with that of Tatian, is already an indication of the synthesis between immortality and resurrection that was to be the orthodox doctrine. Origen's speculations about the preexistence of souls and their eventual salvation were condemned formally in the sixth century, but had been repudiated by most theologians all along. The doctrine of creation was defended by being distinguished from the doctrine of the fall of man: human sin and mortality were not due to some prehistoric fall of the soul and its subsequent incarceration in the body, but to man's first disobedience. Once the doctrine of the immortality of the soul was separated from the notion of the preexistence of the soul, it could be harmonized with the doctrine of the resurrection. The treatise of Ambrose on the resurrection voiced the standard view when it argued that the doctrine of immortality was incomplete without the doctrine of resurrection; resurrection meant the conferral upon the body of that deathless life which the soul already possessed. What the philosophers taught about the immortality of the soul was not incorrect, only incomplete.

The other Christian doctrine whose development was significantly affected by the continuing dominance of Greek thought was the doctrine of God. Implicit in the biblical view of God as the Creator was the affirmation of his sovereign independence: God was not dependent on his creatures as they were on him. But in their assertion of the freedom of God, the prophets emphasized at the same time his involvement with the covenant people in love and wrath. Therefore the Old Testament doctrine of the sovereign freedom of God could not be synonymous with the philosophical doctrine of divine impassibility (ἀπάθεια), which meant first of all that God was free of the changes and sufferings that characterize human life and feeling, although derivatively it could also mean impassivity—that God was indifferent to the changes and sufferings of man. It is significant that Christian theologians customarily set down the doctrine of the impassibility of God as an axiom, without bothering to provide very much biblical support or theological proof. The traditional argumentation is well summarized in a brief treatise, *On the Impassibility and Passibility of God,* by

Pitra 4:103–120,363–76

Tert.*Prax*.29.5 (*CCSL* 2:1202–203)
See pp. 104–5 below

Ath.*Gent*.28 (*PG* 25:56)

Ath.*Gent*.39 (*PG* 25:77)

Didym.*Spir*.9 (*PG* 39:1041)

Thdr.Mops.*Hom.catech*.4.6 (*ST* 145:83)
Thdr.Mops.*Hom.catech*.9.18 (*ST* 145:245)

Cyr.*Inc.unigen*. (*SC* 97:208)

Apoll.*Fid.sec.pt*.12 (Lietzmann 171)

Gr.Nyss.*Apoll*. (Jaeger 3–I:219); Gr.Nyss.*Eun*.3.2.12 (Jaeger 2:51)

Whitehead (1960) 526

Arnob.*Nat*.6.2 (*CSEL* 4:214–15)
Arnob.*Nat*.7.5 (*CSEL* 4:241)

Just. *1 Apol*.25.2 (Goodspeed 42)

Goodenough (1923) 137

Gregory the Wonder-Worker, which has been preserved only in Syriac. Even Tertullian, for all his hostility to metaphysics, argued this way against Praxeas. For Athanasius it was "an admitted truth about God that he stands in need of nothing, but is self-sufficient and filled with himself," as it was "a principle of natural philosophy that that which is single and complete is superior to those things which are diverse." Didymus the Blind took it for granted that the Holy Spirit, as God, had to be "impassible, indivisible, and immutable." According to Theodore of Mopsuestia, "it is well known . . . that the gulf between [the Eternal One and a temporal one] is unbridgeable"; and again, "it is known that variety belongs to creatures and simplicity to the divine nature." Cyril of Alexandria dismissed as "madness" any suggestion that the Logos, as God, could be transformed. Apollinaris summarized the position of Christian theologians, regardless of party, when he declared: "Anyone who introduces passion into the [divine] power is atheistic." For Gregory of Nyssa the very suggestion that God could be passible was too absurd to merit serious consideration and too blasphemous to bear Christian repetition. Whether theologians found Platonic speculation compatible with the gospel or incompatible with it, they were agreed that the Christian understanding of the relation between Creator and creature required "the concept of an entirely static God, with eminent reality, in relation to an entirely fluent world, with deficient reality"—a concept that came into Christian doctrine from Greek philosophy.

Nevertheless, any such concept had to be squared with the assertions of both the Old and the New Testament that God was wrathful against sin, as well as with the confession that Christ the crucified was divine. Some Christian theologians went so far as simply to identify the Christian doctrine of God with the philosophical rejection of anthropomorphism; Arnobius argued that God (the gods) had to be "immune to every disturbance and every perturbation," with no "agitation of spirit" or wrath. Others did not go to this extreme, but maintained that the philosophical doctrine of impassibility was not incompatible with the biblical language about the wrath of God; Justin referred to God as impassible, but also spoke "again and again of God in the most personal language."

Tert.*Prax*.29.5   (CCSL
2:1202–203)

Tert.*Marc*.2.16.7   (CCSL
1:494)

See pp. 229–32 below

Ans.*Cur.d.b*.1.8 (Schmitt
2:59)

Ex. 3:14

Clem.*Paed*.8.71.1 (GCS
12:131)
Or.*Princ*.1.3.6 (GCS 22:57);
Or.*Orat*.24.2 (GCS 3:354)

Hil.*Trin*.1.5 (PL 10:28)
Gr.Naz.*Or*.30.18 (PG 36:125–
28)
Thdr.Mops.*Hom.catech*. 9.10
(ST 145:229)

Philox.*Trin*.1 (CSCO 9:27–28
[10:27])

Aug.*Trin*.7.5 (CCSL 50:261)

Dion.Ar.*D.n*.1.6; 2.1 (PG
3:596; 637)

Jo.D.*F.o*.1.9 (PG 94:836)

Thos.Aq.*S.T*.1.2.3

Marrou (1960) 236–37

Still others seem to have been constrained at least partly by their polemical stance to think through the relation between wrath and transcendence with more awareness of its subtlety; Tertullian contended against Praxeas for the impassibility of God, but Marcion's separation of the God of love from the God of wrath evoked from him the distinction that "God may be wrathful, but he is not irritated." The doctrine of the absoluteness and impassibility of God came to form one of the presuppositions of the trinitarian and christological issues; and the doctrine of the atonement in Anselm of Canterbury was based on the axiom "that the divine nature is impassible, and that it can in no sense be brought down from its loftiness or toil in what it wills to do."

Although the axiom of the impassibility of God did not require conventional biblical proof, one passage from the Old Testament served as the proof text for Christian discussions of ontology: "I am who I am"—the word from the burning bush. To Clement of Alexandria it meant that "God is one, and beyond the one and above the monad itself"; to Origen, that "all things, whatever they are, participate in him who truly is"; to Hilary it was "an indication concerning God so exact that it expressed in the terms best adapted to human understanding an unattainable insight into the mystery of the divine nature"; to Gregory of Nazianzus it proved that "he who is" was the most appropriate designation for God; to Theodore of Mopsuestia it was the mark of distinction between the Creator and all his creatures; to Philoxenus of Mabbug it was the divine way of "expelling the tradition of polytheism"; to Augustine it proved that "essence" could be used of God with strict propriety, while "substance" could not. From these and other sources, such as *On Divine Names* of Dionysius the Areopagite, the ontological understanding of the passage passed into authoritative summaries of Christian doctrine, namely, the *Orthodox Faith* of John of Damascus in the East and the *Summa Theologica* of Thomas Aquinas in the West. It is no exaggeration, therefore, to speak of "a metaphysics of Exodus," with which a church father such as Clement of Alexandria sought to harmonize his Christian Platonism.

Even in the case of the theology of Clement, however, it is misleading to speak of hellenization. For, as Henry

H.Chadwick (1966) 64

Chadwick has stated the paradox, "Clement is hellenized to the core of his being, yet unreserved in his adhesion to the Church." Although theologians quoted Scripture in support of ideas originally derived from philosophy, they often modified these ideas on the basis of Scripture. The tension between biblical and philosophical doctrine is especially visible in those thinkers, such as Origen and Augustine, whose preserved writings include both apologies addressed to pagans and biblical expositions addressed to Christians. This tension, in turn, raises serious doubt about the validity of a distinction between apologetic and kerygmatic theology, whether the distinction be historically or theologically intended. At most, it would appear valid to distinguish between the apologetic and the kerygmatic tasks performed by the same theologians, and in such a distinction to keep the entire picture in view, with all its tensions.

It is even more a distortion when the dogma formulated by the catholic tradition is described as "in its conception and development a work of the Greek spirit on the soil of the gospel." Indeed, in some ways it is more accurate to speak of dogma as the "dehellenization" of the theology that had preceded it and to argue that "by its dogma the church threw up a wall against an alien metaphysic." For in the development of both the dogmas of the early church, the trinitarian and the christological, the chief place to look for hellenization is in the speculations and heresies against which the dogma of the creeds and councils was directed. Speculation there continued to be, even after the dogma had been promulgated. The question of the proper function of philosophy in the exposition of Christian doctrine remained inescapable even for theologians such as Tertullian or Luther, who strove to rule it out of court. Christian doctrine also proved again and again that it could not live by philosophy alone, but had to turn to the word of God in the Old and New Testament.

Harnack (1931) 1:20

Elert (1957) 14

The Expectation of the Nations

The end result of these disputes with Judaism and with classical thought was a schematization of the relation between Christianity and other religions that assured the finality of God's revelation in Christ while acknowledging the partial validity of earlier revelations. "A leader shall

Just. *1 Apol*.32.3–4 (Goodspeed 47)

Just.*Dial*.120.3 (Goodspeed 239)

Iren.*Haer*.4.10.2 (Harvey 2:173–74); Iren.*Dem*.57 (*ACW* 16:85)

Cypr.*Test*.1.21 (*CSEL* 3:54–55)
Hipp.*Antichr*.9 (*GCS* 1–II:10)

not fail from Judah, nor a ruler from his thighs, until that which has been laid up for him shall come; and he shall be the expectation of the nations." This prophecy from Genesis 49:10 (LXX) became a proof text, summarizing all three points of this schematization, namely, the historic mission of Israel, the end of that mission with the coming of Jesus, and the place of Jesus as the divine answer to the aspirations of all the nations. Justin took the prophecy to mean that Judaism had completed its vocation and that the Gentiles now looked to Christ as the one who was to come again; he maintained that the phrase "the expectation of the nations" proved that the passage referred to Christ rather than to Judah himself. Irenaeus saw in it the prophecy that Christ was to be "the hope of the Gentiles," and Cyprian took it as evidence that it would be the Gentiles rather than the Jews who would believe in Christ. With Justin, Hippolytus referred it to the second coming of Christ.

Or.*Cels*.1.53 (*GCS* 2:104);
Or.*Princ*.4.1.3 (*GCS* 22:296–98)

Origen summed up the meaning of the passage for the relation of Christianity to Judaism as well as paganism: "The man who reads the prophecy with an open mind would be amazed at the way in which, after saying that the rulers and leaders of the people would come from the tribe of Judah, he also fixes the time when the rule itself is to come to an end. . . . The Christ of God, for whom are the things which are laid up, has come, the ruler of whom the promises of God speak. He was obviously the only one among all his predecessors and, I would make bold to say, among posterity as well who was the expectation of nations." The prophecy became the theme for the statements of the Christian interpretation of history, as in Eusebius, Augustine, and Sozomen; and it has been cited to prove the finality of Jesus Christ throughout Christian history.

Eus.*H.e*.1.6.1–2 (*GCS* 9:48);
Aug.*Civ*.18.45 (*CCSL* 48:643); Soz.*H.e*.1.1.3 (*GCS* 50:6)

The finality of Christ was interpreted in various ways, but each involved some acknowledgment of the revelations that had gone before. The theme of Clement's *Tutor* was a definition of virtue as "a will in conformity to God and Christ in life, rightly adjusted to life everlasting," but the very terminology of this definition was transposed from Stoicism; and his exposition of the Decalogue as a symbol of the name "Jesus" prompted him to observe that the Greek philosophers had "caught a

Clem.*Paed*.1.13.102.2.4 (*GCS* 12:151)

Clem.*Str*.6.17.149.2 (*GCS* 52:508)

spark from the Sacred Scriptures" but had not apprehended the full truth. The revelation of the will of God in the Decalogue and the investigation of virtue in the philosophers had both been granted by God, but they now had to yield to him whose way they had prepared, the teacher of the good and perfect life. Where the apocalyptic vision predominated, the decisiveness of Christ was seen as an explicitly chronological finality. Tertullian warned his pagan readers of the coming of Christ as judge, "which now impends over the world, now near its close, in all the majesty of Deity unveiled"; but even he had to admit that "in former times the Jews enjoyed much of God's favor" and "special revelations," and that the pagan "philosophers, too, regard the Logos . . . as the Creator of the universe." The coming of Christ was the last and greatest revelation of the will of God, but earlier manifestations had to be accorded at least a temporary importance.

Tert.*Apol*.21.15 (*CCSL* 1:125)

Tert.*Apol*.21.4 (*CCSL* 1:123)

Tert.*Apol*.21.10 (*CCSL* 1:124)

When the cross and suffering of Christ were taken as the primary content of his uniqueness, even these new and unprecedented events were interpreted as the fulfillment of prophecy. For Irenaeus, "Christ is the treasure which was hidden in the field, that is, in the world . . . but the treasure hidden in the [Old Testament] Scriptures is Christ, since he was pointed out by means of types and parables." But the "types and parables" were not merely the words of the prophets, who, as "members of Christ . . . set forth the prophecy" about him; the events and persons of the history of Israel performed this function also, as when "the suffering of the Righteous One was prefigured from the beginning in Abel, also described by the prophets, but perfected in the last times in the Son of God." Abel was a hero of the Christian faith. Abraham was "the chief and the herald [princeps et praenuntiator] of our faith," who "saw in the Spirit the day of the Lord's coming and the dispensation of his suffering"; but with that coming and suffering, the mission of Abraham had reached its goal, and it was right for his followers to "forsake their ship and their father and to follow the Logos." Some ancient Christian writers went further. Origen, defending Christ against the claim of Celsus that "Jesus' message of salvation and moral purity was not sufficient to prove his superiority among men . . .

Iren.*Haer*.4.26.1 (Harvey 2:234)

Iren.*Haer*.4.33.10 (Harvey 2:264–65)

Iren.*Haer*.4.25.2 (Harvey 2:233–34)

Iren.*Haer*.4.25.1 (Harvey 2:233)
Iren.*Haer*.4.5.5 (Harvey 2:157)

Iren.*Haer*.4.5.4 (Harvey 2:156)

Or.*Cels*.2.40–41 (*GCS* 2:164–65)

[because he] should not have died," replied that "if [Celsus] considers as evils poverty, and a cross, and the conspiracy of wicked men, obviously he would say that evil also befell Socrates"; but Socrates "would not have been able to prove that he was pure from all evils," while Christ was. A comparison between the suffering of Christ and that of Socrates seems to have become a common idea in Christian apologetics, which was thus able to find an anticipatory parallel in pagan as well as in Jewish literature for the message of the cross and at the same time to demonstrate the superiority of Christ.

Hipp.*Haer*.10.31.1 (*GCS* 26:287)

In the apologetics against paganism—although not so obviously in that against Judaism—the old age of the Christian Scriptures was a testimony to their credibility. Against Judaism the apologists consistently maintained that the Jews did not understand their own Bible properly because they had not accepted Jesus as the Christ. The Christian attitude toward the Jewish Bible was an ambivalent one. On the one hand, the Old Testament could be regarded as obsolete, now that "he for whom it had been laid up" had come; on the other hand, by means of a "spiritual interpretation," it could be claimed for the church as Christian Scripture. The radical version of the former position seems never to have been taken by the majority of Christians. To be sure, Tertullian did make the intriguing statement that "today" there were more who accepted "our position" that the Old Testament was still a part of the Christian Bible than there were of those who accepted the heretical position of Marcion that the Old Testament had become completely obsolete and devoid of authority with the coming of Christ. But even Harnack was not prepared to conclude any more from this than that "it is not altogether impossible that there was a decade during the second century in which the number of Christians who rejected the Old Testament was greater than the number who accepted it." Nevertheless, the very term "Scripture," which originally referred exclusively to the Old Testament, came to be applied, both in the singular and in the plural, to the entire Christian Bible, comprising the sacred writings that Christianity had inherited from Judaism as well as the Christian writings on the basis of which the Jewish Scriptures were being interpreted. This is the valid basis for Harnack's judgment that the most significant event in the history of the

Tert.*Marc*.5.20.2 (*CCSL* 1:724)

Harnack (1960) 1:206

church between 150 and 250 was that Christianity became

Harnack (1931) 1:395–99

a religion of the two Testaments.

"The authority of the Old Testament," as Nathanael Bonwetsch observes in his comment on Harnack's statement, "was the immediate consequence of the services which the Old Testament had performed, and was still

Bonwetsch (1925) 34

performing, for the church." These services were manifold. To its eighteenth-century author, the theme of *Christianity as Old as the Creation* was primarily the congruence between Christianity and natural religion; but to the early church, this congruence was between Christianity and the Old Testament. When Justin, disputing with Trypho, referred to the Old Testament as "your

Just.*Dial*.29.2 (Goodspeed 123)

Scriptures, or rather not yours, but ours," he was voicing the almost universal Christian claim that the direct line of succession ran from the Old Testament to the church, not to the synagogue. Adam, Noah, Abraham—"all these . . . it would be no departure from the truth to style

Eus.*H.e.*1.4.6 (*GCS* 9:40)

as Christians, in point of fact if not in name." A prominent token of this continuity was the worship of the church. "None of our authorities give us [clear] information on the use of the Psalms and other hymns or chants

Carrington (1957) 2:121

in the primitive church," but we do know from Justin

Just. *1 Apol*.67.3 (Goodspeed 75)

that "the memoirs of the apostles or the writings of the prophets" were read in the Sunday service, and the eucharistic prayer in the *Didache* gives thanks "for the

Did.9.2 (Bihlmeyer 5–6); Clem.*Q.d.s.* 29.4 (*GCS* 17:179)

holy vine of thy son David, which thou madest known unto us through thy Son Jesus." Whether or not the liturgy of the early church included the actual singing of the Psalms, it was certainly replete with allusions to the Old Testament in its prayer, reading, and exhortation.

Yet another service performed by the Old Testament was its contribution to the development of the Christian conception of the apostolic ministry into a priesthood that stood in continuity with the Levitical priesthood of the Old Testament people. Origen, for example, combined the apostolic and the priestly definitions of the Christian ministry when he said that "the apostles and their successors, priests according to the great High Priest . . . know from their instruction by the Spirit for what sins,

Or.*Orat*.28.9 (*GCS* 3:381)

when, and how, they must offer sacrifice." Perhaps as important as the cultic service rendered by the Old Testament to the concrete life of the church was the ethical service provided by the commandments of the Old

Testament, especially by the Decalogue. For despite the strictures on the Jewish law that became a stock argument of anti-Jewish polemics, the Decalogue, as summarized and reinterpreted by the ethical teachings of Jesus, was accorded a special place in the church. Irenaeus said that "the words of the Decalogue . . . remain in force among us"; and even the Gnostic Ptolemy, a follower of Valentinus, distinguished in his *Letter to Flora* between the Decalogue and all the rest of the law of Moses, seeing the former as fulfilled in Christ and the latter as either abolished or spiritualized. It is not clear what role the Decalogue played in Christian worship (although there is some indication that it was recited at certain services) or in Christian education (although certain passages in Augustine give the impression that it was used as a basis for instruction in ethics); but it is clear that the Decalogue was highly valued as a summary of the law of God, both natural and revealed.

In these and other ways, the church took possession of the Old Testament—or, at least, of those portions of the Old Testament that were susceptible of Christian interpretation. Allegorical and typological exegesis were very important in the Christian disputes with Judaism, but the spiritual interpretation of the Old Testament was characteristic also of the theological explanation of the Old Testament for other Christians. Most of what the Christian theologians of the second century and even the third century had to say about the inspiration of the biblical writers pertained to the Old Testament prophets rather than to the authors of the books of the New Testament. With Philo, Athenagoras thought that the prophets "spoke out what they were in travail with, their own reasoning falling into abeyance and the Spirit making use of them as a flutist might play upon his flute." Clement of Alexandria called the prophets "the organs of the divine voice," but distinguished between the ecstasy of false prophets and the inspiration of authentic prophets, which preserved the individuality of the latter. For Origen, the inspiration of the Old Testament precluded imputing unworthy meanings to the text; or, as he argued in another passage, "if therefore [all Scripture] is inspired by God and is profitable, we ought to believe that it is profitable even if we do not recognize the profit." From this Origen drew the conclusion that the profit

Iren.*Haer.*4.16.4 (Harvey 2:192)

ap.Epiph.*Haer.*33.3 (*GCS* 25:450–51)

Aug.*Faust.*15.7 (*CSEL* 25:428–32); Aug.*Serm.*9.9.13 (*PL* 38:85)

Athenag.*Leg.*9.1 (Goodspeed 323)

Clem.*Str.*6.18.168.3 (*GCS* 52:518)

Or.*Ex.*4.2 (*GCS* 29:172–73)

Or.*Jos.*20.2 (*GCS* 30:419)

of the Old Testament could not be found through a literal exegesis, which frequently led to absurd or otherwise unprofitable meanings. For Scripture was to be interpreted according to three senses, the literal, the moral, and the intellectual or spiritual; and the last was the perfect and complete meaning. Although the explicit discussion of Origen's hermeneutical theories and of their application belongs to the history of interpretation rather than to the history of doctrine, the subject does bear mention here as part of the process by which the Christian doctrine of Scripture developed and as the precondition for the development of other doctrines. For, diverge though they did in so many other ways, Origen and Tertullian agreed that, in the words of Tertullian against Marcion, "heretics either wrest plain and simple words to any sense they choose by their conjectures, or else they violently resolve by a literal interpretation words which . . . are incapable of a simple solution." The progressive growth of the allegorical interpretation of the Old Testament was not simply a compensation for the decline in the eschatological expectation of the church, but the explication of the Christian conviction that "the writings of Moses are the words of Christ," and that therefore the term "words of Christ" did not include "only those which he spoke when he became man and tabernacled in the flesh, for before that time, Christ, the Logos of God, was in Moses and the prophets."

On the basis of this conviction it was possible to read the Old Testament as a Christian book and to see "the words of Christ" not only in such passages as Psalm 22, as was explicitly warranted by the New Testament, but also in such books as the Song of Songs. The development of the doctrine of the Trinity, for example, was decisively shaped by the use of Proverbs 8:22–31 (LXX) as a passage dealing with the relation between the preexistent Logos and the Father. And although both the orthodox and the Arians read this passage as a "word of Christ," Newman's generalization is probably an accurate one: "It may almost be laid down as an historical fact, that the mystical interpretation and orthodoxy will stand or fall together." When the mystical interpretation was surrendered or at least seriously qualified, as by Theodore of Mopsuestia, his opponents professed to see a causal connection between his hermeneutics and his christology.

Or.*Jos.*6.1 (*GCS* 30:323);
Or.*Jos.*21.1 (*GCS* 30:429–30)

Tert.*Marc.*4.19.6 (*CCSL* 1:592)

Werner (1941) 151–52

Iren.*Haer.*4.2.3 (Harvey 2:148)

Or.*Princ.*pr.1 (*GCS* 22:7–8)

Matt.27:46
Or.*Cant.*pr. (*GCS* 33:85)

See pp. 186, 191–93 below
Ath.*Ar.*2.18–82
(*PG* 26:184–321)

Newman (1878) 344

See pp. 243–44 below

The christological exegesis of the Old Testament and the dogma of the two natures in Christ supported each other. The declaration of 1 Corinthians 15:3–4, echoed by the Nicene Creed, that the death and the resurrection of Christ had taken place "in accordance with the Scriptures," provided the orthodox tradition with justification for elaborating the statements of the New Testament by additions from the Old.

A good example was Deuteronomy 28:66 (LXX): "You shall see your life hanging before your eyes," which, frequently in conjunction with Jeremiah 11:19 and other passages, came very early to be interpreted as a reference to those who crucified Christ. The heretics who refused to see prophecies of Christ in the Old Testament claimed that "there is nothing easier than to prove that this does not refer to Christ," but is a threat addressed to Israel by Moses. But Irenaeus spoke for the orthodox tradition in challenging the heretics to show who but Jesus Christ could have been meant by such prophecies as this; he and Cyprian linked it with Psalm 22, Isaiah 65:2, and other passages which were considered to be standard prophecies of the cross. Tertullian's version predicted the cross even more explicitly, saying: "Your life will hang on the tree before your eyes," which he explained on the basis of other references to the tree of the cross. Among Western writers, Novatian, Lactantius, and Rufinus all echoed the traditional usage and connected it with the usual passages from the psalms and the prophets. Among Eastern thinkers, Athanasius and Cyril of Jerusalem quoted the passage from Deuteronomy as evidence of the clear language about Christ in the Old Testament. This became the standard interpretation of the passage; its content and the differences between Jews and Christians over its exegesis were seen as proof that the Old Testament had clearly predicted the coming of Jesus Christ but that Judaism had failed to understand the Old Testament correctly. The prophecies of the Old Testament were fulfilled, the religion of the Old Testament was replaced.

The attitude of the church fathers toward classical thought contained a somewhat analogous judgment of its historic role. "Whatever things were rightly said among all men," wrote Justin, "are the property of us Christians." Christianity laid claim to all that was good and noble in the tradition of classical thought, for this had

Symb.Nic.–CP (Schaff 2:57)

Aug.Faust.16.5 (CSEL 25:443–44)

Iren.Haer.4.10 2 (Harvey 2:174)

Iren.Dem.79 (ACW 16:97); Cypr.Test.2.20 (CSEL 3:87)

Tert.Jud.11.9 (CCSL 2:1382) Tert.Jud.13.17–21 (CCSL 2:1388–89)

Nov.Trin.9.47 (Weyer 76); Lact.Inst.4.18 (CSEL 19:358); Rufin. Symb.20 (CCSL 20:158); Ambrosiast. 1 Cor.15:3 (CSEL 81–II:165)

Ath.Ar.2.16 (PG 26:177); Cyr.H.Catech.13.19 (Reischl–Rupp 2:76)

Just. 2 Apol.13.4 (Goodspeed 88)

been inspired by the seminal Logos, who became flesh in Jesus Christ. This meant that not only Moses but Socrates had been both fulfilled and superseded by the coming of Jesus. Some ancient Christian writers were willing to concede a great deal to the preparatory work of the seminal Logos among the Greeks; others were less generous.

None went so far as to designate the history of Greek thought a second Old Testament, although in some of his formulations Clement of Alexandria approached such a designation: "Before the advent of the Lord, philosophy was necessary to the Greeks for righteousness. . . . For God is the cause of all good things; but of some primarily, as of the Old and the New Testament; and of others by consequence, as of philosophy. Perhaps, too, philosophy was given to the Greeks directly and primarily, till the Lord should call the Greeks. For this was a schoolmaster to bring the Greek mind to Christ, as the law brought the Hebrews. Philosophy, therefore, was a preparation, paving the way for him who is perfected in Christ." Here the statement of Paul in Galatians 3:24 became a justification for a positive evaluation of the place of Greek philosophy in the history of salvation, or at least in the history of revelation. But in other passages Clement maintained that the Greeks, unlike the Jews, had no "schoolmaster" to teach them the will of God.

Even this concession to philosophy, however, was aimed at proving that classical thought had represented only a preparatory apprehension of divine truth. In Christian practice, classical thought continued to perform such a preparatory function. For example, Cicero's *Hortensius* "turned my [Augustine's] prayers toward thee, O Lord, and gave me new hope and new desires." Justin had been prepared for Christian revelation by the study of Stoicism, then of Aristotelianism, then of Pythagoreanism, and finally of Platonism. None had satisfied his search for truth, but each had led him progressively closer to those teachers who were "more ancient than all those who have the reputation of being philosophers," the Old Testament prophets. Various apologists seized upon various bits of evidence for the anticipation of revealed truth in the writings of the classical tradition—now in Socrates, now in Cicero, now in other thinkers and writers. Two of the most important sources of such evidence were Vergil's *Fourth Eclogue* and the *Sybilline Oracles*.

Although the apologetic interest in Vergil seems to

Clem.*Str*.1.5.28.1–3 (*GCS* 52:17–18)

Clem.*Paed*.3.2.13.3 (*GCS* 12:244)

Aug.*Conf*.3.4.7 (*CSEL* 33:48)

Just.*Dial*.2 (Goodspeed 91–92)

Just.*Dial*.7.1 (Goodspeed 99)

have been drawn first to the *Aeneid*, it came to concentrate on the fourth of his *Eclogues*. This "messianic eclogue," written in 41 or 40 B.C., prophesied a golden age, the culmination of the centuries, in which a virgin would return and a new offspring, bearing a divine life, would descend from heaven to earth to rule a world transformed by his father's virtues. Augustine believed that these words really referred to Christ, even though "poetically" since the poet had actually spoken them of someone else. Jerome was not willing to "call the Christless Maro a Christian" on the basis of these lines; but the *Oration of Constantine* went much further than Augustine in claiming that Vergil intentionally made his language obscure to avoid persecution, but that he "was acquainted with that blessed mystery which gave to our Lord the name of Savior." With these credentials Vergil became the beloved poet even of Christians who were hostile to classical literature. The medieval West multiplied legends of Vergil's supernatural knowledge and exploits, and it was both for his style and for his content that Dante was able to celebrate Vergil as "my master and my author." Whether Vergil's imagery owed its origins to Hebrew messianism or not, it was "the expression of . . . the profound longing for peace, the unvoiced yearning for a world governed by the goodness of God rather than the conflicting desires of men. . . . It was this longing that prepared the way for the expansion of Christianity," and at least in this sense the *Fourth Eclogue* was "messianic." But to some apologists for Christianity its messianism was considerably more explicit.

Vergil's authority was enhanced by his reference to Cuma in the *Fourth Eclogue*, a reference which Christian writers connected with the Cumaean Sibyl also mentioned in the *Aeneid*. "There is no possession of the Romans, sacred or profane, which they guard so carefully as they do the *Sibylline Oracles*," wrote Dionysius of Halicarnassus; and a modern historian has observed that "the study of the outward and inward effects of the Sibylline books is . . . the real history of religion in the first half of the [Roman] republic." Various interpolations had crept into the Sibylline books already under Roman auspices, but it was especially from Jewish and then from Christian sources that such interpolations came. Josephus cited the authority of the books to substantiate

Verg.*Ecl*.4.4–63

Aug.*Civ*.10.27 (*CCSL* 47:302)

Hier.*Ep*.53.7 (*CSEL* 54:454)

Const.*Or.s.c*.19–20 (*GCS* 7:181–86)

Dant.*Inf*.1.85

Highet (1957) 73

Aug.*Civ*.10.27 (*CCSL* 47:302)

Verg.*Aen*.6.36

Dion.Hal.*Ant.Rom*.4.62.5

Carter (1906) 71

Jos.*Ant*.1.118 (*LCL* 4:56)

Eus.*P.e*.9.15 (*GCS* 43:500)
ap.Or.*Cels*.5.61; 7.53 (*GCS* 3:65; 203)

Just. *1 Apol*.20.1 (Goodspeed 40)

Theoph.*Autol*.2.9 (*SC* 20:120)

Theoph.*Autol*.2.36 (*SC* 20:190–96)

Clem.*Prot*.8.77.3 (*GCS* 12:59)

Lact.*Inst*.7.16; 18 (*CSEL* 19:636–38; 642–44)

Lact.*Inst*.1.6 (*CSEL* 19:23)
Lact.*Inst*.2.11 (*CSEL* 19:154–55)

Lact.*Inst*.4.6 (*CSEL* 19:290)
Aug.*Civ*.18.23 (*CCSL* 48:614–15)

Athenag.*Leg*.30.1–2 (Goodspeed 351); Const.*Or.s.c*.18 (*GCS* 7:179–81)

Just. *1 Apol*.20.1 (Goodspeed 40)

Acts 10:34–35

his apologetic case for Judaism, and Eusebius drew upon Josephus. Several Christian apologists followed his lead, to the point that Celsus ridiculed Christians as "Sibyllists." Justin cited the Sibyl in support of the Christian doctrine "that there is to be a dissolution by God of things corruptible." Theophilus lumped the Sibyl with the Hebrew prophets among the "men of God who were borne along by the Spirit and became prophets, being inspired and made wise by God"; the Sibyl "was a prophetess among the Greeks and the other nations," who had prophesied the eventual conflagration of the world. He quoted from the *Sibylline Oracles* more extensively than did most other Christian writers and may have been the source for some oracles. Clement of Alexandria found the Sibyl "in remarkable accordance with inspiration" but did not accept her oracles uncritically. Lactantius found proof not only, as other fathers had, for Christian eschatology, but for monotheism, for the doctrine of creation, and even, by combining the oracles with Proverbs 8:22–31, for the doctrine that God had a Son; Augustine based his use of the Sibyl at least partly on Lactantius. Other apologists, too, made use of the Sibyl to corroborate Christian teaching. It was an epitome of this apologetic use when the medieval hymn, *Dies irae,* prophesied the coming of the day of wrath on the basis of the dual authority of "David and the Sibyl"—a conflation which more timid Christians vainly tried to modify. Sometimes the references to the Sibyl were combined with citations of "Hystapes," a syncretistic work published under the name of the Persian magus, which provided additional evidence for the claim that pre-Christian paganism had not been devoid of expectations of that which had come in Jesus Christ.

This interpretation of the relation between natural and revealed religion found support in many areas of the life of the church, as did the interpretation of the relation between Christianity and Judaism discussed earlier. The missionary practice of the church was constrained to recognize from the outset that "God shows no partiality, but in every nation any one who fears him and does what is right is acceptable to him," and that therefore the Greek did not have to become a Jew en route to the gospel. From this premise it appeared to follow that Christian missionaries should affirm whatever could be affirmed of the religion prevailing in the nations to which they came and

should represent Christianity as the correction and fulfillment of the expectations at work in those nations.
When Gregory I instructed the missionary Augustine to
adapt both pagan temples and pagan holy days to Christian usage, he was "but following the practice widely
current in the days when the Roman Empire was being
converted." And while it may be an exaggeration to speak
of this approach to the religion of the nations as "the
syncretism of a universal religion," it was based on the
principle that Jesus Christ was the divinely ordained answer to the needs and aspirations of the Gentiles as well
as the fulfillment of the messianic hopes of Israel. Partly
as a consequence of such missionary practice, a similar
view of the relation between natural religion and revealed religion is evident in the development of Christian
piety, as the church led the nations through lower to
higher forms of devotion and worship.

For the development of Christian doctrine, the most
significant area where this principle manifested itself
was probably the relation between philosophy and theology. Most of the generous things which the church
fathers said about paganism applied to the philosophers.
For the religious rituals of Greek and Roman paganism
Christian apologists had only contempt. They did not,
for example, elaborate on the significance of pagan sacrifices for the sacrificial significance of the death of Christ,
as they shared with their pagan opponents a disgust at the
crudities of polytheistic practice. But they took the position that while the priests and professional religionists
of the nations had been perpetuating idolatrous beliefs
and practices, the philosophers had begun the process of
emancipation and rationalization which Christ, the eternal
Reason of God, had now consummated. Both pagan polytheism and Jewish monotheism had now been transcended
by his coming. Gregory of Nyssa summarized the case in
a remarkable passage, echoed by other theologians:
"Truth passes in the mean between these two conceptions,
destroying each heresy, and yet accepting what is useful
to it from each. The Jewish dogma is destroyed by the
acceptance of the Logos and by the belief in the Spirit,
while the polytheistic error of the Greek school is made
to vanish by the unity of the [divine] nature abrogating
this notion of plurality. Yet again, of the Jewish conception, let the unity of the nature stand; and of the Greek,

ap.Bed.H.e.1.30 (PL 95:70-71)

Latourette (1937) 2:68

Harnack (1962) 312

Clem.Prot.3.42.1 (GCS 12:31)

Clem.Str.7.6 (GCS 17:22-27)

Bas.Spir.30.77 (PG 32:213);
Gr.Naz.Or.23.8 (PG 35:1160)

Gr.Nyss.*Or.catech.*3 (*PG* 45:17–20)

only the distinction as to persons. . . . It is as if the number of the Trinity were a remedy in the case of those who are in error as to the One, and the assertion of the unity for those whose beliefs are dispersed among a number of divinities."

In the orthodox doctrine of the Trinity, Christianity articulated its continuity with the Old Testament and its answer to classical thought. Augustine's *On the Trinity* first demonstrated the doctrine of the Trinity from the Scriptures, especially from the Old Testament; it then proceeded to argue that "in the Trinity, Christian wisdom discovers that for which Classicism had so long vainly sought, viz., the *logos* or explanation of being and motion, in other words, a metaphysic of ordered process."

Cochrane (1944) 436–37

The controversies over the doctrine of the Trinity itself and the irrepressible disputes over the propriety of philosophical speculation within the limits of orthodoxy are evidence that the relation of Christian doctrine to Judaism and to classical thought has been a perennial issue in theology. The forms of the issue were largely set by the literature of the first five centuries, but the questions that were left unanswered in the triumph of Christian theology over Judaism and classicism were to take their revenge by reasserting themselves with insistent force when the political, cultural, and ecclesiastical presuppositions of orthodoxy began to wither away in the modern era.

2   Outside the Mainstream

One of the principal concerns of the apologists was to demonstrate the continuity of the gospel with the history of God's revelation in the world. This meant above all the gospel's descent from, and fulfillment of, the Old Testament; but even with other chapters in world history the apologists sought to claim a certain amount of continuity. So overriding was this concern to demonstrate continuity that the distinctiveness of Jesus Christ and the newness of the gospel sometimes seemed to be obscured or even jeopardized. It is significant that although some of the irregular versions of early Christianity overemphasized its continuity with Judaism, the major heresies of the first two or three centuries were those that stressed the radical and unheard-of in the Christian message over against the Old Testament and natural religion. Marcion proclaimed the gospel of a God who, in granting salvation, was wholly other than the Creator and Judge of the Old Testament. The Gnostics held to a secret cosmological wisdom which had been hidden from previous ages and even from the majority of Christians. Montanism laid claim to special revelations of a new prophecy denied to the secularized church. Different though they were not only from what came to be seen as the mainstream of the orthodox development but also from one another, these three heresies all stressed distinctiveness even at the cost of continuity.

History is usually dictated by the victors. As the principal sources of information about the development of Christian doctrine are the writings of orthodox theologians, so most of what has been known about these heresies—at least until the twentieth century—has come from the works of those who combated them. The presupposition of those works was that the primitive deposit of Christian truth had been given by Christ to the apostles and by them in turn to the succession of orthodox bishops and teachers, while the heretics were those who forsook this succession and departed from this deposit. "Heretics," said Origen, "all begin by believing, and afterwards depart from the road of faith and the truth of the church's teaching." With only a few latitudinarian exceptions, both the heretics and the orthodox (although it is misleading to use such terms as though there were some method of determining a priori who were the villains and who the heroes) were agreed throughout the controversies from 100 to 600 that there was only one true doctrine, which each party claimed to possess. The truth was one, and there could be no pluralism in its confession; one's opponents were not merely espousing a different form of Christian obedience, they were teaching false doctrine. The heretics were no less implacable than the orthodox in claiming that only their position was the correct one.

In its earliest Christian use, the term "heresy" was not sharply distinguished from "schism"; both referred to factiousness. But a dominant characteristic of such factiousness was that it created "dissensions and difficulties, in opposition to the doctrine which you have been taught." At least as early as Irenaeus, therefore, "heresy" came to be the term for a deviation from the standard of sound doctrine. It was consistent with this development that Augustine eventually came to define heretics as those who "in holding false opinions regarding God, do injury to the faith itself," as distinguished from schismatics, who "in wicked separations break off from brotherly charity, although they may believe just what we believe." Basil's distinction was only slightly different: heretics were "men who were altogether broken off and alienated in matters relating to the actual faith," and schismatics were "men who had separated for some ecclesiastical reasons and questions capable of mutual solution." But already in the conflict with Montanism, even more in the conflict with Donatism, and above all in the church history of the West since the Reformation, the distinction between heresy and schism has not been easy to maintain with any consistency.

Or.*Cant*.3.4 (*GCS* 33:179); Tert.*Praescrip*. 36.6–8 (*CCSL* 1:217); Tert.*Marc*.1.1.6 (*CCSL* 1:442)

ap.Thdr.Mops.*Phil*.1.18 (Swete 1:208–209)

1 Cor.11:18–19

Rom.16:17

Iren.*Haer*.4.26.2 (Harvey 2:236)

Aug.*Fid.et symb*.10.21 (*CSEL* 41:27); Aug.*Haer*.pr.7 (*CCSL* 46:289)

Bas.*Ep*.188.1 (*PG* 32:665)

I Tim.4:1

Just. *1 Apol.*58.1 (Goodspeed 68)

Tert.*Praescrip.*40.2 (*CCSL* 1:220)

Tert.*Praescrip.*7.3 (*CCSL* 1:192)

ap.Eus.*H.e.*5.28.13 (*GCS* 9:504)

Iren.*Haer.*1.3.6 (Harvey 1:30–31)

Iren.*Haer.*5.35.1 (Harvey 2:423–24)

See pp. 124–25, 129 below

2 Tim.1:13

As a departure from the truth of sound doctrine, heresy was a "doctrine of demons." It was, Justin insisted, the devils who had "put forward Marcion of Pontus" and who continued to produce heresies. Although the demons were the ultimate source of heresy, Tertullian maintained that "heresies are themselves instigated by philosophy," and Hippolytus attacked the heretics because "they seek not for what the Sacred Scriptures declare, but laboriously set themselves to find a form of syllogism which may support their godlessness." Some heresies seem to have retained the conceptual framework and the language of an earlier period, after the development of doctrine had rendered these obsolete; the term "fullness [πλήρωμα]," which came as close as any word to being a technical christological term in the epistles of the New Testament bearing the name of Paul, was vitiated by its association with the Gnosticism of Valentinus, whose use of it, Irenaeus charged, "strives . . . to adapt the good terms of revelation to [its] own wicked inventions" and managed to discredit the term despite its prominence in the New Testament. Yet the same Irenaeus, unswervingly orthodox though he was, had, at another point, failed to anticipate the direction that the development of doctrine would take. For him, a millennial understanding of the kingdom of God was a hallmark of orthodoxy, but such an understanding soon became an aberration from the soundness of "apostolic tradition."

Nevertheless, this discovery that heresy may be a result of poor timing has come only as a consequence of modern historical research: the primitive church was not characterized by an explicit unity of doctrine; therefore heresy could sometimes claim greater antiquity than orthodoxy. But what did characterize primitive Christianity was a unity of life, of fidelity to the Old Testament, of devotion, and of loyalty to its Lord, as he was witnessed to in the Old and New Testament. Heresy was a deviation from that unity; and as the unity came to be transposed into the language of creed and dogma from that of testimony and proclamation, heresy was seen as an aberration from "the pattern of the sound words which you have heard." It is becoming increasingly evident that this "primitive catholicism," with its movement from kerygma to dogma, was already far more explicitly at work in the first century than was once supposed.

Heresy was treated by the early church as the concern not only of doctrinal theology, but also of moral theology, of canon law, and finally of civil law as well. This was not only because of the stock accusation that false doctrine led to "all those kinds of forbidden deeds of which the Scriptures assure us that 'they who do such things shall not inherit the kingdom of God,' " but because of the claim that the invention and especially the propagation of false doctrine were due to "a vainglory that has preoccupied their mind." A heretic, in the later formula of Thomas Aquinas, "no longer adheres to the teaching of the church as to an infallible rule, but to his own will." The formal condemnation of heresy by ecclesiastical authority made it a matter of church law, and the enforcement of orthodoxy by the imperial authority made heresy a matter of civil law as well. "The older methods [of combating heresy] operated through the medium of mutual agreement among bishops toward a commonly desired end, cognizant of binding ecclesiastical law only as expressed in terms of universal tradition. The new methods of administration, on the other hand, operated through the medium of synodical legislation and the establishment of a rule by law, the process being borrowed from civil government and to a degree being forced upon the Church from without." The moral and legal aspects of heresy are relevant to our history of the Christian tradition only as the context within which doctrine developed, but not as the object of special investigation. We are likewise interested only in the Christian careers of the heretical doctrines rather than in their connection with Hellenistic syncretism or in their post-Christian histories.

Iren.*Haer*.1.6.3 (Harvey 1:55)

Iren.*Haer*.2.11.2 (Harvey 1:275)

Thos.Aq.*S.T*.2–II:5.3

Hess (1958) 110

The Separation of Law and Gospel

It is evident that certain forms of Judaism were the origin of the earliest forms of Christian heresy; "to Judaize" was long a term for "to teach false doctrine." Nevertheless, the most important early heresies were not Jewish, but anti-Jewish in their inspiration. Thus, according to Irenaeus, "Cerdo . . . taught that the God proclaimed by the law and the prophets was not the Father of our Lord Jesus Christ. For the former was known, but the latter unknown; while the one also was just, but the other benevolent." Although it had been suggested that "Irenaeus simply transferred Marcion's principal doctrine to Cerdo

Ath.*Decr*.2.1 (Opitz 2–I:2); Gr.Naz.*Or*.38.8 (*PG* 36:320)

Iren.*Haer*.1.27.1 (Harvey 1:214–15)

Harnack (1960) 2:36

Tert.*Marc*.1.2.3 (*CCSL* 1:443)

because he had read in his source that Cerdo, as Marcion's teacher, had influenced him," the testimony of Tertullian and others makes the account of Irenaeus more credible. According to another account, Cerdo not only taught two gods, "one good, the other cruel," but also "repudiates the prophecies and the law; renounces God the Creator; maintains that Christ who came was not the Son of the superior God; affirms that he was not in the substance of flesh; states him to have been only in a phantasmal shape, not to have really suffered, but undergone a quasi passion, and not to have been born at all. A resurrection of the soul merely does he approve, denying that of the body. The Gospel of Luke alone, and that not entire, does he receive. Of the apostle Paul he takes neither all the epistles, nor [those he does accept] in their integrity. The Acts of the Apostles and the Apocalypse he rejects as false." If Cerdo had taught all that this treatise attributed to him, he would have anticipated almost everything taught by Marcion, who would have been thus quite unoriginal in his doctrine; it may have been the intent of this report to disparage the originality of Marcion by transferring his doctrine to Cerdo.

Ps.Tert.*Haer*.6.1 (*CCSL* 2:1408)

Marcion's biography, even as presented by hostile writers, makes it evident that he had come to his basic insights independently of Cerdo. According to these writers, Marcion raised the question of the proper exegesis of statements of Jesus about the new wine and the old wineskins or about the two kinds of trees with their fruit before his excommunication by the church at Rome and before his affiliation with Cerdo. Two of the principal emphases of his theology—the newness of the gospel and the contrast between two sources as an explanation for the antithesis between good and evil in the world—would seem to have been prominent in his thought while he was still in Asia Minor, that is, about 140; they may even have been the occasion for an earlier excommunication, at the hands of the bishop of Sinope, who was his own father. Nevertheless, he does not seem to have systematized his thought until after 144, when he was excommunicated at Rome and went on to found his own church.

Ps.Tert.*Haer*.6.2 (*CCSL* 2:1408)

Tert.*Marc*.1.19.4 (*CCSL* 1:460)

"Marcion's special and principal work," according to Tertullian, was "the separation of the law and the gospel"; his special and fundamental religious conviction was a single-minded dedication to the gospel. "Oh, wonder beyond all wonder or rapture, beyond all power or astonishment it is that one cannot express anything at all about the gospel, nor even think about it, nor compare

ap.Harnack (1960) 2:256

it with anything else at all!" This inexpressible and incomparable wonder of salvation was so overwhelming that it obscured all else in the world—not only in the world as the kingdom of the devil, but in the world as the creation of God. The salvation of man was a more urgent cause than any other and "transcends all others in

Tert.*Res*.2.8 (*CCSL* 2:923)

its importance." It was the key to the proper understanding of other doctrinal issues, such as the resurrection of the body, which had to be interpreted in a manner consistent with the centrality of deliverance, that is, had to

Tert.*Res*.2.12 (*CCSL* 2:923)

be changed into "the salvation of the soul." For it was the purpose of the coming of Jesus to abolish all the works

Tert.*Marc*.5.11.9 (*CCSL* 1:697)
Iren.*Haer*.1.27.2 (Harvey 1:217)

belonging to "this world" and to its Creator, the "ruler of the universe [κοσμοκράτωρ]." Sun and moon, constel-

Tert.*Marc*.5.4.2 (*CCSL* 1:672)

lations and stars, all were overshadowed by his coming. When he came, "he did not come into that which was his

Iren.*Haer*.3.11.2 (Harvey 2:41)

own, but into that which was alien to him." The natural world was made up of "beggarly elements," among which

Tert.*Marc*.1.14.1 (*CCSL* 1:455)

Marcion especially included reptiles and insects. Particularly repulsive to him was the "uncleanliness" of sex and of childbirth, none of which could have anything to do

Tert.*Carn*.4.2 (*CCSL* 2:878); Tert.*Marc*.4.21.10–11 (*CCSL* 1:599–600)

with the salvation of man. An epitome of this elevation of divine deliverance over everything else was the statement of Marcion and his followers that this "one work" of delivering man through the supreme and most excellent

Tert.*Marc*.1.17.1 (*CCSL* 1:458); Tert.*Marc*.1.24.7 (*CCSL* 1:468)

goodness of God was vastly preferable to "the creation of all the locusts."

Or.*Princ*.2.5.4 (*GCS* 22:137)

It was the reality of the world of locusts, crocodiles, and sex that raised for Marcion the "celebrated question" of the meaning of Luke 6:43, "the question of the origin of evil," which was, according to Tertullian, a favorite

Tert.*Marc*.1.2.1–2 (*CCSL* 1:442–43)

preoccupation of heretics. For Marcion, however, it was not primarily a speculative problem, but a religious one. If God were at one and the same time good, all-knowing, and all-powerful, how could he permit the deception and

Tert.*Marc*.2.5.1–2 (*CCSL* 1:479–80)

the fall of man? Since this was precisely what he had done, it followed that God could not be possessed of all three of these attributes. For a good tree did not bear bad fruit. The presence of two kinds of fruits bore witness to the existence of two kinds of trees. To account for the difference between salvation and creation and to

Tert.*Marc*.1.19.4 (*CCSL* 1:460)

Tert.*Marc*.1.6.1 (*CCSL* 1:447)

Tert.*Marc*.1.19.2 (*CCSL* 1:459–60); Tert.*Marc*.4.7.1 (*CCSL* 1:553)

Iren.*Haer*.1.27.2; 3.12.12 (Harvey 1:216; 2:68)

Iren.*Haer*.3.25.3 (Harvey 2:134)

Tert.*Marc*.5.18.12 (*CCSL* 1:720)

Tert.*Marc*.5.13.15 (*CCSL* 1:704)

Blackman (1948) 67

Tert.*Marc*.1.25.2 (*CCSL* 1:468)

Tert.*Marc*.5.4.12 (*CCSL* 1:674)
Tert.*Marc*.4.29.10 (*CCSL* 1:626)

Iren.*Haer*.1.27.2 (Harvey 1:217–18)

Tert.*Marc*.5.4.3 (*CCSL* 1:672)

achieve his "special and principal work," which was "the separation of the law and the gospel," Marcion posited the existence of two gods, "one judicial, harsh, mighty in war; the other mild, placid, and simply good and excellent." The former was the Creator of the world, the God of the Old Testament; the latter was the Father of Jesus Christ, who had descended to earth for the first time in the fifteenth year of the reign of Tiberius Caesar.

According to Irenaeus, Marcion called the Creator "the creator of evils, lustful for war, inconstant in his attitude, and self-contradictory." In another account, however, Irenaeus attributed to Marcion a distinction between a god who was "good" and one who was "judicial." Tertullian suggested that Marcion regarded the Creator as equivalent to the devil, even though he had stated a little earlier that for Marcion "there are two gods, one just and the other good." Thus there is one set of testimonies that Marcion regarded the Creator as "just" and "judicial," but as a lesser divine being than the highest God, while according to another set of testimonies he actually denounced the Creator as "evil." It is not clear how to interpret the contradictions between these two sets of testimonies. It is plausible that Marcion did regard the Creator as evil, while Cerdo did not; or it may be that Marcion avoided the implication that the Creator was actually an evil principle; perhaps the most reasonable interpretation is to suppose that "Marcion indeed started with a plain contrast of good and bad gods, but later accepted Cerdo's teaching that the creator was not altogether evil, but in some respects just."

The attributes of Marcion's good God are more evident. He was said to possess goodness in a pure and simple sense, to be "a Being of simple goodness, to the exclusion of all those other attributes, sensations, and affections, which the Marcionites indeed transfer from their god to the Creator." All contradiction between justice and mercy, between law and gospel, was foreign to him. He could not visit judgment or grow wrathful or take vengeance. He was characterized by "serenity and mildness." While the Creator of the universe was recognized on the basis of his creation, the true God had remained the unknown God until the coming of Jesus. He had "neither any work nor any prophecy, nor accordingly any time, to show himself"; but "although he did not manifest him-ap.Tert.*Marc*.1.19.1 (*CCSL* 1:459)

self from the beginning and by means of the creation, [he] has yet revealed himself in Christ Jesus." To this God and to this Christ, the world fashioned by the Creator was alien, as was the law of Moses. He was wholly other than the God who could be known either from the creation or from Old Testament revelation. So it was that Marcion resolved the tensions within the Christian doctrine of God by a radical separation, which purchased the doctrine of salvation at the cost of the doctrine of the unity of God. The importance of the issue can be gauged by the later struggle to maintain both doctrines at once in the doctrine of the Trinity. Tertullian anticipated that struggle in his trinitarian terminology generally and specifically in his response to Marcion's doctrine of the two gods: "Whatever attributes you require as worthy of God, must be found in the Father, who is invisible and unapproachable, and placid, and (so to speak) the God of the philosophers; whereas those qualities which you censure as unworthy must be supposed to be in the Son, who has been seen, and heard, and encountered, the witness and servant of the Father, uniting in himself man and God, God in mighty deeds, in weak ones man, in order that he may give to man as much as he takes from God. What in your esteem is the entire disgrace of my God, is in fact the

Tert.*Marc*.2.27.6–7 (*CCSL* 1:506–507)

sacrament of man's salvation." Marcion's separation between the two gods was taken up into Tertullian's doctrine of the relation between the eternal, invisible Father and the Son, who had become true man in Jesus Christ.

But Marcion had not been able to take this way out of

Tert.*Marc*.1.15.6 (*CCSL* 1:457)

the dilemma, for his Jesus Christ had not been true man. The Creator, too, had promised a Christ, who had not yet come; but "the Christ who in the days of Tiberius was, by a previously unknown God, revealed for the salvation of all nations, is a different being from him who was ordained by God the Creator for the restoration of the Jewish state, and who is yet to come." Marcion separated his authentic Christ from the political Messiah of the Jews

Tert.*Marc*.4.6.3 (*CCSL* 1:552)

by "a great and absolute difference." This authentic Christ could not have assumed a material body that participated in the created world, for such a body would have been

Tert.*Marc*.3.10.1 (*CCSL* 1:521)

"stuffed with excrement." A material body and a physical birth belonged to the Creator and were unworthy of

Tert.*Marc*.3.11.1 (*CCSL* 1:521–22)

Tert.*Carn*.3.4 (*CCSL* 2:876)

the true Christ. If he had become a man with a material body, this would have meant the end of divinity. Irenaeus

Iren.*Haer*.3.16.1 (Harvey
2:81–82)

Tert.*Marc*.4.21.11 (*CCSL*
1:600)

Tert.*Marc*.3.9.1 (*CCSL* 1:519)

Tert.*Carn*.4.3 (*CCSL* 2:879)

Tert.*Marc*.3.18.1 (*CCSL*
1:531)

Tert.*Marc*.1.11.8 (*CCSL*
1:453)

Tert.*Carn*.5.1 (*CCSL* 2:880)

Tert.*Marc*.4.36.11 (*CCSL*
1:645)

Harnack (1960) 2:262

would seem to have been referring to Marcion (among others) when he attacked certain heretics for teaching that Christ "merely suffered putatively, being naturally impassible."

Human nature, or the condition of having a material body and participating in the change and suffering of the creation, was that from which man had to be delivered, but not that by which he would be delivered. It bound man to this world and to the Creator, but Christ came from the true God and therefore could not have been born of a woman. He was revealed full-grown at once. His body was like the bodies assumed by the angels of the Creator when they met with Abraham and Lot, ate, and worked. It was in such a body that Christ was crucified, to purchase man from the Creator, for man "belonged to another," namely, to the Creator. The Creator would not have exposed his own Son to the curse he had pronounced on anyone who was hanged on a tree; but as the Son of the Supreme God, Christ "brought down upon himself the curse of the Creator" on the cross. Although the manger had been unworthy of the true Christ, the tomb was not. This christology was significantly different from that of other Gnostics, who denied the passion and death of Christ as well as his birth; on the other hand, it was not as different from the teaching of more orthodox theologians at the middle of the second century as their attacks upon it would indicate. And even the christological orthodoxy of the fourth and fifth centuries was to find almost insuperable the task of attributing genuine birth, suffering, and death to the Son of an impassible deity.

Discontinuity was the theme of the relation not only between creation and salvation, the law and the gospel, the Creator and the Father, man and Christ, but also between the Old Testament and the New and between the apostolic community and the apostle Paul. As the God of the Jews was radically separate from the Father of the Lord Jesus Christ, so the deposit of the revelations of the former could not be authoritative for the true disciples of the latter. The Old Testament had not been fulfilled, but abolished. Jesus had come "to subvert the Creator and overthrow the law and the prophets," rather than to establish and fulfill them; in fact, later followers of Marcion even emended Matt. 5:17 to read: "I have not come to fulfill the law but to abolish it." His coming had not

Tert.*Marc*.3.4.3 (*CCSL* 1:512)

been prophesied by the Old Testament, but had been sudden and unforeseen. Where the New Testament referred to the Old Testament as "Scripture" or employed the formula "It is written," Marcion deleted the passage. He accused the Old Testament of "foolishness, weakness,

Tert.*Marc*.5.5.9 (*CCSL* 1:678)

Tert.*Marc*.2.21.1 (*CCSL* 1:499)

dishonor, meanness, and contempt." He criticized various details of its dietary laws, the law concerning the Sabbath, and other prescriptions. Not only the ceremonial law, but the moral law of the Old Testament was unworthy of the true God, who could not, for instance, have commanded

Iren.*Haer*.4:30.1 (Harvey 2:248)

Israel to despoil Egypt at the time of the exodus. At the same time, Marcion did concede to the moral law of the Old Testament a limited and temporary function.

In keeping with this refusal to allow the Old Testament the status of Christian Scripture, Marcion also repudiated the method of nonliteral interpretation. He would not grant that in the Old Testament "very many events are figuratively predicted by means of enigmas and allegories and parables, and that they must be understood

Tert.*Marc*.3.5.3 (*CCSL* 1:513)

in a sense different from the literal description." He insisted that the Old Testament prophecies concerning the

Tert.*Marc*.4.20 (*CCSL* 1:594–95); Tert.*Marc*.3.14.5 (*CCSL* 1:526–27)

Christ of the Creator must be taken literally and that they therefore could not apply to the true Christ. Moreover, the Old Testament had not prophesied that the Christ of

Tert.*Marc*.3.18.1 (*CCSL* 1:531)

the Creator would suffer on the cross. When the Old Testament referred to David's progeny, it meant Solomon,

Tert.*Marc*.3.20.8 (*CCSL* 1:536)

not Christ. There is considerable reason to believe that in this respect and in others Marcion was reflecting the influence of Jewish interpreters. The Old Testament was valid as Jewish Scripture; its historical reports were reliable, and even its moral legislation had been appropriate to its purpose. But that purpose had not been to predict the coming of the true Christ or to prescribe the conduct of the members of his church. As Harnack has said, "It goes without saying that by such an interpretation Marcion was abusing the Old Testament and draining it of its meaning, and that he falls far short of the understanding that was present even among the pious and spiritually advanced Jews of the time. But since everything in this book, inspired and canonical as it was regarded, stood on one level, it is understandable that someone came along who read the book from left to right rather than from right to left and explained the highly developed and won-

Harnack (1960) 1:101–102

derful parts in terms of the primitive ones."

The rejection of the Old Testament was consistent with Marcion's attitude toward the doctrine of creation, whose place in the body of Christian teaching depended on the authority of the Old Testament. For although the doctrine of creation was explicitly taught in many passages of the New Testament, most of these passages were citations or paraphrases of the Old Testament. Similarly, the discussions of the doctrine of creation in the apologists were usually based on such passages as the creation stories in Genesis or Proverbs 8:22–31, which were read as proof that the preexistent Christ had been the agent of creation. Therefore the historical coming of Christ was connected to this prehistoric history. "For it is the God who said, 'Let light shine out of darkness,' who has shone in our hearts to give the light of the knowledge of the glory of God in the face of Christ." From this it followed, Tertullian argued, that Christ as well as the apostles, the gospel as well as Moses, all belonged to that God who was also the Creator of this world rather than to a God who had not said, "Let light shine out of darkness." This continuity Marcion denied, in the name of the newness of the gospel of Christ. Any continuity or sequence (ordo) was unnecessary, for the coming of Christ had been sudden and immediate. The keynote of the teaching of Christ had been its newness. Luke 5:37 meant that the content and the form of that teaching had been different from the law of Moses. But if it was valid to use the Old Testament as a Christian book and to find the details of the life and teaching of Jesus prophesied there, one had to ask: "Then what was there new about what the Lord brought to us when he came?" This was why one could not express anything at all about the gospel, or even think about it, or compare it with anything else at all. The ineffable newness of the gospel would be fundamentally compromised if it were represented as having already been present in the Jewish Scriptures.

Marcion's rejection of the principle of continuity was, however, even more radical. The authentic Christian gospel had to be disengaged not only from the Jewish community, but also from the Christian community, not only from the so-called prophets of the Old Testament but also from the so-called apostles of the New. The apostle Paul was the only one who had transmitted the gospel without adulteration. "Paul alone knew the truth, and to him the mystery was manifested by revelation." The sepa-

2 Cor.4:6

Tert.Marc.5.11.12 (CCSL 1:698)

Tert.Marc.3.3.1 (CCSL 1:510)
Tert.Marc.4.16.2 (CCSL 1:581)

Tert.Marc.4.11.10 (CCSL 1:568)

Iren.Haer.4.34.1 (Harvey 2:269)

Iren.Haer.3.13.1 (Harvey 2:72)

Tert.*Marc*.1.20.1 (*CCSL*
1:460)

Tert.*Marc*.5.2.5 (*CCSL* 1:667)

Tert.*Praescrip*.23.5 (*CCSL*
1:205)

Tert.*Marc*.4.2.4 (*CCSL*
1:548)

Knox (1942) 24;31

2 Pet.3:16

ration of law and gospel had been the theme of the original gospel of Jesus and of Paul, but it had been adulterated by the other apostles and their followers and was now being restored by Marcion. The Epistle to the Galatians had been an attack on such adulterations; the "other gospel" referred to in Galatians 1:8 was the adulterated gospel introduced by the Creator and his apostles. Therefore Paul's teaching that the law of Moses did not apply to believers had not been received from the other apostles, but from a direct personal revelation. The conflict between Peter and Paul provided Marcion with a principle of discrimination by which he could separate the authentic Pauline gospel from the adulterations. These included many passages in the received writings of Paul and in the Gospels. Marcion set about purging the Pauline epistles of such elements as the acknowledgment of the Christian authority of the Old Testament and the identification of the Creator with the Father of the Lord Jesus Christ. In place of the so-called Gospels he put a purified Gospel of Luke, which he took to be the only authentic Gospel and the one most closely connected with Paul. This makes Marcion an important figure not only in the history of the development of doctrine, but also in the history both of the text and of the canon of the New Testament.

The history of the development of doctrine takes account of Marcion's textual emendations only because they embody the theological motifs of his separation of the law and the gospel. His canon, too, belongs in this history. For it has been suggested that "if Marcion's canon was Scripture at all, it was the first distinctively Christian Scripture," and therefore "Marcion is primarily responsible for the idea of the New Testament." He appears to have set his twofold Scripture of "the Lord" (the Gospel of Luke) and "the apostle" (the ten authentic epistles of Paul, namely, and in this order, Galatians, 1 and 2 Corinthians, Romans, 1 and 2 Thessalonians, Ephesians, Colossians, Philippians, and Philemon) in opposition to the twofold Scripture of "the law" and "the prophets." This is not necessarily synonymous with saying that there would not have been a Christian canon of the New Testament except for the opposition to Marcion. There was an increasing tendency to cite apostolic writings as authoritative, and there seem to have been the beginnings of collections of these writings. But regardless of any such tendencies, Marcion's view of the antithesis between the

Old Testament and the pure gospel and his accusation of apostasy against all the apostles except Paul obliged him to expurgate the Christian writings that were in circulation and to organize them into a Christian Scripture that could counterweigh the authority of the Jewish Scripture, which had been foisted upon the church. Even though it is an oversimplification to say that the Christian canon of the New Testament as eventually adopted was the church's answer to Marcion's canon, it does seem accurate to say that Marcion's canon was his answer to the Old Testament.

Marcion did not found a school but a church. During the second half of the second century, the Marcionite church was a noteworthy rival to orthodox Christianity, at least in certain areas. Writing during Marcion's lifetime, Justin admitted that there were many people in every nation who had been persuaded by his heresy. The sheer volume of the antiheretical literature directed against the Marcionite heresy during the second and third centuries is testimony to its continuing importance; this literature was probably voluminous enough to serve as the principal source for Tertullian's treatise against Marcion. Within the Marcionite community the writings of the master were preserved and his name was revered. According to Origen, there were some who taught that Paul was seated at the right hand of Christ in heaven, and Marcion at the left.

But the most significant doctrinal development in the Marcionite movement is that associated with Apelles, who seems to have revised both the master's dualism and his docetism. There was a single divine principle, not two gods, as Marcion had taught; this Apelles declared, not on the basis of proof from prophecy or even of "knowledge," but on the basis of being persuaded of it. Another feature of Marcion's system which Apelles felt obliged to revise was the master's view of the body of Christ. Although he agreed with Marcion that the body had not been born, he went on to teach that it was a real body nonetheless, but a body made up of the elements of stars rather than of ordinary human flesh. In this way he sought to obviate the objection against Marcion that the Savior had delivered mankind by means of a deception when he pretended to have a genuine body in his suffering and death. But Apelles remained a Marcionite in his view of the Old Testament.

Just. 1 Apol.26.5 (Goodspeed 43–44)

Quispel (1943) 22–79

Or.Luc.25.5 (GCS 35:162)

ap.Eus.H.e.5.13.5 (GCS 9:456)

Tert.Carn.6.3 (CCSL 2:883–84)

As these revisions suggest, Marcion's doctrine was not a complete and finished system, but the expression of his fundam‘ental religious beliefs. They also suggest that the doctrines of the unity of God and of the humanity of Christ were—together with the question of authority—the continuing points of divergence between Marcion and his opponents. These two points of doctrine were to constitute the program for the dogmatic conflicts within the doctrinal mainstream of the next several centuries, and the problem of authority was to be the hinge on which many related issues were to turn. Nor was this problem disposed of with the excommunication of Marcion. The Old Testament achieved and maintained its status as Christian Scripture with the aid of spiritual exegesis. There was no early Christian who simultaneously acknowledged the doctrinal authority of the Old Testament and interpreted it literally. For raising the question of the authority of the Old Testament in the Christian community and for compelling at least some clarification of the question, the church's doctrine was indebted to Marcion. It acknowledged the debt by referring to him whenever the question came up. Thus, in the period covered by this volume, Augustine lumped Manes with Marcion in his defense of the Old Testament against the Manicheans, and Jerome attacked Marcion as a representative of the hatred and contempt for the works of the Creator that marked many heretics; that remained the standard attitude toward Marcion. But when the historical and biblical scholarship of the eighteenth and nineteenth centuries reopened the entire problem of the biblical canon, the name of Marcion once more became a cause célèbre. And the publication of Harnack's monograph on Marcion caused Karl Barth to reflect on his "remarkable parallels" to the arch-Paulinist. Comparisons between Marcion and Luther have become as commonplace as they are superficial, but they do illustrate the continuing importance of Marcion's thought.

Aug.*Gest.Pelag.*5.15 (*CSEL* 42:67); Aug.*Pelag.*3.7.20 (*CSEL* 60:510)

Hier.*Jovin.*2.16 (*PL* 23:309)

Knox (1942) 78–81

K.Barth (1933) 13

Systems of Cosmic Redemption

The most important heresies in the early church were those that have been grouped under the name "Gnostic." The name itself is largely the creation of modern historical scholarship. Early Christian writers usually referred to an individual Gnostic group by the name of its founder or eponymous master, and "Gnostic" was a perfectly respectable name for a Christian, who had access to the knowledge (γνῶσις) revealed in Christ. *The Gnostic* (ὁ Γνωστικός) was the title of a book about the ideal monk by Evagrius Ponticus. The term has been applied to so wide a variety of teachers and teachings that it is in danger of losing its usefulness. Since there is no satisfactory alternative term, we shall be dealing here with "Gnosticism," but we shall be dealing with it only as a chapter in the history of the development of Christian doctrine. It is essential for the understanding of early Christian doctrine to see its relation to the religious syncretism of the Hellenistic age, of which various species of Gnosticism are a prime example. Apart from its Christian forms, Gnosticism appeared in three other milieus: the Syrian, the Iranian, and the Jewish. It is not altogether clear whether there was a pre-Christian as well as an extra-Christian Gnosticism and a post-Christian Gnosticism; but it does seem clear that, in Quispel's formulation, "Gnosticism minus Christianity is still Gnosticism."

Viewed as a chapter in the history of Christian doctrine, Gnosticism may be defined as a system which taught the cosmic redemption of the spirit through knowledge. Irenaeus cited certain devotees of Valentinian Gnosticism who taught that "the knowledge of the ineffable greatness is itself perfect redemption. . . . Knowledge is the redemption of the inner man. This, however, is not corporeal, since the body is corruptible; nor is it animal, since the soul is the result of a defect, and is, as it were, the habitation of the spirit. The redemption must therefore be spiritual; for they claim that the inner, spiritual man is redeemed through knowledge, that they possess the knowledge of the entire cosmos, and that this is true redemption." Thus "the cosmic redemption of the spirit through knowledge" includes the principal themes of this system, which are also the themes it shared with most other forms of Christian Gnosticism. The rich growth and extravagant foliation of Gnostic formulas can easily obscure its doctrinal significance, as one recites the passwords and divine names that proliferated in the various Gnostic systems. Or one can attempt to abstract a definition of Gnosticism from the existing documentary evidence and to expound, with the aid of the language of metaphysics or of existentialism, a Gnosticism that has never existed in history but is religiously intelligible. The

ap.Socr.*H.e*.4.23 (Hussey 2:524)

Quispel (1951) 28

Iren.*Haer*.1.21.4 (Harvey 1:186)

surviving evidence—both the heresiologies of the church fathers and Gnostic documents themselves—makes it clear that there was a basis in Gnosticism itself for both these tendencies. Mythology as well as philosophy, speculation combined with magic, were all intertwined in a bizarre and bewildering variety of forms. Gnostics delighted in these as ritual, and orthodox Christians delighted in them as proof of the absurdity of heresy and of its demonic origin. Neither the Gnostic incantations nor the Gnostic affinities with modern philosophy will be our chief concern here. Both the myth and the philosophy were set forth as statements of Gnostic doctrine, and it is to this doctrine that we must pay primary attention.

Although the taxonomy of the Gnostic sects and teachers cannot be our chief concern either, at least a brief catalog must precede a summary of Gnostic teachings; for the variations among these teachings are pertinent to the relation between the doctrines of Gnosticism and those of the church. Much of the origin of Christian Gnosticism lies in Jewish sectarianism and in the eclipse of the apocalyptic vision within Judaism. The earliest Christian Gnostics, therefore, stood on the borders between heretical Judaism and heretical Christianity. Whether "Simon Magus" was one Gnostic teacher or several, Simonian Gnosticism combined certain elements of Jewish speculation with myths from Tyre and with Christian teachings about Jesus, to form a system of redemption from the tyranny of the body and of this earth through the coming of one who was to be the restorer of all things. "He came to free [Helen] from her bonds and to offer men salvation through their recognition of him. For when the angels misgoverned the world, since each of them desired the primacy, he came for the restoration of all things, transformed and made like the principalities and powers. With men he seemed a man, though not a man; he seemed to suffer in Judea, though he did not suffer." Similarly, the Gnosticism of Cerinthus seems to have been based upon the speculations of a heretical form of Jewish Christianity. He taught that there was a distinction between the Supreme God and the Creator, and that at baptism Christ had descended upon Jesus (who until then had been an ordinary man), departing from him once more before his crucifixion. The next step in the development of this species of Gnosticism came with

See pp. 23–25 above

ap.Iren.*Haer.*1.23.3 (Harvey 1:192–93)

Iren.*Haer.*1.26.1 (Harvey 1:211–12)

Saturninus, who elaborated certain rabbinical ideas about
the creation into a sharp dualism between creation and
redemption; Christ descended from heaven in the form

Phil.2:6–11

of a slave to bring the revelation of the redemption from
the created world, from sin and from sex. "Christ came
to destroy the God of the Jews, but to save those who
believe in him, that is, those who have the spark of life in

ap.Iren.Haer.1.24.2 (Harvey
1:197–98)

them."

Concerning the Gnosticism of Simon Magus, Cerinthus, and Saturninus we have only the testimony of the
church fathers, chiefly of Irenaeus. Even he was best in-
formed about, and principally interested in, another species of Christian Gnosticism, that associated with the
name of Valentinus, which also appears to be the form
of Gnostic teaching most thoroughly authenticated by the
direct testimony of the newly discovered Gnostic sources;
much of what we say here about Gnostic doctrine in general will be derived specifically from our information
about Valentinian Gnosticism. There are significant affinities between this form of Gnostic heresy and various
lines of thought in the second century that are acknowledged as more or less orthodox, such as the *Shepherd*
of Hermas, the Christian gnosis of Clement of Alexandria, and the speculations of the apologist Justin.
Whether or not it was the work of Valentinus himself,
the *Gospel of Truth* presented some of the principal
revelations granted to him, and the *Odes of Solomon*
were a liturgical statement of Valentinian doctrine. In
the *Gospel of Truth* the Gnostic revelation was presented
as one of "joy for them who have received the boon,

Ev.Ver.16.31 (Grobel 32)

through the Father of Truth, of knowing it." Eventually
this revelation was developed into a theology further
removed from normative church doctrine. Both the adoption of more myth and the elaboration of more speculation
carried the pupils of Valentinus beyond the boundaries
of that doctrine, as Ptolemy's *Letter to Flora* makes evident.

Approximately contemporary with Valentinus and
Marcion, but apparently coming from Syria and Alexandria, was the other principal Gnostic teacher refuted
by the church fathers, Basilides. According to Hippolytus,
one major difference between Valentinus and Basilides
was that the former "may justly be reckoned a Pythag-

Hipp.Haer.6.29.1 (GCS
26:155)
Hipp.Haer.7.14 (GCS
26:191)

orean and Platonist" while "the doctrines advanced by
Basilides are in reality the clever quibbles of Aristotle."

The summary of the teachings of Basilides given in Hippolytus is contradicted at so many points by that given in Irenaeus that Irenaeus's account seems to be a statement of later developments. We shall be noting both similarities and differences between Valentinian and Basilidian Gnosticism. Although these are the principal species of Gnosticism with which the Christian theologians of the second and third centuries dealt, even this brief catalog would be incomplete without a reference to a similar movement that was to be an important rival of catholic Christianity in the fourth century, Manicheism. It, too, belongs principally to the history of religions rather than to the history of the development of specifically Christian doctrine; for Manes not only borrowed from the teachings of the church, but also elaborated some of the ideas of the followers of Marcion and Basilides. For our purposes, then, Manicheism is a useful source of information, not about the development of Christian doctrine as such, but about the evolution of the syncretistic religions and Christian heresies over against which the church defined its doctrine.

The ontological presupposition of .the Gnostic systems of redemption was a distinctive doctrine of the divine reality and of its relation to the cosmos. Ptolemy, the Valentinian theologian, posited "a perfect preexistent aeon, dwelling in the invisible and unnamable elevations; this is prebeginning and forefather and depth. He is uncontainable and invisible, eternal and ungenerated, in quiet and in deep solitude for infinite aeons. With him is thought, which is also called grace and silence." Apparently the earlier Valentinian teaching made "depth" an attribute of God rather than a distinct being, and the contradictions that eventually emanated as "aeons" were immanent with God. But in the theology of Ptolemy "aeon" became "an emanation from the divine substance, subsisting coordinately and coeternally with the deity." By emanation the aeons came forth from depth and silence, two by two, until there were thirty of them; together with the Supreme God, these constituted the pleroma, the fullness of the divine reality. Their names were the personifications of divine attributes and titles, as well as of other abstractions; in each pair one had a masculine name, the other a feminine one. It appears that the original monotheism evident in the *Gospel of Truth* evolved into a mythological theory in

Iren.*Haer*.1.1.1 (Harvey 1:8–9)

Ev.Ver.22.25 (Grobel 80)

Ev.Ver.23.16 (Grobel 84)

Harvey (1857) cxix

Iren.*Haer*.1.1.3 (Harvey 1:11–12)

later Valentinian Gnosticism. Yet the distinctive emphasis on the tensions within the divine reality itself seems
to be the common element in both the *Gospel of Truth*
and Ptolemy. In the mythological cosmology of Basilides,
it was not only aeons but spiritual beings called "archons"
or "rulers" that carried out this emphasis. The cosmos
did not emanate from God, but was made out of nothing
by a God to whom the category of existence could not
be applied. "The nonexistent God made a nonexistent
cosmos out of the nonexistent." This he did by making a
seed which contained a "tripartite sonship," out of which,
in turn, there came the great archon who created the
cosmos and another archon who made this world.

The distinction between the Supreme God and the
Creator, present also in the teaching of Marcion, under-
lay the Valentinian myths of the emanation of aeons
and the Basilidian doctrine of creation out of nothing.
Between the Supreme God and the created world, according to Ptolemy, was a demiurge, "the Father and God
of everything outside the pleroma." In support of this he
adduced the testimony of the prologue to the Gospel
of John, according to which "a certain principle was first
generated by God . . . in which the Father emitted all
things seminally." Thus "to all the aeons after it the
Logos was the cause of formation and origin." Another
Valentinian exegete, Heracleon, also found support for
his teaching in the Gospel of John, but he taught that
"the aeon and what is in the aeon did not come into
being through the Logos," since the aeon was distinct
from the created world. Although the *Gospel of Truth*
did not attribute the creation of the world to a demiurge
or some other intermediate principle, this was the direction taken by the Valentinian and other Gnostic doctrines
of creation, "the direction of hostility toward the Creator." The God of the Old Testament, who was equated
with the demiurge, was eventually seen as less than
the Supreme God and as an enemy.

Yet the detailed theogonies of the Gnostic teachers
were finally aimed at dealing with the human predicament, not simply at accounting for the origin of the
cosmos. As one Gnostic teacher counseled, "Abandon
the search for God and the creation and other matters
of a similar sort. Look for him by taking yourself as
the starting point. Learn who it is who within you makes
everything his own and says, 'My God, my mind, my

Hipp.*Haer*.7.21.4 (*GCS*
26:197)

Hipp.*Haer*.10.14.2 (*GCS*
26:274–75

Iren.*Haer*.1.5.2 (Harvey 1:43)

Iren.*Haer*.1.8.5 (Harvey
1:76–77)

ap.R.Grant (1961) 195

R.Grant (1959) 137

thought, my soul, my body.' Learn the sources of sorrow, joy, love, hate. Learn how it happens that one watches without willing, rests without willing, becomes angry without willing, loves without willing. If you carefully investigate these matters, you will find him in yourself." Cosmology provided the context for a doctrine of creation and fall, and for an eventual doctrine of redemption. Each in its own way, the Gnostic systems all included a diagnosis of the cosmological descent of the human spirit into matter and sin. In the *Gospel of Truth*, error (represented in a quasi-personal form) conspired against truth, that is, God, and led men astray. Ptolemy's explanation of the fall was characteristically more elaborate. The thirtieth and last of the aeons, wisdom, fell from the perfection of the pleroma through an excess of passion, finally giving birth to a shapeless mass. "And hence they declare material substance had its beginning from [her] ignorance and grief, and fear and bewilderment."

Three kinds of substance came into existence: the material, the psychic, and the spiritual. Corresponding to these were three classes of men, represented by the three sons of Adam—Cain, Abel, and Seth. The truly spiritual men were not in need of salvation, and the material were incapable of it; but the psychic, "those-of-the-middle" as the *Gospel of Truth* called them, were both vulnerable to the fall and capable of redemption. Their creator, the demiurge, "made heaven without knowing heaven; he formed man in ignorance of man; he brought earth to light without understanding earth." This was one of the most explicit statements of the Gnostic doctrine that the creation of man—or at least of all men below the level of the fully spiritual Gnostic—was an act of ignorance on the part of a divine being who was less than the Supreme God, and that therefore the creation of man and the fall of man ultimately coincided.

Frequently this rejection of creation was associated with a revulsion at the processes of human generation and birth, as it was also in Marcion. Other early Christian Gnostics, such as the Encratites, "preached against marriage, thus setting aside the original creation of God, and indirectly blaming him who made the male and female for the propagation of the human race." Saturninus ascribed the origin of marriage and generation to Satan. He also taught that the original man was the creature of the angels rather than of the Supreme God,

Hipp.*Haer*.8.15.1–2 (*GCS* 26:235)

Ev.*Ver*.17.35 (Grobel 46)

Iren.*Haer*.1.2.3 (Harvey 1:16–17)

Iren.*Haer*.1.5.1 (Harvey 1:41–42)

Iren.*Haer*.1.7.5 (Harvey 1:64–65)

Ev.*Ver*.17.34–35 (Grobel 46)

Iren.*Haer*.1.5.3 (Harvey 1:45)

See p. 73 above

Iren.*Haer*.1.28.1 (Harvey 1:220)

Iren.*Haer*.1.24.2 (Harvey 1:198)

but that the Supreme God took pity on man and added the spark of life to what the angels had made; this spark returned to its own after death. Implicit in many Gnostic statements about the cosmological descent of man was a doctrine of the preexistence of man or of his soul; thus according to the Sethian-Ophites, "Adam and Eve previously had bodies that were light, clear, and, as it were, spiritual, as they were at their creation; but when they came into this world, these changed into bodies more opaque, gross, and sluggish. Their soul, too, was feeble and languid, inasmuch as they had received from their creator a merely mundane inspiration."

Although the creation of this world was the work of a being lower than the Supreme Power and the entry of the human soul into this world coincided with the fall of man, humanity even in this world was not bereft of the divine spark. According to Basilides, Romans 5:13–14 meant that "we who are spiritual are sons, who have been left here to arrange, and mold, and rectify, and complete the souls which, according to nature, are so constituted as to continue in this quarter of the universe." In the Valentinian system of Ptolemy, the demiurge made the earthly man and breathed the psyche into him; but unbeknown to him, a product of the higher desire, called "achamoth," was deposited into him, "so that through him it might be sown into the soul created by him and into the material body, might grow and increase in them, and might become ready for the reception of the perfect Logos." This did not refer to the corporeal class of men, who were beyond redemption, but to the spirituals or true Gnostics, who belonged to the true church and through whom the redemption was to be communicated also to the psychics who stood between them and the corporeal.

The presence of this divine element in the world and in part of humanity supplied the point of contact that made redemption possible. Of the three elements, it was to the psychic, which had free will, that he came, in order to save it. "He assumed the primary elements of those beings which he was going to save. From achamoth he took the spiritual, from the demiurge he put on the psychic Christ, and from the constitution of the cosmos he acquired a body which had psychic substance and was constructed by ineffable art so as to be visible, tangible,

Iren.*Haer*.1.24.1 (Harvey 1:197)

Iren.*Haer*.1.30.9 (Harvey 1:235)

Hipp.*Haer*.7.24.2 (*GCS* 26:202–203)

Iren.*Haer*.1.5.6 (Harvey 1:50–51)

Iren.*Haer*.1.6.1 (Harvey 1:52–53)

and subject to passion. He acquired nothing material at all, for matter is not capable of being saved." Both the church fathers and the interpreters of Gnosticism who have simply repeated their accounts have sometimes permitted the confusing proliferation of emanations with names such as Only-begotten, Savior, Logos, Jesus, Christ, and Holy Spirit to obscure the centrality of redemption in Christian Gnosticism; yet this is the leitmotiv evident in the various Gnostic gospels.

Even Irenaeus unwillingly attested to this centrality when he charged that "there are as many schemes of 'redemption' as there are mystagogues of this science." The *Gospel of Truth* announced the message of "the Logos, who has come from the pleroma and who is in the thought and the mind of the Father; he it is who is called 'the Savior', since that is the name of the work which he must do for the redemption of those who have not known the Father. For the name of the gospel is the manifestation of hope." The *Gospel of Thomas* spoke repeatedly of "return" as the content of salvation, meaning thereby "liberation from matter and reunion with the light-world." And even the *Gospel of Philip* declared that "Christ came to ransom some, to save others, to redeem others." It seems clear that the figure of the Savior—which was variously interpreted in the several Gnostic systems—may be used as a way of distinguishing between Christian and non-Christian species of Gnosticism.

Iren.*Haer*.1.21.1 (Harvey 1:181)

Ev.Ver.16.34–17.3 (Grobel 34–36)

Ev.Thos.50 (Grant 156)

Gärtner (1961) 198

Ev.Phil.9 (Wilson 28–29)

It is, however, also a way of distinguishing between Gnostic and non-Gnostic species of Christianity, for one of the characteristics of Gnostic doctrine was its denial that the Savior was possessed of a material, fleshly body; in fact, the very epithet "docetist" seems to have occurred for the first time in reference to the evidence of Gnostic influence on the *Gospel of Peter*. In the strata of Gnostic literature still close to the New Testament, for example in the *Gospel of Truth,* the reality of the body of Jesus and of his sufferings was not denied outright, but the language used there about the resurrected body of Jesus does seem to suggest the beginnings of a docetic tendency. Whatever chariness there may have been about docetism was soon overcome, and an explicit effort to protect the person of the Savior from involvement in matter and in suffering soon became a hallmark of most Christian

Eus.*H.e*.6.12.6 (*GCS* 9:546)

Ev.Ver.20.25–30 (Grobel 64–66)

Ev.Ver.31.5–8 (Grobel 122)

Gnostics. In the theology of Ptolemy, the Savior "remained impassible, for it could not experience passion,
since it was unconquerable and invisible; therefore when
he [Christ] was led before Pilate, that Spirit of Christ
set in him was taken away. . . . What suffered was [only]

Iren.*Haer*.1.7.2 (Harvey
1:61–62)

the psychic Christ." Even this psychic Christ had "passed
through Mary as water passes through a pipe," and the
Savior had descended on him at the time of his baptism.
In the theology which Irenaeus ascribed to Basilides,

Matt.27:32

Simon of Cyrene was crucified instead of Jesus, who did
not and could not undergo death; for salvation pertained

Iren.*Haer*.1.24.4.5 (Harvey
1:200–201)

only to the soul, not to the body. How early the docetic
tendency appeared in at least some Christian groups is
shown by the polemic of Ignatius against the heretical

See p. 174 below

denial of the full humanity of Christ, a polemic which
seems to have been directed at some form of Gnosticism.

Although the body in which the Savior appeared may
not have been real, the cosmic redemption which he
brought was real. His cross "is actually consuming all the
material elements as fire consumes chaff but is purifying

Iren.*Haer*.1.3.5 (Harvey 1:30)

those who are saved as the fan purifies wheat." The
purpose of his passion was to demonstrate in action the
primeval passion of the aeons and thus to reveal the
hidden mystery both of human origins and of human

Iren.*Haer*.1.8.2 (Harvey 1:68)

destiny. In one way or another, redemption seems to have
been equated with revelation; hence the emphasis on
knowledge. The coming of the Savior made possible a
soteriological ascent to undo the damage of the descent
into matter and sin. The descent of Simon Magus was "to
rescue [Helen, the lost sheep] from her bonds, and to

Iren.*Haer*.1.23.3 (Harvey
1:192–93)

offer men salvation through their recognition of him."
That recognition, granted by the Savior, would enable
the saved to ascend as he had descended; he disclosed
to them the way back to their origin and the magical passwords that would let them through the hostile world of
the planets. And so, in the system of Basilides, "the
cosmos remains in this condition until the whole sonship
left below to benefit the souls, in their shapeless state,
and to receive benefit by being refashioned, follows
Jesus and ascends above and comes there after being

ap.Hipp.*Haer*.7.26.10 (*GCS*
26:205)

purified."

The appropriation of this knowledge was not, however, possible for everyone. Those who were corporeal
or material were forever condemned to separation from

the redemption, for what was material ended in corruption. But the saved—or, as they were termed especially in Manichean literature, "the elect"—shared with the Savior in the purity of the restored order of things. Several Gnostic writings spoke of "the man of light" as the one who understood his heavenly origin and destiny. Redemption consisted in the transformation of human life, so that, in the summary description of Puech, one "acquires, with the possession of his 'ego' and his true and ontological being, the meaning of his destiny and the final certainty of his salvation, thus discovering himself as a being who, by right and for all eternity, is saved." This return of the "inner man" from the dungeon of this world to the kingdom of light was accomplished by his "knowledge of who we were and what we have become; where we were and where we have been cast; whither we are hastening, whence we are being redeemed; what birth is, and what rebirth."

As the cosmological descent of the soul through the spheres of the cosmos had carried it further and further from the transcendent God, so its soteriological ascent carried it back through the layers and enabled it to throw off, stage by stage, the accretions that had separated it from its true origin within the divine reality. As the Ophites ascended, they spoke the appropriate passwords at each stage, including this one: "And thou, Ialdabaoth, first and seventh, born to have power with boldness, being ruling Word of a pure mind, a perfect work for Son and Father, I bear a symbol marked with a picture of life, and, having opened to the world the gate which thou didst close for thine eternity, I pass by thy power free again. May grace be with me. Father, let it be with me." The spiritual men would shed their souls and, having become intelligent spirits, would be admitted into the very pleroma; and, continued Ptolemy, "then the fire hidden in the cosmos will shine forth and ignite and become effective in consuming all matter along with itself and finally will become nonexistent." The climax of this Valentinian eschatology was not only the deliverance of the spirit from the tyranny of the flesh and of this world, but the very destruction of the cosmos and of all matter. As for the psychic men, they could be saved, too, but not automatically. The spiritual men would be saved simply because of their spiritual nature, regardless of

Marginal notes (left column):

Iren.*Haer.*1.7.5 (Harvey 1:65)
Aug.*Fort.*3 (*CSEL* 25:84–85); *Act.Archel.*10 (*PG* 10:1445)

Puech (1955) 29

ap.Clem.*Exc.Thdot.*78.2 (*GCS* 17:131)

ap.Or.*Cels.*6.31 (*GCS* 3:101)

Iren.*Haer.*1.7.2 (Harvey 1:59)

Iren.*Haer.*1.6.2 (Harvey 1:54)

their conduct, but the psychic would need to have faith and to practice sexual continence in order to attain to their middle state of salvation.

The redeeming knowledge brought into this world by the Savior was a revelation and, as such, was not generally available to all men. It was not even available to all who styled themselves Christians. Only those who had been inducted into the Gnostic mysteries could have access to it, for it was contained in a special form of the apostolic tradition, which only the Gnostics had received by their own succession. It seems that one of the purposes of composing special gospels was to convey "the secret words which the living Jesus spoke and Didymus Judas Thomas" or some other evangelist (besides Matthew, Mark, Luke, or John) wrote down. As Gärtner has observed, "It is this secret tradition which mediates the truth and is the key to the understanding of the sayings of Jesus, and it is therefore not surprising that Gnostic circles had a definite tendency to assert their own traditions, preserved within their own closed circle, as against those of the Church." Therefore the risen Christ was represented in the *Pistis Sophia* as declaring that now he would hold nothing back but would speak directly, without parables. Parables had been the appropriate means of instructing the psychics and of concealing the deepest gnosis from the corporeal, but after his resurrection he disclosed the full truth to the few in a special apostolic succession.

In the conflict between Gnostic Christians and other Christians, therefore, the Gnostics would declare that "the truth cannot be extracted from [the Scriptures] by those who are ignorant of tradition. For they allege that the truth was not delivered by means of written documents, but viva voce; wherefore also Paul declared, 'But we speak wisdom among those that are perfect, but not the wisdom of this world.'" The "perfect" were, of course, the Gnostic "spirituals," the elect. To them gnosis was delivered from the "few" among the disciples to whom the risen Savior had disclosed it during his sojourn on earth after the resurrection. This reliance on an arcane tradition did not prevent the Gnostics from dealing with the New Testament, as is evident from the interpretations of the Gospel of John by both Valentinus and Heracleon; but it did permit them to argue

ap.Epiph.*Haer.*33.9 (*GCS* 25:457)

*Ev.Thos.*1 (Grant 115)

Gärtner (1961) 80

*Pist.Soph.*6 (*GCS* 45:5)

1 Cor.2:6

Iren.*Haer.*3.2.1 (Harvey 2:7)

Iren.*Haer.*1.30.14 (Harvey 1:239–40)

that the New Testament could not be properly understood except on the basis of the tradition, which supplied the key for the "spiritual" exegesis of the New Testament writings. Thus Basilides claimed access to the secret teachings of Peter, and Valentinus to those of Paul. Only with the help of these secret teachings was it possible to "explain the ambiguous passages of Scripture" as references to the cosmic drama. It was in this sense that the Gnostics claimed "the authority of the Scriptures" and especially of the New Testament.

The attitude of Christian Gnostics toward the Old Testament seems to have been more complicated. They did not, as is sometimes supposed, reject the Old Testament outright. Within the New Testament they saw varying levels of spiritual perception, reflecting different degrees of initiation into the sacred mysteries. The Old Testament manifested even greater variation, for the prophets had spoken their prophecies under the inspiration of different gods. Therefore, although some parts of the Old Testament were the work of the seed of the pleroma planted in this world, many others were the product only of the demiurge, who had also been the one who sent the prophets. According to Simonian Gnosticism, the angels who made the world also inspired the prophets; Saturninus went further and ascribed some of the prophecies to Satan. The story of the creation in Genesis proved to the Simon Magus of the *Clementine Recognitions* that the God who created the world was weak in many ways and that there was a higher God; the preoccupation of Gnostic exegesis with Hebrew names, especially with Elohim, the name for God, suggests that as they ascribed various portions of the Old Testament to various divine and demonic powers, so they found proof in the fluctuations between various divine names that the Supreme Power was not the same as the Creator or the "God of the Jews." Like other Christians, the Gnostics stratified the law of Moses. Ptolemy distinguished three strata: the first was completed by the Savior; the second was entirely destroyed; the third was translated and changed from the literal to the spiritual. But he also asserted that parts of the law had come from men, not from any god.

The ambivalence in the Gnostic treatment of the Old Testament indicates that Marcion's attitude toward it

Clem.*Str*.7.17.106.4 (*GCS* 17:75)

Iren.*Haer*.2.10.1 (Harvey 1:273)

Tert.*Praescrip*.15.2 (*CCSL* 1:199)

Iren.*Haer*.2.35.2 (Harvey 1:384)

Iren.*Haer*.4.35.2 (Harvey 2:274)

Iren.*Haer*.1.23.3 (Harvey 1:193)
Iren.*Haer*.1.24.2 (Harvey 1:198)

Clem.*Recogn*.53.2 (*GCS* 51:83)

See pp. 16–17 above

ap.Epiph.*Haer*.33.5.1–2 (*GCS* 25:453–54)

was both more extreme and more consistent. With him, the other Gnostics shared a deepening hostility to the creation and the Creator, the God of the Jews; but while his literal exegesis of the Old Testament led him to repudiate its scriptural authority, their allegorical interpretation enabled them to ascribe to it a partial validity—which was, after all, the only validity they were willing to assign even to the New Testament. Thus it was both from "the writings of the evangelists and the apostles" and from "the law and the prophets" that they supported their doctrines.

Iren.*Haer.*1.3.6 (Harvey 1:31)

Although the anti-Gnostic fathers would not concede the Gnostics' right to use the Christian Scriptures in that way—or, according to Tertullian, in any other way—the parallels between certain Gnostic doctrines and those that have been acknowledged as orthodox are too striking to be ignored. Two apparent analogies between Gnosticism and orthodoxy have been of particular interest: Gnosticism's connections with the thought of Paul and John and its affinities with the "Christian gnosis" of Clement and Origen. The discovery of the *Gospel of Truth* has raised in a new form the historical problem of the similarities in language, and perhaps also in content, between it and the Gospel of John. John was the favorite Gospel of at least some Gnostic teachers, especially of those who belonged to the Valentinian school; the *Gospel of Truth* contains many echoes of the Gospel of John, and various Valentinian teachers commented on the Fourth Gospel. It seems undeniable that the motifs of descent and ascent appeared in John and that they bore some genetic relation to these motifs in Gnostic speculation. The Savior in John was one who had descended from heaven as the light of the world. He came to judge the world and its prince, the devil, and to restore to the light those who had strayed. Stated in this form, the story of the Gospel of John was one that the Gnostics could have recognized as their own. "Yet it is a story which, though Gnostic and mythological in form, is not Gnostic in content." For the history it recounted had really happened; the protagonist was a real man, with flesh and blood and failings, rather than a phantasm. The emphasis of the Gospel of John on the historicity of its account separated it from the mythopoeic imaginations of even the most Christian among the Gnostics.

R.Grant (1959) 174

Similarly, the Gnostic echoes in the Pauline epistles are quite striking, but not finally decisive, not even if we include as Pauline epistles those to the Ephesians and Colossians. Portions of these latter epistles have been identified, with perhaps some justification, as citations from Gnostic hymns; there is an impressive body of shared terminology between these two epistles and the Gnostic teachers, most strikingly perhaps in the term "fullness [πλήρωμα]," which, although it appeared else-where in the New Testament, acquired what might be called ontological significance only in these two letters.

Eph.1:23; Col.2:9

The Gnostic use of 1 Corinthians 2:6, to which we have already referred, is additional evidence of the affinities between the Pauline and the Gnostic understanding of the elect in the church. Similarly, the Pauline letters to the Corinthians called Satan "the god of this age" and spoke of "the rulers of this age [ἄρχοντες τοῦ αἰῶνος τούτου]" in a terminology resembling that of the Gnostic masters.

2 Cor.4:4

1 Cor.2:8

Yet those very letters provided the final line of demarcation between such language and Gnostic meta-physics: "Although there may be so-called gods in heaven or on earth—as indeed there are many 'gods' and many 'lords'—yet for us there is one God, the Father, from whom are all things and for whom we exist, and one Lord, Jesus Christ, through whom are all things and through whom we exist. However, not all possess this knowledge."

1 Cor.8:5–7

Whatever may have been the existential relation between religious devotees and their "gods" or "lords," there was in fact one God and one Lord: this against all Gnostic mythology and polytheism. Indeed, if Ephesians, Colossians, and the pastoral epistles—or any part of this later corpus—may legitimately be called Pauline, it seems safe to say that "Paul" (whether the apostle himself or his pupils, who felt justified in using his name) regarded incipient Gnosticism as a sufficient threat to the gospel to address specific letters against it and to urge defense of the deposit of the faith in response to its challenge.

The relation between the Gnosticism we have been examining and the "Christian gnosis" of Clement and Origen is considerably more ambiguous. This is not only because, especially in Clement, the term "Gnostic" was used as a title for the Christian intellectual, but be-cause these Alexandrian theologians shared many of the ideas we have been describing. Some passages in the writings of Clement do suggest the preexistence of the human soul, and Origen's doctrine of a prehistoric fall from essence to existence bears more than formal affinities with the Gnostic myth of cosmological descent. More generally, Origen seems to have shared the Gnostic presupposition that "temporal events are an image of what takes place in the world of pure spirits," which determined his way of interpreting biblical history. Origen's eschatology was reminiscent of the soteriological ascent in Gnostic teaching. For him, too, the soul had come down from a purely spiritual state and would eventually be restored to that state; this applied to all spirits, even to the devil. Finally, no one can fail to be reminded of Gnosticism when he reads Clement's claim to possess a secret tradition, neither published in the New Testament nor known to the common people; one of his terms for this secret tradition was "gnosis." On the basis of this substantial body of common teaching between Gnosticism and the thought of the Alexandrian theologians, would one be justified in regarding Clement and Origen as the right wing of Christian Gnosticism rather than as the left wing of Christian orthodoxy?

A consideration of the entire body of their thought makes such an interpretation, however attractive it may be, finally untenable; for at each of the points of similarity, crucial differences appear which set Clement and Origen apart from the Gnostic systems. Quite simply put, "Origen was not a Gnostic because the Bible forbade him to be one." Neither he nor Clement would allow his speculations about aeons or spirits to threaten the oneness of God: the Supreme God was the Creator and the Father of Jesus Christ. Even amid all the allegorization of Old Testament accounts by both Clement and Origen, the historicity of these accounts was not denied; it was simply relegated to a position of secondary importance. Above all, the historical reality of the birth, death, and resurrection of Christ stood firm against any Gnostic docetism. This reality was the guarantee of redemption and the foundation of the church, which was catholic and included all sorts and conditions of men, not merely the spiritual elite. The vigor of the defense against Gnosticism, evident, for example, in Origen's running battle with Heracleon over the exegesis of the Gospel of John, illustrates both the attraction which Gnostic speculation

Daniélou (1955) 194

Hanson (1959) 371

held for Origen and his final inability to square it with the testimony of Scripture as this was believed, taught, and confessed by the church.

Nevertheless, at each of the points we have summarized, Gnosticism served as a reminder of what the theologians of the church, including Clement and Origen, may have been inclined to forget. The myths about the divine abyss counterweighed the oversimplification implicit in the doctrine of divine impassibility, which seemed to reduce the paradox of mercy and wrath to a rational formula. The idea of the cosmological descent of the spirit spoke more meaningfully about man's alienation from the world, from his own true being, and from God than the moralistic anthropology of many church theologians. For all its docetism, the Gnostic picture of the Savior came closer in some ways to certain themes of the New Testament than did the definition of Christ as the giver of the new law. Above all, Christian Gnosticism was a religion of redemption and of the reconciliation of the human spirit with the ineffable greatness of God. It represented a fundamental distortion of Christian doctrine at each of these points, and the church had to resist it. But it also represented a serious effort to come to terms with issues of Christian doctrine from which no theologian, be he orthodox or heretical, could escape.

The New Prophecy

One of the earliest schisms or heresies in the ancient church was that called forth by the work of Montanus, a Phrygian presbyter around the middle of the second century. Surprisingly little is known of his actual teaching, still less of the particulars in his biography; we are not even sure just when his work began, although it was sometime between about 135 and 175. The principal sources available to us today on Montanism stem from its catholic opponents, in whose writings we must make the customary allowances for distortion, and from its later adherent, Tertullian; the reliability of his writings as an index to the original proclamation of the Montanist sect must be subjected to serious question as well. The Montanists produced many sacred writings and evoked other writings directed against them; but most of these have not been transmitted to us.

Working from the existing source material, Nathanael

Hipp.*Haer*.8.19.1 (*GCS* 26:238)

Eus.*H.e*.5.16.1 (*GCS* 9:460)

Bonwetsch defined primitive Montanism as follows: "An effort to shape the entire life of the church in keeping with the expectation of the return of Christ, immediately at hand; to define the essence of true Christianity from this point of view; and to oppose everything by which conditions in the church were to acquire a permanent form for the purpose of entering upon a longer historical development." In the explication of his thesis, Bonwetsch placed the principal stress upon Montanism's attitude toward questions of the Christian life in relation to the world, and he saw it as the first outstanding movement to be called forth by a concern with these questions. Our interest here is in the doctrinal presuppositions and implications of that concern in the Montanists, and in the impact that the Montanist sect had upon the teaching of the greater church.

Bonwetsch (1881) 139

The effort to explain most major phenomena in the early church on the basis of pagan influence has brought about the thesis that for an explanation of Montanism we are to look to the orgiastic religions of Phrygia. For some phenomena in the ancient church (for example, Gnosticism), this effort has produced irrefutable evidence of pagan influence in the early Christian movement. But a meticulous examination of the sources by Wilhelm Schepelern shows, it seems quite conclusively, that though there are traces of general pagan influence in Montanist piety, "Montanism arose from ground soaked with blood —not the blood of the raging slashed adherents of the cult of Cybele, but the blood of Christian martyrs; and Montanism grew in an atmosphere saturated not with Phrygian mystery ideas, but with the apocalyptic conceptions of Judaism and Christianity." Noteworthy in this connection is the absence in the earliest anti-Montanist polemics of any mention of cultic aberrations in the movement, and cultus would seem to have been the first place for the influence of the pagan mysteries to manifest itself.

Schepelern (1929) 162

Specifically, the explanation of the origins of Montanism lies in the fact that when the apocalyptic vision became less vivid and the church's polity more rigid, the extraordinary operations of the Spirit characteristic of the early church diminished in both frequency and intensity. The decline in the eschatological hope and the rise of the monarchical episcopate are closely interrelated phenomena worthy of special treatment; both indicate a process of settling already at work in the second-century church, and perhaps earlier, by which many Christians were beginning to adjust themselves to the possibility that the church might have to live in the world for a considerable time to come. Part of that process of settling was the gradual decline, both in intensity and in frequency, of the charismata that had been so prominent in the earlier stages of the Christian movement.

The *Ascension of Isaiah,* an apocryphal Christian addition to the Book of Isaiah, dating probably from the latter part of the first century or at the latest the early part of the second century of the Christian era, described in quasi-apocalyptic language what was going to happen: "And there will be a great contention about his advent and his coming. . . . And the Holy Spirit will withdraw from many. Nor will there be in those days many prophets or those who speak things confirmed, except a few in a few places. . . . And they will neglect the prophecy of the prophets who were before me, neglecting my visions as well." It would be useful to investigate how long visions, dreams, and apocalypses continued in the church, along with the claim to speak on behalf of the Holy Spirit, and how all of this died out among the laity but continued among the clergy, and especially among the monks. Celsus attested to the presence of "prophets" in Palestine and Phoenicia. Justin Martyr based his case against Judaism partly on the claim that "among us until now there are prophetic charismata," while they had died out among the Jews; and Irenaeus described the many brethren in the church of his day who had these charismata, speaking in tongues by the Spirit, bringing out the secrets of men's hearts and the mysteries of God.

Though not a Montanist, Cyprian contended that the church had a greater share of visions, revelations, and dreams than did they, and Eusebius's anonymous anti-Montanist critic believed that "the apostle declares that the prophetic charisma should continue to be in the entire church until the last parousia." It therefore seems to be correct to note that this type of prophetic speech was at home in the Montanist sect and in the greater church. But the tone of this insistence on the part of the critics of Montanism seems to indicate a certain amount of embarrassment on their part that in practice if not in prin-

*Asc.Is.*3.22–31 (Hennecke 305–306)

ap.Or.*Cels.*7.8 (*GCS* 3:160)

Just.*Dial.*82.1; 88.1 (Goodspeed 194; 201)

Iren.*Haer.*2.32.4 (Harvey 1:374–75)

Cypr.*Ep.*11.3–6 (*CSEL* 3:497–500); Cypr.*Ep.*66.10 (*CSEL* 3:734)

ap.Eus.*H.e.*5.17.4 (*GCS* 9:472)

ciple the charismata were becoming rarer and rarer.
Despite their assertion of the theoretical possibility of
prophecy in the church, the other guarantees of the
presence and work of the Spirit in their midst were becoming so firm in their minds that when Montanism
claimed to actualize this theoretical possibility with a
vengeance, they were put to a severe test.

Such was indeed the claim of Montanism. Montanus
himself seems to have made the claim that the promise

John 14:16; 15:26; 16:7–13

of Jesus concerning the Paraclete had been uniquely fulfilled in him. He was gifted with visions and special
revelations. One of these seems to have been that the
end was near at hand, and that the coming of the Paraclete was the last sign to precede that end. Eusebius's
anonymous source asserted that Montanus "spoke and
made strange sounds, prophesying in a manner different
from that which was traditional in the church from the

ap.Eus.*H.e.*5.16.7 (*GCS*
9:462)

beginning." This may or may not mean that Montanus
was caught up in ecstatic speech, but it does seem clear
that Montanus believed he had inspiration from God.
What is more, he promised this inspiration to his adherents. Notably, it descended upon two of his disciples,
both women, and these prophetesses were filled with the
Holy Spirit and spoke what was revealed to them in this

Eus.*H.e.*5.16.9 (*GCS*
9:462–64)

ecstatic condition. This continued in the Montanist community for some time; Tertullian spoke of a "sister among
us today" who had the charismata of revelation during
worship, conversing with angels, and sometimes even

Tert.*Anim.*9.4 (*CCSL*
2:792–93)

with the Lord himself. The *Passion of Perpetua and
Felicitas,* contemporary with Tertullian if not actually
written or at least edited by him, spoke of acknowledging
and honoring the new prophecies and visions and the
other powers of the Holy Spirit which had come upon

*Pass.Perp.*1.5 (Beek 8)

the church in this latter day.

It is important to note at this point that the central
content of these visions, revelations, prophecies, and
dreams was not doctrinal but ethical. Tertullian insisted
that the Paraclete had come to establish a new discipline,

Tert.*Jejun.*1.3 (*CCSL* 2:1257)

not a new teaching. Hippolytus and the other early
critics of the Montanist movement laid greater stress upon
its moral innovations and rigor than upon any theological

Hipp.*Haer.*8.19.2 (*GCS*
26:238)

aberrations in it, although Montanism was eventually
important on this latter score as well. Specifically, Montanism asserted that the gifts of the Spirit were absent

in the church on account of its moral laxity. The marriage ethic of the church was permitting widows and widowers to remarry, when according to the Montanists the demand of monogamy, stated in the phrase "husband of one wife," forbade multiple marriage in series as well as in parallel, as indeed it had for some earlier Christian writers such as Hermas. The church was growing lax in the enforcement of fasting, but the Montanists insisted that the rapid approach of the end demanded greater strictness than ever in fasting. These questions, together with issues like flight from martyrdom and penitential discipline, formed the principal emphasis of the new prophecy. With a sternness and zeal that has tended to characterize the moral reformers of the church more than its doctrinal or theological reformers, Montanism called the church to repent, for the kingdom of God was now finally at hand.

This would seem to have been the quality in Montanism that attracted men like Tertullian, whose writings are one of our few primary sources for Montanist teaching. His reliability as such a source constitutes a major problem. On the one hand, his Montanism dated from a period almost two generations later than the origins of the movement; and it is almost axiomatic that two generations can and usually do alter the character and emphasis of a movement considerably. On the other hand, Tertullian himself was obviously a man of such strong mind and will as to support the conjecture that he changed Montanism at least as much as he was changed by it. This seems certainly to have been the case with his eschatology, and it may well be true throughout his theology. Not for its theological novelty, if any, was he drawn to it, but for its moral zeal, so that, in Bonwetsch's apt formulation, "what he had previously demanded as a consequence of a pietistic and rigoristic conception of Christianity, he now required as a Montanist on the basis of divine authority." Nevertheless, when it comes to the question of the doctrinal significance of Montanism, it is upon Tertullian's testimony that we must rely in great measure, testing it as well as we can against the other scraps of information that are available. This doctrinal significance is to be sought in two principal areas, in the doctrine of the Trinity and in the concept of the Spirit and of authority in the church.

The problem of the interpretation of the Trinity in

Montanism revolves chiefly around the issue of the Paraclete. It has been suggested that the idea of the Paraclete played a minor role, if any, in the earliest stage of the Montanist movement; against this suggestion stands the traditional notion that Montanism was "a faith in the mission of the Paraclete, incarnate in the person of Montanus." Tertullian's usage of the term "Paraclete" seems to have been quite ambiguous; even Labriolle must grant that there is "a small difficulty" in discovering its meaning in the treatise *Against Praxeas*, finding only one place in that treatise where it was "without doubt" intended to mean Montanus in person.

From our sources it seems likely that when he was caught up in ecstatic rapture, Montanus spoke of the Paraclete in the first person: "I am the Paraclete." According to Epiphanius, Montanus said: "I am the Lord God Almighty, who have descended in a man"; and again: "It is neither an angel nor an elder that has come, but I, the Lord God." Didymus the Blind transmitted another oracle that he had heard attributed to Montanus: "I am the Father and the Son and the Paraclete." On the basis of such oracles some of the later critics of Montanism were moved to maintain that Montanus identified himself with the Holy Spirit in an essential way; so, for example, Cyril of Jerusalem wrote that Montanus "had the audacity to say that he himself was the Holy Spirit." But a comparison between the statements attributed to Montanus in this regard and other similar statements, both Christian and pagan, in those who cultivated the practice of ecstatic speech would seem to indicate that this interpretation is not accurate. It would appear, rather, that such formulas express the sense of passivity as an instrument or mouthpiece of the divine which is characteristic of this practice, not the arrogation to himself by a human being of the claim to deity. Epiphanius also quoted Montanus as saying: "Behold, man is like a lyre." What this practice eventually became in Montanism is perhaps quite another matter, but in the case of Montanus himself and of his immediate successors, it would appear to be the more likely conclusion that the practice had this instrumental nature.

Such a conclusion is borne out also by the fact that through Maximilla, one of the prophetesses, the Spirit said: "I am the Word [ῥῆμα] and the Spirit and the

---

Schepelern (1929) 16

Labriolle (1913) 1:135

Tert.*Prax*.13.5 (*CCSL* 2:1175)
Labriolle (1913) 1:55–56

Epiph.*Haer*.48.11.1 (*GCS* 31:233)

Epiph.*Haer*.48.11.9 (*GCS* 31:235)

Didym.*Trin*.3.41 (*PG* 39:984)

Cyr.H.*Catech*.16.8 (Reischl–Rupp 2:214)

Epiph.*Haer*.48.4.1 (*GCS* 31:224)

Eus.*H.e.*5.16.17 (*GCS* 9:466)

Power." Maximilla did not claim these prerogatives for herself, but for the Spirit that spoke through her. The almost liturgical character of the utterance suggests that this may have been a peculiar Montanist form of the doctrine of the Trinity. In that case, "Word" would refer to the Logos, with more stress on its nature as the spoken word than on the philosophical and cosmological connotations usually implied in the term. Then "Power" would have to refer to the Father. But in much of early

Herm.*Mand.*11.17 (*SC* 53:196–98); Athenag.*Leg.*10.2 (Goodspeed 324)

Christian usage, power was usually connected with the Holy Spirit; in such a passage as Luke 1:35, the two terms seem to be parallel. On the other hand, "Father" did connote power in Christian language, particularly in those writers who came to associate the title with crea-

Just. *1 Apol.*8.2 (Goodspeed 30)

tion, making God the Father of the cosmos and of all men rather than the Father of the Lord Jesus Christ and derivatively of all believers. The possibility does exist that this was a trinitarian formulation; it does not seem plausible that here "the Spirit is defining himself with

Labriolle (1913) 1:69–71

one general term and two others." More significant, however, is the realization that such a formulation as this could have been a quite orthodox doctrine of the Trinity in the second half of the second century.

Eventually, however, Montanism may have gone much farther than did its original founders. This is the impression given by an inscription discovered in Numidia: "Flavius, grandsire of the household. In the name of the Father and the Son [and] of the Lord Muntanus.

ap.Labriolle (1913) 2:195

What he promised, he performed." The inscription is obviously not of pagan origin; at the same time, it would militate against the entire faith and practice of the catholic and orthodox church to insert the name of a saint into the name of the Holy Trinity. Hence the effort to connect the "Muntanus" mentioned here with an orthodox Carthaginian martyr of that name creates considerable difficulty. At most, as in a famous passage of Justin on

Just. *1 Apol.*6.2 (Goodspeed 29)

the angels, such a name might be closely linked to those of Father, Son, and Holy Spirit, but not substituted for one of them. It would seem that this is an inscription from late Montanism. If this is truly the case, then it might follow that sometime in the course of its development—and it seems impossible to date the inscription—Montanism had among its adherents some who took the identification of Montanus with the Paraclete quite literally, including him as the third person in the Trinity. Whether or not one accepts the further reports of the fathers that in the fourth century the Montanists were baptizing in the name of Priscilla or of Montanus, it does seem possible that in this later stage of its development Montanism had parted company with the great church in the doctrine of the Trinity.

Though this was decidedly a later development, still some of it may have been implicit in the movement all along. Hippolytus, while acknowledging in all fairness that some members of the Montanist sect "confess the Father as the God of everything and the Creator of all things, in agreement with the church, and they witness to Christ in accordance with the gospel," reported that there was one party among the Montanists who, in his words, "agreeing with the heresy of the Noetians say that the Father is himself the Son, and that he underwent birth and suffering and death." This is substantiated by the report of Pseudo-Tertullian, *Against All Heresies*. After describing the general blasphemy of the Montanists, who claimed that the Paraclete, speaking through Montanus, had gone beyond the revelation in Christ, this treatise went on to speak of a group following Aeschines, who "add this, that they say that Christ himself is the Son and the Father." In other words, they would seem to have embraced the doctrine that Father, Son, and Holy Spirit were only successive modes of manifestation of the one God. In that case, the manifestation of God as Son in Jesus would have been followed by the manifestation of the one God as Paraclete in Montanus, each in turn. Such language about the Trinity was in itself quite acceptable in the second century, and even later; but when the church went beyond it to formulate the dogma of the Trinity, those Montanists who continued to use this language as a way of including Montanus in the manifestations of God found themselves heretical on this score as well.

It would be a mistake to gather from this that Montanism necessarily implied such a doctrine. On the contrary, the most powerful statement of the case against the doctrine came from the Montanist Tertullian. In his treatise against Praxeas, he accused this Roman presbyter of two errors: "He threw out prophecy and brought in heresy; he put the Paraclete to flight and crucified the Father." The treatise was devoted to a critique of the

Bas.*Ep*.188.1 (*PG* 32:668)

Hipp.*Haer*.8.19.2 (*GCS* 26:238)

Hipp.*Haer*.8.19.3 (*GCS* 26:238)

Ps.Tert.*Haer*.7.2 (*CCSL* 2:1409)

See pp. 176–77 below

Tert.*Prax*.1.5 (*CCSL* 2:1159–60)

doctrine that spoke of the Father as suffering and being
crucified; hence its eventual name "Patripassianism." And
it was Tertullian, writing as a Montanist, who attacked
a doctrine of the identity between the Father and the
Son that some of his Montanist brethren were eventually
to employ as a theological rationale for their system.
There was room for partisans of both brands of trinitarian
theology in the Montanist sect—so long as they did not
remarry after their wives had died.

In any case, the crucial place for an examination of
the significance of Montanism for the history of the doctrine of the Trinity is Tertullian. Is it correct to say that
"what individual adherents of the new prophecy did for
the theological articulation of the doctrine of the Trinity
did not come from their Montanism"? Or is it more
accurate to suggest that Montanism taught Tertullian to
think of the Paraclete in more personal terms than he had
in his early works, so that he came to a more metaphysical
doctrine of the Trinity? With certain reservations, the
second alternative seems preferable, partly for sheer
chronological reasons. The early writings of Tertullian
tended to stress the Father and the Son at the expense
of the Holy Spirit; those which definitely dated from the
Montanist period, on the other hand, did contain a more
metaphysical doctrine of the "Trinity"—a word which
Tertullian seems to have been the first theologian to
employ in Latin. The emphasis in Montanism on the
Spirit is the explanation of this shift that suggests itself
most insistently. The great influence of Tertullian on the
subsequent trinitarian discussion would mean, then, that
while some Montanists held to a naive formula for the
Trinity that was shared by other Christians, Tertullian's
Montanism helped him to insights by which the church
eventually transcended this formula and developed a
more consistent doctrine of the Trinity.

More critical than Montanism's theory of the role of
the Spirit in the Trinity was its conception of the role of
the Spirit in the church, and it was at this point that
the principal doctrinal battle was joined. Montanism
laid claim to supernatural inspiration by the Holy Spirit
as the source of its prophecy, and it pointed to the moral
decline of the church as the main reason for its having
lost this power of the Spirit. Most orthodox writers in
the second and even in the third century maintained that
such inspiration by the Holy Spirit was not only possible,

Aug.*Haer*.41 (*CCSL* 46:308)

Bonwetsch (1881) 75

Loofs (1930) 142

Tert.*Apol*.21.11–14 (*CCSL* 1:124–25)

Tert.*Prax*.3.1 (*CCSL* 2:1161)

See pp. 99–100 above

but present and active in the church. In meeting the challenge of Montanism, they could not, for the most part, take the approach that the age of supernatural inspiration had passed. Among the earliest critics of Montanism, there was no effort to discredit the supernatural character of the new prophecy. Instead, these critics affirmed that the ecstatic seizures of the Montanists were indeed supernatural in origin, but claimed that the supernatural involved was not the Holy Spirit of God but demonic spirits. Yet the decline of genuine prophecy and of the extraordinary functioning of the Spirit among the ranks of the catholic church tended to reduce the effectiveness of this charge that the prophecy of the Montanists was a pseudoprophecy because its supernatural source was demonic.

ap.Eus.*H.e.*5.16.8 (*GCS* 9:462)

There was another way to meet the doctrinal implications of the Montanist challenge, and in the long run that was the way orthodoxy took. The first articulate spokesman of this viewpoint of whom there is record was Hippolytus of Rome, a contemporary of Tertullian. Apparently he recognized that the weakness which Montanism had discovered in the church lay in the church's concept of a continuing prophecy. This concept was of a piece with a vivid eschatology; for apocalyptic has always, as suggested by its very name, which means "revelatory," brought with it the notion of supplementary revelation, by which, among other things, the apocalypticist is convinced that the end has truly come. More consistently than most of the anti-Montanist writers were willing to do, Hippolytus subjected to question the very foundations of the Montanist movement. He was franker than most of his contemporaries in admitting that the church was not necessarily living in the last times, and in opposition to Montanism he defended the process by which the church was beginning to reconcile itself to the delay in the Lord's second coming. As he pushed the time of the second coming into the future, so he pushed the time of prophecy into the past. It had ended with the apostle John, whose Apocalypse Hippolytus maintained was the last valid prophecy to have come from the Holy Spirit. And though John was entitled to claim the inspiration of the Spirit for his prophetic work, later so-called prophets had no such right.

Hipp.*Dan.*4.18.3 (*GCS* 1–I:230)

Hipp.*Dan.*4.19.3 (*GCS* 1–I:234)

Hipp.*Dan.*4.18.7 (*GCS* 1–I:232)

Hipp.*Antichr.*31 (*GCS* 1–II:20–21)
Hipp.*Antichr.*47–48 (*GCS* 1–II:30)

Hipp.*Antichr.*36 (*GCS* 1–II:23)

By setting the authority of the biblical prophets, both

in the Old and in the New Testament, against the claims
of the new prophets, Hippolytus struck at the foundation
of the Montanist movement. But in so doing, Hippolytus
and the theologians that followed him also struck at the
Christian movement that had preceded them. As Schepelern has summarized the situation, "A half century earlier such a movement could still count on ecclesiastical recognition. Between the preaching of judgment by John and
that by Montanus, however, there lies the decisive phase in
the development of the church's organization and ministry, and the free manifestations of the Spirit protest

Schepelern (1929) 162

against their authority in vain." The simple fact was that
in the context of the course that church doctrine was taking by that time, Montanism was obsolete and could not
succeed or survive. Its principal significance for the
development of church doctrine was to serve as an index
to the gradual solidification of the church's message and
work, and to its inevitable need for fixed forms of dogma
and creed.

Montanism was obsolete because the church had begun
to find its most trustworthy guarantees of the presence
and functioning of the Holy Spirit in the threefold apostolic authority taught by Irenaeus rather than in the
ecstasy and prophecy that the Paraclete granted to the adherents of Montanism. In the face of this situation the
apocalyptic spontaneity of Montanism was "an attempt at

Aland (1960) 143

restoration which could not count on any recognition"
and had no place in a church that was soon to make its
peace not only with the empire but with the world as such.
And by the adoption of the threefold norm for the
church's life and teaching, orthodox Christianity fundamentally altered a conception of the activity of the Holy
Spirit that had figured prominently in its earlier history.
To validate its existence, the church looked increasingly
not to the future, illumined by the Lord's return, nor to
the present, illumined by the Spirit's extraordinary gifts,
but to the past, illumined by the composition of the apostolic canon, the creation of the apostolic creed, and the
establishment of the apostolic episcopate. To meet the
test of apostolic orthodoxy, a movement or idea had to
measure up to these norms.

In this way the apostles became a sort of spiritual
aristocracy, and the first century a golden age of the
Spirit's activity. The difference between the Spirit's activ-

ity in the days of the apostolic church and in the history of the church now became a difference not only of degree but fundamentally of kind, and the promises of the New Testament on the coming of the Holy Spirit were referred primarily to the Pentecost event and only through that event, via the apostles, to the subsequent ages of the church. The promise that the Spirit would lead into all truth, which figured prominently in Montanist doctrine, now meant principally, if not exclusively, that the Spirit would lead the apostles into all truth as they composed the creed and the books of the New Testament, and the church into all truth when it was built on their foundation. Here, too, the transition was gradual, and it was not complete. The history of the church has never been altogether without the spontaneous gifts of the Holy Spirit, even where the authority of the apostolic norms has been most incontestable. In the experiences of monks and friars, of mystics and seers, as well as in the underground religion of many believers, the Montanist heresy has carried on a sort of unofficial existence.

John 16:13

Tert.*Fug*.1.1 (*CCSL* 2:1135); Tert.*Prax*.2.1; 30.5 (*CCSL* 2:1160; 1204)

Aug.*Ev.Joh*.96.2–4 (*CCSL* 36:569–72)

Criteria of Apostolic Continuity

In one way or another, each of the three controversies studied in this chapter dealt with the question of continuity. Marcion severed the bond between Christian revelation and the Old Testament; he isolated the apostle Paul from the rest of the apostolic community and attributed the full knowledge of the Christian truth about the relation between law and gospel to Paul alone; and he interpreted the developing catholic Christianity of his day as an apostasy from truly apostolic, that is, Pauline, teaching. The Gnostics radicalized the disjunction between creation and redemption and made of it an ontological principle, rooted within the very nature of the divine reality itself; they attributed to the apostles of Christ a pedagogical accommodation to the erroneous thought patterns of their day, which meant that true gnosis could not be derived directly from the apostolic writings, but was to be discovered there only with the aid of Gnostic hermeneutics; they, too, pitted their Gnostic doctrine, which they had received by true succession, against the catholic teaching of what came eventually to be regarded (thanks in part to these very controversies) as the orthodox mainstream. And the Montanists were, if anything,

ap.Iren.*Haer*.3.5.1 (Harvey 2:19); ap.Tert.*Praescrip*. 25.1–2 (*CCSL* 1:206)

ap.Epiph.*Haer*.33.7.9 (*GCS* 25:457); ap.Iren.*Haer*.3.pr. (Harvey 2:1)

even more explicit than either Marcion or the Valentinians in setting forth the idea of a fall of the church since
the apostolic age, brought on by the worldliness of its
life and the compromises in its teaching; the true succession from the apostles lay with those who, like the apostles, continued to receive the special revelations promised
by Christ to the apostles and by them to the church in all
subsequent generations.

Each of these systems of doctrine asserted that authentic continuity lay with it, and that the catholic claim to
continuity was illegitimate. The question was: What are
the criteria of doctrinal continuity? And if the answer
was "the consanguinity of doctrine with that of the apostles," or the claim that "Christ comes with a message from
God, and the apostles with a message from Christ," this
simply moved the question over one notch, to the issue of
apostolic continuity. It was presumably with some of
these heretical claims in mind that Clement of Alexandria propounded his definition of the true Gnostic as one
who had matured in the Scriptures (that is, of both the
Old and New Testament) and who maintained apostolic
and ecclesiastical orthodoxy in doctrine; this was, he said,
a life of words and actions in conformity with "the tradition of the Lord." This was merely one obiter dictum
among many in the *Stromata;* some of the others laid
claim to secret revelation in a manner reminiscent of the
Gnostics.

A more systematic statement of this doctrine of apostolic continuity is found in the preface to the most important work of Clement's pupil, Origen, *On First Principles.* It has been preserved only in the Latin version of
the book prepared by Rufinus, which has been so dis-
torted in other passages (where there happen to exist
fragments of the Greek original) that scholars have been
extremely skeptical about basing any argument concerning the teaching of Origen only upon passages in Rufinus's translation—especially if such passages set forth the
party line of mainstream orthodox catholic doctrine. For
the purposes of the history of church doctrine, however,
the difficulties created by Rufinus's expurgated text are not
as devastating as they would be if Origen's theology were
our primary focus of interest. If the passage is authentic
Origen, it shows him to have been a champion of emerging catholic orthodoxy; if it is not authentic, but has been

Tert.*Praescrip*.32.6 (*CCSL*
1:213)

1 Clem.42.2 (Bihlmeyer 57)

Clem.*Str*.7.16.104.1–2 (*GCS*
17:73)

Or.*Princ*.pr.1–4 (*GCS*
22:7–11)

doctored by Rufinus, it is still a strikingly complete and accurate summary of how that catholic orthodoxy defined the criteria of apostolic continuity—sufficiently complete and accurate, indeed, to provide an outline for our summary as well.

From the statements of the Gospel of John that "grace and truth came through Jesus Christ" and that Christ was "the truth" in person, it followed that the only reliable source for the Christian life lay in the very words and teachings of Christ. But, continued Origen, the words of Christ did not include only the words which he spoke while he was in the flesh, for Christ had also been the Word of God active in Moses and the prophets. To assert the authority of the word of Christ, therefore, was simultaneously to affirm its continuity with the revelation set down in the Old Testament. This continuity was an essential element in authentic apostolic tradition. It was denied outright by Marcion, and in effect by Valentinus; in Tertullian's formula, "One man perverts the Scriptures with his hand, another their meaning by his exposition." For behind Marcion's denial of continuity between Christ and the Old Testament was his hostility to the Creator and the creation, which was increasingly shared by the Valentinian and other forms of Christian Gnosticism. Montanism does not seem to have cast similar aspersions on the Old Testament, but the newness of the new prophecy certainly implied a diminution of the authority of the old prophecy, whether Christian or Jewish.

So intimate was the apostolic continuity with the Old Testament that the words of the Old Testament could be read as prophecies not only about Christ by the prophets, but also by Christ about "the apostles and all the faithful in succession." The mission of the Christian apostles into the world, their message and their sufferings—all were predicted in the Old Testament. The very boldness of Paul in attacking the authority of the Old Testament law was predicated on a continuity with the Old Testament and on the identity between the God of the law and the God preached in Christ. Because that continuity and identity did not come into question during the lifetime of the apostles, this was truly apostolic doctrine, vindicated as such both materially, by its content, and formally, by its presence within churches of apostolic foundation. Replying to the Marcionites and to the Valentinians, Ire-

John 1:17
John 14:6

Or.*Princ*.pr.1 (*GCS* 22:7–8);
Iren.*Haer*.4.2.3 (Harvey
2:148)

Tert.*Praescrip*.38.7 (*CCSL*
1:219)

Tert.*Marc*.3.22.5 (*CCSL*
1:539)

Tert.*Marc*.1.21.4 (*CCSL*
1:462–63)

Iren.*Haer*.3.12.13 (Harvey 2:68)

Iren.*Haer*.3.12.15 (Harvey 3:71–72); Tert.*Marc*.5.18.11 (*CCSL* 1:719)

Iren.*Haer*.4.32.1 (Harvey 2:254)

Or.*Princ*.pr.8 (*GCS* 22:14)

ap.Iren.*Haer*.1.8.3 Harvey 1:72)
Iren.*Haer*.4.33.1 (Harvey 2:256)

Iren.*Haer*.4.33.15 (Harvey 2:269)

Iren.*Haer*.4.32.2 (Harvey 2:255)

John 5:39

Iren.*Haer*.4.10.1 (Harvey 2:172)

naeus argued that "both the apostles and their disciples" had taught as the church was teaching concerning the difference as well as the unity and harmony between the Old Testament and the New. Since the apostles, whom Christ had designated "witnesses of every action and of every [catholic] doctrine," had treated the law of the Old Testament as the ordinance of the same God whom they had known in Christ, it followed that they stood in continuity with "the first Testament." The anti-Gnostic fathers turned the tables on their opponents by maintaining that the very basis of the Gnostic and especially of the Marcionite case—the polemic of the New Testament, specifically of the apostle Paul, against the law of Moses —served to confirm the case for the authority of the Old Testament within the apostolic tradition. In support of his position on the continuity between the Testaments, Irenaeus also cited a presbyter who had been a pupil of the apostles.

This defense of the Old Testament, however, presupposed the correctness of spiritual interpretation as the method for discovering the Scriptures' deeper meaning. The teaching that the Scriptures had a meaning which was not evident at first sight was, Origen asserted, unanimously accepted throughout the church and belonged to the universally acknowledged content of the ecclesiastical and apostolic tradition. This claim was, however, compromised by the Gnostic use of the allegorical method to interpret not only the Old Testament but the New, not only Genesis but the Gospel of John. This was consistent with the Gnostics' application of the contrast between the psychic and the spiritual man in 1 Corinthians 2:14–15 to the difference between the Gnostic interpreter of Scripture and the catholic. Quoting this very passage from Paul, Irenaeus contended that only the true spiritual could discern the "character of the divine economy" in the Old Testament. There had been two Testaments in the two peoples, but the apostolic doctrine was that the Old Testament contained "types" both of the church and of heaven. To "search the Scriptures" meant to find evidences that the Son of God had been "planted" throughout Moses and the prophets.

Another implication of the apostolic continuity with the Old Testament appeared in the context of the same passage. The continuity between the Old Testament and

Iren.*Haer*.2.9.1 (Harvey
1:271–72)

the New was a corollary of the oneness of God, as the difference between the two Testaments was based on the two dispensations of the one God. The continuity of the New Testament with the Old required a continuity between creation and redemption. "The entire ecumenical church has received from the apostles the tradition" that the one God who was Maker of heaven and earth was also the one who should be addressed as "our Father." From the history of the Old Testament it was evident, Tertullian said against Marcion, that the title "Father of mercies" properly belonged to the Creator and the title "the blessed God" to him who, according to Genesis 1:22, had blessed all things and, according to the Book of Daniel, was blessed by them. The beauties of the creatures showed that it was not unworthy of him to have been their Creator, as even the history of religion outside the Old and New Testament affirmed. Origen summed up this first criterion of apostolic continuity in the confession "that there is one God, who created and arranged all things," "the God of the apostles and of the Old and New Testaments."

Tert.*Marc*.5.11.1 (*CCSL* 1:695)

Tert.*Marc*.1.13.2–5 (*CCSL* 1:454–55)

Or.*Princ*.pr.4 (*GCS* 22:9–10)

Or.*Princ*.pr.4 (*GCS* 22:9); Theoph.*Autol*.3.12 (*SC* 20:228)

A second form of continuity in the apostolic tradition was the continuity of the apostles with one another as the faithful messengers of Christ. Origen spoke in an utterly matter-of-fact way about "the teaching of the apostles," who, like the prophets of the Old Testament, had been inspired by the Holy Spirit. This definition of apostolic continuity was directed against the isolation of one apostle from the apostolic community. Irenaeus described it as a characteristic of heresy that each heretic selected part of the whole apostolic witness and, after adapting it to his system, elevated its authority above that of the other apostles. The Ebionites denied the authority of any Gospel except the Gospel of Matthew; Marcion accepted only the Gospel of Luke; certain other Gnostics, who taught that Jesus had suffered but Christ had not, preferred the Gospel of Mark; and the Valentinians relied on the Gospel of John. It was especially Marcion who denied the continuity of the apostles with one another, asserting that Paul was the apostle who knew the truth, because its mystery had been communicated to him in a special revelation. Marcion or his followers may even have taught that the other apostles could not have been saved, since Paul was the only one who was baptized in the Lord.

Iren.*Haer*.3.11.7 (Harvey 2:45–46)

Iren.*Haer*.3.13.1 (Harvey 2:72)

ap.Tert.*Bapt*.12.2 (*CCSL* 1:287)

Therefore, according to the Marcionites, the polemic of the Epistle to the Galatians against "false apostles" was aimed at Peter, James, and John, and at the forged gospels circulating in the churches; even though Marcion does not seem to have consistently meant the other apostles with the term "false apostles," the conflict between Peter and Paul was a recurring theme of his teaching. For Marcion, Paul was not one apostle among others, but the only apostle, and "he did not follow the preaching of the apostles."

Tert.*Marc*.4.3.2 (*CCSL* 1:548)

Tert.*Marc*.5.2.7 (*CCSL* 1:667–68)

The answer of the church to this elevation of Paul was the ascription of apostolic authority to the entire apostolic community and to the canon of the New Testament, and, consequently, the insistence that there was no conflict between the teaching of Paul and that of the other apostles. "Peter was an apostle of the very same God as Paul was," declared Irenaeus; and Tertullian affirmed that Peter was on the same level with Paul in martyrdom. Since Marcion had not only elevated Paul above the other apostles but elevated the Epistle to the Galatians above the other letters of Paul, placing it first in his collection of the epistles, his catholic critics sought to prove out of Galatians that Paul regarded himself as part of the apostolic community and shared its doctrine. Paul's visit to Peter, referred to in Galatians 1:18, was an acknowledgment of Peter's office and of a shared belief and message; "having been converted from a persecutor to a preacher, he is introduced as one of the brethren to brethren, by brethren—to them, indeed, who had put on faith from the apostles' hands." In effect, this interpreted the Paul of the Epistle to the Galatians on the basis of the Paul of the Book of Acts (not accepted as canonical by Marcion and Cerdo), one of whose themes was the primacy of the twelve apostles and Paul's acknowledgment of their authority. The report in Galatians was said to harmonize, both logically and chronologically, with that in Acts, in fact to be identical with it. In the interests of this harmonization, the text of Galatians 2:5, "To them we did not yield submission even for a moment," seems to have been altered to say that Paul did yield submission—altered, apparently, by the same Irenaeus and Tertullian who attacked Marcion for tampering with the text of the writings of Paul.

Iren.*Haer*.3.13.1 (Harvey 2:72)
Tert.*Praescrip*.24.4 (*CCSL* 1:206)

Tert.*Marc*.4.3.2 (*CCSL* 1:548)

Tert.*Praescrip*.23.6 (*CCSL* 1:205)

Tert.*Marc*.5.2.7 (*CCSL* 1:667); Ps.Tert.*Haer*.6.1 (*CCSL* 2:1408)

Iren.*Haer*.3.13.3 (Harvey 2:74)

Iren.*Haer*.3.13.3 (Harvey 2:74); Tert.*Marc*.5.3.3 (*CCSL* 1:668)

The presupposition for this harmonization was the deepening authority of a normative body of writings, in which not only the Paul of Galatians and the Paul of Acts, not only Paul and Peter, but the entire body of the apostles had expressed the one apostolic faith. From the apostles the entire church throughout the world had had its foundation. It is not clear how early the term "Scripture," as applied to one or more of the books now collected in the New Testament, began to carry some of the connotations of authority it had when applied to the Old Testament. 2 Peter 3:16 suggests that at least certain Pauline epistles were sufficiently invested with these connotations to be subjected to the same distortion as "the other Scriptures." Attacking such distortion, Irenaeus could speak of "the plethora of matters contained in the Scriptures" and, as the context indicates, mean by this not only the Old Testament, but collections of books by the apostles. What the apostles had preached viva voce, they had then "handed down to us in the Scriptures as the pillar and bulwark of our faith." Not to assent to the content of these Scriptures was to hold in contempt those who had had communion with Christ the Lord. In the usage of Irenaeus, "Scripture" could still mean nothing more than the Old Testament, and in almost half of its occurrences it apparently did. But it had also come to include what could, from that time on, be called the canon of the New Testament.

"The canon of the New Testament is authoritative Scripture." For the history of doctrine it is the predicate rather than the subject of this sentence that must be specified. The development of the canon is a fascinating and important area of research, and one whose history demands new investigation in the light of the texts under consideration in this chapter. But it is the doctrine about the authority of Scripture, rather than the process by which the scope and extent of its canon have been determined, that concerns us here. Historically, to be sure, the doctrine and the process have interacted, at the very point with which this section is dealing, the criterion of apostolicity. As John Knox has observed, "Canonicity and apostolicity became almost synonymous terms. . . . The argument moved both ways: II Peter, since it was presumably written by an apostle, must be accorded canonical status; Hebrews, because it obviously deserved canonical status, must have been written by an apostle." The list of these canonical or apostolic books continued to fluctuate for centuries; what did not fluctuate was the

Iren.Haer.3.12.7 (Harvey 2:62)

Iren.Haer.1.1.3 (Harvey 1:13)

Iren.Haer.3.1.1 (Harvey 2:2)

Iren.Haer.3.1.2 (Harvey 2:6)

Knox (1952) 66–67

doctrine, precisely formulated for the first time against the heresies described in this chapter, that in the canon of the New Testament were recorded "the voices of that church from which every church has its origin, the voices of the mother city of the citizens of the new covenant," the voices of the apostles of Jesus Christ.

Yet, as Irenaeus observed, when the Gnostics were confronted with arguments based on these apostolic Scriptures, they would reply that the Scriptures could not be properly understood by anyone who was not privy to "the tradition," that is, the secret body of knowledge not committed to writing but handed down from the apostles to the successive generations of the Gnostic perfect. The catholic response to this claim, formulated more fully by Irenaeus than by any other Christian writer, was to appeal to "that tradition which is derived from the apostles." Unlike the Gnostic tradition, however, this apostolic tradition had been preserved publicly in the churches that stood in succession with the apostles. Or, in the formula of Origen, it was "the doctrine of the church, transmitted in orderly succession from the apostles and remaining in the churches to the present day." Together with the proper interpretation of the Old Testament and the proper canon of the New, this tradition of the church was a decisive criterion of apostolic continuity for the determination of doctrine in the church catholic.

Clearly it is an anachronism to superimpose upon the discussions of the second and third centuries categories derived from the controversies over the relation of Scripture and tradition in the sixteenth century, for "in the ante-Nicene Church . . . there was no notion of *sola Scriptura*, but neither was there a doctrine of *traditio sola.*" At the same time, it is essential to note that doctrinal, liturgical, and exegetical material of quite different sorts was all lumped under the term "tradition," from the christological interpretation of specific passages in the Old Testament to a chiliastic interpretation of the apocalyptic vision; and the process of accretion continued far beyond the ante-Nicene era. Some of the most important issues in the theological interpretation of doctrinal development have been raised by disputes over the content and the authority of apostolic tradition as a source and norm of Christian doctrine and over the relation of this tradition to other norms of apostolicity.

Iren.*Haer.*3.12.5 (Harvey 2:58)

Iren.*Haer.*3.2.1 (Harvey 2:7); Tert.*Praescrip.*22.2 (CCSL 1:203)

Iren.*Haer.*3.2.2 (Harvey 2:7–8)

Or.*Princ.*pr.2 (GCS 22:8)

Outler (1965) 29

Iren.*Haer*.3.9.1 (Harvey 2:30)

Iren.*Haer*.3.10.5 (Harvey 2:40)

Iren.*Haer*.3.pr. (Harvey 2:1)

Iren.*Haer*.3.11.9 (Harvey 2:51)

Iren.*Haer*.3.1.1 (Harvey 2:2)

Iren.*Haer*.3.14.2 (Harvey 2:76)
Iren.*Haer*.3.15.1 (Harvey 2.79)

Iren.*Haer*.3.4.1 (Harvey 2:16)

Iren.*Haer*.3.4.2 (Harvey 2:16–17)

For Irenaeus, God in Christ was both the origin and the content of the tradition. Christ had given the tradition to his disciples that the Father was the one and only God. This one and only God had been announced by the prophets and by the true gospel; he it was whom Christians worshiped and loved with their whole heart. The church had received this gospel tradition from the apostles and had handed it on to her children. Unlike the secret traditions of the Gnostics, which had been transmitted only to the chosen few; unlike the new prophecy of the Montanists, which separated them from communication with the brethren, this apostolic tradition had been proclaimed as by a town crier. It was characteristic of the apostles that what they had learned from Christ, they transmitted openly to all, without discriminating against anyone. The apostolic tradition was a public tradition: the apostles had not taught one set of doctrines in secret and another in the open, suppressing a portion of their tradition to be transmitted through a special succession to the Gnostic elite. So palpable was this apostolic tradition that even if the apostles had not left behind the Scriptures to serve as normative evidence of their doctrine, the church would still be in a position to follow "the structure of the tradition which they handed on to those to whom they committed the churches." This was, in fact, what the church was doing in those barbarian territories where believers did not have access to the written deposit, but still carefully guarded the ancient tradition of the apostles, summarized in the creed—or, at least, in a very creedlike statement of the content of apostolic tradition.

Like the development of the canon of the New Testament, the evolution of Christian creeds is an essential and unavoidable part of the history of early Christian doctrine; almost equally unavoidable is the temptation to document the inclusion and exclusion of individual books from the canon or of particular articles from the creeds. Some amount of such documentation belongs here, but only when (and to the extent that) it truly does serve as an index to the direction of doctrinal development. More immediately relevant here is the claim of the anti-Gnostic fathers that their creedal statements of faith were an integral element in the determination and demonstration of apostolic continuity. These statements were integral for such continuity before, during, and after the establishment of the canon of the New Testament: before, in order that Christians might have the essentials of the faith assured to them; during, so that a principle of discrimination might enable the church to sort out the writings claiming apostolic sanction; and after, because the canon of the New Testament was too long and complex to act as a standard of faith and needed to be condensed into a rule that could be learned and confessed. The term "rule of faith" or "rule of truth" did not always refer to such creeds and confessions, and seems sometimes to have meant the "tradition," sometimes the Scriptures, sometimes the message of the gospel.

A study of the creedal phrases in Irenaeus, Tertullian, and Hippolytus shows there was great variation not only between one Christian writer and another, but between one quotation and another by the same writer, suggesting that the texts of the creeds themselves were far from uniform and that an author adapted and elaborated the texts to suit his purposes. Two elements remain constant through the citations, and one or both of them may safely be said to have formed the outline of most creeds: Father, Son, and Holy Spirit; the life, death, and resurrection of Jesus Christ. These were, according to Origen,

Or.*Princ*.pr.4 (*GCS* 22:9–11)

"the particular points clearly delivered in the teaching of the apostles"; apostolic continuity, he argued, did not preclude discussion of other issues, but this central content was not negotiable. The liturgical evidence supports this interpretation, as do the liturgical echoes in the fathers. Irenaeus spoke of the faith which the church had received from the apostles and from their disciples, and

Iren *Haer*.1.10.1 (Harvey 1:90)

proceeded to quote a creed; Tertullian spoke of a rule of truth which had been handed down from Christ through

Tert.*Apol*.47.10 (*CCSL* 1:164)

his companions. Not only was its content the tradition derived from the apostles, but there developed a tradition that after Pentecost the apostles "assembled in one spot and, being filled with the Holy Spirit, drafted this short summary . . . of their future preaching," the Apostles' Creed, "so that they might not find themselves, widely dispersed as they would be, delivering different mes-

Rufin.*Symb*.2 (*CCSL* 20:134)

sages." This summary was to serve as a guarantee of doctrinal unity and as a criterion of apostolic continuity.

Both doctrinal unity and apostolic continuity were contrasted with the teachings of the Gnostics. Irenaeus spoke of "their variety" and of "their doctrines and succes-

Iren.*Haer*.3.pr. (Harvey 2:1)

Iren.*Haer*.1.10.2 (Harvey 1:92–94)

sions," but claimed that the church, dispersed across the world and speaking many languages, was of one heart and mind, holding the unity of faith. His argument that apostolic tradition provided the correct interpretation of the Old and New Testament, and that Scripture proved the correctness of the apostolic tradition was, in some ways, an argument in a circle. But in at least two ways it broke out of the circle. One was the identification of tradition with "the gospel," which served as a norm of apostolic teaching. The other was the appeal to the churches of apostolic foundation as the warrantors of continuity with the apostles. For when neither Scripture nor tradition could convince the gainsayers, Irenaeus insisted that it lay within the "power of all in every church who may wish to see the truth, to contemplate clearly the tradition of the apostles manifested throughout the whole world; and we are in a position to reckon up those who were by the apostles instituted bishops in the churches,

Iren.*Haer*.3.3.1 (Harvey 2:8–9)

and to [demonstrate] the succession of these men to our times." Chief among these in authority and prestige was the church at Rome, in which the apostolic tradition shared by all the churches everywhere had been preserved. Apostolic foundation and the apostolic succession were another criterion of apostolic continuity.

The orthodox fathers also denied the heretics any legitimate claim to this criterion. Tertullian demanded of Marcion that he produce one Marcionite church that

Tert.*Marc*.1.21.5 (*CCSL* 1:463)

could trace its descent from an apostle. The heretics were said to have come much later than the first generation of bishops to whom the apostles had entrusted their churches. Therefore it was inevitable that the heretics should lose both continuity and unity of doctrine, while the church, possessing the sure tradition of the apostles,

Iren.*Haer*.5.20.1 (Harvey 2:377–79)

proclaimed the same doctrine in all times and in all places. Irenaeus appears to have argued that this apostolic succession of the churches was empirically verifiable, on the basis of the lists of the bishops. This claim was shared by other writers. According to Tertullian (apparently before he became a Montanist), no one was to be received as a preacher without authorization from the churches of apostolic foundation, which were the matrix and fountain of

Tert.*Praescrip*.21 (*CCSL* 1:202–203)

the faith; apostolic tradition was what these churches taught. In this sense and on this basis, all churches that taught rightly could be called primitive and apostolic, be-

Tert.*Praescrip*.20.7 (*CCSL*
1:202)

Cypr.*Unit.eccl*.4 (*CSEL* 3:212)
See p. 159 below

Cypr.*Unit.eccl*.4 (*ACW* 25:46)

Eus.*H.e*.1.1.1 (*GCS* 9:6)

cause they shared the tradition preserved in the churches founded by the apostles. His pupil, Cyprian, took Matthew 16:18, "You are Peter, and on this rock I will build my church," to mean that the church was built on Peter, even though a similar power was entrusted to the other apostles; without retracting this, he seems later to have clarified his meaning by adding that "the other apostles were all that Peter was, endowed with equal dignity and power, but the start comes from him alone." And Eusebius, who summarized much of the development of the third century, wrote his *Ecclesiastical History* to document the proposition stated in his opening words, "the successions from the holy apostles."

Argument in a circle or not, this definition of the criteria of apostolic continuity did propound a unified system of authority. Historically, if not also theologically, it is a distortion to consider any one of the criteria apart from the others or to eliminate any one of them from consideration. For example, when the problem of the relation between Scripture and tradition became a burning issue in the theological controversies of the Western church, in the late Middle Ages and the Reformation, it was at the cost of the unified system. Proponents of the theory that tradition was an independent source of revelation minimized the fundamentally exegetical content of tradition which had served to define tradition and its place in the specification of apostolic continuity. The supporters of the sole authority of Scripture, arguing from radical hermeneutical premises to conservative dogmatic conclusions, overlooked the function of tradition in securing what they regarded as the correct exegesis of Scripture against heretical alternatives.

It is an oversimplification to maintain that the heresies and controversies described here produced these criteria, in the sense that the system of authority would not have developed without them. One can guess, however, that it might not have developed when it did and as it did without them. The Apostles' Creed might not have been obliged to make so explicit the identity of God with the Father, the Almighty, the Maker of heaven and earth; the canonical status of the *Shepherd* may have remained in flux much longer, and that of the pastoral epistles may not have been settled with such dispatch; the validity of revelations and of priestly acts outside the proper channels of the ecclesiastical structure could have been seen as an extraordinary gift of divine generosity rather than as a plot of demonic invention; and the excesses of allegory could have been criticized on orthodox grounds if Marcion had not helped to assure the future of allegory by attacking it. We may entertain any or all these conjectures without necessarily accepting, for example, the extreme judgment that "by his organizational and theological ideas and by his activity Marcion gave the decisive impetus to the creation of the early catholic church and provided it with a model; what is more, he deserves the credit for first grasping and carrying out the idea of a canonical collection of Christian writings, the New Testament."

Harnack (1960) 1:214–15

For it was some decades before Marcion or Montanism that the church was said to have been founded on the apostles and the prophets, Jesus Christ himself being the chief cornerstone: on the prophets, because there was already an acknowledged practice, if not a specified theory, of how to read the prophets; and on the apostles because, as the context in Ephesians suggests, both the apostolic message and the apostolic office were fundamental to the preservation of the Christian gospel. Gnosis and the new prophecy called forth the following definition, as its closing words show; but the content of the definition came from the life, faith, and memory—that is, from the tradition—of the church: "The true gnosis is the doctrine of the apostles, and the ancient constitution of the church throughout the world, and the character of the body of Christ in accordance with the succession of the bishops, by which they have handed on that church which is present in every place and has come down to us, being guarded and preserved, without any distortion of the Scriptures, by a very complete system of doctrine, neither adding nor subtracting anything. It is a reading [of the Scriptures] without forgery, and a lawful and diligent exposition in accordance with the Scriptures, both without danger and without blasphemy. And above all, it is the preeminent gift of love, which is more precious than gnosis, more glorious than prophecy, and which excels all other gifts of love." So it was that "apostolic," "catholic," "traditional," and "orthodox" became synonymous terms: "the apostolic dogmas" was a standard term for that which was believed, taught, and confessed by the orthodox catholic church on the basis of the word of God.

Eph.2:20

Iren.*Haer*.4.33.8 (Harvey 2:262–63)

Thdt.*H.e*.2.31.4 (*GCS* 19:171)

3

The Faith of the
Church Catholic

Against various heresies and schisms, the orthodox and catholic church defined as apostolic doctrine that which it believed, taught, and confessed. This doctrine, so it was presumed, had been believed and taught by the church before heresy demanded that it be confessed. Yet the task of reconstructing it from the existing documents is a complex one. A large part of the Christian literature which has been preserved was preoccupied either with the defense of Christianity against the cultured among its despisers or with polemics against heresy. Hence the interpretation of what was Christian doctrine during the second and third centuries is likely to concentrate on these same issues, at the expense of other doctrinal themes in the belief and piety of the church. The methodological problems in the attempt to uncover those themes in the documents are formidable, but the documents themselves make the attempt both necessary and justifiable. To cite one of the most explicit instances from the second century, Athenagoras opened his apologetic for the doctrine of the resurrection with a distinction between a "plea for the truth," addressed to skeptics and doubters, and an "exposition of the truth," addressed to those who were prepared to accept the truth; he noted that the exposition was more valuable and important, but that pagan hostility to the Christian doctrine of the resurrection of the dead made it necessary for him to give precedence to the plea over the exposition. Athenagoras's distinction justifies the effort to supply as much as possible of the missing "exposition" in defense of which the "plea" was made.

Another set of problems in the study of the state of Christian doctrine in the second and third centuries is

Athenag.*Res.*1 (*TU* 4–II: 48–49)

raised by the literary and historical analysis of the documents. The manuscript tradition of the epistles of Ignatius contains two and even three recensions of his works, varying not only in length and style but also in doctrinal content. How one interprets Ignatius's doctrine of the church and the episcopacy depends upon one's choice from among these recensions, although it has also been true that the decision about the authenticity of one or another version has frequently been shaped by one's doctrinal predilections. Similarly, the garbled transmission of the manuscripts of Cyprian's *Unity of the Church* has raised questions about his doctrine of the primacy of Peter. The chronology of the writings of Tertullian continues to elude precise determination; yet without such determination it is difficult to decide when he was speaking as a catholic and when as a Montanist. Literary analysis of Irenaeus's five books *Against Heresies* has attempted to isolate their several (sometimes contradictory) sources; and even though the attempt has not met with widespread acceptance, it does make an uncritical use of the treatise hazardous. Large parts of Origen's authorship have been preserved only in the Latin translations of Rufinus, which there is reason to regard with suspicion and even with skepticism.

These literary problems, which could be multiplied almost endlessly through these two centuries and well beyond them, jeopardize any history of the early development of Christian doctrine that proceeds from one thinker to the next, tracing origins, influences, borrowings, and divergences. Because we are trying here to listen to the chorus more than to the soloists, some of the problems of text, translation, and authorship recede in importance. Their place is taken by the even more slippery problem of locating a document or its author in the "penumbra" between heresy and orthodoxy, without making such a decision in a dogmatic rather than a historical way, on the basis of what the fourth or the fifth (or the sixteenth or the twentieth) century determined to be orthodox doctrine. Perhaps the only way to cope with this latter problem—or, at least, the way followed here—is to accept and to document the existence of such a penumbra and to seek for lines that may be drawn within it without doing violence to the evidence.

For our purposes, therefore, the importance of Ignatius

See p. 159 below

Turner (1954) 79

Corwin (1960) 29

Bévenot (1957) 8

E.Evans (1948) 79

Harnack (1907) 66

Hanson (1954) 173

lies in "the Christianity presupposed" by his letters; Cyprian's treatise is "a good example of what a dogma can look like while still in an early stage of its development"; even in his Montanism, Tertullian "was in no sense unorthodox, and nowhere makes any claim that the new prophecy supersedes the apostolic faith"; whatever may have been the sources of *Against Heresies*, Irenaeus lived "with all his soul, with his heart and with his head, in the faith of the church"; and in Origen we shall pay attention to what a not uncritical historian has called "his fundamental respect for the Christian tradition of doctrine." We shall also draw upon anonymous liturgical and creedal sources as evidence about the faith of the church catholic.

The Apocalyptic Vision and Its Transformation

Käsemann (1964) 2:100

"Apocalypticism . . . was the mother of all Christian theology." The earliest christology was not expressed in the cool identification of Jesus with the Logos as the rational principle of the universe, but in the fervid vision of the Son of man breaking the power of the demons and ushering in the new aeon with divine judgment and mercy. Baptism was a radical renunciation of the past and of this world, the breaking through of the kingdom into this present age. Each major tenet of primitive Christian belief must be understood in this apocalyptic context: the very charter of orthodoxy, the command of the risen Lord to the apostles to make disciples and to teach them

Matt.28:19–20

Tert.*Praescrip*.8.14 (*CCSL* 1:194)

to observe everything that he had commanded, was predicated on the promise and the prophecy that he would be with them until the consummation of the age. When that consummation was postponed, it could no longer serve as the premise for affirmations of Christian doctrine, which had to be transposed into another key. Of course, the expectation of the end of the world was itself a cardinal tenet of Christian faith, too firmly embedded in the message of Jesus and in the "apostolic doctrine" of the early Christian community to be expunged by such trifles as the details of world history. The place of this expectation as a Christian doctrine and its relevance to the development of other doctrines belong to this summary of the faith of the church.

It would be, however, a gross exaggeration of the evidence to describe the eclipse of the apocalyptic vision as

Werner (1941) 115

"catastrophic" for the generation that followed the apostles. Any such description is based on too simplistic a view of the role of apocalyptic in the teaching of Jesus and in the early church. Nor is it corroborated by later texts, for one looks in vain for proof of a bitter disappointment over the postponement of the parousia or of a shattering of the early Christian communities by the delay in the Lord's return. What the texts do suggest is a shift within the polarity of already/not yet and a great variety of solutions to the exegetical and theological difficulties caused by such a shift. These included the reinterpretation of biblical passages that had carried an eschatological connotation, the reorientation of ethical imperatives toward a more complex description of the life of faith and love within the forms of the present world, and the reconsideration and eventual rejection of certain types of apocalyptic expectation that could claim ancient sanction but were no longer suited to the new stage in the development of Christian eschatology. Here, too, it is important to see the elements of continuity as well as the elements of change.

Indeed, the evidence even suggests that the apocalyptic vision was not eclipsed as quickly or as completely in the church of the second and third centuries as the statements of a few theologians would indicate. One indication of the vision's survival is the tenacity of the millenarian hope, based upon Revelation 20:1–10. Probably the first indication that the prophecy in this chapter was being interpreted to mean an earthly reign of a thousand years following the return of Christ is that associated with the name of Papias. The only doctrinal position definitely attributed to him was the teaching, which he claimed to have derived from "unwritten tradition," that "there will be a millennium following the resurrection of the dead, when the kingdom of Christ is to be established physically on this earth." Irenaeus, with his reverence for "apostolic tradition," described in glowing terms the transformation of the cosmos and the animals during the millennium; as his authority he cited Papias, who was a man of hoary antiquity, had heard the apostle John (writer of the Book of Revelation), and had been associated with Polycarp. The *Epistle of Barnabas*, for all its hostility to Judaism, seems to have appropriated this element of Jewish eschatology.

But there is striking evidence not only that the millen-

ap.Eus.*H.e.*3.39. 11–12 (*GCS* 9:290)

Iren.*Haer.*5.33.4 (Harvey 2:418)

*Barn.*15.4–9 (Bihlmeyer 29)

arian hope continued in the church after the apostolic age, but also that, probably from the beginning, it stood in tension with other descriptions of the reign of Christ, which were not as privy to the details of the timetable for this reign. Although he himself entertained the expectation that Jerusalem would be rebuilt and that the saints of both the Old and New Testament eras would share with Christ in the joys of the new age, Justin admitted that there were other Christian believers, no less pious and orthodox than he, who did not have such an expectation. It would seem that very early in the postapostolic era millenarianism was regarded as a mark neither of orthodoxy nor of heresy, but as one permissible opinion among others within the range of permissible opinions. Although its terminus a quo is set very early, its terminus ad quem is much more difficult to fix. Origen's polemics against millenarianism recounted the exegesis of the literalists on the various promises concerning the kingdom of Christ, but concluded that such an interpretation was "unworthy of the divine promises"; the exegesis of such passages "in accordance with the understanding of the apostles" led to the conclusion that not the body but the soul was the subject of these promises, and that therefore the promised kingdom was a purely spiritual one. But this polemical attack is evidence more for the continuation of millenarianism than for its disappearance, and at least some other indications point to its persistence among Christian believers. Even Methodius, in the very context of an attack on literalistic exegesis, set forth a basically millenarian view of the kingdom; and Commodianus simply took such a view for granted.

Additional evidence for the persistence of primitive eschatology well after the delay in the parousia of Christ comes from the continuing use of apocalyptic imagery and of eschatological motivation, especially in the popular literature of the second and third centuries. There is a surprising amount of such language in the treatises that have survived, and some reason to believe that even these do not indicate how much apocalypticism actually surged within the Christian community. The *Shepherd* of Hermas was regarded by Irenaeus as canonical, by others as dubious, and by Tertullian (in successive periods of his life) as both. Its christology was vague at best, heretical at worst. Nevertheless, it was preserved—and in no less

Just.*Dial*.80.2 (Goodspeed 192)

Or.*Princ*.2.11.2–3 (*GCS* 22:186)

Meth.*Symp*.9.1 (*GCS* 27:113–114) Comm.*Instr*.2.3.6–9; 2.39.15 (*CSEL* 15:63; 111)

Iren.*Haer*.4.20.2 (Harvey 2:213); Eus.*H.e*.3.25.4 (*GCS* 9:252)

Tert.*Orat*.16.1–2 (*CCSL* 1:266); Tert.*Pudic*.10.12 (*CCSL* 2:1301)

prestigious a matrix than the Codex Sinaiticus of the Bible. The author (or authors) of the *Shepherd* used the format of an apocalyptic summons to call the readers to repentance. The vividness of its eschatological language is exceeded only by the decisiveness of its plea. The Lord had not yet returned, and therefore the work of judgment was not yet complete; but it would soon be finished, and then the consummation would come. The doctrinal aberrations in the apocalypses that have been preserved must not be permitted to obscure the evidence they supply about the faith and hope of people who were innocent of any heresy. The impression seems unavoidable that the relation between "already" and "not yet" in Christian apocalyptic raised more problems for philosophical theologians in the early church and for the proponents of "consistent eschatology" among modern exegetes than it did for believers and worshipers in the second and the third century.

That impression is corroborated by the references to the "coming" of Christ in the scraps of early liturgies that have come down to us. For example, the Benedictus of Matthew 21:9 was clearly an affirmation of the coming of the end with the promised arrival of the messianic kingdom. But at least as early as the *Apostolic Constitutions*, and presumably earlier, the liturgical practice of the church employed these same words to salute either the celebrant or the eucharistic presence. For, as Wetter has pointed out in commenting on the prayers of the early liturgies for the "coming" of Christ in the Eucharist, "it is interesting to observe how the epiphany in the cultus is practically amalgamated with the eschatologically oriented parousia. . . . This is evidence how these ideas, too, are connected with primitive Christian belief and perhaps developed from it." The coming of Christ was "already" and "not yet": he had come already in the incarnation, and on the basis of the incarnation would come in the Eucharist; he had come already in the Eucharist, and would come at the last in the new cup that he would drink with them in his Father's kingdom. When the ancient liturgy prayed, "Let grace come [or "Let the Lord come"], and let the world pass away," its eschatological perspective took in both the final coming of Christ and his coming in the Eucharist. The eucharistic liturgy was not a compensation for the postponement of the parousia,

---

Herm.*Sim*.9.5.82 (*SC* 53:298–300)
Herm.*Vis*.5.7.25 (*SC* 53:142–44)

Const.App.7.26.5 (Funk 414)

Wetter (1921) 1:21

Matt.26:29

ap.*Did*.10.6 (Bihlmeyer 6)

but a way of celebrating the presence of one who had promised to return.

The creeds performed some of the same function. While it is true that the addition and the revision of the phrases in the creeds are an index to the evolution of the church's teaching, it is also true that from the very beginning the creeds were a conservative force as well, instructing the candidates and reminding the worshipers of what the church had been believing, teaching, and confessing, which included some doctrinal themes that did not figure as prominently in Christian piety and instruction at one time as they had in another. Even when the consummation of history had failed to materialize as it had been expected, the creed continued to speak of the coming of Christ in both the past and the future tense; even when Platonic theologians were teaching the immortality of the soul as a biblical doctrine, the creed went on confessing the resurrection of the body. It served to counterbalance any oversimplified resolution of the already/not yet in either direction.

Partly because of the conservative influence of the creeds, eschatological language and apocalyptic imagery continued to occupy a prominent place in Christian speech even when the imminent return of Christ was not as vividly expected as it once had been. The writings of Tertullian documented the ebbing of that expectation in some remarkable ways. It is no less remarkable, however, that when he used the word "hope," it was almost without exception related to the great hope of the end of the world, not to lesser hopes this side of the parousia; the same was true of his use of "judgment." The continuing preoccupation with the figure of the Antichrist also indicates the persistence of certain apocalyptic themes. Not only did the figure appear frequently in Tertullian, as might perhaps be expected, but patristic literature dealt with Antichrist often enough to warrant the supposition that piety and preaching continued to make much of this apocalyptic sign. Nor was the sign of Antichrist simply a religious way of expressing the political conflict with Rome. It could be this, as when Commodianus prophesied that Nero would rise from hell and proclaim, "I am Christ, to whom you always pray." But Irenaeus saw in Antichrist the recapitulation of every error and idolatry since the deluge; and, in accordance with the prophecies

Tert.*Marc*.5.16.4 (*CCSL* 1:711); Tert.*Res*.27.6 (*CCSL* 2:956–57)

Comm.*Instr*.1.41.14 (*CSEL* 15:54)

Iren.*Haer*.5.30.1–2 (Harvey 2:406–408)
Hipp.*Antichr*.14 (*GCS* 1–II:11)

Hipp.*Antichr*.27 (*GCS* 1–II:19)

Hipp.*Dan*.4.58 (*GCS* 1–I:332–34)
Hipp.*Antichr*.14; 25 (*GCS* 1–II:11; 18)
See pp. 106–7 above

Buri (1939) 50

Hanson (1959) 354

Harnack (1931) 2:169

Or.*Prin*.pr.7 (*GCS* 22:14)

of both the Old and New Testament, as interpreted by the apostolic tradition of "men who saw John face to face," he believed that Antichrist would be a member of the tribe of Dan. Hippolytus took the same position, and in an entire treatise on Antichrist argued that the prophecies of the Book of Daniel had not all been fulfilled yet and that therefore the end was not immediately at hand; his exposition of Daniel, the oldest extant commentary by a Christian, developed this argument in the context of a full-length exegesis of those prophecies. As Hippolytus's critique of the identification of Antichrist with Caesar makes clear, he did not expect the return of Christ immediately; but his *Commentary on Daniel, Antichrist,* and *Apostolic Tradition* all illustrate how the exegetical, dogmatic, and liturgical tasks of the theologian compelled him to deal with such apocalyptic themes regardless of his own expectations or lack of them.

It was, of course, possible for a theologian so to distort the themes of biblical apocalyptic in the light of his own expectations or lack of them as to make of them something fundamentally different from the church's confession. There is a sizeable body of opinion that just such a distortion appeared in the theological tradition that ran from Clement of Alexandria through Origen to Gregory of Nyssa. Clement is said to "understand by the parousia not an event of the immediate future, as Paul did, but something that has already been fulfilled with the coming of Jesus as the Logos made flesh." Origen's teaching is said to be "not a Platonized form of genuine Christian eschatology, but an alternative to eschatology, indeed an evasion of it." And it is said that "it was only as an apologist of catholic Christianity that Gregory held closely to the historical personality of Christ," but that in his own thought he was a pantheist who had no need either of a historical coming or of a historical second coming of Christ. Such a judgment would apply more to Clement than to Origen, and more to Origen than to Gregory. It is correct to say that Origen, like Clement before him and Gregory after him, took up the idea of the parousia into a schema of world history from prehistory to final restoration. As he himself observed, apostolic tradition had very little to say about the details of eschatology. What it did say, he sought to affirm; but by absorbing it into the cosmic process of a succession of universes, he jeopardized its most fundamental affirmations. This Gregory of Nyssa sought to correct in his mystical and yet biblical eschatology. To Gregory and to the later tradition, Origen's eschatological theories served as a cautionary tale of what an individual theologian was entitled—and was not entitled—to undertake in his private speculations on the basis of tradition.

Most of Origen's eschatological speculation, however, escaped official anathema; so did the millenarianism against which he had reacted with so much vigor. The condemnations of Montanism were not directed principally against its apocalyptic teachings, and the attack against Gnosticism mentioned, but did not concentrate upon, its millenarian tendencies. Eschatology that denied the creed was anathematized as heresy; eschatology that merely went beyond the creed was tolerated as a private opinion (as in the case of the Origenism of Gregory of Nyssa) or as a remnant of earlier and less refined apocalyptic thought (as in the case of millenarian imagery). Eusebius was certainly speaking for a large body of theological opinion in the East when he called Papias's

Eus.*H.e*.3.39.11 (*GCS* 9:290)

millenarianism "bizarre" and "rather mythological." And Augustine set the standard for most catholic exegesis in the West when he surrendered the millenarian interpre-

Aug.*Serm*.259.2 (*PL* 38:1197–98)

tation of Revelation 20, to which he had held earlier, in favor of the view that the thousand years of that text

Aug.*Civ*.20.7 (*CCSL* 48:709)

referred to the history of the church. Nor is it altogether irrelevant to note that Eusebius and Augustine represented, in their interpretations of the future of the world as in their views of its past, the church's new affirmation of the place of universal history in the economy of

See pp. 39–41 above

salvation.

That affirmation had been adumbrated in earlier expressions of Christian concern for the processes and institutions of world history. Perhaps the most dramatic example of the contrast between such concern and the simple fervor of the apocalyptic vision came in Tertullian's *Apology*. Describing the worship of the Christian community, a society knit together by its common confession, its discipline, and its hope, he enumerated some of its petitions: "We pray also for the Caesars, for their ministers, and for all who are in high positions; for the commonweal of the world; for the prevalence of peace." To this rather conventional list he appended one more

Tert.*Apol*.39.2 (*CCSL* 1:150)

petition: "And for the delay of the end." The apologetic context of the statement is significant, but so is its liturgical context. The instructions of I Timothy 2:1–4, echoed in Tertullian's words, were apparently being taken in the liturgy to imply the prayer that the world be spared and that the consummation of the age be postponed. It was another echo of the same New Testament passage when Tertullian claimed—directly after predicting the

Tert.*Scap*.3.3 (*CCSL* 2:1129)
Tert.*Scap*.4.1 (*CCSL* 2:1130)

imminent wrath of God—that Christians were intent on "saving all men." In both statements, Tertullian professed to be speaking for the corporate will and action of the church, not simply to be voicing his private opinions. The same service of worship in which the church prayed for the delay of the end also included the reading of the

Tert.*Apol*.39.3 (*CCSL* 1:150)

Tert.*Praescrip*. 36.4–5 (*CCSL* 1:217); Tert.*Virg.vel*.1.3 (*CCSL* 2:1209)

Scriptures, not, presumably, to the exclusion of their apocalyptic portions; some services included also a recitation of the creeds quoted by Tertullian, including their eschatological affirmations. The prayer for the delay of the end was not a negation of these eschatological hopes, but belonged with them to an eschatology that cannot be classified as either "futuristic" or "realized." It was an eschatology that could go as far as to say that "even if Scripture offered me no hand of celestial hope, I would still have enough of a preliminary judgment of this promise, since I already have the gift on earth and I

Tert.*Marc*.3.24.12 (*CCSL* 1:544)

Tert.*Marc*.3.24.6 (*CCSL* 1:542–43)

could expect something from heaven, from the God of heaven as well as of earth," and at the same time could cast this hope in millenarian terms.

The plain fact was that the categories of an undifferentiated apocalyptic were inadequate to the needs of a faith whose content was a history that had already happened. In the teaching of Jesus its "not yet" had stood in dialectic with the "already" of his visible presence. Both poles of the dialectic appeared in his words and deeds, as these were remembered by the church. When the apocalyptic vision was eclipsed, however, many of those words and deeds appeared enigmatic. Much of the history of the interpretation of the Gospels during the second and third centuries does consist in the effort to make sense of apocalyptic passages when the presuppositions had shifted. The "end" in such passages as Matthew

Tert.*Scorp*.10.17 (*CCSL* 2:1090); Tert.*Fug*.7.1–2 (*CCSL* 2:1144)

10:22 came to refer to the death of the individual, not to the end of the age.

The use of the apocalyptic form in the teaching of

Jesus did not assure it a place in the church's teaching about Jesus. Even more significant than the exegetical readjustments were the doctrinal ones. The doctrine of salvation bore much of the dialectic that had originally been embodied in the apocalyptic vision. The historical figure of Jesus of Nazareth had applied to himself—or had allowed to be applied to him—the otherworldly predicates of the apocalyptic vision of the Son of man. The risen and exalted Lord, present in the church and sovereign over the world, now became the one to whom were applied the thisworldly predicates of the historical portrait of the Son of Mary. Neither the apocalyptic imagery nor the more ontological language of the christological dogma avoided or solved the problem of the relation between the immanent and the transcendent. Similarly, the salvation promised in the teachings of Jesus was described in futuristic terms; and although that con-

Rom.13:11

notation did not disappear from Christian preaching and worship, the dialectic between the achievement of salvation in the death and resurrection of Christ and its completion in his return with glory to judge the quick and the dead had now to make manifest the balance between "already" and "not yet." Only a distinction between two comings of Christ, which was also necessary in sorting out the prophecies of the Old Testament in response to

See p. 19 above

Judaism, could do justice to that balance. To deny the historical character of the first coming, as Gnostic docetism did, or to spiritualize the second coming into a parable of the soul, as Origenistic speculation did, was to subvert apostolic doctrine.

If the teachings of the early church and of Jesus could simply be described as consistent eschatology, we could then trace the decline of such an eschatology as the primary factor in the establishment both of ecclesiastical structures and of dogmatic norms. Neither primitive Christianity nor the church catholic was consistent in so single-minded a way, as each new bit of evidence or new study of old evidence makes clear. But once the dialectic of already/not yet is permitted to emerge from the texts, the magnitude of the change may become visible. It was nothing less than the decisive shift from the categories of cosmic drama to those of being, from the Revelation of St. John the Divine to the creed of the Council of Nicea. Yet it was through that very creed that the human portrait of the Son of Mary was preserved, and by that very creed that the postapocalyptic generations of the church catholic were taught to look for the resurrection of the dead and the life of the age to come.

The Supernatural Order

Christian apocalypticism reflected a supernaturalistic view of the world, which Christian believers shared with other religious men of antiquity. This world view, in turn, formed the presupposition for Christian doctrine. Yet because of its distinctive content, Christianity gave its own special twist to supernaturalism and eventually transcended it through the doctrine of God as Trinity.

Case (1946) 1

"The sky hung low in the ancient world," says Shirley Jackson Case. "Traffic was heavy on the highway between heaven and earth. Gods and spirits thickly populated the upper air, where they stood in readiness to intervene at any moment in the affairs of mortals. And demonic powers, emerging from the lower world or resident in remote corners of the earth, were a constant menace to human welfare. All nature was alive—alive with supernatural forces." With but very few adjustments of vocabulary in one direction or the other, that description of the relation between the natural and the supernatural order could have been recognized by Jews, Christians, and devout pagans in the first century. It formed the common ground on which the apologists for Christian doctrine and their non-Christian opponents stood, as

Tert.*Apol*.22.1–2 (*CCSL* 1:128)

the apologists themselves were frank to concede. The Christian fathers did not attempt to cast doubt on the supernatural character of the phenomena of Greek and Roman religion; instead, they assigned these phenomena to the demonic province of the supernatural world.

For the history of Christian doctrine, the understanding of the supernatural order evident in the faith and life of the first two or three Christian centuries is an essential element in the development of the teaching of the church. Yet it was not itself codified as a dogma of the church. At one level Christianity seems to have done little more than to evidence a universal climate of opinion and, if anything, to have transformed crass supernaturalism into blatant superstition. But we must go on to examine not only the similarities but also the differences between folk piety and church doctrine at each of these points, to see how the church's teaching, shaped by considerations of both its own theological integrity and philosophical enlightenment, finally managed to bend even the most dominant and universal religious sentiment of its time into conformity with the "reasonable service" of the gospel.

Rom.12:1

Pervasive though it was through all of Christian devotion and doctrine, the idea of a supernatural order made itself especially evident at two points: in the conception of angels and demons as beings that somehow stood lower than God but higher than man, and in the use of miracle and prayer as means that interfered with the natural order of things to enlist superhuman aid and to ward off superhuman threats. Of the superhuman beings that caused "the traffic between heaven and earth," those most inseparably connected to the gospel story were angels and demons. Angels had been the heralds of the wondrous birth of Jesus and his miraculous resurrection; they had also been the agents of the annunciation that preceded his birth and were depicted by the Apocalypse as carrying the melody of the church's liturgy during its history on earth and in eternal glory. Here the biblical tradition attached itself to Jewish speculation about angelic beings as well as to the Gnostic cosmologies, one of whose dominant features was an almost infinite series of aeons, mediating for good or ill between the unknown Highest God and humankind. Just how intimate the attachment could become is evident from the polemic of Colossians 2:18 against "worship of angels" and from other hints in the New Testament that some Christians were assigning to angels an importance independent of their function as messengers and servants of God.

Luke 2:11
Mark 16:6
Luke 1:26–38

Rev.11:15–18

Heb.1:5;
1 Pet.1:12

That polemic makes all the more enigmatic a remarkable passage in Justin Martyr, which appears to reflect the liturgical practice and public doctrine of the second-century church. Replying to the charge that the Christians were atheists because they did not worship the official deities of the Roman state, Justin declared: "We concede that we are atheists with regard to such gods, but not with regard to the most true God, the Father of justice and moderation and of all the other virtues, who is beyond all uncleanliness. But we worship and adore him, and the Son who proceeded from him and taught us these things,

Just. *1 Apol.*6
(Goodspeed 29)

Athenag.*Leg.*10.3
(Goodspeed 325)

Crehan (1956) 134

Goodenough (1923) 194

Iren.*Haer.*3.8.3 (Harvey
2:29)

Iren.*Haer.*2.2.1 (Harvey
1:254)

Herm.*Vis.*3.4.1.12 (SC
53:108)

and the host of the other good angels who follow and are made like him, and the prophetic Spirit." Less frequently noticed is the analogous statement of Athenagoras, who, after replying to the same charge of atheism with a recitation of the doctrine of the Trinity, added: "Nor does our doctrine of God [τὸ θεολογικόν] stop there, but we assert a multitude of angels and ministers." Far from "clearing up" Justin's statement about the relation of the angels to the Trinity, this passage merely proves that Justin was not the only Christian teacher to posit some sort of similarity of natures between God and the angels—a similarity substantial enough to justify mentioning the angels in the same breath with the divine Triad. It does not appear unwarranted, therefore, to conclude that there is some cultus of the angels implied in Justin's statement, even though the passage "hangs unsupported in the air."

When we turn from obiter dicta of this sort to the content of the church's teaching and confession, however, the fundamental tenet in the doctrine of the angels is the emphatic insistence that they are not minor deities but creatures. The contrast between church doctrine and the folk piety that seems to speak in Justin's words is quite striking. When the Gnostics read the contradictions of the universe into the divine reality itself and yet tried to screen off the highest God from them by means of a series of aeons, angels, and other demigods, the church's confession sought to make the doctrine of God as Creator unequivocal. From the statement of John 1:3 that without the Logos nothing had been made, Irenaeus concluded that "all things, be they angels or archangels or thrones or dominions, were both established by him who is God over all and created through his Logos." It was a distortion of the relation between Creator and creature to attribute the creation of the world to angels. Hermas seems to have been echoing some such notion but attempting to square it with the doctrine of creation when he spoke of the angels as the first creatures of God, to whom the whole creation had been handed over. In the preface to *On First Principles* Origen found that the express teaching of the church had laid it down as the official tradition that the angels were the servants of God (and, as such, his creatures), but had left the time of their creation and the nature of their existence as matters for investigation

Or.*Princ*.pr.10 (*GCS* 22:16)

Symb.*Nic.–CP* (Schaff 2:60;
Or.*Princ*.4.4.8 (*GCS* 22:359)

Tert.*Marc*.5.19.4 (*CCSL*
1:721); Did.*Spir*.7 (*PG* 39:
1038–39)

Or.*Cels*.5.55 (*GCS* 3:58–59)

Tert.*Idol*.4.2 (*CCSL* 2:1103)

Tert.*Idol*.9.1 (*CCSL* 2:1107)
Tert.*Apol*.35.12 (*CCSL*
1:146–47)
Tert.*Virg.vel*.7.2 (*CCSL*
2:1216)

Tert.*Spect*.8.9 (*CCSL* 1:235)

Tert.*Coron*.6.2 (*CCSL* 2:1047)
Tert.*Cult.fem*.1.2.1 (*CCSL*
1:344)

Min.Fel.*Oct*.26.8 (*CSEL* 2:38)

Athenag.*Leg*.24.5 (Goodspeed
344)

Comm.*Instr*.1.3.15 (*CSEL* 15:7)

and speculation. That official tradition was canonized as dogma when the council of Nicea adopted a confession that went beyond the simple thetical statements of creation in other creeds to specify that God was maker not only of heaven and earth, but of "all things visible and invisible." Speculation about angelology was not cut off, but in its doctrine of creation the church set a limit beyond which such speculation could not be permitted to go.

The same was true of demonology. Because it provided so much of the vocabulary and structure for the doctrine of man as sinner, demonological speculation proved to be even more attractive to the fathers of the second and third centuries than the doctrine of angels. Carrying on the cosmological and exegetical interests of Jewish thought, Christian writers reflected on the nature and deeds of the fallen angels, especially on what was taken to be the first explicit reference to them, in Genesis 6:1–4. It appears to have been from the narrative in this passage that Tertullian took his description of the "angelic apostates" as the "deserters of God, the seducers of women," and the inventors of astrology. Their lust for human virgins had inflamed them to the point that they forsook the presence of God and fell into sin. Thereupon they dedicated themselves to leading men astray. Now Satan and his angels had filled the whole world and had corrupted man and the rest of creation. This picture of the origin of the demons became a commonplace in the literature, as is evident from the statement of Minucius Felix that the erring spirits had been degraded by their lusts and now sought to degrade man; from Athenagoras's rehearsal of what "the prophets" had said about the angels whose lust had brought about their fall; and from the identification of the pagan deities with the fornicating angels.

Christian attention to the dangers of human commerce with demons, fallen angels, and Satan took a sharp upswing with the beginnings of monastic piety, which was also responsible for the development of a new body of Christian literature, the monastic biography. In the first and most influential of such biographies, Athanasius's *Life of Saint Antony,* the conflict between the Christian hero and the demonic powers may be said to be the major theme. Attributing to the demons superhuman

Ath.V.Ant.31 (PG 26:889)
Ath.V. Ant.28; 41 (PG 26:885; 904)
Ath.V.Ant.78; 35 (PG 26:952; 893); Lact.Inst.4.27. 2–4 (CSEL 19:384–85)

perception as well as activity, Antony nevertheless described them as "powerless," especially before the sign of the cross, which prevailed against all magic and sorcery. Not only from the lives of saints and ascetics, but from the comments of less committed observers we know how important the sign of the cross was as a means of warding off evil spirits; the emperor Julian expressed the opinion that "these two things are the quintessence of their [Christians'] theology, to hiss at demons and

Jul.Ep.19 (LCL 3:52)

make the sign of the cross on their foreheads." Although Origen's private demonology was bound up with his ideas about the prehistoric fall, he was certainly summarizing the faith and piety of the church when he warned that evil spirits were lying in wait to lead men astray and that the believer should cultivate the aid of the administering spirits of God to repulse the hostile

Or.Princ.3.2.5 (GCS 22:253–54)

demons.

It is not surprising that when this Christian piety was united with dualistic speculations, as it was in the various Gnostic, Manichean, and Priscillianist systems, the devil and his kingdom became a rival not only to the Christian soul, but to the divine sovereignty. The recurrence of popular dualism and the persistence of satanic arts throughout Christian history seem to prove that Christian doctrine did not succeed in eradicating the long-standing conviction of many Christian believers that

2 Cor.4:4

"the god of this world" really was a god after all. The teaching of the church was, however, plain and unequivocal, already in reaction against Gnosticism and even more in response to the Manichean and Priscillianist dualisms. The monastic anecdotes about the demons also insisted that they were powerless because the cross of Christ had disarmed them. Against Manichean dualism Augustine defined evil in Neoplatonic terms as the

Aug.Mor.Manich.2.4.6 (PL 32:1347)

Aug.Nat.bon.32–33 (CSEL 25:870–71)

absence of good; therefore God was the source of all power, even of the power that was hurtful, and the demons were fallen creatures of the one good God. And against the Priscillianists a council at Braga in 563 decreed: "Whoever denies that the devil was originally a good angel created by God, contending instead that he arose from the chaos and the darkness and has no Creator but is himself the principle and the substance

Mansi 9:775

of evil . . . let him be anathema." Once again, although the reality of the supernatural order was accepted, the oneness of God and the goodness of creation, which Christianity had learned to affirm on the basis of the Old Testament, kept supernaturalism within strict limits, at least in the area of Christian doctrine.

In his conflicts with the demons Antony frequently manifested miraculous powers. He expelled demons from those who were possessed by them, and he was able to heal many of the sick who came to him. Yet Athanasius took pains to point out many times over in his biography that Antony "healed not by giving out commands, but by praying and by calling upon Christ's name, so that it was clear to all that it was not he who did this, but the Lord showing his loving-kindness to men and curing the sufferers through Antony." And there were times when Antony's miraculous powers did not work, because it was not the will of God. There had been earlier claims and accounts about certain Christians who had been endowed with supernatural powers, notably the legend of "the thundering legion." But despite such accounts, the Christian doctrine of miracles was worked out almost completely in the exegesis and the defense of the biblical narratives. When Celsus asserted that God did not will anything that was contrary to nature, Origen countered with the teaching that whatever was done in accordance with the will and word of God could not be contrary to nature; this applied especially to so-called miracles. In his own exegesis of the miracle stories in the Bible, Origen seems to have held to their literal factuality, while in *Against Celsus* and especially in *On First Principles* he argued at length that these stories were not to be taken as they stood, but as mystical statements of spiritual truths. Tertullian, on the other hand, brushed aside the criticism of miracles on the grounds of natural law, since the philosophers who propounded natural law denied the omnipotence of God. Accepting the rule of faith and the inerrancy of the Bible, Tertullian also took the miracle stories as literal truth. In both Origen's doctrine and Tertullian's, the noteworthy element is the restraint which the doctrine of God as Creator put upon the definition of the natural and upon the fascination with the supernatural.

That restraint is even more evident in the development of the patristic doctrine of prayer. Both Origen and Tertullian wrote special treatises on this subject, using the

Ath.*V.Ant.*48; 64 (*PG* 26:913; 933)
Ath.*V.Ant.*56 (*PG* 26:925)

Ath.*V.Ant.*84 (*PG* 26:961)

Ath.*V.Ant.*56 (*PG* 26:925)

Eus.*H.e.*5.5 (*GCS* 9:434–36); Tert.*Apol.*5.6 (*CCSL* 1:96)

Or.*Cels.*5.23 (*GCS* 3:24)
Or.*Matt.*11.2.477–78 (*GCS* 40:35–37); Or.*Matt.* 13.6.577–79 (*GCS* 40:193–96)

Or.*Princ.*4.2.9.15–16 (*GCS* 22:321–23)

Tert.*Anim.*2.7 (*CCSL* 2:785)

Tert.*Praescrip.*44.5–10 (*CCSL* 1:223–24)

Lord's Prayer. For that matter, prayer seems to have been the constitutive element in many of the miracles as well. Perhaps nowhere are the affinities between Christian and pagan supernaturalism more obvious than in their prayer practices; this affinity was so obvious to Tertullian that he found in Roman blessings and curses a "testimony of the soul" for the correctness of Christianity. As Friedrich Heiler has commented, "The close relation between non-Christian and Christian forms of prayer has repeatedly brought astonishment to Christian theologians"; yet he has noted elsewhere that "the history of the Christian life of piety is the most striking proof of the uniqueness and absoluteness of Christianity among the religions of the earth." The task of formulating the Christian doctrine of prayer in such a way as to take account of both these insights fell to the church fathers of the second, third, and fourth centuries. The fact of prayer and the forms which it assumed in the church are the business of the history of piety and the history of liturgy; the meaning and purpose of prayer are a matter for the history of the development of Christian doctrine.

But of course the doctrine began with, and presupposed, the fact of prayer and its forms. A Christian was a man of prayer. In the apologetic literature, the charge that Christianity was seditious was refuted by reference to the prayers that were offered for the empire and for Caesar. With rhetorical vigor Tertullian turned the tables on the critics with the assertion that it was the very refusal of the church to pray to anyone but God alone that supported Caesar and made him great. "I cannot ask this of anyone except the God from whom I know I shall receive it, both because he alone bestows it and because I have claims upon him for his gift." This he set into contrast with the ritualism of Roman sacrifice. Reluctant though they were to expose the sacred mysteries of Christian worship to the blasphemous ridicule of their opponents, the apologists did occasionally feel constrained to describe the postures and gestures of Christian prayer as well as some of the content of the invocation, praise, confession, and thanksgiving spoken in public and in private. Significantly, however, the most complete explanations of the doctrine of prayer were reserved for writings addressed to the church.

Tert.*Test.anim.*2.6 (*CCSL* 1:177); Tert.*Apol.*16.10 (*CCSL* 1:116); Clem.*Str.*7.7 48.5 (*GCS* 17:36)

Heiler (1958) 1212

Heiler (1932) 121

Just. *1 Apol.*65.1 (Goodspeed 74)

Tert.*Apol.*30.5 (*CCSL* 1:141)

Tert.*Apol.*30.6 (*CCSL* 1:142); Tert.*Jejun.*16.5 (*CCSL* 2:1275)

Or.*Orat.*33.1 (*GCS* 3:401)

Athenag.*Leg.*13 (Goodspeed 327–28)

From those writings it is evident that contemporary interpretations of the supernatural provided the Christian doctrine of prayer with two major options for relating the practice of prayer to the teaching of the church. Prayer could be seen as one of the means—together with magic, imprecation, witchcraft, and the like—for making the supernatural order friendly to man; for "the prayer of a righteous man has great power in its effects." Origen observed that one could suppose, in the heat of summer, that by his prayer he could reverse the course of the seasons and bring back the balmy spring. Or the relation between prayer and providence could be the other way around, and prayer could be subordinated so completely to divine sovereignty and predestination as to be rendered objectively useless; for "your Father knows what you need before you ask him." The first of these options beckoned when the writer was exhorting believers to pray and describing the power of prayer, as in Tertullian's treatise; the second when the writer was answering the doubts, his own and those of his readers, arising from the attempt to harmonize the practice of prayer with the doctrine of a wise and sovereign God, as in Origen's treatise. The first option was based on religion, the second on reflection.

Attractive though each of these options was on its own peculiar grounds, neither could satisfy the needs of the Christian doctrine of prayer, because neither could be squared with the doctrine of God as personal and with the doctrine of man as free. If it was legitimate to address God as the Father in heaven, he was beyond manipulation, and prayer could not ask him to act contrary to his will. But this will was one that from eternity had taken into account the actions of man's free will, including his prayers, saying in effect: "I will give ear to this man who prays with understanding on account of the prayer itself which he will utter." Divorced from the doctrine of a personal God and from the doctrine of free will in man, the idea of a supernatural order could lead to either magic or fatalism or both, and in more than one Christian life it evidently did. But the Christian doctrine of prayer, while acknowledging the affinities between the church's practice and prayer as a general religious phenomenon, learned from the Old Testament and especially

Jas.5:16

Or.*Orat*.5.3 (*GCS* 3:309)

Or.*Orat*.5.2 (*GCS* 3:308–309)
Matt.6:8

Tert.*Orat*.29.1 (*CCSL* 1:273–74)

Or.*Orat*.5.1 (*GCS* 3:308)

Tert.*Orat*.4.1 (*CCSL* 1:259)

Or.*Orat*.6.4 (*GCS* 3:314)

Aug.*Ep.*130.11.21 (*CSEL* 44:63–64)

from the Lord's Prayer to transcend both magic and fatalism. The God who had created man with a free will was sovereign also over the supernatural order.

Although the vocabulary and thought of supernaturalism were transcended in Christian doctrine, they continued to provide much of the framework within which Christian doctrine was articulated. The doctrine of the person of Christ and the doctrine of the work of Christ depended on this framework for some of their classic formulations. One of the most notable terms for Christ, and even for the Holy Spirit, in the church's theology be-

See pp. 182–84 below

fore Nicea was "angel." The term was interpreted by some Christian teachers in the light of Jewish speculations about the world of angelic beings and by others in the light of Gnostic speculations about the world of aeons. It was eventually Nicea that "drew the boundary line between God and the world of angels, between Creator and creature," put Christ on the Creator's side of that boundary line, and thus eliminated the mythological el-

Kretschmar (1956) 223

ements of "the [earlier] trinitarian traditions." Similarly, the image of the cross and resurrection of Christ as a

See pp. 149–52 below

"wondrous duel" with the devil could be cast in the form of a thoroughgoing dualism. What saved it from dualism was the consistent application of the doctrine of God as Creator, which meant that the devil had usurped whatever power he had and that therefore Christ was restoring the divinely established order of things.

For this corrective upon the implications that could be drawn from its acceptance of a supernatural order Christian doctrine was indebted to its biblical roots, especially to its retention of the Old Testament. Harnack's exclamation, "What a wealth of religious material, derived from the most variegated stages in the history of religion, is contained in this book!" is certainly borne

Harnack (1931) 2:469

out by the lush religious imagery of the liturgy or by the history of the Christian exegesis of the Song of Solomon. But it utterly overlooks what the Old Testament had done to this "wealth of religious material." A myth that seems originally to have described the discovery of sex

Gen.3:1–7

became the most profound of accounts of the fall, and the Canaanite celebrations of cosmic and human fertility were transformed into festivals of the covenant between the people of Israel and a just and merciful God. The church used, but it did not need, the Old Testament as a resource for the supernaturalism that bound it to the history of religion. But from the Old Testament it learned to redefine the "supernatural," drawing the line of demarcation not between "the spiritual world" and this world, but finally between God the Creator and all his creatures; for it believed, taught, and confessed "that neither death, nor life, nor angels, nor principalities, nor things present, nor things to come, nor powers, nor height, nor depth, *nor anything else in all creation,* will be able to separate us from the love of God in Christ Jesus our Lord."

Rom.8:38–39; Or.*Princ.*3.2.5 (*GCS* 22:252–53)

The Meaning of Salvation

When Irenaeus, in a classical definition, declared that "to follow the Savior is to participate in salvation, and to follow the light is to perceive the light," he was enunciating a Christian belief to every word of which his Gnostic opponents would have willingly subscribed. In Marcion's New Testament no less than in Tertullian's, the gospel was called the power of God for salvation to everyone who has faith, even though Marcion went on to emend the latter part of the verse, deleting the word "first" because it ascribed a priority to Judaism. The gospel was a message of salvation; on this all Christian teachers agreed. But they did not agree about the meaning of the salvation proclaimed by this message.

Iren.*Haer.*4.14.1 (Harvey 2:184)

Rom.1:16

Tert.*Marc.*5.13.2 (*CCSL* 1:702)

Harnack (1960) 2:153

Nor did that meaning become, in the strict sense, a dogma of the church. The creed adopted at Nicea confessed that it had been "for the sake of us men and for the purpose of our salvation" that Christ "came down [from heaven] and was made flesh, was made man, suffered, was raised on the third day, ascended into the heavens, and will come to judge living and dead." But neither it nor later dogmas specified in any detail just how the salvation which was the purpose of Christ's coming was related to these events in his earthly and heavenly states. While the relation of Jesus Christ to God and the relation of the human and the divine within his person became the subject for doctrinal controversy and dogmatic definition, the saving work of Christ remained dogmatically undefined. Yet it was certainly a major constituent of Christian doctrine—if by doctrine we mean what the church believes, teaches, and con-

Symb.*Nic.* (*325*) (Schaff 2:60)

fesses, not only in its polemics and creeds, but also in its liturgy and exegesis.

The very absence of explicit dogmatic and extensive polemical treatment of the meaning of salvation makes it necessary as well as hazardous to find some other scheme for organizing the doctrinal material on this subject. It would be possible, for example, to base a discussion of the development of the doctrine of salvation on the history of the doctrine of sin, noting the relation between the disease and the cure; for that relation has often been a reciprocal one. Or the later flowering of various theories of the atonement could serve as a basis for an examination of their ancestry. Or, since the doctrine of the person of Christ did become a dogma even though the doctrine of the work of Christ did not, the history of doctrine could examine the major alternative theories about the person of Christ with a view toward making explicit the definition of salvation at work in each.

See pp. 290–92 below

Although there is something to be said in favor of each of these methods of systematizing the doctrinal material, we shall follow a procedure that seeks to go beyond them, or more accurately behind them, to the underlying conception of Christ as Savior. For it is "the picture of Christ" as distinguished from "the dogma of Christ" that concerns us in this section; and since much of the material has a liturgical and exegetical context, the organization of the material around the three themes of the life and teachings, the suffering and death, and the resurrection and exaltation of Christ would appear to be legitimate. Such a schema for doctrines of salvation in the second, third, and fourth centuries must not be taken to imply that either the life or the death or the resurrection of Christ was ever seen as the one saving event in utter isolation from the whole of the biblical picture. Repeatedly we shall see the several emphases brought together in one passage. But differences of emphasis do exist and can be identified.

Elert (1957) 12–25

From an examination of how Christian writers of the second century employed materials that are now incorporated into the synoptic Gospels and of how they transmitted other materials that did not find their way into the canon of the New Testament, it is clear that meditation on the life and teachings of Jesus was a major

Clem.*Prot.*1.9–10 (*GCS* 12:9–10)

preoccupation of the piety and doctrine of the church. To cite one of the earliest writers, Clement of Rome ended an extensive catena of biblical quotations about the humility and patience of Christ with the exhortation: "You see, beloved, what the example is that has been given us." Christ as example and Christ as teacher were constant and closely related doctrinal themes, but precisely because salvation, however it may have been defined, was the fundamental truth of the gospel, the imitation of Christ as example and the obedience to Christ as teacher must be seen in their close connection with it.

1 Clem.16.17 (Bihlmeyer 44)

Where that connection is not noted, the doctrines of Christ as teacher and Christ as example can be interpreted as evidence of a moralism bereft of the idea of salvation. For one critic of *First Clement,* "It is difficult to see any place for Christ in the Christian salvation beyond that of a preacher of the 'grace of repentance.'"

Torrance (1959) 46

"The most astonishing feature" of all the apostolic fathers, he states in summary, "was the failure to grasp the significance of the death of Christ." Even more open to this criticism were the apologists. "Only Justin provides anything resembling an answer. . . . Undoubtedly the principal purpose of the incarnation, when he views the matter as a philosopher, strikes him as having been didactic." Some of the other apologists did not even make much of a point of that. Bent as they were upon proving that Christianity was the fulfillment of the intuitions and expectations of all the nations, not only of the Jews, the apologists represented Christ as God's answer to the ideas and aspirations of the Greek philosophers. In their treatises, therefore, salvation could be equated with the gift of this answer. But it is a mistake to read their treatises in isolation from what the church was believing, teaching, and confessing. As one of the most influential and most critical of the interpreters of Justin pointed out, "It is equally certain that Justin's own faith was nourished more by that which the congregation confessed and taught concerning Christ its Lord than by that which he himself interpreted in a theoretical way." He was, after all, ready to lay down his life for Christ; and his martyrdom speaks louder, even doctrinally, than does his apologetics.

Torrance (1959) 137

Kelly (1958) 168

See pp. 62–67 above

Engelhardt (1878) 186

The writings of the apologists, even those of Justin, were addressed to readers on the outside. Is there any reason to assume that in the doctrine of the church "on the inside" the cruciality of Christ as teacher and example ran deeper than the rather vapid expressions of Justin and the other apologists would indicate? The answer to that difficult question is bound up with the interpretation of Irenaeus's doctrine of recapitulation. If that doctrine was completely a piece of his private speculation, then it cannot serve as proof that the church's doctrine went beyond the theories of the apologists; but then it would also prove that Irenaeus was unbelievably more of an individualistic religious genius than his own doctrine of the criteria of apostolic continuity would have permitted either him or any other Christian teacher except a Valentinian heretic to be. Liturgical sources and the writings of other church fathers suggest that in this doctrine of recapitulation, as in his teaching generally, Irenaeus was reflecting the mind of the Christian community, even though his own mind may have elaborated and embellished the seminal ideas present in the belief, teaching, and confession of the church. Even the artificial

Loofs (1930) 357–74

literary theories regarding the sources of Irenaeus lead to the same conclusion.

Irenaeus's doctrine of recapitulation can be read as the most profound theological vindication in the second and third centuries of the universal Christian ideal of the imitation of Christ. For Irenaeus, the imitation of Christ by the Christian was part of God's cosmic plan of salvation which began with Christ's imitation of the Christian or, more precisely, with Christ's imitation of Adam. The

Iren.*Haer*.5.16.2–3 (Harvey 2:367–68)

Logos "assimilated himself to man and man to himself" in his life and in his passion. After his incarnation he passed through every stage of human growth, hallowing each and redeeming each by "being made for them an

Iren.*Haer*.2.22.4 (Harvey 1:330)

example of piety, righteousness, and submission." The disobedience of the first Adam was undone through the complete obedience of the second Adam, so that many

Iren.*Haer*.3.18.7 (Harvey 2:101–102)

should be justified and attain salvation. He summed up in himself the entire continuity of the human race and

Iren.*Haer*.3.18.1 (Harvey 2:95)

provided man with salvation in a concise summary. "So the Word was made flesh, in order that sin, destroyed by means of that same flesh through which it had gained the mastery and taken hold and lorded it, should no longer be in us; and therefore our Lord took up the same first formation for an incarnation, that so he might join battle on behalf of his forefathers, and overcome through Adam what had stricken us through Adam." Christ became the example for men, as Adam had been the example for Christ; being the Logos of God, Christ was not only the example, but the exemplar and prototype of the image of God according to which man had been created. The origin of this parallelism in the Pauline discussions of the first and the second Adam, Irenaeus's quotation from a lost work of Justin where the parallelism appeared, and the echoes of it in other writers all bear out the impression that the term "example" in the doctrine of salvation carried connotations not exhausted by its rather superficial exposition at the hands of the apologists.

The same is true of the term "imitation" of God or of Christ. It was laden with connotations which it had acquired in Platonic usage, where imitation had come to mean "the process by which the poet or actor assimilates himself . . . to the person whom he is portraying and thereby extinguishes his own personality for the time being" and where the imitation of God was the ideal. Echoing some of Tertullian's eschatological ideas, Cyprian admonished his readers to "imitate" what they would some day be. Philo had combined the Platonic aspiration toward the imitation of God with biblical ideas, and on this basis Clement of Alexandria developed one of the fullest doctrines of imitation. The statement of the Sermon on the Mount, "Be merciful, even as your Father is merciful," provided biblical warrant for describing the mature Christian as an imitator of God; for "the [Old Testament] law calls imitation 'following,' and such 'following' to the limits of one's power makes one like the model." This assimilation to Christ would produce incorruptibility and salvation. After a series of quotations from Plato, supported by a series from the Old Testament, Clement found his definition of imitation summed up in I Corinthians 11:1, which he took to mean that "assimilation to God, so that as far as possible a man becomes righteous and holy with wisdom, [Paul] lays down as the aim of faith, and the end to be that restitution of the promise which is effected by faith." Platonic and highly idiosyncratic though Clement's doctrine of imitation quite unabashedly was, both it and Irenaeus's doctrine of recapitulation act as a corrective on

Iren.*Dem.*31 (*ACW* 16:68)

Iren.*Haer.*5.16.2 (Harvey 2:367)

Tert.*Marc.*3.9.5 (*CCSL* 1:520); Tert.*Jud.*13.11–19 (*CCSL* 2:1387–88); Hipp.*Dan.*4.11.5 (*GCS* 1–1:212–14)

Hipp.*Antichr.*26 (*GCS* 1–II:19)

Jaeger (1945) 2:403

Cypr.*Domin.orat.*36 (*CSEL* 3:294)

Luke 6:36

Clem.*Str.*2.19.100.4 (*GCS* 52:168) Clem.*Paed.*1.5.20.4 (*GCS* 12:102)

Clem.*Str.*2.22.136.6 (*GCS* 52:188)

any reductionism in the interpretation of what was meant by salvation through obedience to the teachings of Christ and through imitation of his example.

Yet the language of Irenaeus and Clement also shows that neither the teachings nor the example of Christ could be isolated from the message of the cross. According to Irenaeus, it was not only by recapitulating each stage of human development that Christ brought salvation, but especially by the obedience of his passion, which on the tree of the cross undid the damage done by the tree of disobedience. And even Clement, though he could speak almost glibly of Christ's "acting out the drama of human salvation" and not so much as mention the cross in this connection, went on a little later to declare that Christ had "transformed sunset into sunrise and by his crucifixion turned death into life." It is significant that this confession follows a passage that sounds like a quotation from the church's worship. For there is reason to believe that the saving power of the suffering and death of Christ was more explicitly celebrated in the liturgy of the second century than formulated in its theology.

There are certainly liturgical echoes audible in some of the language of the church fathers describing Christ's death as a sacrifice, which was a term borrowed from pre-Christian worship, both Jewish and pagan, and adopted very early for Christian worship. Just how early the idea of sacrifice was applied to Christian worship, specifically to the Eucharist, is the subject of controversy. But by the date of the *Didache*—although that date is itself a controversial issue—the application of the term "sacrifice" to the Eucharist seems to have been quite natural, together with the identification of the Christian Eucharist as the "pure offering" commanded in Malachi 1:11. But even without an answer to the question of the Christian sacrifice, the description in the Epistle to the Hebrews of the death of Christ as a sacrifice seems to have been based on the Jewish liturgy. When the Jewish liturgical context of this sacrificial language could no longer be taken for granted among Christian hearers and readers, the Christian liturgies were already using similar language about the offering of the prayers, the gifts, and the lives of the worshipers, and probably also about the offering of the sacrifice of the Mass, so that the

Iren.*Haer*.5.16.3 (Harvey 2:368)

Clem.*Prot*.10.110.2 (*GCS* 12:78)

Clem.*Prot*.11.114.4 (*GCS* 12:80)

Clem.*Prot*.11.114.1 (*GCS* 12:80)

See pp. 168–69 below

Did.14.1 (Bihlmeyer 8)

Richardson (1935) 101;
Corwin (1960) 172

Barn.8.2 (Bihlmeyer 20)

Cypr.Ep.63.16 (CSEL 3:714)

Cypr.Ep.63 (CSEL 3:701–17)

Scorp.7.5–6 (CCSL 2:1081–82)

Tert.Jud.13.21 (CCSL
2:1388–89)

See pp. 156–58 below

Tert.Paenit.7.14 (CCSL 1:334)

Tert.Paenit.8.9 (CCSL 1:336)

Tert.Paenit.5.9 (CCSL
1:328–29)

Hil.Ps.53.12–13 (CSEL
22:144–45)

sacrificial interpretation of the death of Christ never lacked a liturgical frame of reference. When Barnabas, perhaps alone among the apostolic fathers, identified Jesus with the sacrificial victim of Old Testament worship, this accorded with his view of the Old Testament. And when, somewhat more than a century later, Cyprian described Christ as offering the sacrifice of his suffering, it was in the context of the most extensive discussion of the celebration of the Eucharist in the third century. Between Barnabas and Cyprian, we find Tertullian speaking of Christ "offering himself up [to God] for our offenses" and citing the sacrifices of pagan worship in defense of the appropriateness of such an idea; and in a contrast between the "sacraments" of the Old Testament and those of the New, he spoke of Christ as a "sacrifice for all the Gentiles."

Yet the development of the doctrine of the death of Christ was to be shaped by another term, "satisfaction," which Tertullian seems to have introduced into Christian language but which was to find its normative exposition only in the Middle Ages. Tertullian's doctrine of "satisfaction" may have come from Roman private law, where it referred to the amends one made to another for failing to discharge on obligation, or from Roman public law, which enabled the term to be interpreted as a form of punishment. In the language of the church, "satisfaction" was a term for the reparation made necessary by sins after baptism, within the context of the developing doctrine of penance. Tertullian's treatise on repentance spoke of God as "one to whom you may make satisfaction" and of confession as motivated by a desire to make satisfaction. One who repented was "making satisfaction to the Lord," one who lapsed after repentance was "making satisfaction to the devil." The momentous consequences of the introduction of "satisfaction" into Christian vocabulary did not become evident until later.

The first to apply the term to the death of Christ seems to have been Hilary, who equated "satisfaction" with "sacrifice" and interpreted the cross as Christ's great act of reparation to God on behalf of sinners. Although the actual use of Tertullian's term "satisfaction" for the death of Christ cannot be traced to Tertullian himself, it was a fuller exposition of such statements of his as this:

"Who has ever redeemed the death of another by his own, except the Son of God alone? . . . Indeed, it was for this purpose that he came—to die for sinners." And the term adds its own weight to the impression that many of the themes in which theologians eventually expressed their discussions of the saving power of the death of Christ came from the liturgical and sacramental life of the church.

Tert.Pudic.22.4 (CCSL 2:1328–29)

One such term, however, was certainly not liturgical, but exegetical in its basis, the term "ransom." The basis was provided both by the sayings attributed to Jesus, which spoke of the Son of man "giving his life as a ransom for many," and by the more frequent use of this idea in the Old Testament, especially in Isaiah 53:5–6, a passage that was claimed by Christians, beginning with the writers of the New Testament, as an explicit prophecy of Christ's passion. The *Epistle to Diognetus* was apparently repeating the language of the Bible when it said that God "himself parted with his own Son as a ransom for us, the holy for the lawless, the guileless for the evil." But neither this statement nor the biblical passages on which it was based specified to whom the ransom had been paid. Because of the prominence of demonology in Christian piety and theology, the Christian thinkers who dealt with the idea of ransom usually took it to be a ransom paid to the devil to set man free. Irenaeus does not seem to have had this conception in mind in his exposition of the idea of the ransom, but Origen clearly did. Origen's biblical commentaries, where "his doctrine [was] much nearer to the common ecclesiastical Christianity," repeatedly referred to the idea of Christ's being handed over by his Father to the hostile powers. Since the devil had the power of death, the way man was rescued from devil and death was for the Son to be delivered by the Father into the devil's hands, and by him in turn into the hands of the enemies of Christ. "To whom did he give his soul as a ransom for many? Certainly not to God! Then why not the devil? For he had possession of us until there should be given to him the ransom for us, the soul of Jesus." Only in the fourth century, in the thought of such men as Gregory Nazianzus, did this notion of a ransom paid to the devil yield to further theological reflection. That reflection shared with the notion it rejected a basic recognition of the place of the cross in the Chris-

Matt.20:28

See pp. 18–19 above

Diogn.9.2 (Bihlmeyer 147)

Wingren (1959) 129

Franks (1918) 1:54

Or.Matt.13.8–9 (GCS 40:203–204)

Or.Matt.16.8 (GCS 40:498)
Gr.Naz.Or.45.22 (PG 36:653)

tian understanding of salvation; together with the sacrifice, the idea of ransom sustained that recognition in the thought of Origen.

Yet when a modern Western Christian turns to the Christian writers of the second and third centuries for their understanding of salvation in Christ, it is neither their attention to the teachings and example of Christ (which he may, rather superficially, identify with that of Protestant liberalism) nor their preoccupation with the passion and death of Christ (which he may, with some justification, see as an ancestor of the orthodox doctrine of vicarious atonement), but their emphasis on the saving significance of the resurrection of Christ that he will find most unusual. So great was that emphasis in the soteriology of many church fathers that the definition of salvation through Christ's victory over man's enemies has been called "the classic" theory of the atonement. To be sure, other ways of speaking about the atonement were too widespread even among the Greek fathers to permit us to ascribe exclusive or even primary force to any one theory, but Christ as victor was more important in orthodox expositions of salvation and reconciliation than Western dogmatics has recognized.

Aulén (1969) 4–7

It was apparently in defense of what he thought the church believed and taught, not merely in defense of his own speculations, that Origen asserted, in opposition to Celsus, the proposition that it was not enough for Christ, as a "wise and perfect man," to provide "an example of the way to die for the sake of religion," but that by his death he had begun the overthrow of the devil's dominion over the whole earth; and "it was he who dwelt in the apparently human Jesus who said that he was the resurrection." The "baptism" spoken of in Luke 12:50 was not merely the suffering of Christ, but his "leading captivity captive." The church doctrine described here by Origen was developed more fully by Irenaeus, with two biblical passages, Genesis 3:15 and Matthew 12:29, supplying the basis for his exposition. The promise of the woman's seed in Genesis 3:15 described the conflict between Christ and the devil as one in which the devil would win temporarily but Christ would triumph eternally. It required that the champion of mankind himself be a man who would do battle with Adam's conqueror and vanquish him, granting the palm of victory over

Or.*Cels*.7.16–17 (*GCS* 3:168–69)

Or.*Joh*.6.56–57.291–92 (*GCS* 10:165)

Iren.*Haer*.5.21.1–2 (Harvey 2:380–81)

Iren.*Haer*.3.23.7 (Harvey 2:129–30)

Iren.*Haer*.2.20.3 (Harvey 1:322–23)

Iren.*Haer*.5.21.3 (Harvey 2:384)

Iren.*Haer*.3.18.6 (Harvey 2:100)

Cypr.*Domin.orat*.34 (*CSEL* 3:292)

Connolly (1906) 213–14

Rufin.*Symb*.16 (*CCSL* 20:152–53)

Just.*Dial*.72.4 (Goodspeed 182)

Iren.*Haer*.3.20.4 (Harvey 2:108–09)

Or.*Cels*.2.39 (*GCS* 2:163–64)

Ephr.*Carm.Nis*.35.19 (*CSCO* 102:7[103:5])

death to those who had been captive to death and the devil. The woman's seed, the conquering Christ, crushed the head of the serpent and destroyed the last enemy, death; man was set free, and "his salvation is death's destruction." Christ, by his suffering, destroyed death and error, corruptibility and ignorance, and he endowed believers with incorruption. The words of Jesus in Matthew 12:29 meant that Satan would be bound with the very chains with which he had bound man and would be led captive. Paraphrasing the passage, Irenaeus said: "He [Christ] fought and was victorious; for he was man doing battle for the fathers, and by his obedience utterly abolishing disobedience. For he bound the strong man, liberated the weak, and by destroying sin endowed his creation with salvation."

From these statements of Irenaeus and Origen it is evident that not only the resurrection of Christ, but especially his passion and death belonged to the description of salvation as the victory of Christ over the enemies of man. Another event sometimes associated with that victory was the descent into hell. The earliest references to this event seem to have been in Syriac materials, where it probably was synonymous with his death and burial; some later references to it seem to have kept this meaning. But in Justin it had already come to acquire additional connotations, thanks to one of the passages which Justin accused the Jews of expunging from the Old Testament: "The Lord God remembered his dead people of Israel who lay in their graves, and he descended to preach to them his own salvation." Quoted also by Irenaeus, this passage seemed to interpret Christ's "descent into the realm of the dead" as a liberation of the patriarchs of the Old Testament. The only passage of the New Testament that could incontrovertibly be applied to this event was 1 Peter 3:19, where, however, it was not the patriarchs, but "the spirits in prison" to whom Christ descended to preach. This could be taken to refer to pagan spirits who had not heard him in the days of his flesh, but whose expectation of him made their paganism a preparation for the gospel. Ephraem Syrus represented the demons as exclaiming at the "odious sign" when Christ captured their cities. But it was in the West that the descent acquired creedal status with its incorporation into the final text of the Apostles'

Creed, no earlier than 370. By that time, however, Western theology was interpreting the atonement as a sacrifice and increasingly as an act of satisfaction offered by the death of Christ. The descent into hell then assumed the function which the Greek fathers had assigned to the death and resurrection, the triumph celebrated by Christ over the devil and his legions. As "the harrowing of hell," the descent played a significant part in the arts as well as in the church's teaching, but it was not until the Middle Ages and the Reformation that it became an issue of dogmatic debate.

Certainly the boldest version of the idea that salvation was a triumph over the devil was Origen's speculation about "the restoration of all things [ἀποκατάστασις πάντων]." From his theory of the preexistence and the prehistorical fall of the soul he drew a corollary about its ultimate destiny; for "the end is always like the beginning." The decisive text for his picture of this "end" was 1 Corinthians 15:24–28, which prophesied the eventual subjection of all enemies, including death, to Christ, and the delivery of the kingdom by Christ to the Father. Then God would be "all in all." The pedagogical process by which this subjection was to be carried out would achieve "salvation," and Origen was prepared to believe "that the goodness of God, through his Christ, may recall all his creatures to one end, even his enemies being conquered and subdued"—not only "the last enemy," death, but also the devil, who held the world in his dominion. God would not truly be "all in all" until "the end has been restored to the beginning, and the termination of things compared with their commencement. . . . And when death shall no longer exist anywhere, nor the sting of death, nor any evil at all, then truly God will be all in all." In voicing this speculation, Origen believed himself to be thinking within the confines of ecclesiastical orthodoxy, which had not pronounced on these eschatological questions. Eventually, in the sixth century, it did pronounce on them, condemning this version of universalism. The version of it propounded by Gregory of Nyssa, disengaged from Origen's idea of preexistence but grounded in Gregory's definition of the vision of God as an eternal process in which "one never reaches satiety in his yearning for God," was not condemned, at least not formally; but it was also not made a dogma. A temporal creation

Acts 3:21

Or.*Princ*.1.6.2 (*GCS* 22:79–80)

Or.*Orat*.25.2 (*GCS* 3:358)

Or.*Princ*.1.6.1 (*GCS* 22:79)
Or.*Cels*.7.17 (*GCS* 3:169)

Or.*Princ*.3.6.3 (*GCS* 22:284)

Or.*Princ*.pr.7 (*GCS* 22:14)
See pp. 337–38 below
Daniélou (1940) 328–47

Gr.Nyss.*V.Mos*.2 (Jaeger 7–1:116)

and a temporal end of history were part of the church's official doctrine, as was Christ's victory over death and the devil. It was left to theology to ponder the various theories about how the reconciliation of God with the world was achieved in the life, death, and resurrection of Christ, as well as the various speculations about how the victory assured by this reconciliation would eventually be actualized in history and beyond history.

Roughly corresponding to these three themes of the life and teachings, the suffering and death, and the resurrection and exaltation of Christ as the means by which salvation was achieved were three ways of defining the content of the salvation which he brought: revelation of the truth; forgiveness of sins and justification; immortality and deification. These definitions are, if anything, even less discrete in the literature than are the atonement themes we have just examined. Nor is the correspondence between each of the definitions and its counterpart an exact one. There is, in fact, an even deeper, though largely unexamined, ambiguity in the doctrine of salvation through Christ, running through both the atonement themes and the definitions of salvation. Was the work of Christ to be thought of as having accomplished the reconciliation between God and the world or as having disclosed a reconciliation that had actually been there all along?

That ambiguity was especially palpable when the work of Christ was represented as that of the exemplar and teacher who brought the true revelation of God's will for man. His prophecies had come true in the past, Justin argued, and the reasonable man should therefore believe his teachings. To be a Christian meant to live in accordance with these teachings. When Clement of Rome referred to Christ as "our salvation, the high priest who offers our gifts, the patron and helper in our weakness," he went on to specify the content of that salvation: "Through him the eyes of our heart were opened. Through him our unintelligent and darkened mind shoots up into the light. Through him the Master was pleased to let us taste the knowledge that never fades." Although the doctrine of the eternal Logos gave this emphasis upon Christ as the imparter of saving revelation a depth that went beyond the simple designation of Jesus as the greatest of prophets, it served only to accentuate the stark con-

Just. 1 Apol.12.10 (Goodspeed 33)
Just. 1 Apol.16.14 (Goodspeed 37-38)

1 Clem.36.1-2 (Bihlmeyer 55)

trast between what the apologists said about the person of Christ and what they said about the work of Christ: He did not have to be identified that intimately with God if his chief vocation as Savior was to teach men the truth about monotheism and the moral life.

These same apologists also spoke often about the crucifixion of Jesus. Their theories of its effect on the relation between God and man were far more rudimentary than were their ideas about the enlightenment in Christ's teachings, but in the liturgy of the church and in its biblical imagery they found so high an esteem for the cross that they had to include it even if they had no adequate systematic formulas to describe its importance for salvation.

He who was bound to the wood of the cross of Christ, Clement of Alexandria promised his pagan readers, would be delivered from destruction. Christ was "the purifier [from sin], the Savior, and the bringer of peace." As God, Christ forgave sins; as man, he trained his followers not to sin. The application of Isaiah 53 to Christ frequently shaped the connection between the death of Christ and the forgiveness of sins. Origen quoted almost the entire chapter in his defense of the doctrine that those who had once been sinful had been "healed by the passion of the Savior." But as many of the passages from the fathers which we have quoted make clear, the definition of salvation as revelation and the definition of it as forgiveness were repeatedly linked with what seems from the surviving documentary evidence to have been by far the most widespread understanding of salvation in the church catholic of the second and third centuries, namely, salvation from death and the attainment of everlasting life.

Liturgical sources from widely scattered areas attest to the universal importance of this understanding. One of the earliest of Christian prayers thanked God for "the knowledge, faith, and immortality, which thou hast made known through thy servant, Jesus"; similar prayers appeared in other liturgies. The doctrine of salvation as rescue from the power of death, expressed in these liturgies, was carried over into the literature of apologetics, exegesis, and instruction. If it were not for the knowledge of God that had come in Christ, wrote Minucius Felix to the pagans, what substantial happiness could there be, since death was inevitable? Christians, declared Justin

Clem.*Prot.*12.118.4 (*GCS* 12:83)
Clem.*Prot.*10.110.1 (*GCS* 12:78)

Clem.*Paed.*1.3.7.1 (*GCS* 12:94)

Or.*Cels.*1.54–55 (*GCS* 2:105–106)

ap.*Did.*10.2 (Bihlmeyer 6)

Wetter (1921) 1:45

Min.Fel.*Oct.*37.8(*CSEL* 2:53)

in response to Trypho, were able to rejoice in death because they expected to be raised free of corruption, change, and death. The love spoken of in the Song of Solomon, said Origen in his commentary, "alone possesses immortality," and therefore it alone could make believers immortal. The fire unquenchable threatened everlasting death, wrote Ignatius to the Ephesians, but Christ had breathed incorruption upon the church. This definition of the meaning of salvation, which reached its consummate expression in the theology of Athanasius, was the common property of catholic Christianity.

Just.*Dial*.46.7 (Goodspeed 144)

Or.*Cant*.pr. (*GCS* 33:70)

Ign.*Eph*.16–17 (Bihlmeyer 87)

See pp. 205–6 below

Frequently it was bound up with the continuing though flagging hope for the speedy return of Christ. The expressions of that hope, however, were also frequently tied to the assurance that the substance of the infinite bliss of heaven was already the possession of the church on earth. Tertullian's recourse to such assurance is particularly significant in view of his importance for the development of eschatological doctrine. His graphic description of the great spectacle on the day of judgment, when poets, philosophers, and rulers would receive their long-delayed recompense, concluded with the observation that by faith believers could have the joy of this spectacle even now. He taunted Marcion for teaching a deliverance that was imperfect because it lay exclusively in the future. In language and thought closely related to Tertullian's, Minucius Felix boasted that Christians "both rise again in bliss and are already living in contemplation of the future." And Tertullian's disciple Cyprian assured his readers of salvation from death here and hereafter because the Savior, "who once conquered death for us, is continually conquering it in us."

See pp. 129–30 above

Tert.*Spect*.30.7 (*CCSL* 1:253)
Tert.*Marc*.1.24.7 (*CCSL* 1:468)

Min.Fel.*Oct*.38.4 (*CSEL* 2:54)

Cypr.*Ep*.10.3 (*CSEL* 3:492)

An important element of this salvation from death was salvation from sin. A proof text for the definition of the relation between salvation from death and salvation from sin was the healing of the paralytic in Matthew 9:2–9, as interpreted by the Greek fathers. According to Irenaeus, this passage meant that the only Son of God had come from God for the salvation of man. Through his Son, he against whom man had sinned came to grant the forgiveness of sins. Because disease was one of the consequences of sin, it was appropriate that the bringer of "salvation [σωτηρία]" be the bringer of "health [σωτηρία]," and against the Gnostics Irenaeus insisted that the bringer of

Iren.*Haer*.5.17.3 (Harvey 2:371)

salvation from sin and the bringer of salvation from disease had to be the same. Therefore when Jesus remitted sins, he healed man, and also manifested who he himself

Mark 2:7

was. No one could forgive sins but God; the salvation of healing and forgiveness which Jesus brought demonstrated that he was the very Logos of God, so that while it was as man that he suffered for man, it would be as God that he had mercy on man and forgave him his sin. Or, as Clement of Alexandria said in summarizing the same pericope, the good tutor, the Logos, healed the body and soul, granting restoration of health to the sick and for-

Clem.*Paed*.1.2.6.1 (*GCS* 12:93)

giveness to the sinners; and to both he was "the Savior."

For the Greek patristic tradition, especially in its mystical forms, the final goal and result of this saving knowledge, this forgiveness, and this rescue from death was "deification [θέωσις]." The appeal of Clement of Alexandria to the Greeks was that "the Logos of God had become man so that you might learn from a man how a man

Clem.*Prot*.1.8.4 (*GCS* 12:9)

may become God." Origen took the petition of the Lord's Prayer for daily bread to mean that those who were nour-

Or.*Orat*.27.13 (*GCS* 3:371–72)

ished by God the Logos would thereby be made divine. In many other places, too, he defined salvation as the attainment of the gift of divinity. Identification with Christ would lift the believer through the human nature of Christ to union with his divine nature and thus with God

Or.*Cels*.3.28 (*GCS* 2:226)

and thus to deification. The full clarification of the term "deification" had to await the resolution of the conflict over the deity of Christ; the church could not specify what it meant to promise that man would become divine until it had specified what it meant to confess that Christ had always been divine. But even from the writings of Irenaeus, Clement, and Origen, for all the differences between them, we can conclude that the church could not regard "salvation" as simply a restoration of what had been lost in the first Adam, the original creation; it had to be an incorporation into what had been vouchsafed in the second Adam, a new creation.

The Church and the Means of Grace

Historically, the relation between the doctrine of grace and the doctrine of the means of grace has been ambiguous. The doctrine of grace as justification and forgiveness developed slowly and unsteadily; the doctrine of the means of grace, on the other hand, developed very rapidly.

A high estimate of the means of grace was not necessarily incompatible with a low estimate of grace itself; that is, it was possible to emphasize the sacraments as something which a man did, at the expense of grace as something which God gave. A theologian did not have to be very specific about the content of the means of grace to insist that they were essential.

In one sense, of course, the use of "means of grace" as a plural is deceptive, for the church was itself the primary means of grace. Irenaeus was expressing a common conviction when he said: "Where the church is, there is the Spirit of God; and where the Spirit of God is, there is the church, and every kind of grace." But he did go on in the next sentence to speak of "the fountain that issued from the body of Christ," apparently referring, on the basis of the tradition reflected in John 19:34 and in 1 John 5:6–8, to baptism or to the Eucharist or perhaps even to both. The doctrine of the church and the doctrine of the sacraments were corollaries, for both described the divinely instituted means through which grace was communicated. The church, the Scriptures, the priesthood, the sacraments —all were called "holy," both because they were holy in themselves and because they made men holy by the sanctifying grace whose instruments they were. To Origen, for instance, the Eucharist was "a certain holy body which sanctifies those who partake of it with a pure intention."

The term "holy" applied with special force to the church. It was used already in the New Testament; and of the four classic notes of the church defined in the Nicene Creed—one, holy, catholic, and apostolic—it appeared in more creeds and in earlier creeds than did any of the others. In the present connection, the notes of holiness and unity are of immediate relevance, for by their intimate and intrinsic association with the doctrine of the sacraments—an association evident already in 1 Corinthians—they helped to shape that doctrine and were shaped by it in turn. This association was especially decisive for the doctrine of the holiness of the church, as an early liturgical formula suggested when it invited the communicants with the words: "If any man is holy, let him come; if any man is not, let him repent." It was also over the definition of the holiness of the church and over its implications for baptism and penance that some of the earliest ecclesiological controversies arose.

Iren.*Haer*.3.24.1 (Harvey 2:132)

Tert.*Bapt*.16.1 (*CCSL* 1:290)

Iren.*Haer*.4.33.2 (Harvey 2:257–58)

Or.*Cels*.8.33 (*GCS* 3:249)

Symb.Nic.–CP (Schaff 2:58)

Schaff 2:55

Did.10.6 (Bihlmeyer 6)

There was no controversy over the absolute requirement that the church be holy; that was universally assumed
and unanimously asserted, by catholics, schismatics, and
heretics alike, as can be seen from the witness of Tertullian. Writing as a catholic, Tertullian boasted that the
members of the church alone were without crime; writing
as a Montanist schismatic, he scorned the moral compromise which supposed that a member of the church
could become superior in holiness through self-indul-
gence; and he quoted Marcion the heretic as demanding
celibacy for sanctity in his church. Hippolytus warned that
if anyone wanted to become a citizen of the church but
lacked the fear of God, it would be of no benefit to him
to congregate with the saints. The church was holy because Christ was present in it; therefore it was called "the
spouse of Christ" or "the body of Christ" or even "the
body of Father, Son, and Holy Spirit." But the holiness
that was the gift of the indwelling Christ also had to be
an attribute of the members of the church. Susanna was
"a figure of the church" for Hippolytus, exhibiting the
freedom from the sins of the flesh that belonged to the
true holiness of the church and of its members; Cyprian,
too, read the story of Susanna as an allegory of the church
and its purity, both doctrinal and moral.

Yet both Hippolytus and Cyprian became involved in
grave doctrinal controversies about the holiness of the
church. Hippolytus clashed with Callistus, bishop of
Rome, over the latter's willingness to define the holiness
of the church in such a way that men who had "indulged
in sensual pleasures" were not completely excluded if they
were properly penitent. Whether or not Callistus was
being accused of violating the church's stand on absolution after proper penance and whether or not this accusation was fair—both highly mooted questions—it seems
obvious that Hippolytus, for his part, was defending a
definition of the holiness of the church as "the holy as-
sembly of those who live in accordance with righteousness." In opposition to him Callistus argued on the basis
of two biblical proofs: the parable of the wheat and the
tares, which was to become dominant in the later catholic
defense of the idea of the church as a "composite body
(corpus permixtum)" made up of saints and sinners; and
the ancient typology of the ark of Noah, which included
unclean animals together with the clean. These were taken

Tert.*Apol*.45.1 (*CCSL* 1:159)

Tert.*Jejun*.17.4 (*CCSL* 2:1276)
Tert.*Marc*.1.29.1 (*CCSL* 1:472–73)

Hipp.*Dan*.4.38.2 (*GCS* 1–I:284–86)

Cypr.*Unit.eccl*.6 (*CSEL* 3:214)
Tert.*Marc*.5.19.6 (*CCSL* 1:722)
Tert.*Bapt*.6.2 (*CCSL* 1:282)

Hipp.*Dan*.1.14.5 (*GCS* 1–I:24)

Cypr.*Ep*.43.4 (*CSEL* 3:593)

Hipp.*Haer*.9.12.20 (*GCS* 26:249)

Hipp.*Dan*.1.17.7 (*GCS* 1–I:28)

Matt.13:30

ap.Hipp.*Haer*.9.12.22–23 (*GCS* 26:250)

to imply that the definition of the holiness of the church would have to be based on forgiveness rather than on the empirical sanctity of its members. The tares were, Callistus maintained, "the sinners in the church." As Hamel has summarized the conflict between the two, "For Hippolytus the church is the congregation of saints, whose holiness is guaranteed by the unconditional purity of its members from sins of the flesh. But according to Callistus, the church does not lose its character as 'church catholic' even

Hamel (1951) 75

when unworthy members remain within it."

Cyprian's conception of the holiness of the church was both more profound and more complex. It was called forth by two distinct though related crises in the life of the Latin-speaking church, the controversy over the readmission of the "lapsed"—those guilty of apostasy dur-

Cypr.Laps.16 (CSEL 3:248–49)

ing persecution—into the communion of the church and the controversy over the rebaptism of those who had been

Cypr.Ep.70–71 (CSEL 3:766–74)

baptized by heretics. Both of these controversies were to reach, with their repercussions, into the doctrinal debates

See pp. 308–13 below

of the fifth century and even beyond. Therefore the evolution of Cyprian's attitude toward the issue of readmission, while principally a part of the history of church discipline, was crucial for the entire development of the doctrine of the church as well. On the one hand, the gradual relaxation of the conditions for readmission involved the concession that the ideal of a pure church had to yield to the concept of the church as the place where purity was to be

Cypr.Ep.59.15–16 (CSEL 3:684–86)

pursued; on the other hand, Cyprian continued to argue against the wholesale application of the parable of the

Cypr.Ep.54.3 (CSEL 3:622–23)

wheat and the tares to the doctrine of the church. Cyprian's resolution of this tension between two definitions of the holiness of the church came in the course of his controversy with the bishop of Rome over the validity of baptism outside the church. Although he had been compelled, in the controversy over the lapsed, to concede that the presence of sinful members did not invalidate the holiness of the church, he would not permit that to mean that the church could tolerate sinful clergy. For the people could not be free of the contagion of sin if they communi-

Cypr.Ep.67.3 (CSEL 3:737)

cated with a sinful priest. Cyprian seems to have concluded that the very condition of the church as a mixed body required that the bishops and clergy be pure, so that they might administer the sacraments by which the members of the church could become pure.

This reinterpretation of the holiness of the church was to become one of the chief issues in the Donatist controversy. But it also served to give additional force to Cyprian's view of the church as the institution outside of which there was no salvation. Noah's ark, which to Callistus meant that both clean and unclean could be saved, meant to Cyprian that only those within the church could be saved; he cited it as a self-evident axiom that there was no salvation outside the church. Hence it was imperative that the unity of the church be preserved, and Cyprian devoted his most famous treatise to this theme. The unity of the church, like its holiness, was to be found in the bishops, in their unity with one another, affirmed by the words of Jesus to Peter in Matthew 16:18–19. No passage in Cyprian's writings has received more detailed attention than the two versions of the exegesis of these words in chapter 4 of his *Unity of the Church:* one version seems to assert the primacy of Peter as prerequisite to unity among the bishops, while the other seems to treat the primacy of Peter as only representative of that unity. It seems that the first of these versions came first, chronologically, while the second was a clarification of it issued by Cyprian himself, because Rome was making more of his words than he had intended. But the debate over the "papal" vs. the "episcopal" exegesis of Matthew 16:18–19 should not obscure the more fundamental point shared by both kinds of exegesis: the indispensability of the empirical unity of the church, "this holy mystery of oneness, this unbreakable bond of close-knit harmony . . . portrayed in the Gospel by our Lord Jesus Christ's coat, which was not divided or cut at all. . . . [For] that man cannot possess the garment of Christ who rends and divides the church of Christ."

In making such an issue of the empirical unity of the church, Cyprian was expressing the conviction of the church catholic from the beginning. Heresy and schism were closely related because both of them violated the unity of the church. It is interesting that in all seven epistles of Ignatius the church was explicitly called "holy" only once, while the unity of the church in the bishop was one of the overriding preoccupations of all the epistles, so much so that it seems accurate to conclude that "the most important aspect of the church for the apostolic fathers is its unity." It has also been observed that the

Cypr.*Ep*.75.15 (*CSEL* 3:820)
Cypr.*Ep*.73.21 (*CSEL* 3:795)

Cypr.*Unit.eccl*.4 (*CSEL* 3:212–13)

Cypr.*Unit.eccl*.7 (*CSEL* 3:215)

Ign.*Trall*.inscr. (Bihlmeyer 92)

R.Grant (1964) 1:137–38

Ign.*Phil.*7.2 (Bihlmeyer 104)

Or.*Orat.*31.5 (*GCS* 3:399)

Or.*Joh.*6.59.301 (*GCS* 10:167)

1 *Clem.*32.2; 40.5 (Bihlmeyer 52; 57); *Did.*13.3 (Bihlmeyer 7)

See p. 25 above

See pp. 117–18 above

Iren.*Haer.*4.8.3 (Harvey 2:167)
Iren.*Haer.*4.34.3 (Harvey 2:422)

Tert.*Castit.*7.5–6 (*CCSL* 2:1025–26)

Tert.*Castit.*4.5 (*CCSL* 2:1021)

Tert.*Castit.*7.3 (*CCSL* 2:1024–25)

noun "unity" occurred eleven times in Ignatius and the verb six times, but that neither was found anywhere else in the apostolic fathers. For both Ignatius and Cyprian, moreover, the bishop was the key to authentic unity, and schism was identified as party spirit in opposition to him. Therefore the efforts to superimpose upon the second or third centuries the distinction made by Augustinism and especially by the Reformation between the visible and the invisible churches have proved quite ineffectual, even in interpreting the thought of Origen, whose dichotomy between the heavenly and the earthly churches might seem to have tended in that direction; but on earth there was only one church, and it was finally inseparable from the sacramental, hierarchical institution. This church was, in a striking phrase of Origen, "the cosmos of the cosmos, because Christ has become its cosmos, he who is the primal light of the cosmos."

For another distinction of Augustinism and the Reformation, however, there is considerable support in the teaching of the second- and third-century fathers: the distinction between the hierarchical priesthood and the priesthood of all believers. Already in Clement of Rome and in the *Didache* the attributes of the Levitical priesthood of the Old Testament were being applied to the ministers of the church. Yet the conception of the priesthood of believers remained alongside this development, as is evident from quite divergent lines of tradition. Irenaeus was the most articulate defender of the thesis that the continuity of the church was guaranteed by the apostolic office of the men who held the apostolic sees; yet it was also Irenaeus who, perhaps more explicitly than any of his contemporaries, affirmed that "all the righteous have a priestly order" and that therefore "all the disciples of the Lord are Levites and priests." The Montanism of Tertullian represented an attack upon the structures of ecclesiastical order, including that of the clerical priesthood, in the name of the manifestations of the Spirit through the new prophecy, which transcended the distinction of clergy and laity; yet it was also Tertullian who, in the same Montanist treatise, formulated the principle that while all believers could say with the apostle in 1 Corinthians 7:40, "I think that I have the Spirit of God," this did not make all believers apostles; the distinction between clergy and laity was still to be observed.

The earliest formula of ordination to have survived, that which is preserved in the *Apostolic Tradition* of Hippolytus, prayed that God would pour out upon the bishop the power of the Holy Spirit, which Christ had bestowed on the apostles, and would endow him with the authority to intercede on behalf of the people and to ab-

Hipp.*Trad.ap.*3 (SC 11:27–30)

solve them of their sins. The surviving liturgical information and canonical legislation also reinforce the impression of great variety of usage, as well as of nomenclature, in the relation between the offices of priest (or presbyter) and bishop, which seem to have been interchangeable in some places but not in others; but these sources also document the general and deepening doctrinal agreement on the sacramental understanding of the priesthood as dispenser of the means of grace, on its continuity with the apostles, and on its function as the assurance of unity.

One means of grace associated with the ecclesiastical office, though not exclusively, was the word of God. "Word of God" was, of course, one of the most impor-

See pp. 186–89 below

tant technical terms for Jesus Christ in his relation to the Father; and when "the Gospel" or "Scripture" was equated with the "word of God," the presence of Christ in this means of grace was seen as in some way analogous to his presence in the flesh. The translation of λόγος with "sermo," speech or discourse, seems to have been widespread in early Christian Latin: Christ was the preaching of God. It suggests the teaching that, through his presence in the preached word, Christ the personal Word gave instruction to the church and conferred the power to be-

Or.*Princ.*3.1.15 (GCS 22:222–23)

lieve and obey that instruction. When Origen spoke of "the divine word" promising to take away wickedness from those who heeded it, he was referring to Christ as the Word but also to Scripture as the word and to the proclamation of the word. The old man who converted Justin to Christianity kindled in his soul a love for the prophets and for the disciples of Christ. The words of Christ, he found, "have in themselves something of dreadful majesty, and are enough to put to shame those that turn out of the right way, while rest most delightful

Just.*Dial.*8.2 (Goodspeed 99)

comes to those who carry them out in practice."

A special version of the doctrine of the word as means of grace came in the claim that the Scriptures could convert a reader, even apart from such instruction or proclamation. Tertullian maintained that anyone who "listened to" (which in the context seems to have meant "read") the Old Testament would find God there, and that if he took the trouble to understand it he would be brought to faith. Tatian maintained that while he was pondering the religious practices and philosophical ideas of paganism he chanced upon the Old Testament, whose literary style, prophetic vision, moral force, and doctrine of providence caused him to believe it, to give obedience to the words of God, and in this way to be delivered from the tyranny of the rulers of the cosmos. Similarly, Theophilus described how, while he was still an unbeliever, he had encountered the prophets of the Old Testament and had been converted; therefore he urged his reader to pay reverent attention to the prophetic Scriptures. The providential encounter with just the right admonition or exhortation of Scripture became a convention in the literature of conversion: for example, in the account of Antony's hearing of Matthew 19:21 and Matthew 6:34; in the related narrative of Augustine's reading of Romans 13:13, which drove away his doubt and enlightened him with complete certainty; in the story of a chance reading of a psalm at Mass, vindicating Martin of Tours; and in the legend that Francis of Assisi made the sign of the cross over the Bible and then opened it to the three passages in the Gospels that spoke to his condition. The attention to the sacraments in dogmatic theology has failed to do justice to the place of the doctrine of the word of God, proclaimed but also written, within the total doctrine of the means of grace during the second and third century.

In this same period, the doctrine of the means of grace did refer primarily to the sacraments, although the term "sacrament" frequently did not refer only to what later centuries of the church called sacraments. From the writings of Tertullian and Chrysostom it is clear what a great variety of Christian usages and teachings, far beyond anything termed sacramental in modern dogmatic terms, the Latin "sacramentum" and the Greek μυστήριον could cover; in the New Testament the Greek word does not seem ever to refer explicitly to "sacraments." Nor did early Christian theology treat in detail the question of sacraments in general; rather, its sacramental doctrine emerged from the concrete teaching and practice of the church. Baptism and Eucharist were linked as early as 1

Tert.*Apol*.18.9 (*CCSL* 1:119)

Tat.*Or*.29–30 (*TU* 4–I:29–31)

Theoph.*Autol*.1.14 (*SC* 20:88–90)

Ath.*V.Ant*.2–3 (*PG* 26:841–45)

Aug.*Conf*.8.12.29 (*CSEL* 33:194–95)

Sulp.Sev.*Mart*.9.5–7 (*SC* 133:272)

Corinthians 10:1–4 and perhaps John 19:34 and 1 John 5:6, but there could not be a doctrine of the sacraments before the doctrines of baptism, the Eucharist, penance, and whatever other sacraments had developed. The definition of a doctrine of sacraments in general and the determination of their number at seven came only with the beginnings of scholastic theology in the Latin West, and they seem to have been adopted by the Greek East on the basis of their Western development.

Although references to the doctrine of baptism are scattered throughout the Christian literature of the second and third centuries, only one extant treatise from that period is devoted exclusively to the subject, that of Ter-

Tert.*Bapt.* (*CCSL* 1:277–95)

tullian. And the most succinct statement by Tertullian on the doctrine of baptism actually came, not in his treatise on baptism, but in his polemic against Marcion. (It was a similar polemical need that called forth Irenaeus's sum-

See p. 167 below

mary of the catholic doctrine of the Eucharist.) Contending against Marcion's dualism between the Creator and the Redeemer, Tertullian argued that none of the four basic gifts of baptism could be granted if that dualism were maintained. The four gifts were: the remission of sins, deliverance from death, regeneration, and the be-

Tert.*Marc.*1.28.2 (*CCSL* 1:472)

stowal of the Holy Spirit. All of these would be vitiated on the basis of Marcion's presuppositions. It is noteworthy that Tertullian, regardless of how much a Montanist he may have been at this point, was summarizing what the doctrine of the church was at his time—as well as probably before his time and certainly since his time. Tertullian's enumeration of the gifts of baptism would be difficult to duplicate in so summary a form from other Christian writers, but those who did speak of baptism also spoke of one or more of these gifts.

Baptism brought the remission of sins; the doctrine of baptism was in fact the occasion for many of the references to forgiveness of sins in the literature of these centuries. The Lord had commanded in Matthew 28:19–20, said Cyprian, that the nations be washed in the name of the Father and of the Son and of the Holy Spirit and that

Cypr.*Ep.*27.3 (*CSEL* 3:543)

their past sins be remitted in baptism. Hippolytus described those who were cleansed and who, by faith in the word of truth, put off the filth of their sins, as those who

Hipp.*Dan.*4.59.4 (*GCS* 1–I:336)

would receive the Holy Spirit. For Irenaeus, the story of the cleansing of Naaman the leper in 2 Kings 5 was a

Iren.*fr*.33 (Harvey 2:497–98);
Or.*Job*.6.48.250 (*GCS* 10:157)

Mark 1:4

Tert.*Bapt*.10.5–6 (*CCSL* 1:285)

Clem.*Str*.2.13.58.1 (*GCS* 52:144)

Ps.82:6

Clem.*Paed*.1.6.26.1–2 (*GCS* 12:105)

Const.*App*.2.32.3 (Funk 115)

Just 1 *Apol*.61.12 (Goodspeed 71)

Didym.*Trin*.2.1 (*PG* 39:452)

type of baptism; for "as we are lepers in sin, we are made clean by means of the sacred water and the invocation of the Lord, from our old transgressions, being spiritually regenerated as newborn babes." The baptism of John the Baptist was a baptism "of repentance for the forgiveness of sins"; but this meant, according to Tertullian, that John announced a forgiveness that was to come, while in Christ and in the baptism which he instituted the forgiveness and sanctification were actually conferred. Being baptized for (literally, into) the forgiveness of sins meant, warned Clement of Alexandria, a break with the pagan way of life and a substitution of faith for sin; this was what made sin after baptism such a grave offense, and "second repentance" a privilege not to be dealt with triflingly.

Clement also attached remission of sins in baptism to "deliverance from death," which was probably the most widely disseminated term for the content of salvation through Christ. In a description of the baptism of the Christian as an imitation of the "model [ὑπογραφή]" of Christ's baptism, he enumerated its effects: "Being baptized, we are illuminated; illuminated, we become sons; being made sons, we are made perfect; being made perfect, we are made immortal. 'I say,' says he, 'you are gods, sons of the Most High, all of you.' This work is variously called gift of grace, illumination, perfection, and washing: washing, by which we wash away our sins; grace, by which the penalties accruing to transgressions are remitted; and illumination, with which that holy light of salvation is beheld, that is, by which we see God clearly." Illumination as deliverance from darkness was a familiar metaphor for this deliverance from death through baptism, as Hebrews 6:4 and 10:32 suggest. When Justin explained the metaphor as signifying that those who were baptized were illuminated in their understanding, this seems to have been an apologetic reduction of the meaning given to illumination in the church's teaching; for other instances of the term bear out Clement's understanding of it as a synonym for deliverance. Another metaphor for this deliverance was "seal," as when Hermas spoke of the water of baptism as a seal, by means of which those who were to be saved ascended from the deadness of their former life to be made truly alive; even the descent into hell was interpreted to mean that the apostles had descended into the abode of the dead to preach and

Herm.*Sim*.9.16.3–5.93 (*SC* 53:326–28)

Const.App.7.43.3 (Funk 448)

Meth.*Symp*.3.8.72 (*GCS* 27:36)

Tert.*Bapt*.5.1; 6 (*CCSL* 1:280; 282)

See pp. 291–92 below

Cypr.*Ep*.64.2; 5 (*CSEL* 3:718; 720)

Luke 9:56

Or.*Cels*.1.64 (*GCS* 2:116–18)

Or.*Princ*.1.3.2 (*GCS* 22:50)

See pp. 211–19 below

Matt.3:11; Mark 1:8; Luke 3:16; John 1:33

Acts 1:5

to grant this seal of baptism, which would deliver them from death.

With deliverance from death came a new life and regeneration. The phrase "washing of regeneration" in Titus 3:5 was synonymous with "the baptism of regeneration." Weaving together Titus 3:5 and the creation story from Genesis, Methodius of Olympus developed the idea that the church, through intimate union with the Logos, gave birth to the faithful by means of the regeneration granted in baptism; "the illuminated receive [from the Holy Spirit], and by [him] they are rightly begotten into immortality." While he was aware that pagan baptismal rites had the supposed purpose of achieving "regeneration and release from punishment," Tertullian contrasted such rites with Christian baptism, which truly destroyed death by washing away sins. The practice of infant baptism contributed to the development of a more precise doctrine of original sin by Cyprian. His argument was based on the idea that baptism conferred the remission of sins and grace; for "the Son of man came not to destroy men's lives but to save them." Therefore Origen could point to the regeneration and renewal of life that had been effected by the "washing of regeneration" as proof of the transforming power of the gospel and of its superiority to pagan philosophy.

But it does seem that for Origen, as for church doctrine generally, the most distinctive gift of baptism was the gift of the Holy Spirit. As Origen's words suggest, the doctrine of baptism was frequently the context within which the doctrine of the Holy Spirit as the gift of baptism came up for discussion; and since this was long before the dogmatic determination of the doctrine of the Holy Spirit, this tendency to speak of the Holy Spirit in less than "personal" terms may well have held back the development of the full form of the doctrine of the Trinity. Conversely, an earlier settlement of the doctrine of the Holy Spirit within the doctrine of the Trinity might have affected the development of the doctrine of baptism, but in fact this settlement came too late to matter significantly. The association of Christ's baptizing with the gift of the Holy Spirit was attributed to John the Baptist in all four Gospels and appeared in Acts as well; it had established itself early in Christian teaching. Ignatius may have been contrasting the gift of the Holy Spirit through the water of baptism with the promise of the Spirit in other ritual washings when he referred to "eloquent water"; elsewhere, too, he linked baptism and the Holy Spirit. The conferral of the Holy Spirit in conjunction with baptism was the principal doctrinal point in Tertullian's *On Baptism*, where the story of the angel descending on the pool became the occasion for a description of the cleansing in baptism, which was followed by anointing and then by the imposition of hands, through which (rather than through baptism itself) the Holy Spirit was granted. The liturgical evidence in the *Apostolic Tradition* of Hippolytus about the granting of the Holy Spirit to the baptized is garbled in textual transmission and remarkably equivocal on the very question whether baptism itself or some other part of the ritual conferred the Spirit. Although the question cannot be answered from Hippolytus's own teaching either, it is evident that in some way he connected the "washing of regeneration" in Titus 3:5 with the breath of the Holy Spirit, and made the gift of the Holy Spirit contingent on a "cleansing" that came in baptism. Whatever the precise moment of the coming of the Holy Spirit may have been thought to be, Cyprian was expressing a catholic doctrine when he wrote that "water alone is not able to cleanse away sins, and to sanctify a man, unless he also has the Holy Spirit. Therefore it is necessary that they [his opponents on the question of rebaptizing heretics] should grant the Holy Spirit to be there, where they say that baptism is; or else there is no baptism where the Holy Spirit is not, because there cannot be baptism without the Spirit." Tertullian's summary of these four gifts makes it clear "that by the end of the second century, if not fifty years earlier, the doctrine of baptism (even without the aid of controversy to give it precision) was so fully developed that subsequent ages down to our own have found nothing significant to add to it."

The same cannot be said in any sense about the doctrine of the real presence of the body and blood of Christ in the Eucharist, which did not become the subject of controversy until the ninth century. The definitive and precise formulation of the crucial doctrinal issues concerning the Eucharist had to await that controversy and others that followed even later. This does not mean at all, however, that the church did not yet have a doctrine of the Eucharist; it does mean that the statements of its doctrine must

Ign.*Rom*.7.2 (Bihlmeyer 100)

Ign.*Eph*.18.2 (Bihlmeyer 87)

John 5:4

Tert.*Bapt*.5.5 (*CCSL* 1:281)

Tert.*Bapt*.8.1 (*CCSL* 1:283)

Lampe (1956) 128–42

Hipp.*Antichr*.59 (*GCS* 1–II:39–40)

Hipp.*Dan*.4.59.4 (*GCS* 1–I:336)

Cypr.*Ep*.74.5 (*CSEL* 3:803)

E.Evans (1964) xxix

not be sought in polemical and dogmatic treatises devoted to sacramental theology. It means also that the effort to cross-examine the fathers of the second or third century about where they stood in the controversies of the ninth or sixteenth century is both silly and futile.

Perhaps the best illustration of such futility is the controversy that has been carried on, at least since the sixteenth century, over the eucharistic teaching of Irenaeus, especially over one passage. Since it unites the basic themes of eucharistic doctrine, this passage may serve the same function in this discussion of the Eucharist that was served by the passage from Tertullian in our summary of the doctrine of baptism. Arguing, just as Tertullian did, against a dualistic disparagement of creation, Irenaeus used the sacramental practice and teaching of the church to refute Gnostic claims; it was over bread which belonged to the creation that Christ had pronounced his blessing and said, "This is my body." The church had received this tradition from the apostles, and all over the world it made this offering to God: "We offer to him the things that are his own, consistently announcing and confessing the fellowship and unity of flesh and spirit. For as the bread taken from the earth, when it has received the consecration from God, is no longer common bread but is the Eucharist, which consists of two realities, earthly and heavenly; so also our bodies, when they receive the Eucharist, are no longer corruptible, but have the hope of the resurrection into eternal [life]." In the light of the controversy over these words it does seem an exaggeration to say that "nothing can be more express and clear than the language of the fathers upon this point."

Yet it does seem "express and clear" that no orthodox father of the second or third century of whom we have record either declared the presence of the body and blood of Christ in the Eucharist to be no more than symbolic (although Clement and Origen came close to doing so) or specified a process of substantial change by which the presence was effected (although Ignatius and Justin came close to doing so). Within the limits of those excluded extremes was the doctrine of the real presence. Fundamental to that doctrine was the liturgical recollection (ἀνάμνησις) of Christ. It was, according to Justin Martyr, a "recollection of [Christ's] being made flesh for the sake of those who believe in him" and of "the suffering which

*Iren.Haer.*4.17.5 (Harvey 2:197–99)

*Iren.Haer.*4.18.5 (Harvey 2:205–208)

Harvey 2:206

1 Cor.11:24–25

Just.*Dial.*70.4 (Goodspeed 181)

Just.*Dial*.41.1; 117.3
(Goodspeed 138; 235)

Clem.*Str*.2.10.70:4 (*GCS*
52:228)

Or.*Cels*.2.9 (*GCS* 2:136–37);
Or.*Cels*.5.12 (*GCS* 3:13)

Or.*Ex*.13.3 (*GCS* 29:274)

Ign.*Smyrn*.7.1 (Bihlmeyer 108)

Ign.*Rom*.7.3 (Bihlmeyer 100–
101)

Tert.*Marc*.3.19.4 (*CCSL*
1:533);Tert.*Marc*.4.40.1 (*CCSL*
1:656)

Tert.*Res*.8.3 (*CCSL* 2:931)

Just.*Dial*.117.3 (Goodspeed
235); Just.*Dial*.41.1 (Goodspeed 138); Just. *1 Apol*.13
(Goodspeed 33–34)

he underwent" to deliver men from their sins and from the power of evil. But in the act of remembrance the worshiping congregation believed Christ himself to be present among them. That he was also present among them apart from the Eucharist, they affirmed on the basis of such promises as Matthew 18:20, which Clement of Alexandria applied to matrimony, and Matthew 28:20, which Origen cited against Celsus as proof that the presence of God and of Christ was not spatial. Yet the adoration of Christ in the Eucharist through the words and actions of the liturgy seems to have presupposed that this was a special presence, neither distinct from nor merely illustrative of his presence in the church. In some early Christian writers that presupposition was expressed in strikingly realistic language. Ignatius called the Eucharist "the flesh of our Savior Jesus Christ, which suffered for our sins," asserting the reality of Christ's presence in the Eucharist against docetists, who regarded his flesh as a phantasm both in the incarnation and in the Eucharist; Ignatius combined the realism of his eucharistic doctrine with a symbolic implication when he equated the "bread of God" with "the flesh of Jesus Christ," but went on to equate "his blood" with "incorruptible love." Tertullian spoke of the eucharistic bread as a "figure" of the body of Christ, but he also taught that in the Eucharist the flesh of the communicant fed on the flesh and blood of Christ. The theologians did not have adequate concepts within which to formulate a doctrine of the real presence that evidently was already believed by the church even though it was not yet taught by explicit instruction or confessed by creeds.

As Irenaeus's reference to the Eucharist as "not common bread" indicates, however, this doctrine of the real presence believed by the church and affirmed by its liturgy was closely tied to the idea of the Eucharist as a sacrifice. Many of the passages we have already cited concerning the recollection and the real presence spoke also of the sacrifice, as when in several ambiguous passages Justin contrasted the sacrifice of Judaism with the sacrifice offered up in the "remembrance effected by the solid and liquid food" of the Christian Eucharist. One of the most ample and least ambiguous statements of the sacrificial interpretation of the Eucharist in any ante-Nicene theolo-

See p. 25 above

gian was that of Cyprian, who is also one of the earliest authorities for the sacerdotal interpretation of the Christian ministry. In the course of a discussion of liturgical problems, Cyprian laid down the axiom: "If Jesus Christ, our Lord and God, is himself the chief priest of God the Father, and has first offered himself a sacrifice to the Father, and has commanded this to be done in commemoration of himself, certainly that priest truly discharges the office of Christ who imitates that which Christ did; and he then offers a true and full sacrifice in the church to God the Father, when he proceeds to offer it according to what

Cypr.*Ep*.63.14 (*CSEL* 3:713)

he sees Christ himself to have offered." This was based on the belief that "the passion of the Lord is the sacrifice

Cypr.*Ep*.63.17 (*CSEL* 3:714)

which we offer." The sacrifice of Christ on Calvary was a complete offering; the sacrifice of the Eucharist did not add anything to it, nor did it "repeat" it, as though there were more than the one sacrifice. But as the sacrifice of

Gen.14:18
Cypr.*Ep*.63.4 (*CSEL* 3:703)
Cypr.*Ep*.63.14 (*CSEL* 3:713)

Melchizedek the priest "prefigured the sacrament of the sacrifice of the Lord," so the eucharistic sacrifice of the church was performed "in commemoration" of the sac-

Cypr.*Ep*.63.9 (*CSEL* 3:708)

rifice of Good Friday and in "celebration with a legitimate consecration." In other liturgical discussions, too, Cyp-

Cypr.*Laps*.25–26 (*CSEL* 3:255)
Ps. 51:17
Cypr.*Ep*.76.3 (*CSEL* 3:830–31)

rian made it clear that "sacrifice" was an appropriate way of speaking about the Eucharist; but he also insisted that "the sacrifice of a broken spirit" was "a sacrifice to God equally precious and glorious."

Another prominent theme of eucharistic doctrine was the belief that participation in the Lord's Supper would prepare the communicant for immortality. Perhaps the most familiar statement of this theme came in the words of Ignatius, describing the bread of the Eucharist as "the medicine of immortality, the antidote against death, and everlasting life in Jesus Christ." The much-debated words

Ign.*Eph*.20.2 (Bihlmeyer 88)

of Justin about the "transmutation [μεταβολή]" taking

Just. *1 Apol*.66.2 (Goodspeed 74–75)

place in the Eucharist may be a reference either to the change effected in the elements by their consecration or to transformation of the human body through the gift of immortality or to both. Irenaeus explicitly drew a parallel between these two transformations when he declared that the bodies that had received the Eucharist were no longer corruptible, just as the bread that had received the conse-

Iren.*Haer*.4.18.5 (Harvey 2:207–208)

cration was no longer common. On the other hand, it is not self-evident that every echo of this theme was an explicit reference to the Eucharist. When Clement of Alexandria spoke of "the medicine of immortality" as "magnificent," there does not seem to have been any eucharistic overtone in his words. And when Origen, interpreting the petition of the Lord's Prayer for "supersubstantial bread [ὁ ἄρτος ὁ ἐπιούσιος]," defined it as "that [bread] which is most adapted to the rational nature and is akin to its very substance, bringing to the soul health and well-being and strength, and giving to him that eats of it a share of its own immortality," it is not obvious that he was describing the effects of consuming the eucharistic bread. Perhaps his added comment that "the Logos of God is immortal" may serve to explain his language about immortality through the "supersubstantial bread" and much of the language about sacrifice in such writers as Justin, for both themes were ultimately derived from the teaching that Christ the Logos was the true sacrifice and the true gift of immortality.

Both themes, moreover, seem to presuppose the teachings of the church and its liturgical practice. Liturgical evidence suggests an understanding of the Eucharist as a sacrifice, whose relation to the sacrifices of the Old Testament was one of archetype to type, and whose relation to the sacrifice of Calvary was one of "re-presentation," just as the bread of the Eucharist "re-presented" the body of Christ. It would also seem that the spiritualization of material reality in the theology of Clement of Alexandria and Origen went as far as it could without verging on Gnostic heresy; therefore their noneucharistic use of such eucharistic notions as "medicine of immortality" and "bread that confers immortality" would seem to suggest how prominent such notions were in the doctrine that was being expressed by the liturgy and piety of the church. They were spiritualizing what seem to have been prevalent modes of describing the meaning of the Lord's Supper. Those modes of speaking, prevalent in widely scattered remains of the literature, are more important for the development of church doctrine than the spiritualization that was dependent upon them. Great theological refinement was needed before these modes of speaking could be built up into a eucharistic theology; above all, the doctrine of the person of Christ had to be clarified before there could be concepts that could bear the weight of eucharistic teaching. But even with concepts that bent

Clem.*Prot*.10.106.2 (*GCS* 12:76)

Or.*Orat*.27.9 (*GCS* 3:369)

Tert.*Marc*.1.14.3 (*CCSL* 1:455)

under the weight, the church went on celebrating and believing, teaching and experimenting with metaphors, defending and confessing. In its doctrine as in its liturgy, it recalled One who was present in its celebration, and in its corporate experience it was united to that sacrifice by which the promise of eternal life became real.

In many ways it is inappropriate to speak of other "sacraments" in the teaching of the ante-Nicene church, except in the case of penance, whose development during these centuries we have sketched in our discussion of the attribute of holiness in the doctrine of the church, and perhaps also in the case of holy orders, whose indispensability as a prerequisite for the valid celebration of the Eucharist helped to endow holy orders with sacramental status. It was only after the conflict between Augustine and the Donatists that Western theology was able to begin constructing a full-blown theory about the nature and the number of the sacraments, and it was not until the Middle Ages that such a theory was evolved. But the early centuries in the development of doctrine had the assignment of clarifying the function of the church as the means of grace; this clarification was the prerequisite for any understanding of the word of God and the sacraments.

See pp. 156–58 above

See pp. 308–13 below

4

The Mystery
of the Trinity

The climax of the doctrinal development of the early church was the dogma of the Trinity. In this dogma the church vindicated the monotheism that had been at issue in its conflicts with Judaism, and it came to terms with the concept of the Logos, over which it had disputed with paganism. The bond between creation and redemption, which the church had defended against Marcion and other Gnostics, was given creedal status in the confession concerning the relation of the Father to the Son; and the doctrine of the Holy Spirit, whose vagueness had been accentuated by the conflict with Montanism, was incorporated into this confession. The doctrine believed, taught, and confessed by the church catholic of the second and third centuries also led to the Trinity, for in this dogma Christianity drew the line that separated it from pagan supernaturalism and it reaffirmed its character as a religion of salvation.

Such a statement about the relation of the Nicene dogma of the Trinity to the centuries preceding it could, however, give the superficial impression of a greater smoothness than the facts warrant, for the formulation and reformulation of the dogma were called forth by a doctrinal debate more vigorous than any the church had ever experienced. The central question in that debate has been concisely stated as follows: "Is the divine that has appeared on earth and reunited man with God identical with the supreme divine, which rules heaven and earth, or is it a demigod?" The controversy over that question occupied most of the fourth century. Dominating the history of the controversy was the career of Athanasius,

Harnack (1905) 192

172

who became bishop of Alexandria and champion of orthodoxy in 328, three years after the Council of Nicea, and died in 373, only eight years before the Council of Constantinople. Instead of following the controversy in a rigidly chronological way, however, we shall concentrate on the doctrinal issues, the conflicting positions, and the creedal settlements. Such a concentration will also preclude any but the briefest references to the nontheological factors in the debate, many of which seemed ready again and again to determine its outcome, only to be countermanded by other forces like unto themselves. Doctrine often seemed to be the victim—or the product —of church politics and of conflicts of personality. When we turn to a study of the development of the doctrine of the Trinity in its own terms, we are not relegating such factors to a position of unimportance, but only delegating them to another area of historical research.

Christ as Divine

Amid the varieties of metaphor in which they conceived the meaning of salvation, all Christians shared the conviction that salvation was the work of no being less than the Lord of heaven and earth. Amid all the varieties of response to the Gnostic systems, Christians were sure that the Redeemer did not belong to some lower order of divine reality, but was God himself. The oldest surviving sermon of the Christian church after the New Testament opened with the words: "Brethren, we ought so to think of Jesus Christ as of God, as of the judge of living and dead. And we ought not to belittle our salvation; for when

2 *Clem.*1.1–2 (Bihlmeyer 71)

we belittle him, we expect also to receive little." The oldest surviving account of the death of a Christian martyr contained the declaration: "It will be impossible for us to forsake Christ . . . or to worship any other. For

*M.Polyc.*17.2–3 (Bihlmeyer 129–30)

him, being the Son of God, we adore, but the martyrs . . . we cherish." The oldest surviving pagan report about the church described Christians as gathering before sun-

Plin.*Ep.*10.96.7

rise and "singing a hymn to Christ as though to [a] god." The oldest surviving liturgical prayer of the church was

1 Cor.16:22

a prayer addressed to Christ: "Our Lord, come!" Clearly it was the message of what the church believed and taught

Nov.*Trin.*13.71 (Weyer 98)

that "God" was an appropriate name for Jesus Christ. But before this belief and teaching developed into the confession of the Trinity and the dogma of the person of Christ, centuries of clarification and controversy had to intervene, and the relation of this belief to the full range of Christian doctrine had to be defined.

For the one whom the church was calling God was also the one whose suffering and death on the cross were the burden of the church's witness, as the context of several of these very quotations also shows. The claim that he who was God had suffered called forth some of the earliest doctrinal controversy in the church. Speaking for pagan critics of the gospel, Celsus made this claim the object of his attack, and he contended that "the body of a god would not have been born . . . [nor] eat." The Marcionites, citing the words "likeness of sinful flesh" from Romans 8:3, protested against a picture of Christ as a man with a material, suffering body; Simonian Gnosticism taught that Simon "seemed to suffer in Judea, though he did not suffer"; for Ptolemy, the Savior "remained impassible"; and the Gnostic gospels sought to put a screen between the person of the Savior and the pain and suffering described in the canonical Gospels. But the historical principle that the line of demarcation between orthodoxy and heresy must not be drawn prematurely or too precisely is borne out by the evidence that such docetism was not confined to Gnostics and other heretics, but was sufficiently widespread within the churches to evoke the reiterated warnings of early Christian writers. Although the overt assertion that "his suffering was but a make-believe" was the teaching of Gnostics and was early and easily identified as heretical, the example of Clement of Alexandria shows that docetizing tendencies, even among orthodox believers, must be seen as one way to "think of Jesus Christ as of God." That it was a way which gave up too much for the sake of this confession was recognized above all by Ignatius. He insisted that Christ "was really born, and ate and drank, was really persecuted by Pontius Pilate, was really crucified and died . . . really rose from the dead." Yet the very existence of docetism is also a testimony to the tenacity of the conviction that Christ had to be God, even at the cost of his true humanity.

The problems raised by docetism were somewhat premature, for the more subtle and profound implications of these problems had to await the creation of a christological terminology that was equally subtle. They also had

2 *Clem*.1.2 (Bihlmeyer 71);
M.Polyc.17.2 (Bihlmeyer 129)

See pp. 75–76, 89–90 above

Or.*Cels*.2.16 (*GCS* 2:145)
·Or.*Cels*.1.69–70 (*GCS* 2:124)

Tert.*Marc*.5.14.1 (*CCSL* 1:705)

Iren.*Haer*.1.23.3 (Harvey 1:193)

Iren.*Haer*.1.7.2 (Harvey 1:61)

ap.Ign.*Trall*.10 (Bihlmeyer 95)

See p. 47 above

Ign.*Trall*.9 (Bihlmeyer 95)

to await the clarification of the more fundamental problem, which was not the relation of the divine in Christ to his earthly life but the relation of the divine in Christ to the divine in the Father. In the formula of Athanasius, "How is it possible for someone not to err with regard to the incarnate presence [of the Son] if he is altogether ignorant of the genuine and true generation of the Son from the Father?" Consideration of the doctrine of Christ clarified the thought and language of the church about that previous problem, and then, with the help of some of the very same language, returned to the issue of the "twofold proclamation" concerning Christ as both God and man.

*Ath.Ar.*1.8 (*PG* 26:28)

Ps.Ath.*Apoll.*1.10 (*PG* 26:1112)

In the Christian effort to provide biblical grounding and theological definition for the doctrine that Christ was God we may discern at least four sets of Old Testament passages which, when interpreted by the proper method and combined with their counterparts in the New Testament, spoke of Christ as divine: passages of adoption, which, by identifying a point in time at which he became divine, implied that the status of God was conferred on the man Jesus Christ at his baptism or at his resurrection; passages of identity, which, by speaking of Yahweh as "the Lord," posited a simple identification of Christ with God; passages of distinction, which, by speaking of one "Lord" and of another "Lord," drew some difference between them; and passages of derivation, which, by referring to the Father as "the greater" or using such titles as angel, Spirit, Logos, and Son, suggested that he "came from" God and was in some sense less than God.

The first group of passages provided the basis for what Harnack defined as an adoptionist christology: "Jesus is regarded as the man whom God has elected for his own, the one in whom the Deity or the Spirit of God dwelt, and who, after being tested, was adopted by God and endowed with full dominion." Significantly, Harnack adds: "Only one work that explicitly states the adoptionist christology has been preserved for us in its entirety, the *Shepherd* of Hermas." The claim that the *Shepherd* was adoptionist in its doctrine is difficult to prove or disprove, because of the confusing language of the book and because of the literary problems of determining its origin and composition. Such New Testament declarations as the words of Peter in Acts 2:32–36 could be read as

Harnack (1931) 1:211

adoptionism. A widespread tradition of the text of the New Testament, supported by evidence from manuscripts, versions, and early citations from orthodox fathers, rendered the word from the cloud at the baptism of Jesus as the decree of Psalm 2:7: "You are my Son, today I have begotten you"; the Ebionites likewise read the text that way, in support of their teaching that Jesus was a man endowed with special powers of the Spirit.

The baptism of Jesus was apparently regarded as the decisive event in his divine sonship also by Paul of Samosata. Although it seems impossible to reconstruct his teaching from the surviving fragments, he does seem to have called Jesus "Christ" only after the baptism, at which the Logos took up his abode in the man Jesus through the conferral of the Holy Spirit. He also forbade "psalms . . . addressed to our Lord Jesus Christ." This is the valid meaning of the report that Paul "espoused low and mean views as to Christ, contrary to the church's teaching, namely, that he was in his nature an ordinary man," and that he taught that "Jesus Christ is from below." Therefore the union between Jesus and the Logos was not an ontological one, but was analogous to the union between the Christian and the "inner man" or between the prophets of the Old Testament and the inspiring Spirit. Paul's rendition of this doctrine appears to have been more careful than earlier versions of the theory had been. While Theodotus the Cobbler had been condemned for teaching "that Christ was a mere man," Paul incorporated a doctrine of the Logos into his theories and gave them a more adequate exegetical basis. Christian orthodoxy at the middle of the third century did not yet possess a theological formula to "think of Jesus Christ as of God," much less a formula to describe the relation between the divine in him and his days on earth. But orthodoxy was clear enough in its own mind to identify the teachings of Paul of Samosata as "low and mean views" of Christ in his relation to God.

Although adoptionism is today more commonly called "adoptionist Monarchianism" or "dynamic Monarchianism," the label "Monarchian" seems to have been invented by Tertullian to designate those who, declaring that "we maintain the monarchy," protected the "monarchy" of the Godhead by stressing the identity of the Son with the Father without specifying

Just.*Dial*.103.6 (Goodspeed 219)

Luke 3:22

Hipp.*Haer*.7.35.2 (*GCS* 26:222)

Eus.*H.e*.7.30.10 (*GCS* 9:710)

Eus.*H.e*.7.27.2 (*GCS* 9:702)
Eus.*H.e*.7.30.11 (*GCS* 9:710)

Eus.*H.e*.5.28.6 (*GCS* 9:502);
Hipp.*Haer*.7.35 (*GCS* 26:222)

Tert.*Prax*.10.1; 10.6 (*CCSL* 2:1169; 1170)

Tert.*Prax*.3.1 (*CCSL* 2:1161)

Bousset (1913) 312

Mel.*fr*.13–14 (*SC* 123:238–40)

Ign.*Polyc*.3.2 (Bihlmeyer 111)
Tat.*Or*.13 (*TU* 4–I:15)
See pp. 241–42 below

Tert.*Marc*.2.16.3 (*CCSL* 1:493)

Iren.*Dem*.88 (*ACW* 16:102);
Iren.*Haer*.3.20.4 (Harvey
2:108); Tert.*Marc*.4.22.11
(*CCSL* 1:603; Tert.*Carn*.14.6
(*CCSL* 2:900); Cypr.*Test*.2.7
(*CSEL* 3:72)

See pp. 19–20 above

Tert.*Jud*.10.11 (*CCSL*
2:1378)

Tert.*Marc*.3.19.1–3 (*CCSL*
1:533)

the distinction between them with equal precision. In the same treatise, however, Tertullian admitted that "the simple people . . . who are always the majority of the faithful . . . shy at the economy," that is, at the distinction between Father and Son. He conceded that even orthodox believers could speak of the relations within the Trinity in such a way as to emphasize the monarchy at the expense of the economy. This judgment is substantiated by the sources, especially if one pays attention to what has been called the "hymnological theology of the congregation, whose characteristic it is to revel in contradiction." Whether or not they were actually quoting hymns and liturgies, many of the passages in ancient Christian writers which sound like modalistic Monarchianism also sound like snatches from the language of adoration. "He who is impassible suffers and does not take revenge, he who is immortal dies and does not answer a word," said Melito of Sardis; and again: "He who appeared as a lamb, remained the Shepherd." In some of the same words Ignatius praised "the Invisible, who for our sake became visible, the Impassible, who became subject to suffering on our account and for our sake endured everything." Such phrases as "God is born," "the suffering God," or "the dead God" had so established themselves in the unreflecting usage of Christians that even Tertullian, for all his hostility to the Monarchians, could not avoid speaking this way.

This liturgical language found its echo in the exegesis of the passages of identity. The salvation accomplished by Christ was the work of God, as Isaiah 63:9 (LXX) said: "Not an intercessor, nor an angel, but the Lord himself" in a simple and undifferentiated sense was the Savior; Christ as Lord was Yahweh. The amplification of Psalm 96:10 by means of a "Christian midrash" to read "The Lord reigns from the tree" was interpreted to mean, in opposition to Jews, that the Lord had already come and was reigning from the cross, and, in opposition to heretics, that the one who had come in Christ and was reigning from the cross was no one less than the Supreme God himself. Even while claiming the titles "God" and "Lord" for Christ without qualification, Christians also insisted, in what they taught one another within the community and in what they confessed over against paganism and Judaism, that the oneness of God had not been compromised, but on the contrary vindicated, by what had happened in the coming of "our God," Jesus Christ. In a derivative or a metaphorical sense—as passages like Psalm 82:6, interpreted through John 10:34, showed—the term "god" could be applied to creatures. But when the church applied it to Christ, it was contending "not for the name 'God,' for its sound or its written form, but for the substances to which the name belongs."

"In reference to the historical human appearance of Christ," such formulas were "intelligible and, interpreted religiously, even intelligent; but isolated from the historical appearance of Jesus Christ, they sound like the babbling of an idiot." As a liturgical utterance or even as an exegetical tool, the simplistic identification of Jesus Christ as God could be said to make a certain kind of Christian sense. Great difficulties arose, however, when the identification was transposed from belief to teaching, even greater difficulties when it was transposed from teaching to confession. One could speak this way while kneeling to pray, but it was harder to do so when standing to teach or sitting to write. That became evident in modalistic Monarchianism, which may be defined as an effort to provide a theology for the language of devotion. Alleging biblical passages such as those just cited and "making use only of one class of passages," namely, those which made no distinction between the Father and the Son, the modalistic Monarchians contended that "there exists one and the same Being, called Father and Son, not one derived from the other, but himself from himself, nominally called Father and Son according to the changing of times; and that this One is he that appeared [to the patriarchs], and submitted to birth from a virgin, and conversed as man among men. On account of his birth that had taken place he confessed himself to be the Son to those who saw him, while to those who could receive it he did not hide the fact that he was the Father." Both monotheism and the deity of Christ were safeguarded, but there remained no distinction between Father, Son, and Holy Spirit. This theory "thinks it impossible to believe in one God unless it says that Father and Son and Holy Spirit are one and the same." Creation and salvation were the work of one and the same God, who, according to the mode and time of

Iren.*Haer*.3.6.1 (Harvey 2:22); Tert.*Prax*.13.4 (*CCSL* 2:1174)

Tert.*Marc*.1.7.3 (*CCSL* 1:448)

Loofs (1930) 172

Hipp.*Noët*.3 (*PG* 10:805)

Hipp.*Haer*.9.10.11 (*GCS* 26:244–45)

Tert.*Prax*.2.3 (*CCSL* 2:1161)

his appearing, could be called Father or Son or Holy Spirit.

Taken as it stands, that is, as Hippolytus and Tertullian have reported it, this doctrine of the relation between Christ and God turns out to have been a systematization of popular Christian belief. It also turns out to have been rather naïve. A somewhat more subtle version of it appeared, if we are to believe later reports, in the theology of Sabellius, from whom it takes its usual name, Sabellianism. Sabellius is said to have advanced beyond the simpleminded language of Noetus and Praxeas by positing a more precise succession of the manifestations of Father, Son, and Holy Spirit. "What shall we say?" Epiphanius quoted the Sabellians as saying, "Do we have one God or three?" If one, then the words of Isaiah 44:6 applied also to Christ: "Thus says the Lord, the King of Israel and his Redeemer, the Lord of hosts: 'I am the first and I am the last; besides me there is no God.'" Sabellius designated this one God as "Sonfather [υἱοπάτωρ]." Attaching his doctrine to the idea of God as light and the Son of God as radiance, he was said to have used the image of the sun, conceived as one essence with three energies (the light-giving, the warming, and the astrological [σχῆμα]), as an analogy for his Trinity. He was also quoted as saying: "As there are 'diversities of gifts, but the same Spirit,' so also the Father is the same, but is expanded into Son and Spirit." If this somewhat dubious report is accurate, the notion of expansion would seem to have been a way of avoiding the obvious disadvantages in any theory of the relation between Christ and God which lacked a device for distinguishing between them.

That disadvantage was the burden of the polemic against this position, from Tertullian and Hippolytus to Epiphanius and the Pseudo-Athanasian *Fourth Oration against the Arians*. The basic point of the polemic was stated by Tertullian: "As though the one [God] were not [Father, Son, and Holy Spirit] in this way also, that they are all of the one, namely, by unity of substance, while nevertheless the mystery of that economy is protected which disposes the unity into trinity, setting forth Father and Son and Spirit as three, three however not in quality but in sequence, not in substance but in aspect, not in power but in [its] manifestation." Or, more succinctly,

Epiph.*Haer*.62.2.6 (*GCS* 31:391)

Epiph.*Haer*.62.2.2 (*GCS* 31:390)

Ar.*Ep.Alex.* (Opitz 3:12); Didym.*Trin*.3.18 (*PG* 39:881)

1 Cor.12:4

Ps.Ath.*Ar*.4.25 (*PG* 26:505)

Tert.*Prax*.2.4 (*CCSL* 2:1161)

Tertullian accused Praxeas of driving out the Paraclete

Tert.*Prax*.1.5 (*CCSL* 2:1160) and crucifying the Father. This effort to clarify the relation between Christ and God seems to have foundered at the very place where its bête noire, the pluralistic speculation of Marcion and the Gnostics, did: the crucifixion and death of the one who was called God.

Such a teaching utterly contradicted the impassibility

See pp. 52–54 above of God. According to Hippolytus, Noetus reasoned thus: "I am under necessity, since one [God] is acknowledged, to make this One the subject of suffering. For Christ was God, and suffered on account of us, being himself the

Hipp.*Noët*.2 (*PG* 10:805) Father, that he might be able to save us." This was, Hippolytus responded, a "rash and audacious dogma [that] the Father is himself Christ, himself the Son, himself was born, himself suffered, himself raised him-

Hipp.*Noët*.3 (*PG* 10:808) self." Carrying the modalist position to its unavoidable consequences, Tertullian argued that, contrary to their intentions, the Monarchians ended up separating one God from another even as they abolished the distinction

Rom.8:11 between Father and Son; for "he who raised up Christ and is also to raise up our mortal bodies will be as it were another raiser-up than the Father who died and the Father who was raised up, if it is the case that Christ

Tert.*Prax*.28.13 (*CCSL* 2:1202) who died is the Father." Tertullian's comment, immediately following, was: "Let this blasphemy be silent, let it be silent. Let it be enough to say that Christ the Son

Tert.*Prax*.29.1 (*CCSL* 2:1202) died, and this [only] because it is so written." It was difficult enough to ascribe suffering and death to the Son of God, so that in the absence of overwhelming biblical evidence one would shrink even from that; but it was sheer blasphemy to ascribe them to the Godhead in an undifferentiated sense. It also implied that the curse of the cross, pronounced by the Father on the Son for the sake of mankind, would now be pronounced on the Father himself; for "just as a thing said of anyone of whom it may appropriately be said is said without blasphemy [that is, of Christ], so what is not appropriate is

Tert.*Prax*.29.4 (*CCSL* 2:1202) blasphemy if it is said [that is, of the Father]." The Father could not share in the suffering of the Son.

The Monarchian teaching collided no less directly with the main body of Christian exegesis. For although passages of identity such as Isaiah 63:9 (LXX) meant that "not an intercessor, nor an angel, but the Lord himself" had acted to save man in the cross of Christ, Christian exegesis paid special attention to passages of distinction in the Old Testament, where one "Lord" was discriminated from another "Lord" or some other distinction was posited which, while not negating the appropriateness of such titles as "Lord" or even "God" for Christ, still provided a warrant for transcending the simpleminded identification of the Father with the Son. Genesis 19:24 meant to Justin that there had to be some distinction between "the Father and Lord of all" and "the Lord" who was Christ, and again between "the Lord who received a commission" and "the Lord who [remains] in heaven"; to Irenaeus it meant that neither the Holy Spirit nor the apostles would use the title "Lord" for anyone "except God the Father ruling over all, and his Son who has received dominion from his Father over all creation"; to Tertullian it was proof for a distinction between Father and Son. Justin, Irenaeus, and Tertullian all linked Genesis 19:24 more or less closely with Psalm 110:1; both passages meant that "since the Father is truly Lord, and the Son truly Lord, the Holy Spirit has fitly designated them by the title of Lord." Even the most explicit identification of Christ as God in the New Testament—Romans 9:5, "who is God, blessed forever," which Noetus and Praxeas seem to have quoted in support of the Monarchian position—did indeed mean that the name "God" could rightly be applied to Christ, but it implied no less that there was a distinction. Whether or not the so-called Monarchian prologues to the Gospels were in fact composed with this tendency in view, Monarchian exegesis had a difficult time squaring itself with the use of the second and third person permeating the language of Christ about the Father in the New Testament and attributed to Christ in the orthodox interpretation of the Old.

Despite its attempt to validate its orthodoxy by reference to the usage of Christian devotion, therefore, the Monarchian resolution of the problem was condemned as heresy, first by the all but unanimous verdict of the defenders of orthodoxy (a notable exception being Zephyrinus, bishop of Rome) and then formally by such gatherings as the sixth-century Synod of Braga, which decreed: "If anyone does not confess that the Father and the Son and the Holy Spirit are three persons of one essence and virtue and power, as the catholic and apos-

Just.*Dial*.127.5 (Goodspeed 249)

Just.*Dial*.56.23 (Goodspeed 160)

Iren.*Haer*.3.6.1 (Harvey 2:20–21)

Tert.*Prax*.16.2 (*CCSL* 2:1181)

Iren.*Haer*.3.6.1 (Harvey 2:21)

Hipp.*Noët*.6 (*PG* 10:812)

Tert.*Prax*.15.7 (*CCSL* 2:1180)

Hipp.*Haer*.9.11.3 (*GCS* 26:246)

tolic church teaches, but says that [they are] a single and solitary person, in such a way that the Father is the same as the Son and this One is also the Paraclete Spirit, as Sabellius and Priscillian have said, let him be anathema." The very date of that synod, however, indicates that though the Monarchian position may have been anathema, the question it raised and the intuition it represented could not be dismissed so easily.

Later forms of christological speculation must also be read as efforts to involve the God of Jesus Christ in the cross of Jesus Christ; for here again Isaiah 63:9 (LXX) was taken to mean that "not an intercessor, nor an angel, but the Lord himself has saved us, and not by the death of someone else nor by the intervention of an ordinary man, but by his own blood." And in the Theopaschitic controversy, one of the fundamental issues was the one already at stake here, so that those who employed the liturgical formula "Holy is God, he who was crucified for us" had to defend themselves against the charge of reviving the Sabellian heresy. In other ways, too, the Monarchian position has continued to crop up even after its condemnation. For throughout Christian history "men have been frequently condemned for denying the deity of Christ but rarely for denying the distinction between the Father and the Son. To deny the former has generally seemed unchristian; to deny the latter only unintelligible."

Developing alongside the Monarchian hypothesis and interacting with it and with one another were various ways of speaking about Christ as divine, based on what we have called the passages of derivation. These passages eventually became the key to the orthodox understanding both of the passages of identity and the passages of distinction. Some of the titles taken from them proved to be inadequate or misleading and virtually disappeared from the language of the church. To others the future belonged, especially as they caught up the connotations of those that had been discarded.

Among the titles of derivation tried, evaluated, and finally rejected was the designation of the divine in Christ as angel. It came, at least in part, from those passages of the Old Testament in which "the angel of the Lord" was identified by Christian exegesis with the preexistent Christ. Justin Martyr, in the same discourse from his *Dialogue with Trypho* in which he emphasized the distinction implied by the words, "the Lord rained brim-

Mansi 9:774

Cyr.Chr.un. (SC 97:472)

See pp. 270–71 below

McGiffert (1947) 1:275

stone and fire from the Lord" in Genesis 19:24 and the distinction made between "the Lord" and "my Lord" in Psalm 110:1, also proved from the epiphany at Mamre that of the three angels who appeared to Abraham "one is God and is called 'angel,' because he brings messages." This designation of Christ as "angel" frequently appeared in a liturgical context. It seems to have been especially prominent in the *Shepherd* of Hermas—seems, we have to say, not only because precise interpretation of the *Shepherd* is difficult, but also because this same book has been regarded as the chief extant expression of adoptionism and has also been taken as a primary source for those who posit the existence of binitarianism alongside trinitarianism. Not only did several of the references to angels in the *Shepherd* evidently mean the preexistent Christ, but Christ was also identified with the archangel Michael, "who has the power over this people and is their captain. For this is he that puts the law into the hearts of believers."

On the strength of these passages and a few others like them, an "angel christology" has been set forth as the standard theory about the person of Jesus Christ in primitive Christianity, indeed, as the only hypothesis that can explain why christology simply did not yet constitute a theological issue. "If, for the Jewish Christianity of the primitive apostolic community as well as for Paul, the Christ is interpreted, in accordance with late Jewish apocalypticism, as a being of the higher angelic world, created and chosen by God for the task of inaugurating the new aeon of the kingdom of God at the end of time in a battle with the spiritual powers of the existing world; then there is no need for any new problem to arise at all with regard to the relation of the Christ to God." But the evidence from surviving sources appears considerably more ambiguous. The references to Christ as "angel" in Justin must be seen in context, as, for example: "Christ is king, and priest, and God, and Lord, and angel, and man, and captain, and stone, and a Son born, and first made subject to suffering, then returning to heaven, and again coming with glory, and he is preached as having the everlasting kingdom." Significantly, Christ continued to be called "prince of angels" by orthodox theologians—Greek, Latin, and Syriac—in the third and even the fourth centuries. Of course, it may be that other remnants of an angel christology, together with the other

Gen.18:2

Just.*Dial*.56.4 (Goodspeed 156)

See p. 175 above

Herm.*Sim*.8.3.3.69 (*SC* 53:266–68)

Werner (1941) 311

Just.*Dial*.34.2 (Goodspeed 128)

Cyr.H.*Catech*.10.10 (Reischl-Rupp 1:272); Nov.*Trin*.11.57 (Weyer 84); Lact.*Inst*.4.14.17 (*CSEL* 19:328); Ephr.*Serm*. 1.36 (*CSCO* 88:2[89:2])

remnants of adoptionism, have been deleted by later
orthodox expurgations; but even with the discovery of
Gnostic and other texts, the existence of such remnants
remains at least as much "an altogether unprovable
hypothesis" as is the "latent christological problematic

Werner (1941) 311

of primitive Christianity."

Considerably more evidence exists for the hypothesis
that "Spirit" was a term widely used in ante-Nicene
Christian doctrine for the divine in Christ. The distinction between "according to the flesh" and "according to
the Spirit" in Romans 1:3–4 may well be called one of the
oldest of christological formulas. Whether or not it may
also be called one of the oldest of trinitarian formulas is,
however, quite another matter; for when combined with
2 Corinthians 3:17, it can be taken as one of the earliest

Macholz (1902)

"traces of a binitarian mode of thinking," that is, of a
theory of the divine nature according to which only two,
rather than three, forms of the divine were to be distinguished: the Father and the Son-Spirit. Ignatius,
for example, employing the distinction of Romans
1:3–4, described Christ as "one physician, both car-

Ign.*Eph*.7.2 (Bihlmeyer 84)

nal and spiritual, born and unborn"; from this it
has been concluded that the "unborn," eternal, and pre-

Loofs (1930) 199–200

existent in him was the Spirit. Some of the most striking statements of this identification occurred in Hermas,
for example: "The holy preexistent Spirit, which created
the whole creation, God made to dwell in flesh that he

Herm.*Sim*.5.6.5.59 (*SC*
53:238)

desired," namely, the flesh of Jesus. Celsus thought he
was giving an account of Christian belief when he said
that, according to the church, God "thrust his own Spirit
into a body like ours, and sent him down here, that we

ap.Or.*Cels*.6.69 (*GCS* 3:139)

might be able to hear and learn from him." And the
works of Tertullian, at least before his Montanist period
and the treatise *Against Praxeas,* contained many passages
in which Christ and the Spirit were equated, as in the
opening words of his treatise *On Prayer:* "The Spirit of
God, and the Word of God, and the Reason of God—
Word of Reason, and Reason and Spirit of Word—Jesus
Christ our Lord, namely, who is both the one and the
other. . . . Our Lord Jesus Christ has been approved as
the Spirit of God, and the Word of God, and the Reason
of God: the Spirit, by which he was mighty; the Word,

Tert.*Orat*.1.1–2 (*CCSL* 1:257)

by which he taught; the Reason, by which he came." In
Aphraates also, a "Spirit christology" has been found,

although mistakenly; and even Clement of Alexandria, despite his general reluctance to speak even of God as Spirit, could speak of "the Lord Jesus, that is, the Word of God, the Spirit incarnate, the heavenly flesh sanctified."

From these and similar passages it is clear that in what it believed and taught intramurally the church did not hesitate to use the term "Spirit" as a more or less technical term for the preexistent divine in Christ. It should also be noted that the readiness to address hymns and prayers to Christ was not matched by a similar readiness with regard to the Holy Spirit; even in medieval liturgical usage, *Veni Creator Spiritus* and *Veni Sancte Spiritus* were among the few prayers to the Spirit, as distinguished from many prayers for the Spirit. The question of the place of the Holy Spirit within the Trinity was raised, debated, and dogmatically adjudicated, all within a decade or two, and it was left to the medieval debates between East and West to probe the matter more deeply. So persistent was the connection between Spirit and Christ, moreover, that in the so-called Niceno-Constantinopolitan creed, in the recension quoted in the acts of the Council of Chalcedon of 451, the article on the Holy Spirit read: "And in the Holy Spirit, the Lordly, the life-giving," where "Lordly [κύριον]" was not a noun but an adjective relating the Spirit to the Son as Lord. And the use of "Lord" for the Spirit in 2 Corinthians 3:17 continued to require explanation even after the trinitarian issues appeared settled.

Yet as this creedal formulation suggests, the process of giving confessional and theological expression to what it believed and taught compelled the church to clarify the confusion between the Spirit and the divine in Christ. It does seem peremptory to shrug the problem off with the comment that "if from the middle of the first century the same people were both Binitarians and Trinitarians, their Binitarianism cannot have amounted to much in actual fact. . . . Christ is constantly described as a 'spirit' by the Fathers, in virtue of His divine nature; but this usage has nothing to do with an identification between Him and 'the Holy Spirit.'" But the substance of the comment is valid. The use of "Spirit" for the divine in Christ was most prominent in those early Christian writings which still showed marks of the Jewish origins of Christianity; at the same time even these writings also

Clem.*Paed*.1.6.43.3 (*GCS* 12:116)

See pp. 211–19 below

Symb.Nic.–CP (Schaff 2:57)

Hil.*Trin*.2.32 (*PL* 10:72–73); Aug.*Trin*.2.10.19 (*CCSL* 50:105–106)

Prestige (1956) xxiii

echoed the trinitarian language of the church. The conflict with Stoicism seems to have been a significant force
in inhibiting the unreflective use of "Spirit" as a term
for the divine in Christ, even, in fact, as a term for God.
The distinction between "according to the flesh" and
"according to the Spirit" in Romans 1:3–4 was originally
a way of speaking about the relation between the divine
and the human in Christ (for which it was to prove
useful again), not about the relation between the divine
in Christ and the divine in the Father and the Holy
Spirit. As the encounter with Greek paganism and the
conflict with heresy made greater precision of thought
and terminology an absolute necessity, "Spirit" was no
longer an adequate way of identifying the divine in
Christ.

It was replaced by two titles of derivation which had
been present in Christian language since the New Testament, but which largely took over the functions of all
the titles we have been discussing: Logos and Son of
God. In the apologists, as well as in the apologetic writings of theologians such as Origen and Tertullian who
also spoke to the church, "Spirit" was largely, if not
completely, displaced by "Logos" as the technical term
for the divine in Christ. Particularly among the latter
group of theologians, "Logos" never lost the Old Testament connotations which, despite the term's eventual role
as an apologetic device, had originally been the basis
of its appearance in the Christian vocabulary. In fact,
if we concentrate on the entire body of Christian literature rather than on the apologetic corpus, it becomes
evident that the basis for the fullest statement of the
Christian doctrine of the divine in Christ as Logos was
provided not by its obvious documentation in John 1:1–
14 but by Proverbs 8:22–31 (LXX)—which may, for
that matter, have been more prominent in the background
of the Johannine prologue than theologians have recognized. Even in the apologetic work of Justin, for example,
the notion of the Logos did not play a significant role
despite its place in the usage of the church. The doctrine
of the Logos was peculiarly suited to the task of expressing what the church believed and taught even as it also
came to summarize what the church was obliged to
confess.

One indication of the presence within Christian teaching of a doctrine of the Logos not primarily determined by Greek cosmological speculation was the translation of the term as "sermo" in some of the earliest Latin versions of the New Testament. For Tertullian—who also

Tert.*Apol.*21.10 (*CCSL* 1:124)

employed the term "verbum," for example in his *Apology* —"sermo" was the term for the Logos used most often in

Tert.*Prax.*6.3–4 (*CCSL* 2:1163–64); Tert.*Herm.*20.4 (*CCSL* 1:414) Cypr.*Domin.orat.*1 (*CSEL* 3:267)

his specifically christological writings, the treatises against Hermogenes and against Praxeas. Christ as "Word of God" was, according to Cyprian, "the sermo of God, who was in the prophets,""the sermo of God, our Lord

Cypr.*Test.*2.3 (*CSEL* 3:64–65)

Jesus Christ," or even the "verbum sermo." By the time of Novatian, "sermo," while still referring principally to "an immanent conception of the relations between Father and Son," was also being interpreted "as a timeless and

Kriebel (1932) 64

therefore eternal substantia in God." And even Jerome still employed "sermo" (interestingly, in a translation of

Hier.*Hom.Orig.in Luc.*5 (*PL* 26:229)

Origen) for the Logos. Of course, the continuity between Christ as the Logos and the speaking of God in the Old Testament prophets was a theme not confined to the Latin fathers and their use of "sermo." Ignatius, for example, "meant by Logos the Spoken Word, not indwelling Reason. . . . The fact that for Ignatius the connotations of the term 'Logos' are those which contrast it with

Corwin (1960) 126

speech shows he is not using it in a philosophical sense." While Irenaeus could speak of the Logos glorifying the

Iren.*Haer.*4.14.1 (Harvey 2:184)

Father before the foundation of the world, such a state-

Schmaus (1927) 42

ment, for all its "Augustinian" overtones, is not primarily a speculative doctrine of the Logos as a cosmological principle, but a definition of the Logos as the divine agent of revelation. Although Irenaeus was not unacquainted with the apologetic doctrine of the Logos, he made relatively little use of it. The use of the idea of Logos in Revelation 19:13 should have shown that there was a place in the language of the church for a conception of this idea which owed very little to philosophical speculation.

It is, nevertheless, the Christian adaptation of the Greek idea of the Logos for the purposes of apologetics and philosophical theology that has figured most prominently in the secondary literature, and for a good reason. The idea of the seminal Logos provided the apologists with a device for correlating Christian revelation not only with the message of the Old Testament, but also with the glimpses of the truth that had been granted

See pp. 31–32 above

to classical philosophers. As is evident from John 1:3 and its background in Proverbs 8:30, the doctrine of the preexistent Logos was also a means of correlating the redemption accomplished in Jesus Christ with the doctrine of creation. Creation, revelation both general and special, and redemption could all be ascribed to the Logos; the presupposition for each of these activities was the transcendence of God, who "cannot be contained, and is not found in a place, for there is no place of his rest; but his Logos, through whom he made all things, being his power and wisdom" was the agent through whom God had dealt with mankind, achieving his purpose of creation and revealing his will. In his defense of the divinity of Christ in the *Apology,* Tertullian described how his miracles while on earth "prove that he was the Logos of God, that primordial first-begotten Word, accompanied by power and reason, and based on the Spirit; that he who was now doing all things by his word and he who had done that of old were one and the same."

Theoph.*Autol.*2.22 (*SC* 20:154)

Tert.*Apol.*21.17(var.) (*CCSL* 1:125)

The Logos who eventually appeared in Jesus Christ, then, was the "principle [ἀρχή]" of creation; God "had this Logos as a helper in the things that were created by him, and by him he made all things. He [the Logos] is called principle because he rules, and is Lord of all things fashioned by him." But as Logos, he was also the principle of rationality, in God and in the rational creatures. The Christians, so Athenagoras insisted, were not atheists; for they taught a God "who is apprehended by the understanding only and the reason," who, "as the eternal mind, had the Reason within himself, being from eternity endowed with reason." As the radiance of the glory spoken in Hebrews 1:3, the Logos both irradiated "the partial radiances of the remaining rational creation" and transcended them. As the principle of rationality, he became, in turn, the principle of speech or discourse; for "God is not discursive from the beginning but is rational even before the beginning." So, in turn, the Logos was the principle of revelation. He had "come down upon the prophets, and through them spoken of the creation of the world and of all other things." And now this very Logos, principle of creation and of rationality, of speech and of revelation, had become incarnate: "The Logos is to be contemplated by the mind. . . . An idea is a conception of God; and this the barbarians have

Theoph.*Autol.*2.10 (*SC* 20:122)

Athenag.*Leg.*10.1 (Goodspeed 324)

Or.*Jo.*32.28.353 (*GCS* 10:474)

Tert.*Prax.*6.3 (*CCSL* 2:1164)

Theoph.*Autol.*2.10 (*SC* 20:122)

termed the Logos of God. . . . The Logos issuing forth was the cause of creation. Then also he generated himself, when the Word became flesh, that he might be seen."

There is one function of the Logos doctrine to which we have not referred directly; it served as a way of giving respectability to the more usual title of derivation for the divine in Christ, namely, "Son of God." Celsus accused Christians of "sophistry when they say that the Son of God is the very Logos himself," for "although we proclaim the Son of God to be Logos we do not bring forward as evidence a pure and holy Logos, but a man who was arrested most disgracefully and crucified." In allusion to the accusation stated by Celsus—that crucifixion was unworthy of the Logos—and in explicit response to the accusation that Christianity was reintroducing crude notions of divine sonship into the idea of the divine, Athenagoras warned: "Let no one laugh at the idea of God having a Son! This is not a case of the myths of the poets who make the gods out to be no better than men; we have no such idea about God the Father or the Son. The Son of God is the Logos of the Father in thought and in power." Theophilus, too, explained that "the Logos of God is also his Son." Similarly, both Ignatius and Irenaeus expressed the simple equation of the Logos with the Son. Although it cannot be determined statistically, there is reason to believe that when Christians spoke to fellow Christians about the divine in Christ, they ordinarily called him "Son of God."

In a baptismal creed that found its way into a textual variant of the New Testament there was the confession: "I believe that Jesus Christ [or simply 'Jesus'] is the Son of God." It has become part of the conventional scholarly wisdom that in the New Testament "Son of God" had referred to the historical person of Jesus, not to a preexistent being. Therefore "the transfer of the concept 'Son' to the preexistent Christ is the most significant factor in the pluralistic distortion of the Christian doctrine of God . . . and the monstrosities of the Monophysitic christology." Whether or not we accept this interpretation of the New Testament, the development of doctrine attached itself to "the view that saw the divine sonship grounded in preexistence. . . . Christology acquired the contours which henceforth were normative for theological

Clem.*Str.*5.3.16.1–5 (*GCS* 52:336)

Hipp.*Noët.*15 (*PG* 10:821)

Or.*Cels.*2.31 (*GCS* 2:158)

See pp. 28–29 above

Athenag.*Leg.*10.1–2 (Goodspeed 324)
Theoph.*Autol.*2.22 (*SC* 20:154)

Ign.*Magn.*8.2 (Bihlmeyer 90–91); Iren.*Haer.*4.20.3 (Harvey 2:214)

Acts 8:37

Loofs (1924) 314–15

explication and in whose framework its further development took place." By what may be called "a collation of
images" the title Son of God was able to take up into
itself not only the content of other titles of derivation
such as Logos, but also the connotations of almost all the
other sets of passages for the divine in Christ, each of
which contributed something to the eventual understanding of the content of "Son," whether or not this had
originally belonged to this title.

Among the various passages of adoption, Psalm 2:7
had a special place, the baptism of Jesus or his resurrection being interpreted as the point at which he was
adopted or "designated" Son of God. With the discovery
that the "today" in the decree of the psalm did not refer
to any day in the earthly life of Jesus, but that it antedated the foundation of the world, indeed, that these
words were spoken "unconditionally and without regard
to time," this and other passages of adoption were no
longer a source of embarrassment to trinitarian orthodoxy.
Isaiah 63:9 (LXX) epitomized the passages of identity,
and Monarchian exegesis took advantage of its lack of
any distinction; but even this passage could be accommodated to the eternal sonship of Christ. "Not an ambas-
sador, nor an angel, but the Lord himself saved us. Therefore we also bless thee, O Lord; thou with the Father and
the Holy Spirit art blessed before the ages and forever."
Among the passages of distinction between "Lord" and
"Lord," none was more prominent than Psalm 110:1,
in which there was, to be sure, no reference to any kind
of derivation of one Lord from another; but when this
passage was conflated with a passage of adoption such as
Psalm 2:8, it could form part of the biblical proof for the
thesis that "the rule of truth teaches us to believe, after
the Father, also in the Son of God, Christ Jesus, the Lord
our God, but the Son of God." So it was that as "Son
of God" Jesus was at the same time everything else that
all the other passages of the Old Testament said he was—
not less than any of these, but more than all of them. Yet
even the dual designation of him as Logos and Son of
God, as set forth in the passages of derivation, left un-
clarified his oneness with the one eternal God, as set
forth in the passages of identification and even in the
passages of distinction. The specification of what this
implied was called forth by the Arian challenge.

F.Hahn (1963) 315

Just.*Dial*.88.8 (Goodspeed 203); Tert.*Prax*.7.2 (*CCSL* 2:1165)

Meth.*Symp*.8.9 (*GCS* 27:91)

Ps.Meth.*Palm*.6 (*PG* 18:396)

Nov.*Trin*.9.46 (Weyer 74)

Christ as Creature

The use of the titles Logos and Son of God to interpret and correlate the passages of adoption, passages of identity, passages of distinction, and passages of derivation was a theological tour de force accomplished by the theologians of the second and third centuries, including Tertullian and Novatian in the West, and above all Origen in the East. In Origen's doctrine of the Logos, however, there were "two sets of ideas. From the oscillation between them proceeds the ambiguity, characteristic of the Logos theology of Origen, that Christ the Logos is thought of in a thoroughly personal way and [yet possesses] many impersonal features. [The two sets of ideas] are the idea of the indwelling of Christ in the heart, derived from Holy Scripture, and its speculative interpretation, taken over from the Greek doctrine of

Lieske (1938) 114

the Logos." Even more important for the development of doctrine was a related ambiguity in Origen, and not only in Origen. In one sense, the logic of Origen's anti-Sabellian exegesis led to the insistence that the Logos was distinct from the Father, but eternal, so that none

Or.*Princ*.4.4.1 (*GCS* 22:349); Ath.*Dec*.27.2 (Opitz 2:23)

could "dare to lay down a beginning for the Son, before which he did not exist." But at the same time Origen interpreted the passages of distinction and especially the passages of derivation in such a way as to make the Logos

Or.*Princ*.4.4.1 (*GCS* 22:349)

a creature and subordinate to God, "the firstborn of all creation, a thing created, wisdom." And in support of this latter interpretation his chief proof was Proverbs 8:22–31 (LXX).

The trinitarian and christological exegesis of this passage of distinction had used it to specify how the pre-existent Logos was to be distinguished from the creatures. For Athenagoras, it meant that God, being eternally "endowed with reason [λογικός]," had the Logos within himself eternally, and that therefore the Son, as Logos,

Athenag.*Leg*.10.2 (Goodspeed 324)

"did not come into existence" but was eternal. Hippolytus

Hipp.*Haer*.6.14.3 (*GCS* 26:139)

paraphrased the passage to read: "He begot me before all ages." Identifying the Logos as "Spirit of God and principle of creation and wisdom and power of the Most High," Theophilus attributed to him the inspiration

Theoph.*Autol*.2.10 (*SC* 20:122)

of the Old Testament prophets. The prophets had not existed before the world began, but the Wisdom that was in God and the Logos that was present with God had, as Proverbs 8:27 proved. There appears to have been a confusion between the preexistent Logos and the Spirit not only in this passage from Theophilus, but in other trinitarian interpretations of Proverbs 8:22–31. Irenaeus, having supplied several biblical proofs "that the Logos, that is, the Son, was always with the Father," went on to prove from the discussion of wisdom in Proverbs 3:19–20 that the same was true of the Spirit. This was then followed by long quotations of Proverbs 8:22–25, 27–31, leaving it unclear whether it was the eternal preexistence of the Son or that of the Spirit or both that was thought

Iren.*Haer*.4.20.3–4 (Harvey 2:214–15)

to be demonstrated by these passages. Proverbs 8:22–31 served to distinguish not only between Christ and the creatures, but also between the Logos and the Father. In the classic statement of the latter distinction, the *Against Praxeas* of Tertullian, the text from Proverbs

Tert.*Prax*.7.3 (CCSL 2:1165–66)

occupied a dominant place; and Tertullian supplied what would be a proper paraphrase of the text if his Monarchian opponents were right: "I, the Lord, founded myself as the beginning of my own ways for the sake of my

Tert.*Prax*.11.3 (CCSL 2:1171)

works." The distinctness of the Logos both from the creature and from the Father had already been seen in the text by Justin in his polemic against Judaism; for Proverbs 8:22–25 meant "that this offspring was begotten by the Father before all creatures, and that what is begotten is

Just.*Dial*.129.4 (Goodspeed 251)

another in number than the one who begets."

Ironically, as Hilary observed about the Arian use of Proverbs 8:22–31, "these weapons, granted to the church in its battle against the synagogue," came to be used

Hil.*Trin*.12.36 (PL 10:454)

"against the faith set forth in the church's proclamation." As a "passage of distinction," Proverbs 8:22–23 easily became a passage of subordination; for it said: "The Lord created me" and "before the age he established me." We have already noted Origen's exegesis of the passage against the Sabellian blurring of the distinction between the Logos and the Father. Origen's pupil, Dionysius of Alexandria, carried this anti-Sabellian exegesis even further, declaring "that the Son of God is a creature and something made, not his own by nature, but alien in essence from the Father. . . . Being a creature,

ap.Ath.*Dion*.4.2 (Opitz 2:48)

he did not exist before he came into being." From the surviving fragments of his writings it seems that the word "created" in Proverbs 8:22 was the proof, as

ap.Ath.*Dion*.10–11 (Opitz 2:53–54)

Sabellianism was the provocation, of this doctrine. His

namesake and contemporary, Dionysius of Rome, without identifying his target by name, inveighed against the "absurdities" of such an exegesis of the word "created." Those who claimed, on the basis of Proverbs 8:22, "that the Son is a work," had "missed the truth completely" and were setting forth an exegesis that was "contrary to the meaning of the divine and prophetic Scripture." In this passage "he created" did not mean the same as "he made"; it meant being begotten, not being made. Athanasius, to whom we owe the preservation of the passages from both the Roman and the Alexandrian Dionysius, used the words of Dionysius of Rome to exonerate Dionysius of Alexandria of the charge of paternity for Arianism and to prove that the Arian exegesis of Proverbs 8:22–31 could not claim continuity with the fathers.

Although the transmission of the documents of Arianism is even more confused than that of other heretical literature, it does seem clear that the Arian controversy broke out over the exegesis of Proverbs 8:22–31. According to the emperor Constantine, it came when Bishop Alexander of Alexandria called upon several presbyters, especially Arius, to give an account of their opinions "about a certain passage in the divine law," which was "presumably Proverbs 8:22ff." The terminology of this passage is certainly prominent in the few surviving documents of Arianism. In his letter to Eusebius, Arius wrote, quoting Proverbs 8:22–23: "Before he was begotten or created or ordained or established, he did not exist." In the confession which he and his colleagues addressed to Alexander, he quoted the same verbs in asserting that the Son had been "begotten timelessly by the Father and created before ages and established." In his account of Arian doctrine, Hilary said that "they maintain that [Christ] is a creature, because of what is written" in Proverbs 8:22. Indeed, of all the Arian arguments which, according to Hilary, threatened shipwreck to the orthodox faith, this passage was "the greatest billow in the storm they raise, the big wave of the whirling tempest." And Didymus called it "the primary objection," as well as "the most irreligious and absurd," put forth by the heretics.

Yet Constantine's diagnosis of the origins of Arianism spoke not only of the "passage in the divine law" over

ap.Ath.*Decr*.26.5 (Opitz 2:22)

Ath.*Dion*.6 (Opitz 2:49–50)

Ath.*Dion*.27 (Opitz 2:66–67)

ap.Eus.*V.C*.2.69.1 (GCS 7:68)
Schwartz (1938) 3:157

Ar.*Ep.Eus*.5 (Opitz 3:3)

Ar.*Ep.Alex*.4 (Opitz 3:13)

Hil.*Trin*.4.11 (*PL* 10:104)

Hil.*Trin*.12.1 (*PL* 10:434)

Didym.*Trin*.3.3 (*PG* 39:805)

whose exegesis there had been controversy, but also of an "unprofitable question" raised by Arius which had led him to speculations that were better left alone. It was, then, the exegesis of Proverbs 8:22–31 in the light of a particular set of theological a prioris which produced the Arian doctrine of Christ as creature. At least some of these may be reconstructed from the fragmentary evidence. One such a priori which may be identified is a special version of the absoluteness of God. The fundamental idea in the Arian doctrine of God was "one and only [μόνος]." God was "the only unbegotten, the only eternal, the only one without beginning, the only true, the only one who has immortality, the only wise, the only good, the only potentate." Even "one and only" was not absolute enough; it had to be raised to a superlative, so that God was "without beginning and utterly one [ἄναρχος μονώτατος]." God was "a monad [μονάς]." There had always been a divine monad, but a dyad had come into being with the generation of the Son and a triad with the production of the Spirit or wisdom. Therefore "the triad is not eternal, but there was a monad first." No understanding of the Logos as divine could be permitted in any way to compromise this arithmetical oneness of God, who "alone" created his "only" Son. Originally and fundamentally, then, "God was alone."

So stark a monotheism implied an equally uncompromising view of divine transcendence. The metaphor of the Son's derivation from the Father "as a torch from a torch" was rejected both by the Arians and by their opponents: by the anti-Arians because it implied that "the substance [of the Father and the Son] is something separate from either person"; by the Arians for the very opposite reason, because it suggested a continuity of ousia (essence) between the Father and the Son, which violated the transcendence of God. No action of God, neither the creation of the world nor the generation of the Logos, could be interpreted in such a way as to support the notion that "the Father had deprived himself of what he possesses in an ungenerated way within himself, for he is the source of everything." God was "the monad and the principle of creation of all things," and he did not share this with anyone, not even with the Logos. Any other conception of God would, according to Arius, make the Father "composite and divisible and mutable and a body." But "the

ap.Eus.V.C.2.69.1 (GCS 7:68)

ap.Didym.Trin.3.16 (PG 39:865)

Ar.Ep.Alex.2 (Opitz 3:12)

Ar.Ep.Alex.4 (Opitz 3:13)

ap.Ath.Syn.15.3 (Opitz 2:243)
ap.Ath.Ar.1.17 (PG 26:48)

Ath.Ar.2.24 (PG 26:197)
ap.Ath.Ep.Aeg.Lib.12 (PG 25:565)

Ar.Ep.Alex.3 (Opitz 3:13)

Hil.Trin.6.12 (PL 10:166);
Ath.Decr.23.3 (Opitz 2:19)

Ar.Ep.Alex.5 (Opitz 3:13)

bodiless God" must at all costs be represented in such a way that he did not suffer the changes affecting a body. This meant that God in his transcendent being had to be kept aloof from any involvement with the world of becoming. His "unoriginated and unmitigated essence" transcended the realm of created and changeable things so totally that there was not, and ontologically could not be, a direct point of contact between them. Such a total transcendence was necessary not only for the sake of the utter oneness of God, but also because of the fragility of creatures, which "could not endure to be made by the absolute hand of the Unoriginate."

It was incompatible with this definition of divine oneness and transcendence to speak of the divine in Christ as God in the unequivocal sense of that title. Alleging Deuteronomy 6:4 and related passages of exclusive monotheism, the Arians demanded: "Behold, God is said to be one and only and the first. How then can you say that the Son is God? For if he were God, [God] would not have said, 'I alone' or 'God is one.' " The point at which the Arian understanding of God called forth a controversy was, then, not in the doctrine of God as such, but in the doctrine of the relation between God and the divine in Christ. In asking a question about Christ, Arius was really asking the question about God, as the exchanges between the Arians and their opponents also made clear. The Arian poems confessed: "God has not always been a Father," and again, "Once God was alone, and not yet a Father, but afterwards he became a Father." If the Son had a beginning, it followed that before that beginning the Father was not Father. And the converse also seemed to follow, namely, that if God had always been Father and the divine paternity was coeternal with him, the divine sonship likewise had to be coeternal with the Son. To accept such an implication would have meant to blaspheme against the deity of God.

Proverbs 8:22–31 was well adapted to this Arian theology. It explicitly stated that God had "created" wisdom, and that he had done so "for the sake of his [other] works." This had been "before the age" and before the creation of the earth and the abyss and the mountains. Hence both Logos and Son of God, the two titles which summarized the meaning of the divine in Christ, were taken to refer to a created being. Arius declared: "The

ap.Ath.*Ar*.2.26 (*PG* 26:201)

ap.Ath.*Ar*.2.24 (*PG* 26:200);
ap.Ath.*Decr*.8.1 (Opitz 2:7)

ap.Ath.*Ar*.3.7 (*PG* 26:333)

ap.Ath.*Ar*.1.5; 9 (*PG* 26:21; 29)

Hil.*Trin*.12.23 (*PL* 10:447);
Didym.*Trin*.1.15 (*PG* 39:320)

ap.Ath.*Ar*.1.14 (*PG* 26:41)

ap.Ath.*Dion*.23.1 (Opitz
2:63)

Ath.*Ar*.2.37 (*PG* 26:225)

ap.Ath.*Ar*.1.6 (*PG* 26:24)

ap.Ath.*Ar*.1.13 (*PG* 26:40)

Ath.*Ar*.1.14 (*PG* 26:41)

Prov.8:22
Ar.*Ep.Alex*.2 (Opitz 3:12)

ap.Ath.*Ar*.1.5 (*PG* 26:21)

Ath.*Decr*.7.1 (Opitz 2:6)
Bas.*Eun*.2.20–21 (*PG*
29:616–20)

Logos . . . is only called Logos conceptually, and is not
Son of God by nature and in truth, but is merely called
Son, he too, by adoption, as a creature." Indeed, it seems
from some of the evidence that in such statements as
these, Arian theology drew a distinction between the
Logos and the Son, identifying the Logos as the one
through whom God had also made the Son. Whether or
not this latter distinction was actually a consistent Arian
tenet, the creaturely status of the Logos (and of the Son
of God) was a cardinal doctrine. The Logos was "alien
and unlike in all respects to the essence and selfhood of
the Father"; he was ranged among the things originated
and created, all of which were fundamentally different
from God in essence. In the ontological distinction between Creator and creature, the Logos definitely belonged
on the side of the creature—yet with an important qualification.

Other creatures of God had their beginning within
time, but the Logos began "before times." The declaration upon which the opponents of Arianism fastened,
that "there was a then when he did not exist," explicitly
avoided saying that "there was a time when he did not
exist," in order to distinguish between the Logos and
other creatures. Proverbs 8:23 specifically identified the
"establishing" of wisdom as something that had happened "before the age." Yet because the Arians insisted
upon "certain intervals, in which they imagine he was
not," their avoidance of the term "time" was dismissed
as sophistry. According to Proverbs and according to the
Arian exegesis of it, the Logos had been established "before the age" for a purpose: to be "the principle of creation of his ways for the sake of his works." Although the
Logos was a creature, he was "not as one of the creatures,"
for they were created through him while he was created
directly by God. He was "made out of nothing." According to Athanasius, it was part of their original doctrine
(but according to Basil a later refinement by the Anomoeans) to argue: "We consider that the Son has this prerogative over others, and therefore is called Only-Begotten, because only he was brought into being by God alone,
while all other things were created by God through the
Son." This was in keeping with the Arian doctrine of
God, according to which the creatures "could not endure
the untempered hand of the Father and be created by

ap.Ath.*Ar*.2.24 (*PG* 26:200)

Didym.*Trin*.1.8 (*PG* 39:276–77)
Ath.*Decr*.8.2 (Opitz 2:7);
Ath.*Ar*.2.26 (*PG* 26:201);
Epiph.*Haer*.76.6.2 (*GCS* 37:346)

Ath.*Ar*.1.26 (*PG* 26:65)

See pp. 182–84 above

Ath.*Ar*.1.53 (*PG* 26:121)

Ath.*Ar*.1.56 (*PG* 26:129)
Iren.*Haer*.1.22 (Harvey 1:189)

Hil.*Trin*.4.17–21 (*PL* 10:110–13)

Aug.*Trin*.12.6.6–7 (*CCSL* 50:360–62)

Barn.6.12 (Bihlmeyer 17)

Just.*Dial*.62.3 (Goodspeed 168)
Tert.*Anim*.23.5 (*CCSL* 2:815)

Tert.*Res*.5.2 (*CCSL* 2:926)

Ath.*Ar*.2.31 (*PG* 26:213)

Ath.*Ar*.1.62 (*PG* 26:141)

him" and therefore needed a mediator to call them into being. The orthodox replied either that, consistently, no mediator should be needed, or that this presupposition, carried to its conclusion, would require an infinite regress of mediators, each cushioning the shock for the next. This was, however, the particular office of the Logos in Arian cosmology: to be the instrument through which the Creator fashioned the universe and all that is therein.

Of special interest in the Arian vocabulary about the relation of the Son of God as creature to God the Creator was their use of the title "angel." This title could claim a distinguished lineage in the liturgical, exegetical, and apologetic usage of the church. It was also well suited to the needs of Arian theology. The interpretation of Proverbs 8:22–31 could be combined with the words of Hebrews 1:4 to show that the preexistent one belonged to the category of the angels, although, to be sure, he was preeminent among them. According to the apostle Paul in Galatians 3:19, the law of Moses had been "ordained by angels through an intermediary." Various theologians, both Jewish and Christian—chiefly Gnostics, however, as Athanasius charged—had assigned to the angels an intermediary role in the creation of the world and of man. "Let us make man" in Genesis 1:26–27 was ordinarily used as a passage of distinction, as when Hilary argued on the basis of it that God could not be conceived of as "solitary," but that he had always had a "companion"; for Augustine the passage became the basis for the idea that man was created in the image of the entire Trinity, not merely in that of the Father or the Son. But already in Barnabas and then at greater length in Justin, Christian interpretation of the passage had to take account of the exegesis, said by Justin to be maintained "among you" Jews (or, in a variant reading, "among us" Christians), by which God was thought to be speaking to angels. In response to this exegesis, which he attributed to Platonic influence, Tertullian reminded his readers nevertheless that the "angels rank next to God." This mediatorial role of the angels could be broadened to include the Logos as the chief among them. And so in Arian terminology it would be proper either to call the angels sons of God or to call the Son of God an angel. To this extent it is right to see Arianism as "a final, mighty upheaval" of an angel christology that had come down from late Jewish and early Christian apocalypticism and was making its last stand "against the new, hellenized christology," even though the evidence for the universality of this form of speaking about the divine in Christ is less convincing than that judgment assumes.

Even on the basis of the scraps of information about Arianism handed on principally by its opponents, we may recognize in the Arian picture of this Logos-Son, who was less than God but more than man, a soteriological as well as a cosmological intermediary. The absoluteness of God meant that if the Logos was of the same essence with the Father, the Logos had to be impassible. The orthodox found it blasphemous when the Arians, also in the interest of the absoluteness of God, described the Logos as one possessed of a mutable nature and therefore not of the same essence with the Father. "He remains good," the Arians said, "by his own free will, so long as he chooses to do so," rather than by virtue of his oneness of essence with God. And so, according to Arius, God, foreknowing that the Logos would resist temptation and remain good, bestowed on him proleptically the glory which, as man, he would eventually attain by his own virtue. The Logos became "the pioneer of salvation" by first enduring in his own name and then enabling those who followed him to do likewise. "By his care and self-discipline" he had triumphed over his mutable nature. His "moral progress [προκοπή]" had won for him the title Son of God, according to Paul of Samosata; and Arius seems to have taught something similar. From what can be known of Arian teaching about salvation, it does not seem overly harsh to comment that "the men who had replaced the Father in heaven by an abstract ὄν would naturally confess a mere minister of creation rather than a conqueror of death and sin." The ultimate outcome of the Arian system was a Christ suspended between man and God, identical with neither but related to both: God was interpreted deistically, man moralistically, and Christ mythologically.

Whether angel or Son of God, the Arian Logos, though subordinate to the Father and not of the same ousia with him, was nevertheless worthy of worship. The Arians shared with other Christians the usage of paying to the Son of God an adoration that by right belonged to God alone. The usage itself was so persistent that, for ex-

Werner (1941) 34

ap.Ath.*Ar*.1.5 (*PG* 26:21)
Heb.2:10

ap.Thdt.*H.e*.1.4.13 (*GCS* 44:11)

Ath.*Syn*.26.4.2 (Opitz 2:252)

Gwatkin (1882) 23

Gr.Nyss.*Apoll*. (Jaeger 3–I:206)

Or.*Orat.*15.1 (*GCS* 3:333)
Jay (1954) 126–27

Or.*Cels.*5.4 (*GCS* 3:4)

Ath.*Ar.*1.8 (*PG* 26:28)

Ambr.*Fid.*1.11.69 (*CSEL* 78:30)

Ath.*Ar.*3.12 (*PG* 26:345–48)

Or.*Cels.*5.5 (*GCS* 3:4–5)

Didym.*Trin.*3.23 (*PG* 39:928–29)

Gr.Naz.*Or.*40.42 (*PG* 36:417–20); Cyr.*Inc.unigen.* (*SC* 97:276)

Ath.*Ar.*1.34 (*PG* 26:81–84)

ample, Origen, despite his carefully documented insistence that "properly, prayer is to be addressed to God the Father alone," himself addressed prayers to Christ; and in opposition to a pagan critic he championed the appropriateness of "petitions to the very Logos himself," consisting of intercessions and thanksgiving, so long as the distinction between prayer in the absolute sense and prayer in the relative sense was observed. The Arians found prayer to the Logos an unavoidable element of Christian worship. Yet by this inconsistency between their dogmatic principle and their liturgical practice the Arians were saying, in effect: "Abandon the worship of the creation, and then draw near and worship a creature and a work." From the attacks of orthodox writers like Ambrose it is clear that the Arians refused to abandon the practice of worshiping Christ; "else, if they do not worship the Son, let them admit it, and the case is settled, so that they do not deceive anyone by their professions of religion." There is some indication that they may have justified their usage by reference to the worship of angels, even though Origen, in the defense of prayers to the Logos just cited, had explicitly ruled out the worship of angels. Apparently some Arian groups may have revised the Gloria Patri to read: "Glory be to the Father through the Son in the Holy Spirit."

The Arians also continued the practice of baptizing in the name not only of the Father, but also of the Son and of the Holy Spirit; Gregory of Nazianzus, in a treatise on baptism, took advantage of this to argue that if one worshiped a creature or were baptized into a creature, this would not bring about the divinization promised in baptism. Athanasius, too, argued on the basis of the universal baptismal practice accepted also by the Arians that baptism was "not into the name of Unoriginate and originate, nor into the name of Creator and creature, but into the name of Father, Son, and Holy Spirit." In short, both the Arians and their opponents addressed themselves to Christ in a manner that assumed some special divinity in him. The question was how what the church taught in its exegetical and catechetical work and what it confessed in its apologetics toward Jews or pagans and in its creeds was to be related to what it believed in its prayers. It was an acknowledgment of this relation between what was believed, taught, and confessed when the opponents of

Ath.Ar.3.16 (PG 26:353–56);
Hil.Trin.8.28 (PL 10:256–57);
Marc.fr.129 (GCS 14:215);
Boeth.Trin.1 (LCL 6)

Arianism, from Athanasius and Hilary through Marcellus of Ancyra and Boethius, accused it of being polytheistic despite its rigid monotheism; for by worshiping as divine one whom they refused to call divine, they would "certainly be going on to more gods" and would "lead into a plurality" of divine beings.

In many ways Arianism was more aware of the nuances of the trinitarian problem than its critics were. It compelled them, in turn, to avoid the oversimplifications to which church theology was prone. It also made it more difficult to fob off speculation as exegesis, or exegesis as speculation. As the official doctrine of the church proceeded to settle the question of the relation of Christ to God by means of the formula "homoousios," it was Arianism that helped, through its demand for precision, to rescue that formula from the heretical, Gnostic incubus that afflicted it. And by reminding the early leaders of Alexandrian theology—whose successors were to make such problems unavoidable for the entire church—that the earthly biography of the Logos in his life, death, and resurrection was an inescapable element of the "double

Ath.Ar.3.29 (PG 26:385)

proclamation," Arianism helped to keep churchly doctrine both honest and evangelical.

Christ as Homoousios

The Arian doctrine of Christ as creature collided with the tradition of describing him as God; but the Arian use of the titles Logos and Son of God, which together had come to summarize the central meaning of that tradition, made the collision between the two quite ambiguous. In fact, it is misleading to speak of "the two" as though Arianism and orthodoxy were such obvious alternatives throughout the controversy. For while the tradition of describing Christ as God was indeed the basic doctrinal and liturgical issue at stake in the controversy from the beginning, it was only in the course of the debate that the proper formula for that tradition, together with the implications of any such formula, became evident.

After various personal and administrative gambits had failed to silence the Arians, a regional council held at Antioch early in 325, drawing upon an epistle of Alexander, bishop of Alexandria, promulgated a lengthy statement of "the faith" in Christ as divine; it anathematized "those who say or think or preach that the Son of God is a crea-

ture or has come into being or has been made and is not
truly begotten, or that there was a then when he did not

*Symb.Ant.*13 (Opitz 3:39)   exist." In its positive section the statement of faith described Christ as "not made but properly an offspring,
but begotten in an ineffable, indescribable manner," as
one who "exists everlastingly and did not at one time not

*Symb.Ant.*9 (Opitz
3:38–39)   exist." It had many verbatim citations from Arian theology, even though it did not mention Arius by name, and
it affirmed the "orthodox faith concerning Father and
Son," which Alexander had announced with the formula:
"These we teach, these we preach, these are the apostolic

*Alex.Tom.*3 (Opitz 3:30)   dogmas of the church." And the council excommunicated
the three men who had refused to sign the creed.

Later in the same year the doctrine set forth in this
creed was elaborated and promulgated for the entire imperial church at Nicea: "We believe in one God, the Father Almighty, maker of all things visible and invisible;
And in one Lord Jesus Christ, the Son of God, begotten
from the Father, only-begotten, that is, from the ousia
of the Father, God from God, light from light, true
God from true God, begotten not made, homoousios with
the Father, through whom [namely, the Son] all things
came into being, things in heaven and things on earth,
who for the sake of us men and for the purpose of our
salvation came down and became incarnate, becoming
man, suffered and rose again on the third day, ascended
to the heavens, and will come to judge the living and the
dead; And in the Holy Spirit. But as for those who say,
'There was a then when he did not exist,' and, 'Before
being born he did not exist,' and that he came into existence out of nothing, or who assert that the Son of God
is of a different hypostasis or ousia, or is created, or is
subject to alteration or change—these the church catholic

Symb.Nic.(325) (Schaff 2:60)   anathematizes."

The basis of the creed of Nicea was not, as scholars believed for a long time on the basis of the letter of Eusebius

*Eus.Ep.Caes.*2 (Opitz 3:43)   describing the Council of Nicea, the baptismal creed of
his church in Caesarea; the most that modern research
has been able to determine is that this was "some local
baptismal creed, of Syro-Palestinian provenance" and
that "to go beyond this and attempt to identify the under-

Kelly (1950) 229   lying formula would be an unprofitable exercise." For the
history of doctrine, as distinguished from the history of
creeds, it is less important to identify the original text that

formed the basis for the creed promulgated at Nicea than it is to specify the additions made by the council. Initially, it seems, the council had wanted to adhere to the ipsissima verba of Scripture, such as that the Son was "from God"; but when passages like 1 Corinthians 8:6 and 2 Corinthians 5:17 were adduced to prove that "all things are from God" in the sense of being created by him, the bishops at the council "were forced to express more distinctly the sense of the words 'from God.' " This they did especially in two formulas: "only-begotten, that is, from the ousia of the Father"; and "homoousios." In the Gospel of John and in 1 John—especially if, as many fourth-century theologians supposed, the variant reading "the only-begotten one, God" is the correct one in John 1:18—the term had something of the quality of a technical title; at the very least, it had stressed the uniqueness of the "begetting" of Christ by God. But in his confession of faith addressed to Alexander, Arius had explained it to mean, among other things, "a perfect creature of God, but not as one of the creatures." Asterius had declared that though Christ was called "the power of God," nevertheless "there are many of those powers which are one by one created by him [God], of which Christ is the firstborn and only-begotten."

The creed at Nicea, therefore, called the Son "only-begotten, that is, from the ousia of the Father," in a sense quite different from the way all (other) creatures could be said to be "from God." It was also an attack on Arius —in fact, a direct turning upon him of the very weapon he had brought—when the creed designated Christ as homoousios. According to Eusebius of Caesarea, the term was added at the urging of Constantine; and it usually has been attributed to Western sources, mediated through Ossius of Cordova. The variety of its meanings and its previous association with Gnosticism—and, as Arius had pointed out, with Manicheism—made it suspect to the orthodox; its identification with the condemned ideas of Paul of Samosata was to be a source of embarrassment to its defenders long after Nicea. But at Nicea, the doctrine it expressed was "that the Son of God bears no resemblance to the genetos creatures [that is, those that have a beginning], but that He is in every way assimilated to the Father alone who begat Him, and that He is not out of any other hypostasis and ousia, but out of the Father."

Ath.*Decr*.19.2 (Opitz 2:16)

Gr.Nyss.*Tres dii* (Jaeger 3–I:55); Didym.*Trin*.1.32 (PG 39:429); Thdr.Mops.*Hom. catech*.4.3 (ST 145:79) Didym.*Trin*.3.2–3 (PG 39:788–89)

Ar.*Ep.Alex*.2 (Opitz 3:12); Ammon.*Joh*.3 (PG 85:1412)

Ath.*Syn*.18.6 (Opitz 2:246); Didym.*Trin*.3.4 (PG 39:828)

Amph.*Ep.syn*. (PG 39:96)

Eus.*Ep.Caes*.7 (Opitz 3:44)

Ar.*Ep.Alex*.3 (Opitz 3:12)

See p. 176 above Hil.*Syn*.81; 86 (PL 10:534; 538–39)

Prestige (1956) 211

The anti-Arian polemic of these two additions was made even more explicit by the closing anathemas of the creed, which read like a summa of Arian dogmatics. They condemned any and all of the various formulas by which Arius and his supporters had attempted to range Christ on the other side of the line separating Creator from creature. It would not do to say that he was created, or that he had come into being out of things that do not exist, or that his hypostasis or ousia was different from that of the Father, or, in the most familiar of Arian mottoes, that "there was a then when he did not exist." Condemned out of his own mouth, Arius refused to sign the creed; in this act of heroism and honesty he was joined, apparently, by only two of the council fathers. All the rest saluted the emperor, signed the formula, and went right on teaching as they always had. In the case of most of them, this meant a doctrine of Christ somewhere between that of Arius and that of Alexander.

Yet it was to the doctrine espoused by Alexander, as refined after further clarification and violent controversy, that the palm was given, and it was in the light of this doctrine that the creed of Nicea came to be interpreted. We can summarize this doctrine at the present point in our narrative, even though, as will become clear later in this section, it represented anything but theological unanimity at the time of the Council of Nicea itself, much less during the half-century that followed. Among the expositors of the "faith of Nicea," Athanasius, everyone agrees, should have pride of place; but Amphilochius and especially Didymus in the East, and Ambrose and Hilary in the West, deserve to be ranged alongside him, if for no other reason than because of the intricate web of intellectual and literary relations among them.

The faith confessed at Nicea, both in its own original formulation and in its interpretation by its defenders, was a cosmological confession and a soteriological confession simultaneously. Underlying it was the conviction that only he who had created the universe could save man, and that to do either or both of these he himself had to be divine and not a creature. The Logos was present in all of creation as the one through whom it had come into being. Because God, in his generosity, was unwilling to begrudge the gift of being, "he has made all things out of nothing through his own Logos, Jesus Christ our

Ath.*Ep.Aeg.Lib.*6 (*PG* 25:552); Ath.*Tom.*3 (*PG* 26:800)

Ath.*Inc.*17.1 (Cross 26)

Ath.*Inc*.3.3 (Cross 5)

Didym.*Trin*.1.15 (PG 39:300)
Ath.*Fug*.14.1 (Opitz 2:78)

Didym.*Trin*.1.15 (PG 39:308–309)

Ath.*Ar*.2.51 (PG 26:253)

Ath.*Dec*.19 (Opitz 2:15–16)

See pp. 35–37 above

Ath.*Inc*.4.6 (Cross 7)

Ath.*Ar*.3.63 (PG 26:456)
See p. 54 above

Ath.*Gent*.41 (PG 25:81–84)

Ath.*Ar*.3.33 (PG 26:393)

See pp. 286–92 below

Lord." He who was "in the beginning" did not have a beginning himself, but was the principle of creation of all things; they were his creatures, but he was the Creator. He was the creator of the times. "And if he, when there was no other energy, created the ages, which are made up of times, and provided the principle of creation for all things," it followed that he was not temporal but eternal. In opposition, therefore, to the Arian equation of "only-begotten" with "firstborn of the creatures," namely, the first creature among creatures, the Nicene confession insisted that the creation of man and of the cosmos could not be understood apart from him as Creator, but that he had to be seen apart from his creatures. The creatures came "from God" in the sense that their origin was not to be attributed to chance, but the Logos came "from God" in the sense that he was "of the ousia of the Father."

The conflict with paganism had given prominence to the Christian insistence that the creatures had come into existence "out of nothing." The conflict with Arianism made that insistence even more crucial. For "man is by nature mortal, since he is made out of what is not." He was therefore constantly being drawn back down into the nonbeing out of which he had been called by the creating power of the divine Logos. Because God was "he who is [ὁ ὤν]," by the standard exegesis of Exodus 3:14, his creatures could be delivered from annihilation only by participation in the image of the Creator. God "saw that all created nature, if left to its own principles, was in flux and subject to dissolution. To prevent this and to keep the universe from disintegrating back into nonbeing, he made all things by his very own eternal Logos and endowed the creation with being." Man's fall into sin made him "mortal and corruptible," the victim of his own nature and its propensities. To a considerable degree, the definition of sin in church doctrine appears to have developed a posteriori, by a process which, proceeding from the salvation in Christ and from infant baptism, made the diagnosis fit the cure. But it was essential for Nicene orthodoxy to speak of sin in relation to the creation out of nothing, so that the Logos who had been the agent of creation might also be identified as the agent of salvation.

That identification was central to the faith of Nicea as interpreted by its defenders. "A man is altogether irreligious and a stranger to the truth," said Amphilochius,

Amph.*fr.*16 (*PG* 39:116)

Ath.*Ar.*2.76 (*PG* 26:308)

Ath.*Inc.*4 (Cross 6–7)

Didym.*Trin.*3.1 (*PG* 39:780)

Hil.*Trin.*3.10 (*PL* 10:81)

Didym.*Trin.*3.3 (*PG* 39:805–17)

Ambr.*Fid.*3.7.46 (*CSEL* 78:124–25)

Didym.*Trin.*3.3 (*PG* 39:817); Hil.*Trin.*12.44–45 (*PL* 10:460–63)

Matt.26:39
Matt.24:36
Amph.*fr.*6 (*PG* 39:104); Didym.*Trin.*3.22 (*PG* 39:915–21)

Matt.17:5
Didym.*Trin.*1.9 (*PG* 39:288–89)

See pp. 152–55 above

Bas.*Spir.*8.18–19 (*PG* 32:97–104)

Luke 10:30–37

"if he does not say that Christ the Savior is also the Maker of all things." It was not appropriate, Athanasius argued, that created life should be founded in any except "the Lord who is before the ages and through whom the ages came into existence, so that, since it was in him, we also might be able to inherit that eternal life." Only he who had called men out of nonbeing into being would be able to recall them after they had fallen back into the nothingness that threatened them. According to Didymus, the fundamental mistake of the Arians was not to understand what Scripture said "about the Redeemer, God the Logos, the originator of all things." The Logos-Son had become incarnate, so that he might be glorified in his humiliation and crucifixion. It was to the incarnate one and to the reality of his created nature as man that the defenders of Nicea applied those passages of subordination on the basis of which the Arians had called the preexistent one a creature. This meant, above all, that "he created me" in Proverbs 8:22 either had to be using "created" in an improper sense or had to be speaking of the created humanity of the incarnate Christ. The latter was the easier solution, taking the words to mean "that the Lord Jesus was created from the Virgin in order to redeem the works of the Father." "He created," then, was synonymous with "he established"—established not only above the cherubim but also in the manger. Other passages of this sort, too, could be explained as applying to his created humanity. The prayer in the garden of Gethsemane had to be interpreted this way, according to Amphilochius; so did Christ's confession of ignorance about the last day. The word from the cloud, which was the proof text for an adoptionist christology, applied not to the preexistent Christ, but to the incarnate one.

All of this was "for the sake of us men and for the purpose of our salvation," as the Nicene confession affirmed. The content of this salvation, to be sure, was variously defined. The same theologians who refused to brook any divergence from the norm of trinitarian and christological orthodoxy were quite willing to manipulate soteriological theories and images without similar compunction. But regardless of the atonement metaphor employed, the christological implication was that Christ was homoousios. Ambrose used, among other images, that of the Good Samaritan who had taken pity on fallen man; but

Ambr.*Fid.*2.11.89–99 (*CSEL* 78:89–93)

John 4:1–30; Amph.*Hom.*4.2; 4.5 (*PG* 39:69; 73–76)

Amph.*Mesopent.* (*PG* 39:124)

Hil.*Ps.*53.13–14 (*PL* 9:345–46)

Ath.*Ar.*2.69–70 (*PG* 26:293–96)

Didym.*Trin.*1.29 (*PG* 39:413)

Ath.*Inc.*40.5 (Cross 63); Amph.*Hom.*1.1 (*PG* 39:36); Didym.*Trin.*3.27 (*PG* 39:944)

Didym.*Trin.*1.34 (*PG* 39:437)

Matt.2:11

Amph.*fr.*3 (*PG* 39:100)

to be this, Christ had to be "incarnate" and at the same time have his "deity" acknowledged. Amphilochius was fond of the familiar medical imagery, applying it also to the story of the Samaritan woman; but this imagery implied that healing was to be obtained only from the incarnate Christ, who was "the Maker of the senses and the Creator of the creatures." Hilary used the picture of Christ as the sacrificial victim, but immediately went on to explain that this did not mean a diminution in "his eternal possession of unchangeable deity." Athanasius was the spokesman for the Eastern tradition that God the Logos had become man in order that men might become God; but if this was to be the gift of his incarnation and if man was to be rescued from the corruption that so easily beset him, it was indispensable that "the Logos not belong to things that had an origin, but be their framer himself." Didymus, too, could speak of the Savior in various ways, as "judge of the living and the dead, that is, of the righteous and of the sinners, the one who grants forgiveness of sins to those who believe in his name, the one who saves us by his own glory and graciousness"; but "because he is by nature merciful and the Savior, he is in no way subordinate to the merciful and saving God and Father." Any of the various definitions of the meaning of salvation was taken to require that—in the words of Isaiah 63:9 (LXX), the passage of identity quoted by Athanasius and in a Christmas sermon of Amphilochius and by Didymus —it be neither a messenger nor an angel, but God himself who saved mankind. And the formula that guaranteed this requirement was homoousios.

By the homoousios, so interpreted and defended, the expositors of Nicene doctrine attempted to safeguard the soteriological and liturgical concerns of the church, for which it was mandatory that Christ be divine. There was nothing left for the deniers of homoousios, Didymus charged, but "to change the name of the Father in their liturgies," as well as to remove the names of the Only-Begotten and of the Spirit; for it was characteristic of Jewish worship to adore only the Father, and of pagan worship to adore a plethora of lesser beings which differed from God in essence. Like the worship of the church, the offerings of the Magi could be exonerated of the charge of idolatry only if the Christ child was king and God. Writing before Nicea, Athanasius, without any

Ath.*Gent*.47 (PG 25:96);
Ath.*Inc*.49.6 (Cross 78–79)

Ath.*Ar*.2.23–24 (PG
26:193–200)

Ambr.*Fid*.1.16.104 (*CSEL*
78:45)

Ath.*Ep.Serap*.2.5 (PG
26:616);
Ath.*Decr*.20 (Opitz 2:16–17)

Soz.*H.e*.3.1.1 (*GCS* 50:101)

sense of inconsistency, denounced paganism for "serving the creature rather than the Creator" and then for refusing to "worship the Logos, our Lord Jesus Christ the Savior." After Nicea, when he was involved in the Arian controversy, he made use of this contrast to argue that the worship of Christ by men and angels proved his essential difference from all creatures, including angels; only if he was not a creature, but true God by nature, could such worship be proper. Ambrose echoed many of these arguments when he called upon the Arians to stop worshiping one whom they regarded as a creature or else to call him a creature even when they worshiped him; for as things stood, their theological position and their liturgical practice were irreconcilable.

As we have mentioned, however, the consensus suggested by such an exposition of "the Nicene faith" is an illusion—albeit an illusion fostered by the official accounts of the developments after 325. Sozomen, for example, dated the beginning of public divergence from "the doctrine which had been promulgated at Nicea" with the death of Constantine on 22 May 337. Even before that time "this doctrine did not have universal approval," but only with Constantine's death did open opposition to it break out. The story of this opposition has been told often, though not always well. Many accounts of the development of doctrine during the half-century from Nicea to Constantinople lose themselves in chronology and political history. As we indicated at the beginning of this chapter, the political history of these decades is in many ways more important—and in most ways more interesting—than the doctrinal history. Yet a development of doctrine there is, and one which can (keeping as much of the chronology in view as can safely be determined from the documents) be traced in its own terms.

Even in the interpretation which we have just summarized, the Nicene formulation left certain fundamental doctrinal questions unanswered and certain lingering suspicions unallayed. And as the interpretation and defense of Nicea thickened, the questions of the gainsayers became ever more insistent and their suspicions increasingly difficult to dismiss as baseless. The furor over Marcellus proved an embarrassment to Nicene orthodoxy. One of the signers in 325 and a fellow exile with Athanasius at Rome in 339, Marcellus of Ancyra asserted the unity of the Godhead, on the basis of the passages of identity, in terms that compelled him to interpret the passages of distinction as only temporary and "economic": Son and Spirit were not eternal in the Godhead, but "Son" was the name properly given only to the incarnate one. Against the identification of Son and Logos, Marcellus insisted that only "Logos" was an appropriate title for the preexistent one, and that even this referred to a Logos immanent in God and internal to him rather than to an eternally subsisting Logos. He did not use homoousios in the fragments of his works that have been preserved, though it was used in a statement of faith which may have come from Marcellus, attacking the Sabellians for their denial of the doctrine. Nevertheless, it is safe to see in his theology a version of the homoousios according to which the unity of God was safeguarded before the incarnation by the complete immanence of the Logos and after the incarnation by the surrender of the kingdom of the Son to the Father, that God might be all in all. It was in response to this latter contention that the final recension of the "Nicene" creed eventually came to incorporate the clause, "of his [Christ's] reign there will be no end." But more important for the development of the trinitarian dogma is how this crypto-Sabellianism of Marcellus vindicated the charge of his opponents that the Nicene formula needed revision and amplification to clarify what was meant by the One in God.

They were, if anything, even more critical of the inadequacy of the Nicene formula as a statement of the complementary doctrine of the Three in God, and with good reason. Marcellus had declared that "it is impossible for three existing hypostases to be united by a monad unless previously the trinity has its origin from the monad." This made it clear to Eusebius that Marcellus was merely setting forth a sophistic form of Sabellianism. Even opponents of the homoousios more moderate than Eusebius, Acacius, and the Homoeans were concerned that it was wiping out any ontological distinction between Father, Son, and Holy Spirit. Nicea had appeared to equate hypostasis and ousia in its anathemas. The Greek term "hypostasis" was, moreover, a precise equivalent of the Latin "substantia," so that Western theologians, in speaking of one substantia in the Godhead, seemed to be oblit-

Marc.fr.43 (GCS 14:192)

Marc.fr.109 (GCS 14:208)

Marc.fr.43 (GCS 14:192)

Ps.Ath.Exp.fid.2 (PG 25:204)

1 Cor.15:28;
Marc.fr.116 (GCS 14:209–10)

Didym.Trin.1.31 (PG 39:421–25)

Marc.fr.66 (GCS 14:197)

Eus.E.th.3.4 (GCS 14:157)

Hil.Syn.25 (PL 10:499)

Gr.Naz.*Or*.21.35 (*PG* 35:1124–25)

Ar.*Ep.Alex*.4 (Opitz 3:13)

ap.Epiph.*Haer*.73.12 (*GCS* 37:284–85)

Gummerus (1900) 124

ap.Epiph.*Haer*.73.13.1 (*GCS* 37:285)

Gibbon (1896) 2:352

Ath.*Syn*.54.3 (Opitz 2:277)

erating the threeness of hypostases; as Gregory Nazianzus observed, they avoided speaking of "three hypostases." To be sure, Arius had declared in his creed addressed to Alexander that "there are three hypostases." Thus the formula "three hypostases" was tarred with the brush of Arianism—but no more so than the formula "homoousios" with the brush of Sabellianism, Gnosticism, and Paul of Samosata. But the "Origenists" or "homoiousians," no less opposed to Arianism than to Sabellianism, came nevertheless to be called "Semi-Arians" because of their insistence on "three hypostases" and their opposition to homoousios. Faced with the distinction between Son and Logos in Marcellus, they urged that Son be seen as the highest and most appropriate designation, while Logos should be put on a level with life, resurrection, and bread as a metaphor for the Son. In this doctrine, therefore, "Logos and Son stand as mutually complementary titles . . . except that in this passage only the one side, the 'hypostatic' self-subsistence, is emphasized," as it had not, in their judgment, been sufficiently emphasized in the Nicene formula of homoousios and in its authorized exponents.

As a substitute for homoousios, therefore, they proposed homoiousios, "of a similar ousia," or, more aptly and precisely, "like [the Father] in every respect," rather than merely "like the Father" but not in ousia. The antithesis between "Nicene" and "Semi-Arian" has, consequently, come to be interpreted as the struggle between homoousios and homoiousios, with the result, in Gibbon's memorable phrase, "that the profane of every age have derided the furious contests which the difference of a single diphthong excited between" them. Like most controversies over terminology, however, this was no mere logomachy, as Athanasius recognized, punning on the word "logomachy" as "a battle about the Logos." At stake were fundamental questions both of Christian doctrine and of theological methodology. It had been the wish of the bishops at Nicea to confine themselves to the simple words of Scripture, but this proved bootless. Repeatedly throughout the half-century after the council, protagonists of one or another position voiced the same wish. As Constantine had proposed the homoousios in 325, so his son Constantius intervened on the opposite

Hil.Const.16 (PL 10:594)

side with the ruling: "I do not want words used that are not in Scripture." But behind the mutual accusations of using words not in Scripture was the recognition which developed on all sides that such words were unavoidable and that it was inconsistent to voice the accusation against the opponent's position while using such words in defense of one's own position.

Ath.Decr.18.4 (Opitz 2:15);
Gr.Naz.Or.31.23 (PG
36:157–60)

But among nonscriptural words, what was so sacrosanct about homoousios? Athanasius, for example, made surprisingly little use of it and wrote his longest defense of the concept, the three *Orations against the Arians,* almost without mentioning it. And at the very end of his treatise on the councils, Hilary, "calling the God of heaven and earth to witness," swore that he had not so much as heard of the Council of Nicea until he was about to go into exile in 356, but that he regarded homoousios and

Hil.Syn.91 (PL 10:543–45)

homoiousios as synonymous. They were not synonymous to begin with, but they eventually converged—not principally through such orthodox suasions, but through the recognition by the adherents of both terms that the threat to what they believed most deeply was coming from the extreme of the Arian position: Christ the Logos was "unlike the Father" or, more moderately, "like the Father but not in ousia." Speaking doctrinally rather than politically, the homoousios was saved by the further clarification of the unresolved problems of the One and the Three and by the recognition of a common religious concern between the partisans of homoousios and those of homoiousios. The spokesman for that recognition, after various kinds of hesitation, was Athanasius himself, who ultimately asserted his unwillingness to attack the Homoiousians "as Ariomaniacs, or as opponents of the fathers; but we discuss the issue with them as brethren with brethren, who mean what we mean and are disputing only about terminology." By saying that Christ was "of the ousia" of the Father and "like [the Father] in ousia," they were, he continued, "setting themselves in opposition

Ath.Syn.41.1 (Opitz 2:266)

to those who say that the Logos is a creature." And this was finally the doctrinal interest for which homoousios had been a symbol—coined by Gnostic heretics, dictated by an unbaptized emperor, jeopardized by naive defenders, but eventually vindicated by its orthodox opponents.

The Three and the One

The form in which the homoousios was vindicated and the identification of Christ as God was codified was the dogma of the Trinity, as it was hammered out during the third quarter of the fourth century. And the issue that brought the homoousios to a head and thus helped to formulate the doctrine that Christ was divine was not so much the doctrine of Christ as the doctrine of the Holy Spirit.

At Nicea the doctrine of the Holy Spirit had been disposed of in lapidary brevity: "And [we believe] in the Holy Spirit." Nor does there seem to have been a single treatise dealing specifically with the person of the Spirit composed before the second half of the fourth century. It may be that Montanism was responsible for some development in the direction of a more "personal" understanding of the Holy Spirit in Tertullian, and through him in the evolving trinitarianism of the third century; but even this possibility is tenuous. Once the question of the Holy Spirit was raised, its absence from the earlier discussions itself became a question. Gregory of Nazianzus explained the absence by a theory of development of doctrine, according to which "the Old Testament proclaimed the Father manifestly, and the Son more hiddenly. The New [Testament] manifested the Son, and suggested the deity of the Spirit. Now the Spirit himself is resident among us, and provides us with a clearer explanation of himself." The obscurity of the Old Testament references to the Trinity provided the occasion for other analogous theories of development. But Amphilochius of Iconium, in addition to proposing that the One was manifest in the Pentateuch, the Two in the prophets, and the Three only in the Gospels, also provided, in his synodical letter of 376, a simpler and more plausible explanation of the vagueness of the doctrine of the Holy Spirit in the creed adopted at Nicea: "It was quite necessary for the fathers then to expound more amply about the glory of the Only-Begotten, since they had to cut off the Arian heresy, which had recently arisen. . . . But since the question about the Holy Spirit was not being discussed at the time, they did not go into it at any greater length."

See p. 105 above

Gr.Naz.*Ep*.58 (*PG* 37:113–17)

Gr.Naz.*Or*.31.26 (*PG* 36:161)

Didym.*Trin*.1.18 (*PG* 39:348)

Amph.*fr*.17 (*PG* 39:116)

Amph.*Ep.syn.* (*PG* 39:96)

It was not only the Council of Nicea that was silent about the deity of the Holy Spirit, however. Scripture itself, one had to concede, did not "very clearly or very often call him God in so many words, as it does first the Father and later on the Son." This silence was a source of considerable embarrassment. Similarly, the liturgical usage of the church did not seem to provide instances of worship or prayer addressed to him. It was, of course, to be expected that those who refused the title God to the Son should also demur at calling the Spirit God and should describe the Spirit as created out of nothing. But there were also some who, having broken with the Arians on the question of Christ as creature, nevertheless "oppose the Holy Spirit, saying that he is not only a creature, but actually one of the ministering spirits, and differs from the angels only in degree." Others ascribed to the Holy Spirit an essence less than that of God, but more than that of a creature. He possessed a "middle nature" and was "one of a kind." On the basis of the surviving sources it seems virtually impossible to determine with any precision the relation between the several groups variously called Pneumatomachi, Tropici, and Macedonians by the theologians and historians of the fourth and fifth centuries; modern efforts at reclassification have not proved to be very helpful, either.

While this hesitancy in calling the Holy Spirit God could be attacked for "denying the Arian heresy in words but retaining it in thought," it was symptomatic of a basic lack of clarity in both the words and the thought of the theologians of the church, including those who professed to be orthodox and anti-Arian. Marcellus of Ancyra, for example, seems to have denied that the Holy Spirit had his own hypostasis. He did not distinguish between the eternal or "immanent" proceeding of the Spirit and the temporal or "economic" sending of the Spirit—a distinction that was to figure in the medieval debates between East and West. Therefore with the second coming of Christ the Spirit would no longer "have any functions to discharge." The inadequacies of such a conception of the Spirit became evident when the doctrine received closer attention. But what also became evident was the state of theological reflection about it, as Gregory of Nazianzus conceded as late as 380 when he admitted

Gr.Naz.Or.31.21 (PG 36:157)

Gr.Naz.Or.31.12 (PG 36:145)

Ath.Ar.3.15 (PG 26:353)

Ath.Ep.Serap.1.1 (PG 26:532)

ap.Cyr.Dial.Trin.7 (PG 75:1076–77)

Socr.H.e.2.45 (Hussey 1:365–69);
Soz.H.e.4.27.5 (GCS 50:184)

Gr.Naz.Or.31.13 (PG 36:148)
Ath.Tom.3 (PG 26:800)

Bas.Ep.263.5 (PG 32:981)

Marc.fr.67 (GCS 14:197–98)

Bas.Spir.16.40 (PG 32:141)

Meth.Symp.3.8.72 (GCS 27:36)

Gr.Naz.*Or*.21.33 (*PG* 35:1121)

that "to be only slightly in error [about the Holy Spirit] was to be orthodox." In a remarkable summary of the controversy within the orthodox camp, composed in the same year, he declared: "Of the wise men among ourselves, some have conceived of him [the Holy Spirit] as an activity, some as a creature, some as God; and some have been uncertain which to call him. . . . And therefore they neither worship him nor treat him with dishonor, but take up a neutral position." He did add, however, that "of those who consider him to be God, some are orthodox in mind only, while others venture to be so with the

Gr.Naz.*Or*.31.5 (*PG* 36:137)

lips also." It was apparently not only "careful distinctions, derived from unpractical philosophy and vain de-

Bas.*Spir*.3.5 (*PG* 32:76)

lusion" that could be blamed for this confusion, but also the undeveloped state of the doctrine of the Holy Spirit in relation to the Son in the Trinity.

The relation between the Son and the Holy Spirit was, to be sure, one rather quick and simple way to dispose of the confusion. Cyril of Alexandria suggested that "the identity of nature [ἡ φυσικὴ ταυτότης]" between the Son and the Spirit was enough to prove that the Spirit was God, but this was, as he himself recognized, begging the

Cyr.*Dial.Trin*.7 (*PG* 75:1104)

question. Athanasius had tried many years earlier to argue that if the relation of the Spirit to the Son was the same as that of the Son to the Father, it followed that neither the

Ath.*Ep.Serap*.1.21 (*PG* 26:580)

Son nor the Spirit could be described as a creature. But this provoked the not unwarranted taunt that the Holy

Ath.*Ep.Serap*.4.1 (*PG* 26:637); Gr.Naz.*Or*.31.7 (*PG* 36:140)

Spirit would then have to be interpreted as the son of the Son and hence the grandson of the Father. The same argument could, of course, take a somewhat more respectable form. Athanasius, for example, sought to elevate it to the status of a methodological principle: "If we must take our knowledge of the Spirit from the Son, then it is appropriate to put forward proofs which derive

Ath.*Ep.Serap*.3.4 (*PG* 26:629)

from him [the Son]." The argument had, after all, worked in the opposite direction. Athanasius had maintained that since the Holy Spirit was the gift of no one less than God himself and since the Son conferred the

Ath.*Ar*.2.18 (*PG* 26:184)

Spirit, it followed that the Son was God. The metaphor of the Son as "light from light," especially as employed in Hebrews 1:3, helped to guarantee the deity of the

Ath.*Ep.Serap*.1.19 (*PG* 26:573)

Spirit, too, for Christ, the radiance of God, enlightened the eyes of the heart by the Holy Spirit.

Comparison suggests that Athanasius, having developed the main lines of his theology in the debate over Christ as homoousios, found it sufficient proof for the assertion that the Holy Spirit was homoousios to relate the Spirit to the Son, while others, notably Didymus, had to relate the Spirit to the entire Trinity. Didymus, too, could argue on the basis of the assertion that "the Holy Spirit is inseparable from Christ." Perhaps the most striking illustration for the use of the analogy of Son and Spirit was the recurrence here of the passage of identity, Isaiah 63:7–14 (LXX), which had proved to be so important for the assertion that Christ was divine. To Athanasius Isaiah 63:14, "the Spirit of the Lord," was proof that, paraphrasing Isaiah 63:9, not an angel but the Spirit himself had given rest, and that therefore "the Spirit of God is neither angel nor creature, but belongs to the Godhead." For Didymus, too, the words of Isaiah were proof that the believers in the Old Testament had received grace from none less than "the Spirit, who is inseparable from the Father and the Son." From the same passage he also showed that a sin against the Spirit was a sin against the Holy One of Israel; therefore the Spirit was God. Summarizing this exegesis, Cyril of Alexandria saw in Isaiah 63:9–14 a proof for the identity of ousia between the Holy Spirit and God, just as the exegetical tradition had seen there a proof for the identity between the Logos and God.

The other analogy that suggested itself for an understanding of the relation between the Holy Spirit and God was, obviously, the analogy of the relation between the human spirit and the human self. The analogy had explicit biblical warrant in the words of 1 Corinthians 2:11. Athanasius used it to demonstrate that the divine impassibility which he found attested in James 1:17 applied also to the Holy Spirit, so that "the Holy Spirit, being in God, must be incapable of change, variation, and corruption." Basil professed to find far more in the analogy, elevating it to the status of "the greatest proof of the conjunction of the Spirit with the Father and the Son." But in his actual argument it played a relatively minor role. Although it is not clear precisely why the analogy between divine Spirit and human spirit, despite the extravagant words of Basil, did not bulk as large as the analogy between the divine Spirit and the divine Son,

Didym.*Spir.*40 (*PG* 39:1069)

See pp. 177, 206 above

Ath.*Ep.Serap.*1.12 (*PG* 26:561)

Didym.*Spir.*43 (*PG* 39:1071)

Didym.*Spir.*47 (*PG* 39:1074)

Cyr.*Dial.Trin.*7 (*PG* 75:1104–1105)

Gr.Naz.*Or.*23.11 (*PG* 35:1161); Thdr.Mops.*Hom.catech.*10.8 (*ST* 145:257–59)

Ath.*Ep.Serap.*1.26 (*PG* 26:592)

Bas.*Spir.*16.40 (*PG* 32:144)

one plausible explanation is that pressing the former analogy at all forcefully could easily lead to a Sabellian understanding of the Spirit, contrary to that view of hypostases in the Trinity which had indeed been developed principally on the basis of the distinction between Father and Son, but had now to be applied as well to that between the Spirit and both the Father and the Son.

Epiph.*Haer.*62.1.4 (*GCS* 31:389)

Another exploitation of the arguments in favor of the deity of the Son in the case for the deity of the Spirit was the repetition of the point that the attribution of divine titles, qualities, and operations amounted to an admission of deity. "What titles which belong to God," asked Gregory of Nazianzus, "are not applied to [the Holy Spirit], except only 'unbegotten' and 'begotten'?" and he followed his question with a list of divine titles that were in fact ascribed to the Spirit. One such title for the Holy Spirit was, of course, the term "holy" itself. It was applied to him as "the fulfillment of [his] nature," for he was spoken of as sanctifying, not as sanctified. And so he was holy not "by participation or by a condition having its source outside him," but "by nature and in truth." Similarly, the declaration that the Spirit was "from God" was clarified by the same arguments that had been used to distinguish the christological confession that Christ was "from God" from the general affirmation that all things were "from God" because they were the creatures of God; as a predicate of the Holy Spirit, "from God" meant that he "proceeds from God, not by generation, as does the Son, but as the breath of his mouth." The very title "spirit" seemed to Basil to connote a nature uncircumscribed by change and variation. Because he was "the fullness of the gifts [or good things] of God," he was to be acknowledged as their transcendent source and therefore as also different in kind from the incorporeal creatures. This transcendent source of all created good was "unapproachable by thought"; therefore he had to be God. Even so problematical a title for him as "the place of those who are being sanctified" meant that he was Creator rather than creature.

Gr.Naz.*Or.*31.29 (*PG* 36:165)

Bas.*Spir.*19.48 (*PG* 32:156)
Gr.Naz.*Carm.*2.1.630–34 (*PG* 37:1017); Gr.Naz.*Or.*41.9 (*PG* 36:441)

Cyr.*Dial.Trin.*7 (*PG* 75:1121)

See p. 202 above

Bas.*Spir.*18.46 (*PG* 32:152)

Bas.*Spir.*9.22 (*PG* 32:108)

Didym.*Spir.*4 (*PG* 39:1036)
Bas.*Spir.*22.53 (*PG* 32:165)

Bas.*Spir.*26.62 (*PG* 32:181)

Perhaps even more decisive than the titles of the Holy Spirit were his works. The Holy Spirit was God because he did what only God could do. If the creatures were the objects of his renewing, creating, and sanctifying activity, he could not belong to the same class of beings as they,

Didym.*Trin.*2.7 (*PG* 39:560–600); Thdr.Mops. *Hom.catech.*9.15 (*ST* 145:237)
Apoll.*Fid.sec.pt.*8 (Lietzmann 170)
Ath.*Ep.Serap.*1.23 (*PG* 26:584–85)

but had to be divine. He who filled all creatures had to
Didym.*Spir*.8 (*PG* 39:1040) be "of a different *substantia* than are all the creatures."
Specifically, as the one who justified sinners and per-
Cyr.*Dial.Trin*.7 (*PG* 75:1101); Gr.Naz.*Or*.40.44 (*PG* 36:421) fected the elect, the Holy Spirit did what was appropriate
"only to the divine and supremely exalted nature." Be-
cause he possessed "the power to make alive," Cyril
continued a little later, he could not be merely a creature,
Cyr.*Dial.Trin*.7 (*PG* 75:1116) but had to be God. Yet salvation was not merely vivifica-
See p. 155 above tion but deification. This was the gift of the Holy Spirit,
and therefore he was God. "By the participation of the
Spirit," Athanasius formulated the axiom, "we are knit
Ath.*Ar*.3.24 (*PG* 26:373) into the Godhead." Enumerating the gifts of the Spirit,
Basil affirmed that from him "comes foreknowledge of
the future, understanding of mysteries, apprehension of
what is hidden, distribution of good gifts, the heavenly
citizenship, a place in the chorus of angels, joy without
end, abiding in God, the being made like to God—and
Bas.*Spir*.9.23 (*PG* 32:109) highest of all, the being made God." But, Cyril insisted,
if "the Spirit that makes us God" were of a nature dif-
Cyr.*Dial.Trin*.7 (*PG* 75:1089;1097) ferent from that of God, all hope would be lost. Thus
the soteriological argument, adapted to the special func-
tioning of the Spirit, was no less prominent in the case
for his deity than it had been in the case for the deity
of the Son.

A special form of the soteriological argument, and one
especially appropriate to the doctrine of the Holy Spirit,
was the proof from baptism; this was especially appropriate, though not uniquely so, for the defenders of Nicea
had previously made good use of the baptismal formula
in Matthew 28:19 to charge Arianism with commingling
Ath.*Ar*.2.42 (*PG* 26:237); Thdr.Mops.*Hom.catech*.9.15 (*ST* 145:237) Creator and creature. Athanasius presented his own
trinitarian interpretation: "When baptism is given, whom
the Father baptizes, him the Son baptizes; and whom the
Ath.*Ar*.2.41 (*PG* 26:236) Son baptizes, he is consecrated with the Holy Spirit." But
that very interpretation suggested the peculiar connec-
tion between baptism and the Holy Spirit. For if the
Spirit did not belong properly to the Godhead, "how
Gr.Naz.*Or*.31.28 (*PG* 36:165) can he deify me by baptism?" This argument from
baptism, in refutation of the denial of the deity of the
Ath.*Ep.Serap*.4.7 (*PG* 26:648) Holy Spirit, was for Athanasius "the supreme instance"
and the most persuasive demonstration of how noxious
such a denial was; "for to reject this or to misinterpret it,
Shapland (1951) 163 is to stake salvation itself." Regeneration through the
grace given in baptism was the divine way of salvation,

Bas.*Spir*.10.26 (*PG* 32:113)

Bas.*Spir*.29.75 (*PG* 32:209)

Ath.*Ep.Serap*.1.29 (*PG* 26:596);
Amph.*Ep.syn*.(*PG* 39:96–97)

Cyr.*Dial.Trin*.7 (*PG* 75:1080); Thdr.Mops.*Hom. catech*.9.3 (*ST* 145:219)

Gr.Naz.*Or*.6.22 (*PG* 35:749); Gr.Naz.*Or*.33.17 (*PG* 36:236–37); Amph.*Ep.syn*. (*PG* 39:96)

Didym.*Spir*.24 (*PG* 39:1054)

Bas.*Spir*.10.24 (*PG* 32:109–12)

Bas.*Spir*.10.26;11.27 (*PG* 32:113;116); Amph.*Ep.syn*. (*PG* 39:97)

Gr.Naz.*Or*.8.23 (*PG* 35:817)
Bas.*Spir*.1.3 (*PG* 32:72)

Bas.*Spir*.25.59 (*PG* 32:177)

Bas.*Spir*.7.16 (*PG* 32:96)

Bas.*Spir*.25.58 (*PG* 32:176)

Gr.Nyss.*V.Macr.* (Jaeger 8–I: 398–99)

Bas.*Spir*.29.73 (*PG* 32:205)

Basil argued, so that rejecting the deity of the Holy Spirit meant casting away the meaning of salvation itself; and on the day of judgment he would defend himself by this. This regeneration took place through baptism "into the name of the Father and of the Son and of the Holy Spirit." If the last named was a creature, "the rite of initiation which you reckon to perform is not entirely into the Godhead." But to be Christian meant to be set free from the worship of creatures and to be baptized into the one Godhead of the Trinity, "not into a polytheistic plurality."

Not only the gift of baptism, but the baptismal formula itself constituted a proof. Without the name of the Holy Spirit the formula would be incomplete and therefore the baptism invalid. Basil was especially vigorous in claiming that it was not orthodoxy in its trinitarianism, but Christ in the baptismal formula, that was guilty of "ranking the Holy Spirit alongside the Father and the Son." He therefore urged his opponents "to keep the Spirit undivided from the Father and the Son, preserving, both in the confession of faith and in the doxology, the doctrine taught them at their baptism." His reference to the doxology was provoked by an attack upon him for using, in the liturgy, both the form "Glory be to the Father with [μετά] the Son together with [σύν] the Holy Spirit" and the form "Glory be to the Father through [διά] the Son in [ἐν] the Holy Spirit." It was the phrase "with the Holy Spirit" that seemed an innovation, for it placed the Spirit on the same level as the Father and the Son. Basil replied that this was precisely the reason that had "led our fathers to adopt the reasonable course of employing the preposition 'with,' " and that this had been preserved in the liturgical language of the common people. If liturgical usage was to be authoritative for dogmatic confession, it was unwarranted to make an exception in this instance. Nor, for that matter, was this doxology the only example of a liturgical doctrine of homoousios; for in the hymn that was sung each evening at the lighting of the lamps, the people had preserved the ancient form when they sang: "We praise Father, Son, and God's Holy Spirit."

Yet the processes we have just described, by which the doctrine of the deity and homoousia of the Holy Spirit developed, simultaneously presupposed and compelled development of a more nearly adequate doctrine of the Trinity itself. Therefore Athanasius could put the question: "If there is such a coordination [συστοιχία] and unity within the holy Triad, who can separate either the Son from the Father, or the Spirit from the Son or from the Father himself?" Using the same philosophical term for a coordinate series and applying it to the baptismal formula in Matthew 28:19, Basil maintained that the relation of Spirit to Son was the same as that of the Son to the Father, and that this coordination expressly ruled out any notion of ranking. Such argumentation appeared to derive the deity of the Holy Spirit by logic, as a direct corollary from the doctrine of the Trinity: "If the One was from the beginning, then the Three were so too," and therefore the Spirit was divine. Athanasius, by contrast, made very little use of the doctrine of the Trinity in presenting his defense of the deity of the Son; and the most fully developed formulation of trinitarian teaching anywhere in the Athanasian corpus—still a very brief one—was evoked from him in the course of arguing for the deity of the Holy Spirit. The apparent inconsistency of Didymus's first arguing that there was a correlation between the operation of Father, Son, and Holy Spirit and their ousia, and then maintaining that one could not conclude a difference of nature between them on the basis of the diversity of their operations, could not be clarified without a full-scale doctrine of the Trinity, in which both the unity and the diversity could be precisely formulated within a systematic theory and with a technical terminology adequate to obviate misunderstanding or equivocation. Development of such a doctrine was the achievement of the same men whose doctrine of the Holy Spirit we have been considering, especially of the so-called Cappadocians, Basil, Gregory of Nazianzus, and Gregory of Nyssa.

In this way the development of the doctrine of the Holy Spirit reopened and brought to a head many of the issues that had supposedly been settled at Nicea. For not only had Nicea and its expositors disposed of the problem of the Holy Spirit with a formula which said everything and nothing; but because homoousios left the question of the One unanswered and the creed neglected to codify a term for the Three, the adjudication of the deity of the Holy Spirit made it necessary to

Ath.*Ep.Serap*.1.20 (*PG* 26:576–77)

Bas.*Spir*.17.43 (*PG* 32:148); Didym.*Trin*.2.10 (*PG* 39:640)

Gr.Naz.*Or*.31.4 (*PG* 36:137)

Ath.*Ep.Serap*.1.28 (*PG* 26:596)

Didym.*Spir*.17 (*PG* 39:1049–50); Gr.Nyss.*Tres dii* (Jaeger 3–1:48–49)

Didym.*Spir*.27 (*PG* 39:1058)

develop and to deepen the Nicene Creed. Both the absence of a formula for the One and the tone of the defense of Nicea, in particular the exegesis of the passages of identity and the stock metaphors that were employed, left the Nicene position open to charges of blurring the distinction between Father, Son, and Holy Spirit, after the fashion of the Sabellians. What was needed was a term for the One and another for the Three. A term at hand for the latter was hypostasis, which had been used this way at least since Origen; an obvious term for the former, hallowed not only by long usage but by its association with the Christian exegesis of Exodus 3:14, was ousia. And, in the event, these were the terms in which the relation between the One and the Three came to be formulated: one ousia, three hypostases.

Part of the difficulty was that ousia and hypostasis seemed to be equivalent, if not quite identical; they had, in fact, been so used in the Nicene Creed itself. Athanasius, too, had used ousia as a way of explaining the meaning of hypostasis. Elsewhere he insisted that "hypostasis is ousia and means nothing else but simply being." Indeed, the two terms continued to be used almost interchangeably even after the distinction between them as technical terms had become a standard trinitarian formula. On the basis of the Nicene formula, opponents of the distinction between the two terms such as Marcellus could insist that loyalty to Nicea implied rejection of the notion of distinct hypostases. Besides, the only use of hypostasis in the New Testament as a "trinitarian" technical term, in Hebrews 1:3, seemed to be speaking of the divine ousia which Christ as homoousios shared with the Father, not of the hypostasis which was peculiar to the Father. This appeared to present biblical evidence against the formulation of one ousia, three hypostases; and Basil had to argue, in defense of the formulation, that the passage in Hebrews was not intended to distinguish among the hypostases. It was, then, both an obdurate tenacity about the terminology employed at Nicea and a quasi-Sabellian resistance to the notion of distinct hypostases that stood in the way of the new version of Nicene trinitarian doctrine.

Basil summarized this resistance as follows: "Many persons, in their treatment of the mystical dogmas, fail to distinguish that which is common to the ousia from

ap.Bas.*Ep.*210.5 (*PG* 32:776–77)

Or.*Cels.*8.12 (*GCS* 3:229)

See p. 54 above

Symb.*Nic.* (Schaff 2:60)

Ath.*Ar.*3.66 (*PG* 26:461)
Ath.*Ep.Afr.*4 (*PG* 26:1036)

Epiph.*Haer.*69.72 (*GCS* 37:220–21)

Bas.*Ep.*125.1 (*PG* 32:548)

Bas.*Hom.*24.4 (*PG* 31:608)

Bas.*Ep.*38.6–7 (*PG* 32:336–37)

Bas.*Ep.*210.5 (*PG* 32:776–77)

'the meaning of the hypostases.' They think that it makes no difference whether one says ousia or hypostasis. Therefore to some of those who accept ideas about this subject uncritically it seems just as appropriate to say one hypostasis as one ousia. On the other hand, those who assert three hypostases suppose that it is necessary, on the basis of this confession, to assert a division of ousias into the same number." It was in response to such thinking that a way had to be found that "the hypostases are confessed and the pious dogma of the monarchy does not collapse." The only way to dispel the confusion was to come up with a definition of hypostasis that set it apart from ousia and made it a fit instrument for the specification of what was distinctive in the Father, in the Son, and in the Holy Spirit. The hypostasis, then, had to be "that which is spoken of distinctively, rather than the indefinite notion of the ousia." Coupled with hypostasis in the identification of the distinctiveness of each member of the Triad was another technical term, "mode of origin [τρόπος τῆς ὑπάρξεως]." It seems first to have been used of the Son and the Spirit, the former as begotten and the latter as proceeding from the Father; then it was applied to the Father as well, but in a negative way, namely, that he was unbegotten and did not proceed. Theologians varied in their designations for the mode of origin of each hypostasis, as well as in their degree of emphasis upon the individuality of each; but individuality, howsoever defined, was now to be predicated of Father, Son, and Holy Spirit.

This conception of three hypostases effectively removed the taint of Sabellianism from the Nicene confession, but it did so by raising another specter, at least equally terrifying to Christian faith—the threat of tritheism. Gregory of Nyssa voiced the natural reaction of many upon hearing that Christian faith in God required the confession of three hypostases: "Peter, James, and John are called three humans, despite the fact that they share in a single humanity. And there is nothing absurd in using the word for their nature in the plural, if those who are thus united in nature be many. If, then, general usage grants this, and no one forbids us to speak of two as two, or of more than two as three, how is it that we in some way compromise our confession, by saying on the one hand that the Father, the Son, and the Holy Spirit

Bas.*Ep*.38.1 (*PG* 32:325)

Bas.*Spir*.18.47 (*PG* 32:153)

Bas.*Ep*.38.3 (*PG* 32:328)

Bas.*Spir*.18.46 (*PG* 32:152)

Ps.Bas.*Eun*.4.1 (*PG* 29:681)

have a single godhead, and by denying on the other that we can speak of three gods? For in speaking of the mysteries [of the faith], we acknowledge three hypostases and recognize there is no difference in nature between them." Each of the hypostases was "one" in the complete sense of the word; therefore the confession of the "one God" was not compromised by positing three hypostases. The other Cappadocians were also troubled by the question, and Basil may be the author of a treatise sometimes ascribed to him, *Against Those Who Falsely Accuse Us of Saying That There Are Three Gods.* The monotheistic confession of Deuteronomy 6:4, which Christianity had inherited from Judaism, seemed to be at stake once more, as it had been, in a different sense, in the controversy over whether the Christ whom Christians worshiped could nevertheless be called a creature.

The defense of the Cappadocians against this charge took several forms. None has received greater notoriety than their adaptation to trinitarian theology of a Platonic doctrine, which, following a usage that went back to Plato himself, they called "the universal [τὸ κοινόν]." Gregory of Nazianzus quite unabashedly drew a parallel between the Christian doctrine of the unity of God and the theory of "the more advanced philosophers" among the Greeks about "one Godhead." And elsewhere he formulated the principle that what was common or universal to Father, Son, and Holy Spirit was their "not having come to be and the Godhead"; he then went on to specify "the distinctive" in each. Going even beyond this identification of the Godhead or ousia as a kind of Platonic universal, Gregory of Nyssa answered his own question by declaring that it was, strictly speaking, inaccurate even to speak of Peter, James, and John as "three humans," since "human" was a term for the nature which they had in common; in the case of the three hypostases in the Trinity, however, such a plural was not only inaccurate, but downright dangerous. No one could conclude from the phrase "three humans" that there were three humanities, but it was clear from the history of religion that just such a conclusion had been drawn from the use of the plural for the divine. And so "the divine, simple, and unchangeable nature transcends any sort of diversity according to ousia, in order to be [truly] one." The divine ousia was far more real and far more truly one

Gr.Nyss.*Tres dii* (Jaeger 3–I:38)

Gr.Nyss.*Eun.*1 (Jaeger 1:113–14)

PG 31:1488–96

Bas.*Spir.*18.45 (PG 32:149)
Gr.Nyss.*Tres dii* (Jaeger 3–I:42)

Ath.*Syn.*49.4 (Opitz 2:273)

Gr.Naz.*Or.*31.15 (PG 36:149)

Gr.Naz.*Or.*25.16 (PG 35:1221)

Gr.Nyss.*Tres dii* (Jaeger 3–I:54–55)

than other universals. Basil, too, recognized that his emphasis upon the unity of the divine ousia above and beyond the three hypostases might seem to elevate it to a superior position and thus to depress the reality of the hypostases. Although he rejected any such inference as "irreligion" and blasphemy, it is clear that if the identification of the divine ousia as a universal were the only means of safeguarding the unity of God, that unity would have been in serious jeopardy.

Bas.Ep.52.1 (PG 32:393);
Bas.Hom.24.4 (PG 31:605)

Significantly, the defense of the dogma of the Trinity did not rely primarily on this metaphysical identification. Even Gregory of Nyssa, philosophically the most brilliant and bold of the three Cappadocians, stopped short of providing a speculative solution for the relation of the One and the Three or of the distinction between the properties of the One and those of the Three. Despite his great debt to Middle Platonism, Gregory did not assign to the Platonic doctrine of universals a determinative place in his dogmatics, which was finally shaped by what the church believed, taught, and confessed. His fundamental axiom was: "Following the instructions of Holy Scripture, we have been taught that [the nature of God] is beyond names or human speech. We say that every [divine] name, be it invented by human custom or handed on to us by the tradition of the Scriptures, represents our conceptions of the divine nature, but does not convey the meaning of that nature in itself." And the specific "name" to which he was applying this stricture was "Godhead [θεότης]" itself, the very title he used in his accommodation to Greek theism.

Holl (1904) 217

Gr.Nyss.Tres dii (Jaeger
3–I:42–43)

There was perhaps one exception to the rule that all such "names" were descriptive only of human comprehensions of God. That exception pertained to a mystery that was, if anything, even more ineffable than the mystery of God's relation to the world, namely, the relations within the divine Triad. In opposition to the danger that the distinctiveness of the three hypostases would dissolve in a Platonically defined ousia, the Cappadocians, with varying degrees of emphasis, found the guarantee of the unity of the Godhead in the Father. For Basil, the Father was "a certain power subsisting without being begotten or having an origin," in whom both the Son and the Spirit, each in his way, had their origin. Gregory of Nazianzus went so far as to call the Father "greater" in

Bas.Ep.38.4 (PG 32:329);
Apoll.Fid.sec.pt.18 (Lietzmann 173)

the sense that "the equality and the being" of the equals,
Son and Spirit, came from him. And Gregory of Nyssa
identified the Father as "the source of power, the Son
as the power of the Father, the Holy Spirit as the Spirit
of power." Specifically on the question of distinctions
among the Three, he identified causality as the only real
point of distinction, stating that one was the cause,
namely, the Father, and that the Son and the Spirit were
derived from him, but eternally. In this one cause was the
guarantee of the unity of the Three.

This puzzling, indeed frustrating, combination of
philosophical terminology for the relation of One and
Three with a refusal to go all the way toward a genuinely
speculative solution was simultaneously typical of the
theology of the Cappadocians and normative for the
subsequent history of trinitarian doctrine. Formulas such
as homoousios, three hypostases in one ousia, and mode
of origin were metaphysically tantalizing; but the adjudication of their meaning was in many ways a defiance
not only of logical consistency, but of metaphysical coher-
ence. How, for example, could the Father be the source
of Son and Spirit within the Trinity and yet fatherhood
be a property not only of his hypostasis, but of the divine
ousia as such? Or, to put it in liturgical terms, was the
Lord's Prayer addressed only to the hypostasis of the
Father as "our Father" and the Father of the Son, or
to the entire ousia of the Godhead? Basil's answer to this
and to any such difficulty was to declare that what was
common to the Three and what was distinctive among
them lay beyond speech and comprehension and therefore beyond either analysis or conceptualization. For
all the identification of the mode of origin, the distinction
between the generation of the Son and that of the Spirit,
Didymus admitted, remained "an unknown mode."
Gregory of Nyssa was willing to look for rational supports in his reflection on the One and the Three; but if
none were forthcoming, it was most important to "guard
the tradition we have received from the fathers, as ever
sure and immovable, and seek from the Lord a means of
defending our faith." The dogma of the Trinity was
enshrined in the liturgy and, if one read them aright,
documented in the Scriptures. Now it was the task of
theology to defend it, to reflect upon it. In one sense,
the dogma of the Trinity was the end result of theology,

Marginal references (left column):

Gr.Naz.*Or*.40.43 (*PG* 36:420)

Gr.Nyss.*Maced*.13 (*PG* 45:1317)

Gr.Nyss.*Tres dii* (Jaeger 3–I:55–56)

Ath.*Decr*.31.2–3 (Opitz 2:27)

Bas.*Ep*.38.4 (*PG* 32:333)

Didym.*Trin*.1.9 (*PG* 39:281)

Gr.Nyss.*Tres dii* (Jaeger 3–I:39)

for it brought together many of the themes of the preceding development. But in another sense, it was the starting point.

Throughout the following centuries of the history of doctrine, this dogma was dominant. In fact, one of the reasons for the contrast between the more corporate emphasis of the early history and the more individualistic emphasis of later periods lies in this very dogma. Having become the official teaching of the church, it provided the virtuoso with the limits beyond which his speculation dared not stray as well as with the riddle over which it could puzzle. "The theologian" became, in a special sense, the title for a man who defended the deity of Christ in the context of the trinitarian dogma. The speculations of Augustine's *On the Trinity* enabled him to identify himself with the church catholic and yet to press the believing reason to the very limits of its powers. It was the trinitarian dogma, especially its notion of the divine "energies," that provided the Hesychastic theology of fourteenth-century Byzantium with a foundation for its speculations about the relation between the created and the uncreated light of God. As one of the principal transmitters of patristic doctrine to the Latin Middle Ages, Boethius codified trinitarianism in a form that was to shape the theology of Thomas Aquinas. And the declaration of independence of liberal Protestant theology was most typically expressed in Schleiermacher's relegation of the trinitarian dogma to an appendix in his *Christian Faith*. The distinctive features of the trinitarianism of each of these men and movements deserve individual attention. At this point it bears mentioning that the unresolved contradictions evident in the Cappadocian theology presented a challenge to each of them also; but that meanwhile the church went on believing, teaching, and confessing the dogma in its liturgies and sermons, its catechisms and commentaries.

At the same time, the shape taken by Cappadocian trinitarianism served to move the discussion from the relation between the One and the Three to the relation between the divine and the human in Christ, with which, in one way, the controversy had begun. For granted that it was appropriate to call Christ divine and to assert that he was homoousios with the Father, what did this mean for his also being homoousios with man—and with man

Gr.Presb.*V.Gr.Naz.* (*PG* 35:288)

the creature? Some of the very considerations with which the discussion had opened were bypassed by the solutions which the trinitarian dogma sought to provide for them. But they were too fundamental to the gospel to remain in obscurity, and the form of the trinitarian solution made a reopening of the christological issue unavoidable, particularly for those who had formulated their trinitarian orthodoxy in such a way that their christology became suspect.

5

The Person
of the God-Man

The dogma of the Trinity was developed as the church's
response to a question about the identity of Jesus Christ.
Was he, or was he not, equal in his divine existence with
the Creator and Lord of heaven and earth? The answer
of orthodox Christian doctrine to that question was the
confession that he was "from the ousia of the Father" and
"homoousios with the Father." For all the problems
there were in this answer, the formulation traditionally
identified with the Council of Nicea (although in a somewhat later recension) was the version of the doctrine of
the Trinity which came to be acknowledged as the faith
of the church. And except for the questions—speculative,
liturgical, exegetical, and constitutional—raised in the
course of debates between East and West about the
procession of the Holy Spirit, this was the interpretation
of the doctrine of God in relation to the person of Christ
that was to survive the fall of the Roman Empire, the
schism between Eastern and Western Christendom, and
the upheavals of Renaissance and Reformation, to be
rejected by the critical intelligentsia only in the period of
the Enlightenment and of nineteenth-century Protestant
liberalism. But "a few decades after Nicea the theme of
the formation of dogma shifted completely. . . . Now
the theme is not the preexistent Son of God, but the
incarnate one. Not the relation of God to God is now at
issue, but the relation of God to man in the person of
Elert (1957) 21
the earthly Christ, who dwelt among men." Or, to quote
again the question of Athanasius, "How is it possible
for someone not to err with regard to the incarnate
presence [of the Son] if he is altogether ignorant of the

226

Ath.*Ar*.1.8 (*PG* 26:28)

genuine and true generation of the Son from the Father?"

Now that the meaning of this "genuine and true generation" had been defined at the Council of Nicea and clarified in the half-century after the council, the locus of the issue was transferred to the person of Jesus Christ himself. Ranged against each other in the debate over this issue were the theological traditions represented by Alexandria and by Antioch, whose rivalry in church politics shaped their conflict in christological doctrine and was in turn shaped by it. It is understandable that, coming as it did in the wake of the trinitarian debates, the problem of christology was sometimes treated as though it were susceptible of solution by some of the same means employed in the solution of the questions of the Trinity. For example, one proof for the full deity of the Son was the argument that if the Son were not God, one would be

See p. 199 above

baptized into a creature. The same argument was then pressed into service to support the deity of the Holy

See pp. 216–17 above

Spirit. But now that the question was the relation between the divine and the human in the person of the incarnate Son, a theologian such as Cyril of Alexandria, who maintained that this relation was one of an intimate and inseparable union, was faced with the disturbing question: "Have we, then, been baptized into a man, and shall we

Cyr.*Inc.unigen.* (*SC* 97:276)

admit that this is true?" It is significant that Cyril and his fellow Alexandrians employed in their christology many of the same technical terms that had been mined and minted, largely by previous generations of Alexandrians, during the trinitarian discussion, terms such as "to be joined together [συναφθῆναι]," "unity [ἕνωσις]," "inseparable [ἀδιαίρετος]," and the like. Moreover, some of the same passages of identity that had been so useful for trinitarian doctrine were introduced into the discussion of christological doctrine, as when Cyril of Alexandria, quoting Isaiah 63:9 (LXX), insisted that "it was not an elder, nor an angel, but the Lord himself who saved us, not by an alien death or by the mediation of an ordinary man,

Cyr.*Chr.un.* (*SC* 97:472)

but by his very own blood." In keeping with such argumentation, some modern interpreters have claimed that Cyril's Antiochene opponents in the christological debate, especially Nestorius, were operating with "an insuffi-

Camelot (1951) 229

ciently developed trinitarianism."

But these attempts, ancient and modern, to treat the christological question as a subtopic of the trinitarian one, while partially valid, obscure both the profundity and the poignancy of the evolution of christology: theologians who shared an uncompromising loyalty not only to the letter of Nicea but to the Nicene orthodoxy of Didymus and the Cappadocians were nevertheless on opposite sides when the question of Christ and God became the question of God and man in Christ. Not "an insufficiently developed trinitarianism," but the neglect of the christological question during the discussion of the trinitarian question was responsible for the impasse. Theologians on both sides of the christological debate sought to impugn the trinitarian orthodoxy of their opponents.

Cyril drew an analogy between the Arians and the Antiochenes: the former blasphemed the preexistent Logos, the latter the incarnate. The outstanding exegetical scholar of the Antiochene school, Theodore of Mopsuestia, on the other hand, was attacking the Apollinarist extreme of Alexandrian teaching when he charged that "the partisans of Arius and Eunomius . . . say that [the Logos] assumed a body but not a soul, and that the nature of the Godhead took the place of the soul." The trinitarian development had not really prepared the church for the problematics of the christological issue, and no one was entitled to draw a simple christological inference from either the content or the method of the Nicene and post-Nicene discussions. Yet before the christological controversy was over, it had managed to raise again some of the problems that had supposedly been disposed of in the dogma of the Trinity.

Presuppositions of Christological Doctrine

In at least one respect, there was a close analogy between the doctrine of the Trinity and the doctrine of the person of Christ. Each doctrine drew together many of the motifs of the development that had preceded its formulation. Formally stated, these motifs could be called the common property of all orthodox Christians; yet the different conclusions drawn from common presuppositions suggest that even in these shared beliefs there were divergent emphases. Various of the common presuppositions were variously interpreted, and the relation among the several presuppositions was variously conceived.

The creed of Nicea had followed its statement of the "divinity" (God in himself) with one about "economy"

Cyr.*Chr.un.* (SC 97:306)

Thdr.Mops.*Hom.catech.*5.9 (*ST* 145:111); Nest.*Baz.*1.1.47 (Bedjan 56)

Thdr.Mops.*Hom.catech.*5.3 (*ST* 145:103)

(God in his plan of salvation) in the confession that "for the sake of us men and for the purpose of our salvation" Christ had come down, had become incarnate, had suffered and risen again on the third day, had ascended to the heavens, and would come again to judge the living and the dead. This confessional statement could, with one or another modification or addition, be matched by affirmations in many of the ancient creeds. Each of its components, however, required careful scrutiny for its christological implications; each of them had also been the subject of earlier development. To attach this capsule account of the earthly deeds of Jesus Christ to the affirmation of his divinity was to raise the question of the relation between the divine nature and the events of his life and death. Moreover, if he had come "for the sake of us men and for the purpose of our salvation," it was necessary to specify the connection between his person and his saving work. And by affirming that he was worthy of worship, the church put its teaching and confession about him into the context of its liturgy, where it was the incarnate one who was adored in his sacramental presence and power.

As the Son and Logos of God, Christ was the revelation of the nature of God; in the formula of Irenaeus, "the Father is that which is invisible about the Son, the Son is that which is visible about the Father." If, in a phrase that Irenaeus quoted from an even earlier source, "the Son is the measure of the Father," one would expect that the Christian definition of the deity of God would be regulated by the content of the divine as revealed in Christ. In fact, however, the early Christian picture of God was controlled by the self-evident axiom, accepted by all, of the absoluteness and the impassibility of the divine nature. Nowhere in all of Christian doctrine was that axiom more influential than in christology, with the result that the content of the divine as revealed in Christ was itself regulated by the axiomatically given definition of the deity of God. No one wanted to be understood as setting forth a view of Christ in which this definition was in any way compromised or jeopardized. To Theodore of Mopsuestia the divine transcendence meant that "it is not possible to limit and define the chasm that exists between the one who is from eternity and the one who began to exist at a time when he was not. What possible resem-

Iren.*Haer*.4.6.6 (Harvey 2:160–61)

Iren.*Haer*.4.4.2 (Harvey 2:153)

See pp. 52–54 above

Thdr.Mops.*Hom.catech*.4.6
(*ST* 145:83)

blance and relation can exist between two beings so widely
separated from each other?" At the other end of the christological spectrum, Apollinaris also insisted that the presence of the "sufferings belonging to the flesh" could not

Apoll.*Fid.sec.pt*.11 (Lietzmann 171)

in any way impair the impassibility of the divine nature;
therefore he attacked anyone who would attribute to the
divinity in Christ such "human things" as "development

Apoll.*Fid.sec.pt*.3 (Lietzmann
168)

and suffering."

In their doctrine of God, Alexandrians such as Apollinaris appear to have stressed the notion of impassibility
without compromise. This is borne out by an examination
of Cyril of Alexandria. Confronted by the statement of
such passages in the Psalms as 94:22 and 90:1 (LXX)
that God had "become" man's refuge, Cyril asked the
rhetorical question whether this meant that God had
ceased being God and had become something that he had
not been in the beginning. Of course not, for "being unchangeable by nature, he always remains what he was and
ever is, even though he is said to have 'become' a refuge."
In fact, the very mention of the word "God" made the
interpretation of "become" as applied to God "stupid and
altogether wicked" if it supposed that this could refer to

Cyr.*Chr.un.*(*SC* 97:312–14)

any sort of change in the unchangeable God. Elsewhere
Cyril amplified this metaphysical contrast between the
nature of God the Creator and that of creatures. The nature of God was firmly established, maintaining its unchangeable permanence; it was characteristic of created
existence, on the other hand, to be given over to time and
therefore to be subject to change. Anything that had taken
a beginning had changeability implanted within it. "But
God, whose existence transcends all reason and who rises
above all beginning and all passing away, is superior to
change." Quoting Baruch 3:3 (LXX), "Thou art enthroned for ever, and we are perishing for ever," Cyril
concluded that the divine could not be changed by any

Cyr.*Inc.unigen.* (*SC* 97:208);
Cyr.*Joh*.1.9(ad 1:9) (*PG*
73:125–29); Cyr.*Is*.4.5(ad
51:6) (*PG* 70:1117); Cyr.
Dial.Trin.7 (*PG* 75:1112)

time, or shaken by any sufferings, while created nature
was incapable of being endowed with essential immutability.

As this last statement suggests, however, the purpose
of Cyril's abstract disquisition on the absoluteness and
immutability of God was to deal with the mystery of the
divine Logos. It would not do to speak of his "being
transformed into the nature of flesh" in such a way that

Cyr.*Inc.unigen.* (*SC* 97:208)

his divine immutability was impaired. "He was the Logos

also in the beginning, and proceeding from the eternal
and immutable God and Father, he also had in his own

Cyr.*Inc.unigen.* (*SC* 97:290)

nature eternity and immutability." This attribute of being
"ancient and unchangeable" could not be set aside even
in the incarnation. Although he was said to suffer in the
flesh, impassibility continued to be characteristic of him

Cyr.*Chr.un.* (*SC* 97:472)

insofar as he was God. He was incapable of suffering but
took on a flesh that could suffer, so that the suffering of

Cyr.*Chr.un.* (*SC* 97:474)

his flesh could be said to be his own. But then the question was: "In what sense does not [the impassible Logos]
himself suffer?" Cyril replied that it was "by suffering in

Cyr.*Chr.un.* (*SC* 97:504);
Cyr.*Joh.*12(ad 19:26–27)
(*PG* 74:664)

his own flesh, but not in the nature of his deity," in a manner that transcended all reason and all language. Even
the Alexandrian insistence upon the reality of his sufferings and upon the unity of divine and human in his person could not be allowed to qualify or endanger the essential impassibility of the nature of God.

On this issue the Antiochenes were no less firm; indeed,
it has been suggested that "it was the question of divine
impassibility which took more of the attention of the

H.Chadwick (1951) 158

Antiochenes." Cyril himself may have been acknowledging this when he attributed to them the fear that if human
qualities and experiences were ascribed to the Logos, who
was begotten from above and who transcended all things,
this would be blasphemy; therefore they sought to prevent
any jeopardy to the divine and impassible nature of the

Cyr.*Chr.un.*(*SC* 97:430)

Logos himself. Theodore represented the Logos as saying
that "it is impossible that I myself should be destroyed,
as my nature is indestructible, but I will allow this [body]
to be destroyed because such a thing is inherent in its

Thdr.Mops.*Hom.catech.*8.6
(*ST* 145:195)

nature." It was permissible, according to Nestorius, to
call the impassible Christ passible because he was "impassible according to his divinity but passible according to

Nest.*Ep.Cyr.*2.4 (*ACO*
1–I–1:30)

the nature of his body." He took the homoousios of the
Nicene Creed to mean that the attributes of the divine
nature were those of the Logos, to be by nature impas-

Nest.*Baz.*2.1 (Bedjan 249)

sible, immortal, and eternal. His critics, he said, were
charging him with blasphemy "because I have said that
God is incorruptible and immortal and the quickener of

Nest.*Baz.*2.1 (Bedjan 318)

all"—"God" meaning here the divine Logos. At the same
time, Nestorius maintained that the fusion (or confusion) of the divine and the human in Alexandrian christology not only jeopardized the impassibility of the Logos,
but also made meaningless the possibility of the man

Luke 22:43

Nest.*fr*.24 (Loofs 333); Thdr.
Mops.*Hom.catech*.15.25 (*ST*
145:505)

Jesus. Such an account in the Gospels as that of the angel
strengthening Jesus in the garden would then have to be
no more than a parable, "for he who suffers impassibly
has no need of anyone to strengthen him." From what
seemed to be a shared presupposition about the absoluteness of God there came radically divergent theories about
the person of Jesus Christ.

Yet it was not only of God that impassibility was to be
predicated. One could also speak of "the hope of the life
to come, [where we shall] abide immortal and impassible

Thdr.Mops.*Gal*.1.2–3 (Swete
1:8)

and free of all sin." Impassibility could also be described
as the gift of salvation. God had waited to make Jesus
Christ "immortal, incorruptible, and immutable" until
his resurrection "because he was not the only one whom
he wanted to make immortal and immutable, but us as

Thdr.Mops.*Hom.catech*.6.11
(*ST* 145:151)

well who are associated with his nature." It was in the
resurrection of Christ that both he and those whom he
came to save acquired "an immortal and impassible na-

Thdr.Mops.*Phil*.3.10 (Swete
1:237)

ture." Athanasius of Alexandria, on the opposite side,
had described the "settled character" of the saved person, in this case of the monk Antony, whose "soul was

Ath.*V.Ant*.67 (*PG* 26:940)

imperturbed, and so his outward appearance was calm."
Antony, he meant to say, "possessed in a very high degree Christian ἀπάθεια—perfect self-control, freedom
from passion—the ideal of every true monk and ascetic
striving for perfection. Christ, who was free from every
emotional weakness and fault—ἀπαθὴς Χριστός—is his

R.Meyer (1950) 126

model." The Antiochene and the Alexandrian traditions
were in agreement that salvation was the purpose of the
coming of Christ and that immortality and impassibility
were the consequence of that salvation. It was also agreed
on all sides that there had to be a theological congruence
between the doctrine of the person of Christ and the doctrine of the work of Christ; or, to state it negatively, that
no christological doctrine could be accepted if it militated
against the office of Jesus Christ as Savior. "The main
point of our salvation is the incarnation of the Logos,"

Apoll.*Fid.sec.pt*.11 (Lietzmann
170–171)

Nest.*Baz*.1.1.88 (Bedjan
116–17)

said Apollinaris. The incarnation had to take place as it
did, Nestorius argued, or Satan would not have been
vanquished. In his treatise *On the Incarnation of the
Only-Begotten*, Cyril, for his part, examined the soteriological implications of the christological theories under
discussion and refuted each theory on the grounds that if
it were correct, the saving work of Christ would have been

impossible; other arguments came and went from one theory to another, but this argument was applicable to each. Even to be only a spokesman and a revelation of the divine nature, a task for which it might seem that it would have been enough for him to be "the carpenter's son," he had to be the one who had descended from heaven and the "God who appeared to us, being the Lord" Jesus Christ. This had already been a standard weapon in the arsenal of the Alexandrian and Cappadocian defenders of Nicea.

But when Cyril, together with most of those defenders of Nicea, came to specify the content of this salvation whose integrity had to be maintained in any christological doctrine, it became evident that within the general presupposition presumably shared by all there were pronounced differences. For Cyril attached his understanding of the meaning of the salvation of man to the tradition that had defined it as deification, which he took to be the only means of conferring impassibility on man. Apollinaris had summarized the tradition in the confession: "We declare that the Logos of God became man for the purpose of our salvation, so that we might receive the likeness of the heavenly One and be made God after the likeness of the true Son of God according to nature and the Son of man according to the flesh, our Lord Jesus Christ." Cyril's version of the concept of deification laid special emphasis on the salvation and transformation of the flesh through the incarnation of the immutable and impassible Logos. Defining the purpose of the incarnation, Cyril asserted that "the Only-Begotten became a perfect man in order to deliver our earthly body from a foreign corruption," and that by doing so Christ had "dyed the soul of man with the stability and unchangeability of his own nature," making it a participant in his impassible divinity. Using the identical formulas in another passage, Cyril added that the Only-Begotten had delivered the earthly body from corruption by making his own soul more powerful than sin and endowing the human soul with his own "stability and immutability as wool is imbued with a dye."

If there was to be a congruence between soteriological and christological doctrine, the relation between the divine and the human in the person of Christ had to be adequate to effect this through a transformation in the

Cyr.*Inc.unigen.* (*SC* 97: 196–202)

Cyr.*Chr.un.* (*SC* 97:458–60)

See pp. 205–6 above

See p. 155 above

Apoll.*Fid.sec.pt.*31 (Lietzmann 179)

Cyr.*Inc.unigen.* (*SC* 97:230)

Cyr.*Thds.*20 (*ACO* 1–I–1:54)

very nature of man. And more than the nature of man had to be transformed and saved. A theory of the relation between divine and human in Christ that protected the impassibility of God by attributing suffering and death only to a man whom the Logos had assumed narrowed the doctrine of salvation. For if it were true, "how then can he be said to have become the Savior of the cosmos, and not rather [only] of man, as a pilgrim and traveler

Cyr.Chr.un.(SC 97:356)

through whom we have also been saved?" But since he was to be the one through whom the world was saved, the connection between the man Jesus and the Logos (through whom the world had been created) had to be more intimate than the doctrine of the assumption of a man by the Logos would allow. For if, according to Hebrews 2:14–15, the Savior was to "destroy him who has the power of death, that is, the devil," it had to be "the Creator of the universe, the Logos of God rich in mercy"

Cyr.Inc.unigen. (SC 97:202)

who emptied himself and was born of a woman. No mere association, nothing less intimate than a union between the Logos-Creator and the one who was born and crucified would have been sufficient to liberate those who had been given over to lifelong bondage through their fear of death. If salvation was to be the gift of impassibility and immortality, the Savior had to be the Logos himself, not only a man assumed by the Logos.

It was possible to interpret every one of these themes in quite another way, and therefore to derive quite another christology from them. Despite the rhetorical question just quoted from Cyril, Theodore did teach that Christ had saved the world, not merely man—but that he had saved the world by saving man. The universe was made up of the invisible, rational beings such as angels, and of the visible, material things, composed of the four elements of earth, air, water, and fire. Man was related to the invisible through his soul, to the visible through his

Thdr.Mops.Eph.1.10 (Swete 1:129)

body. He was the one link between the various orders of the created universe, and his sin and death jeopardized the unity of that universe. Christ was the Savior of the entire world in the sense that the salvation of man, the microcosm, also effected the salvation of the macrocosm. "Therefore the connection between all things is also reestablished on the basis of our renewal. The first fruit of this is he who is Christ according to the flesh, in whom there is accomplished a very good and, so to speak, a compendious new creation of all things." So it came that "the agreement and harmony and connection of all existing things will be saved for incorruptibility" through the salvation of man by the man Christ. The salvation of the cosmos lay in the reintegration of the only creature in whom all the constituent parts of the cosmos were represented, that is, man—in his reintegration, not in an ontological transformation of his nature into something more than human and therefore less than human.

In Theodore's view of human nature, three factors were interrelated: the fall into sin, susceptibility to change, and mortality. Sometimes he could follow the conventional, though by no means universal, Christian teaching that mortality was simply the result of sin, and that "death was introduced when we sinned." In consonance with this view he could say that in this life "we suffer many changes, as those who are by nature mortal." But he also reversed the connection between sin and death, as when he described life in heaven: "Because we shall be made immortal after our resurrection, we shall no longer be able to sin; for it follows from our being mortal that we sin." And the impassibility conferred through salvation meant deliverance from mutability, which was not to be identified with either sin or death but was to be related to both; for "it would be possible to save the body from death and corruption if we first made the soul immutable and delivered it from the passions of sin, so that by acquiring immutability we would also obtain deliverance from sin." No simple causal relation would be adequate. "Mortality is chronologically prior to sin, but sin is logically prior to mortality"; but it should perhaps be added that passibility was a factor in some sense distinct from both. Death had entered into human life through sin, but now it had weakened human nature and aggravated its tendency to sin. To be restored to authentic humanity, man needed to be saved from all of these; salvation meant "second birth, renewal, immortality, incorruptibility, impassibility, deliverance from death and servitude and all evils, the happiness of freedom, and participation in the ineffable good things which we are expecting," as well as deliverance from the punishment and damnation deserved by human sins.

This restoration of authentic humanity was the work of Christ the man in his life, death, and resurrection. Only

Thdr.Mops.*Col*.1.16 (Swete 1:269)

Thdr.Mops.*Eph*.1.10 (Swete 1:129)

Thdr.Mops.*Gal*.2.15–16 (Swete 1:26)

Thdr.Mops.*Col*.3.5 (Swete 1:299)

Thdr.Mops.*Hom.catech*.5.11 (*ST* 145:117)

Norris (1963) 184

Thdr.Mops.*Hom.catech*.12.8 (*ST* 145:335)

Thdr.Mops.*Hom.catech*.14.17 (*ST* 145:439)
Thdr.Mops.*Eph*.2.5 (Swete 1:145)

Thdr.Mops.*Hom.catech.*7.13
(*ST* 145:181)

Thdr.Mops.*Eph.*1.6 (Swete
1:125)

Thdr.Mops.*Gen.*49.10 (*PG* 66:
645); Thdr.Mops.*Pecc.orig.*
(Swete 2:335)

Thdr.Mops.*Hom.catech.*7.4
(*ST* 145:167)

See pp. 149–52 above

Thdr.Mops.*Col.*2.15 (Swete
1:291)

Norris (1963) 209

Durand (1964) 279

because he had been "one of us, who came from out of our race" and our nature, could he achieve this salvation. What had been accomplished through him and in him as the first fruit of the human race "had all been done to him for [our] common salvation." Although a true and complete man, he had not taken death upon himself as a punishment as other men do; being "more excellent," he had passed through death to immortality and incorruptibility and could now confer these gifts on his brethren. His life and death were part of his saving work, but the decisive event in the economy of salvation was his resurrection, which was "the principal object of all the reforms wrought by him, as it is through it that death was abolished, corruption destroyed, passions extinguished, mutability removed, the inordinate emotions of sin consumed, the power of Satan overthrown, the urge of demons brought to nought, and the affliction resulting from the law wiped out." The dramatic interpretation of the death and resurrection of Christ as a victory over the demonic powers that held man in their sway, which was a prominent motif in the ante-Nicene tradition, became in Theodore's hands the statement of Christ's triumph over the "principalities and powers . . . which would have no power over us if we could avoid sinning." But whatever motif Theodore selected as he commented upon the imagery suggested in this or that text, he customarily referred it to "his insistence upon the active agency of Christ's humanity in the work of redemption." This insistence led to "a definite christological dualism," a radical distinction between the divine Logos and the man whom he had assumed, because of what Christ had to be in order to save as Theodore said he did. He and Cyril held many of the themes of soteriology and christology in common; but the differences between them, while less obvious, proved to be more decisive.

It has been pointed out that "the predilection of St. Cyril for the soteriological approach to the problems becomes evident with special prominence in his discussions of the Eucharist." Here, too, a common ground of shared teaching about the sacraments led to a divergence in christological formulation. Theodore set forth the doctrine of the real presence, and even a theory of sacramental transformation of the elements, in highly explicit language. When Christ gave the bread, Theodore argued, "he did not say, 'This is the symbol of my body,' but 'This is my body' "; for the elements "were so transformed by the descent of the Holy Spirit." He could even connect this transformation of the elements to the traditional idea of the Eucharist as the medicine of immortality: "At first it is laid upon the altar as a mere bread and wine mixed with water, but by the coming of the Holy Spirit it is transformed into body and blood, and thus it is changed into the power of a spiritual and immortal nourishment." These and similar passages in Theodore are an indication that the twin ideas of the transformation of the eucharistic elements and the transformation of the communicant were so widely held and so firmly established in the thought and language of the church that everyone had to acknowledge them. Even if this eucharistic doctrine was inconsistent with Theodore's general theological method, he continued to teach in his theology what the church believed and taught in its liturgy about the Eucharist.

The difference between Theodore and Cyril was that Theodore did not base a christology upon this eucharistic doctrine, but Cyril did. The key to Cyril's christological interpretation of sacramental theology lay in his emphasis upon the life-giving and transforming power of salvation in Christ, a power conveyed by the sacraments, especially the Eucharist. Baptism was also a channel for this power. By baptism, Cyril said, "we are reshaped into the divine image in Jesus Christ," adding that it would be absurd to think of this as a "bodily re-formation." Elsewhere, however, particularly when speaking about the change effected by eating the body and blood of Christ in the Lord's Supper, he seems to have been far less reluctant to ascribe "bodily re-formation" to the working of sacramental grace. His proof text for the doctrine of the Eucharist was not the account of its institution in the synoptic Gospels and 1 Corinthians (although he did, of course, comment also on these passages), but the sixth chapter of the Gospel of John: "Unless you eat the flesh of the Son of man and drink his blood, you have no life in you." These words meant, he said, that Christ "as God makes us alive, not merely by granting us a share in the Holy Spirit, but by granting us in edible form the flesh which he assumed." Commenting on these same words elsewhere, he insisted that the body given in the Eucharist could not be

---

Thdr.Mops.*Hom.catech*.15.10
(*ST* 145:475)

See pp. 169–70 above

Thdr.Mops.*Hom.catech*.16.36
(*ST* 145:593)

Cyr.*Inc.unigen*. (*SC* 97:274)

Cyr. *1 Cor*.10.1 (*PG* 74:880)

Cyr.*Joh*.4.2(ad 6:48–50) (*PG* 73:560–85)

John 6:53

Cyr.*Inc.unigen*. (*SC* 97:278)

Cyr.*Chr.un.* (SC 97:510)

life-giving unless it had become "the very flesh of the Logos who gives life to everything." The body received in the Eucharist was like a "vivifying seed," by which the communicant was intimately joined with the Logos himself and made to be like the Logos, immortal and incorruptible.

Cyr.*Luc.*22.19 (PG 72:909–912)

In the course of developing this understanding of the Eucharist, Cyril made explicit his rejection of the suggestion that the words of John 6:53 could refer to "the precious body and blood, not of God the Logos, but of a man joined to him" in the incarnation. This represented an erroneous view of the Eucharist and of the person of Christ. There is reason to believe that in the Antiochene tradition, despite the formulas of transformation quoted earlier from Theodore, the Eucharist came to be thought of as consisting, in the formula of Irenaeus, of an earthly and a heavenly substance, each of which retained its nature. Eutherius of Tyana, a partisan of Nestorius, appears to have taught that objectively "the mystical bread is of the same nature" as earthly bread, but that by faith it subjectively became the body of Christ to the believer. And Nestorius argued that by the words of institution, "This is my body," Christ "says not that the bread is not bread and that his body is not a body, but he has said demonstrably bread and body, which is in the ousia." We may conjecture that in the course of controversy the Antiochenes discovered an inconsistency between Theodore's eucharistic doctrine and his christological doctrine, and that they eventually adjusted the former to the latter; in any case, it is clear that the Alexandrians formulated and defended a christology that was conformable to the eucharistic piety in which they believed.

Cyr.*Chr.un.* (SC 97:508)

See p. 167 above

ap.Ficker (1908) 20–21

Nest.*Baz.*2.1 (Bedjan 449)

This christology was, the Alexandrians argued, conformable also to the liturgical practice of the church, and they insisted that the christology of their opponents was not. The admonition of *Second Clement* to think of Jesus Christ as of God also implied that Jesus Christ was deserving of that worship which was properly paid to God alone. In the controversy with Arianism, Nicene orthodoxy had made much of the inconsistency between the Arians' practice of worshiping Jesus Christ and their refusal to acknowledge that he was God in the fullest and most unambiguous sense of the word; the same argument had been used, on the basis of the doxologies, in support of the deity of the Holy Spirit. At this point more than

2 *Clem.*1.1 (Bihlmeyer 71)

See pp. 198–200 above

See p. 217 above

at any other, the application to the christological controversy of an argument invented during the trinitarian controversy proved to be effective. For the defenders of Nicea refused to distinguish between the worship appropriate to the Father and that appropriate to the Son. The *Detailed Confession* of Apollinaris, which summarized Nicene orthodoxy without getting into the speculations about the human soul of Christ for which the author was later condemned, was speaking for the main body of the tradition when it attacked an interpretation of the Trinity that would lead to "three dissimilar and diverse systems of worship, [contrary to the institution of] a single legal way of religious observance." There was, he wrote elsewhere, "nothing that is to be worshiped and nothing that saves outside the divine Trinity." The Christian worship of God was properly addressed to the Trinity of Father, Son, and Holy Spirit, without any distinction at all as to degree or kind. Such was the orthodox interpretation of the Nicene decree and the clear outcome of the post-Nicene development, as eventually stated in the formula that the Holy Spirit was "the one who with the Father and the Son is worshiped and glorified."

Now that the point of discussion was not the relation of the Son and the Spirit to the Father, but the relation of the humanity to the divinity in the incarnate Son, the issue became more complex. Was the humanity of the Logos, too, the object of worship? The Arians had been accused by Athanasius of practicing the worship of a man, because they made the Logos less than God. But could not the charge of "anthropolatry" be directed with equal validity against the descendants of Athanasius? For example, Apollinaris went on, in the creedal statement just quoted, to declare: "We confess . . . a single worship of the Logos and of the flesh which he assumed. And we anathematize those who render diverse acts of worship, one divine and one human, and who worship the man born of Mary as being different from him who is 'God from God.' " The Christian adoration of Christ had to be "the worship of the Son of God including the human likeness." Worship was addressed to the incarnate one, divine and human; "to him we properly bring our worship, and his flesh is not excluded from the worship. . . . For whoever does not worship this flesh, does not worship him." The Christian cultus required the worship of the entire incarnate Logos in the undiscriminated unity

Apoll.*Fid.sec.pt.*1 (Lietzmann 167)

Apoll.*Fid.inc.*5 (Lietzmann 195)

Symb.Nic.—CP (Schaff 2:57–58)

Ath.*Ar.*3.32 (PG 26:392)

Apoll.*Fid.sec.pt.*28 (Lietzmann 177)

Apoll.*fr.*6 (Lietzmann 205)

Apoll.*Fid.inc.*6 (Lietzmann 197)

Apoll.*fr*.9 (Lietzmann 206–207)

Euther.*Confut*.5 (*PG* 28:1349–53)

Cyr.*Inc.unigen.* (*SC* 97:258)

Matt.1:23

Thdr.Mops.*Phil*.2.10–11 (Swete 1:222–23)

Thdr.Mops.*Hom.catech*.5.6 (*ST* 145:107)

Thdr.Mops.*Eph*.1.21 (Swete 1:138)

Thdr.Mops.*Hom.catech*.7.13 (*ST* 145:181)

Cyr.*Chr.un.* (*SC* 97:392)

1 Tim.3:16

Cyr.*Chr.un.* (*SC* 97:356)

Nest.*Serm*.1 (Loofs 262)

Nest.*Baz*.2.1 (Bedjan 328)

Nest.*Null.det.* (Loofs 249)

of his person, as implied by the liturgical practice of the church. Any worship of the incarnate one that separated his humanity from his divinity would be equivalent to replacing the divine Triad by a tetrad of Father, Son, Holy Spirit, and the man Jesus. Therefore it was untenable to imply that "we worship Emmanuel as a man."

In the acknowledgment that Emmanuel, the God-man who was "God with us," was deserving of worship, all who accepted the Nicene definition were agreed; it was demanded not only by Nicea, but by Philippians 2:6–11. These words of the apostle meant, according to Theodore, that "because of the link he has with the Only-Begotten," Jesus, the man assumed by the Logos, had been highly exalted and given a name above every name; this could not have been given to the Logos, for he had always had it and had never lost it. After the resurrection, when this glory had been conferred on the man assumed by the Logos, "all men adore him and all men confess Jesus Christ to be God to the glory of God the Father." The man Jesus had been raised to the right hand of God, "and he constantly receives adoration from all creation because of his close union with God the Logos." His sitting at the right hand of the Father meant that the man assumed by the Logos had become a participant in the glory of the Logos, so that "because of the nature of God the Logos dwelling in him, he is to be adored by all." Likewise, the authority to judge the quick and the dead belonged to the man assumed. Even Theodore's opponents were forced to recognize that he ascribed "the dignity and honor" of the Logos to the man Jesus, although they maintained that "the mystery of religion" was dissolved by his interpretation of how the Logos was to be worshiped. To Nestorius, Philippians 2:6–11 meant that one adored Jesus the man on account of the Logos who bore him, and that "on account of the One who is hidden I worship the one who appears. . . . I distinguish the natures, but I unite the worship." It was the assumed man "who endured death three days, and him I adore with the divinity. . . . On account of him who is clothed I adore the clothing." Or, as Nestorius put it in a single formula, "Let us confess the God in man, let us adore the man who is to be worshiped together with God because of the divine conjunction with God the Creator." The Christian worship of Jesus Christ was an assumed presupposition on both sides, and nothing in the debate caused either side to question its propriety. Theology had to come to terms with liturgy.

Of special interest in the liturgy was the language being used about the Virgin Mary, who had come to be called "Theotokos [θεοτόκος]." Despite the effort to find evidence of it elsewhere, there is reason to believe that the title originated in Alexandria, where it harmonized with and epitomized the general Alexandrian tradition. The earliest incontestable instance of the term Theotokos was in the encyclical of Alexander of Alexandria directed against Arianism in 324. Later in the fourth century, the emperor Julian, in his polemic against the "Galileans," asked the Christians: "Why do you incessantly call Mary Theotokos?" But the sources of the idea of Theotokos are almost certainly to be sought neither in polemics nor in speculation, but in devotion, perhaps in an early Greek version of the hymn to Mary, *Sub tuum praesidium;* here, too, theology had to come to terms with liturgy. In the conflicts with Gnosticism Mary had served as proof for the reality of the humanity of Jesus: he had truly been born of a human mother and therefore was a man. But as Christian piety and reflection sought to probe the deeper meaning of salvation, the parallel between Christ and Adam found its counterpart in the picture of Mary as the Second Eve, who by her obedience had undone the damage wrought by the disobedience of the mother of mankind. She was the mother of the man Christ Jesus, the mother of the Savior; but to be the Savior, he had to be God as well, and as his mother she had to be "Mother of God." In popular devotion these themes were interwoven with other speculations about the manner of Christ's birth and about the later life of the Virgin, but in its fundamental motifs the development of the Christian picture of Mary and the eventual emergence of a Christian doctrine of Mary must be seen in the context of the development of devotion to Christ and, of course, of the development of the doctrine of Christ.

For it mattered a great deal for christology whether or not one had the right to call Mary Theotokos. Arians and others may have used the term without drawing from it conclusions agreeable to Athanasian orthodoxy. But once the Nicene formula had been established and clarified, those who stood in the succession of Athanasius—and

Alex.*Ep.Alex.*54 (Opitz 3:28)

Jul.*Gal.*262D (*LCL* 3:398)

Iren.*Haer.*5.1.2 (Harvey 2:316)

Iren.*Dem.*33 (*ACW* 16:69)

Ath.*Ar*.3.29 (*PG* 26:385)

perhaps Athanasius himself—found in this title an apt
formula for their belief that in the incarnation deity and
humanity were united so closely that, by what came to be
known as "the communication of properties," neither
birth nor crucifixion nor salvation could be attributed to
one nature without the other. It was a way of speaking
about Christ at least as much as a way of speaking about
Mary. Since it was permissible to speak of Christ as "the

See p. 177 above

suffering God," as the piety and the proclamation of the
church did, Alexandrian christology could also take advantage of the liturgical term Theotokos to support its
emphasis on the unity of the person of Christ.

Its opponents correctly saw the implications of the
term. Nestorius objected that it had not been used by the

Nest.*Baz*.2.1 (Bedjan 220)

fathers and that it was a calumny to attribute it to them.
If he actually advocated Anthropotokos [mother of a
human being] as a substitute, he did not, as his opponents charged, mean this as a reversion to the long-repudi-
ated heresy that Christ was a mere man. His own preferred
term was Christotokos, which he set against both Theotokos and Anthropotokos, because it "both removes the
blasphemy of [Paul of] Samosata . . . and avoids the evil

Nest.*Ep.Cael*. (Loofs 182)

of Arius and Apollinaris": Mary was the bearer of Jesus
Christ, the man in whom God the Logos dwelt, not of the
Deity. Eventually, Nestorius found it possible to reconcile himself even to Theotokos, not only because there
was a sense in which he could accept its orthodoxy, but
perhaps also because its position in Christian worship
was so firmly established as to be unassailable.

Within these several presuppositions the doctrine of
the person of Christ developed. The presuppositions included what the church believed, taught, and confessed:
what in its apologies and creeds it confessed about God;
what in its preaching and exposition it taught about salvation; what in its piety and liturgy it believed about the
coming of God in Christ. As controversy forced the teachers of the church in various parties to clarify what they
believed, taught, and confessed, they turned to biblical
exegesis and to philosophical-theological speculation for
answers. The dogmatic legislation of the church did not
supply such answers; instead, it sought to identify the
orthodox premises for the exegesis and to draw the proper
boundaries within which the speculation and further controversy were to be carried on. In the sense that these

premises and boundaries had not been specified with any real precision before, the formulation of the doctrine of the person of Christ involved genuine novelty. But in the sense that the presuppositions were already present, that formulation could claim to be, in the opening words of the Chalcedonian decree, "following the holy fathers."

Symb.Chalc. (Schaff 2:62);
Cyr.Inc.unigen. (*SC* 97:298)

Alternative Theologies of the Incarnation

Decisive though they were in many ways, the presuppositions just analyzed did not of themselves produce a christology. For the content of the doctrine of the person of the God-man was supplied by the words and deeds of Jesus Christ and by the witness of all of Scripture to him. Apollinaris was expressing a common opinion when he spoke of "innumerable teachings supplied everywhere throughout the divine Scriptures, all of them together bearing witness to the apostolic and ecclesiastical faith." We are, said Cyril, "obliged in every way to the truth, eager to track down what seems right in accordance with the Sacred Scriptures, and loyal in following the opinions of the fathers." All sides accepted this authority; all sides affirmed that the Logos had become man and were compelled to acknowledge that their opponents affirmed the same; all sides professed obedience to the entire apostolic faith as set forth in the Bible. Yet it was difficult, indeed impossible, for any single theology of the incarnation to do equal justice to all these "innumerable teachings" about Christ. When, for example, Hilary made the Pauline and then Nicene phrase "in accordance with the Scriptures" a refrain in his apostrophe to the death and resurrection of Christ, this led him to the formula that "the only-begotten God suffered the things that men can suffer," which would not have been acceptable without qualification to various participants in the christological controversy.

In part, the variations in the use of Scripture to construct a doctrine of the person of Christ can be attributed to differences of opinion about the validity and the limits of allegorical exegesis. In what way was the Old Testament a proper source of data for christology? Directing his criticism against the allegorical method of Origen and his followers, Theodore of Mopsuestia sought to curb the tendency to read the Old Testament and the New as "words of Christ" in the same sense of the term. One was

*Apoll.Fid.sec.pt.*43 (Lietz-mann 184)

Cyr.Inc.unigen. (*SC* 97:298)

*Hil.Trin.*10.67 (*PL* 10:394-95)

*Iren.Haer.*4.2.3 (Harvey 2:148)

Thdr.Mops.*Eph*.arg. (Swete 1:117)

Or.*Cels*.4.44 (*GCS* 2:317)

Thdr.Mops.*Gal*.4.24 (Swete 1:73–74)

Thdr.Mops.*Gal*.4.29 (Swete 1:86)

Thdr.Mops.*Gal*.4.24 (Swete 1:79)

Thdr.Mops.*Eph*.4.8 (Swete 1:166)

Thdr.Mops.*Gal*.4.27 (Swete 1:84)

Ps.110:1; Heb.1:13

Ps.22:1; Matt.27:46

CCP (553) *Anath*.3 (Mansi 9:377)

not to read Scripture in an "absolute" or "simple" way, that is, "without reference to the occasion and historical connection" of the passage. The most explicit and detailed allegory in the New Testament was that contained in Galatians 4:21–31, which was used by the proponents of the method as justification for applying it to other narratives of the Old Testament as well. This was, Theodore insisted, an "abuse of the apostle's term"; for "the apostle does not abolish the history nor dissolve the things that happened in the past, but he accepts them as they had happened then and applies the history of the things that happened to his own understanding." The apostle retained the historicity of these events as "things that had really happened." A proper allegory, then, was one that "compared [and applied] events that happened in the past to the present." For example, the use of Psalm 68:19, "When he ascended on high he led a host of captives," in Ephesians 4:8 did not mean that the verse in the Psalms had been "spoken prophetically"; it was simply an allusion like those used in sermons. Similarly, the use of Isaiah 54:1 in Galatians 4:27, in the very context of the allegory of Sarah and Hagar, was not intended to prove that these words had been "spoken prophetically about the resurrection, but he abused the statement [that is, applied it in a sense different from its intended one] because of the word 'barren.'" Theodore and his followers were far more restrained than the Alexandrians in employing Old Testament passages as constituent elements in the doctrine of the person of Christ.

More decisive than the question of whether to apply passages of the Old Testament to the doctrine of Christ was the question of how to combine the disparate statements about him that appeared in both the Old Testament and the New. The Psalter spoke of his being enthroned at the right hand of God; it was also the source of his cry of dereliction on the cross. The Second Council of Constantinople in 553 recognized the key issue in the christological controversy when it anathematized anyone "who says that God the Logos who performed the miracles is one, and that the Christ who suffered is another." The relation of Christ the miracle-worker to Christ the crucified could be defined as simply the relation of the divine in him to the human in him, but this oversimplification really satisfied no one. There was, for example, the mir-

Matt.14:25

Nest.*Capit.* (Loofs 218–19)

Leo M.*Tom.*4 (*ACO* 2–II–1:29)

ap.Eust.Mon.*Ep.* (*PG* 86:924)

Matt.9:18–25
Luke 7:11–15

Cyr.*Joh.*4(ad 6:64) (*PG* 73:604)

Cyr.*Chr.un.* (*SC* 97:422)

Cyr.*Chr.un.* (*SC* 97:320)

Matt.27:46

Ambr.*Luc.*10.127 (*CCSL* 14:381)

Ath.*Ar.*3.56 (*PG* 26:441)

Ath.*Ar.*3.57 (*PG* 26:444)

acle of Christ's walking on the water. Nestorius, responding "to him who asks, 'Who is it that walked on the water?' " declared: "It was the feet that walked, and the concrete body through the power that dwelt in him. That is a miracle. For if God walks on the water, that is not amazing." Leo, by contrast, made the flat assertion: "To walk on the back of the sea with feet that do not sink and to still the rising of the waves by rebuking the winds —this is, unambiguously, divine." As Severus pointed out, it was not characteristic of the divine to walk at all, nor characteristic of the human to walk on water. Therefore Cyril insisted that in such miracles as the raising of Jairus's daughter or of the widow's son at Nain both the divine and the human were involved; the hand of Christ touched the person to demonstrate the "single operation" of Logos and flesh. For if Christ had performed his miracles only by virtue of an "indwelling" of the divine Logos, he would have been no different from the prophets, who did the same. Therefore one must say that the Source of life was hungry, that the All-Powerful grew tired.

The critical problem was his suffering, crucifixion, and death. Who "cried with a loud voice, 'Eli, Eli, lama sabachthani?' " Without taking account of all the consequences of his language, Ambrose explained these words to mean that "it was the man who cried out as he was about to die by separation from the divinity. For since the divinity is immune to death, there could not have been any death unless life had withdrawn; for the life is the divinity." Athanasius, too, attributed the cry of dereliction to the humanity of Christ, since "the Lord cannot be forsaken by the Father, being ever in the Father, both before he spoke and when he uttered this cry." This was evident from the miraculous changes in nature that accompanied his death, such as the darkening of the sun and the raising of the dead, immediately after the report of the cry of dereliction. It followed, therefore, according to Athanasius, that "human were the sayings, 'Let the cup pass' and 'Why hast thou forsaken me?' and divine the act by which he himself caused the sun to grow dark and the dead to rise." Cyril saw in the cry the voice of "the human nature in him," which was sinless but which, as the second Adam, bespoke and rescued the human condition. With this he contrasted the view of the

Cyr.*Chr.un.* (SC 97:438)

Thdr.Mops.*fr.* (Swete 2:325)

Thdr.Mops.*Hom.catech.*5.6
(ST 145:107)

Cyr.*Chr.un.* (SC 97:494)

Cyr.*Ep.*46.5 (ACO
1–1–6:161–62)

Thdr.Mops.*Phil.*2.8 (Swete
1:220)

Thdr.Mops.*Ps.*8.5 (ST 93:47)

Antiochenes, as he understood it, who claimed that "these sounds are those of the assumed man," not of the Logos incarnate. Theodore was quoted as teaching that "the deity was separated from him who suffered according to the experience of death, for it was not possible for it [the deity] to undergo the experience of death." But he also asserted that "He [the Son of God] was not separated from him [the assumed man] in his crucifixion, nor did He leave him at death, but He remained with him until He helped him to loose the pains of death." The specter of Gnostic and other forms of docetism made it imperative for all to affirm the reality of the sufferings of Christ and of his agony in the garden; the specter of Patripassianism made it impossible to attribute these to the divine nature.

The problem of attributing both the divinity and the humanity, both the miracles and the crucifixion, to the same subject could have been resolved if the New Testament itself had been more precise in its language. As in other cases, the transmission and translation of the biblical text introduced a greater precision than the text itself had possessed. There were, for instance, two Syriac translations, perhaps even two Greek texts, of Hebrews 2:9; one of them read, "Because he, God, by his grace tasted death for every man," while the other read, "Apart from God he [Jesus] tasted death." The first preserved the oneness of the divine and the human, even in his death; the other preserved the divine against the passibility of the human, especially in his death. Even those who wanted to do the latter had to acknowledge that Scripture, in speaking of Christ, "speaks as of a single person, and gathers together into one those things that are different in force according to the division of the natures." But this had to be explained in such a way that "when we hear Scripture saying either that Jesus has been honored or glorified or that something has been conferred on him or that he has received dominion over all things, we must not understand [this to refer to] God the Logos, but to the man who has been assumed." And on the other hand, those who were bent upon preserving the unity of the divine and human in the one Christ were nevertheless careful to specify that, while "the statements and deeds in the Gospels and in the apostolic proclamation" were not to be sorted out into those that pertained to the divine and those that pertained to the human, it was essential to observe that they did not apply "to the naked and not yet incarnate" Logos, but only to the incarnate one in the

Cyr.*Chr.un.* (SC 97:448)

concreteness of his total life.

It was, then, difficult for any one theology of the incarnation to encompass in an integrated whole the "innumerable teachings supplied everywhere throughout the

Apoll.*Fid.sec.pt.*43 (Lietzmann 184)

divine Scriptures." Instead, each theology found certain passages about Christ congenial to its own central emphasis, and certain passages difficult to account for. Since it was around the explanation of such passages that so much of the doctrinal development moved, an identification of the proof text and of the crux of interpretation may serve to clarify the alternative positions. For from the proof texts came the root metaphors in the light of which all other predications were viewed. By examining these passages and their metaphors, together with those that became problematical, we may identify the two conflicting christologies as the doctrine of "the hypostatic union" and the doctrine of "the indwelling Logos"— even though each side not only tried to account for all biblical passages in its system, but also tried to come to terms with the formulas characteristic of its opponents. This makes it all the more desirable to classify the doctrines on another basis than that of the patriarchal parties, Alexandrian and Antiochene, usually arrayed against each other in the standard accounts of the controversy.

The locus classicus or "starting-point" for the theology

Kelly (1958) 284

of the hypostatic union was John 1:14: "And the Word became flesh." The connection between Logos and flesh was the principal subject for both debate and development, but "became" was a problem in its own right. For how could the Logos, coequal with the Father in his eternal and immutable being, become something else? Conflicting as it did with the self-evident axiom of divine immutability, such a suggestion was, Cyril asserted, "nothing other than sheer sophistry and trumpery" and "the fabrication of a deranged mind." Psalm 94:22 read: "The Lord has become my stronghold"; and Psalm 90:1 (LXX) read: "Lord, thou hast become a refuge to us from generation to generation." Did this mean that God had ceased to be God and had been transformed into a refuge, "changed in his nature into something he had not been before?" But he "is unchangeable according to

Cyr.*Chr.un.* (SC 97:312–14)

nature, remains completely what he was and ever is."
To those who were curious about the meaning of the incarnation, John 1:14, when correlated with Philippians
2:5–8 and Hebrews 1:3, declared that "God from God,
being by nature the only-begotten Logos of God, the
radiance of the glory and the express image of the person
of him who begot him, became man, but was not changed

Cyr.*Chr.un.* (SC 97:314–16)
Cyr.*Inc.unigen.* (SC 97:228)

into flesh." Therefore Cyril insisted that "becoming
flesh" was synonymous with "becoming man"; if the opposing position was correct, "the incarnation, or to be
more specific, the humanization of the Logos is done away

Cyr.*Chr.un.* (SC 97:322)

with." John 1:14 required that the various titles attached
to Jesus Christ should not be sorted out, but on the contrary should be brought together "into an indivisible

Cyr.*Chr.un.* (SC 97:370–72)

unity."

So overriding was this concern for an indivisible unity
in the theology of the hypostatic union that, if need be,
the symmetry of the relation between the divine and
the human in Christ could be sacrificed to it. What later
generations have labeled as the Apollinarian heresy was
a consistent, if oversimplified, application of this fundamental perspective. Athanasius, in his own language
about the relation between the divine and the human in
Christ, habitually employed formulas that spoke of the
Logos "also" taking up flesh. "He who is the Son of God

Ath.*Ar.*1.45 (PG 26:105)

became also the Son of Man," he wrote; again, "We invoke the natural and true Son from God, him who also

Ath.*Ar.*3.32 (PG 26:392)

became man." Quoting John 1:14, Athanasius taught
that "he bore flesh and became man," neither affirming
nor denying but simply ignoring the presence of a human

Ath.*Ar.*3.35 (PG 26:397)

soul in the incarnate one. This danger of sacrificing the
integrity of his humanity to the unity of his person became
a reality when Apollinaris set forth the position that
"incarnation, as it must be envisaged in Christ, only comes
about if divine pneuma [spirit] and earthly sarx [flesh]
together form a substantial unity in such a way that the
man in Christ first becomes man through the union of

Grillmeier (1965) 222

these two components." The divine and the human in
Christ could not be thought of as equal components of
his incarnate being; rather, the Logos, by uniting himself
with a body, was still "one nature [μία φύσις]," as John
1:14 also made clear when it called his coming from
heaven a "tabernacling" and asserted that "the Word

Apoll.*fr.*2 (Lietzmann 204)

became flesh," but did not add "and soul."

It would, however, be a mistake to regard this denial of a soul or a spirit in the incarnate one as a necessary corollary of the theology of hypostatic union. Here as elsewhere, Syriac theology exhibited the possibility of transcending (or of ignoring) the conventional theological polarization. It used the same word, *kyânâ,* to mean either "nature" or "person" and could therefore attribute to the incarnate Christ one *kyânâ* or "two"; when it spoke of two, it referred to the divine and the human, "the sublime and the humble," but when it spoke of the one, it referred to the concrete person of Jesus Christ as the incarnate Logos. Although his own early writings showed an indifference to the question of the integrity of the humanity of Christ, Cyril came eventually to a similar insistence upon the concrete person of Jesus Christ as the proper subject for christological predications. "For my part," he stated in an axiom, "I say that it is appropriate neither for the Logos of God apart from the humanity, nor for the temple born of the woman not united to the Logos, to be called Christ Jesus." It is clear from the commentary of Cyril on the Gospel of John and from his other treatments of Gospel material that, even in the course of a theological polemic about the preincarnate Logos, he concentrated upon the concrete incarnate one as the object of Christian devotion and as the bringer of salvation. His true and full deity needed to be defended against Arianism, his true and full humanity against Apollinarianism; but it was the one incarnate Logos, truly and fully both God and man, who was the Savior.

At the same time, it was necessary to face up to the usage of Scripture, which did not consistently speak of him this way. For example, 1 Timothy 2:5, contradicting Cyril's axiom, referred to "the man Christ Jesus" and called him "the one mediator between God and man." Was this a "fitting" way of speaking about him, as Theodore maintained, or did the very term "mediator" imply, as Theodoret argued, that he "united in himself distinct qualities by the unity of natures, that is, of deity and of humanity"? The theology of the hypostatic union came to terms with such passages as this by noting that in myriad sayings of Scripture the properties of the two natures were interchanged, so that "the Logos is not consumed" but "both are taken together into one." Or, as Cyril had summarized the point earlier in the same

E.Beck (1949) 56–58

Cyr.*Inc.unigen.* (*SC* 97:250)

Cyr.*Joh.*12(ad 20:28) (*PG* 74:733)

Cyr.*Luc.*6.12 (*PG* 72:580–81)

Thdr.Mops. *1 Tim.*2.5 (Swete 2:88)

Thdt.*Eran.*2 (*PG* 83:121)

Cyr.*Inc.unigen.* (*SC* 97:280–82)

treatise, "he is proclaimed by Holy Scripture, sometimes as being an entire man, with his deity passed over in silence, for the sake of the divine economy, and sometimes again as God, with his humanity passed over in silence; but he is not treated unjustly by either way of speaking, on account of the conjunction of the two [natures] into

Cyr.Inc.unigen. (SC 97:252)

a unity." In the prophecy of the birth of Christ in Micah 5:2 (LXX) he was called a Bethlehemite, but the same verse also said that his "origin is from eternity." Where a particular passage of Scripture did not observe this balance explicitly, it nevertheless intended it. And the eternity of which Micah spoke was to be ascribed also to the flesh of Christ, that is, "to a flesh united with God by nature, and the good things of his own [divine nature]

Cyr.Inc.unigen. (SC 97:292)

he customarily communicates to his own body." A communication of properties was a characteristic not only of biblical language, however, but of the person of the incarnate one.

This communication was demanded by the work of Jesus Christ as Savior and by the history of the life, death, and resurrection through which he had accomplished that work. If the reality and totality of the incarnation were denied, "this is the emptying of faith and the undoing of the cross, which is the salvation and the life of the uni-

Cyr.Inc. unigen. (SC 97:200)
Durand (1964) 415

verse." The writings of Cyril, both exegetical and polemical, were filled with references to "the concrete scenes of the Gospel," such as the story of the confronta-

Matt.16:13–20; Cyr.Dial. Trin.4 (PG 75:865)

tion between Jesus and Peter at Caesarea Philippi. The subject of the words and deeds recorded in the Gospels had to be none other than the incarnate Logos. "Who is it then who both underwent death and was raised in glory and is from Nazareth, except Jesus Christ, that is, he who was ineffably born of the Father before all ages . . .

Cyr.Inc.unigen. (SC 97:270)
Cyr.Inc.unigen. (SC 97:296)

and bodily of a woman?" Reviewing the life of Jesus, his temptation and hunger, his suffering and death, Cyril insisted that all these had to be attributed to the one incarnate Logos, who used his flesh as an instrument for

Cyr.Inc.unigen. (SC 97:232)
Heb.5:7

his miracles and for his sufferings. The "prayers and supplications, with loud cries and tears" of Christ in his temptation were ascribed to "the natural and true Son, possessing the glories of the deity," who had humbled

Cyr.Chr.un. (SC 97:436–40)
Matt.17:5
Cyr.Inc.unigen. (SC 97:272)

himself to save those who were tempted. The voice from the cloud identified the one incarnate Logos, divine and human, as "my beloved Son." And so through all the various concrete scenes of the life of Jesus, the theology of the hypostatic union found substantiation for its insistence upon the one Lord Jesus Christ as the subject.

Yet this insistence contradicted some of those concrete scenes, notably those that attributed growth and development to Jesus. If John 1:14 was the proof text for this theology of the hypostatic union, its crux of interpretation was Luke 2:52: "And Jesus increased." Taunting his opponents with this passage, Nestorius asserted: "He is brought to perfection who increases little by little, about whom Luke also exclaims in the Gospels: 'Jesus increased in stature and in wisdom and in grace.'" Cyril responded to such challenges with the suggestion that the Logos could have brought his body to perfection immediately and that he could easily have endowed it with wisdom immediately. But this would have been "a monstrous affair and a violation of the words of the economy [of salvation]." Therefore the incarnate Logos, who in his divinity could not increase or change, took our nature upon himself to such an extent that he did increase. If Cyril's opponents were even more concerned to safeguard the absoluteness and immutability of the divine nature than he was, his embarrassment at the "increasing" of Christ was understandable. The theology of the hypostatic union could do justice to the predominant tendency of the Bible, which was to speak quite indiscriminately of the divine or the human in Christ while retaining the same subject; it could not do justice to those passages in which this tendency was replaced by language about the growth of Jesus. Or, to put it in the terminology of its proof text, this theology ran the danger of changing the incarnation into a theophany by reading John 1:14 as follows: "And the Word became flesh . . . and we beheld his glory."

The missing words, "and dwelt among us," made even John 1:14 amenable to interpretation in quite other terms, as part of the theology of the indwelling Logos. Then the incarnation taught in that passage could be paraphrased to mean: "This one we understand to be one Lord who is of the divine nature of God the Father, who for our salvation put on a man in whom he dwelt and through whom he appeared and became known to mankind." The theology of the indwelling Logos may be defined as an interpretation of the relation between the divine and the human in Jesus Christ that sought to pre-

Nest.*Hom.in Heb.3:1* (Loofs 235–36); Nest.*Baz*.2.1 (Bedjan 338)

Cyr.*Chr.un.* (SC 97:454)

Thdr.Mops.*Hom.catech*.3.5 (ST 145:59)

serve the distinction between them by describing their union as the indwelling of the Logos in a man whom he had assumed. This theology could not only quote John 1:14, but even speak of a "personal union" of godhead and manhood in Christ—"personal" because it was neither a union according to ousia, as was the union in the Trinity, nor a union according to nature, as was the union of soul and body. Either of these definitions of union would obliterate the distinction between the divine and the human, produce a monstrosity, and make salvation through Christ impossible. It was, rather, a third kind of union, according to "person [πρόσωπον]," which was the "convenient non-technical and non-metaphysical expression to describe the permanent and objective forms or Persons in which the godhead is presented alike to human vision and to the divine self-consciousness." The divine and the human in Christ, according to Nestorius, coincided in their appearance and so were one. Yet "appearance" was not synonymous with "illusion," for there was a genuine indwelling of the divine Logos in the man Jesus, and in this sense a genuine incarnation.

Prestige (1956) 162

The proof text for this theology of the incarnation was John 2:19: "Jesus answered them, 'Destroy this temple, and in three days I will raise it up.' " Quoting these words of Christ about his body, Nestorius asked: "Am I, then, the only one who calls Christ 'double'? Does he not designate himself both as a temple that can be destroyed and as a God that raises up? If, however, it was God who was destroyed . . . the Lord would have said: 'Destroy this God, and in three days he will be raised up.' " The relation between the Logos as active and the humanity as passive, set forth in John 2:19, served in turn as a key to those passages which seemed to predicate both divine glory and human passibility of the same divine-human subject. It was evident that "obedient unto death, even death on a cross" could be applied only to the man, as John 2:19 proved. And so "the temple created by the Holy Spirit is one, and the God who hallows the temple is another." The words of Christ referred to the temple of his body in the third person and to the Logos in the first person; "he called the man who was assumed his temple while showing that he himself was dwelling in that temple, and through his dwelling he clearly showed us his power when he delivered it [his dwelling] to the destruc-

Nest.Serm.Theot.1 (Loofs 259)

Thdr.Mops.Phil.2.8 (Swete 1:219)

Nest.fr.256 (Loofs 331)

Thdr.Mops.*Hom.catech*.8.5
(*ST* 145:193)

ap.Cyr.*Apol.Thdt*.1 (*ACO*
1–I–6:109)

Grillmeier (1965) 218

Thdr.Mops.*fr.inc.* (Swete
2:293–95)

Cyr.*Chr.un.* (*SC* 97:380)

Cyr.*Chr.un.* (*SC* 97:420)

Nest.*Hist.* (Loofs 206)

tion of death, according to his desire, and then raised it by the greatness of his might." Supplementing the testimony of John 2:19 was that of such a passage as Colossians 2:9: "In him [the man who was assumed] the whole fullness of deity dwells bodily."

From this proof text came the metaphor of indwelling, which "goes on to become the distinguishing mark" of this christology. In a treatise on the incarnation, of which only fragments have been preserved, Theodore sought to define the precise nature of this indwelling by distinguishing it from other forms of the divine presence in a creature. It was different from the general omnipresence of God, which was according to his "essence and operation," while the incarnation was an indwelling according to his "good pleasure." Yet such an indwelling according to his good pleasure could also be predicated of his presence in the church, but the difference was that the latter was dependent on the former; only in Jesus did the divine "dwell totally, equipping him by assigning to him all the honor in which the indwelling Son shared by nature." Did this doctrine mean, as its critics charged, that since the Logos "dwells in us ourselves," not only in Jesus, the Logos had not become flesh, but only a "dweller in man" or an "inhabitant of man"? Nestorius, like Theodore, insisted that the doctrine did not mean this, but that indwelling had a unique sense when it was applied to the incarnation of the Logos. For "if we speak of indwelling with regard to Christ or of the temple of the Godhead and the descent of the grace of the Holy Spirit [upon him], we do not mean the same kind of indwelling as came upon the prophets, nor the same as is celebrated in the apostles, nor even the same as there is in the angels, who [by the Spirit] are strengthened for the service of God. For Christ is the Sovereign, even according to the flesh the Lord of all." In this way the proponents of the theology of the indwelling Logos sought to disengage their position from the earlier christological heresies, such as adoptionism, with which it was so easy to identify it.

Clearer than its pedigree is the religious intent of the doctrine of the indwelling Logos: to take seriously the fact of moral development in the man Christ Jesus and thus to guarantee his status as simultaneously Redeemer and example. Therefore "the main thing is that the Logos in the form of a servant brought into existence a sinless man; hence the stress is laid on the moral and religious development of Jesus." When the Gospels described the baptism of Christ, for example, this was "symbolically drawn to the pattern of ours." If the New Testament had referred only to the deity or only to the humanity of Christ in its description of his suffering and obedience, it would have failed to make its point; only by involving both could it "draw from both what was appropriate for the purpose of exhortation." It was as man that Christ fulfilled the law "for us" as men. Such a phrase in the sayings of Christ as "my God and your God," while difficult for the proponents of the theology of the hypostatic union to explain, suited this theology very well; for it showed that the man who had been assumed by the Logos could, as man, call God his Father and his God and that therefore the believer, as man, could do likewise. The form of biblical exhortation required, then, that "although Christ had the divine nature in himself, still with great humility he wanted to suffer everything for our salvation. Therefore he says that this is 'worthy of the calling,' in the sense that, imitating the humility of Christ, they mutually sustain one another." This perfect obedience and innocence of the man who had been assumed by the Logos achieved the salvation of men.

Hence the human and the divine had to be united closely enough to achieve the salvation, but not so closely as to render it irrelevant to man as man—or to involve the divine in the suffering of the cross. In Theodore's formula, "the Godhead was separated from the one who was suffering in the trial of death, because it was impossible for him to taste the trial of death if [the Godhead] were not cautiously remote from him, but also near enough to do the needful and necessary things for the [human] nature that was assumed by it." Wherever there was a reference to the cross and death of Christ or to his "blood" as the instrument of salvation, this meant the man who had been assumed by the Logos, not the indwelling Logos himself, who was, as God, impassible. Conversely, when the one who was assumed was called "Son [of God]," this was "because of the close union that he had with the One who assumed him." And therefore it was necessary to note that in many passages of the New Testament there was a distinct transition from the one way of speaking to the other. In Colossians 1:15–18 the

Loofs (1914) 88

Thdr.Mops.*Hom.catech*.14.24 (*ST* 145:451–53)

Thdr.Mops.*Phil*.2.8 (Swete 1:221–22)
Thdr.Mops.*Gal*.3.13 (Swete 1:42)
John 20:17

Cyr.*Chr.un.* (*SC* 97:334–36)

Thdr.Mops.*Eph*.1.3 (Swete 1:121)

Thdr.Mops.*Eph*.4.2 (Swete 1:163)

Thdr.Mops.*Hom.catech*.12.9 (*ST* 145:335–37)

Thdr.Mops.*Hom.catech*.8.9 (*ST* 145:199)

Thdr.Mops.*Eph*.1.7 (Swete 1:126–27)

Thdr.Mops.*Hom.catech*.8.16 (*ST* 145:209)

apostle moved back and forth from the One in whom all things were created, the Logos, to the one who was "the firstborn of the dead," the assumed man, all the while speaking of him "as of one." At the same time, however, the apostle made clear that "in him [the man who had been assumed] all the fullness of God was pleased to dwell." It was not surprising that the New Testament formulated its predications this way, for this was its common practice in the Gospels and in the Epistles. On the other hand, it was no less necessary to note that certain predications could not be applied to the man in whom the Logos dwelt, but only to the eternal Logos himself. While the phrase of the creed, "and he ascended into heaven," meant that the man who had been assumed had become a partaker of the grace of the Logos and that therefore believers could also become so, the phrase "and he shall come again with glory" could only be referred to the Logos, since the Logos had come to dwell in the man who had been assumed, but the man had not "come" from heaven but had been born on earth, and therefore could not come "again."

Some passages, however, were difficult to explain away by any such principle of double predication. Judging from the frequency of their attempts to deal with it, one such crux of interpretation for the proponents of the theology of the indwelling Logos was 1 Corinthians 2:8: "they . . . crucified the Lord of glory," not merely the man in whom the Lord of glory dwelt. Eustathius was typical in asserting that since it was impossible to attribute suffering to the deity, Paul must have been referring to the man assumed by the Logos. Another crux was Hebrews 13:8: "Jesus Christ is the same yesterday and today and forever"; for the subject of this passage was "Jesus Christ," not merely Christ or the Logos, and yet eternity and identity, which were appropriate only to the Logos, were predicated also of the man in whom the Logos dwelt. Therefore the passage was often quoted against this theology. A special place was occupied by Philippians 2:6–11; for although it has been maintained that "the idea of Nestorius is most easily understood by us, if we look at" this passage, it seems in many ways to have been both a proof text and a crux of interpretation for the theology of the indwelling Logos: a proof text because it spoke of that which was "given" to the man who had

Thdr.Mops.*Col.*1.15–18
(Swete 1:272–74)

Thdr.Mops.*1 Tim.*3.16 (Swete 2:137–38)

Thdr.Mops.*Hom.catech.*7.6–7
(ST 145:171)

Thdr.Mops.*Hom.catech.*7.14
(ST 145:183)

ap.Thdt.*Eran.*3 (PG 83:288)

Loofs (1914) 82–83

Thdr.Mops.*Hom.catech*.6.5
(*ST* 145:139–41)

Thdr.Mops.*Phil*.2.6–11
(Swete 1:220)

been assumed, and because it made his earthly life and obedience the subject for an exhortation to imitate him; a crux of interpretation because in it, as in other passages, the apostle "speaks as though of one person and combines into one those things that by the division of natures are different in force." Because it did not easily suit the extremes of either of these alternative theologies, Philippians 2:6–11 was well suited to the needs of a position that sought to transcend both extremes.

The Dogma of the Two Natures in Christ

The dogmatic future belonged to a theology of preexistence, kenosis, and exaltation, which, on the basis of such passages as Philippians 2:6–11, was in a position to affirm a hypostatic union of the divine and the human in Christ as well as a permanent distinction between the divine and the human also after the incarnation. The term "kenosis" is taken from the phrase "emptied himself" in that passage. As the theology of the hypostatic union was chiefly identified with Alexandria and the theology of the indwelling Logos with Antioch, so this theology was associated with the thought of the Latin West. It found its most characteristic spokesman in Hilary, its most creative interpreter in Augustine, its most influential advocate in Leo, its most authoritative formulation in the decree of Chalcedon. Yet it was no more exclusively regional in its origin than either of the others. From the point of view of the others, especially of the theology of the hypostatic union, it achieved its conceptual clarity and its evangelical simplicity by ignoring the deeper issues of biblical exegesis as well as of christological speculation; but this very quality was its strength as a compromise formula uniting the partisans of opposing theories and as a basis for continuing development.

As the title "preexistence, kenosis, and exaltation" indicates, this christology took its departure not only from the relation between "natures," but also from the relation between "states"; not only from the being of Christ as God and man, but from his history as well. Identifying three states in the history of the person of Christ, Hilary spoke of his being only divine before the incarnation (ante hominem Deus), both divine and human during his kenosis (homo et Deus), and still completely man and completely God in his exaltation (post hominem et

Hil.*Trin*.9.6 (*PL* 10:285)

Deum totus homo totus Deus). These states needed to be clearly distinguished. For "it is one thing, that he was God before he was man, another that he was man and God, and another, that after being man and God, he was perfect man and perfect God. Do not then confuse the times and natures in the mystery of the dispensation, for according to the attributes of his different natures, he must speak of himself in relation to the mystery of his humanity, in one way before his birth, in another while he was yet to die, and in another as eternal." The theology of the indwelling Logos manifested the tendency (or danger) of equating "times" and "natures" by insisting that kenosis and exaltation applied only to the man who had been assumed by the Logos; the theology of the hypostatic union threatened to lose sight of the times altogether, and perhaps, by its preoccupation with the ontological questions raised by the union between the two natures, even to construct the monstrosity of a preexistent human nature. But this was a theology in which both times and natures belonged to "the mystery of the dispensation" and both had to receive their due. The relation between the two natures could not be specified without attention to the three times. Biblical predications were to be sorted out not only, as the theology of the indwelling Logos emphasized, on the basis of the distinction between the two natures, but also on the basis of the history of the one person, Jesus Christ, in his preexistence, kenosis, and exaltation.

By attempting to have it both ways, this theology linked "a static doctrine of two natures with a dynamic soteri-

Grillmeier (1965) 467

ology." Its underlying soteriology required that Christ as Savior be both divine and human, so that he could effect the exchange between himself and the sinner by which he assumed the sins of the world and the sinner became holy. The kenosis of Christ established a new covenant between

Ambr.*Ps*.118.14.46 (*CSEL* 62:329)
Ambr.*Fid*.3.7.52 (*CSEL* 78:127)

God and man. By his humiliation he taught men humility, so that they could be exalted with him. "We were raised because he was lowered; shame to him was glory to us. He, being God, made flesh his residence, and we in return

Hil.*Trin*.2.25 (*PL* 10:67)

are lifted anew from the flesh to God." The cross of Christ was the mystery of salvation by which the power of God achieved its redemptive purpose, as well as an ex-

Leo M.*Serm*.72.1 (*SC* 74:129)

ample by which men were aroused to humility. "By a wonderful exchange he entered into a bargain of salvation, taking upon himself what was ours and granting us

Leo M.*Serm*.54.4 (*SC* 74:33)

what was his." Most metaphors of the atonement that were transmitted by the tradition appeared in this theology as well, often in combination, as in Augustine's words about his mother: "She knew that [at the altar] the holy sacrifice was dispensed by which the handwriting that was against us is blotted out; and that enemy vanquished who, when he summed up our offenses and searched for something to bring against us, could find nothing in Him, in

Aug.*Conf*.9.13.36 (*CSEL* 33:225)

whom we conquer." In such statements as this, the relation between the imitation of the humility of Christ, the sacrifice of the blood of Christ, the victory of Christ over the enemies of mankind, the ransom paid either to God or to the devil, and various other ways of describing the achievement of salvation was not worked out very precisely. What was clear, however, was that each was taken to require a christology of preexistence, kenosis, and exaltation, a christology of two natures in one person.

Drawing upon this tradition, Leo concluded that the kenosis or "emptying" of Philippians 2:7 had to be interpreted as "the bending down of compassion, not the failing of power." Therefore, "while the distinctness of both natures and substances is preserved, and both meet in one person, lowliness is assumed by majesty, weakness by power, mortality by eternity." A passible humanity was joined to an impassible divinity, so that Christ would "from one element be capable of dying, and from the

Leo M.*Tom*.3 (*ACO* 2–II–1:27)

other be incapable." This was the meaning of the stories in the Gospels, all of which, both the evidences of kenosis and the proofs of continuing divine power, had to be accounted for in a christological doctrine: both the lowliness of the swaddling clothes and the glory of the angels' song; both the vulnerability to Herod and the adoration

Leo M.*Tom*.4 (*ACO* 2–II–1:28); Leo M.*Serm*.55.3 (*SC* 74:38)

of the Magi; both "being pierced with nails and opening the gates of Paradise to the faith of the thief" on the cross. And so "the rhythm of his language swings to and fro like a pendulum, from the divine side to the human side, from the transcendence of God to the immanence of our earthly history. The latter should be noted. Despite all his predilection for a static treatment of the nature of Christ, corresponding to the doctrine of the two natures, Leo again and again shows his love for a salvation-histor-

Grillmeier (1965) 466

ical approach." He dealt both with "times" and with "natures" in his exposition of the mystery of the dispensation.

When this christology of preexistence, kenosis, and exaltation was addressed to the conflict over the relation between the two natures, it manifested certain affinities with the theology of the hypostatic union. It seemed to have even more affinities with the theology of the indwelling Logos; this was partly because Leo intervened in the conflict to condemn what he understood to be the Eutychian extreme of the doctrine of hypostatic union. Removed from the arena of that controversy, the actual doctrinal relation between the theology of the hypostatic union, the theology of the indwelling Logos, and the theology of preexistence, kenosis, and exaltation may perhaps be seen more clearly. The congeniality of the third position with the second was evident. Both were intent on preserving "the distinctness of both natures" and substances and on protecting the unchangeable divine nature from contamination by the vicissitudes that befell the human nature. Therefore "each 'form' does the acts which are appropriate to it, in communion with the other, the Logos, that is, performing what is appropriate to it, and the flesh carrying out what is appropriate to the flesh." It is understandable that the advocates of the theology of the indwelling Logos saw this position as a vindication of their own. Yet when its polemically conditioned overtones have been subtracted from it, this theology is seen to have manifested a concern for the oneness of Jesus Christ in his person and saving acts that sets it apart from the theology of the indwelling Logos no less than its stress upon the distinctness of the natures sets it apart from the theology of the hypostatic union. For it was none other than the Lord of glory who had been crucified, as 1 Corinthians 2:8 asserted. And by virtue of the relation between divine and human in him, it did not matter "according to which substance Christ is spoken of." Therefore Mary was Theotokos, for she was the mother of the one Christ who was both God and man.

Nevertheless, this position above the battle was achieved at the cost of ignoring many of the most serious issues. Despite such occasional formulations as the assertion that believers were, through union with the incarnate Lord, made to be like him and thus deified, the yearning for the transformation of the finite, passible human nature into an eternal, impassible, and divine nature was foreign to the thought, if not always to the language, of the theory we have been describing. On the other hand,

Leo M.*Tom*.3 (*ACO* 2–II–1:27)

Leo M.*Tom*.4 (*ACO* 2–II–1:28)

Leo M.*Tom*.5 (*ACO* 2–II–1:29)

Leo M.*Ep*.124.7 (*ACO* 2–IV:162)

Leo M.*Ep*.124.2 (*ACO* 2–IV:159)

Leo M.*Serm*.50.6–7 (*SC* 74:83–84)

its readiness to speak of the trials and temptations of
Jesus—Matthew 4:1–11 was the Gospel lesson for the

Leo M.*Serm*.39.3 (*SC* 49:29)

first Sunday in Lent—must not be taken to mean that the
moral struggles and growth of the Lord could have issued
in anything but a foregone conclusion; for Christ permitted himself to be tempted, not for his own sake, but so
that he might support men in their temptations not only
by his aid but also by his example. Neither the metaphysical profundity of the one alternative nor the moral ear-
nestness of the other was decisive for this theology, although it was in many ways more moral than metaphysical
in its own orientation. But in the dynamics of the polemical situation it was this christology of preexistence, kenosis, and exaltation that provided the vocabulary for a solution that was almost automatically declared to be orthodox
even though it was almost immediately acknowledged to
be inadequate.

The encounter between the theology of the hypostatic
union and the theology of the indwelling Logos took
place in the arena of the Council of Ephesus in 431. Instead of coining a new dogmatic formula in response to
the conflict between christological systems, Ephesus reaffirmed the authority of the confession of the Council of

CEph.(431)*Act*.43 (*ACO*
1-I-2:12-13)

Nicea—as a christological, not only as a trinitarian, formula. This was not simply archaism or evasion (although
neither of these factors was altogether absent), but the
recognition that the Nicene Creed did answer the fundamental issue at stake between the alternative theologies
of the incarnation. For it did not sort out either his attributes or his deeds on the basis of the distinction between the two natures, but simply declared a faith "in one
Lord Jesus Christ" and then proceeded to predicate of
that one Lord both that he was homoousios with the
Father and that he "suffered" in the crucifixion. It is not
clear that the Nicene formula, which had been directed
to the question of the relation between the divine in
Christ and the divine in the Father, was intended as a
statement of the relation between the divine in Christ
and the human in Christ, but Ephesus declared "that
no one is permitted to bring forward, or to write,
or to compose a different creed besides that which was
set down by the holy fathers who were gathered together

CEph.(431) (*ACO* 1-I-7:105)

with the Holy Spirit at Nicea." The phrase "different
creed" would seem to refer to content rather than to

form, although this canon has sometimes been taken to mean that it was unlawful to compose any additional creeds or to add to the creed of Nicea.

The reaffirmation of the Nicene Creed at Ephesus was, however, arranged to constitute a vindication of Cyril's theology of the hypostatic union and a condemnation of Nestorius's theology of the indwelling Logos. After the reading of the Nicene Creed, the second and most important of Cyril's letters against Nestorius was read to the fathers, who affirmed one after another that Cyril's letter was "orthodox and without fault" and accorded with the faith of the 318 fathers of Nicea; when Nestorius's response to that letter was read, on the other hand, it was decided that this diverged from the creed and was therefore to be condemned as "wholly alien from the apostolic and evangelical faith, sick with many and strange blasphemies." In intent if not in all details, the fathers joined themselves to the position that "the Logos from God the Father was united to the flesh in a hypostatic way [καθ᾽ ὑπόστασιν], and that with his own flesh he is the one Christ, the same one simultaneously God and man." It was wrong to assign some of the statements of Christ about himself, or those of the saints about him, to one or the other hypostasis rather than to the single Christ. It was the Logos himself who "suffered in the flesh and was crucified in the flesh and tasted death in the flesh"; indeed, "as God he is both life and the life-giving one," and yet this same Christ had become through the resurrection "the firstborn from the dead." The council approved the second letter of Cyril, with its formula of a hypostatic union; "but we should surely not look for a philosophical definition in this expression, [which] ... is merely meant to express the reality of the union in Christ in contrast to a purely moral and accidental interpretation which the Synod presumed to be the teaching of the other side." At one point the legislation of Ephesus did establish precision in terminology: assembled in the great double church of St. Mary at Ephesus, the synod proclaimed Mary Theotokos.

That was anything but the end of the christological controversy. As soon became clear, the Ephesian resolution of the conflict was not acceptable to anyone and had itself to be resolved in one or another direction. The narrative of the two decades after Ephesus in many ways

CEph.(431)*Ep.Cael.*5 (*ACO* 1–I–3:6); CEph.(431)*Act.* (*ACO* 1–I–2:13–31)

CEph.(431)*Ep.Cael.*5 (*ACO* 1–I–3:7); CEph.(431)*Act.* (*ACO* 1–I–2:31–35)

Cyr.*Ep.Nest.*3.12.2 (*ACO* 1–I–1:40)

Cyr.*Ep.Nest.*3.12.4 (*ACO* 1–I–1:41)

Cyr.*Ep.Nest.*3.12.12 (*ACO* 1–I–1:42)

Grillmeier (1965) 416–17

CEph.(431)*Ep.Cael.*4 (*ACO* 1–I–3:6)
Cyr.*Ep.Nest.*2.7 (*ACO* 1–I–1:28)

belongs more to the history of imperial or ecclesiastical politics than to the history of the Christian message; nevertheless, the inner dynamics of the doctrine of the person of Christ continued to be at work, and it is to this that we must give attention here. After 431 there were several directions in which the doctrine could develop, each of which had its fierce partisans and its political opportunity, but also its own logical validity within the evolution of christological doctrine. The theology of the indwelling Logos, at least as represented by Nestorius, had been condemned at Ephesus, not quite without a hearing but certainly without an understanding of its primary intent; and some appeal to a higher court, or perhaps to another session of the same court, seemed to be called for. Eastern delegates to the council of 431, led by John of Antioch, accused the council of "Apollinarian, Arian, and Eunomian heresies" and demanded that those who had approved Cyril's theology "accept anew the Nicene faith without foreign additions [and] anathematize the heretical propositions of Cyril." Even if the Nestorian cause itself could no longer be defended as a theological position, the distinction between the two natures, as a widely held theological teaching, seemed to be threatened by the blanket approval of Cyril.

CEph.*Gest.Orient.*15 (*ACO* 1–I–5:122)

On the other hand, the theology of the hypostatic union had certainly been vindicated when its designation of "one and the same Christ" as the subject of all christological predicates, including deity and crucifixion, had been acknowledged as identical with the creed of Nicea. Yet nothing had become more obvious from the christological controversies during the century after Nicea than the inadequacy of the Nicene—or, for that matter, of the Athanasian—conceptual structure for any serious attention to the problem of the divine and the human in Christ. The vindication at Ephesus would be hollow unless it were accompanied, or at any rate followed, by a far more elaborate statement of how the person of the God-man was unqualifiedly one after the incarnation. But there appeared to be inherent in this theology of the hypostatic union a tendency to achieve any statement of this sort by affirming, with Eutyches: "I confess that before the union our Lord had two natures, but after the union I confess one single nature." And therefore a synod of 449, con-

ap.CChalc.*Act.*527 (*ACO* 2–I–1:143)

CEph.(449) ap.CChalc.*Act.*
492–93 (*ACO* 2–I–1:140)

trolled by this position, could declare: "Whoever teaches two natures, let him be anathema." Could the hypostatic union be salvaged without going to this extreme?

Both precedent and prudence seemed to call for some sort of compromise, and despite the polarization of dogmatic positions there were adherents of each position who recognized this. The spokesmen for the theology of preexistence, kenosis, and exaltation, having excommunicated Nestorius at a Roman synod in 432, approved the action of the synod at Ephesus; but various papal documents—including even the rescript of Pope Celestine, who had commissioned Cyril to carry out the excommunication and deposition of Nestorius—made it clear that there was still hope of asserting an "apostolic" solution that would reconcile, if not the extremists, then at least the main body of believers and theologians. Theodoret, who in many ways assumed the mantle of Nestorius as the defender of the theology of the indwelling Logos, found it possible to formulate a compromise document in which it was affirmed that "a union of two natures has taken place, and therefore we confess one Christ, one Son, one Lord" and that consequently "in accordance with this concept of the union without confusion we confess that

ap.Joh.Ant.*Ep.Cyr.*3 (*ACO*
1–I–4:9)

the Holy Virgin is Theotokos." In some way, Cyril found it possible to sign this document, to the chagrin of many of his partisans. Yet neither in theological finesse nor in political timing did this confession succeed in providing the right formula for the right time. That was done by the principal interpreter of the theology of preexistence, kenosis, and exaltation, Pope Leo, in his *Tome to Flavian,* which, with judicious additions from other theological traditions, came to serve as the formula of reconciliation for most, though by no means all, of the parties at Chalcedon in 451. The text of the Chalcedonian formula—fundamental ever since to the christological development of all of the Latin West, much of the Greek East, and some of the Syriac East—read:

"Following therefore the holy fathers, we confess one and the same our Lord Jesus Christ, and we all teach harmoniously [that he is] the same perfect in godhead, the same perfect in manhood, truly God and truly man, the same of a reasonable soul and body; homoousios with the Father in godhead, and the same homoousios with us in manhood, like us in all things except sin; begotten before ages of the Father in godhead; the same in the last days for us and for our salvation [born] of Mary the Virgin Theotokos in manhood, one and the same Christ, Son, Lord, unique; acknowledged in two natures without confusion, without change, without division, without separation [ἐν δύο φύσεσιν ἀσυγχύτως, ἀτρέπτως, ἀδιαιρέτως, ἀχωρίστως]—the difference of the natures being by no means taken away because of the union, but rather the distinctive character of each nature being preserved, and [each] combining in one person and hypostasis—not divided or separated into two persons, but one and the same Son and only-begotten God, Logos, Lord Jesus Christ; as the prophets of old and the Lord Jesus Christ himself taught us about him, and the symbol of the fathers has handed down to us."

Symb.Chalc. (Schaff 2:62–63; ACO 2–I–2:129–30)

The genealogy of this decree makes clear that "the formula is not an original and new creation, but like a mosaic, was assembled almost entirely from stones that were already available." Specifically, its sources were the so-called Second Letter of Cyril to Nestorius, the Letter of Cyril to the Antiochenes together with the union formula of 433, and the Tome of Leo; the phrase "not divided or separated into two persons" appears to have come from Theodoret. Even though it may be statistically accurate to say that "the majority of the quotations come from the letters of St. Cyril," the contributions of Leo's Tome were the decisive ones, in the polemic against what were understood to be the extreme forms of the alternative theologies of the incarnation as well as in the reduction of the problem to the positive affirmations on which general, though by no means universal, agreement could be achieved. The formula, like the Tome, condemned any notion of hypostatic union that would jeopardize "the differences of the natures" or would violate the rule that the union was accomplished "without confusion." At the same time it insisted that Christ not be "divided or separated into two persons," setting itself apart from any theology of the indwelling Logos that would make the Logos one person and the man assumed by him another person.

Urbina (1951) 398

Urbina (1951) 400

It is, of course, quite another question whether these interpretations of the christological alternatives represented a fair and accurate reading of the various theolo-

gies. The insistence that Christ not be divided or separated into two persons did not really strike the center of
its intended target, which was the need to affirm that the
birth, suffering, and death of Christ were real, and simultaneously to protect the Godhead from compromise by
them. To say that the difference of the natures was not
taken away by the union could mean that the activities
and properties appropriate to each nature were to be
predicated ontologically only of that nature, even though
verbally it might be permissible to predicate them of "one
and the same Christ." "Without confusion" could likewise be interpreted in support of the thesis that, since the
incarnation no less than before it, the human was the human and the divine was the divine. Even more explicitly,
"without change," which applied to the human nature
since it was taken for granted by both sides that the divine
nature was unchangeable, could be read as an attack on
the notion that because the salvation of man consisted in
the transformation of his human nature into a divine one,
the human nature of Christ had begun the process of salvation by its union with the divine nature. Although the
Chalcedonian formula did not in fact say any of these
things unequivocally, it did seem to allow room for them;
hence it could even be, and indeed was, taken as a vindication of the Nestorian position.

If anything, the relation of the formula to the other alternative was even less clear and certainly less reassuring
in the long run. It was undeniable that the formula taught
a hypostatic union of sorts: "combining in one person and
hypostasis." It also referred to the Virgin as Theotokos
and required that, though there be two natures, they be
acknowledged as "without division, without separation."
For the theology of the hypostatic union, this was a good
beginning, but no more than a beginning. The really difficult problems were either ignored or disposed of by equivocation. It was not clear, for example, who the subject
of suffering and crucifixion was, for these events in the
history of salvation were not so much as mentioned. Presumably, the references to "one and the same" near the
beginning and near the end would indicate that he, in the
concreteness of his total person both divine and human,
was the subject, but this was not specified. Conversely, all
the warnings against any confusion of the two natures left
the proponents of the hypostatic union unsatisfied on their

fundamental soteriological point: that the ultimate deification of man had its inception in the union of the humanity of Christ with his divinity in an intimate and inseparable wholeness of person. And perhaps the most crucial problem of all, evident in almost any creedal statement but especially obvious in this one, was the hermeneutical one. The creed opened with the claim that it was "following the holy fathers" and concluded with specific references not only to the prophets of the Old Testament and to the teachings of Jesus in the New Testament, but also to the authority of "the symbol of the fathers." In the light of the deliberations at Ephesus and the issues in the controversy, this almost certainly referred to the creed of Nicea. But everyone laid claim to that authority; and, depending on which of the "holy fathers" one cited, Nicea, and now Chalcedon, could be interpreted in any of several ways.

It was, then, an agreement to disagree. But it was more than this: it was basically a statement of the theology of preexistence, kenosis, and exaltation, formulated in such a way as to transcend the speculative alternatives by going beyond (or beneath) them to the truth of the Gospels— pure, clear, and simple. But the truth, even the truth of the Gospels, is never pure and clear, and rarely simple. The Chalcedonian christology set the terms for the theology and devotion of the Latin church at least until the Reformation, and even then the various contending doctrines of the person of Christ vied with one another in their protestations of loyalty to Chalcedon. But in the Greek and Syriac portions of the church, the ambiguity of this christology made it considerably less successful. Whether it was regarded as evasive or only as naïve, it settled very little in the East, providing the terms for subsequent controversies rather than the solution for past ones and in the process alienating large segments of Christendom which, even after a millennium and a half, are still not reconciled either to the Council of Chalcedon or to the churches that accept it.

The Continuing Debate

Even more than the christological controversies before Chalcedon the continuing debate after Chalcedon was shaped by nontheological factors, ranging from mob rule and athletic rivalry to military promotions and the domes-

tic intrigues of the imperial household. The patriarch of
Alexandria, Proterius, was lynched during Holy Week
457 for his christological position; conflicting views of
Chalcedon were reflected in the competition between the
Blues and the Greens in the circus of Constantinople; an
imperial edict of 7 February 452 threatened to strip of his
rank any army officer who opposed the orthodox dogma
promulgated the previous year; and the empress Theo-
dora, hailed by the Monophysites as "a Christ-loving
woman," connived to change the dogmatic policies of her
husband.

Nevertheless, the religious, liturgical, and dogmatic
import of the debate must not be minimized because of
any of this. For the post-Chalcedonian conflicts made it
clear that as the settlement of the dogma of the Trinity at
Nicea and Constantinople had reopened the christological
question, so the settlement of the dogma of the two natures in Christ at Ephesus and Chalcedon reopened the
trinitarian question, as well as the other fundamental presupposition of christological doctrine, the question of
soteriology. The controversy had come full circle. The
vehemence of the opposition to Chalcedon and the prominence of these two presuppositions in the controversy
were expressed in a passionate denunciation by an Egyptian monk in the sixth century: "Anathema to the unclean Synod of Chalcedon! Anathema to everyone who
agrees with it! Anathema to everyone who denies the redemptive suffering of Christ! . . . As for us, to our dying
breath we believe in the Father, the Son, and the Holy
Spirit, the coequal Trinity which is also a single Godhead." From many theologians and parties who agreed on

ap.Cramer (1951) 328

little else came this recognition of the centrality of the
dogma of the Trinity and of the doctrine of salvation to
further christological development.

The Nestorian party, condemned at Ephesus in 431,
continued to claim that it, not the decision of 431 identifying the christology of Cyril with that of Nicea, represented the legitimate tradition of "the holy fathers, 318
in number, who gathered in Nicea, and the 150 who met

Syn.Sel.(585) (Chabot 394)

in Byzantium," that is, the councils of Nicea in 325 and
of Constantinople in 381. This it could do by setting forth
an interpretation of the person of Christ which safeguarded the place of the Logos within the Trinity by
erecting every possible buffer between him and the suffer-

ings of the crucified. "If God the Logos suffered in his flesh . . . he has completely lost his impassibility, and his homoousia with the Father and the Holy Spirit, and [his] eternal nature, which is in the one ousia." To use such expressions as "one of the Trinity suffered in the flesh" meant either that the Father and the Holy Spirit also suffered or that the Logos was separated from them; either of these conclusions was heretical. Over against Arians past and present, this theology of the indwelling Logos declared: "In your ungodly defense of the hypostatic union you deny the assumption [of the man by the Logos] . . . and by your hypostatic and composite union you make the divinity suffer . . . so that God is not God and man is not man. You are alienated from the whole tradition of the church and anathematized by all under heaven who are orthodox." Christology, then, was determined by the dogma of the Trinity and was not to be developed in its own terms except as this trinitarian framework allowed. For example, the christological creed adopted by the East Syrian "Nestorian" synod of Seleucia-Ctesiphon near the end of the sixth century declared that the Logos "became flesh without changing. . . . He assumed without adding, because in his being and in his assuming his ousia remained free of change and addition: Jesus Christ, the Son of God, God the Logos, light from light." The doctrine of the hypostatic union, even in the form adopted at Chalcedon, compromised the relation of the divine hypostases within the Trinity and threatened the impassibility of the Logos and therefore of the entire Godhead.

The principal opponents of orthodoxy in the continuing debate after Chalcedon, however, were not the remnants of Nestorianism, but the several parties of "Monophysites," who opposed the formula of the council because it had not gone far enough in affirming the hypostatic union. We shall turn to a fuller exposition of Monophysite teaching in a later volume. Under the Monophysite label were included theologies that diverged from one another more than some of them did from Chalcedon— especially from Chalcedon as it eventually came to be interpreted, thanks largely to the conflict with these theologies. After Chalcedon, as after Nicea, the epithets and nicknames proliferated, as the various theological parties were identified by the absurd or heretical conclusions that appeared to flow from their positions. These party nick-

Bab.*Un.*7 (*CSCO* 80:210 [79:258–59])

Bab.*Un.*7 (*CSCO* 80:210–11 [79:260])

Bab.*Un.*7 (*CSCO* 80:247 [79:306–307])

Syn.Sel.(585) (Chabot 454)

names, which fill the accounts of the controversy, both primary and secondary, often serve largely to obscure the doctrinal issues. Similarly, the technical terms of the trinitarian and christological dogmas were variously understood by various parties and schools, with the result that the accusation of logomachy, so often made against theological controversy and so seldom accurate, would seem to fit the latter half of the fifth century and the first half of the sixth century better than it does most periods in the history of Christian doctrine.

At stake within and behind the logomachy and the polemical epithets were the trinitarian and the soteriological implications of the doctrine of the person of Christ. Severus of Antioch charged that his opponents "said that it was in his ousia that the Logos of God endured the saving cross and took upon himself the passion on our behalf," and that they "would not consent to call the one Lord and our God and Savior Jesus Christ homoousios with us in the flesh." And Theodosius of Alexandria wrote to him in turn that "he who is one of the Holy Trinity, the hypostatic Logos of God the Father, united to himself hypostatically a flesh homoousios with us and, like us, capable of suffering." The parallelism of "homoousios with the Father" and "homoousios with us," deceptively simple and ultimately imprecise, did at least make clear the two foci for a reconsideration of christology.

The battle against the doctrine of the two natures in Christ after the incarnation, as formulated at Chalcedon, led to a reopening of the problem of the Trinity in at least two ways. The relation between the One and the Three had been clarified, or at any rate adjudicated, at the end of the fourth century with the adoption of the formula "one ousia, three hypostases." The second member of the Trinity was one hypostasis of the three. In the critique of the Chalcedonian doctrine, some Monophysites identified hypostasis with "nature," asserting that, as one hypostasis, the Logos after the incarnation could still be possessed of only one nature. But this seemed to lead to the conclusion that each hypostasis of the Trinity had a nature and was an ousia in and of itself. Then the unity of the Father, Son, and Holy Spirit would be found in the Godhead which they shared. This was an effective argument against the Chalcedonian doctrine of two natures,

Sev.Ant.*Ep*.6.5.6 (Brooks 2–II:315)

Thds.Al.*Ep*. (*CSCO* 103:4 [17:9])

ap.Joh.D.*Haer*.83 (*PG* 94:745–53)

but one that proved to be theologically expensive. It was quickly labeled tritheism, for its Aristotelian interpretation of the key trinitarian terms, hypostasis and ousia, seemed to lead to a surrender of any unity in the Godhead except the most abstract. It was therefore at least as much from other Monophysites as from the supporters of Chalcedon that the answer came. Those who said that "if each hypostasis, when it is considered in and of itself, is an ousia and a nature, then since there are three hypostases of the Holy Trinity, there are therefore also three ousias and three natures, should know that they demonstrate ignorance more than others do." The proper way to define the doctrine of the Trinity and yet to make the anti-Chalcedonian point was to declare that "there was not a union of ousias and natures which are generic and common—that is, of the nature which contains the Trinity of the divine hypostases, Father, Son, and Holy Spirit, and of the nature which includes the entire human race of all men—but there was merely a union of God the Logos and his own flesh, endowed with a rational and intellectual soul, which he united to himself in a hypostatic way." The orthodox trinitarianism of Nicea and Constantinople was preserved in this way, and yet its implications were drawn in opposition to the theory of two natures in the incarnate Logos. One of the Three in the Trinity became incarnate, suffered, and died.

This did not mean that it was permissible to say: "The Trinity has become incarnate through one of its hypostases." Here again the Monophysite concern led to controversy over the dogma of the Trinity. The locus of the controversy, as could have been expected, was in the liturgy. If it was liturgically traditional and dogmatically proper to call Mary Theotokos and by this title to predicate birth of the Second Person of the Trinity, the sufferings of the cross could also be legitimately attributed to him. A few years after Chalcedon, therefore, the Sanctus or Trisagion was revised in the liturgy at Antioch to read: "Holy God, holy and mighty, holy and immortal, thou who wast crucified for us, have mercy on us." The revision could be rejected simply because it was a liturgical innovation, but it also raised a fundamental dogmatic question: "Did one of the Trinity suffer in the flesh?" Because the impassibility of God was a basic presupposition of all christological doctrine, any formula that seemed to

Thds.Al.Or.5 (CSCO 103:44 [17:64])

Thds.Al.Or.6 (CSCO 103:51–52[17:74])

Jac.Bar.Ep. (CSCO 103:121 [17:174])

Ps.Fel.Ep.Petr.Full.71 (CSEL 35:162–69); Evagr.H.e.3.44 (PG 86:2697–2700)

Leont.H.Nest.7 (PG 86:1757–68)

Vaschalde (1902) 37

Cyr.S.*Sab*.32 (*TU* 49–II:118)

See pp. 241–42 above

Horm.*Ep*. (*PL* 63:496)

Procl. *Arm*.19–21 (*ACO* 4–II: 191–92)

CChalc.*Act*. (Mansi 6:741)

Ps.Leont.B.*Sect*.5.1 (*PG* 86:1228)

tend toward jeopardizing this impassibility was suspect. Various compromises were suggested, including the insertion of "Christ the king," so as to remove the ambiguity. Eventually the formula failed of acceptance, and even those who were theologically sympathetic to the close identification between suffering and "one of the Trinity" were resolved "to sing in accordance with the ancient tradition of the catholic church and not with this innovation." Yet the liturgical quarrel brought into sharp focus the need to bring christological titles (such as Theotokos) and christological theories (such as the communication of properties) into harmony with the dogma of the Trinity. The emperor Justinian spoke for many when he expressed this need, writing to Hormisdas, the pope: "It seems to us that it is correct to say that our Lord Jesus Christ, the Son of the living God, born of the Virgin Mary, he whom the chief of the apostles proclaims as having 'suffered in the flesh' reigns as one in the Trinity together with the Father and the Holy Spirit." Or, in the formula of Proclus, "God the Logos, one of the Trinity, was incarnate"; therefore "he himself both works miracles and suffers."

Although these controversies over the dogma of the Trinity were in many ways the most dramatic occasioned by the Monophysites, more attention was drawn by the question of the relation of Christ to mankind than by the question of his relation to the Trinity. Here again it is important to keep in mind that the Monophysite movement was the source not only of the extreme views of this relation that arose, but also of their refutation. Thus Eutyches was reported to have declared: "Until this very day I have never said that the body of our Lord and God is homoousios with us." But even the opponents of the Monophysite position conceded that it "anathematizes both the synod [of Chalcedon] and Eutyches because he refused to say that the body of Christ is homoousios with us." Even most of the extremists among the opponents of Chalcedon were able to affirm in some sense that the humanity or the body of Christ was "homoousios with us" or with "the human"; but such an affirmation was highly ambiguous, for it did not specify whether it referred to the human before the fall of Adam, the human in its present fallen state, or the human as through the redemption of Christ it would become. The concept of the communication of properties was responsible for the debate over the title "Theotokos" and over the phrase "one of the Trinity suffered in the flesh," for it affirmed the propriety of ascribing to the total person of the God-man actions and attributes of his humanity. But it also moved in the opposite direction. Worship was appropriately addressed to the total person of the God-man, too, not only to his divinity, for by the communication of properties the entire person was worthy of adoration.

Did this concept apply to all the properties of divinity, and, if so, did the communication of properties invalidate the teaching that the humanity of Christ was "homoousios with us"? Three such properties of divinity became especially problematical in the post-Chalcedonian controversies: freedom from corruption, omniscience, and uncreatedness. All of them were, by a self-evident axiom, properties of the divine nature, therefore of the divine Logos not only before the incarnation, but also (since he was, by the same self-evident axiom, unchangeable) after the incarnation. Freedom from corruption was, moreover, the content of the salvation for which he became incarnate, therefore a property of the transformed human nature which men shared through him. But humanity, since the fall and before redemption, was characterized by corruption, together with weaknesses which, while not sinful in themselves, were the inevitable concomitants of a corruptible and fallen human nature, weaknesses such as weeping or being susceptible to hunger and thirst. Christ had wept for Lazarus; in the days of his flesh he had suffered hunger; he had thirsted on the cross; he had also eaten after the resurrection. It was generally agreed on all sides that the "body of glory" which he had after the resurrection transcended not only the limitations of time and space, but also the necessities of ordinary physical existence, and that therefore his eating then was not to satisfy his hunger but to reveal himself to the disciples. But Julian of Halicarnassus and other Monophysites arose to teach that "his body was free of corruption from the moment of union" rather than only from the resurrection. "Even though Christ wept over Lazarus," said one, "it was His incorruptible and divine tear that raised him from the dead." Therefore Christ subjected himself to these weaknesses not because of "the necessity of nature" but for the sake of the "economy" of redemption. Already in the days of his flesh

Jo.D.F.*o*.3.28 (*PG* 94:1100)

John 11:35

Matt.4:2
John 19:28
Luke 24:43; John 21:13

ap.Ps.Leont.B.*Sect*.10.1 (*PG* 86:1260)

ap.Anast.S.*Hod*.23 (*PG* 89:301)

Leont.B.*Nest.et Eut*.2 (*PG* 86:1329)

he was free from the "corruption" that infected all flesh;
for as the Son of man, he was homoousios with Adam
before the fall, not with man in his present fallen state.

Inevitably, this doctrine seemed to suggest analogies
to the Gnostic docetism of an earlier century, which had
taught that the humanity of Christ, especially his body,
was apparent rather than real. The principal refutation
of it came from other opponents of Chalcedon, notably
from Severus. "We do not have the right," he said, "because of the brilliance of the divine miracles and of the
things that transcend the law of nature, to deny that his
sufferings of redemption and his death occurred in accordance with the laws of human nature. He is the Logos
incarnate without being changed. He performed the
miracles as is appropriate for God, and he voluntarily permitted the laws of the flesh to operate in his parts while
he bore his sufferings in a human way." The hunger of
Christ after his fast of forty days in the wilderness was
"for us" and one that he "voluntarily accepted when he
gave place to temptation by the Slanderer," so that he
might "be victorious when he fights on the side of God,
who gives food to all flesh, and might become weak and
able to conquer on our behalf." Men could restrain their
appetites, for he proved that they did not live by bread
alone. In the hour of his passion his soul was sorrowful
to the point of death, and "his fear was greater than that
of anyone. . . . He experienced anguish and sorrow and
disturbance of mind more than anyone else. . . . He cried
'I thirst.' " Although it was uncomfortable for a Monophysite like Severus to be in the position of saying that
those who worshiped Christ in the days of his flesh were
worshiping his corruptible body, this seemed to be required by the reality of the hypostatic union, as Athanasius had already sought to show in explaining away the
tears, hunger, and sorrow of the incarnate Logos.

The other two properties of divinity over whose communication to the entire God-man in the days of his flesh
there was controversy, omniscience and uncreatedness,
were dealt with in much the same way. But the former
raised certain exegetical problems, and the latter certain
metaphysical problems, that required special attention.
The explicit statements of the New Testament in John
11:34 and especially in Mark 13:32 seemed to some of
the supporters of Severus clear evidence not only that

Paul.Ant.*Ep.syn.* (*CSCO*
103:228–29[17:327])

See pp. 75–76, 89–90 above

Paul.Ant.*Ep.syn.* (*CSCO*
103:228–29[17:327])

Sev.Ant.*Ep.Thds.* (*CSCO*
103:13–14[17:22–23])

Philox.*Hom.*11.432 (*SC*
44:382)

John 19:28
Philox.*Inc.*1 (*CSCO* 10:140–
41[9:186–89])

Ath.*Ar.*3.54–55 (*PG* 26:436–
40)

Christ in the days of his flesh had indeed participated in weaknesses such as hunger and sorrow, but that he had also been ignorant of certain facts, notably of the hour of the last judgment. This seemed, in turn, to require even of a Monophysite position some distinction between the omniscience of God the Logos and the ignorance of the Son of man. It is an indication of the theological confusion of the time that this theory set forth by certain Monophysites was condemned not only by other Monophysites, but also by no less an adherent of Chalcedon than Gregory I, who took Mark 13:32 to mean that "the Son says that he does not know the day, which he himself causes to be unknown, not because he himself does not know it, but because he does not allow it to be known." Among the opponents of Severus, on the other hand, the logic of the right-wing Monophysite position was carried to its ultimate conclusion when (if the report is to be believed) they maintained that from the moment of the union and incarnation the body of Christ had been not only uncorrupted, but uncreated. Here, too, it was Monophysite theology that refuted the extremes to which its own position seemed to be moving, by affirming that the humanity of Christ was "homoousios with us" in the most fundamental sense of all, namely, in being a creature.

If these Monophysite responses to Monophysite extremes suggest some narrowing of the theological gap, though not of the ecclesiastical schism, between the defenders and the opponents of Chalcedon, such a narrowing is to be found at least as much in the Chalcedonian party itself, which, during the century between the Council of Chalcedon in 451 and the Second Council of Constantinople in 553, moved steadily toward an interpretation of Chalcedon in terms of Cyril and therefore nearer (though never quite near enough to heal the schism) to the Monophysite doctrine. The first stage in this theological process, launched immediately after the council, reached its formal doctrinal (and political) articulation in the Henotikon of the emperor Zeno, issued in 482; this document was an attempt to resolve the dogmatic impasse by major concessions, amounting to capitulation, to the Monophysite position. The only binding statement of dogmatic orthodoxy was affirmed to be the creed adopted by the 318 fathers of the Council of

ap.Phot.*Cod*.230 (*PG* 103:1080–84)

Gr.M.*Ep*.10.21 (*MGH* 2:257)

Tim.CP *Haer*. (*PG* 86:44)

ap.Evagr.*H.e*.3.14 (*PG* 86:2620–25)

Nicea—but as interpreted by the Councils of Constantinople and Ephesus and above all by the twelve anathemas of Cyril. Both Nestorius and Eutyches were declared anathema, but so was "anyone who taught or teaches otherwise, now or in the past, at Chalcedon or at any other synod." The trinitarian dispute growing out of the post-Chalcedonian controversies was resolved with the formula: "The Trinity remains Trinity, even after one of the Trinity, God the Logos, became flesh." Christ was "homoousios with the Father according to his divinity and homoousios with us according to his humanity," but this did not in any way mollify the strict insistence that "there is only one Son, not two." Politically, the Henotikon failed to appease the Monophysites but managed to precipitate a schism with Rome. Dogmatically, it was, however, a somewhat exaggerated version of the eventual accommodation of Chalcedonian orthodoxy to an almost completely Cyrillian interpretation of the decree of 451.

This "Neo-Chalcedonianism" was the doctrinal issue at stake in "the most wearisome controversy in Church history," the power struggle brought on by Justinian's condemnation of "the three chapters" (a term originally applied to chapters of writings, then to their authors): a letter of Ibas of Edessa mediating between the Cyrillian and the Nestorian alternatives; the attack of Theodoret on Cyril; and the person and work of Theodore of Mopsuestia. The exoneration of the first two of these in the decrees of Chalcedon was, politically, one of the grounds for the charge that the council had made concessions to the Nestorians; theologically, it meant that there was some justification for interpreting the Chalcedonian formula in a mediating manner that still appeared to be soft on Nestorianism. In 544 or 545 Justinian anathematized the three chapters (in a treatise that has since been lost), and in 551 he issued a comprehensive statement of what he took to be the orthodox faith. It opened with a reaffirmation of the dogma of the Trinity, explicitly ruling out the idea that "the Trinity is one person with three names [ἓν πρόσωπον τριώνυμον]." God the Logos was declared to be "one of the Holy Trinity, homoousios with God the Father according to divinity, homoousios with us according to humanity; passible as to the flesh, and yet the same One is also impassible as to the divinity." Therefore it was wrong to say

Wigram (1923) 129

Justn.*Conf.* (*PG* 86:995)

Justn.*Conf.* (*PG* 86:995)

that God the Logos had performed the miracles and that only Christ had suffered. "God the Logos himself gave his body for us." On the crucial question of one nature or two in the incarnate Logos, the confession equivocated. In one sentence it spoke of him as "one Christ synthesized from both natures [ἐξ ἑκατέρας φύσεως . . . σύνθετον]," but in the very next it went on to speak of acknowledging "one Lord in each nature." Neither confusion of natures nor separation was to be inferred from these declarations. There was, rather, "a hypostatic union," as taught in Philippians 2:6–7. Such was "the teaching concerning the orthodox faith above all of St. Cyril." This implied, as Cyril himself had confessed, that there was "one Lord Jesus Christ, perfect in divinity, and the same perfect in humanity, one who did not suffer in his divine nature but in his earthly nature."

But when this mediating position specified in detail which theologies of the incarnation it intended to condemn, it became clear that the primary target of its polemic was a continuation, even though a refinement, of the theology of the indwelling Logos. For Christ was within himself "one hypostasis, or one person, and had the perfection of the divine and uncreated nature and the perfection of the human and created nature." Little more than a slap on the wrist was administered to those who, for the sake of this unity, introduced the analogy of the relation between soul and body in man. For they, following the example of Gregory of Nyssa, "united in [divine] mercy" what had to be distinguished in understanding. There was no one in the communion of catholic Christianity who "dared to say that there are three natures in the divine Trinity as there are three hypostases." Not only the Councils of Nicea, Constantinople, and Ephesus, but also "the holy fathers who gathered in Chalcedon" were affirmed as holy confessors. Nevertheless, the anathemas attached to the confession made it obvious where its direction lay. These condemned anyone who taught two Christs or who denied the Theotokos or who denied the unity of Christ in (and despite) the two natures. And therefore "if anyone defends Theodore of Mopsuestia . . . who set forth such blasphemies, and if he does not anathematize him and whatever is ascribed to him, and those that have reasoned similarly to him or still do, let him be anathema." The same applied to

Justn.Conf. (PG 86:997)

Justn.Conf. (PG 86:999–1001)

Justn.Conf. (PG 86:1003)

Justn.Conf. (PG 86:1003)

Justn.Conf. (PG 86:1009)

Justn.Conf. (PG 86:1013)

Theodoret's support of Nestorius: "If anyone defends the remembered writings of Theodoret and does not anathematize them, let him be anathema." This was addressed not only to the partisans of those here condemned, but also and above all to the Monophysite critics of Chalcedon; for it was being asserted here that this interpretation of its decrees, rather than the obvious (and Western and, indeed, Nestorian) interpretation, was the valid one. For "the catholic church condemns this false teaching not against 'the temple' and against the indwelling [Logos] in the temple, but against the one Lord Jesus Christ, the incarnate Logos of God."

The imperial condemnation of the three chapters met with some resistance from various ecclesiastical authorities, including the bishop of Rome, but eventually it was approved and reinforced by the Second Council of Constantinople in 553. The council condemned anyone who maintained that "God the Logos who performed miracles was another than Christ who suffered." It reaffirmed the Theotokos and rejected a mere Christotokos. Its first anathema was a restatement of the orthodox dogma of the Trinity, and it declared that "the Holy Trinity did not undergo the addition of a person or hypostasis when one of the Holy Trinity, God the Logos, became incarnate." In addition to the usual catalog of heretics and heresies to be condemned—including Arius, Eunomius, Macedonius, Apollinaris, Nestorius, and Eutyches—the council devoted special canons to anathemas pronounced upon each of the three chapters. For good measure, the name of Origen was added to the roster; the condemnation of various doctrines attributed to Origen, which Justinian had issued in 543, is often included with the acts and minutes of the council, although it does not seem to have been officially adopted there. Chalcedon was vindicated as a "holy synod" and one that had acted "devoutly," but the entire tone of the construction put on Chalcedon was the one given to it by the imperial theology that prevailed. The christological problem was not settled at the Second Council of Constantinople much more effectively than it had been at Chalcedon, and during the seventh century the controversy over whether Christ had one will or two continued to rage.

Justn.*Conf.* (*PG* 86:1017)

Justn.*Conf.* (*PG* 86:1019)

Justn.*Conf.* (*PG* 86:1021)

CCP(553)*Anath.*3 (Mansi 9:377)
CCP(553)*Anath.*6 (Mansi 9:380)

CCP(553)*Anath.*1 (Mansi 9:376–77)

CCP(553)*Anath.*5 (Mansi 9:380)

CCP(553)*Anath.*11 (Mansi 9:384)

CCP(553)*Anath.*12–14 (Mansi 9:384–88)

CCP(553)*Can.* (Mansi 9:396–400)

CCP(553)*Anath.*6 (Mansi 9:380)

Nature and Grace

The trinitarian and christological dogmas together make up the basic content of normative church doctrine as it developed in the course of the emergence of the catholic tradition between 100 and 600. All three of the so-called ecumenical creeds—the Apostles', the Nicene, and the Athanasian—were essentially formulations of these two dogmas, with a few statements appended about other doctrinal themes. "Whoever wants to be saved," read the third of these, "must, above all else, hold the catholic faith. . . . This is the catholic faith: that we worship one God in Trinity, and Trinity in unity. . . . Furthermore, it is necessary to everlasting salvation that he also believe faithfully the incarnation of our Lord Jesus Christ. . . . This is the catholic faith; unless a man believes it truly and firmly, he cannot be saved."

Symb.Ath. (Schaff 2:66–70)

Despite various references to what was done "for the sake of us men and for the purpose of our salvation," the creeds were basically concerned with the divine ousia and with its relation to the events of the life, death, and resurrection of Jesus Christ. Most of the references to the human condition in these creeds occurred in that context; for example, the question of the relation between soul and body in man (not to mention the relation of soul, spirit, and body) was touched on in passing as an analogy, though an imperfect one, for the relation of the divine and the human in Christ. But trinitarian and christological orthodoxy was not enough for the question of human nature and its relation to the grace given in Christ. On the one hand, what made the incarnation of the divine Logos possible? How could the situation of man be described in a way that would not make it incongruous for the Second Person of the Trinity to take upon himself the very human nature that flesh was heir to? On the other hand, could the coming of the Logos into flesh be described in such a way as to make clear, indeed vivid, why it was necessary that he become incarnate? Without forgetting the wonder of creation and the dignity of incarnation, could the Christian doctrine of man also speak about the fall into sin and the need for salvation?

Many of these issues had been involved in earlier theological discussions, but under other rubrics. Theologians could not consider the Christian doctrine of God as Trinity without raising at some point the question of man as the one to whom the revelation of the Trinity had been vouchsafed. If one affirmed, as all orthodox and even most semiorthodox theologians did, that the incarnate Logos was "homoousios with us according to his humanity" just as he was "homoousios with the Father according to his divinity," it became necessary to specify the referent of the former as well as of the latter. For reasons whose ultimate cultural origins go beyond the scope of this book, it fell to Western Christianity to be the primary locus of this doctrinal controversy, apart from, and to a considerable degree in spite of, the Eastern tradition.

The State of Christian Anthropology

"The Christian doctrine of sin in its classical form," Reinhold Niebuhr has written, "offends both rationalists and moralists by maintaining the seemingly absurd position that man sins inevitably and by a fateful necessity but that he is nevertheless to be held responsible for actions which are prompted by an ineluctable fate." Only seldom in Christian history have the spokesmen for the Christian tradition been confronted with equal force by those who denied that sin was inevitable and by those who denied that man was responsible. Martin Luther, for example, one of the most eloquent interpreters of the inevitability of sin, did not face opponents whose fatalism would have made a mockery both of moral responsibility and of salvation; and therefore he was able to ignore the potentially fatalistic implications of his own one-sided formulations. Most of the doctrinal development in the

R.Niebuhr (1941) 1:241

first four centuries had, like Luther, faced only one option; but in this instance it was the deterministic alternative that constituted the major opposition, with the result that Christian anthropology, as formulated in the course of the ante-Nicene and immediately post-Nicene debates, leaned noticeably to one side of the dilemma, namely, the side of free will and responsibility rather than the side of inevitability and original sin. Why was this so?

Augustine's own answer was to note that "before this heresy [Pelagianism] arose, they did not have the necessity to deal with this question, so difficult of solution.

Aug.*Praed.sanct.*14.27 (PL 44:980); Aug.*Persev.*2.4 (PL 45:996)

They would undoubtedly have done so if they had been compelled to respond to such men." That is, both the attacks upon Christianity from without and the distortions of it from within had tended in the same direction, the deterministic explanation of the human predicament, with the result that the defenders of the faith were obliged to define man's responsibility for his condition much more carefully than they did the inevitability of the condition itself. One horn of the dilemma of Christian anthropology, that of responsibility, seemed to be the one demanded by the polemical situation. Yet in the long run the other alternative, that of inevitability, was the one to which the interpretation of Christian doctrine was obliged to give its primary attention. To explain this development, we must look at the anthropological implications of the history we have traced so far.

Both responsibility and inevitability had been prominent in the classical understanding of man. In the Homeric poems "destiny [μοῖρα]" was a power which the Olympian gods could not dominate; but at the same time it is true to say that "chthonian powers are not so much absent from the *Odyssey* as they are subdued or brought into his service by the hero's extraordinary feats

C.Taylor (1963) 94

of will and intelligence," so that neither the presence of destiny nor that of the gods vitiated the importance of human virtue. There was not in Homer any systematic formula for the relation between destiny and the gods, a relation which was bequeathed as a problem to later Greek thinkers. With the loss of confidence in the gods of Olympus, fortune or fate became increasingly prominent, and men "tended more and more to resign themselves to fate." Aeschylus sought to balance the three

Jaeger (1945) 3:278

forces—the tyranny of fate, the power of the gods, and the responsibility of man—concluding the *Oresteia* trilogy with the words: "There shall be peace forever between these people / of Pallas and their guests. Zeus the all-seeing / met with Destiny to confirm it." And Plato, although he seemed in the *Timaeus* to elevate necessity to the status of an overriding force and in the *Laws* quoted the tradition that even God could not oppose necessity, attempted to maintain some similar balance between divine governance, "luck [τύχη]," "timing [καιρός]," and "skill [τέχνη]."

Aesch.*Eum*.1044–46

Pl.*Ti*.48

Pl.*Leg*.741a

Pl.*Leg*.709b–c

The Romans, too, were impressed with the power of destiny. Ovid represented Jupiter as acknowledging to the other gods that both he and they were ruled by the fates. But in the period of the empire this consciousness of fate grew even more dominant, as the Stoic doctrine of necessity coincided with the incursion of the Chaldean astrologers. "Reason compels us to admit," Cicero asserted, "that all things take place by fate. . . . namely, the order and series of causes." Stoicism identified fate with the divine will, but in the process had to surrender the freedom of the human will. According to Pliny, the goddess Fortune was being invoked everywhere, even though there were those who, with Juvenal, insisted that it was human beings who had made Fortune a goddess. In the popular mind, not Stoic theories of necessity, but the predetermination of the stars undercut human freedom and responsibility. "Fate has decreed as a law for each person the unalterable consequences of his horoscope," said a pagan contemporary of the Christian apologists. And even the emperor Tiberius stopped paying homage to the gods because everything was already written in the stars.

Ov.*Met*.9.433–34

Cic.*Div*.1.56.127

Plin.*HN*2.5.22

Juv.*Sat*.10.365–66; Lact. *Inst.* 3.29.17 (*CSEL* 19:270–71)

ap.F.Grant (1953) 60

Suet.*Tib*.69

In the conflict of Christian theology with classicism it was chiefly this sense of fate and necessity that impressed itself upon the interpreters of the gospel as the alternative to their message, rather than, for example, the Socratic teaching that with proper knowledge and adequate motivation a man could, by the exercise of his free will, overcome the tendency of his appetites toward sin. With very few exceptions the apologists for the gospel against Greek and Roman thought made responsibility rather than inevitability the burden of their message. Justin Martyr felt constrained to make clear that the

Christian understanding of the fulfillment of Old Testament prophecy in Christ did not mean that what happened had been fated. The only unavoidable fate was the rule that reward was based on the actions of a man's free will, whether good or evil. This God foreknew, and he decreed that the recompense of an action should be commensurate with its virtue. Tertullian denounced astrology because "men, presuming that we are disposed of by the immutable arbitrament of the stars, think on that account that God is not to be sought after." Origen, opposing himself to those who denied the freedom of the will, defined the purpose of prayer in such a way as to insure both human freedom and divine providence; for divine foreknowledge was not the cause of man's actions, which he performed in freedom and for which he was accountable. Origen rejected the opinion of those who said that temptations to sin could not be resisted. Refuting various Greek doctrines about the cyclical nature of history, he asserted the Christian teaching "that the universe is cared for by God in accordance with the conditions of the free will of each man, and that as far as possible it is always being led on to be better, and . . . that the nature of our free will is to admit various possibilities." And Augustine's City of God, as part of its statement of the Christian case against paganism, disengaged the Christian understanding of divine omnipotence and human freedom from the "sacrilegious and impious" audacity of reason, as represented by the speculations of Cicero, and asserted simultaneously "that God knows all things before they happen, and that by our own will we do whatever we know and feel could not be done by us unless we willed it."

Not only the Greco-Roman critics of the faith, but also its heretical opponents seemed to err chiefly on the side of emphasizing the inevitability of sin at the expense of the responsibility for sin; in fact, Athanasius linked the heretics with "some of the Greeks" on this issue. It would perhaps be an exaggeration to say that the most explicit doctrines of original sin in the second century were taught not by the church fathers, but by the Gnostics; it is also misleading to speak of a "doctrine of original sin" in church fathers such as Irenaeus. Nevertheless, the theories of cosmic redemption in the Gnostic systems were based on an understanding of the human predicament

Just. *1 Apol*.43 (Goodspeed 55–56)

Just. *1 Apol*.44.11 (Goodspeed 57)

Tert.*Idol*.9.1 (*CCSL* 2:1107)

Or.*Orat*.6.3; 29:13 (*GCS* 3:313; 387–88)

Or.*Orat*.6.3–4 (*GCS* 3:313–14) Or.*Princ*.3.1.4 (*GCS* 22:198–99)

Or.*Cels*.5.21 (*GCS* 3:23)

Aug.*Civ*.5.9 (*CCSL* 47:138)

Ath.*Gent*.6 (*PG* 25:12–13); Iren.*Haer*.2.14.4 (Harvey 1:295)

Orbe (1969) 277–314

in which man's incapacity to avoid sin or to evade destiny was fundamental. The division of the human race into three classes was not due to any action of their free will for which they could be held responsible, but to a pre-determined destiny—even though one class of men, the "psychics," could transcend the nature with which they were born. So rigid was the determination of necessity, according to some of the Gnostics, that "everything passes away by necessity into that state out of which it was created. And they make God himself the slave of this necessity, so that he cannot add immortality to that which is mortal." Simon Magus was accused of teaching that those who were to be saved would receive salvation by grace alone, irrespective of their moral actions, so that moral responsibility was meaningless. So far did this determinism go that the "aspect of the cosmos in which to the Gnostics its character was pre-eminently revealed is the *heimarmene,* that is, universal fate." In one way or another, the various schools of Gnosticism depicted man as the victim and slave of forces over which he had no control, and therefore they diagnosed sin as inevitable.

The response of the anti-Gnostic fathers was to deny the inevitability of sin and to insist that God "sets before man good and evil, life and death. The entire order of discipline is arranged through precepts, as God calls, threatens, and exhorts. This could not be so if man were not free, endowed with a will capable of obedience and resistance." If man were subject to the bondage of evil, it would be unjust of God to base rewards and punishments on human conduct. Only "a spontaneous commission of transgression" could be called to account this way. Rejecting the Gnostic stratification of humanity, Irenaeus insisted that "all men are of the same nature, able both to hold fast and to do what is good, and, on the other hand, having also the power to cast it from them and not to do it." The rebukes and exhortations of the prophets presupposed man's capacity to obey, as did the ethical teachings of Jesus, all of which documented the "self-determination [τὸ αὐτεξούσιον]" of man. If, as the Gnostics maintained, "it were not in our power to do or not to do these things, what reason did the apostle have, and much more the Lord himself, to give us counsel to do some things, and to abstain from others? But because man is possessed of free will from the beginning, and

Hipp.*Haer.*10.9 (*GCS* 26:268)

Iren.*Haer.*2.14.4 (Harvey 1:294–95)

Iren.*Haer.*1.23.3 (Harvey 1:193)

Jonas (1963) 254

Tert.*Marc.*2.5.7 (*CCSL* 1:480–81)

Tert.*Marc.*2.6.7 (*CCSL* 1:482)

Iren.*Haer.*4.37.2 (Harvey 2:286–87)

Iren.*Haer.*4.37.3 (Harvey 2:288)

Iren.*Haer*.4.37.4 (Harvey 2:289)

God is possessed of free will, in whose likeness man was created, advice is always given to him to keep fast the good, which is done by means of obedience to God." And those who fled from the eternal light of God were themselves the cause for their dwelling in eternal darkness. In sum, "those who have apostatized from the light given by the Father, and transgressed the law of liberty, have done so through their own fault, since they have been created free agents, and possessed of power over themselves."

Iren.*Haer*.4.39.4 (Harvey 2:300)

This insistence seemed the only way to preserve both the Christian doctrine of the goodness of the Creator and the Christian doctrine of the responsibility of the creature, in opposition to a theology that denied them both by subjecting God and man to the slavery of an all-powerful fate.

Man did have the freedom to sin or not to sin; otherwise he could not be commanded or rebuked or exhorted —or summoned to account. As a spokesman for the Christian faith in response to the heathen and the heretics, Clement of Alexandria delivered just such an exhortation: "As far as we can, let us try to sin as little as possible." Only God could avoid sin altogether; but wise men were able to avoid voluntary transgressions, and those who were properly trained in Christianity could at

Clem.*Paed*.1.2.4.1-3 (*GCS* 12:91-92)

least see to it that they fell into very few.

This direction of Christian apologetics and of Christian polemics found its counterpart in certain emphases within Christian dogmatics, especially within the christological debates. The definition of "human" was a part of the presupposition of christological doctrine, and that in at least three ways: the understanding of the human condition and its need for salvation; the definition of the human nature of Christ; and the picture of a human race redeemed and transformed by his coming. The two principal options in the doctrine of the incarnation contained, each in its own distinctive manner, elements that served to preclude a full investigation of the inevitability of sin. The proponents of the hypostatic union could certainly never be accused of taking the human predicament lightly. As the anthropology of Athanasius demonstrated in vivid detail, these theologians set the coming of the Logos into flesh against the somber background of the human condition of sin, corruption, and death. By turning away from God in disobedience, men "became the cause of their own corruption in death." This state, moreover, was deteriorating progressively, and men had become "insatiable [ἀκόρεστοι] in sinning." Not satisfied with the first sin, men "again filled themselves with other evils, progressing still further in shamefulness and outdoing themselves in impiety." Neither sun nor moon nor stars had fallen away from God; only man was vile. Viewed against this background, the incarnation of the Logos was seen as the only means of rescue for fallen mankind.

Despite all this strong language about sin, however, the fundamental problem of man was not his sin, but his corruptibility. The reason the incarnation was necessary was that man had not merely done wrong—for this, repentance would have sufficed—but had fallen into a corruption, a transiency that threatened him with annihilation. As the agent of creation who had called man out of nothing, the Logos was also the one to rescue him from annihilation. This the Logos did by taking flesh. For this theology, it was the universality of death, not the inevitability of sin, that was fundamental. The statement of Romans 5:14, that "death reigned from Adam to Moses, even over those whose sins were not like the transgression of Adam," was taken to prove that there were many who had been "pure of every sin," such as Jeremiah and John the Baptist. It was death and corruption that stood in the way of man's participation in the divine nature, and these had to be overcome in the incarnation of the Logos.

The theory of the indwelling Logos was even less helpful in working out a doctrine of sin and the fall. This theory's emphasis on the moral progress of Jesus as the man assumed by the Logos had as its counterpart a doctrine of man that stressed his capacity to imitate this progress. It is too facile to dismiss this as "Pelagianism before Pelagius," for it did not really fit into the categories of the Western development. But it is clear from some fragments that have survived of a treatise *Against the Defenders of Original Sin* by Theodore of Mopsuestia that he "reiterates in effect that it is only *nature* which can be inherited, not sin, which is the disobedience of the free and unconstrained will." Despite their fundamental differences, the theory of the hypostatic union and the theory of the indwelling Logos both con-

Ath.*Inc*.5.3 (Cross 8)

Ath.*Gent*.8 (*PG* 25:17)
Ath.*Inc*.43.1 (Cross 67)

Ath.*Inc*.7.3 (Cross 11)
Ath.*Gent*.41 (*PG* 25:81)

Ath.*Ar*.3.33 (*PG* 26:393)

Ath.*Ar*.3.40 (*PG* 26:409)

Thdr.Mops.*Pecc.orig*. (Swete 2:332–37)

Norris (1963) 179

Thdr.Mops.*Hom.catech.* 12.8
(*ST* 145:335)

Cyr.*Inc.unigen.* (*SC* 97:230)

Thdr.Mops.*Job.*1.29 (*CSCO* 116:29[115:42])

Reuter (1887) 32

centrated on death rather than on sin. Theodore often attributed sin to the fact of man's mortality, although he sometimes reversed the connection; Cyril insisted upon the perfect humanity of Christ because only this would "deliver our earthly body from a foreign corruption." Cyril did sometimes speak of human sin in a way that suggested a doctrine of original sin, and Theodore could say that "since sin was reigning in our mortality, and conversely death was growing stronger in us on account of sin, our Lord and Savior Jesus Christ came . . . and having destroyed death by his death, he also destroyed the sin which was rooted in our nature by reason of its mortality." Yet the detailed implications of these positions for the definition of sin had not been drawn in the course of the christological controversies.

Not from the tendencies evident in the theological controversies of the first four centuries, whether with pagans or with other Christians, but from the direction of the life and practice of the church, there came the material out of which a fuller statement of the relation between nature and grace was to be formulated. For "the predominant anthropology of the second and third centuries stood in partial contradiction with the supernaturalism of the cultus" of the church. Two themes from the cultus probably deserve to be singled out for their bearing upon the dilemma of Christian anthropology: the confession of the virgin birth of Christ and the practice of infant baptism. It was upon these that Christian doctrine, especially in the West, drew for support, inferring from them a more complete explanation of the relation between the inevitability of sin and responsibility for sin than had been set forth by the spokesmen of orthodoxy. Both themes were present in the life and language of the church before they were ever exploited for their anthropological import; at least there appears to be little or no warrant, on the basis of evidence available now, to argue that they were derived from a previously defined theory of the fall and original sin. But given their increasingly secure place in cultus and confession, they became the premises from which conclusions could be drawn about the fall and original sin.

The assertion of the virgin birth of Jesus Christ—or, more precisely, of his virginal conception—originated in the New Testament itself, being found in the Gospels

of Matthew and Luke, but nowhere else. In the first
of these "the Virgin Birth story is theologically mute, no
christological argument or insight is deduced from this

Stendahl (1960) 103

great divine intervention." The narrative in Luke was
somewhat more specific in identifying the significance
of the intervention, for the angel said to Mary: "The
Holy Spirit will come upon you, and the power of the
Most High will overshadow you; therefore the child to

Luke 1:35

be born will be called holy, the Son of God." The word
"therefore [διό]" indicated "that the inference is self-

Arndt (1957) 197

evident" and thus that the holiness and the divine sonship of the child had some connection, perhaps a causal
one, with the special circumstances of his conception. Yet
even Luke did not elaborate on this suggestion in the rest
of his Gospel or in the Book of Acts. For that reason
the doctrine of the virgin birth, even when it had been
enshrined in the creeds, did not carry with it any unambiguous indication of its own meaning. Not only was it
absent from all of the New Testament writers except
Matthew and Luke, but among the apostolic fathers the
only one to refer to it was Ignatius. For him, Christ was

Ign.*Eph*.7.2 (Bihlmeyer 84);
Ign.*Trall*.9.1 (Bihlmeyer 95)

Ign.*Smyrn*.1.1 (Bihlmeyer 106)

"Son of Mary and Son of God" and therefore both "flesh
and spirit": the birth from the Virgin Mary was a guarantee of the true humanity. But it was more: "Hidden
from the prince of this world were the virginity of Mary
and her childbearing and likewise also the death of the
Lord—three mysteries to be cried aloud—which were

Ign.*Eph*.19.1 (Bihlmeyer 87)

wrought in the silence of God." Here the function of
the miraculous conception and birth of Christ was to
show that "our God, Jesus the Christ, was conceived
in the womb by Mary according to a dispensation, of the

Ign.*Eph*.18.2 (Bihlmeyer 87)

seed of David but also of the Holy Spirit." The intent
of the doctrine was christological, certainly not "mariol-
ogical"; much less was it anthropological.

The doctrine "was not formulated for the sake of a
theological line of thought; it was simply a supposedly
'apostolic' piece of biblical tradition that was handed
down. It was not defense, but interpretation, with which
the early Church saw itself confronted in relation to this

Campenhausen (1964) 24

piece of doctrine." Part of that interpretation was some
systematic reflection on what it meant for the Christian
understanding of the person of Christ; and this, in turn,
was bound to have implications for the doctrine of man.
An intriguing example of such reflection is the history

of John 1:12–13 from the second to the fifth centuries—
both its textual transmission and its exegesis: "To all
who received him [the Logos], who believed in his name,
he gave power to become children of God; who were
[textual variant: "who was"] born, not of blood nor of
the will of the flesh nor of the will of man, but of God."
Many, perhaps even most, of the quotations of this passage in the Christian writers of the second and third centuries contained the reading "who was" (which also appeared in some Latin and Syriac codices of the New Testament), which would seem to be an explicit reference to
the virgin birth of Jesus. Irenaeus quoted it to say that
"in the last times, not by the will of the flesh, nor by the
will of man, but by the good pleasure of the Father, his
hands formed a living man, in order that Adam might be

Iren.Haer.5.1.3 (Harvey 2:317)

created [again] after the image and likeness of God."
His other quotations of the passage also read it in the
singular, as a reference to the special circumstances of

Iren.Haer.3.16.2; 3.19.2
(Harvey 2:83; 103)

Christ's birth. Tertullian went so far as to label the plural
reading a Gnostic distortion of the passage, insisting that
the passage proved that Christ was the Logos made flesh,
but that "as flesh, he is not of blood, nor of the will of the

Tert.Carn.19.2; 24.2 (CCSL
2:907; 915–16)

flesh, nor of man" because he was born of a virgin.
This causal connection between the virgin birth and
the holiness of Jesus Christ was reinforced by the growth
of Christian asceticism. The narrative of that growth belongs to the history of institutions and of spirituality
rather than to the history of doctrine, but in the development of the doctrine of man and in the rise of a doctrine
of Mary this connection seems to have played a theological role. Already in the New Testament there was
evidence of the teaching that "it is well for a man not

1 Cor.7:1

to touch a woman" and of the idea that the redeemed
saints were those "who have not defiled themselves with

Rev.14:4

women, for they are virgins." Some parts of the early
church seem to have required celibacy as a condition of
baptism and membership. Tertullian represented the extreme form of a considerably more widespread notion
when he asserted that "marriage and fornication are different only because laws appear to make them so; they are
not intrinsically different, but only in the degree of their

Tert.Castit.9 (CCSL 2:1027–28)

illegitimacy." Although the mainstream of patristic asceticism eschewed the outright condemnation of marriage
and of sex espoused by Tertullian, it did share his posi-

tive appreciation of virginity as a higher way of life. Its most articulate and influential spokesman, arguing on the basis of Revelation 14:4 and related biblical passages, asserted that "all those who have not remained virgins, following the pattern of the pure chastity of angels and that of our Lord Jesus Christ himself, are polluted"; and this included married couples as well as widows. Christ and Mary were the models of true chastity, that is, of virginity; for it was Mary's virginity that made her worthy of becoming the mother of Jesus, and Christ, "as a virgin himself, consecrated the first fruits of his virgins in his own virgin self." Jerome was too good a textual scholar to accept "who was born" as the proper reading in John 1:13; but his ascetical theology, which praised marriage because it was the way virgins were brought into the world, put such a premium on virginity, that of Christ and Mary and that of their imitators, that he no longer needed this reading of the verse to make the point.

It is probably to Ambrose, who in turn became the mentor of Augustine on these matters, that we should attribute the definitive establishment of a firm "causal relation between the virginal conception and the sinlessness of Christ. . . . the combination of the ideas of the propagation of original sin through sexual union and of the sinlessness of Christ as a consequence of his virginal conception." To be free from sin, Christ had to be free from the normal mode of conception: this was the conclusion that Ambrose seemed to draw from Isaiah 53:8 (Vulg.): "Who will tell the story of [enarrabit] his having been begotten [generationem]?" The chief proof text was, however, Psalm 51:5: "Behold, I was brought forth in iniquity, and in sin did my mother conceive me." These words were spoken by David, "who was regarded as righteous beyond others." If Christ was to be called truly righteous, it had to be "for no other reason than that, as one who was born of a virgin, he was not bound in any way by the ordinances against a guilty mode of having been begotten." Combining Psalm 51:5 and the variant text of John 1:13, Ambrose summarized the relation between sin and the virgin birth of Christ: "Even though he assumed the natural substance of this very flesh, he was not conceived in iniquity nor born in sin— he who was not born of blood nor of the will of the flesh nor of the will of a man, but of the Holy Spirit from a

Hier.*Jovin*.1.40 (*PL* 23:269)

Hier.*Ep*.22.38.3 (*CSEL* 54:203)

Hier.*Jovin*.1.39 (*PL* 23:266)

Aug.*Jul.op.imperf*.6.21 (*PL* 45:1549)

Huhn (1954) 79–80

ap.Aug.*Pelag*.4.11.29 (*CSEL* 60:560)

ap.Aug.*Pelag*.4.11.29 (*CSEL* 60:560–61)

virgin." The prerogative of the virgin birth meant that Christ was different from all other men by virtue of his having been protected from the "natural taint" of sin. But it was a simple and unavoidable logical inversion to conclude that those who were conceived and born in the normal manner were therefore subject to that taint and could not be freed of it except through Christ the virgin-born. "That one sin," said Augustine, "was itself so great that by it, in one man, the whole human race was originally and, so to say, radically condemned. It cannot be pardoned and washed away except through 'the one mediator between God and men, the man Christ Jesus,' who alone could be born in such a way as not to need to be reborn."

Another force working in the same direction was infant baptism. Like the virgin birth, infant baptism rested on biblical warrants that were somewhat ambiguous: the story of Jesus blessing the children in Mark 10:13–16 and parallels; the formula in the Book of Acts according to which a "household" was said to have been baptized; the analogy between circumcision in the Old Testament and infant baptism in the New. Whatever its origins or its spread during the second century, the first incontestable evidence for the practice appeared around the end of that century, in the writings of Tertullian. Attacking the practice as a novelty, he asked: "Why should innocent infancy be in such a hurry to come to the forgiveness of sins? Let them come while they are maturing, while they are learning, while they are being taught what it is they are coming to. Let them be made Christians when they have become able to know Christ." Tertullian also spoke of the fall of Adam in a way that seemed to be "a short step . . . to the doctrine of original sin." Adam was called "the pioneer of our race and of our sin." "Man," he said, "is condemned to death for having tasted the fruit of one miserable tree, and from it proceed sins with their penalties; and now all are perishing who have never even seen a single bit of Paradise." Yet this language about the fall stopped short of a genuine doctrine of original sin; indeed, Tertullian "could hardly have taken this attitude [toward infant baptism] . . . unless he had held lightly to the doctrine of original sin."

In the writings of Origen, on the other hand, the cus-

Or.*Rom*.5.9 (PG 14:1047)

tom of infant baptism was taken to be of apostolic origin. He maintained that there was "a tradition of the church from the apostles" to administer baptism also to infants. But even though it was apostolic, the custom remained problematical for him. If infants were completely devoid of anything that called for forgiveness and pardon, baptismal grace would seem superfluous. Why, then, was it

Or.*Lev*.8.3 (*GCS* 29:398)

the custom of the church to administer baptism to them? Attempting to draw together these various considerations, he proposed as a tentative answer: "Infants are baptized 'for the remission of sins.' Of which sins? Or at what time have they sinned? Or how can there exist in infants that reason for washing, unless in accordance with the idea that no one is clean of filth, not even if his life on earth has only been for one day? And because the filth of birth is removed by the sacrament of baptism, for that reason infants, too, are baptized; for 'unless one is born again of water and the Spirit, he cannot enter the

Or.*Luc*.14.5 (*GCS* 49:87–88)

kingdom of heaven.' " Although Tertullian seemed to have the makings of a doctrine of original sin, he did not have its necessary corollary, the practice of infant baptism; while Origen, on the other hand, affirmed the apostolic origin of infant baptism, he did not formulate an anthropology adequate to account for it.

The achievement of a correlation between the practice of infant baptism and the doctrine of original sin was first made visible in Cyprian. It had apparently been a custom for some parts of the church to baptize infants on the eighth day after their birth, but Cyprian insisted that this was too long to wait: "If, when they subsequently come to believe, forgiveness of sins is granted even to the worst transgressors and to those who have sinned much against God, and if no one is denied access to baptism and to grace; how much less right do we have to deny it to an infant, who, having been born recently, has not sinned, except in that, being born physically according to Adam, he has contracted the contagion of the ancient death by his first birth! [The infant] approaches that much more easily to the reception of the forgiveness of sins because the sins remitted to him are not his own, but those of an-

Cypr.*Ep*.64.5 (*CSEL* 3:720–21)

other." Cyprian did not in fact elaborate these sentiments into a full-scale theory about the origin and the propagation of "the contagion of the ancient death." But he did invoke a doctrine of original sin to account for a practice about whose apostolic credentials and sacramental validity he had no question whatever.

Augustine, who learned from Ambrose to draw the anthropological implications of the doctrine of the virgin birth, learned from Cyprian—and specifically from the epistle just quoted, which he called Cyprian's "book on the baptism of infants"—to argue that infant baptism proved the presence in infants of a sin that was inevitable, but a sin for which they were nevertheless held responsible. "The uniqueness of the remedy" in baptism, it could be argued, proved "the very depth of evil" into which mankind had sunk through Adam's fall, and the practice of exorcism associated with the rite of baptism was liturgical evidence for the doctrine that children were in the clutches of the devil. Cyprian's teaching showed that this view of sin was not an innovation, but "the ancient, implanted opinion of the church." On the basis of Cyprian's discussion of infant baptism and of Ambrose's interpretation of the virgin birth, Augustine could claim that "what we hold is the true, the truly Christian, and the catholic faith, as it was handed down of old through the Sacred Scriptures, and so retained and preserved by our fathers and to this very time, in which these men have attempted to overthrow it." This faith he expressed in his theology of grace.

The Paradox of Grace

In Augustine of Hippo Western Christianity found its most influential spokesman, and the doctrine of grace its most articulate interpreter. It has been said that although he may not have been the greatest of Latin writers, he was almost certainly the greatest man who ever wrote Latin. In any history of philosophy he must figure prominently; no history of postclassical Latin literature would be complete without a chapter on him; and there is probably no Christian theologian—Eastern or Western, ancient or medieval or modern, heretical or orthodox—whose historical influence can match his. Any theologian who would have written either the *Confessions* or the *City of God* or *On the Trinity* would have to be counted a major figure in intellectual history. Augustine wrote them all, and vastly more. He was a universal genius. Yet genius is not so rare as all that—and, more importantly,

Aug.*Nupt.et concup.*2.29.51 (*CSEL* 42:308)

Prosp.*Coll.*9.3 (*PL* 51:237–38)

Aug.*Pecc.merit.*3.3.6 (*CSEL* 60:132)

Aug.*Pelag.*4.12.32 (*CSEL* 60:568)

not so pertinent as all that to the history of the development of Christian doctrine as that which the church believes, teaches, and confesses on the basis of the word of God.

It was, however, characteristic of this genius that, more perhaps than any other theologian deserving of that ambiguous designation, he was also a teacher of the church in his private writings and individual speculations, and this in at least two ways. The theological opinions of Augustine were stated in the matrix of the doctrines of the church. In his most speculative formulation of Christian thought, *On the Trinity*, he was determined to speak in the name of catholic orthodoxy: "This is also my faith, inasmuch as this is the catholic faith." Even when they exceed the limits of the development that had preceded him, some of these opinions (for example, the Filioque, the doctrine of the procession of the Holy Spirit from the Father and the Son rather than only from the Father) went on to set the lines for the doctrinal history that was to follow him. Other theories (for example, his doctrine of double predestination) were repudiated in later generations, but even the repudiation was formulated in Augustinian terms. In a manner and to a degree unique for any Christian thinker outside the New Testament, Augustine has determined the form and the content of church doctrine for most of Western Christian history.

The role of Augustine in the evolution of Christian thought and teaching affected the history of every doctrine and was not confined to the issue of nature and grace, which has been so inseparably associated with his name. Augustine's *City of God* is the logical treatise with which to conclude any study of the history of early Christian apologetics, for in it he caught up most of the themes of his Greek and Latin predecessors and synthesized them into a grand historical design. Although his trinitarian speculations, especially the Filioque, represented anything but a dogma of the universal church, they do form so integral a part of the history of the doctrine of the Trinity in Christian antiquity that any narrative of that history is obliged to deal with them repeatedly. And his reflections on the person and work of Jesus Christ significantly shaped the entire Western christological method and thus contributed to the dogmatic settlement at Chalcedon. Almost anywhere one touches the history

Aug.*Trin*.1.5.7 (*CCSL* 50:36)

See pp. 327–29 below

of early Christian doctrine, Augustine is there either as a synthesizer or as a creator or as both. Almost no doctrinal emphasis was alien to him.

Yet the Latin church was correct when it designated him not only a "doctor of the church," but specifically the "doctor of grace." For if there was a doctrinal accent that bound together most of what he said and wrote, it was divine grace. As Albert C. Outler has well said, "The central theme in all Augustine's writings is the sovereign God of grace and the sovereign grace of God. Grace, for Augustine, is God's freedom to act without any external necessity whatsoever—to act in love beyond human understanding or control; to act in creation, judgment, and redemption; to give his Son freely as Mediator and Redeemer; to endue the Church with the indwelling power and guidance of the Holy Spirit; to shape the destinies of all creation and the ends of the two human societies, the 'city of earth' and the 'city of God.' Grace is God's unmerited love and favor, prevenient and occurrent. It touches man's inmost heart and will. It guides and impels the pilgrimage of those called to be faithful. It draws and raises the soul to repentance, faith, and praise. It transforms the human will so that it is capable of doing good. It relieves man's religious anxiety by forgiveness and the gift of hope. It establishes the ground of Christian humility by abolishing the ground of human pride. God's grace became incarnate in Jesus Christ, and it remains immanent in the Holy Spirit in the Church."

Outler (1955) 14–15

The grace of God was sovereign because God was sovereign. His creatures might accept his will or defy it, but that did not threaten his sovereignty; for "however strong the wills either of angels or of men, whether good or evil, whether they will what God wills or will something else, the will of the Omnipotent is always undefeated." The wisdom and power of God were such that even the evil deeds of evil men in defiance of his will eventually contributed to the achievement of his good and just purposes. The very name Omnipotent meant simply that God had the power to do everything he willed. It was above all in the mystery of creation that divine sovereignty made itself evident. Heaven and earth were subject to change and decay because they had been made out of nothing. "We exist," they would have to say, "only because we have been made; we did not exist

Aug.*Enchir*.26.102 (*CCSL* 46:104)

Aug.*Civ*.22.2 (*CCSL* 48:807)

Aug.*Civ*.21.7 (*CCSL* 48:769); Aug.*Corrept*.14.45 (*PL* 44:943–44)

Aug.*Conf*.11.4.6 (*CSEL* 33:284)

Aug.*Enchir*.28.107 (*CCSL* 46:107)

Aug.*Civ*.8.6 (*CCSL* 47:223)

Scheel (1901) 145

Aug.*Soliloq*.1.4.9 (*PL* 32:874)

Aug.*Conf*.8.2.3 (*CSEL* 33:171)

Alfaric (1918) 1:399

Aug.*Mag*.38 (*CSEL* 77:47)

Aug.*Vera relig*.4.7 (*CCSL* 32:192)

before we came to be so that we could have made ourselves." Among the creatures, man was preeminently the object of the Creator's gracious intent. His creation was an act of sheer grace. "But unless grace is gratis, it is not grace. . . . Therefore man was made upright in such a way that he could not have remained in that uprightness without divine help." For the Creator, there could not be a distinction between his being and his life, nor between either of these and his understanding, nor between any of these and his state of blessedness; "but for him to live, to understand, to be blessed—these are to be," as the Platonic philosophers had already understood.

Such references as these to the Platonic tradition suggest the possibility that "Augustine's doctrine of grace is merely a consequence of his Neoplatonism and of the concept of God that emerged from this, in which the idea of absolute causality and omnipotence is raised to a position of greater importance than the Father's love." Especially in his early writings Augustine seemed to identify the biblical doctrine of God as Creator with "what Plato and Plotinus have said about God." He himself quoted Simplicianus, one of his early mentors in the gospel, as advising him that "in the Platonists, at every turn, the pathway led to belief in God and in his word." On the basis of these early writings it has been claimed that "morally as well as intellectually, he was converted to Neoplatonism rather than to the gospel." It is appropriate here to observe how consistently Platonic was Augustine's early doctrine of knowledge in the soul, which identified the work of Christ as the divine teacher with the idea of recollection (ἀνάμνησις), so that "we do not consult a speaker who utters sounds to the outside, but a truth that presides within. . . . Christ, who is said to dwell in the inner man—he it is who teaches." It would require only "the change of a few words and sentiments" for Plato and his followers to "become Christians." Nevertheless, the doctrine of God in another of Augustine's mentors, the Neoplatonist and Christian Marius Victorinus, must make us hesitate before accepting any simplistic view of Augustine's conversion. For even in Victorinus, philosophical doctrines of God, including Neoplatonic doctrines, were set into contrast with the doctrine of Scripture, which "both declares that he is God and that there is nothing before him—he who combines in himself both being and activity [qui et id est quod est esse et id quod operari]. This is the God whom we confess and worship." Neither in Victorinus nor a fortiori in Augustine was there a mere identification of Christianity with Neoplatonism; rather, a study of the early treatises suggests "that Augustine in 386 accepted Christianity without reservation and in opposition to the Neo-Platonist, Porphyry, who had most helped him, perhaps, at this stage. At the same time he looked to Neo-Platonism for help in the understanding of problems."

The ancestry of Augustine's doctrine on the sovereignty of the God of grace cannot be ascribed to Plotinus or Porphyry without taking into account the biblical view of God as Creator, which formed a major preoccupation of his thought, not only in his several commentaries on Genesis, but throughout his works. For "while Plotinus sees the process [of creation] beginning in the hierarchy of 'things divine' and completing itself in the external world of sense, Augustine draws his line firmly and finally between the one Maker and the many things made." It is quite another question whether this doctrine of the Creator was determined in its fundamental content by the christocentric perspective which Augustine espoused in principle. When he came to speak of the divine essence, it was usually defined in relation to absoluteness and impassibility rather than on the basis of the active involvement of God in creation and redemption. Biblical language that spoke about this involvement, as, for example, Exodus 20:5, "I the Lord your God am a jealous God," was an analogy and an accommodation to the childish understanding of men; "but Scripture rarely uses terms which are spoken unmetaphorically [proprie] about God and which are not found in any creature," as it did in Exodus 3:14. Book 4 of *On the Trinity* was given over to an extensive dissertation on the saving effect of the incarnation and death of Christ. But even this was connected to the preceding book by the statement that "the essence of God, by which he is, has nothing changeable" in it, and was connected to the following book by the declaration that "he who is God is the only unchangeable substance or essence, to whom certainly being itself [ipsum esse], from which the noun 'essence' comes, most especially and truly belongs." The dogma of the Trinity and the drama of the redemption must be in-

Mar.Vict.*Ar*.1.33 (*SC* 68:288)

O'Meara (1950) 197

Burnaby (1960) 163

Aug.*Trin*.1.1.2 (CCSL 50:29)

Aug.*Trin*.4 pr. (*CCSL* 50:160)

Aug.*Trin*.5.2.3 (*CCSL* 50:208)

terpreted in a manner that would be consistent with this a priori definition of the deity of God. Neoplatonic elements were unmistakably present in this definition, but in setting it forth Augustine believed himself to be—and he was—expressing the catholic creed.

What was distinctive about his version of that creed was his awareness of the sovereignty of divine power and divine grace. This awareness took the form of a doctrine of predestination more thoroughgoing than that of any major orthodox thinker since Paul. He defined predestination as "God's arrangement of his future works in his prescience, which cannot be deceived and changed." As part of the apologetics in his *City of God,* Augustine sought to distinguish the Christian-Pauline understanding of predestination from pagan fatalism, arguing that the decisions of the human will were part of the "order of causes" included in the divine prescience. But even in this book he came eventually to include the human will in the order of effects of the divine predestination; for "according to that will of his [God's] which is as eternal as his prescience, certainly he has already done in heaven and on earth all the things that he has willed—not only things past and present, but even things still future."

In some ways more important than the relation between prescience and predestination was the connection between predestination and grace; the only difference between them was that predestination was the preparation for grace, while grace was the bestowal of the gift itself. Since grace was sovereign, those whom God had predestined would be saved. "As the one who is supremely good, he made good use of evil deeds, for the damnation of those whom he had justly predestined to punishment and for the salvation of those whom he had kindly predestined to grace." Even in the case of the damned, the omnipotence of God achieved its purpose and the will of God was done on earth as it is in heaven. Why then did God create those whose fall he foreknew? To manifest his wrath and to demonstrate his power. Human history was the arena for this demonstration, in which the "two societies of men" were predestined, the one to reign eternally with God and the other to undergo eternal suffering with the devil. But double predestination applied not only to the city of God and the city of earth, but also to individuals. Some were predestined to eternal life, others to eternal death; and

Aug.*Persev.*17.41 (*PL* 45:1019)

Aug.*Pelag.*2.5.10 (*CSEL* 60:469)

Aug.*Civ.*5.9 (*CCSL* 47:138)

Aug.*Civ.*22.2 (*CCSL* 48:808)

Aug.*Praed.sanct.*10.19 (*PL* 44:974)

Aug.*Enchir.*26.100 (*CCSL* 46:103)

Aug.*Gen.ad litt.*11.8 (*CSEL* 28:341)

Aug.*Civ.*15.1 (*CCSL* 48:453)

Aug.*Anim*.4.11.16 (*CSEL* 60:396)

G.Nygren (1956) 265–66

Aug.*Anim*.4.11.16 (*CSEL* 60: 395–96)

Aug.*Pelag*.4.6.16 (*CSEL* 60:539)

Aug.*Spir.et litt*.34.60 (*CSEL* 60:221)

Warfield (1897) 134

Aug.*Corrept*.12.33 (*PL* 44:936)

Aug.*Civ*.14.26 (*CCSL* 48:449)

among these latter were infants who died without baptism.

Therefore "the doctrine of double predestination, to heaven and to hell, has . . . the last word in the theology of Augustine." It was an inescapable corollary of his view of God the Creator as the sovereign God of grace. Even in his most explicit statements about double predestination, however, Augustine spoke of that grace as a mystery. He preferred ignorance to rashness, as he said in the passage just cited about the damnation of infants. It was ultimately an unfathomable mystery why one should receive grace and another should not receive it, when neither of them deserved to receive it. The words of Romans 11:33 were his consistent reply to those who wanted the mystery resolved. And "if this answer displeases someone, let him seek more learned [theologians], but let him beware lest he find [more] presumptuous ones!" It was not appropriate to attempt to discern the intention of God from the external and observable facts of human behavior. The basis of eternal predestination was not human merit, but divine grace; and even in the case of those who were predestined to damnation, the will of God was good and just, for they received the damnation which they—and the saved as well—deserved. But this led back to the sovereignty of grace, which was the real stumbling block to the gainsayer. "What men object to is gratuitous and sovereign grace: and to this no additional difficulty is added by the necessary assumption that it was foreknown and prepared for from eternity."

Underlying this theory of predestination and this definition of grace was not only a doctrine of God as the omnipotent and sovereign Creator whose will was always accomplished, but also a doctrine of man as the fallen and sinful creature whose will had been turned against God. Man had been created with the ability not to sin (posse non peccare) and not to die, although not with the inability to sin (non posse peccare) and to die. Adam "lived in Paradise as he wanted to, and for as long as he wanted what God had commanded. He lived enjoying God, from whom, the Good, he also was good; and he lived without lacking anything, having it in his power to live this way forever." To this end Adam had been endowed with the qualities requisite to being human, such as rationality, as well as with the special gifts of grace necessary for obeying the will of God. "He did not need grace to receive good, because he had not yet lost it; but to abide in it he needed the aid of grace [adjutorium gratiae], without which he could not do this at all."

Aug.*Corrept.*11.32 (*PL* 44:936)

Aug.*Corrept.*11.29 (*PL* 44:933–34)

Adam had the grace of God in great measure, but not as sinners have it today. The grace given to him did not include a confirmed perseverance in good, but the choice between good and evil was left to the decision of his free will. The angels, too, were created in such a way that the same act of creation that constituted their nature endowed them with grace; but they also were capable of falling. Yet this did not imply that the creation of man was anything other than "very good." Even the tree whose mortal taste caused man to fall was not blameworthy in itself, but good. Against any disparagement of the creation or of the Creator Augustine insisted that "being is good simply because it is being [esse qua esse bonum est]"; therefore the sinner was of God insofar as he was a living creature, and not of God insofar as he was a sinner. The grace given to Adam in the state of integrity was the grace of innocence, but not yet the grace of perfection: innocence was appropriate to the alpha-point of human history, but perfection could come only at the omega-point.

Aug.*Corrept.*12.37 (*PL* 44:938–39)

Aug.*Civ.*12.9 (*CCSL* 48:363)

Aug.*Gen.ad litt.*11.21 (*CSEL* 28:353); Aug.*Pecc.merit.*2.21. 35 (*CSEL* 60:107)

Aug.*Nat.bon.*36 (*CSEL* 25:872–73)

Aug.*Duab.anim.*9 (*CSEL* 25:62)

Adam lost this grace of innocence through his fall into sin. He fell when his soul refused to obey God and when, as a result of the disobedience in his soul, his body also disobeyed. The body was the instrument of the disobedience, not its source. Yet once the disobedience had taken place, the body also became its bearer—and its transmitter. For in the sin of Adam the entire human race sinned. In Augustine's Latin Bible Romans 5:12 read: "Sin came into the world, and death through sin, and so death spread to all men, through one man, in whom all men sinned [in quo omnes peccaverunt]." Although this last clause really meant "because [ἐφ'ᾧ] all men sinned," the translation "in whom all men sinned" had led an earlier Westtern theologian to conclude that "all have sinned in Adam, as it were in the mass, for he himself was corrupted by sin, and all whom he begot were born under sin." Quoting these words, Augustine insisted that "all men are understood to have sinned in that first man, because all men were in him when he sinned." Just how they

Aug.*Pecc.merit.*1.16.21 (*CSEL* 60:20–21)

Ambrosiast.*Rom.*5.12.3 (*CSEL* 81:165)

Aug.*Pelag.*4.4.7 (*CSEL* 60:528)

Aug.*Pecc.merit.*1.15.19 (*CSEL* 60:19)

Aug.*Pecc.merit.*1.15.20 (*CSEL* 60:20)

Aug.*Pecc.merit.*1.9.10 (*CSEL* 60:12)

Aug.*Nupt.et concup.*1.18.20 (*CSEL* 42:232)

Aug.*Nat.et grat.*53.62 (*CSEL* 60:279)

Aug.*Conf.*3.6.11; 3.11.20 (*CSEL* 33:52–53; 61–62)

Aug.*Faust.*24.1 (*CSEL* 25:718)

ap.Aug.*Jul.op.imperf.*2.32; 3.67; 5.25 (*PL* 45:1155; 1278; 1462)

ap.Aug.*Nupt.et concup.*2.29.49 (*CSEL* 42:304)

Aug.*Spir.et litt.*28.48 (*CSEL* 60:202)

were in Adam and sinned in Adam, he usually explained by referring to the "carnal begetting" by which their lives began. For "by the begetting of the flesh . . . that sin is contracted which is original" as distinguished from that which a man committed himself. Sin and death had been transmitted to all men from one man "by the propagation" of the human race. A variant reading of Luke 20:34, "The sons of this age beget and are begotten," meant that even Christian parents begot "sons of this present age," who were born of the lust of the flesh and to whom therefore its contagion was passed on. Because it was transmitted by natural propagation, original sin was as universal and inevitable as life itself. "Behold," wrote Augustine in summary, "what harm the disobedience of the will has inflicted on human nature! Let him be permitted to pray that he may be healed [orare sinatur, ut sanetur]. Why should he presume so much on the capacity of his nature? It is wounded, hurt, damaged, destroyed. It needs a true confession, not a false defense. It needs the grace of God, not that it may be created, but that it may be restored."

The use of such a term as "destroyed" rather than only "damaged" to describe human nature after the fall of Adam could lead to the impression that as a result of sin man had ceased being man and was now being created, at least partly, in the image of the devil rather than in the image of God. Such had been Augustine's personal belief during the nearly nine years that he was a Manichean. For the Manicheans had taught that the begetting of men took place in the "madness and intemperance" of sexual lust and that therefore it was blasphemous to suppose that "God forms us according to his own image" through the madness and lust of our parents. Augustine's theory of the transmission of sin from generation to generation through "carnal begetting," as though this were some sort of venereal disease, seemed suspiciously reminiscent of the Manichean doctrine, enough so to prompt the charge of one of his contemporaries that "anyone who defends [the doctrine of] original evil is a thoroughgoing Manichean." For Augustine as an orthodox Christian, the image of God had not been lost through the fall and man had not ceased being God's good creature: God created man according to his image, "not as regards the possession of a body and of physical life, but as regards the possession of a rational mind by which to know God." He distinguished his view of innate and radical evil from the Manichean by holding two doctrines together which the Manicheans (as well as the Pelagians) treated as mutually contradictory. Man had "a good creation but a corrupt propagation, confessing for his goods a most excellent Creator and seeking for his evils a most merciful Redeemer." The nature of man as a creature of God remained even after the fall into sin, which, as a turning away from God to evil, did not mean the creation of another and evil nature but the corruption of that nature which had already been created good; for "although there was a fault present in nature, yet nature was not itself a fault." It still possessed life, senses, and intellect as gifts of the Creator. And therefore man was neither created in the image of the devil nor degraded to the level of the brutes. "For man has such excellence [even after the fall] in comparison with the brute that what is a fault in man is nature in the brute. Still man's nature is not changed into the nature of the brute. God, therefore, condemns man because of the fault by which his nature is disgraced, not because of his nature, which is not abolished through its fault."

Nature had not been destroyed, but it had been gravely wounded and needed to be healed by divine grace, which had been lost in the fall but was now restored in Christ. Grace was more than nature, more than free will, more even than the forgiveness of sins and the gift of God's commandments; it was the divinely given power to avoid and conquer sin. There were very few biblical passages which Augustine quoted more frequently or more fervently than Romans 5:5: "The love of God has been shed abroad in our hearts by the Holy Spirit, who has been given to us." Neither free will of itself nor instruction in the law and will of God would suffice to achieve righteousness, for free will was good only for sinning unless a man knew the law, and even after he knew it he still lacked a love for it and a delight in it; this came only through the love of God shed abroad, "not by the free will whose spring is in ourselves, but through the Holy Spirit." The traditional picture of Christ as the physician and of salvation as divine healing was incorporated into

Aug.*Faust*.24.2 (*CSEL* 25:721)

Aug.*Pelag*.4.4.4 (*CSEL* 60:524)

Aug.*Grat.Christ*.19.20 (*CSEL* 42:141)
Aug.*Nat.et grat*.3.3 (*CSEL* 60:235)

Aug.*Pecc.orig*.40.46 (*CSEL* 42:204)

Aug.*Gest.Pelag*.31.56 (*CSEL* 42:110)

Aug.*Ep*.177.4 (*CSEL* 44:672)

Aug.*Spir.et litt*.3.5 (*CSEL* 60:157)

Augustine's doctrine of grace. Christ "took up sinners to heal and restore them . . . being himself physician and medicine both in one." This grace was not based upon any preceding merit or works of man; for man could not love God unless God first loved him, and he could not have any merits when he did not yet love God. The love of God shed abroad, or grace, brought it about "not only that we learn to know what ought to be done, but also that we do what we have learned." Grace, then, preceded and followed man's life of love: preceded it in order that we might be healed, followed it that we might become healthy and strong. The doctrine of preceding (or prevenient) grace was most clearly seen in the baptism of infants, who in receiving grace had no will, no preceding merit; for if they had, grace would no longer be grace. As this was true of infants, who lacked not only merit but actual sin as well, it was true even more of adults, for whom both original and actual sin had to be remitted by grace.

In Augustine's theology of grace infant baptism proved not only the universal necessity of grace, but also the objective mediation of grace. If the grace of God was sovereign in its predestinating efficacy, God could not be said to be absolutely bound *by* the church and the sacraments; but he was bound *to* them. The mystery of grace was not resolved by simply determining who belonged to the external fellowship of the church or who had been baptized. It was necessary to "distinguish the visible holy sacrament, which can exist both in the good and in the bad . . . from the invisible unction of charity, which is the peculiar property of the good." Yet the same mystery that precluded empirical judgments about who was or was not predestined also obliged the believer to wait upon the ordinances of the church; for the prescience and the predestination of God extended not only to the end he had in view, the salvation of the elect, but also to the means whose bestowal made possible a righteous life. Therefore the doctrine of predestination, even of double predestination, did not undercut the sacramental doctrine of Augustine, as it has that of some theologians. His doctrine of the church was more seriously affected by his view of predestination than was his doctrine of the sacraments. It was by no means self-evident that those who "participate physically in the sacraments" were to be regarded as members of the body of Christ, the church. For "in the ineffable prescience of God, many who seem to be on the outside are in fact on the inside, and many who seem to be on the inside are nevertheless in fact on the outside"; therefore the true church consisted of "the fixed number of the saints predestined before the foundation of the world," even though some of them were now wallowing in heresy or vice. These belonged to the city of God, predestined and elected by grace, aliens here below but citizens above. When the church was defined this way, it was valid to say that God had none who were outside the communion of the church.

This definition of the church as the "number of the predestined" was to figure prominently in the polemics of the late Middle Ages and the Reformation against the institutional church, but in Augustine's theology it had precisely the opposite function. It enabled him to accept a distinction between the members of the empirical catholic church and the company of those who would be saved, while at the same time he insisted that the empirical catholic church was the only one in which salvation was dispensed; "for it is the church that gives birth to all." Although God predestined, "we, on the basis of what each man is right now, inquire whether today they are to be counted as members of the church." It was to the church as now constituted that one was to look for grace, for guidance, and for authority. Those who accepted "the authority of the Scriptures as preeminent" should also acknowledge "that authority which from the time of the [earthly] presence of Christ, through the dispensation of the apostles and through a regular succession of bishops in their seats, has been preserved to our own day throughout the world." This authority of orthodox catholic Christendom, "inaugurated by miracles, nourished by hope, enlarged by charity, established by antiquity," was so powerful as even to validate the very authority of the Bible. "For my part," Augustine declared, "I should not believe the gospel except as moved by the authority of the catholic church." At the same time, he distinguished sharply between the authority of the Bible, which never needed to be corrected but only obeyed, and that of later bishops, who needed to be corrected by it. Someone who failed to support his position from the Bible "need not detain us very long." But between the authority of the Bible and

Aug.*Bapt.*5.27.38 (*CSEL* 51: 294–95); Aug.*Corrept.*7.16 (*PL* 44:925)

Aug.*Civ.*15.1 (*CCSL* 48:454)

Aug.*Bapt.*4.10.14 (*CSEL* 51: 239)

Aug.*Bapt.*1.15.23 (*CSEL* 51: 167)

Aug.*Bapt.*4.3.4 (*CSEL* 51: 225)

Aug.*Faust.*33.9 (*CSEL* 25:796)

Aug.*Ep.fund.*4 (*CSEL* 25:196)

Aug.*Ep.fund.*5 (*CSEL* 25:197)

Aug.*Bapt.*2.3.4 (*CSEL* 51: 178)

Aug.*Bapt.*7.48.95 (*CSEL* 51: 367)

the authority of the catholic church (which was present within, but was more than, the authority of its several bishops past and present) there could not in a real sense be any contradiction. Here one could find repose in "the resting place of authority," not in the unknown quantity of the company of the elect, but in the institution of salvation that could claim foundation by Christ and succession from the apostles.

In that institution of salvation the principal channels of grace were the sacraments. It was characteristic of any religious society, whether true or false, that in it men were gathered together by "a sharing of signs or visible sacraments [aliquo signaculorum vel sacramentorum visibilium consortio]"; these were of inestimable importance, for without them piety could not be made perfect. This applied in a special sense to the church, which maintained as part of its tradition that no one could be admitted to its altar unless he had been baptized. Echoing the understanding set forth by Tertullian, Augustine ascribed to baptism the traditional effects: a washing away of "absolutely all sins, whether of deeds or words or thoughts, whether original or added, whether committed unconsciously or permitted consciously"; the assurance that "one may hope for an unending life when he dies"; a regeneration through "the washing of regeneration," as a beginning of complete and eternal regeneration; and the gift of the Holy Spirit, even though it was also true that "it is possible for baptism to exist without the [Holy] Spirit." All of these effects were conferred through baptism on infants, who could not have either the kingdom of heaven or eternal life "if they do not have the Son [of God], whom they are able to have only through his baptism." Therefore the church did not shrink from calling them worthy of the title "believer," which no truly faithful Christian would be willing to deny them. The words of Jesus to Nicodemus in John 3:5, amplified by the words of Paul in Titus 3:5, meant that "no one can enter into the kingdom of God unless he has been bathed in the washing of regeneration." The Punic Christians of Augustine's North Africa "very fittingly call baptism nothing else than 'salvation,' and the sacrament of the body of Christ nothing else than 'life.' "

Augustine's doctrine about "the sacrament of the body in Christ" was less explicit than his doctrine about bap-

Aug.*Bapt*.2.8.13 (*CSEL* 51:189)

Aug.*Faust*.19.11 (*CSEL* 25:510)

Aug.*Bapt*.2.14.19 (*CSEL* 51:195)
See pp. 163–66 above

Aug.*Pelag*.3.3.5 (*CSEL* 60:490)
Aug.*Pecc.merit*.2.31.50 (*CSEL* 60:121)

Aug.*Pecc.orig*. 39.44 (*CSEL* 42:202)
Aug.*Nat.et grat*.53.61 (*CSEL* 60:278)

Aug.*Bapt*.5.24.34 (*CSEL* 51:291)

Aug.*Pecc.merit*.1.27.42 (*CSEL* 60:40–41)
Aug.*Pecc.merit*.3.2.2 (*CSEL* 60:130)

Aug.*Pecc.merit*.1.25.38 (*CSEL* 60:37)

Aug.*Anim*.3.11.17 (*CSEL* 60:373)

Aug.*Pecc.merit*.1.24.34 (*CSEL* 60:33)

tism, not because he spoke of it less often (though he probably did), but because he did not specify its content with equal detail. Even those interpreters of Augustine who maintain that he taught the real presence of the body and blood of Christ in the Eucharist so explicitly that his language is "inexplicable unless he not only employed realistic formulas, but understood them in a realistic way" have been obliged to acknowledge that "certain formulas are found in Augustine which can hardly be explained easily." It was certainly "realistic language" when Augustine, speaking of miracles performed by angels, drew a parallel with the presence of the body and blood of Christ on the altar. The presence in the sacrament was sufficiently "objective" to imply that Judas, as well as more recent unworthy communicants, received "the body of the Lord and the blood of the Lord nonetheless." In the incarnation Christ "took upon himself earth from earth, because flesh is from the earth, and he received flesh from the flesh of Mary. . . . He walked here in that very flesh and gave us that very flesh to eat for our salvation." But in the same paragraph he went on to paraphrase John 6:63 to mean: "Understand spiritually what I have said. You are not to eat this body which you see, nor to drink that blood which will be shed by those who are to crucify me." Augustine's famous formula, "Why are you preparing your teeth and your stomach? Believe, and you have already eaten," does not, in its context, seem to have been referring specifically to the Eucharist; but shortly thereafter he does seem to have had it in mind when he asserted that Christ, in "explaining what it means to eat his body and to drink his blood," intended that "for a man to eat this food and to drink this drink means to abide in Christ and to have Christ abiding in him." Similarly, he could speak of "the figure [figura] of his body and blood" as the content of what Christ had committed and delivered to his disciples in the institution of the Lord's Supper.

It is incorrect, therefore, to attribute to Augustine either a scholastic doctrine of transubstantiation or a Protestant doctrine of symbolism, for he taught neither—or both—and both were able to cite his authority. It is scarcely less idle to debate whether Augustine counted seven sacraments, as the scholastics eventually did, or only two, as Protestants did. He used the term "sacra-

Moriones (1961) 591; 599

Aug.*Trin*.3.10.21 (*CCSL* 50: 149)

Aug.*Bapt*.5.8.9 (*CSEL* 51: 270)

Aug.*Ps*.98.9 (*CCSL* 39:1385)

Aug.*Ps*.98.9 (*CCSL* 39:1386)

Aug.*Ev.Joh*.25.12 (*CCSL* 36:254)

Aug.*Ev.Joh*.26.18 (*CCSL* 36:268)

Aug.*Ps*.3.1 (*CCSL* 38:8)

Aug.*Doctr.christ*.2.1 (*CCSL* 32:32)

Aug.*Ep*.138.7 (*CSEL* 44:131)
Aug.*Serm*.228.3 (*PL* 38:1102)

Aug.*Pecc.merit*.3.12.21 (*CSEL* 60:149)

Aug.*Pecc.merit*.1.24.34 (*CSEL* 60:34)

Aug.*Spir.et litt*.27.48 (*CSEL* 60:202)

mentum" more or less synonymously with "signum" and "signaculum." A sign was "a thing which, over and above the impression it makes on the senses, causes something else to come into the mind as a consequence of itself"; but when signs pertained to divine things, they were called sacraments. The Lord's Prayer, for example, could be called a sacrament. What was important about the sacraments was neither their definition nor their number, but their divinely appointed function as conveyers of grace. "There is no other valid means of making Christians and remitting sins, except by causing men to become believers by the institution of Christ and the church, and through the sacraments," and "no man can hope for either salvation or eternal life without baptism and the Lord's body and blood."

To interpret Augustine as a partisan of either scholastic or Protestant doctrine about grace and the means of grace would resolve the inconsistencies of his thought and language, but it would also resolve the paradox of grace. The sovereignty of grace, with its inevitable corollary in the doctrine of predestination, could make the means of grace incidental to the achievement of the divine purpose. The necessity of grace, with its recognition that even the virtues of the ungodly did not secure eternal life, could relativize the demand for a righteous life and sever the moral nerve. The mediation of grace, with its emphasis on the obligation to attend upon the services and sacraments of the church, could substitute a righteousness based on works of piety for a righteousness based on works of morality. Each of these possibilities was present in the theology of Augustine, and each has manifested itself in the subsequent history of Augustinism. But Augustine managed to hold together what Augustinians have often tended to separate. In his piety and preaching, if not always in his theology, the paradox of grace as sovereign, as necessary, and as mediated transcended the alternatives inherent in it. And so he could write: "By the law is the knowledge of sin, by faith the acquisition of grace against sin, by grace the healing of the soul from the fault of sin, by the health of the soul the freedom of the will, by free will the love of righteousness, by love of righteousness the accomplishment of the law. Thus as the law is not made void but established through faith, since faith obtains the grace by which the law is fulfilled; so free will is not made void but established through grace, since grace cures the will, by which righteousness is loved freely." These disparate elements could be held together because "all the stages which I have here connected together in their successive links have severally their proper voices in the sacred Scriptures," and Augustine sought to be as comprehensive as the Scriptures themselves. He acknowledged the limitations of theology as an expression of this comprehensiveness. The speculation and polemics of his book on the Trinity could, he said, be "better concluded with a prayer than with a disputation." Yet in his theology, too, this was the goal, and it was especially in the course of theological disputation that he was compelled to examine and defend, but also to refine and develop, his view both of grace and of the means of grace.

Aug.*Spir.et litt.*30.52 (*CSEL* 60:208)

Aug.*Trin.*15.27.50 (*CCSL* 50:533)

Grace and Perfection

The outline of Augustine's teaching on grace just presented could give an impression of greater consistency and of a more symmetrical structure than were in fact the case. When pressed in controversy, he himself sometimes claimed that from the time of his conversion he had always taught as he was teaching now. But there were many inconsistencies and changes in his thought. His own *Retractations*, written about four years before his death, contained not only a defense of many of his works, but also a correction of various ideas and formulations that had appeared in them. Even in the heat of battle he disclaimed any desire "to think or say that my writings are free from every kind of error," and he admitted having previously been in error on so vital an issue as whether faith was a gift of God or not. He changed his mind on many questions as a result of more careful examination; "it is characteristic of Augustine that every new stage of his development is inaugurated by a renewed and deepened study of Scripture." But no less potent a force in the refinement of his thought were the various theological controversies, large and small, in which he became involved. He recognized that a personal polemic could make it almost impossible "to engage without bitterness in the discussion of scriptural doctrine"; but he also exhorted heretics to join him in a search for truth "as if it were unknown to both of us," and he knew from the

Aug.*Jul.*6.12.39 (*PL* 44:843)
Aug.*Retract.* (*CSEL* 36)

Aug.*Bapt.*5.17.23 (*CSEL* 51:282)

Aug.*Praed.sanct.*3.7 (*PL* 44:965)

Hofmann (1933) 77–78

Aug.*Ep.*73.1 (*CSEL* 34:264)

Aug.*Ep.fund.*3 (*CSEL* 25:195)

Aug.Ep.185.2 (CSEL 57:2)

Aug.Haer. (CCSL 46:286–345)

Bible that there had to be heresies in the world "so that we might be instructed among our enemies."

Of the many "heresies" against which Augustine defended the Catholic faith, the two most virulent were Donatism and Pelagianism, both of which dealt with the doctrine of grace, and specifically with the relation between grace and perfection. Donatism charged that the mediation of grace through the church and the sacraments was vitiated when the administrator of the sacraments had lost his Christian perfection through a serious fall into sin. Pelagianism maintained that man still faced the same choice faced by Adam between sin and perfection, and that therefore grace was helpful, but not necessary in the sense in which Augustine taught. Chronologically, the two controversies scarcely overlapped at all. Augustine's case against Donatism had been stated fully and repeatedly and had become official church teaching at the Conference of Carthage in May 411, and the first of his many treatises against Pelagianism, *On the Merits and the Remission of Sins,* was written in 411 or 412. Not only chronologically, but also logically, the connection between the two controversies was tenuous. "The doctrine of sin and grace and the doctrine of the church developed in complete independence of each other. . . . In the books that were composed before the beginning of the Donatist controversy . . . the church is nowhere emphasized as the sphere of salvation in a special sense; nowhere in the anti-Donatist writings is the doctrine of original sin employed in a special way in the interest of the doctrine of the church." There was a striking lack of cross-references between the two. Of the handful of references to Donatism in the anti-Pelagian writings, there appears to have been only one that drew a significant parallel: "Pelagius was accused of having said: 'The church here [on earth] is without spot or wrinkle.' It was on this very issue that the Donatists, too, were constantly in conflict with us at our conference. In their case, we used to lay special stress on the mixture of evil men with the good, like that of the chaff with the wheat, an idea to which we were led by the metaphor of the threshing floor. We might apply the same illustration in answer to our present opponents [the Pelagians]."

The relation between grace and perfection was differently defined, and differently debated, in Augustine's

Reuter (1887) 15

Aug.Anim.3.2.2 (CSEL 60:360); Aug.Jul.1.3.7; 3.1.5 (PL 44:644; 704)

Aug.Gest.Pelag.12.27 (CSEL 42:80)

polemics against Donatism than it was in his polemics against Pelagianism. Beyond the many questions of church organization, religious persecution, and even social and tribal rivalry raised by Donatism, the central doctrinal question was: What is the causal connection between grace and perfection, or between the unity of the church and the holiness of the church? The Donatist answer to the question was simple and, at least upon first examination, consistent. "By doing violence to that which is holy," said Petilian, "you cut asunder the bond of unity." Donatism was no less insistent than Augustine that there could be only one church. The Donatists also laid claim to the title "catholic," which they denied to anyone else. But they made the unity and the catholicity of the church contingent upon its prior holiness. Therefore they demanded that the church be purged of those among its clergy and bishops who had been guilty of betraying the faith under persecution. Only that church was a true church in which the "communion of saints" was a communion of genuine, perfect saints. And the only church that met this qualification was the Donatist community; it alone had true unity, for it alone had true holiness. Likewise, it alone had the sacraments. "There is," said one Donatist bishop, "one baptism, which belongs to the church; and where there is no church, there cannot be any baptism either." The moral pollution of the church's bishops by the mortal sin of apostasy invalidated the ordinations they performed, canceled the efficacy of the baptism administered by their clergy, deprived the church of its requisite holiness, and thereby brought on the fall of the church. In the name of this demand for holiness, the Donatists felt obliged to separate themselves from the vast body of those who called themselves catholic Christians; for there could be no fellowship between the church of Christ (the Donatists) and the synagogue of Satan (the catholics).

One answer that Augustine addressed to this charge was to emphasize the mystery of predestination, by which some who were not empirically part of the one church "already are what they are to be eventually." It was part of his doctrine of predestination that here and now Christians were to look for signs that someone did or did not belong to the true church, in which grace was dispensed. But the holiness and perfection of clergy and bishops

ap.Aug.*Petil*.2.105.240 (*CSEL* 52:155)

Aug.*Petil*.2.58.132 (*CSEL* 52:94)

ap.Aug.*Bapt*.7.31.60 (*CSEL* 51:360)

Aug.*Bapt*.7.24.46 (*CSEL* 51:357)

See pp. 297–98 above

Aug.*Bapt*.4.3.4 (*CSEL* 51:225)

could not be such a sign, as the North African tradition believed. Almost two dozen times in the space of a few chapters of his treatise against Petilian the Donatist, Augustine asked: "If the conscience of the one who gives in holiness is what we look to, what means are to be found to cleanse someone who receives baptism when the conscience of the giver has been polluted without the knowledge of the one who is to receive the sacrament at his hands?" Until the end of history and the conquest of death, "the time will not come for the church as a whole when it will be utterly without spot or wrinkle or any such thing." Therefore no one could become perfect and holy "so long as he is separated from the unity of the body" of Christ. And so, "as there is in the catholic church something that is not catholic, so there may be something that is catholic outside the catholic church." Neither the presence of unholiness in the empirical catholic church nor the possibility of righteousness apart from it could excuse "the enemies of Christian unity throughout the world" for perpetuating the schism.

At the same time, the possession of catholic unity did not excuse the church from the responsibility of working toward that degree of perfection which it was possible for grace to create under the conditions of historical existence. Augustine did not want his words to be taken to mean "that church discipline should be set aside and that everyone should be permitted to act just as he pleases without any control over him." In opposition to various specific charges of immorality among catholic bishops, Augustine maintained that the Donatist accusations remained unsubstantiated; in fact, that the large number of deposed bishops and clergy who had been suspended by the catholic church for various sins was proof of the excommunication still being practiced by "constant, diligent, and prudent ministers of Christ." But in effect Augustine assigned excommunication—and thus the question of the morality of the members of the church, including its bishops and clergy—to the area of discipline rather than of doctrine. Private or public sins were indeed harmful to the church. But the loss of personal perfection by a bishop did not invalidate the grace being mediated by his sacraments, for, strictly speaking, they were not his sacraments at all but belonged to the church —and to Christ. The church had not fallen and baptism

Aug.*Petil*.3.15.18 (*CSEL* 52: 176)

Aug.*Ep*.185.38 (*CSEL* 57:34)

Aug.*Ep*.185.42 (*CSEL* 57:36)

Aug.*Bapt*.7.39.77 (*CSEL* 51: 363)

Aug.*Petil*.1.18.20 (*CSEL* 52: 16)

Aug.*Petil*.3.4.5 (*CSEL* 52:166)

Aug.*Petil*.2.36.84 (*CSEL* 52:69)

Aug.*Petil*.3.37.43 (*CSEL* 52: 197)

had not fallen and baptism had not been destroyed, even though that baptism was administered by a fallen bishop. The universal church went on praying in the Lord's

Aug.*Ep*.185.39 (*CSEL* 57:35)

Prayer: "Forgive us our debts."

The perfection and holiness of the church was not the holiness of its individual members or clergy, but the holiness of the grace dispensed in its sacraments. As Optatus, Augustine's predecessor in anti-Donatist polemics, formulated the argument, "the church is one, and its holiness is produced by the sacraments. It is not to be

Optat.*Donat*.2.1 (*CSEL* 26:32)

considered on the basis of the pride of individuals." Augustine was quite prepared to carry this point to its logical consequences. Baptism "belongs to Christ, regard-

Aug.*Bapt*.6.10.15 (*CSEL* 51: 309)

less of who may give it." He preferred to leave certain casuistic questions to the decision of a regional or an ecumenical council; but if he were pressed for his own opinion, he "would not hesitate to say that all men possess baptism who have received it in any place, from any sort of man, just so long as it was consecrated with the words of the Gospel and was received by them with-

Aug.*Bapt*.7.53.102 (*CSEL* 51: 373–74)

out deceit and with some degree of faith." This interpretation made the holiness of the church objective and divine, a gift of sacramental grace that transcended the perfection of the minister and even of the recipient; "the genuineness and holiness of the sacrament [does not depend upon] what the recipient of the sacrament believes

Aug.*Bapt*.3.14.19 (*CSEL* 51: 208)

and with what faith he is imbued." In other words, perfection as a moral condition was not constitutive of the church, but was derivative from its ground in the grace of God.

Unity, on the other hand, was not the final result of a long process of growth, but the immediate and necessary corollary of grace. "If baptism is the sacrament of grace while the grace itself is the abolition of sins, then the grace of baptism is not present among heretics [although baptism is]. Thus there is one baptism and one

Aug.*Bapt*.7.19.37 (*CSEL* 51: 355)

church, just as there is one faith." The one sin that threatened the church was not the adultery or even the

Aug.*Petil*.3.32.37 (*CSEL* 52: 192)

private apostasy of a bishop, but schism. Punning on the Latin word "traditor," which meant "one who hands over," whether as a traitor or as a transmitter, Augustine argued that the true successor of Judas the traitor, "who delivered up Christ," was not the bishop who in time of persecution had handed over a Bible to Roman soldiers, but someone "who had not given himself up to Christ in company with the whole world" and who therefore was a genuine "traditor," that is, one who had betrayed the catholic unity of the church. The proper locus for a concern about perfection was a commitment to grace as it was mediated through the church and its sacraments. Within the unity of this church there was enough to be done to bring the "spotted actuality" of the empirical church closer to the church as it was in the perfection that belonged to the mind and will of God. Or, as Augustine put it rhetorically in a peroration that summarized his theology of grace and perfection as this related to the church and its sacraments: "Come back to the church. Those whom you have wounded, bring to be healed by the medicine of grace. Those whom you have killed, bring to be revived by the life of charity. Fraternal concord has great power to propitiate God. The Lord says: 'If two of you agree on earth about anything, it will be done for them.' If this is true of two individuals, how much more of two peoples! Let us prostrate ourselves together before the Lord. You share with us our unity; let us share with you your contrition; and let charity cover the multitude of sins."

During this conflict over the relation between sacramental grace and perfection "the problem [of church and sect] first appears clearly in the opposition between the sacramental-hierarchical church conception of Augustine and the Donatists." And it was solved by a doctrine of the objectivity of grace that was to be normative in catholic Christianity, especially Western Christianity, for more than a millennium. If perfection was attainable for anyone in this life, it would come through that grace which was mediated by the church and its sacraments, so that a severing of the unity of the church for the sake of the holiness of the church was altogether self-defeating. The Augustinian theology of grace was thus obliged, before the relation between nature and grace had been raised as a major doctrinal issue, to commit itself to the principle that the efficacy of the sacraments, and especially of baptism, was assured "ex opere operato," by the sheer performance of the act, rather than "ex opere operantis," by the effect of the performer upon the act. From one perspective, this assured the priority of the divine initiative; for it was God, not the bishop or the priest, who did the baptizing, ordaining,

Aug.*Petil*.2.8.20 (*CSEL* 52:32)

K.Adam (1954) 223

Matt. 18:19

Aug.*Bapt*.2.13.18 (*CSEL* 51:194)

Troeltsch (1960) 333

and dispensing of sacramental grace. At the same time, it was the recipient, whether he be the communicant or the candidate for baptism or ordination, who took the initiative of presenting himself for the administration of the sacrament and for the dispensation of its grace. From another perspective, therefore, the initiative had been his (except in the instance of infant baptism). And, as medieval theology was to demonstrate repeatedly, the doctrine of ex opere operato could become the basis for assigning to the human initiative the decisive role in the determination of the relation between God and man; the perfection of man's readiness to accept the sacraments could determine the grace he received.

In Pelagianism Augustine was confronted by a theology which seemed to give man the capacity of self-determination by asserting the possibility of achieving sinless perfection in this life without grace; and his stance in the Pelagian controversy has affected the Western view of the necessity of grace as profoundly as his stance in the Donatist controversy has affected the Western view of the mediation of grace. Of the three leaders of Pelagianism, Pelagius himself "to a great degree lacked an interest in dogma"; Julian of Eclanum served as the "architect" of "the Pelagian dogma" and was "the last and probably the most formidable" of Augustine's opponents; and Celestius seemed to Augustine to be declaring openly what was Pelagius's real but unacknowledged doctrine. The religious and moral concerns of Pelagius must be distinguished from their distortions in the writings of Augustine, and the differences between Pelagius and Pelagians must be kept in view. Nevertheless, it was Pelagianism as a doctrinal option that determined the anti-Pelagian polemics of Augustine and the dogmatic formulations of the Latin church. An injustice may have been done, here as in other dogmatic debates, but it was an injustice that made history.

The relation between grace and perfection was fundamental to the Pelagian doctrine of man, and nothing less than perfection was commanded in such biblical precepts as Matthew 5:48, "an injunction which [Christ] would not have issued if he had known that what he enjoined was beyond achievement." The issuance of a commandment implied an ability on the part of the hearer to obey the commandment. Not only the Sermon on the Mount, but the moral preachments of the Old

Loofs (1904) 764

Aug.*Jul*.6.11.36 (*PL* 44:842)

Bonner (1963) 344

Aug.*Pecc.orig*.6.6 (*CSEL* 42:170)

ap.Aug.*Pecc.merit*.2.15.22 (*CSEL* 60:94)

ap.Aug.*Perf.just*.3.6 (*CSEL* 42:7)

Testament made it explicit that "every man shall be put
to death for his own sin" and that a man was able to
respond to the commandments of God and could be held
personally responsible if he failed to do so. In this
emphasis upon responsibility, faith assumed a prominent role. God "proposed to save by faith alone those
about whom he foreknew that they would believe." Faith
was accounted for righteousness because it granted forgiveness for past sins, justified in the present, and prepared one for good works in the future. God justified
the wicked man whom he intended to convert "sola fide,"
by faith alone, and forgave his sins "sola fide." The
commandments and warnings of Scripture were supported
also by the examples of the saints, "who not only lived
without sin, but are described as having led holy lives,"
from Abel and Enoch to Joseph and John. The Virgin
Mary was a special case, "for of her we are obliged to
grant that her piety had no sin it it." Augustine, too, was
obliged to grant this, refusing "out of honor to the
Lord" even to raise the question of sin where she was
involved; "for from him we know what abundance of
grace for overcoming sin in every particular was conferred upon her who had the merit to conceive and bear
him who undoubtedly had no sin."

The Pelagian resolution of the paradox of grace was
based on a definition of grace fundamentally different
from the Augustinian definition, and it was here that
the issue was joined. Pelagius was rumored to be "disputing against the grace of God." His treatise on grace
gave the impression of dwelling "on scarcely any other
topic than the faculty and capacity of nature, while he
makes God's grace consist almost entirely in this." It
seemed from this book that "with every possible argument
he defended the nature of man against the grace of God,
by which the wicked man is justified and by which we
are Christians." Pelagius was accused of failing to acknowledge that grace "which is neither nature with its
free will nor the knowledge of the law nor merely the
remission of sins, but that which is necessary in all our
actions." To this accusation his response was to attribute
the capacity of not sinning to "the necessity of nature"
and therefore to God as "the Author of nature." "How,
then, can that be regarded as spoken without the grace
of God which is shown to belong to God in a special
way?" Grace was necessary for every hour and every

Deut.24:16

ap.Aug.*Jul.op.imperf*.3.13
(PL 45:1252)

Pelag.*Rom*.8.29 (Souter 2:68)

Pelag.*Rom*.4.6 (Souter 2:37)

Pelag.*Rom*.4.5 (Souter 2:36)

Pelag.ap.Aug.*Nat.et grat*.36.42
(CSEL 60:263); Pelag.ap.
Aug.*Grat.Christ*.48.53 (CSEL
42:164)

Aug.*Nat.et grat*. 36.42 (CSEL
60:263–64)

Aug.*Persev*.20.53 (PL
45:1026)

Aug.*Gest.Pelag*.22.46
(CSEL 42:100)

Aug.*Grat.Christ*.35.38 (CSEL
42:154)

Aug.*Retract*.2.68 (CSEL
36:180)

Aug.*Gest.Pelag*.31.56 (CSEL
42:110)

Pelag.ap.Aug.*Nat.et grat*.51.59
(CSEL 60:276)

Pelag.ap.Aug.*Grat.Christ*.2.2
(*CSEL* 42:125)

Pelag.ap.Aug.*Grat.Christ*.7.8
(*CSEL* 42:131–32)

ap.Aug.*Jul.op.imperf*.1.94
(*PL* 45:1111)

ap.Aug.*Jul.op.imperf*.3.189;
3.196 (*PL* 45:1330; 1331–32)

Aug.*Grat.Christ*.3.4–4.5
(*CSEL* 42:127–28)

ap.Aug.*Jul.op.imperf*.1.38
(*PL* 45:1064)

ap.Prosp.*Ep.Ruf*.3.4 (*PL*
51:79); ap.Aug.*Pelag*.2.5.10
(*CSEL* 60:469)
ap.Aug.*Jul.op.imperf*.3.188;
3.208 (*PL* 45:1329; 1335)

ap.Aug.*Jul.op.imperf*.2.74
(*PL* 45:1173)

ap.Aug.*Jul.op.imperf*.4.93
(*PL* 45:1393)
ap.Aug.*Jul.op.imperf*.1.91
(*PL* 45:1108)

ap.Aug.*Jul.op.imperf*.1.78
(*PL* 45:1102)

minute of life, indeed for every act, and those who denied this were to be anathematized.

Grace had a fourfold content for Pelagius: doctrine and revelation; disclosure of the future, with its rewards and punishments; demonstration of the snares of the devil; and "illumination by the manifold and ineffable gift of heavenly grace." This grace was not identical with nature or the law or creation, but all of these were major constituents of it. "We confess a manifold grace of Christ. Its first gift is that we have been created out of nothing, its second that by our reason we are superior to those who live by their senses." Any disparagement of nature was simultaneously a disparagement of grace. Both positions spoke of grace as necessary for perfection; but Augustine saw in grace the knowledge of the good, the joy in doing the good, and the capacity to will the good, while for Pelagius "the ability [posse]" came from God, but both "willing [velle]" and "acting [esse]" depended on the free decision of man.

Where grace and nature, perfection and righteousness, were interpreted this way, the doctrine of original sin was absurd and unjust. It was an affront to divine justice "without which there is no deity." Under the guise of grace it was in fact teaching a new doctrine of fate, since man could do nothing but sin unless God infused a new inclination into him against his will. But this view of sin made man incapable of redemption. Not by Adam's fall, transmitted through the propagation of the race by marriage and sex, was sin to be explained. For sin "is carried on by imitation, committed by the will, denounced by the reason, manifested by the law, punished by justice"; and none of these would be true if the doctrine of original sin prevailed. The doctrine of original sin was self-contradictory. "If sin is natural, it is not voluntary; if it is voluntary, it is not inborn. These two definitions are as mutually contrary as are necessity and [free] will." Even after sin the will remained as free as it had been before sin was committed, for man continued to have "the possibility of committing sin or of refraining from sin." This doctrine of sin was conveniently summarized in a series of six propositions of Celestius: "Adam was created mortal and would have died whether he had sinned or not sinned; the sin of Adam injured only him, not the human race; the law leads to the kingdom [of heaven], just as the gospel does; even before the coming of Christ there were men without sin; newborn infants are in the same state in which Adam was before his transgression; the whole human race does not die through the death and transgression of Adam, nor does it rise again through the resurrection of Christ."

ap.Aug.*Gest.Pelag*.11.23 (*CSEL* 42:76); ap.Aug.*Pecc. orig*.11.12 (*CSEL* 42:173–74)

Much of this could claim support from the tradition as well as from contemporary Eastern theologians. What is more, it was combined with an impeccable trinitarian orthodoxy. Pelagius confessed: "I believe in the Trinity of the one substance, and I hold all things in accordance with the teachings of the holy catholic church." Before the outbreak of the controversy on grace and sin he had written a treatise *On the Faith of the Trinity*. Pelagius had a reputation for teaching "the right faith." Celestius, too, could wholeheartedly recite the creed, "from the Trinity of the one Godhead all the way to the kind of resurrection of the dead that there is to be." If the touchstone of orthodoxy was adherence to the true faith concerning the Trinity and the person of Christ, it was incorrect to call this doctrine of sin and grace a "heresy." Those who held to erroneous doctrines in this area were to be anathematized "as fools, not as heretics, for there is no dogma." The questions under discussion were not matters of officially promulgated dogma, but still lay in the area of permissible difference. "If any questions have arisen beyond the compass of the faith," Celestius declared, "on which there might be perhaps dissension on the part of a great many persons, in no case have I presumed to pronounce a decision on any dogma, as if I possessed a definitive authority in the matter myself; but whatever I have derived from the fountain of the prophets and the apostles, I have presented for approbation . . . so that if any error has crept in among us, human as we are, through our ignorance, it may be corrected." Such issues were "a matter of question, but not of heresy [quaestionis, non haeresis]." Among these open questions were such problems as the transmission of sin through the propagation of the race.

ap.Aug.*Gest.Pelag*.11.25 (*CSEL* 42:79–80)

ap.Aug.*Gest.Pelag*.19.43 (*CSEL* 42:99)

Gennad.*Vir.ill*.43 (*TU* 14–I:77); Aug.*Ep*.186.1 (*CSEL* 57:45)

Aug.*Pecc.orig*.23.26 (*CSEL* 42:185)

ap.Aug.*Gest.Pelag*.34.59 (*CSEL* 42:115)

ap.Aug.*Gest.Pelag*.6.16 (*CSEL* 42:69)

ap.Aug.*Pecc.orig*.23.26 (*CSEL* 42:185)

ap.Aug.*Pecc.orig*.4.3 (*CSEL* 42:169)

But the standard of trinitarian orthodoxy, the Nicene Creed, also contained the statement: "We confess [in the Latin text: "I confess"] one baptism for the forgiveness of sins." And by the first part of the fifth century this meant, as a rule, the baptism of infants. So much

Symb.Nic.–CP (Schaff 2:58)

was this the rule that both sides in the dispute over grace and perfection had to affirm the validity, indeed the necessity, of the practice. To Augustine infant baptism was "what the universal church holds as handed down by tradition." To Julian of Eclanum, too, it was absolutely necessary; Celestius declared, perhaps "under duress": "I have always said that infants need baptism and ought to be baptized"; and it was probably Pelagius who stated that "infants are to be baptized in order that they may be with Christ in the kingdom of God." But when these statements of support for the practice of infant baptism became more specific, the difference between the two positions was obvious. It was apparently the circulation of the proposition "that infants are baptized not for the purpose of receiving remission of sin, but that they may be sanctified in Christ," which first aroused the suspicion of Augustine that something was awry in the doctrine of some people about original sin. Later Pelagius reaffirmed his support of infant baptism in the rhetorical question: "Who is so wicked as to want to exclude infants from the kingdom of heaven by prohibiting their being baptized and born again in Christ?" Julian of Eclanum taught that infants were to be baptized even though they were created good, for this would make them better through renewal and adoption as children of God.

And so, as Augustine noted, "not even they have ever denied the impossibility of infants entering the kingdom of heaven without baptism. But this is not the question; what we are discussing concerns the obliteration of original sin in infants." Attaching himself to the interpretation of infant baptism enunciated by Cyprian, Augustine insisted that only his doctrine of original sin would do justice to the implications of the practice. In the controversy over Christ as divine, both sides had acknowledged the legitimacy of paying worship to Christ, but they differed over the content of the divinity ascribed to him by such homage; eventually it was concluded that the only way to justify such worship without shipwreck to biblical monotheism was the confession that "he is homoousios with the Father." Similarly, the Pelagians' acceptance of infant baptism for "redemption" was fundamentally inconsistent with their anthropology, while the Augustinian theory provided a theological justification for an unchallengeable sacramental practice. The doctrine of

Aug.*Bapt.*4.24.31 (*CSEL* 51:259)
ap.Aug.*Jul.op.imperf.*3.149 (*PL* 45:1308)

Aug.*Ep.*157.22 (*CSEL* 44:471)

ap.Aug.*Pecc.orig.*4.3 (*CSEL* 42:169)

ap.Aug.*Pecc.merit.*1.30.58 (*CSEL* 60:57)

Aug.*Pecc.merit.*3.6.12 (*CSEL* 60:139)

ap.Aug.*Pecc.orig.*18.20 (*CSEL* 42:180–81)

ap.Aug.*Jul.op.imperf.*3.151 (*PL* 45:1308)

Aug.*Pecc.orig.*19.21 (*CSEL* 42:181)

Aug.*Ep.*175.6 (*CSEL* 44:660–62); Aug.*Pecc.orig.*19. 21 (*CSEL* 42:181)

Aug.*Serm.*294 (*PL* 38:1335–48)

original sin, of the fall, of the transmission of sin, and of the necessity of grace appeared to make sense of infant baptism and to account for the statistical regularity with which men who supposedly faced Adam's possibilities always made Adam's choice. Perfection was not possible without grace, and even with grace it was a goal rather than an achievement. Therefore among the eight canons of the Synod of Carthage, 1 May 418, against Pelagianism, was the decree: "Anyone who denies that newborn infants are to be baptized or who says that they are baptized for the remission of sins but do not bear anything of original sin from Adam which is expiated by the washing of regeneration, so that as a consequence the form of baptism 'for the remission of sins' is understood to be not true but false in their case—let him be anathema." And in the person of Celestius, Pelagianism was condemned by the Council of Ephesus in 431 as a heresy.

Syn.Carth.(418) Can. (Mansi 3:811)

CEph.(431)Anath. (ACO 1–I–3:27)

Natural Endowment and Superadded Gift

The official condemnation of Pelagianism did not imply an unconditional endorsement of Augustinism, which had in many ways gone beyond even the Western theological tradition (not to mention the Eastern tradition) by positing a doctrine of predestination, including predestination to damnation, and of the irresistibility of grace. Even those who joined in the opposition to Pelagius refused to go along with the extreme form taken by this doctrine of predestinating grace. The penchant for tagging every doctrinal position with a party label has led to the invention of the name Semi-Pelagianism, which is even less useful than most such designations. Augustine himself acknowledged that those who were disagreeing with him on predestination were "brethren of ours," whose acceptance of the doctrines of original sin and grace "abundantly distinguishes them from the error of the Pelagians." These brethren taught that salvation was not "through one's own works but through the grace of God." They were admirers and followers of the Augustinian teaching in every issue of doctrine except the issues relating to predestination. Indeed, they were "members of the same body and participants with us in the grace of Christ [concorporales et comparticipes gratiae Christi]." They were, they said, steering between Scylla and Charybdis, and they insisted that their position was not to be confused

Faust.Rei.Grat.1.1 (CSEL 21:6–12)

Aug.Praed.sanct.1.2 (PL 44:961)

Prosp.Ep.Aug.3 (PL 51:69)

Prosp.Ep.Aug.9 (PL 51:74)

Prosp.Coll.1.2 (PL 51:217)
Faust.Rei.Grat.1.1 (CSEL 21:7)

with "the profane notion of some who attribute everything to free will and lay down that the grace of God is dispensed in accordance with the desert of man," for they asserted without qualification "that the grace of God is superabounding." Critics of Augustine though they were, they did not deny that in the fall of Adam human nature had lost its powers (virtutes) and could regain them only by grace.

Cassian.*Coll.*13.16 (*SC* 54:176)

Prosp.*Resp.Gen.*3 (*PL* 51:190)

The opposition to Augustine earned this position the title "Semi-Pelagian" in the sixteenth century, but already in the fifth century the partisans of Augustine were calling it "the remnants of the Pelagian heresy [Pelagianae pravitatis reliquiae]." The term is used to cover a group of theologians from the fifth and the sixth centuries, the most prominent of whom were John Cassian, Vincent of Lérins, and Faustus of Riez. To the defenders of Augustine against these men it seemed incongruous at one and the same time to assert that grace was necessary because of original sin and yet to reject the corollary doctrine of predestination. "Do they intend to hold none of the things that were condemned and nevertheless to reject some aspects of what was defended?" This was precisely what they intended. Identifying as catholic not only what had been affirmed by church councils but also the individual theories of Augustine, Prosper of Aquitaine found that such a position was "in harmony neither with the heretics nor with the catholics," but was a tertium quid that disagreed with both. From this he drew the consequence that two such incompatible interpretations of grace could not exist side by side. "If both these doctrines must be preached within the one church in such a way that neither of them excludes the other but both must yield to each other mutually, then it may come to pass that we accept what the Pelagians hold and that the Pelagians accept what we hold." But such a compromise would mean not that the Pelagians had become catholics but that the catholics had become Pelagians. And yet these "remnants of Pelagianism" taught, with Augustine and against Pelagius, "that when Adam sinned every man sinned." The difference between them lay in the inference being drawn from the doctrine of original sin for the doctrine of predestination: if the Augustinian view of predestination was right, his critics argued, it would follow from the

Prosp.*Ep.Aug.*7 (*PL* 51:72)

Prosp.*Coll.*1.2 (*PL* 51:217)

Prosp.*Coll.*3.1 (*PL* 51:221)

Prosp.*Coll.*18.2 (*PL* 51:264)

Prosp.*Ep.Aug.*3 (*PL* 51:69)

invitation of Christ to all those who labor and are heavy laden that "not all are heavy laden with original or actual sin" and that therefore Romans 5:12, which served Augustine so well as a proof text against Pelagianism, could not be true.

See pp. 299–300 above
Cassian.*Coll*.13.7 (*SC* 54:156)

Fundamentally, the objection was that Augustine had resolved the paradox of inevitability and responsibility at the expense of responsibility, and that he glorified grace by belittling nature and free will. "If you pay careful attention, you will recognize clearly and abundantly how through the pages of the Scriptures sometimes it is the power of grace and at other times it is the assent of the human will that is asserted." Grace and freedom stood in a kind of antinomy, which had been resolved first in favor of freedom and was now being resolved in favor of grace, but which "the rule of the church's faith" did not permit one to resolve at all. It was a violation of the rule of faith and of the teaching of the fathers to teach, as Augustine did, that God called only the elect in accordance with his decree. The Augustinian doctrine was opposed to the authority of tradition. By asserting a special grace of God which would provide for the elect without any effort on their part, it was echoing the words of the devil to Jesus, "Throw yourself down," and tempting believers to repudiate the universal and ancient faith of the catholic church in favor of a novel and heretical idea.

Faust.Rei.*Grat*.1.13 (*CSEL* 21:44)

Cassian.*Coll*.13.11 (*SC* 54:163)

ap.Prosp.*Ep.Aug*.2 (*PL* 51:68)

Matt.4:6

Vinc.Ler.*Comm*.26.37 (Moxon 107–110)

But the Augustinian doctrine was not merely novel and heretical, it was finally heathen. It was a "fatalistic theory [fatalis persuasio]." It spoke a great deal about grace, but "in the name of grace [Augustine] preaches fatalism." Predestination was simply a euphemistic way of reintroducing a pagan notion of fatal necessity. The Augustinian doctrine appeared to be epitomized in the thesis that "by God's predestination men are compelled to sin and driven to death by a sort of fatal necessity." But fatalism, even under the guise of the Christian doctrine of predestination, would lead to conclusions that any Christian would find repugnant. When Romans 1:28 spoke of God giving men over to a base mind, this was not to be interpreted fatalistically; for "someone who is cut off for reasons that have gone before is not being pressed down by fate but condemned by a judgment" that was just. It was a reductio ad absurdum of the Augustinian view of absolute predestination to conclude that

Faust.Rei.*Grat*.1.16 (*CSEL* 21:50)

ap.Prosp.*Ep.Ruf*.3 (*PL* 51:79)
ap.Prosp.*Ep.Aug*.3 (*PL* 51:69)

ap.Prosp.*Resp.Gall*.1.1 (*PL* 51:157)

Faust.Rei.*Grat*.2.10 (*CSEL* 21:87)

ap.Prosp.*Resp.Vinc*.8 (*PL* 51:182)

ap.Prosp.*Resp.Vinc*.10–11 (*PL* 51:182–83)

Faust.Rei.*Grat*.2.3 (*CSEL* 21:63–65)

Faust.Rei.*Grat*.2.2 (*CSEL* 21:61)

Aug.*Corrept*.14.44 (*PL* 44:943)

Aug.*Praed.sanct*.8.14 (*PL* 44:971)

Aug.*Enchir*.27.103 (*CCSL* 46:104)

Aug.*Corrept*.15.46–47 (*PL* 44:944–45)

ap.Prosp.*Resp.Gall*.1.8 (*PL* 51:162)

"God does not wish all catholics to persevere in the faith but wants a great number of them to apostatize." Similarly, one could argue that if this view were right, adultery, incest, and murder all happened because it was the will of God that they should. Did God's foreknowledge of such sins imply that they had been committed by his willing? What was needed to correct and clarify the Augustinian doctrine was a more precise definition of predestination that would distinguish it from prescience. For "what God wills is one thing, what God permits is another thing. Therefore he wills the good, and permits the evil, and foreknows both; he assists righteous deeds with his goodness, he permits unrighteous deeds in accordance with the freedom of the [human] will."

What was at stake was not only the standard Christian defense of both divine providence and human responsibility against the charge of fatalism, but the Christian doctrine of salvation itself. Augustine's teaching that the will of God must always, in sovereign grace, achieve its intended purpose was not easy to harmonize with the biblical assertion that universal salvation was the will of God. If not all men were saved, did this mean that God had not willed it or that the saving will of God had been frustrated? Augustine resorted to various devices to square his position with 1 Timothy 2:4: "who desires all men to be saved and to come to the knowledge of the truth." "All men" meant all the predestined, because every kind of human being was represented among them. These were taught by God to come to Christ, for he "wills all such [the elect] to be saved"; if he had willed the salvation of those who now despised the word, "they undoubtedly would have come also." The passage did not say "that there is no man whose salvation [God] does not desire, but that no one is saved unless God desires it." Stated as it was as part of an admonition of prayer, the passage could even be interpreted to mean "that in our ignorance of who is to be saved, God commands us to desire that all those to whom we preach this peace may be saved. . . . [1 Timothy 2:4] may also be understood in this sense, that God desires all men to be saved by making us desire this."

But then Augustine's critics were right in summarizing his doctrine: "God does not desire all men to be saved, but only the fixed number of the predestined." And it did not really resolve the ambiguities of Augustine's position to resort to the secret counsels of God and to speak of "the reasons for a division [between the elect and the nonelect] which God's wisdom keeps hidden in the mystery of his justice," in spite of which somehow "we must believe sincerely and profess loudly that 'God desires all men to be saved.'" Regardless of such believing and professing, Augustinian predestinarianism did seem to vitiate any universalism. For "how," asked Augustine's critics, "can we imagine without grievous blasphemy that he does not desire all men in general, but only some rather than all to be saved? Those who perish, perish against his will."

It was a grievous blasphemy also against the means of grace to ascribe salvation and damnation to the hidden decrees of divine predestination. For then it would have to follow that in the case of those who had not been predestined, the grace of baptism did not wipe away original sin. It would be of no use to such to be regenerated through baptism or to live a pious life. "Yet all men without exception are offered the reconciliation which Christ merited by the mystery of his death, in such a manner that whoever wishes to come to the faith and to receive baptism can be saved." In the New Testament it was the practice that when one came to baptism, "first there was an inquiry into the desire of the one who was coming, and then the grace of the regenerating One followed." During the conflict with the Donatists over perfection and grace, Augustine himself had contended for the position that even a heretic who had been baptized in the name of the Trinity did not need to repeat the baptism if he became orthodox and that therefore his baptism had been efficacious. How then could it be that, because he was not predestined, baptism would not be efficacious to someone who came of his own free will and was properly baptized? To be consistent with the Augustinian position against Donatism, one had to acknowledge that a baptism was "a true baptism also in those who are not to persevere in the truth and who for that reason were not predestined for eternal life." But in their instance baptism seemed "true" in a somewhat hollow sense.

Hollow, too, was the call to repentance when this call was issued to the nonelect. Any such call presupposed both divine grace and human freedom, because a man could desire virtue but could not receive it without the

Prosp.*Resp.Vinc*.2 (*PL* 51:179)

Cassian.*Coll*.13.7 (*SC* 54:156)

ap.Prosp.*Resp.Gall*.1.2 (*PL* 51:157)

ap.Prosp.*Resp.Gall*.1.3 (*PL* 51:158)

ap.Prosp.*Ep.Aug*.3 (*PL* 51:69)

Faust.Rei.*Grat*.2.10 (*CSEL* 21:84)

See p. 311 above

Faust.Rei.*Grat*.1.14 (*CSEL* 21:47)

Prosp.*Resp.Gall*.2.2 (*PL* 51:170)

ap.Prosp.*Resp.Vinc*.15 (*PL* 51:185)

Cassian.*Coll.*13.9 (*SC* 54:160)

Cassian.*Coll.*13.13 (*SC* 54:169)

Aug.*Corrept.*7.14 (*PL* 44:925)

ap.Prosp.*Ep.Aug.*6 (*PL* 51:72)

Faust.Rei.*Grat.*1.3 (*CSEL* 21:15–17)

Faust.Rei.*Grat.*1.16 (*CSEL* 21:52)

Cassian.*Coll.*13.4 (*SC* 54:152)

Rom.2:14

Prosp.*Coll.*10.2 (*PL* 51:240)

Prosp.*Coll.*12.4 (*PL* 51:246)

Prosp.*Coll.*13.3 (*PL* 51:248)

Faust.Rei.*Grat.*2.10 (*CSEL* 21:86)

help of God. So it was in the case of David, when he acknowledged his guilt after being admonished. But Judas, after being admonished, betrayed his Lord. Did this mean, as Augustine did not stop short of declaring, that Judas had been "elected to a work for which he was fitted," and that the other disciples "were elected by mercy, but he by judgment, they to inherit the kingdom [of Christ], he to shed [Christ's] blood"? What, then, was the point of evangelizing unbelievers or of admonishing believers? In fact, what was the use even of prayer if all had already been determined by the secret predestinating decree of God? In sum, the Augustinian doctrine of the will of God appeared to overlook the revealed will of God, which desired all men to be saved, and to have constant recourse to the hidden will of God, into which it was illegitimate to inquire.

This doctrine appeared to be no less cavalier in its treatment of the will of man, which it called free even as it denied any genuine freedom. Man was "a kind of unfeeling and inept material that had to be moved from one place to another." But this did not accord either with the undeniable moral achievements of the free will outside the church or with the way of salvation inside the church. In the face of evidence of virtue in heathens, "how can we think that the freedom of their will is taken captive?" The New Testament itself acknowledged that "Gentiles who have not the law do by nature what the law requires." This proved to Augustine's critics the continuing power of nature, but to Augustine's supporters it applied to Gentiles who had been converted to Christ. Yet this evasion obviously did not hold, and so it was necessary to declare that while Greek learning and Roman eloquence could, through the exercise of reason, achieve a kind of virtue that gave decency (*honestare*) to life in this world, this had nothing to do with life eternal. In the souls of unbelievers there could be no genuine virtues. But if this was the case, how was it possible to say, as Romans 1:20 did, that "they are without excuse," when their inability to achieve virtue was the result of their not having been predestined?

Even while asserting that without divine assistance none of these virtues could attain perfection, Augustine's critics still insisted that "it cannot be doubted that there are by nature some seeds of goodness in every soul im-

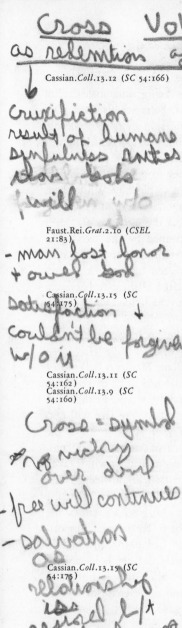

Cross Vol 2 as redemption of humanity

Cassian.*Coll.*13.12 (*SC* 54:166)

Cruxifiction result of humans sinfulness enter don bolo forbidden ydo

Faust.Rei.*Grat.*2.10 (*CSEL* 21:83)

- man lost favor + owed bol

Cassian.*Coll.*13.15 (*SC* 54:175)

Satisfaction + couldn't be forgiven w/o it

Cassian.*Coll.*13.11 (*SC* 54:162)
Cassian.*Coll.*13.9 (*SC* 54:160)

Cross = symbol of victory over devil
- free will continues
- salvation

Cassian.*Coll.*13.15 (*SC* 54:175)

relationship restored b/t God + humans

Cassian.*Coll.*13.18 (*SC* 54:181)

- God remained faithful

planted by the kindness of the Creator." This did not detract from the glory of redemption. If it was said "that one should not pay attention to what is good by nature because before the coming of Christ, the Gentiles obviously did not attain to salvation," the reply was the axiom: "Anyone who denies that nature is to be proclaimed in its good qualities, simply does not know that the Author of nature is the same as the Author of grace," and that therefore "since the Creator is the same as the Restorer, one and the same is celebrated when we praise either work." Praising the free will of man meant praising its Creator and did not detract from his grace.

This was evident from the Bible itself, where "the bounty of God is actually shaped according to the capacity of man's faith." Sometimes, for example in the conversion of Paul or of Matthew, divine grace had preceded any desire or good will on the part of man. But in other instances, for example in the account of Zacchaeus or of the thief on the cross, the free will of man had taken some initiative. By the goodness of the Creator there still remained the capacity to initiate the will for salvation. The mistake was to reduce the complex and diverse operations of God to a single formula such as Pelagian synergism or Augustinian predestinarianism. God's calls were varied, as those whom he called were varied. "And so the manifold wisdom of God grants salvation to men with manifold and inscrutable kindness. It imparts to each one according to his capacity the grace of His bounty, so that He wills to grant His healing not according to the uniform power of His majesty but according to the measure of the faith in which He finds each one, or as He Himself has imparted it to each one." Since the defeat of Pelagianism, no one was attacking the sovereignty of divine grace. It was by grace that each stage of conversion was effected: the desire for the good, although with free will; the capacity to perform virtue, although still with a free choice; and persistence in the goodness already acquired, although without a surrender of freedom.

The Augustinian tradition was not well equipped to deal with this challenge, which did not, as the Pelagian challenge was at least understood to do, detract from the role of divine grace, but on the contrary glorified it. What it found objectionable in the Augustinian theology

[handwritten marginalia: Abelard Vol 2 — 6 methods to n writings + why reliable; methods value possibility dialogue w/ opponents; what kind of agreement is ... found in sources; temporarily solve problems]

Aug.*Persev.*13.33 (PL 45:1012–13)

Prosp.*Ep.Aug.*7 (PL 51:72)

Fulg.*Ep.*15.15 (CCSL 91:455)

Aug.*Praed.sanct.*19.38 (PL 44:988)

Prosp.*Coll.*21.3 (PL 51:272–73)

1 Tim.2:4

Prosp.*Ep.Ruf.*13 (PL 51:85)

of grace was not the doctrine of grace at all, but the identification of the primacy of grace with a particular and idiosyncratic theory of predestination. For Augustine as a theologian, such an identification may have been necessary. It was less clear that it was necessary for the church's affirmation of the Augustinian doctrine of grace, which from 418 onward was no longer a matter of his private beliefs but of the church's doctrinal intentions. Initially, the importance of the doctrine of grace in Christian dogmatics seemed to imply that any attack upon the Augustinian view amounted to a recrudescence of Pelagianism, or at any rate of its vestigial remnants. The defense of grace likewise implied a defense of predestinarianism without any qualifications whatever. For example, Fulgentius of Ruspe could follow Augustine in the problematical exegesis of 1 Timothy 2:4 and affirm: "All those are predestined whom God desires to be saved and to come to the knowledge of the truth. They are called 'all' because they are saved from both sexes, from all kinds, classes, ages, and conditions of men. The will of God Almighty is always fulfilled, because his power is never defeated." Initially, the argument was prepared to assert, with Augustine, that what God foresaw in predestinating men was not their reaction but his own sanctifying work, so that he made his choice not because men were to believe but so that they might. For the defenders of Augustinism at this stage, there was no distinction to be made between his various opponents, and those who objected to his predestinarianism were on the same plane as the Pelagians themselves had been. Even the Augustinian evasion of the implications of the doctrine that God "desires all men to be saved and to come to the knowledge of the truth" had to be accepted and reinforced. The objection was dismissed as "trite" because it was constantly being raised, for it was only a lack of understanding that would conclude that it contradicted the doctrine of predestination. Beyond this there was only "the secret counsel of God" as an explanation of the difference between those who were predestined and those who were not.

In the long run, this identification of the anti-Pelagian view of grace with an absolute predestination would not work. For one thing, it was obliged to recognize the great gulf fixed between any brand of Pelagianism and this "anti-Augustinism." It was not simply that the most explicit and articulate spokesman of the opposition could nevertheless refer to Augustine, with perhaps only a touch of sarcasm, as "the most blessed prelate [beatissimus pontifex]," who had expressed himself in a "most learned sermon." It was something more profound. Here grace was not acknowledged grudgingly, but celebrated enthusiastically. In Cassian there was "absolute dependence upon grace. . . . There is no minimizing of the meaning of grace. The Pelagians referred grace to externalities like the law or the preaching of the Gospel. In Cassian grace possessed its full Augustinian meaning, an interior working of God within the soul." And therefore it was unavoidable that the defense of essential Augustinism reexamine his exegesis of 1 Timothy 2:4 with a view to asserting the universal will of God for salvation, and that it distinguish more sharply between doctrine as that which was believed, taught, and confessed by the church and theology as that which was maintained by individual teachers in the church.

To affirm the doctrine of the universal will of God for salvation it was necessary to develop more fully the idea that those who were damned were "without excuse" because they had all, in some meaningful way, been given the opportunity to respond to the call of God and had refused it. If Augustine held to any such idea, he had not made it very explicit in most of his writing. But further reflection and debate compelled Augustinism to concede that "there is no one to whom either the preaching of the gospel or the commandments of the law or the voice of nature does not transmit God's call." A consideration of the gifts distributed by the providence of God to all mankind without distinction showed them to be "so general in the past and in the present that men find in their testimony sufficient help to seek the true God"; unbelievers could not use the excuse that the light of truth had been denied them. Therefore it was wrong to refer their unbelief and damnation to the decrees of God. It was his prescience that they would not believe which prompted him to condemn them. And so "the reason why they were not of the predestined is that God foreknew they would be impenitent through their own fault." Prescience effectively removed the objections to the doctrine of predestination, although embedding the definition of the

Faust.Rei.*Grat*.2.9 (CSEL 21:81)

O.Chadwick (1968) 113

Rom.1:20

Prosp.*Resp.Gall*.1.8 (PL 51:164)

Prosp.*Vocat*.2.25 (PL 51:710–11)

Prosp.*Vocat*.2.29 (PL 51:715)

Prosp.*Resp.Gall*.1.14 (PL 51:169)

Prosp.*Resp.Gall*.1.3 (PL 51:158)

Prosp.*Vocat*.2.29 (*PL* 51:715)

Prosp.*Vocat*.2.19 (*PL* 51:706)

Prosp.*Vocat*.1.25 (*PL* 51:686)

Prosp.*Auct*.10 (*PL* 51:211–12)

Prosp.*Vocat*.1.12 (*PL* 51:664)

Prosp.*Vocat*.2.37 (*PL* 51:722)

Prosp.*Sent*. (*PL* 51:427–96)

CAraus.(529)Can. (*CCSL* 148–II:55)

Aug.*Ev.Joh*.19.19 (*CCSL* 36:202)

elect in a doctrine of prescience removed the doctrine of predestination itself from any central position. The term "God's changeless will from eternity" now referred not to the eternal predestinating will by which God had chosen some and rejected others, but to the will spoken of in 1 Timothy 2:4, that all men be saved. This, and not predestination, was now to be called an "essential element of faith [pars fidei]" and a "rule of apostolic doctrine." As for predestination, it was one of those "more profound and more difficult points" of theology which it was not necessary to go into in an exposition of the doctrine of grace.

Prosper's *Call of All Nations* did not so much as use the word "predestination," nor for that matter did it refer explicitly to Augustine himself. What it sought to assert was no longer the private theology of Augustine, but the teaching of the church: the teaching that grace was gratuitous and the teaching that God desired the salvation of all men. To this the church was bound, in its prayer as well as in its doctrine. "Let, then, holy church pray . . . for God, who desires all men to come to the knowledge of the truth, cannot repel anyone without a just reason." In addition to his *Call of All Nations*, Prosper compiled a *Book of Sentences from the Works of St. Augustine*, containing almost four hundred quotations, a compendium of Augustine's teaching on a variety of issues, but especially on those most recently in controversy. This compilation became the source from which the Synod of Orange in 529 drew the bulk of its decrees on nature and grace; the other chief source was the Augustinian theology of Caesarius of Arles, summarized in a brief treatise, *On Grace*. Point by point, the criticisms of Augustine summarized above were raised and answered by the canons and decrees of Orange, and essential Augustinism was vindicated.

To the charge that the Augustinian doctrine of grace represented an innovation without adequate precedent in the tradition, Orange set forth its teaching as one "gathered by the ancient fathers from the books of Sacred Scripture." The accusation of fatalism was met with an apposite quotation from Augustine: "When men do what is displeasing to God, they perform their own will, not God's." Like Augustine himself, his vindicators took an ambiguous position on the relation between predestina-

Passages of Adoption, Identity, Derivation, Distinction

time when Christ becomes divine

tion and the universal saving will of God. Caesarius could write: "Perhaps you say: 'God does indeed desire that all would believe in him, but not all are willing. Why? Because they are unable to do so without his grace.' At this point I ask you whether [you meant that] the human will has power to contradict the divine will rather than that the power of God is able to convert human wills to itself. ... If he has done whatever he has willed, whatever he has not done he has not willed—by a hidden and profound and yet a just and incomprehensible judgment." This would seem to lead ineluctably to a doctrine of double predestination. Yet it did not, and in his role as a spokesman for the teaching church rather than as an individual theologian Caesarius confessed: "In accordance with the catholic faith we ... not only do not believe that some men have been predestined to evil by the power of God, but if there is anyone who wants to believe something so evil, we declare that he is utterly anathema." The same confession asserted the catholic faith "that after receiving baptism all those who have been baptized ... are able to fulfill what pertains to the salvation of their souls."

JC + Yahweh same person

one God speaking along another

"begotten not made"

Caes.Arel.Gr.(Morin 2:162)

CAraus.(529) Def.fid. (CCSL 148–II:63)

Father as Son

CAraus.(529) Can.9 (CCSL 148–II:60)

Against the extollers of heathen virtue Orange quoted the flat assertion of Augustine that the fortitude of Gentiles had its source in worldly greed, while the fortitude of Christians had its source in the love shed abroad in their hearts by the Holy Spirit. And in response to the argument that there was a diversity of operations by which in some cases men took the initiative and in others God took the initiative, the synod condemned as "alien to the true faith" anyone who taught that "some have come to the grace of baptism by mercy, but others by free will." Citing the specific biblical examples that had been used in support of this teaching, Caesarius affirmed that the conversion of Zacchaeus and of the thief on the cross had also been "not achievements of nature, but gifts from the generosity of divine grace." The "beginning of faith" was always due to the inspiration of the Holy Spirit.

CAraus.(529) Can.8 (CCSL 148–II:58)

CAraus.(529) Def.fid. (CCSL 148–II:63)

In this adjudication of the controversy, the paradox of grace, which had lain at the center of Augustine's theology, was not resolved; and it seems an oversimplification to assert that "this 'Augustinism' is basically almost as close to Semi-Pelagian synergism as to the particularistic and predestinarian monergism of Augustine." For

Loofs (1959) 357

here, as in Augustine, grace was sovereign, necessary, and mediated—but none of these without the others. In keeping with Augustine, the effort to mitigate the necessity of grace by ascribing some initiative in salvation to the will of man was rejected. On the other hand, the opposite extreme, to which the anti-Pelagian Augustine had sometimes seemed willing to go, asserting the sovereignty of grace by ascribing damnation to the will of God, was also anathematized. In this sense it is true that Orange condemned some of Augustine's theology, but this was a gentle rebuke compared with the condemnation not only of Pelagius but also of those whom Prosper had called "the remnants of the Pelagian heresy." Rome solemnly confirmed the action of the synod and attested that "we approve your confession . . . as in harmony with the catholic rules [of faith] of the fathers." Shorn of its predestinarian elements and in this sense harmonized with his anti-Donatist sacramentalism, Augustine's anti-Pelagian doctrine of grace became the official teaching of Latin Christianity. The natural endowments of man, even of the heathen man, were not to be minimized, but saving grace was a superadded gift of the unmerited generosity of God, mediated through the church and its sacraments. This distinction between natural endowment and superadded gift could attach itself to the explicit teaching of Augustine himself. Even in his swan song on predestination he had been prepared to attribute to nature "that grace by which we are distinguished from cattle" as well as "that grace by which, among men themselves," various distinctions of intelligence and beauty were visible. But this "natural endowment" was to be distinguished from "that good gift which pertains to a holy life," which did not come from nature, but was superadded by God. "The capacity to have faith, as the capacity to have love, belongs to men's nature; but to have faith, even as to have love, belongs to the grace of believers."

Such was the Augustinism that prevailed through the work of Prosper and of Caesarius and through the legislation of Orange, and that went on to set the terms for the development of medieval doctrine. It was not Orange itself that was usually cited, however, but the condemnation of Pelagianism at Ephesus. Gregory I, for example, spoke of Pelagius as one "who was condemned at the Synod of Ephesus" and asked, in reaction to an apparent

Bon.II.*Ep.Caes.Arel.*2 (*CCSL* 148–II:68)

Aug.*Praed.sanct.*5.10 (*PL* 44:967–68)

Gr.M.*Ep.*6.14 (*MGH* 1:393)

recrudescence of Pelagian tendencies, "Since Celestius and Pelagius were condemned in that synod [Ephesus], how is it possible for those teachings whose authors were condemned now to be approved?" Yet the official Augustinism of Gregory also contained the possibility for subtle shifts from the doctrine of the sovereignty and necessity of grace, by way of the doctrine of the mediation of grace, to a reintroduction of the notions of merit and human initiative; on the other hand, the thought of Augustine always contained the possibility for a shift back in the direction of predestinarianism. Much of Western theology since Orange has oscillated between these two poles, and we shall have to write its history (to paraphrase Whitehead's epigram about Plato) as "a series of footnotes" to Augustine. The first important predestinarian controversy of the Middle Ages, in the ninth century, was cast in Augustinian concepts, and even in Augustinian language, on both sides. The assertion of a double predestination, to eternal life or to eternal death, invoked the authority of Augustine; its opponents took it upon themselves "to collect testimonies from the holy father Augustine so that the prudent reader may recognize that he did not in any way teach two predestinations, not a single predestination with two parts, nor a double predestination." And once again it was this Augustine, doctor of grace but opponent of double predestination, who was celebrated as "the clearest and sweetest of authors" and as "that man of divine genius."

Later controversy, too, took its start from issues that had been raised by Augustine or against Augustine. When, for example, penance rather than infant baptism was taken as the paradigm for the way God and man interacted in the relation of grace, Cassian's description of the penance of David (who was taken to be the writer of Psalm 51, "Miserere mei," the portion of Scripture sung, recited, and expounded most frequently in penitential literature) could be echoed by Christian preaching and exhortation: "It was his own doing that he was humbled and acknowledged his guilt; but that in a very short interval of time he was granted pardon for such sins, this was the gift of the merciful Lord." Nothing seems more Augustinian than introspective meditation upon the meaning of sin and repentance; yet the "psychological impact" of such feelings of humility and contrition could lead late

Gr.M.Ep.9.153 (MGH 2:134)

Whitehead (1960) 63

Scot.Er.Praed.14.1 (PL 122:408)

Serv.Lup.Ep.4–5 (PL 119:444–46)

Cassian.Coll.13.13 (SC 54:169)

medieval theology to a doctrine of justification that "is essentially Pelagian."

Such was the authority of the Augustinian view of nature and grace that even those who relapsed into Pelagian forms of teaching had to do so in Augustine's terms. The Reformation of the sixteenth century has repeatedly, and to some degree accurately, been interpreted as a movement in which the anti-Pelagian doctrines of Augustine about the necessity of grace were used to attack the anti-Donatist doctrines of Augustine about the mediation of grace. The *Augustinus* of Cornelis Jansen, published posthumously in 1640, showed that even within post-Reformation Roman Catholicism the problem had not been settled; to compile it Jansen was said to have read all of Augustine ten times, but the anti-Pelagian treatises thirty times. In each of these theological controversies both sides claimed to be defending the Augustinian heritage and to be recovering the true Augustine. Both sides were right, and both were wrong.

[margin handwritten notes:]

Oberman (1963) 160; 177

- author of tradition
- attack against Augustine
- universality antiquity consensus
  Councils
  bishops
  priests
  liturgy
- criteria predestination

① was it universal
② Can it be found in scripture
③ do we find it in leadings of 4

In Dwelling Logos
- divine + human natures
- distinction preserved b/t
  the logos + the man assumed
- logos can move in and out of
  NO Union
- person of christ not
  divine till resurrection
  weakness - 4 people need of
  trinity

7 The Orthodox Consensus

During the fifth and sixth centuries, christology and mystagogy in the East, and anthropology and ecclesiology in the West, brought together much of the dogmatic development of the preceding centuries and laid the foundations for later constructions of Christian doctrine. After a century of controversy following Augustine's death in 430, the Synod of Orange in 529 codified Augustinism in a form that made it acceptable to Western theology; and after a century of controversy following the Council of Chalcedon in 451, the Second Council of Constantinople in 553 undertook to define the teachings of the fathers and the decrees of the councils as the standard for the teaching of the entire church, but especially for Eastern theology. In addition to these conciliar actions, which brought to a settlement, at least for a while, the debates over the person of the God-man and over nature and grace, the sixth century was also the time when, each in its own way, the East and the West articulated an orthodox consensus about what was to be regarded as normative. There were noteworthy bodies of Christians who did not share in this consensus. Donatists in North Africa, Arian Lombards in Italy, Nestorians in Persia, and Monophysites in Egypt, Syria, and Armenia—all had been excluded from the body of orthodox Christendom, even though the history of doctrine in those communions, particularly in those of the East, will continue to be part of our account. Yet it must be chiefly with the orthodox consensus that we concern ourselves, interpreting it in relation to the development of doctrine in the ancient church and in relation to the Byzantine and the medieval developments for which it provided the dogmatic starting point.

Ubique, Semper, Ab Omnibus

Fundamental to the orthodox consensus was an affirmation of the authority of tradition as that which had been believed "everywhere, always, by all [ubique, semper, ab omnibus]." The criteria for what constituted the orthodox tradition were "universality, antiquity, and consensus." This definition of orthodox Catholic tradition was the work of Vincent of Lérins, writing under the pseudonym Peregrinus. The immediate purpose of his treatise seems to have been to attack the predestinarianism of Augustine and his supporters for being an innovation and a deviation from the tradition of orthodoxy. As a statement of catholic authority Vincent's rule was thoroughly Augustinian; it also summarized, better than Eastern Christian writers themselves had done, a canon of church teaching which, formally at any rate, the Greeks shared with the Latins. At the time of Vincent's writing, in 434, the attempt to specify the material content of this orthodox tradition would have been premature both in the East and in the West. His rule did state, however, that understanding of orthodoxy which the theologians and church councils of the fifth and sixth centuries were to canonize for the centuries that followed, as affirmed, for example, a century later in the treatise *On the Catholic Faith* attributed to Boethius: "This catholic church, then, spread throughout the world, is known by three particular marks: whatever is believed and taught in it has the authority of the Scriptures, or of universal tradition, or at least of its own and proper usage."

The criterion of universality required that a doctrine, to be recognized as the teaching of the church rather than a private theory of a man or of a school, be genuinely catholic, that is, be the confession of "all the churches . . . one great horde of people from Palestine to Chalcedon with one voice reechoing the praises of Christ." In one dogmatic conflict after another, this argument had been used, with lesser or greater appropriateness, to refute heresy. Hilary had cited various Eastern creeds as evidence of the universality of what he was defending in the West

Vinc.Ler.*Comm*.2.3 (Moxon 10)

Vinc.Ler.*Comm*.2.3 (Moxon 10–11)

Boeth.*Fid.cath.* (*LCL* 70)

Hier.*Vigil*.5 (*PL* 23:343)

Hil.*Syn*.30 (*PL* 10:503–504)

Ath.*Apol.sec*.30.1 (Opitz 2:109)

Aug.*Parm*.3.4.24 (*CSEL* 51:131)

Gr.M.*Mor*.17.29.43 (*PL* 76:30)

Gr.M.*Mor*.16.55.68 (*PL* 75:1153)

Gr.M.*Mor*.35.8.13 (*PL* 76:756–57)

Gr.M.*Mor*.19.18.27 (*PL* 76:115)

Gr.M.*Mor*.20.2.2 (*PL* 76:136)

Gr.M.*Mor*.8.5.7 (*PL* 75:805)

Gr.M.*Mor*.18.11.18 (*PL* 76:47)

as the Nicene faith; Athanasius had vindicated his position by referring to "so many bishops in unanimity" with him, including Western bishops; and Augustine, writing against the Donatists, had coined the formula, "the judgment of the whole world is reliable [securus judicat orbis terrarum]." Catholicity was a mark both of the true church and of the true doctrine, for these were inseparable. "The churches, although many, make up one catholic church, diffused throughout the world," as Gregory I phrased it. Or, in a fuller explanation, "because states derive their names from the peoples who live together in them, it is fitting that the churches of the true faith should be called states, which, although located in various parts of the world, make up one catholic church, in which all those who believe correctly about God live together in harmony." To identify orthodox doctrine, one had to identify its locus, which was the catholic church, neither Eastern nor Western, neither Greek nor Latin, but universal throughout the civilized world (οἰκουμένη).

This church was the repository of truth, the dispenser of grace, the guarantee of salvation, the matrix of acceptable worship. Only here did God accept sacrifices, only here was there confident intercession for those who were in error, only here were good works fruitful, only here did the powerful bond of love hold men together, and "only from the catholic church does truth shine forth." It was characteristic of heretics that they erred in one extreme or the other, denying either the One or the Three, either despising marriage or denigrating virginity. "But the church, by contrast, proceeds with ordered composure midway between the quarrels on both sides. It knows how to accept the higher good in such a way as simultaneously to venerate the lower, because it neither puts the highest on the same level with the lowest nor on the other hand despises the lowest when it venerates the highest." Although the church was "oppressed by tribulations from heretics and from carnal men," its faithful disciples paid heed to its direction as those who were called upon "not to judge but to obey." Because the church was universal, unlike the heretics, it did not teach one thing in public and another in private; but it confessed and taught as it believed, and it lived in accordance with its confession. Therefore "holy church does not conceal anything of the truth." Yet in presenting the truth to those who were in error, the church, "instructed by the teaching of humility, does not command as though by authority, but persuades by reason." What this apparently meant was not that the church lacked authority but that, like Christ, "who knew all things but in his manner of speaking took our ignorance upon himself," it declined to invoke its authority but relied upon its powers of persuasion instead.

A special mark of the universality and of the authority of the church was the ecumenical councils. The Second Council of Constantinople pledged its allegiance to "the things which we have received from Holy Scripture and from the teaching of the holy fathers and from the definitions of one and the same faith by the four sacred councils"—Nicea in 325, Constantinople in 381, Ephesus in 431, and Chalcedon in 451. "These four councils," according to Justinian, "which took place and were confirmed, are authoritative in the church of God." When, at the end of the century, there were those who maintained "that in the times of Justinian of pious memory something was subtracted from the faith of the holy synod of Chalcedon" as a concession to the Monophysites, Gregory insisted that "with all faith and all devotion we venerate" the Council of Chalcedon. And he added: "In like manner all the four synods of the holy universal church we receive as we do the four books of the holy Gospels." Elsewhere, too, he drew a parallel between the four Gospels and the four ecumenical councils. Although this parallel may be interpreted as nothing more than a pleasant suggestion, there are grounds for reading into it the conviction of Gregory that one and the same truth of divine revelation, which had been vouchsafed to the church universal, was present both in the four Gospels and in the four councils, just as the ark of the covenant in the Old Testament symbolized the holy church, which "being extended to the four parts of the world, is declared to be equipped with the four books of the Gospels." The parallel was confirmed negatively by the tendency of heretics to teach doctrines that were not contained either in Scripture or in tradition. But the church of the four Gospels and the four councils was faithful to Scripture and to tradition and was universal both in its outreach and in its authority.

It was fundamental to this definition of authority, however, that there be a universality in time as well as a uni-

Gr.M.*Mor*.8.2.3 (*PL* 75:803)

Gr.M.*Mor*.1.23.31 (*PL* 75:542)

Justn.*Monoph.* (*PG* 86:1145)

CCP (553) *Sent.* (Mansi 9:375)

Justn. *Ep.Thdr.Mops.* (*PG* 86:1039)

Gr.M.*Ep*.3.10 (*MGH* 1:170)
Gr.M.*Ep*.1.24 (*MGH* 1:36)

Gr.M.*Past*.2.11 (*PL* 77:49)

Gr.M.*Mor*.18.26.39 (*PL* 76:58)

versality in space: antiquity was an essential component
of tradition. Indeed, in Vincent's definition this criterion
appears to have been the most decisive; "the interpretations that obviously were maintained by our saintly fore-
bears and fathers" were normative, and a doctrine such
as that of Augustine on predestination which deviated
from them was to be rejected. In the usage of Eusebius,
the terms orthodox, ancient, and ecclesiastical were almost
interchangeable. On the basis of the consistent claim of
ecclesiastical theologians that the saints before Christ
were to be included in the definition of the Christian
church, the demand that doctrine conform to antiquity in
order to be orthodox implied that "the passion of the
church began with the blood of Abel, and the church of
the elect is one," whether the elect came before or after
Christ. Hence "the holy church in the integrity of its
faith" and doctrine included the saints of both the Old
Testament and the New. Even the patriarchs, who lived
before the giving of the law to Moses, "knew that the
one Almighty God is the Holy Trinity, but did not preach
very much publicly about the Trinity whom they knew."
The saints of the Old Testament could not have loved
God truly unless they had received the grace of "that very
Trinity, who is God." And since the doctrine of catholic
Christianity could simply be designated as "the mystery
of the Holy Trinity" or as "the faith of the Trinity," this
doctrine must have been believed not only everywhere
throughout Christendom but also always throughout the
ages before and after Christ.

But as a norm of orthodoxy, the requirement that a
doctrine be one that has been always believed referred
with special force to "the doctrines of the fathers who
spoke of God [τὰς τῶν θεηγόρων Πατέρων διδασκαλίας],"
from which it was wrong to deviate. Those who claimed
to be wise in their own learning overlooked "the ancient
labors of the holy fathers," and against them it was necessary to cite the authority of "the witness of the ancients."
One could define a heretic as someone who by his own
wicked ideas sought to destroy the the teachings of the
fathers. A heretic would "bring forth as something new
what is not contained in the old books of the ancient fathers" or in the Bible. It was inconceivable to the exponents of the orthodox consensus that there could be any
contradiction between Scripture properly interpreted and

Vinc.Ler.Comm.2.3 (Moxon
11)

Eus.H.e.5.27 (GCS 9:498)

Gr.M.Ezech.2.3.16 (PL
76:966)

Gr.M.Ezech.2.3.17 (PL
76:967)

Gr.M.Ezech.2.4.10 (PL
76:979)

Gr.M.Ezech.2.4.4 (PL
76:975)

Gr.M.Ezech.2.4.11 (PL
76:980)
Gr.M.Mor.33.10.20 (PL
76:684)

Leont.B.Nest.et Eut. 1 (PG
86:1305)

Leont.B.Nest.et Eut.pr. (PG
86:1268–69)
Leont.B.Nest.et Eut.pr. (PG
86:1272)

Gr.M.Mor.16.53.66 (PL
75:1152)

Gr.M.Mor.18.26.39 (PG
76:58)

the tradition of the ancient fathers; or, more precisely, Scripture was properly interpreted only when it was seen as standing in agreement with tradition. An Eastern synod in 691 defined the orthodox consensus succinctly: "If any controversy is raised in regard to Scripture, let [the clergy and the bishops] not interpret it otherwise than as the lights and the doctors of the church in their writings have expounded it, and in these let them glory rather than in making things up out of their own heads, lest through their lack of skill they depart from what is proper." It was imperative to recognize the continuity between the teaching of Scripture and the doctrine of the orthodox fathers. "What [the apostles] spoke in brief form, that [the orthodox theologians of the church] expanded to greater length . . . by gathering together the statements of many who had gone before and expanding these more profoundly in what they added to them." The apostles had ruled the church by their proclamation, and now their place had been taken by others who continued to rule by the same proclamation. The succession was uninterrupted and the continuity unbroken.

Yet the norm of antiquity did not automatically elevate to authoritative status every theologian of the past, regardless of what he taught. In his defense of the catholic faith against Manicheism, Augustine had rejected "all the testimony you can bring in favor of your book from antiquity or tradition" so long as it did not agree with "the testimony of the catholic church . . . supported by a succession of bishops from the original sees of the apostles to the present time." Vincent, for his part, insisted that the prestige of the theologians of the church, including that of Augustine himself, defer to "the decisions of antiquity." A prime instance of this requirement was the case of Origen, who, although an ornament of the church for his piety and his learning, fell into error and corrupted the ancient faith. Vincent's judgment of Origen was made official at the Second Council of Constantinople, at the urging of Justinian. Justinian cited the authority of "the holy fathers who, following the inspired Scriptures, condemned such doctrines [as the preexistence of the soul], together with Origen, who made up such myths." By his doctrines Origen had "forsaken the divine Scriptures and the holy fathers whom the catholic church of God regards as its teachers and through whom

CTrull.*Can*.19 (Mansi 11:952)

Gr.M.*Mor*.27.8.14 (*PL* 76:406)

Gr.M.*Mor*.4.3.62 (*PL* 75:671)

Aug.*Faust*.11.2 (*CSEL* 25:315)

Vinc.Ler.*Comm*.24.34 (Moxon 101)

Vinc.Ler.*Comm*.17.23 (Moxon 66–74)

Justn.*Or*. (*ACO* 3:197)

Justn.Or. (ACO 3:189)

every heresy everywhere was driven out and the orthodox faith was explained." Within antiquity, then, some teachers were to be preferred to others; there was ancient heresy as well as ancient orthodoxy, and any teaching was to be condemned despite its age if it deviated from what had always been taught by the true succession of orthodox bishops and theologians. In Augustine's case, there was probably no possibility of anything so drastic as a formal condemnation by a duly constituted synod of the church. Instead, later Augustinism discreetly eliminated what was objectionable in Augustine even as it celebrated his authority. Antiquity was vindicated and orthodoxy was preserved.

The third norm of orthodox tradition was for it to have been believed "by all." In the passage against Manicheism quoted earlier, Augustine added to the authority of the bishops a reference to "the consensus of so many

Aug.Faust.11.2 (CSEL 25:315)

nations." Vincent of Lérins qualified the requirement that it be believed "by all" with the condition that "in antiquity itself we adhere to the consensus of the definitions and determinations of all—or at least of almost all—

Vinc.Ler.Comm.2.3 (Moxon 11)

priests and doctors." Not everyone had equal weight in the determination of what had been taught by all; priests counted for more than laymen, bishops for more than priests, synods and councils for more than individual bishops. The church also possessed the means to enforce its definition of orthodoxy. Those upon whom a council pronounced excommunication and anathema were to be rejected, for the councils, "having been constituted by a

Gr.M.Ep.1.24 (MGH 1:36–37)

universal consensus," were binding upon all. In addition, God had put into the hands of the secular rulers "solicitude for the peace of the faith" as this was defined by the

Gr.M.Mor.31.6.8 (PL 76:576)

orthodox church. Banishment of heretics was another way to insure consensus. Cassian put the case for consensus perhaps more completely than any other theologian of the fifth and sixth centuries: "There has never been anyone who quarreled with this faith without being guilty of unbelief, for to deny what has been proved to be right is to confess what is wrong. The consensus of all ought then of itself to be enough to refute heresy; for the authority of all shows indubitable truth, and a perfect reason results where no one disputes it. Therefore if a man seeks to hold opinions contrary to these, we should, at the very outset, condemn his perversity rather than listen to his assertions.

For someone who impugns the judgment of all announces his own condemnation beforehand, and a man who disturbs what had been determined by all is not even given a hearing. For when the truth has been established by all men once and for all, whatever arises contrary to it is by this very fact to be recognized at once as falsehood, because it differs from the truth."

It would be an exaggeration to claim, however, that the consensus was an exclusively clerical prerogative. The people had their ways of expressing doctrine, even though they did not use the erudite terms of theology. Especially important in the fifth and sixth centuries was the doctrinal authority of Christian devotion and liturgy, as the victory of the idea of Theotokos made clear. Augustine, faced with the relative silence of earlier generations of theologians about such issues as original sin and predestination, had recourse to this argument. Although the theological discourses of the church had not spoken extensively on these matters, the prayers of the church from the beginning had been far more explicit, pleading with God for forgiveness and for the gift of perseverance. Here the "all" of the praying church were to be given precedence over what seemed to be the consensus of the church's theologians. Prosper formulated this principle in the axiom that "the rule of prayer should lay down the rule of faith [ut legem credendi lex statuat supplicandi]." In every catholic church all over the world prayers were offered in conformity with apostolic tradition. This was a rule for discovering the orthodox consensus. So was the life of Christian believers past and present. From the lives of the holy fathers, Gregory I maintained, it was possible to derive principles for the proper interpretation of Scripture, so that the practice (actio) helped to make sense of the preaching (praedicatio). To understand what had been believed by all, it was necessary to consult the silent in the land and to read off the doctrine which they believed even at a time when the church had not yet begun to teach it in theology or to confess it in creed.

Catholic Orthodoxy in the East

Orthodox doctrine was, by definition, the doctrine taught everywhere in the church, and in principle this was true. Both the East and the West had contributed to the trinitarian dogma, and both were committed to its correctness.

Cassian.*Nest*.1.6 (*CSEL* 17:245)

See pp. 241–42 above

Aug.*Persev*.23.63 (*PL* 45:1031–32)

Prosp.*Auct*.8 (*PL* 51:209)

Gr.M.*Ezech*.1.10.38 (*PL* 76:901)

Moreover, even the doctrinal emphases and dogmatic issues peculiar to one portion of the church had received attention from the universal church: Pelagianism was condemned not only by Latin-speaking synods, but by the

Justn.Conf. (PG 86:1033)

Council of Ephesus; Monophysitism was almost completely an Eastern problem, but popes from Leo to Vigilius and Gregory participated in its settlement. It was technically accurate, therefore, to speak of the one orthodox faith as the doctrine professed by all of Christendom. Nevertheless, the condemnation of Pelagianism represented anything but the dominant thought of Eastern Christendom, and the Western role in christological developments after the Council of Chalcedon became less and less significant. By the end of the sixth century, Greek Christianity and Latin Christianity, still parts of one and the same church, were clearly going their separate ways, not only liturgically, administratively, and culturally, but also doctrinally.

Among Christian doctrines, it continued to be the christological that claimed the attention of Eastern Christians. The armistice of Chalcedon and the compromise of Second Constantinople did not even seriously interrupt the conflict between the opposing and enduring forces of those who saw the salvation of the human race assured only by the most intimate of associations between the divine and the human in the person of the God-man and those who saw this salvation threatened by any association in which one nature—and this always meant the human nature—was foreshortened by the very definition of the incarnation. The decrees of 553 momentarily provided a respite among conflicting theories: it was affirmed that Christ had to have two natures in order to save the human; but the "three chapters," all of them directed toward a sharper distinction between the two natures than the dominant tendency of Eastern devotion and doc-

See pp. 275–77 above

trine would allow, were condemned. This was too much for the remaining partisans of the theology of the indwelling Logos; they maintained, with some justification, that the decree of the Council of Chalcedon had also acknowledged the validity of this theology. On the other hand, the condemnation was not nearly enough for the adherents of the theology of the hypostatic union. Having failed to achieve dogmatic status for the theory that the union had brought about one nature of the incarnate

Logos, Alexandrian christology was eventually to go on to argue that at any rate there was only one will in the incarnate Logos. This controversy, which belongs to the period following the one recounted in the present volume, continued and redefined the terms of the post-Chalcedonian struggle; but for a while, at least some participants in the struggle thought they had reason to believe that the conflict had been transcended by a theology which, refusing to "know or to teach" the extremes of any position, could "set forth in an orthodox fashion the religion of the holy fathers." The hope of peace was illusory, as the East was to learn during the controversies that led up to the Third Council of Constantinople in 680; it was also to learn, in the course of its negotiations with Pope Honorius I, that neither the question nor its answer could be expected to find understanding in depth by the Western church.

In many ways the most representative spokesman for catholic orthodoxy in the East was Justinian—not only because a Christian emperor was regarded as "Christ-loving [φιλόχριστος]," but because in Justinian, "as hardly ever again in a Byzantine emperor, politics, administration, and theology are combined. . . . Nevertheless, certain areas can be identified in which the theologian won out over the ruler and the politician. In these there becomes evident a theology of a Neo-Chalcedonian coinage which is more original than has been assumed hitherto." The theology of Justinian not only pointed the direction in which the reinterpretation of Chalcedon would have to move if its decrees were to be made acceptable to the partisans of the theology of the hypostatic union. It also manifested the reverence for tradition that lay at the heart of Greek Christianity; and it affirmed that close bond between the faith believed in the divine liturgy and the doctrine taught in theology and confessed in dogma which, while present also in the Latins, has been an especially powerful force in the life and thought of the East.

Such an affirmation of the authority of tradition could, of course, be duplicated from the writings of many others. Although he did not use the formula, Justinian could have claimed that what had been taught "ubique, semper, ab omnibus" was to be normative doctrine in the church. But his formulation of the principle had special force,

Leont.B.*Nest.et Eut.*4.9 (*PG* 86:1669)

Ath.*Apol.Const.*3 (*PG* 25:600)

H.Beck (1959) 377

and his constant reiteration of it showed how fundamental it was to his piety and faith. His opponents, usually labeled "enemies of the truth," were accused of "following neither the prophets nor the evangelists nor the proclamation of the apostles," all of these being equated with the orthodox tradition. The enemies of the truth were "violating all the doctrines of the fathers." Those who, out of loyalty to Cyril, opposed Chalcedon were guilty of disloyalty to the unanimous testimony of the orthodox fathers, including Cyril. For "Cyril, before the condemnation of Nestorius, in the condemnation, and after the condemnation, did not cease to proclaim the confession of the two natures in the one Christ. But Severus, the enemy of the truth, understanding none of this, calls the fathers by the name 'fathers,' but denies the dogmas which they have handed down to the church in the orthodox tradition [τὰ παρ' αὐτῶν ὀρθῶς τῇ Ἐκκλησίᾳ παραδεδομένα δόγματα]. He does not know that while Nestorius was condemned for his irreligion, the doctrine of the fathers was also denied by him. If then, according to the madness of Severus, the statements which the holy fathers made in an orthodox sense are to be repudiated because the heretics distort them, he will also have to abolish Holy Scripture, from which all heretics claim to find support for their diseased ideas. It is evident, therefore, that according to his foolish position, both the Holy Scriptures and the traditions of the fathers must be rejected." Even while he was giving a decidedly Cyrillian cast to Chalcedon and interpreting Philippians 2:5-7 on the basis of passages from the polemical writings of Cyril, he continually professed his unwavering fidelity to "the dogmas of the catholic church, the traditions of the fathers, the men who have been outstanding in their time within the holy church of God, and those assembled in the four sacred councils." Although Byzantine theology after the sixth and seventh centuries did not become as petrified as the caricatures of it suggest, it was characterized by a distinctive subservience to the past even in its most original and creative periods of theological discussion.

The emperor was also a patron of the liturgical theology of the East. For the construction of St. Sophia in Constantinople, "both God and the emperor are magni-

Justn.*Monoph.* (PG 86:1121)
Justn.*Monoph.* (PG 86:1112)

Justn.*Monoph.* (PG 86:1136-37)

Justn.*Monoph.* (PG 86:1109)

Justn.*Monoph.* (PG 86:1144-45)

Paul.Sil.*Soph.*2 (PG 86:2119)

Paul.Sil.*Soph*.31–32 (*PG* 86:2121)

Paul.Sil.*Soph*.709–711; 803 (*PG* 86:2146; 2150)

Justn.*Ep.Thdr.Mops.* (*PG* 86:1037)

Justn.*Or.* (*ACO* 3:204)

See pp. 236–38 above

Justn.*Ep.Thdr.Mops.* (*PG* 86:1053–55)

See pp. 270–71 above

Justn.*Monoph.* (*PG* 86:1141)
Prosp.*Auct.*8 (*PL* 51:209)

See pp. 198–200 above
See p. 217 above

fied," God for his gift of victory and the emperor for his "magnanimity, intelligence, and faith." Here the worship of God and the cult of the Theotokos had received their fitting artistic statement. This liturgical and architectural tribute had its counterpart in Justinian's theology. He recognized the liturgical origin of theological formulations, acknowledging that "almost our entire controversy over the faith arose from our insisting that Mary is Theotokos." Conversely, where there was false doctrine, there would also be false worship. Therefore Justinian made the quite unsubstantiated charge that Origen "in the very time of his martyrdom denied Christ and paid his worship to the many gods of the Greeks." Recalling earlier eucharistic arguments for the theology of the hypostatic union, Justinian defined the members of the catholic church as those who, "confessing that God the Logos, being one of the Trinity, became flesh and was made man, eat his body and blood for the forgiveness of sins and for life everlasting," as John 6:54 promised.

The phrase, "one of the Trinity," was an echo of the liturgical and dogmatic controversy over the proper form of the Trisagion, in which the intimate connection between worship and doctrine had been evident. According to Justinian, Severus had presumed to say that the Trisagion was addressed only to the Son, rather than to the Father and the Holy Spirit as well. "Supposing that they are worshiping the Son, they offend him in their ignorance by not worshiping him with the same worship that is addressed to the Father and the Holy Spirit." The fathers had handed down the interpretation of the original Trisagion, Isaiah 6:3, as a "doxology of the Holy Trinity." The rule of prayer, as Prosper had said, was to lay down the rule of faith. This was true throughout the church and had been a decisive factor in the trinitarian controversies, where the worship which was addressed to Christ and the trinitarian doxology which included the Holy Spirit had helped to clinch the case for Christ and the Holy Spirit being homoousios with the Father. But the iconoclastic controversy of the eighth and ninth century was to show again how constitutive of Eastern doctrine this congruity between the rule of prayer and the rule of faith continued to be.

One distinctive feature of the doctrinal history of Greek Christianity for which Justinian was not especially

important was the role of mysticism; for although he used
Justn.*Or.* (*ACO* 3:197) such a term as "mystagogy [μυσταγωγία]," he meant by it
the dying words of Peter of Alexandria to the church, not
the principles of the practice of mysticism. These principles had many of their roots in Origen and, behind him,
in his Platonic heritage. They had been worked out by
the pupils of Origen, particularly by Gregory of Nyssa
and Evagrius Ponticus. It was Evagrius who gave them
the form they had in the literature of Egyptian monasticism. Most of this material belongs to the history of Christian spirituality and to the history of ascetic practice, but
it shaped the history of church doctrine when it spoke of
the vision of God and of the union between the soul and
God in a manner that caught up many of the themes of
Greek Christianity.

Mysticism became a major doctrinal force with the
composition of the works that were published under the
pseudonym of Dionysius the Areopagite, described in
Acts 17:34 as one of the few Athenians who joined Paul
and believed. Arising about 500, probably in the
Monophysite circles of Syria, the Dionysian corpus soon
achieved wide acceptance as a subapostolic exposition of
how the celestial hierarchy of God and the angels was
related to the ecclesiastical hierarchy of bishops and
priests with their sacraments. Here the mystical speculations of Neoplatonism and the spirituality of Origen were
integrated into Eastern dogma in a way that was to shape
the subsequent evolution of doctrine through such movements as the Hesychasm of the fourteenth century. It also
shaped medieval Western theology, for the writings of
Dionysius formed the basis for the mystical thought of
Bernard of Clairvaux and Thomas Aquinas. These developments belong to later periods in the history of Christian doctrine and will be treated there, but the Dionysian
system of mystical doctrine is itself an essential part of the
story of catholic orthodoxy in the Greek church of the
sixth century.

The point at which the dogmas of orthodoxy and the
tenets of mysticism intersected most significantly was the
definition of salvation as deification or, in the Dionysian
Panillo (1965) 121–22 schema, "creation, deification, restoration." This Greek
Christian definition provided Dionysius with a point of
contact to which he could attach his doctrine of mystical
union with God. It was the purpose of a hierarchy,

whether celestial or ecclesiastical, to achieve, "as much as
attainable, assimilation to God and union with him

Dion.Ar.*C.h.*3.2 (PG 3:165)
[ἡ πρὸς θεὸν, ὡς ἐφικτὸν, ἀφομοίωσίς τε καὶ ἕνωσις]." This
definition was amplified elsewhere: "Reasonable salvation . . . cannot occur otherwise than by the deification of
those who are saved. Now deification [θέωσις] is, as much

Dion.Ar.*E.h.*1.3(PG
3:373–76)
as attainable, assimilation to God and union with him."
It meant attaining to perfection in divine things and
elevating what was lower to participation in the nature of

Dion.Ar.*E.h.*1.2 (PG 3:372)
God. "The principle of deification [ἡ ἀρχὴ τῆς θεώσεως]"
was the beatitude of God himself, that by which he was
God; his goodness conferred the gift of salvation and

Dion.Ar.*E.h.*1.4 (PG 3:376)
deification on all rational and intelligent beings. The ·
words of John 1:13, which, in a variant reading, had

See pp. 287–90 above
helped to interpret the virgin birth of Christ, were put
to use here to describe that birth of believers from God
by which, through the coming of Christ, earthlings could

Dion.Ar.*E.h.*2.1 (PG 3:393)
be united to him and receive deification. Such statements
as these suggest, perhaps more in their connotations than
in their denotations, that the definition of salvation as
deification had undergone a change by being identified
with the goal awaiting the true mystic at the end of the
three steps of purification, illumination, and union. Although the idea of deification in the Greek fathers had
run the danger of obscuring the distinction between
Creator and creature, the pressure of the controversy over
Christ as creature had acted to restrain any pantheistic
tendencies that may have been present in it. Now that
the pressure was coming not from the trinitarian dogma,
but from the mystical theories of Neoplatonism, these
tendencies seemed to be asserting themselves with new
vigor.

This also became evident in the sacramental theology
of Dionysius. The sacraments, especially the Eucharist,
had long been interpreted as the means by which human
nature was transformed and man was made fit to participate in the impassible and incorruptible nature of

See pp. 236–38 above
God; this interpretation had been a prominent element
in the theology of the hypostatic union. The docetic and
even pantheistic possibilities which the supporters of the
theology of the indwelling Logos claimed to discern in
the doctrine of the hypostatic union may have been responsible for their drawing back from an elaborate
eucharistic theology. Dionysius was laboring under no

Dion.Ar.E.h.7.6 (PG 3:561)

Dion.Ar.E.h.5.3 (PG 3:504)

See pp. 164–65 above

Dion.Ar.E.h.2.1 (PG 3:392)

Dion.Ar.E.h.7.11 (PG 3:565)

Dion.Ar.E.h.2.7 (PG 3:404)

Dion.Ar.E.h.3.1 (PG 3:428)

Dion.Ar.C.h.1.3 (PG 3:124)

Dion.Ar.E.h.3.7 (PG 3:433)

Dion.Ar.E.h.4.12 (PG 3:485)

Dion.Ar.E.h.3.1 (PG 3:428)

Dion.Ar.Ep.9.1 (PG 3:1108)

such inhibitions and was free to adapt the traditional theology of the sacraments, which he cited as his authority, to the uses of his mystical version of the doctrine of deification.

For Dionysius the ecclesiastical hierarchy had as its purpose the achievement of the three steps of mystical ascent, and to this end it administered baptism, the Eucharist, and anointing. Baptism had long been identified as the sacrament of cleansing, and a favorite patristic term for it was illumination. Dionysius called it "the tradition of our holy and divine regeneration." Through it even little children, who were incapable of grasping divine things, were made participants in a divine birth, sharing in the sacramental signs of communion with God. Trine immersion in baptism represented the three days and nights of Christ's sojourn in the grave and the resurrection by which he had accomplished this divine birth. But it was the Eucharist to which Dionysius devoted primary attention as the sacrament of deification. The Eucharist was a divine participation and a peaceful sharing in bread and wine, a commemoration of the divine supper of participation in God. A brief definition of it was "participation in Jesus, the communion of the most divine Eucharist." Through such communion one was permitted to share in "the most perfect forms of deification," which enabled him to ignore any but the most basic demands of the body and to grow, by means of this sublime deification, into a temple of the Holy Spirit. This perfection, which was the gift of baptism and of the Eucharist, reached its consummation here on earth in the administration of anointing, which could be called simply "making perfect [τελετή]," a technical term for various rites in the mystery religions and in Christianity. The use of such a term suggests that Dionysius regarded the Christian sacraments, specifically the Eucharist, as "the chief symbol" of mystical truth; for "Jesus taught theology in parables and handed down the deifying sacraments through a symbolic setting of the table."

In such a system of mystical doctrine, Jesus himself could become no more than a "chief symbol" for the transcendent reality of man's union with God through mystical ascent. The Dionysian writings referred to Jesus in many different ways that sought to establish his relation to the processes of purification, illumination, and union. It was the content of the instruction received from "divine knowledge" to know that "the Godlike life has already begun for us in Christ." Again, Dionysius could refer to the goal of both hierarchies as deification and add that Jesus was "both the principle of creation and the consummation of all the hierarchies." Nevertheless, neither the recitation of such formulas nor the repetition of the name of Jesus Christ—even the repetition in the continual "prayer to Jesus" practiced by some of Dionysius's predecessors and successors in Eastern Christian mysticism—was a genuine index to the doctrinal significance of Christ for this theology. For regulating all such practices and ideas was a picture of God in which the doctrine of the incarnation, as well as the understanding of immanence and transcendence underlying this doctrine, threatened to be swallowed up in the One and the All. Positive statements about God and analogies with light by which he was described were "more solemn" and seemed to convey revelations about the divine reality. But the transcendence of God meant that such statements fell far short of describing God and that negative statements were "more valid" and "more appropriate." Therefore it was better to say "not what He is, but what He is not."

This theology of negation implied more than the transcendence of the Creator over any and all of his creatures. Eventually, even the terms and concepts that had been central to the Christian doctrine of God had to fall before the principle that the ultimate divine reality could not be properly spoken of except by saying what he was not. For all the formal trinitarian orthodoxy of the writings of Dionysius, neither the One nor the Three of earlier trinitarian theology could be maintained in the conventional terms. The One was "a unity that transcends oneness [ὑπερηνωμένη ἑνάς]," so that to call God one was not strictly proper unless it was made clear that unity did not mean here what it meant anywhere else. For in fact God transcended all number, since "number participates in being" and God was "One beyond being," who "determines all number." He was the "principle and cause and number and order" of all things, even of numbers themselves. "Therefore the Deity that is above all things is worshiped both as a Unity and as a Trinity, but is neither a unity nor a trinity in the sense in which we know them.

Dion.Ar.*E.h.*7.2 (*PG* 3:553)

Dion.Ar.*E.h.*1.2 (*PG* 3:373)

Dion.Ar.*C.h.*2.3 (*PG* 3:140–41)

Dion.Ar.*Myst.*3 (*PG* 3:1032–33)

Dion.Ar.*D.n.*13.3 (*PG* 3:980)

Dion.Ar.*D.n.*2.1 (*PG* 3:637)

Dion.Ar.D.n.13.3 (PG 3:980–81)

. . . With the trinitary and the unitary divine name we name Him who is above names; with things that are [we name] Him who is above being." So transcendent was this God that he was above not only incarnation and Trinity, but godhead itself, as Dionysius explained in a remarkable letter which summarized the doctrines both of deity and of deification: "How does He who transcends all things exist beyond the principle of deity and the principle of goodness? If you understand deity and goodness to be the matter of being made good and the gift of deification, and the inimitable imitation of Him who is above God and above the Good, by which we are deified and made good. For if this is the principle of 'deification and of being made good for those who are deified and made good, then He who is the principle above principles, including the principle of so-called deity and goodness, transcends the principles both of deity and of goodness. And since He is inimitable and incomprehensible, He surpasses the imitations and the comprehensions of those who imitate [the divine nature]

Dion.Ar.Ep.2 (PG 3:1068–69)

and participate in it."

There is both historical significance and theological irony in the chronological coincidence between the condemnation of Origen and the rise of Dionysian mysticism, for most of the doctrines on account of which the Second Council of Constantinople anathematized Origen were far less dangerous to the tradition of catholic orthodoxy than was the Crypto-Origenism canonized in the works of Dionysius the Areopagite. Anyone who copied the books of Severus or Nestorius ran the risk of having his hand

Justn.Sev. (ACO 3:122)

amputated, but the books of the Areopagite, a convert of Paul, could claim an authority that was all but apostolic. Because it set the pattern for the reinterpretation of the christological development while still affirming the continuity of the orthodox tradition, even as it bequeathed the Dionysian corpus to subsequent centuries in the East and in the West, it is correct to say that the century of Justinian "has, also when it is evaluated in its significance for the history of dogma, the conclusive character which it appears to have in so many other fields" such as law. And so "under Justinian the dogma of the ancient Greek

Loofs (1887) 37; 53

church came to a conclusion." More precisely, under Justinian there was handed on to the Byzantine theology that followed him a congeries of doctrinal ideas that was more monolithic in appearance than the orthodoxy of Nicea and Chalcedon had ever been, but that carried within it the seeds of its own development and gradual, though sometimes almost imperceptible, transformation. *The Spirit of Eastern Christendom,* volume 2 of *The Christian Tradition,* will deal with this development.

Orthodox Catholicism in the West

In that section of the church over which Gregory I ruled as "last of the church fathers and first of the popes," the development of catholic orthodoxy was closely associated with the rise of papal hegemony. In many ways Gregory and Boethius may be said to have occupied together a place in the Latin church analogous to that held by the combination of Justinian and Dionysius in Greek Christianity, for both pairs of sixth-century thinkers caught up the distinctive themes of their respective traditions and passed them on in a form that was to frame the theology of the subsequent centuries. Like Dionysius, Boethius provided orthodox Christian sanction for ideas whose non-Christian origin might otherwise have disqualified them. But Boethius was important for the medieval West also as the translator of Aristotle and as the transmitter of the trinitarian and christological dogmas in a collection of theological opuscula that were to be the basis of commentaries for a millennium. Grabmann has maintained that "of all the Latin writers of the patristic era, Boethius is second only to Augustine in his influence on scholasticism, especially on the development of the scholastic method." His treatises *On the Holy Trinity* and *Against Eutyches and Nestorius* were thoroughly orthodox in their doctrine, but formulated the questions in such a way as to compel examination of the relation between revelation and reason as means of finding religious truth.

It was the purpose of his tractate on the Trinity, he said in the preface, to investigate the question of the mind's capacity to grasp the mystery of the Trinity, and in his conclusion he expressed the hope that he had "furnished some support in an argument [from reason] to an article which stands by itself on the firm foundation of faith." In his exposition of christological orthodoxy, Boethius intended to expound what "catholics confess in accordance with reason [rationabiliter]," and elsewhere

Grabmann (1957) 1:148

Boeth.*Trin*.pr. (*LCL* 2–4)

Boeth.*Trin*.6 (*LCL* 30)

Boeth.*Eut*.6 (*LCL* 112)

Boeth.*Divin.* (*LCL* 36)

Boeth.*Eut.*6 (*LCL* 116)
Boeth.*Divin.* (*LCL* 32)

Boeth.*Fid.cath.* (*LCL* 52)

See pp. 42–44 above

Boeth.*Eut.*pr.; 5 (*LCL* 76; 100)

Boeth.*Eut.*7 (*LCL* 118)

Boeth.*Trin.*pr. (*LCL* 4)

Gr.M.*Ep.*10.16 (*MGH* 2:251)

Dudden (1905) 2:294

R.Seeberg (1953) 3:45

he bade his reader: "If possible, reconcile faith and reason." There was, of course, no question what this faith and confession included. Boethius held unwaveringly to "the true and solid content of the catholic faith," which was "the surest source of all truth." The Boethian authorship of the treatise *On the Catholic Faith* has been disputed but is now usually accepted; on this issue at least, its affirmation of "this our religion which is called Christian and catholic" was consistent with the position of the other theological opuscula of Boethius. And if the defense of orthodoxy undertaken by Boethius is understood to have been motivated by the desire "if possible, to reconcile faith and reason," there appears to have been a certain kind of consistency also between all the opuscula and the *Consolation of Philosophy.* In a positive way, the providence celebrated in that masterpiece of prison literature can be read as a generalized version of the concept of the divine economy presented in Boethius's extended paraphrase on the Credo, *On the Catholic Faith;* and negatively, the reliance on reason in the *Consolation* can be read as the catholic via media over against the extreme positions taken by heresy, for it was characteristic both of true doctrine and of rational moral philosophy to occupy a middle place between extremes.

To justify his consideration of reason as part of his defense of the orthodox dogma of the Trinity, Boethius expressed the hope that he was bringing to fruition "the seeds of reason from the writings of blessed Augustine." In this respect, too, he was typical as well as influential, for during his time Latin theology was working out the reinterpreted Augustinism that was, and to a considerable degree still is, the orthodox consensus of Western Christianity about the catholic tradition. Gregory spoke for that consensus when he called his own writings "chaff" compared with the "wheat" in those of Augustine; his biographer has suggested that "perhaps there has never been an author who owed more to the writings of another." The great prestige of the works of Boethius and Gregory served only to enhance still further the unique eminence of Augustinism as the official way of stating Christian doctrine in the West. It is perhaps too much to say of Gregory that "almost everything in him has its roots in Augustine, and yet almost nothing is genuinely Augustinian"; but to understand Gregory as a theologian and to relate the seventh, eighth, and ninth century to him it is necessary to see his formulations of doctrine as Augustinian traditionalism. When, a generation after his death, he was celebrated by Ildefonso as wiser than Augustine, more eloquent than Cyprian, and more pious than Antony, this too had the effect of leading medieval theology through Gregory to Augustine—or, at any rate, to the Augustinism which, thanks to the Synod of Orange and Gregory, had spared Augustine the fate of Origen.

Ildef.*Vir.ill.*1 (*PL* 96:198)

A convenient and authoritative compendium of the catholic consensus in the West seems to have come into existence at about this time: the so-called Athanasian Creed, for which the first unquestionable testimony comes from Caesarius of Arles. The theology of the Athanasian Creed has been called "codified and condensed Augustinianism . . . traditional, almost scholasticized Augustinianism." Here the trinitarian argumentation of Augustine was given creedal form. The affirmation of the Athanasian Creed that "the Father is omnipotent, the Son is omnipotent, and the Holy Spirit is omnipotent; yet there are not three omnipotents, but one omnipotent" was taken almost verbatim from Augustine's *On the Trinity*, where such statements had occurred more than once. In its christological paragraphs, the Athanasian Creed was directed chiefly against the Nestorian version of the theology of the indwelling Logos and against the Nestorian criticism of the doctrine of the hypostatic union. The declaration near the end of the creed that all men would "have to give account for their own works" could perhaps be interpreted as Semi-Pelagian polemic against Augustine, but there were many similar formulations in Augustine himself. On the other hand, "the markedly Augustinian tone of its theology generally is no obstacle to its having been composed in a Semi-Pelagian environment, for however much the Semi-Pelagians of south Gaul detested Augustine's teaching about grace and predestination, they yielded to none in their admiration for his Trinitarian and Christological doctrines"; and it was these latter doctrines, rather than the points at issue between Augustine and the Semi-Pelagians, that formed the core of the Athanasian Creed, which, despite its official name, could more aptly have been called "the Augustinian Creed."

Kelly (1964) 80–81

*Symb.Ath.*13–14 (Schaff 2:67)

Aug.*Trin.*5.8.9; 8.1.2 (*CCSL* 50:215; 269)

*Symb.Ath.*34–36 (Schaff 2:69)

*Symb.Ath.*42 (Schaff 2:69)

Kelly (1964) 119

Although the Athanasian Creed opened and closed with

an affirmation of the authority of "the catholic faith," it did not refer, even implicitly, to the form in which that authority was clothed and through which it was exerted in Western Christendom, namely, the primacy of the pope of Rome. The origins and growth of the papacy as an institutional structure do not properly belong to the history of doctrine; neither does the tangled account of the relations of the pope to other rulers, temporal and spiritual. Church history and the history of canon law have the task of telling all of that story. But it was characteristic of the papacy, as it had already been much earlier of the episcopacy, that it was not only a practical system of ecclesiastical governance subject to adjustment and compromise, but also a doctrine that was to be believed, taught, and confessed by the church on the basis of the word of God. Only in this sense is the papacy of direct interest to us here. Although earlier pontiffs, notably Leo I, had set forth much of the content of the doctrine of papal primacy and authority, there is probably no exaggeration in the conventional view, which sees the teaching and practice of Gregory I as the significant turning point for the papacy, not only jurisdictionally but also theologically. In the course of exercising his office he established the doctrinal foundation for his administrative decisions, and in one of his letters he summarized the doctrine:

"To all who know the Gospel it is obvious that by the voice of the Lord the care of the entire church was committed to the holy apostle and prince of all the apostles, Peter. . . . Behold, he received the keys of the kingdom of heaven, the power to bind and loose was given to him, and the care and principality of the entire church was committed to him. . . . Am I defending my own cause in this matter? Am I vindicating some special injury of my own? Is it not rather the cause of Almighty God, the cause of the universal church? . . . And we certainly know that many priests of the church of Constantinople have fallen into the whirlpool of heresy and have become not only heretics but heresiarchs. . . . Certainly, in honor of Peter, the prince of the apostles, [the title 'universal'] was offered to the Roman pontiff by the venerable Council of Chalcedon." The proof text for the doctrine of the primacy of Peter among the apostles, and therefore for the doctrine of the primacy of the pope

Gr.M.Ep.5.37 (MGH
1:321–22)

See p. 159 above

Gr.M.*Ep*.7.37 (*MGH*
1:485–86)

Gr.M.*Mor*.26.26.45 (*PL*
76:376)

Tert.*Pudic*.13.20 (*CCSL*
2:1306); Hipp.*Antichr*.59
(*GCS* 1–II:39); Cypr.*Ep*.30.2
(*CSEL* 3:550)
Gr.M.*Mor*.17.26.37 (*PL*
76:28)

in the one, holy, catholic, and apostolic church, was the
saying of Jesus to Peter in Matthew 16:18: "And I tell
you, you are Peter [Πέτρος], and on this rock [πέτρα]
I will build my church." The question of the proper
meaning of these words and of their applicability to the
relation between Rome and other churches had been a
matter of confusion and controversy at the time of
Cyprian, but Gregory had no hesitation in quoting them
here, together with John 21:17 and Luke 22:31, as a
proof text. He quoted the same catena of passages from
the Gospels elsewhere to prove that the "holy church
has been established in the solidity of the prince of the
apostles, whose firmness of mind has been carried over
to his name." The commission of Christ meant that "by
the authority of God, Peter holds principality in the
church." Using the metaphor of the church as a ship,
which went back at least to Tertullian, Hippolytus, and
Cyprian, Gregory saw the bark of Peter mentioned in
Luke 5:3 as "the church, which has been committed
to Peter."

Such statements as these were not intended primarily
to exalt the place of Peter among the twelve apostles
of the first century, but to affirm the place of the bishop
of Rome among the bishops of the sixth century. Peter
had been the first bishop of Rome, and the pope was
his successor. To be sure, Peter had also been in Alexandria and in Antioch, and Gregory sometimes put forth
the idea that these two patriarchs shared with him the
primacy given to Peter: Rome was the see where Peter
had died, Alexandria the see to which he had sent Mark,
and Antioch the see which he himself had occupied
for seven years. There was one see of Peter in three

Gr.M.*Ep*.7.37 (*MGH* 1:485)

places. But this touch of whimsy about the apostle did
not have any far-reaching implications for Gregory's
concrete doctrine of primacy in the church. Everybody
knew that the see of Peter was Rome. When the legates
at Chalcedon in 451 responded to the reading of Leo's
Tome with the exclamation, "Peter has spoken through

CChalc. (*ACO* 2–I–2:81)

the mouth of Leo!" they were simply giving voice to this
general assumption. For the early church, primacy had

Iren.*Haer*.3.12.5 (Harvey
2:58)

belonged in a special way to Jerusalem, the mother city
of all believers. But it had moved from the capital city of
the old Israel to the capital city of the world, which
became the capital city of the new Israel. The story of

the Book of Acts began with the return of the apostles,
Peter being the first listed, to Jerusalem; but it closed with
the simple and portentous sentence: "And so we came
to Rome." The "we" in that sentence were presumably
Paul and Luke, and no mention was made of Peter. But
Rome was where both Peter and Paul had been
martyred and were buried, and this had given the church
of Rome a unique eminence as early as the time of Tertullian. Citing the events of 451, Gregory declared that
"the prelates of this apostolic see, which by the providence
of God I serve, had the honor offered to them of being
called 'universal' by the venerable Council of Chalcedon."
This title "universal [οἰκουμενικός]" could not therefore
be claimed by Constantinople, even though it was the new
Rome. The church of Rome was the mother of other
churches in the Latin West, which were subject to it.

The churches of the Greek East, too, owed a special
allegiance to Rome. As far as the church of Constantinople was concerned, "who would doubt that it has been
made subject to the apostolic see," that is, of course, to
Rome? By hailing the authority of Leo, the fathers at
Chalcedon gave witness to the orthodoxy of Rome. One
see after another had capitulated in this or that controversy with heresy. Constantinople had given rise to
several heretics during the fourth and fifth centuries,
notably Nestorius and Macedonius, and the other sees
had also been known to stray from the true faith occasionally. But Rome had a special position. The bishop of
Rome had the right by his own authority to annul the
acts of a synod. In fact, when there was talk of a council
to settle controversies, Gregory asserted the principle
that "without the authority and the consent of the apostolic see, none of the matters transacted [by a council]
have any binding force." Although he was willing to
draw a parallel between the four Gospels and the four
ecumenical councils, he was already beginning to formulate a doctrine of the dogmatic authority of Rome, based
on the primacy of Peter and corroborated by a record
and reputation for doctrinal orthodoxy. This doctrine,
however, was not to achieve complete definition as a
dogma until many centuries later. Although he held
tenaciously to the authority of tradition and the teachings
of the fathers, the see of Rome had a special assignment
to defend that tradition. As another bishop wrote to

Acts 1:12

Acts 28:14

Tert.*Praescrip*.36 (*CCSL*
1:216–17)

Gr.M.*Ep*.5.44 (*MGH* 1:341)

Gr.M.*Ep*.9.26 (*MGH* 2:59)

Gr.M.*Ep*.9.26 (*MGH* 2:60)

Gr.M.*Ep*.5.44 (*MGH*
1:338–43)

Gr.M.*Ep*.9.156 (*MGH* 2:158)
See p. 335 above

Gregory, "I know what a grave matter it is to transgress the limits that have been set for us by the fathers. . . . Therefore I take my refuge in the bosom and the lap of your most sacred Roman church." The particular issue involved here was episcopal ambition rather than dogma, but even matters of church administration had to be adjudicated on the basis of doctrine, namely, on the basis of the doctrine of the primacy of the pope.

In the development of several other doctrines as well, "Gregory is throughout prefigurative of the Middle Ages." As a loyal Augustinian, he repeated many of his master's ideas, together with the general patristic heritage which he had received. For example, he took over from earlier theology the image of the devil as the Leviathan of Job 41:1, whom Christ lured into swallowing him by baiting the hook of his divinity with his humanity. When the hook of Christ's divinity sank in, the devil could not hold the bait but expelled Christ the man, together with the human race, and thus redemption was achieved. But some of the elements in the patristic heritage were reworked in Gregory's thought. Two such were the doctrine of purgatory and the doctrine of the sacrifice of the Mass. Neither of these doctrines may be said to be uniquely Western, for there are equivalents to both in the Greek theologians; but Latin theology, as it was systematized by Gregory, gave them definitive form. The origins of the idea of purgatory may be traced to the widespread hope, expressed by Origen, that the power of the saving will of God extended beyond the limits of this earthly life, granting men a further opportunity for purification and eventual salvation even after death. Augustine, while opposing himself to the speculations of Origen about the universal salvation of all men and of the devil, nevertheless believed that there were "temporary punishments after death" and that it was appropriate to pray that some of the dead be granted remission of sins. These suggestions about purgatorial fire, made tentatively and in passing, became "something that has to be believed [credendus]" in Gregory. Again, "it has to be believed [credendum est]" that the prayers of the faithful availed in obtaining release from purgatorial fire for those who had sinned "not out of malice but out of the error of ignorance." Such men were "somewhat deficient in perfect righteousness," but could be aided

Gr.M.*Ep*.3.66 (*MGH* 1:228–29)

H.Taylor (1938) 1:102

Rufin.*Symb*.14 (*CCSL* 20:151–52)

Gr.M.*Mor*.33.7.14 (*PL* 76:680–81)

See pp. 151–52 above

Aug.*Civ*.21.23 (*CCSL* 48:787–89)

Aug.*Civ*.21.13 (*CCSL* 48:779)

Aug.*Civ*.21.24 (*CCSL* 48:789)

Gr.M.*Dial*.4.39 (*PL* 77:396)

Gr.M.*Dial*.4.40 (*PL* 77:397)
Gr.M.*Dial*.4.25 (*PL* 77:357)

by the intercession of the departed saints and of the faithful here on earth.

A special kind of intercession was the sacrifice of the Mass. "If guilty deeds are not beyond absolution even after death, the sacred offering of the saving Victim consistently aids souls even after death, so that the very souls of the departed seem sometimes to yearn for this." The liturgy and the theology of the church had long believed and taught that the Eucharist was a sacrifice of the body and blood of Christ. But in the course of the disquisition on purgatory just quoted, Gregory stated the sacrificial interpretation of the Eucharist with new definiteness and detail: "We ought to immolate to God . . . the daily sacrifices of our tears, the daily offerings of His flesh and blood. . . . For who among the faithful can have any doubt that at the very hour of the immolation, in response to the voice of the priest, the heavens are opened and the choirs of angels are present in this mystery of Jesus Christ?" On the nature of the eucharistic presence, by contrast, Gregory was far less specific, repeating Augustinian formulas that left it quite vague. He spoke of "His body and blood in our sacrament" in language that would seem to teach the real presence, but made very little more of it. Only in the ninth century did the doctrine of the real presence become a matter of controversy; meanwhile, however, thanks at least partly to Gregory, the doctrine of the sacrifice of the Mass was established teaching. When the former doctrine did come up for discussion, therefore, the latter was the presupposition of the discussion, and theologians debated about the presence of that body and blood which, by common consent, was offered sacrificially in the celebration of the sacrament.

Between the theology of the Greek fathers and its reinterpretation by Augustine, on the one hand, and the Augustinian traditionalism that led to scholasticism, on the other hand, stood the doctrinal consolidation that took place in the Latin church during the sixth century. For a thousand years after Gregory, the fundamental assumption underlying almost all the doctrinal treatises and biblical commentaries of Western theologians was the teaching authority of the bishop of Rome. The limits of that authority were often a matter of debate, and specific decisions a matter of challenge, but everyone was obliged

Gr.M.Dial.4.55 (PL 77:416–17)

See pp. 146–47, 168–69 above

Gr.M.Dial.4.58 (PL 77:425–28)

See pp. 304–6 above

Gr.M.Ev.14.1 (PL 76:1127)

to avow his loyalty to the pope. Doctrinal orthodoxy throughout Christendom meant wholehearted acceptance of the dogmas whose development has been traced in this book, but in the catholic West it came to mean more —or perhaps less: obedience to the holy see. Even the decisions of ecumenical councils had to be ratified by Rome, and eventually the codification of the dogmas from the beginning was attributed to Roman authority. Prosper of Aquitaine, addressing himself to the conflicts over the doctrine of grace after Augustine, stated the consensus of orthodox catholicism in the Latin church: "For a profession of faith in the doctrine of the grace of God . . . we consider quite sufficient what the writings of the apostolic see . . . have taught us. Anything that is contrary to these propositions we cannot regard in any way as consistent with the catholic faith." Medieval thought accepted this normative definition; it reexamined the Augustinian formulation of apostolic teaching; it reopened the Boethian consideration of Aristotelian philosophy; and in all these ways it reinterpreted the Gregorian consensus on orthodox catholic doctrine. Volume 3 of *The Christian Tradition, The Growth of Medieval Theology,* will describe these developments.

Prosp.*Auct.*10 (*PL* 51:212)

Selected
Secondary Works

GENERAL

Adam, Alfred. *Lehrbuch der Dogmengeschichte.* Gütersloh, 1965–. The first volume deals with the early church, the second with the Middle Ages and the Reformation. The third volume will treat the period since the Reformation.

Altaner, Berthold. *Kleine patristische Schriften.* Edited by Günther Glockmann. Berlin, 1967. Especially important for the relation of Augustine to the Greek tradition.

Arndt, William F., and Gingrich, F. Wilbur. *A Greek-English Lexicon of the New Testament and Other Early Christian Literature.* Chicago, 1957. Based on Walter Bauer's *Wörterbuch.*

Beck, Hans-Georg. *Kirche und theologische Literatur im byzantinischen Reich.* Munich, 1959.

Blaise, Albert. *Dictionnaire latin-français des auteurs chrétiens.* Strasbourg, 1954.

Bolotov, Vasilij Vasilievič. *Istorija cerkvi v period vselenskich soborov: Istorija bogoslovskoj mysli* [History of the church in the period of the ecumenical councils: History of theological thought]. Petrograd, 1918. This is the fourth and last volume of Bolotov's *Lekcii po istorii drevnej cerkvi* [Lectures on the history of the ancient church], edited after Bolotov's death by A. Brilliantov. It covers not only the doctrinal development narrated here in our first volume, but also some of that to be described in our second volume.

Bornkamm, Heinrich. *Luther und das Alte Testament.* Tübingen, 1948.

Calhoun, Robert L. "Lectures on the History of Christian Doctrine." Mimeographed. New Haven, 1947.

Campenhausen, Hans von. *The Fathers of the Greek Church.* Translated by Stanley Godman. New York, 1959.

———. *Men Who Shaped the Western Church.* Translated by Manfred Hoffmann. New York, 1964. Perceptive essays on the character, life, and thought of the principal church fathers, East and West.

Carrington, Philip. *The Early Christian Church.* 2 vols. Cambridge, 1957.

Cochrane, Charles Norris. *Christianity and Classical Culture: A Study of Thought and Action from Augustus to Augustine.* London and New York, 1944. Although confined largely to Latin writers, both classical and Christian, Cochrane's interpretation is pertinent to every chapter of this book.

Daniélou, Jean. *The Development of Christian Doctrine before the Council of Nicaea.* Translated by John A. Baker. London, 1964–. Because of its concentration on the relation of Christian thought to Judaism (vol. 1) and to Hellenistic culture (vol. 2), Daniélou's work is especially important for the first two chapters of this book.

Elert, Werner. *Der Ausgang der altkirchlichen Christologie: Eine Untersuchung über Theodor van Pharan und seine Zeit als Einführung in die alte Dogmengeschichte.* Edited by Wilhelm Maurer and Elisabeth Bergsträsser. Berlin, 1957. This posthumously published volume includes Elert's provocative lecture, "Die Kirche und ihre Dogmengeschichte."

Florovskij, Georgij Vasilievič. *Vostočnye otci IV-go vjeka* [The Eastern fathers of the fourth century]. Paris, 1931.

―――――. *Vizantijskie otci V-VIII* [The Byzantine fathers of the fifth to the eighth (centuries)]. Paris, 1933. These two works are basic to our interpretation of the trinitarian and christological dogmas.

Flückiger, Felix. *Der Ursprung des christlichen Dogmas: Eine Auseinandersetzung mit Albert Schweitzer und Martin Werner.* Zurich, 1955.

Funk, Robert W. *A Greek Grammar of the New Testament and Other Early Christian Literature.* Chicago, 1961. Based on the German work of Blass-Debrunner.

Gibbon, Edward. *The History of the Decline and Fall of the Roman Empire.* Edited by J. B. Bury. 7 vols. London, 1896–1900. Filled with insight, prejudice, and learning, especially in its treatment of Christianity and of "the triumph of barbarism and religion."

Grabmann, Martin. *Die Geschichte der scholastischen Methode nach gedruckten und ungedruckten Quellen.* 2 vols. 1909–11. Reprint. Graz, 1957.

Hägglund, Bengt. *History of Theology.* Translated by G. Lund. Saint Louis, 1968.

Hahn, August, ed. *Bibliothek der Symbole und Glaubensregeln der Alten Kirche.* 3d ed., rev. 1897. Reprint. Hildesheim, 1962.

Harnack, Adolf von. [*Grundriss der*] *Dogmengeschichte.* 4th ed., rev. Tübingen, 1905. The first edition was translated into English as *Outlines of the History of Dogma* by Edwin Knox Mitchell in 1893. Reprinted with an introduction by Philip Rieff. Boston, 1957.

―――――. *Lehrbuch der Dogmengeschichte.* 3 vols. 5th ed. Tübingen, 1931–32. English translation of the third German edition by Neil Buchanan, *History of Dogma.* 7 vols. Reprint. New York, 1961. Superseded but never surpassed, Harnack's work remains, after more than eighty years, the one interpretation of early Christian doctrine with which every other scholar in the field must contend.

Hauck, Albert, ed. *Realencyklopädie für protestantische Theologie und Kirche.* 22 vols. 3d rev. ed. Leipzig, 1896–1908. Together with its French Roman Catholic counterpart (see under "Vacant" below), indispensable as a source of information and bibliography on most of the men and ideas discussed here.

Hefele, Karl Joseph. *Histoire des conciles d'après les documents originaux.* Translated and revised by Henri Leclercq. 11 vols. Paris, 1907–52.

Heick, Otto W. *A History of Christian Thought.* 2 vols. Philadelphia, 1965–66.

Holl, Karl. *Gesammelte Aufsätze zur Kirchengeschichte.* 3 vols. Tübingen, 1928. The first volume, on Luther, is the most celebrated, but Holl was also an eminent patristic scholar, as many of the articles in the second and third volumes demonstrate.

Kelly, John N. D. *Early Christian Doctrines.* New York, 1958. The most careful and readable account in English of this period.

Ladner, Gerhart B. *The Idea of Reform: Its Impact on Christian Thought and Action in the Age of the Fathers.* Cambridge, Mass., 1959. A work of enormous erudition and great range.

Lampe, Geoffrey William Hugo. *A Patristic Greek Lexicon.* Oxford, 1961–69.

Lohse, Bernhard. *Epochen der Dogmengeschichte.* Stuttgart, 1963. An English translation, entitled *A Short History of Christian Doctrine,* was prepared by F. Ernest Stoeffler (Philadelphia, 1966).

Loofs, Friedrich. *Leitfaden zum Studium der Dogmengeschichte.* Edited by Kurt Aland. Tübingen, 1959. Dependent upon Harnack for its general conception, but strikingly original in judgments and hypotheses.

McGiffert, Arthur Cushman. *A History of Christian Thought.* 2 vols. Reprint. New York, 1947.

Prestige, George Leonard. *Fathers and Heretics: Six Studies in Dogmatic Faith with Prologue and Epilogue.* London, 1948. Deceptively simple, profound analyses of the relation between orthodoxy and heresy in the early church.

Quasten, Johannes. *Patrology.* Westminster, Md., 1951–. Judicious quotations and complete bibliographies.

Schwartz, Eduard. *Gesammelte Schriften.* 5 vols. Berlin, 1938–63. While unsympathetic to any history of Christian doctrine divorced from a study of its total context, Schwartz was able, by strict philological scholarship, to illumine every aspect of doctrinal history he touched.

Seeberg, Reinhold. *Lehrbuch der Dogmengeschichte.* 4th rev. ed. 4 vols. Basel, 1953–54. The counterpole to Harnack's history, simultaneously more cautious and less interesting, but never negligible.

Taylor, Henry Osborn. *The Mediaeval Mind: A History of the Development of Thought and Emotion in the Middle Ages.* 4th ed. 2 vols. London, 1938.

Tillich, Paul. *A History of Christian Thought.* Edited by Carl E. Braaten. New York, 1968. While it often tells more about Tillich than about the history of doctrine, this account always calls attention to significant issues.

Tixeront, Joseph. *Histoire des dogmes dans l'antiquité chrétienne.* 3 vols. 11th ed., rev. Paris, 1930. An English translation of an earlier edition was published: *History of Dogmas.* 3 vols. St. Louis, 1910–16.

Troeltsch, Ernst. *The Social Teaching of the Christian Churches.* 2 vols. Introduction by H. Richard Niebuhr. Translated by Olive Wyon. New York, 1960. The most articulate statement of the thesis that Christian doctrine cannot be interpreted—as it has been interpreted in our work—in isolation from its social and cultural setting.

Urbina, Ignazio Ortiz de. *Patrologia syriaca.* Rome, 1958. The standard manual for the study of the Syriac fathers, who are anything but "standard" sources for the history of early Christian doctrine.

Vacant, Jean-Michel-Alfred, et al., eds. *Dictionnaire de Théologie Catholique.* 15 vols. Paris, 1903–50. No portion of our account has remained unaffected by this massive compendium of scholarly synthesis.

Werner, Martin. *Die Entstehung des christlichen Dogmas problemgeschichtlich dargestellt.* Bern, 1941. The one attempt—misguided in our judgment—to get beyond Harnack's definition of the problem.

Whitehead, Alfred North. *Process and Reality.* Reprint. New York, 1960.

Wiles, Maurice. *The Making of Christian Doctrine: A Study in the Principles of Early Doctrinal Development.* Cambridge, 1967. A brief but solid discussion of the problem of development of doctrine, with special attention to the relation between Scripture and worship as factors in shaping church doctrine.

Wolfson, Harry A. *The Philosophy of the Church Fathers.* Cambridge, Mass., 1956–.

SOME DEFINITIONS

Atkins, Anselm. "Religious Assertions and Doctrinal Development." *Theological Studies* 27 (1966): 523–52.

Baur, Ferdinand Christian. *Introduction to Lectures on the History of Christian Dogma. Ferdinand Christian Baur on the Writing of Church History.* Edited and translated by Peter C. Hodgson. New York, 1968. Before Harnack, Baur was probably the most exciting historian of doctrine in the nineteenth century.

Chadwick, Owen. *From Bossuet to Newman: The Idea of Doctrinal Development.* Cambridge, 1957. A careful examination of the ironic shift between Roman Catholicism and Protestantism on the idea of development of doctrine.

Dilthey, Wilhelm. *Briefwechsel zwischen Wilhelm Dilthey und dem Grafen Paul Yorck von Wartenburg 1877–1897.* Halle, 1923.

Gilson, Étienne. "Doctrinal History and Its Interpretation." *Speculum* 24 (1949): 483–92.

―――. "Historical Research and the Future of Scholasticism." In *A Gilson Reader.* Edited by Anton C. Pegis, pp. 156–67. Garden City, N. Y., 1957.

Glick, G. Wayne. *The Reality of Christianity: A Study of A. von Harnack as Historian and Theologian.* New York, 1967. The first full-length study in English of Harnack's historical and theological thought.

Hodgson, Peter C. *The Formation of Historical Theology: A Study of Ferdinand Christian Baur.* New York, 1966.

Krüger, Gustav. *Was heisst und zu welchem Ende studiert man Dogmengeschichte?* Freiburg i. Br., 1895.

Lovejoy, Arthur O. *The Great Chain of Being: A Study of the History of an Idea.* Cambridge, Mass., 1936. In addition to its substantive discussion of many developments germane to our study the work contains Lovejoy's introductory chapter on "The Study of the History of Ideas."

―――. "The Historiography of Ideas." In *Essays in the History of Ideas,* pp. 1–13. Reprint. New York, 1955.

McKeon, Richard P. "Truth and the History of Ideas." In *Thought, Action, and Passion,* pp. 54–88. Chicago, 1954.

Newman, John Henry. *An Essay on the Development of Christian Doctrine.* Rev. ed. London, 1878. First published in 1845, Newman's *Essay on Development* moved the question of development of doctrine to the center of theological debate and historical research.

Pauck, Wilhelm. *Harnack and Troeltsch: Two Historical Theologians.* New York, 1968. Vignettes of Harnack and Troeltsch, with an essay on each by the other.

Pelikan, Jaroslav. *Development of Christian Doctrine: Some Historical Prolegomena.* New Haven, 1969.

―――. *Historical Theology: Continuity and Change in Christian Doctrine.* New York, 1971. These two monographs provide historical background and state methodological assumptions of the present work.

Rahner, Karl. "The Development of Dogma." In *Theological Investigations,* 1:39–77. Baltimore and London, 1961–.

———. "Considerations on the Development of Dogma." In *Theological Investigations,* 4:3–35. Rahner's is perhaps the most important of present-day theological interpretations of the issue.

Ritschl, Albrecht. "Über die Methode der ältern Dogmengeschichte." In *Gesammelte Aufsätze,* 1:147–69. Frankfurt, 1893–96.

Schleiermacher, Friedrich. *Der christliche Glaube, nach den Grundsätzen der evangelischen Kirche im Zusammenhang dargestellt.* Edited by Martin Redeker. 2 vols. Berlin, 1960. Defining systematic theology as a historical discipline, Schleiermacher shaped much of the method of the history of doctrine as well.

Smith, Page. *The Historian and History.* New York, 1964.

Wolf, Ernst. "Kerygma und Dogma? Prolegomena zum Problem und zur Problematik der Dogmengeschichte." In *Antwort: Karl Barth zum siebzigsten Geburtstag,* pp. 780–807. Zurich, 1956. A recent attempt at a redefinition of the field.

1. PRAEPARATIO EVANGELICA

Alföldi, Andrew. *The Conversion of Constantine and Pagan Rome.* Oxford, 1948.

Banner, W. A. "Origen and the Tradition of Natural Law Concepts." *Dumbarton Oaks Papers* 8(1954): 51–92.

Bigg, Charles. *The Christian Platonists of Alexandria.* Oxford, 1886. A classic statement of the thesis that the theology of Clement and Origen was determined by their philosophical presuppositions.

Blumenkranz, Bernhard. *Die Judenpredigt Augustins: Ein Beitrag zur Geschichte der jüdisch-christlichen Beziehungen in den ersten Jahrhunderten.* Basel, 1946.

Bousset,Wilhelm. *Jüdisch-christlicher Schulbetrieb in Alexandrien und Rom.* Göttingen, 1915.

Callahan, John F. *Four Views of Time in Ancient Philosophy.* Cambridge, Mass., 1948.

Carter, Jesse Benedict. *The Religion of Numa, and Other Essays on the Religion of Ancient Rome.* London, 1906.

Chadwick, Henry, ed. Origen. *Contra Celsum.* Cambridge, 1953. Both for its rendering and for its annotation, a model translation.

———. *Early Christian Thought and the Classical Tradition: Studies in Justin, Clement, and Origen.* New York, 1966.

Cherniss, Harold Fredrik. *The Platonism of Gregory of Nyssa.* Berkeley and Los Angeles, 1930.

Courtonne, Yves. *Saint Basile et l'hellénisme: Étude sur la rencontre de la pensée chrétienne avec la sagesse antique dans l'Hexaeméron de`Basile le Grand.* Paris, 1934. A fundamental and pioneering monograph.

Daniélou, Jean. *Platonisme et théologie mystique: Essai sur la doctrine spirituelle de saint Grégoire de Nysse.* 2d ed. Paris, 1954. An attempt to disengage the mysticism of Gregory of Nyssa from its philosophical framework.

———. *Origen.* Translated by Walter Mitchell. New York, 1955. The standard apologia for Origen as a churchman and, in intention if not in achievement, an orthodox theologian.

———. *From Shadows to Reality: Studies in the Biblical Typology of the Fathers.* Translated by Wulstan Hibberd. Westminster, Md., 1960.

Diestel, Ludwig. *Geschichte des Alten Testaments in der christlichen Kirche.* Jena, 1869. No one since Diestel has attempted to pull together this important material.

Dix, Gregory. *Jew and Greek.* London, 1953.

Fortin, Ernest L. *Christianisme et culture philosophique au cinquième siècle: La querelle de l'âme humaine en Occident.* Paris, 1959. "God and the soul, the soul and God" between Christianity and classicism.

Geffcken, Johannes. *Zwei griechische Apologeten.* Leipzig, 1907.

Glawe, Walther Karl Erich. *Die Hellenisierung des Christentums in der Geschichte der Theologie von Luther bis auf die Gegenwart.* Berlin, 1912.

Goodenough, Erwin R. *The Theology of Justin Martyr.* Jena, 1923. Still the best monograph on the subject.

Grant, Robert M. *The Letter and the Spirit.* New York, 1957. Christian allegorism in its cultural setting.

Grillmeier, Aloys. "Hellenisierung-Judaisierung des Christentums als Deuteprinzipien der Geschichte des kirchlichen Dogmas." *Scholastik* 33 (1958): 321–55; 528–58.

Hanson, Richard Patrick Crosland. *Origen's Doctrine of Tradition.* London, 1954. Distinguishes between Origen and Clement of Alexandria, but raises the question of Origen's relation to Gnosticism.

Harnack, Adolf von. *Judentum und Judenchristentum in Justins Dialog mit Trypho.* Leipzig, 1913.

———. "Sokrates und die alte Kirche." In *Reden und Aufsätze,* 1:27–48. Giessen, 1906.

———. *The Mission and Expansion of Christianity in the First Three Centuries.* Reprinted with an introduction by Jaroslav Pelikan. Translated by James Moffatt. New York, 1962.

Harris, J. Rendel. *Testimonies.* 2 vols. Cambridge, 1916–20.

Hatch, Edwin. *The Influence of Greek Ideas on Christianity.* Reprinted with an introduction by Frederick C. Grant. New York, 1957.

Hering, Jean. *Étude sur la doctrine de la chute et de la préexistence des âmes chez Clément d'Alexandrie.* Paris, 1923.

Highet, Gilbert. *The Classical Tradition: Greek and Roman Influences on Western Literature.* Reprint. New York, 1957.

Jaeger, Werner. *Paideia: The Ideals of Greek Culture.* Translated by Gilbert Highet. 3 vols. New York, 1945.

———. *Early Christianity and Greek Paideia.* Cambridge, Mass., 1961. This small volume, published just a week before the author's death, relates the themes of his three-volume work to his lifelong interest in the Greek church fathers, especially Gregory of Nyssa.

Koch, Hal. *Pronoia und Paideusis.* Berlin, 1932. Christian and classical motifs in the thought of Origen.

Labriolle, Pierre de. *La réaction païenne: Étude sur la polémique antichrétienne du Ier au VIe siècle.* Paris, 1934. The pagan opponents of the Christian apologists and their critiques.

Latourette, Kenneth Scott. *A History of the Expansion of Christianity.* Vol. 1. *The First Five Centuries.* New York, 1937.

Lightfoot, Joseph Barber. "Eusebius of Caesarea." In *A Dictionary of Christian Biography, Literature, Sects and Doctrines,* 2:308–48. London, 1880.

Lortz, Joseph. *Tertullian als Apologet.* 2 vols. Münster, 1927–28.

Marrou, Henri-Irénée, ed. *Clément d'Alexandrie. Le Pédagogue, Livre I.* Sources chrétiennes, no. 70. Paris, 1960. Introduction and notes make this the most helpful guide to Clement's thought.

Meijering, Eginhard Peter. *Orthodoxy and Platonism in Athanasius: Synthesis or Antithesis?* Leiden, 1968.

Molland, Einar. *Clement of Alexandria on the Origin of Greek Philosophy.* Oslo, 1936.

Mondésert, Claude. *Clément d'Alexandrie: Introduction à l'étude de sa pensée religieuse à partir de l'Écriture.* Paris, 1944.

Momigliano, Arnaldo, ed. *The Conflict between Paganism and Christianity in the Fourth Century.* Oxford, 1963. Especially pertinent are the essays by the editor on "Pagan and Christian Historiography in the Fourth Century" (pp. 79–99) and by Pierre Courcelle on "Anti-Christian Arguments and Christian Platonism: from Arnobius to St. Ambrose" (pp. 151–92).

Niebuhr, H. Richard. *Christ and Culture.* New York, 1951. Discussions of Tertullian, Clement of Alexandria, and Augustine, as well as of later theologians.

Norden, Eduard. *Die antike Kunstprosa, vom 6. Jahrhundert vor Christo bis in die Zeit der Renaissance.* 2 vols. Leipzig, 1898.

———. *Die Geburt des Kindes: Geschichte einer religiösen Idee.* Leipzig, 1924. Vergil's "messianic Eclogue" and the Christmas story in history.

Osborn, Eric Francis. *The Philosophy of Clement of Alexandria.* Cambridge, 1957.

Pelikan, Jaroslav. *The Shape of Death: Life, Death, and Immortality in the Early Fathers.* New York, 1961. Chapters on Tatian, Clement of Alexandria, Cyprian, Origen, and Irenaeus.

Peterson, Erik. *Die Kirche aus Juden und Heiden.* Salzburg, 1933.

Pines, Salomon. *The Jewish Christians of the Early Centuries of Christianity according to a New Source.* Jerusalem, 1966.

Prümm, K. "Das Prophetenamt der Sibyllen in kirchlicher Literatur mit besonderer Rücksicht auf die Deutung der vierten Ekloge Virgils." *Scholastik* 4 (1929): 54–77; 221–46; 498–533.

Rand, Edward Kennard. *Founders of the Middle Ages.* Cambridge, Mass., 1929.

Rohde, Erwin. *Psyche: The Cult of Souls and Belief in Immortality among the Greeks.* Translated by W. B. Hillis. New York, 1925.

Ruether, Rosemary Radford. *Gregory of Nazianzus: Rhetor and Philosopher.* Oxford, 1969. Contains analysis of Gregory's oratorical works and relates his theology to his oratory.

Schoeps, Hans Joachim. *Theologie und Geschichte des Judenchristentums.* Tübingen, 1949.

———. *The Jewish-Christian Argument: A History of Theologies in Conflict.* Translated by David E. Green. New York, 1963.

Simon, Marcel. *Verus Israel: Étude sur les relations entre Chrétiens et Juifs dans l'Empire romain (135–425).* Paris, 1948.

Smith, Joseph P., ed. St. Irenaeus. *Proof of the Apostolic Preaching.* Ancient Christian Writers, no. 16. Westminster, Md., 1952.

Stakemeier, Eduard. *Civitas Dei: Die Geschichtstheologie des heiligen Augustinus als Apologie der Kirche.* Paderborn, 1955.

Stauffer, Ethelbert. "Zum Kalifat des Jakobus." *Zeitschrift für Religions- und Geistesgeschichte* 4 (1952): 193–214.

Thieme, Karl Otto. *Kirche und Synagoge: Die ersten nachbiblischen Zeugnisse ihres Gegensatzes im Offenbarungsverständnis.* Olten, 1945. A study of Barnabas and Justin Martyr.

Vasiliev, Alexander A. *History of the Byzantine Empire 324–1453.* 2 vols. Reprint. Madison, Wis., 1958.

Wendland, Paul. *Die hellenistisch-römische Kultur in ihren Beziehungen zu Judentum und Christentum.* Tübingen, 1907.

Williams, Arthur Lukyn. *Adversus Judaeos: A Bird's-Eye View of Christian Apologiae until the Renaissance.* Cambridge, 1935.

2. OUTSIDE THE MAINSTREAM

Aland, Kurt. "Bemerkungen zum Montanismus und zur frühchristlichen Eschatologie." In *Kirchengeschichtliche Entwürfe,* pp. 105–48. Gütersloh, 1960.

Barth, Carola. *Die Interpretation des Neuen Testaments in der valentinianischen Gnosis.* Leipzig, 1911.

Barth, Karl. *The Epistle to the Romans.* Translated by Edwyn C. Hoskyns. London, 1933.

Bartsch, Hans Werner. *Gnostisches Gut und Gemeindetradition bei Ignatius von Antiochien.* Gütersloh, 1940.

Bauer, Walter. *Rechtgläubigkeit und Ketzerei im ältesten Christentum.* 2d ed. Edited by Georg Strecker. Tübingen, 1964. Stresses the doctrinal heterogeneity of early Christianity and therefore the inappropriateness of such concepts as orthodoxy and heresy. Bauer's thesis has shaped an entire generation of scholars since its first appearance in 1934.

Blackman, Edwin Cyril. *Marcion and His Influence.* London, 1948.

Bonwetsch, G. Nathanael. *Geschichte des Montanismus.* Erlangen, 1881.

————, ed. *Texte zur Geschichte des Montanismus.* Bonn, 1914.

Bousset, Wilhelm. *Hauptprobleme der Gnosis.* Göttingen, 1907.

Burkitt, Francis Crawford. *Church and Gnosis.* Cambridge, 1932.

Campenhausen, Hans von. *Die Entstehung der christlichen Bibel.* Tübingen, 1968. The first major attempt in several decades at an account of the rise of the biblical canon.

————. *Ecclesiastical Authority and Spiritual Power in the Church of the First Three Centuries.* Translated by J. A. Baker. Stanford, Calif., 1969. The transition from charisma to office.

Cullmann, Oscar. *The Earliest Christian Confessions.* London, 1949.

Eynde, Damien van den. *Les normes de l'enseignement chrétien dans la littérature patristique des trois premiers siècles.* Paris, 1933.

Festugière, André Marie Jean. *La révélation d'Hermès Trismégiste.* 4 vols. Paris, 1944–54. Essential for an understanding of Gnosticism and syncretism.

Flesseman-Van Leer, Ellen. *Tradition and Scripture in the Early Church.* Assen, 1954.

Gärtner, Bertil. *The Theology of the Gospel of Thomas.* Translated by Eric J. Sharpe. New York, 1961.

Grant, Robert M. *Gnosticism and Early Christianity.* New York, 1959.

————, ed. *Gnosticism: A Source Book of Heretical Writers from the Early Christian Period.* New York, 1961. Taken together, Grant's monograph and his collection of primary sources offer a fine introduction to Gnosticism as a Christian movement.

Hanson, Richard Patrick Crosland. *Allegory and Event: A Study of the Sources and Significance of Origen's Interpretation of Scripture.* London, 1959.

Harnack, Adolf von. *Marcion, das Evangelium vom fremden Gott: Eine Monographie zur Geschichte der Grundlegung der katholischen Kirche.* 2 vols. *Neue Studien zu Marcion.* Reprint. Berlin, 1960. Harnack first wrote an interpretation of Marcion at Dorpat in 1870, but did not publish his monograph until 1920.

Hess, Hamilton. *The Canons of the Council of Sardica, A.D. 343: A Landmark in the Early Development of Canon Law.* Oxford, 1958.

Hilgenfeld, Adolf. *Ketzergeschichte des Urchristentums, urkundlich dargestellt.* Leipzig, 1884. Still a useful source book.

Jonas, Hans. *The Gnostic Religion: The Message of the Alien God and the Beginnings of Christianity.* 2d ed. rev. Boston, 1963. The most successful of modern attempts to systematize and interpret Gnosticism.

Kelly, John N. D. *Early Christian Creeds.* London, 1950. Learned and reliable.

Knox, John. *Marcion and the New Testament.* Chicago, 1942.

————. *Criticism and Faith.* New York, 1952.

Labriolle, Pierre de. *La crise montaniste. Les sources de l'histoire du Montanisme: Textes grecs, latins, syriaques.* Paris, 1913. The most comprehensive treatment of Montanism and of its significance.

Outler, Albert. "The Sense of Tradition in the Ante-Nicene Church." In *The Heritage of Christian Thought: Essays in Honor of Robert Lowry Calhoun,* pp. 8–30. Edited by Robert E. Cushman and Egil Grislis. New York, 1965.

Pelikan, Jaroslav. *The Finality of Jesus Christ in an Age of Universal History: A Dilemma of the Third Century.* London, 1965.

Puech, Henri-Charles. *Le Manichéisme: Son fondateur, sa doctrine.* Paris, 1949.

————, et al. *The Jung Codex: A Newly Recovered Gnostic Papyrus.* London, 1955.

Quispel, Gilles. *De bronnen van Tertullianus' Adversus Marcionem* [The sources of Tertullian's *Against Marcion*]. Leiden, 1943. A bold hypothesis about the composition and revision of our most important source of information concerning Marcion.

————. *Gnosis als Weltreligion.* Zurich, 1951.

Sagnard, François M. M. *La Gnose valentinienne et le témoignage de saint Irénée.* Paris, 1947. Examination of the reliability of Irenaeus as a reporter of Gnostic teaching.

Schepelern, Wilhelm. *Der Montanismus und die phrygischen Kulte: Eine religionsgeschichtliche Untersuchung.* Translated by W. Baur. Tübingen, 1929.

Seeberg, Alfred. *Der Katechismus der Urchristenheit.* Leipzig, 1903.

Weinel, Heinrich. *Die Wirkungen des Geistes und der Geister im nachapostolischen Zeitalter bis auf Irenäus.* Tübingen, 1899.

Widengren, Geo. *Mesopotamian Elements in Manichaeism: Studies in Manichaean, Mandaean, and Syrian-Gnostic Religion.* Uppsala, 1946.

3. THE FAITH OF THE CHURCH CATHOLIC

Adam, Karl. *Der Kirchenbegriff Tertullians.* Paderborn, 1907.

Aleith, Eva. *Paulusverständnis in der Alten Kirche.* Berlin, 1937.

Alès, Adhémar de. *La théologie de Tertullian.* Paris, 1905.

Altendorf, Erich. *Einheit und Heiligkeit der Kirche: Untersuchungen zur Entwicklung des altchristlichen Kirchenbegriffs im Abendland von Tertullian bis zu den antidonatistischen Schriften Augustins.* Berlin, 1932. A study of North African ecclesiology.

Atzberger, Leonhard. *Geschichte der christlichen Eschatologie innerhalb der vornicänischen Zeit.* Freiburg, 1896.

Aulén, Gustaf. *Christus Victor: An Historical Study of the Three Main Types of the Idea of Atonement.* Translated by A. G. Hebert. Reprinted with an introduction by Jaroslav Pelikan. New York, 1969.

Bardy, Gustave. *La théologie de l'église de saint Clément de Rome à saint Irénée.* Paris, 1945. The crucial developments of the second century.

Benkö, Istvan. *Sanctorum Communio: Eine dogmengeschichtliche Untersuchung über das Symbolglied.* Basel, 1951.

Benoit, André. *Le baptême chrétien au second siècle: La théologie des pères.* Paris, 1953.

————. *Saint Irénée. Introduction à l'étude de sa théologie.* Paris, 1960.

Bévenot, Maurice. *Saint Cyprian's "De Unitate," Chapter IV, in the Light of the Manuscripts.* Rome, 1937. Settled, to the satisfaction of most, the relation between the two "primacy texts."

————, ed. St. Cyprian. *The Lapsed. The Unity of the Catholic Church.* Ancient Christian Writers, no. 25. Westminster, Md., 1957.

Boer, S. de. *De anthropologie van Gregorius van Nyssa.* Assen, 1968. Interesting discussion of "de participitie aan de goddelijke natuur [participation in the divine nature]" (pp. 89–102), based on Gregory's exegesis of 2 Peter 1:4.

Bonwetsch, G. Nathanael. *Die Theologie des Methodius von Olympus.* Göttingen, 1903.

————. *Die Theologie des Irenaeus.* Gütersloh, 1925.

Bornhäuser, Karl. *Die Vergottungslehre des Athanasius und des Johannes Damascenus.* Gütersloh, 1903.

Bousset, Wilhelm. *Der Antichrist.* Göttingen, 1895.

Braun, René. *"Deus Christianorum": Recherches sur le vocabulaire doctrinal de Tertullien.* Paris, 1962. A massive philological analysis with important theological consequences.

Buri, Fritz. *Clemens Alexandrinus und der paulinische Freiheitsbegriff.* Zurich, 1939.

Case, Shirley Jackson. *The Origins of Christian Supernaturalism.* Chicago, 1946.

Connolly, Richard H. "The Early Syriac Creed." *Zeitschrift für die neutestamentliche Wissenschaft und die Kunde der älteren Kirche* 7 (1906):202–23.

Corwin, Virginia. *St. Ignatius and Christianity in Antioch.* New Haven, 1960.

Crehan, Joseph Hugh, ed. Athenagoras. *Embassy for the Christians. The Resurrection of the Dead.* Ancient Christian Writers, no. 23. Westminster, Md., 1956.

Cumont, Franz. *Astrology and Religion among the Greeks and Romans.* New York, 1912.

Daniélou, Jean. "L'apocatastase chez Grégoire de Nysse." *Recherches de science religieuse* 30 (1940):328–47. Seeks to differentiate between Origen's universalism and Gregory's.

Dibelius, Martin. *Die Geisterwelt im Glauben des Paulus.* Göttingen, 1909. Similarities and differences between Christian supernaturalism and that of its milieu.

Elert, Werner. *Abendmahl und Kirchengemeinschaft in der Alten Kirche, hauptsächlich des Ostens.* Berlin, 1954. The real presence and the doctrine of the church in early Christianity.

Engelhardt, Moritz von. *Das Christentum Justins des Märtyrers: Eine Untersuchung über die Anfänge der katholischen Glaubenslehre.* Erlangen, 1878.

Evans, Ernest, ed. *Tertullian's Treatise against Praxeas.* London, 1948.

————. *Tertullian's Homily on Baptism.* London, 1964. Perhaps no other early Christian writer has been as well served by his translator into English as has Tertullian by Ernest Evans.

Fittkau, Gerhard. *Der Begriff des Mysteriums bei Johannes Chrysostomus: Eine Auseinandersetzung mit dem Begriff des "Kultmysteriums" in der Lehre Odo Casels.* Bonn, 1953.

Franks, Robert S. *A History of the Doctrine of the Work of Christ in Its Ecclesiastical Development.* 2 vols. New York, 1918.

Grant, Robert M. *Miracle and Natural Law in Graeco-Roman and Early Christian Thought.* Amsterdam, 1952. Especially important for Origen and Tertullian.

————, ed. *The Apostolic Fathers: A New Translation and Commentary.* New York, 1964–.

Greenslade, Stanley Lawrence. *Schism in the Early Church.* London, 1953.

Gross, Jules. *La divinisation du chrétien d'après les péres grecs: Contribution historique à la doctrine de la grace.* Paris, 1938. More sympathetic to the idea of "deification" than Bornhäuser and de Boer, but less so than Popov.

Hamel, Adolf. *Kirche bei Hippolyt von Rom.* Gütersloh, 1951.

Harnack, Adolf von, ed. *Des heiligen Irenaeus Schrift zum Erweise der apostolischen Verkündigung.* Leipzig, 1907. The first edition of the Ἐπίδειξις of Irenaeus, with notes by Harnack that are still valuable.

Heiler, Friedrich. *Prayer: A Study in the History and Psychology of Religion.* Translated by S. McComb and J. E. Park. New York, 1932.

————. "Gebet." *Die Religion in Geschichte und Gegenwart,* 2:1209–13. 3d ed. Tübingen, 1958.

Hoh, Josef. *Die kirchliche Busse im II. Jahrhundert: Eine Untersuchung der patristischen Busszeugnisse von Clemens Romanus bis Clemens Alexandrinus.* Breslau, 1932.

Käsemann, Ernst. "Die Anfänge christlicher Theologie." In *Exegetische Versuche und Besinnungen,* 2:82–104. Göttingen, 1964.

Koch, Hugo. *Cyprianische Untersuchungen.* Bonn, 1926.

————. *Cathedra Petri: Neue Untersuchungen über die Anfänge der Primatslehre.* Giessen, 1930.

Kolping, Adolf. *Sacramentum Tertullianeum.* Münster, 1948.

Lampe, Geoffrey William Hugo. *The Seal of the Spirit: A Study in the Doctrine of Baptism and Confirmation in the New Testament and the Fathers.* London, 1956. Despite its polemical accent, a balanced and positive study.

Lietzmann, Hans. *Mass and Lord's Supper: A Study in the History of the Liturgy.* Translated by Dorothea H. G. Reeve. Leiden, 1953.

Linton, Olof. *Das Problem der Urkirche in der neueren Forschung: Eine kritische Darstellung.* Uppsala, 1932. A fine summary of a large body of literature.

Loofs, Friedrich. *Theophilus von Antiochien adversus Marcionem und die anderen theologischen Quellen bei Irenaeus.* Leipzig, 1930. A novel theory about the sources and the theology of Irenaeus, which has not gained wide acceptance.

Lubac, Henri de. *Histoire et esprit: L'intelligence de l'Écriture d'après Origène.* Paris, 1950. Origen as "homme d'église," especially in his allegorism.

Lundberg, Per Ivar. *La typologie baptismale dans l'ancienne église.* Uppsala, 1942.

Molland, Einar. *The Conception of the Gospel in the Alexandrian Theology.* Oslo, 1938. A fundamental study.

Norris, Richard Alfred. *God and World in Early Christian Theology.* New York, 1965.

Plumpe, Joseph C. *Mater Ecclesia: An Inquiry into the Nature of the Church as Mother in Early Christianity.* Washington, 1943.

Popov, Ivan V. "Ideja oboženija v drevne-vostočnoi cerkvi" [The idea of deification in the early Eastern church]. *Voprosi filosofij i psychologij* 97 (1909):165–213.

Quasten, Johannes, ed. *Monumenta eucharistica et liturgica vetustissima.* Bonn, 1935–37. A unique collection of source material.

Richardson, Cyril C. *The Christianity of Ignatius of Antioch.* New York, 1935.

Rush, Alfred C. *Death and Burial in Christian Antiquity.* Washington, 1941.

Simpson, Robert L. *The Interpretation of Prayer in the Early Church.* Philadelphia, 1965. Based chiefly on various expositions of the Lord's Prayer.

Solano, Jesus, ed. *Textos eucaristicos primitivos.* 2 vols. Madrid, 1962–64. Although the pertinence of some texts may be questioned, the checkered history of the doctrine can be studied with the aid of these quotations.

Torrance, Thomas F. *The Doctrine of Grace in the Apostolic Fathers.* Reprint. Grand Rapids, Mich., 1959. Exaggerated but brilliant.

Turner, Henry Ernest William. *The Patristic Doctrine of Redemption: A Study of the Development of Doctrine during the First Five Centuries.* London, 1952.

———. *The Pattern of Christian Truth: A Study in the Relations between Orthodoxy and Heresy in the Early Church.* London, 1954. An answer to Walter Bauer.

Völker, Walther. *Das Vollkommenheitsideal des Origenes: Eine Untersuchung zur Geschichte der Frömmigkeit und zu den Anfängen christlicher Mystik.* Tübingen, 1931. A turning point in the interpretation of Origen.

Wetter, Gillis P. *Altchristliche Liturgien.* 2 vols. Göttingen, 1921–22.

Wingren, Gustaf. *Man and the Incarnation: A Study in the Biblical Theology of Irenaeus.* Translated by Ross Mackenzie. Philadelphia, 1959.

4. THE MYSTERY OF THE TRINITY

Aulén, Gustaf. *Den kristna gudsbilden genom seklerna och i nutiden en konturteckning* [An outline of the Christian picture of God through the centuries and in the present day]. 2d ed. Stockholm, 1941. A German translation of the 1927 edition was published in 1930.

Barbel, Joseph. *Christos Angelos: Die Anschauung von Christus als Bote und Engel in der gelehrten und volkstümlichen Literatur des christlichen Altertums.* Bonn, 1941.

Bertrand, Frédéric. *Mystique de Jésus chez Origène.* Paris, 1951. The problem of the place of the historical Jesus in Origen's piety.

Bethune-Baker, James Franklin. *The Meaning of Homoousios in the "Constantinopolitan" Creed.* Cambridge, 1901. A refutation of the hypothesis that Nicea was compromised by its defenders.

Bousset, Wilhelm. *Kyrios Christos: Geschichte des Christusglaubens von den Anfängen des Christentums bis Irenaeus.* Göttingen, 1913.

Chevalier, Irénée. *S. Augustin et la pensée grecque: Les relations trinitaires.* Fribourg, 1940.

Cross, Frank Leslie. *The Study of St. Athanasius.* Oxford, 1945.

Dörries, Hermann. *De Spiritu Sancto: Der Beitrag des Basilius zum Abschluss des trinitarischen Dogmas.* Göttingen, 1956. Basil on the Three and the One.

Galtier, Paul. *Le Saint-Esprit en nous d'après les péres grecs*. Rome, 1946. Subjective and objective elements in the patristic doctrine of the Holy Spirit.

Grant, Robert M. *The Early Christian Doctrine of God*. Charlottesville, Va., 1966.

Gummerus, Jaakko. *Die Homöusianische Partei bis zum Tode des Konstantius: Ein Beitrag zur Geschichte des Arianischen Streites in den Jahren 356–361*. Helsinki, 1900.

Gwatkin, Henry Melvill. *Studies of Arianism, Chiefly Referring to the Character and Chronology of the Reaction which Followed the Council of Nicaea*. Cambridge, 1882. Helps to sort out parties and positions.

Hahn, Ferdinand. *Christologische Hoheitstitel: Ihre Geschichte im frühen Christentum*. Göttingen, 1963.

Holl, Karl. *Amphilochius von Ikonium in seinem Verhältnis zu den grossen Kappadoziern*. Tübingen, 1904. Despite its unprepossessing title, a splendid introduction to the thought of Basil and the two Gregorys.

Houssiau, Albert. *La Christologie de saint Irénée*. Louvain, 1955.

Ivancov-Platonov, A. M. *Religioznija dviženija na christianskom vostoke v IV i V vekach: Kritiko-istoričeskija zamečanija* [Religious movements in the Christian East during the fourth and fifth centuries: critical-historical observations]. Moscow, 1881. Especially penetrating in its analysis of the origins of Arianism in the left wing of the Origenist school.

Jay, Eric George, ed. *Origen's Treatise on Prayer*. London, 1954.

Kretschmar, Georg. *Studien zur frühchristlichen Trinitätstheologie*. Tübingen, 1956. Stresses liturgical background of trinitarian thought.

Kriebel, Martin. *Studien zur älteren Entwicklung der abendländischen Trinitätslehre bei Tertullian und Novatian*. Marburg, 1932.

Krüger, Gustav. *Das Dogma von der Dreieinigkeit und Gottmenschheit in seiner geschichtlichen Entwicklung dargestellt*. Tübingen, 1905.

Lebreton, Jules. *History of the Dogma of the Trinity from Its Origins to the Council of Nicaea*. Translated by Algar Thorold. London, 1939. A translation of the first volume of the original French edition.

Lieske, Aloisius. *Die Theologie der Logosmystik bei Origenes*. Münster, 1938. Origen's trinitarian ideas as the source both of Arian and of Nicene teaching.

Lonergan, Bernard. *De Deo Trino*. 2 vols. 2d and 3d ed. Rome, 1964. Contains (2:42–53) a defense of the historical method in the study of the dogma of the Trinity, as well as much historical material (1:17–112).

Loofs, Friedrich. *Paulus von Samosata: Eine Untersuchung zur altchristlichen Literatur- und Dogmengeschichte*. Leipzig, 1924.

Macholz, Waldemar. *Spuren binitarischer Denkweise im Abendlande seit Tertullian*. Jena, 1902.

Murray, John Courtney. *The Problem of God Yesterday and Today*. New Haven, 1964. The second chapter is a capsule account of the history of the Christian doctrine of God.

Newman, John Henry. *The Arians of the Fourth Century*. 3d ed. London, 1871. Includes Newman's essay, "The Orthodoxy of the Body of the Faithful during the Supremacy of Arianism."

Otis, B. "Cappadocian Thought as a Coherent System." *Dumbarton Oaks Papers* 12 (1958):95–124.

Pelikan, Jaroslav. *The Light of the World: A Basic Image in Early Christian Thought*. New York, 1962. The metaphor of light in Athanasius, especially his concept of Christ as "the radiance of the Father."

Prestige, George Leonard. *God in Patristic Thought.* 2d ed. London, 1956. Patristic terminology as a key to trinitarian theology.

Rawlinson, Alfred Edward John, ed. *Essays on the Trinity and the Incarnation by Members of the Anglican Communion.* London, 1928.

Riedmatten, Henri de. *Les actes du procès de Paul de Samosate: Étude sur la Christologie du IIIe au IVe siècle.* Fribourg, 1952.

Ruesch, Theodor. *Die Entstehung der Lehre vom Heiligen Geist bei Ignatius von Antiochia, Theophilus von Antiochia und Irenäus von Lyon.* Zurich, 1952.

Schermann, Theodor. *Die Gottheit des Heiligen Geistes nach den griechischen Vätern des vierten Jahrhunderts.* Freiburg, 1901.

Schindler, Alfred. *Wort und Analogie in Augustins Trinitätslehre.* Tübingen, 1965. Important for an understanding of the second half of Augustine *On the Trinity.*

Schmaus, Michael. *Die psychologische Trinitätslehre des heiligen Augustinus.* Münster, 1927. Has determined modern discussion of the problem.

Shapland, C. R. B., ed. Athanasius. *Letters concerning the Holy Spirit.* London, 1951.

Smulders, Pierre. *La doctrine trinitaire de S. Hilaire de Poitiers.* Rome, 1944. Hilary was a transmitter of trinitarian theology between the Greek East and the Latin West.

Spasskij, A. *Istorija dogmatičeskich dviženij v epochu vselenskich soborov (v sviazi s filosofskimi učeniami togo vremeni)* [History of the dogmatic movements in the age of the ecumenical councils (in conjunction with the philosophical teachings of that time)]. Sergiev Posad, 1914. The only volume to appear of this work, Spasskij's monograph is restricted to the fourth century, closing with the Council of Constantinople in 381.

Stülcken, Alfred. *Athanasiana: Literar- und dogmengeschlichtliche Untersuchungen.* Leipzig, 1899.

Urbina, Ignazio Ortiz de. *Die Gottheit Christi bei Afrahat.* Rome, 1933. Despite the absence of technical terms, whether Greek or Latin, Syriac theology shared the orthodox doctrine of Christ as divine.

Verhoeven, Th. L. *Studien over Tertullianus' Adversus Praxean.* Amsterdam, 1948. Together with the notes of Ernest Evans, Verhoeven's analysis of Tertullian's language illumines the origins of Latin trinitarianism.

Williams, George Huntston. "Christology and Church-State Relations in the Fourth Century." *Church History* 20–III(1951):3–33; 20–IV:3–26. Correlates political and dogmatic parties.

5. THE PERSON OF THE GOD-MAN

Beck, Edmund. *Die Theologie des heiligen Ephraem.* Rome, 1949.

Bethune-Baker, James Franklin. *Nestorius and His Teaching.* Cambridge, 1908. An early effort to set the record straight.

Burghardt, Walter J. *The Image of God in Man according to Cyril of Alexandria.* Washington, 1957.

Callewaert, Camillus. *S. Léon le Grand et les textes du Léonien.* Bruges, 1954.

Camelot, Thomas. "De Nestorius à Eutychès: l'opposition de deux christologies." *Das Konzil von Chalkedon,* 1:213–42. (See Grillmeier and Bacht, below.) A sober analysis of the issues.

Chabot, Jean Baptiste, ed. *Documenta ad origines monophysitarum illustrandas.* 2 vols. Louvain, 1952–55. While more significant for the second than for the first volume of our work, Chabot's collection of Syriac sources with Latin translations and notes is vital to an understanding of 451.

Chadwick, Henry. "Eucharist and Christology in the Nestorian Controversy." *Journal of Theological Studies,* 2d ser. 2 (1951):145–64.

Cramer, Maria, and Bacht, Heinrich. "Der antichalkedonische Aspekt im historisch-biographischen Schrifttum der koptischen Monophysiten (6–7. Jahrhundert)." *Das Konzil von Chalkedon,* 2:315–38. (See Grillmeier and Bacht, below.)

Devreesse, Robert. *Essai sur Théodore de Mopsueste.* Rome, 1948. Special attention to the exegesis of Theodore, defense of his essential orthodoxy.

Draguet, René. *Julien d'Halicarnasse et sa controverse avec Sévère d'Antioche sur l'incorruptibilité du corps du Christ.* Louvain, 1924.

Durand, G. M., ed. Cyrille d'Alexandrie. *Deux dialogues christologiques.* Sources chrétiennes, no. 97. Paris, 1964.

Ficker, Gerhard. *Eutherius von Tyana.* Leipzig, 1908.

Galtier, Paul. "Saint Cyrille d'Alexandrie et saint Léon le Grand à Chalcedoine." *Das Konzil von Chalkedon,* 1:345–87. (See Grillmeier and Bacht, below.)

Glubokovskij, Nikolai Nikanorovič. *Blaž. Feodorit, ep. Kirrskij: Ego žizn' i literaturnaja dejatel'nost'* [St. Theodoret, bishop of Cyrrhus: his life and literary activity]. 2 vols. Moscow, 1890. More than a biography, this comprehensive work places Theodore's thought, especially his christological thought, into the context of his time.

Greer, Rowan A. *Theodore of Mopsuestia: Exegete and Theologian.* Westminster, 1961.

Grillmeier, Aloys, and Bacht, Heinrich, eds. *Das Konzil von Chalkedon: Geschichte und Gegenwart.* 3 vols. Würzburg, 1951–52. Truly deserves the overworked label "monumental," even though one may—or must—dissent from some of its conclusions.

Grillmeier, Aloys. *Christ in Christian Tradition: From the Apostolic Age to Chalcedon (451).* Translated by J. S. Bowden. New York, 1965. Translation and expansion of Grillmeier's key essay in the symposium of 1951.

Kerrigan, Alexander. *St. Cyril of Alexandria: Interpreter of the Old Testament.* Rome, 1952.

Koch, Günter. *Die Heilsverwirklichung bei Theodor von Mopsuestia.* Munich, 1965.

Lebon, Joseph. *Le monophysisme sévérien: Étude historique, littéraire et théologique sur la résistance monophysite au concile de Chalcédoine jusqu'à la constitution de l'église jacobite.* Louvain, 1909. The basic study in the reinterpretation of the "Monophysite" position.

———. "La christologie du monophysisme syrien." *Das Konzil von Chalkedon,* 1:425–580. The fruit of a half-century of historical research.

Liébaert, Jacques, and Lamarche, P. *Christologie: Von der apostolischen Zeit bis zum Konzil von Chalkedon (451).* Freiburg, 1965.

Loofs, Friedrich. *Nestorius and His Place in the History of Christian Doctrine.* Cambridge, 1914.

Manoir, H. de. *Dogme et spiritualité chez saint Cyrille d'Alexandrie.* Paris, 1944.

Meyendorff, John. *Christ in Eastern Christian Thought.* Washington, 1969. Perhaps the only satisfactory study in a Western language of the crucial developments during and after the period of the present volume.

Meyer, Robert T., ed. St. Athanasius. *The Life of Saint Antony.* Ancient Christian Writers, no. 10. Westminster, Md., 1950.

Moeller, Charles. "Le chalcédonisme et le néo-chalcédonisme en Orient de 451 à la fin du VIe siècle." *Das Konzil von Chalkedon,* 1:637–720. A new framework for the interpretation of events after the Council of Chalcedon.

Norris, Richard Alfred. *Manhood and Christ: A study in the Christology of Theodore of Mopsuestia.* Oxford, 1963.

Pelikan, Jaroslav, ed. *The Preaching of Chrysostom: Homilies on the Sermon on the Mount.* Philadelphia, 1967.

Raven, Charles Earle. *Apollinarianism: An Essay on the Christology of the Early Church.* Cambridge, 1923.

Roldanus, J. *Le Christ et l'homme dans la théologie d'Athanase d'Alexandrie: Étude de la conjonction de sa conception de l'homme avec sa christologie.* Leiden, 1968. Human nature and incarnation in Athanasius.

Romanides, John S. "Highlights in the Debate over Theodore of Mopsuestia's Christology and Some Suggestions for a Fresh Approach." *Greek Orthodox Theological Review* 5 (1959/60):140–85.

Samuel, Vilakuvel Cherian. "The Council of Chalcedon and the Christology of Severus of Antioch." Ph.D. dissertation, Yale University, 1957. A clarification of "Monophysite" doctrines, largely on the basis of Syriac materials.

Sellers, Robert Victor. *Two Ancient Christologies: A Study in the Christological Thought of the Schools of Alexandria and Antioch in the Early History of Christian Doctrine.* London, 1940.

———. *The Council of Chalcedon: A Historical and Doctrinal Survey.* London, 1953. Both of these studies by Sellers strive to be fair to all the alternative theologies of the incarnation.

Sullivan, Francis Aloysius. *The Christology of Theodore of Mopsuestia.* Rome, 1956. Defends traditional view that Theodore was a Nestorian.

Urbina, Ignazio Ortiz de. "Das Glaubenssymbol von Chalkedon—sein Text, sein Werden, seine dogmatische Bedeutung." *Das Konzil von Chalkedon,* 1:389–418.

Vaschalde, Arthur Adolphe, ed. *Three Letters of Philoxenus, Bishop of Mabbogh (485–519).* Rome, 1902.

Weigl, Eduard. *Untersuchungen zur Christologie des heiligen Athanasius.* Paderborn, 1914.

———. *Die Christologie vom Tode des Athanasius bis zum Ausbruch des nestorianischen Streites.* Munich, 1925.

Wigram, William Ainger. *The Separation of the Monophysites.* London, 1923.

6. Nature and Grace

Adam, Karl. *Die Eucharistielehre des heiligen Augustin.* Paderborn, 1908.

———. *The Spirit of Catholicism.* Translated by Justin McCann. Garden City, N. Y., 1954.

Alfaric, Prosper. *L'évolution intellectuelle de saint Augustin.* Vol. 1. *Du Manichéisme au Néoplatonisme.* Paris, 1918. The early "Christian" writings of Augustine are more Neoplatonic than Christian.

Andresen, Carl, ed. *Bibliographia Augustiniana.* Darmstadt, 1962.

Arnold, Carl Franklin. *Caesarius von Arelate und die gallische Kirche seiner Zeit.* Leipzig, 1898.

Barth, Heinrich. *Die Freiheit der Entscheidung im Denken Augustins.* Basel, 1935. The freedom of the will between Manicheism and Pelagianism.

Bohlin, Torgny. *Die Theologie des Pelagius und ihre Genesis.* Uppsala, 1957.

Bonner, Gerald. *St. Augustine of Hippo: Life and Controversies.* London, 1963. A balanced and highly readable summary.

Bourke, Vernon J. *Augustine's Quest of Wisdom.* Milwaukee, 1945.

Boyer, Charles. *Christianisme et Néoplatonisme dans la formation de saint Augustin.* Paris, 1920. An answer to Alfaric.

Bruckner, Albert Emil, ed. *Quellen zur Geschichte des pelagianischen Streites.* Tübingen, 1906.

————. *Julian von Eclanum, sein Leben und seine Lehre: Ein Beitrag zur Geschichte des Pelagianismus.* Leipzig, 1897.

Burnaby, John. *Amor Dei: A Study of the Religion of St. Augustine.* Reprint. London, 1960.

Campenhausen, Hans von. *The Virgin Birth in the Theology of the Ancient Church.* Translated by Frank Clarke. London, 1964.

Chadwick, Owen. *John Cassian: A Study in Primitive Monasticism.* 2d ed. London, 1968. A leading critic of Augustinian predestinarianism.

Dinkler, Erich. *Die Anthropologie Augustins.* Stuttgart, 1934.

Evans, Robert Franklin. *Four Letters of Pelagius.* New York, 1968.

————. *Pelagius: Inquiries and Reappraisals.* New York, 1968. New insight into "one of the most maligned figures in the history of Christianity."

Frend, William Hugh Clifford. *The Donatist Church: A Movement of Protest in Roman North Africa.* Oxford, 1952. The role of "nontheological factors."

Gaith, Jérome. *La conception de la liberté chez Grégoire de Nysse.* Paris, 1953.

Grant, Frederick C., ed. *Hellenistic Religions: The Age of Syncretism.* New York, 1953.

Gross, Julius. *Entstehungsgeschichte des Erbsündendogmas: Von der Bibel bis Augustinus.* Munich, 1960.

Henry, Paul. *Plotin et l'Occident: Firmicus Maternus, Marius Victorinus, Saint Augustin et Macrobe.* Louvain, 1934.

Hofmann, Fritz. *Der Kirchenbegriff des heiligen Augustinus in seinen Grundlagen und in seiner Entwicklung.* Munich, 1933.

Holl, Karl. "Augustins innere Entwicklung." *Gesammelte Aufsätze,* 3:54–116.

Huhn, Joseph. *Ursprung und Wesen des Bösen und der Sünde nach der Lehre des Kirchenvaters Ambrosius.* Paderborn, 1933.

————. *Das Geheimnis der Jungfrau-Mutter Maria nach dem Kirchenvater Ambrosius.* Würzburg, 1954. Ambrose was more influential in the history of doctrine than has usually been assumed.

Karpp, Heinrich. *Probleme altchristlicher Anthropologie: Biblische Anthropologie und philosophische Psychologie bei den Kirchenvätern des dritten Jahrhunderts.* Gütersloh, 1950. The doctrine of man in Tertullian, Clement of Alexandria, Lactantius, and Origen.

Loofs, Friedrich. "Pelagius und der pelagianische Streit." *Realencyklopädie für protestantische Theologie und Kirche,* 15:747–74. Learned and profound.

Marrou, Henri-Irénée. *Saint Augustin et la fin de la culture antique.* 4th ed. Paris, 1958. Augustine as thinker and man of letters.

Moriones, Franciscus, ed. *Enchiridion theologicum Sancti Augustini.* Madrid, 1961.

Niebuhr, Reinhold. *The Nature and Destiny of Man.* 2 vols. New York, 1941–43.

Nygren, Gotthard. *Das Prädestinationsproblem in der Theologie Augustins.* Lund, 1956.

Oberman, Heiko Augustinus. *The Harvest of Medieval Theology: Gabriel Biel and Late Medieval Nominalism.* Cambridge, Mass., 1963.

O'Meara, John J., ed. St. Augustine. *Against the Academics.* Ancient Christian Writers, no. 12. Westminster, Md., 1950.

Orbe, Antonio. *Antropología de San Ireneo.* Madrid, 1969. Systematic, perhaps overly systematic, exposition of Irenaeus on the doctrine of man.

Outler, Albert C., ed. Augustine. *Confessions. Enchiridion.* Library of Christian Classics, vol. 7. Philadelphia, 1955.

Pegis, Anton C. "The Mind of St. Augustine." *Mediaeval Studies* 6 (1944):1–61.

Portalié, Eugène. *A Guide to the Thought of Saint Augustine.* Translated by R. J. Bastian. Chicago, 1960. Sound learning and historical perspective mark this extremely useful survey.

Rahner, Karl. "Sünde als Gnadenverlust in der frühchristlichen Literatur." *Zeitschrift für katholische Theologie* 60 (1936):471–510.

Ratzinger, Joseph. *Volk und Haus Gottes in Augustins Lehre von der Kirche.* Munich, 1954. Gives attention to noninstitutional aspects of Augustine's ecclesiology.

Reuter, Hermann. *Augustinische Studien.* Gotha, 1887. Reuter influenced many later interpretations of Augustine's doctrine of the church.

Romanides, John S. Τό προπατρικόν ἁμάρτημα [Ancestral sin]. Athens, 1957. Analysis of patristic doctrines of "original sin" that did not develop as Augustine's did.

Scheel, Otto. *Die Anschauung Augustins über Christi Person und Werk.* Tübingen, 1901.

Scholz, Heinrich. *Glaube und Unglaube in der Weltgeschichte: Ein Kommentar zu Augustins De Civitate Dei.* Leipzig, 1911.

Soden, Hans von, ed. *Urkunden zur Entstehungsgeschichte des Donatismus.* 2d ed. Edited by Hans von Campenhausen. Berlin, 1950. Scattered documents brought together into a handy collection.

Stendahl, Krister. "Quis et unde? An Analysis of Mt 1–2." *Judentum Urchristentum Kirche: Festschrift für Joachim Jeremias,* pp. 94–105. Edited by Walther Eltester. Berlin, 1960. The virgin birth in Matthew.

Struker, Arnold. *Die Gottesebenbildlichkeit des Menschen in der christlichen Literatur der ersten zwei Jahrhunderte: Ein Beitrag zur Geschichte der Exegese von Gen. I.26.* Münster, 1913.

Taylor, Charles H., ed. *Essays on the Odyssey: Selected Modern Criticism.* Bloomington, Ind., 1963.

Troeltsch, Ernst. *Augustin, die christliche Antike und das Mittelalter.* Munich, 1915. The significance of Augustine and of Augustinism for later centuries.

Warfield, Benjamin Breckenridge. *Two Studies in the History of Doctrine.* New York, 1897.

Weigel, Gustave. *Faustus of Riez.* Philadelphia, 1938. Is Faustus rightly termed a "Semi-Pelagian"?

Williams, Norman P. *The Ideas of the Fall and of Original Sin.* London, 1927.

Willis, Geoffrey Grimshaw. *Saint Augustine and the Donatist Controversy.* London, 1950.

7. THE ORTHODOX CONSENSUS

Alivisatos, Hamilcar S. *Die kirchliche Gesetzgebung des Kaisers Justinian I.* Berlin, 1913. Deals with Justinian's ecclesiastical legislation, including that against heresy, but introduces this with a summary evaluation of Justinian as theologian.

Chevallier, Philippe, ed. *Jésus-Christ dans les oeuvres du Pseudo-Aréopagite*. Paris, 1951.

Courcelle, Pierre. *Histoire littéraire des grandes invasions germaniques*. Paris, 1964.

————. *Late Latin Writers and Their Greek Sources*. Translated by Harry E. Wedeck. Cambridge, Mass., 1969. Both of these works by Courcelle, but especially this one, put the entire history of Western thought during this period into a new light.

Diekamp, Franz. *Die origenistischen Streitigkeiten im sechsten Jahrhundert und das fünfte allgemeine Konzil*. Münster, 1899.

Dudden, Frederick H. *Gregory the Great: His Place in History and Thought*. 2 vols. London, 1905.

Frickel, Michael. *Deus totus ubique simul: Untersuchungen zur allgemeinen Gottesgegenwart im Rahmen der Gotteslehre Gregors des Grossen*. Freiburg, 1956.

Guillaumont, Antoine. *Les "Kephálaia Gnostica" d'Evagre le Pontique et l'histoire de l'origénisme chez les grecs et chez les syriens*. Paris, 1962. Systematizer of Origen's theology, Evagrius was condemned at Constantinople in 553.

Hathaway, Ronald F. *Hierarchy and the Definition of Order in the "Letters" of Pseudo-Dionysius: A Study in the Form and Meaning of the Pseudo-Dionysian Writings*. The Hague, 1969. An original contribution.

Holl, Karl. *Enthusiasmus und Bussgewalt beim griechischen Mönchtum*. Leipzig, 1898. The distinctive place of monastic piety and theology in the patristic and early Byzantine period.

Kelly, John N. D. *The Athanasian Creed*. New York, 1964. Definitive study.

Koch, Hugo. *Pseudo-Dionysius Areopagita in seinen Beziehungen zum Neuplatonismus und Mysterienwesen*. Mainz, 1900.

Loofs, Friedrich. *Leontius von Byzanz und die gleichnamigen Schriftsteller der griechischen Kirche*. Leipzig, 1887. Almost certainly mistaken in its identifications, this monograph nevertheless contains many brilliant suggestions.

McClain, J. P. *The Doctrine of Heaven in the Writings of St. Gregory the Great*. Washington, 1956.

Marić, Joseph. "Pseudo-Dionysii Areopagitae formula christologica celeberrima de Christi activitate theandrica." *Bogoslovska smotra* 20 (1932):105–73.

Meyendorff, John. "Justinian, the Empire and the Church." *Dumbarton Oaks Papers* 22 (1968):43–60. Stresses Justinian's awareness of "the unavoidable limitations of his power in doctrinal matters" and sympathetically assesses his reinterpretation of Chalcedon.

Oksiuk, M. "Feopaschitskie spory" [The theopaschite controversies]. *Trudy Kievskoi duchovnoi akademij* [Transactions of the Spiritual (Theological) Academy of Kiev] 1 (1913):529–59.

Panillo, José Ramon Bada. *La doctrina de la mediación dinámica y universal de Cristo, Salvador Nuestro, en el "Corpus Areopagiticum."* Zaragoza, 1965.

Patch, Howard Rollin. *The Tradition of Boethius: A Study of His Importance in Medieval Culture*. New York, 1935.

Richardson, Cyril C. "The Condemnation of Origen." *Church History* 6-I (1937): 50–64.

Roques, René. *L'univers dionysien: Structure hiérarchique du monde selon le Pseudo-Denys*. Paris, 1954. Basic for any study of metaphysics in Pseudo-Dionysius.

Schurr, Viktor. *Die Trinitätslehre des Boethius im Lichte der "skytischen Kontroversen."* Paderborn, 1935.

Schwartz, Eduard. "Zur Kirchenpolitik Justinians." *Gesammelte Schriften*, 4:276–328.

Viller, Marcel, and Rahner, Karl. *Aszese und Mystik in der Väterzeit*. Freiburg, 1939.

Index

Biblical

377

General

Abraham, 14–15, 25, 57, 59
Adam. *See* Man
Adoptionism. *See* Christ, defined as
   adopted
Aeons, Gnostic doctrine of, 85–87
Aeschines, ca. 200, Montanist in Rome,
   104
Aeschylus, d. 456 B.C., Greek dramatist,
   280–81
Africa, North, 304, 310
Alexander, d. 328, bishop of Alexandria,
   193, 200–201, 241
Alexandrians: on the doctrine of Christ,
   227, 247–51; the Eucharist, 236–38;
   God, 227, 230–32; Mary, 241–42;
   salvation, 233–34. *See also* Athanasius;
   Clement of Alexandria; Cyril of
   Alexandria; Origen
Allegory. *See* Scripture, defined as
   allegorical
Ambrose, d. 397, bishop of Milan
—on the doctrine of Christ, 245, 257;
   immortality and resurrection, 52;
   the virgin birth, 289–90
—relation of, to: Arianism, 199;
   Augustine, 289; Nicea, 203–7; paganism, 35; Plato, 33
Ambrosiaster, unknown author of
   commentaries ascribed to Ambrose, 299
Amphilochius, d. 395, bishop of Iconium,
   203–7, 211
Anastasius of Sinai, d. ca. 700, abbott of
   monastery of St. Catherine, 272
Angels, doctrine of, 103, 133–35, 140,
   197, 299. *See also* Christ, defined
   as angel
Anomoeans, left-wing Arians of the
   fourth century, 196, 228
Antichrist. *See* Eschatology
Antioch, 200–201, 270–71
Antiochenes: on the doctrine of Christ,
   227, 251–56; the Eucharist, 236–38;

God, 231–32; Mary, 242; salvation,
   234–36. *See also* Nestorius; Theodore
   of Mopsuestia
Antiquity of Christian doctrine, 34–35
Antony, d. 356, Egyptian hermit, 135–37,
   162, 232
Apelles, second-century Gnostic, 80
Aphraates, fourth-century Syriac writer,
   184–85
Apocalypticism. *See* Eschatology
Apollinaris, d. ca. 390, bishop of Laodicea:
   on the doctrine of Christ, 228, 239–40,
   248; God, 53, 230; salvation, 232, 233;
   Scripture, 243
Apollinarism. *See* Apollinaris
Apologetics, and apologists, 27–41, 45
Apostles, and apostolicity. *See* Bishops;
   Church, defined as apostolic;
   Scripture; Tradition
Apostles' Creed, 117, 119, 150–51. *See
   also* Creeds
Apostolic Constitutions, early collection
   of canon law, perhaps from fourth
   century, 126
Archons, Gnostic doctrine of, 86, 95
Arianism. *See* Arius
Aristobulus, Jewish writer of second
   century B.C. in Alexandria, 33
Aristotle, d. 322 B.C., Greek philosopher:
   relation of, to Basilides, 84; Boethius,
   42, 349; Monophysites, 269–70;
   Tertullian, 50; transubstantiation, 44
Arius, d. ca. 336, priest in Alexandria. *See
   also* Athanasius; Nicea
—on the doctrine of: angels, 197–98;
   baptism, 199–200; Christ, 195–200;
   God, 193–97; prayer to Christ,
   198–99; salvation, 198
—relation of, to: Alexander, 200–203;
   Antiochenes, 228; Apollinarism,
   228; Nicea, 203; Semi-Arianism,
   209

THE CHRISTIAN TRADITION, Volume 1

Designed by Joseph Alderfer.
Composed by Typoservice Corporation
in Linotype Garamond with display lines
in Foundry American Garamond.
Printed by Photopress Inc.
on Warren's Olde Style.
Bound by A. C. Engdahl Co. in Joanna Arrestox Vellum
and stamped in red and gold.
The symbol on the cover is a Chrismon with
the Alpha and Omega.
It is adapted from a bronze cross of the fifth century,
the original of which is in the
Kunsthistorisches Museum
in Vienna, Austria.